American Library History

American Library History

A Comprehensive Guide to the Literature

Donald G. Davis, Jr.
University of Texas at Austin

John Mark Tucker
Purdue University

Santa Barbara, California
Oxford, England

Library of Congress Cataloging-in-Publication Data

Davis, Donald G.
   American library history : a comprehensive guide to the literature
 / by Donald G. Davis, Jr., and John Mark Tucker.
   Includes bibliographies and indexes.
   ISBN 0-87436-142-7
   1. Library science—United States—History—Bibliography.
 2. Libraries—United States—History—Bibliography. I. Tucker,
John Mark. II. Title.
   Z731.D38 1989   027.073—dc20   89-33480

ISBN 0-87436-142-7 (alk. paper)

96 95 94 93 92 91 90 89   10 9 8 7 6 5 4 3 2 1

ABC-CLIO, Inc.
130 Cremona Drive, P.O. Box 1911
Santa Barbara, California 93116–1911

Clio Press Ltd.
55 St. Thomas' Street
Oxford, OX1 1JG, England

This book is Smyth-sewn and printed on acid-free paper ∞ .
Manufactured in the United States of America

For
Avis Jane
and
Barbara Ann

Contents

Foreword

When I wrote the foreword to the first edition of this bibliography, I noted that American library historians had "long been frustrated by the lack of a good, standard bibliography." The appearance of the first edition of *American Library History: A Bibliography* remedied that deficiency. The 1978 edition was a boon not only to the senior historian, but also to the aspiring historian. Along with the *Dictionary of American Library Biography,* published at the same time, *American Library History* has proved its worth many times over during the ensuing decade. When combined with the *DALB* and our research journal, *Libraries & Culture* (formerly the *Journal of Library History*), the new *American Library History* assures library historians working today that they have a first-rate bibliography, biographical dictionary, and scholarly journal, both for basic research and for keeping up to date with results of the latest and best scholarship our field has to offer.

What of this second edition, compiled and edited by two of the profession's most accomplished American library historians?

One is tempted to call the bibliography *exhaustive,* a term that few librarians use anymore in describing their collections or their scholarship. The proliferation of newsletters, journals, and monographs threatens to overwhelm the scholar, even one working in a very small area of scholarship. *Information overload* and *surfeit of information* are terms most historians know all too well. One can only note that the second edition, renamed *American Library History: A Comprehensive Guide to the Literature,* more than doubles the number of entries from the first edition, and that within a short decade. Davis and Tucker do not need to be reminded that *exhaustive* and *complete* are terms that bibliographers use at their peril. Nonetheless, so impressed am I with the incredible number of sources included in this bibliography that I have no problem with their use of *comprehensive* as an appropriate descriptor.

As the authors indicate, historians of American librarianship have been increasingly productive during the past two decades. They have also become more sensitive to trends in the larger world of scholarship, particularly in changing approaches to historical interpretation and in new areas of historical research. The reader will note with approval the appearance of separate sections on the history of archives and on women in librarianship. But if we congratulate ourselves on the progress of library history, we also note how far we have to go. As gender studies and women's studies have become more prominent, we cannot help noting the absence of substantive works on biographies of women librarians. This writer checked the biographical section in vain for essays on women librarians in land-grant colleges and universities for one of his students. Alas, at this point in our history, the essays don't exist. Such an absence should be seen not as a cause for despair, but as a gap that both senior and junior historians should fill before the next edition of *American Library History* makes its appearance.

The general user of this guide will be especially impressed with the introductory essays to the fifteen sections. Davis and Tucker have been judicious in their appraisals, though not everyone will agree with their assessments of individual titles. They are sensitive to changes in historical methodology as well as to the newer interpretations mentioned above.

The authors have not included every item *about* libraries, but only those works where the historical intent was clear. Fortunately, the entries include many items that are not, strictly speaking, "research" but items that may provide important information subsequent historians can use for their own research. As most practicing historians know, establishing a useful chronology of events, or even interpreting a person's contributions to a profession, is sometimes difficult; even laudatory or celebratory essays can often be helpful. This historian is especially grateful that such items on the "essential facts about past people, places, events, institutions, and ideas" have been included.

Access to the entries is enhanced not only by three indexes but also by rearrangement of the articles in each section chronologically. That rearrangement, which enables the researcher to trace the development of a topic by years, is especially helpful. Also, a spot check of the comprehensive index to the bibliographic essays and of the author and institution indexes revealed how carefully the indexing has been done.

As I have often remarked to my students, "The place to begin your research is with *American Library History*." Now it will be a pleasure to say to them, "Don't forget to start with Davis's and Tucker's *American Library History: A Comprehensive Guide to the Literature*."

Students, scholars, reference librarians, and librarians generally will welcome this revised scholarly bibliography, which will continue to make a substantial contribution to the improvement of research and publication in American library history.

On behalf of all future users of *American Library History*, I not only congratulate the authors on their splendid achievement; I also thank them for making our future research easier and more productive.

Edward G. Holley

William Rand Kenan, Jr., Professor
School of Information and Library Science
The University of North Carolina at Chapel Hill

Preface

In *American Library History: A Bibliography*, Michael H. Harris and Donald G. Davis, Jr. called attention to a "new emphasis on the nature and dissemination of ideas" in the history of the United States, an emphasis that encouraged scholars to pay closer attention to the impact of the printed word than they had previously. Bearers of the printed word—books, newspapers, periodicals, and microforms—and repositories of those publications—libraries—have taken on fresh historical significance. "As a result, the study of the origins, contents, and evolution of private and public libraries now plays an important part in the writing of American intellectual history."

The study of books and libraries in their cultural context has gained momentum during the past decade. Important historical treatments of literacy, reading, book culture, and information usage have signified the potential for a better understanding of the history of librarianship. Representative among these are papers presented at Library History Seminars VI (1980) and VII (1985) and many of the articles and monographs evaluated by Wayne A. Wiegand in bibliographic essays published in the *Journal of Library History* the renaming of which to *Libraries & Culture* itself recognizes a new breadth of scope and audience. Moreover, a growing number of writers regard the history of libraries and librarianship as well as the history of books, reading, printing, and publishing as topics that rightly encompass common territory. Although library historical studies remain comparatively youthful, they are flourishing. New perspectives on the relationships between library history and similar social and cultural phenomena, as well as the history of ideas, have resulted in greater historical interest.

In addition to scholars who might be expected to value the history of libraries, others working in interdisciplinary fields have come to recognize the significance of exploiting to the full the collected memory of society and its subgroups. For example, those associated with the American Studies movement in the United States and around the world have discovered that archival collections and libraries not only hold the keys to basic research in their broadly conceived discipline, but that the histories of the institutions themselves provide valuable clues to the quality of the communities and societies that have supported these institutions. The ability to access the manuscript and printed archive of a culture is an essential foundation for solid scholarship.

While one purpose of this guide, then, is to meet the research needs of cultural, social, and intellectual historians and American Studies specialists, a second goal is to meet the information needs of practicing librarians. The library and information science community must serve and instruct its clientele in an increasingly complex and rapidly changing environment. The value of a continual dialogue on the philosophical and social origins of librarianship should be apparent to professional librarians as well as to historians. The historical literature, as an essential resource for that dialogue, holds forth the potential for revision and clarification of the ethics and philosophies that underlie daily practice. Pierce Butler's claim, that librarians without a "clear historical consciousness" are "quite certain at times" to serve their communities "badly," remains as compelling today as when he published those words in his classic, *An Introduction to Library Science* (University of Chicago Press, 1933).

The culture of librarianship also includes library and information science educators, trustees and political supporters, publishers, association officers, consultants, and a number of others who produce and consume library and information services—all of whom may find in this compilation a source of interpretations that lend continuity, direction, or special meaning to current practice. Thus, with these various scholarly and professional groups in mind, we compiled this bibliographical guide.

The present volume, a revised and expanded version of *American Library History: A Bibliography* (University of Texas Press, 1978), represents work conducted over a period of more than two decades. It is intended as a comprehensive bibliographic record of historical publications issued through 1986 about libraries and closely related subjects in the United States. Readers interested in publications appearing after 1986 may consult *Libraries & Culture* for biennial bibliographic essays that serve as supplements to the present volume.

Our attempt at compiling a thorough bibliographic record has not resulted in a definitive list of works *about* libraries. An effort of that magnitude would produce a multivolume work identifying tens of thousands of descriptive items. Rather, we have sought to identify publications written *consciously* as history, a criterion retained from the earlier version. This seemingly elusive standard has, we believe, proven effective in assembling a comprehensive bibliography of more than 7,150 entries to which researchers and practitioners could turn for the most authoritative historical writing and the essential biographical sources. Thus, for example, annual or periodic reports from individual libraries or library agencies do not appear. We included a number of publications, particularly in our chapter on biography, that are somewhat brief. Brevity of presentation did not preclude entry. Therefore, some of the publications mentioned in our entries offer only the barest of historical details, yet they have in common an effort by their authors to establish a meaningful chronology and to inculcate in librarianship a vigorous historical consciousness. These authors met our historical criteria by presenting essential facts about past people, places, events, institutions, and ideas. Not a few, however, included interpretive frameworks and conclusions as well.

Various types of material appear in the body of this work. In addition to monographs and journal articles, entire issues of serial publications, chapters of monographs and collected works, short commemorative pieces, and various forms of unpublished research receive attention. Abbreviations for journals and reference works cited five times or more appear following this preface. In addition to dissertations and master's theses, the present bibliography also includes less formal master's and research papers accessible primarily, though not exclusively, at schools of library and information science. Such material has proven valuable by focusing on otherwise little known people and institutions and by providing a depth of initial detail. When a substantial portion or a comprehensive summary of a dissertation or thesis has appeared in print, we excluded the original work in order to limit replication of citations. Duplication of entries (less than one percent) occurred only when we determined that the breadth of subject matter necessitated an added entry. Parenthetically, we regret the loss to ongoing basic library research due to the demise of sustained research assignments at the master's level in schools of library and information science.

The sources drawn upon for this compilation constitute the major reference and bibliographic sources in American librarianship. They include Cannons's *Bibliography of Library Economy, Dictionary Catalog* of the Columbia University School of Library Service, *Dictionary of American Library Biography, Encyclopedia of Library and Information Science, Libraries in American Periodicals Before 1876* by Barr, McMullen, and Leach, *Library & Information Science Abstracts,* and *Library Literature.* We also consulted prepublication drafts of Wayne Wiegand's bibliographic essays and Arthur P. Young's *American Library History: A Bibliography of Dissertations and Theses;* we gratefully acknowledge the cooperation of Wiegand and Young in this enterprise.

General reference sources also proved useful, especially *America: History and Life, Biography Index, Current Biography, Dictionary of American Biography, Humanities Index,* and *Reader's Guide to Periodical Literature,* as well as the *Bibliographies of New England History* and *Writings on American History.* We searched these sources either manually or online. As we anticipated, the general reference sources often led us to other, more specialized sources. (For example, entries in the *Encyclopedia of Library and Information Science* frequently included bibliographies of books, articles, or unpublished sources; we followed the pattern of moving from general to more specialized references many times over.)

As the title suggests, *American Library History: A Comprehensive Guide to the Literature* is not complete but, rather, *comprehensive.* Although we systematically examined numerous library science sources and general reference sources, other, more specialized works were not consulted. For example, users interested in biographical references to librarians and library benefactors may wish to consult, in addition to our Chapter 15, "Biographies of Librarians and Library Benefactors," any of several recent scholarly reference sources, such as *Dictionary of American Religious Biography* (1977), *Biographical Dictionary of American Educators* (1978), *Biographical Dictionary of American Science* (1979), *Dictionary of American Negro Biography* (1982), and the new series just initiated, *Encyclopedia of American Business History and Biography*.

The present volume represents a special effort to recognize the historically significant role of women in American librarianship. Consequently, we consulted reference sources such as *Notable American Women* and *Women in American History: A Bibliography*, publications that identified useful contributions. However, in our search for materials about women in librarianship, we were most richly rewarded by Kathleen Heim's and Kathleen Weibel's landmark anthology, *The Role of Women in Librarianship, 1876–1976: The Entry, Advancement, and Struggle for Equalization in One Profession*. This collected work includes a lengthy annotated bibliography, serving as an excellent beginning point for further research. The results of our efforts appear in Chapter 14, "Women in Librarianship," a new feature of this compilation.

Similarly, we sought to ensure that blacks would not be underrepresented as they have been in some reference works in the past. Thus, we turned to the *Index to Periodical Articles by and about Blacks* and its bibliographical predecessors. Likewise, we consulted the book catalogs of major black research institutions, including those of the Moorland Collection of Negro Life and History at Howard University, the Negro Collection of the Fisk University Library, and the Schomburg Collection of Negro Literature and History of the New York Public Library. Additional standard sources consulted include Monroe N. Work's classic, *Bibliography of the Negro in Africa and America*, and the recent compilation, *In Black and White: A Guide to Magazine Articles, Newspaper Articles, and Books Concerning More than 15,000 Black Individuals and Groups*. We discuss the roles of blacks and black collections in American librarianship in the bibliographic essays that introduce Chapter 2, "General Studies" and Chapter 15, "Biographies."

The *archival enterprise* in American library history is another area we felt warranted bibliographic treatment. Chapter 10 represents an effort to identify important sources in the history and development of archives and archival collections. We were fortunate to persuade Professor Frederick J. Stielow (of Catholic University of America, Washington, D.C.) to contribute this chapter to the bibliography. Stielow has emerged as an authority on oral history archives and is widely respected as a consultant in the field of archives and records management. To assist him, he chose an accomplished archival historian, James Gregory Bradsher. Stielow and Bradsher add substantially to an understanding of the difficulties inherent in defining terms such as "library," "archives," and related concepts.

Another significant change from *American Library History: A Bibliography* is the deletion from Chapter 3 of entries relating to the book trade. This related and vast field deserves more thorough treatment than the present work can provide. Scholars who work more closely with the literature of the history of the book and of publishing have begun to fill this gap in bibliographic access. We mention some of the standard sources that serve as beginning points for these related subjects in the bibliographic essay that introduces Chapter 3, "Private Libraries and Reading Tastes."

The arrangement of the expanded second edition replicates that of the earlier version except for the aforementioned alterations. We regard the classified approach as an effective device for locating information about types of libraries or about libraries in particular states. Categories such as private libraries, public libraries, academic libraries, special libraries, and others remain as widely accepted terms in contemporary practice. The use of such categories also indicates a historical significance, and their meanings have, occasionally, changed over time. We underscore those changes, as well as complementary coverage in other chapters, in our introductory bibliographic essays which draw freely from the earlier work. The challenge of identifying "classic" studies from among recent literature proved to be an intriguing but quite difficult task.

In an effort to facilitate use of the present volume as a truly historical bibliography, we have arranged chapter entries chronologically by year of publication (although alphabetically by author within each year). This device should assist readers to follow the historical development of a topic and to identify periods when a particular issue came in or out of favor as a matter of historical interest. The boundaries of the chronological divisions, where they appear, coincide generally with pivotal years or periods in American library history—the establishment of organized American librarianship, the first issue of *Library Journal*, the birth of the American Library Association, and the appearance of the U.S. Bureau of Education's massive report on libraries (1876); the impact of World War I on the expanded role of American libraries and the bureaucratization of the American Library Association (1919–1920); the reordering of American librarianship and library education, with its new master's degree programs following World War II (1949–1950); and another reorientation of the American library profession, exemplified in the rejuvenation of the Library History Round Table and new accreditation standards for professional schools (1971–1972). We have employed these benchmarks in the lengthier chapters.

Three indexes further enhance access to entries: (1) the author index identifies the individual or group responsible for each contribution; (2) the institution index locates entries about particular institutions such as libraries, library schools, associations, government bureaus, and other groups; and (3) the index to the bibliographic essays serves as a comprehensive alphabetical index to the authors, titles, and subjects mentioned in the introductory narratives that begin each chapter.

Without the help of many people, this project would not have been completed. Marilyn Redmond created the database format and entered many of the citations, as did Tammy Weiner, Vivian Carlson, William Bishop, and Neva Smith. Judith Briden, who gave of herself to the project unselfishly for eighteen months, provided general editorial oversight and assistance in the final preparation in addition to data entry responsibilities. David Smith, the computer programming consultant, helped throughout the project but especially in the final bringing of various parts and entries together. Without his and Judith's support, this work would still be in progress. Among others at the University of Texas at Austin who deserve thanks are Vice President and Graduate Dean William S. Livingston, who provided a research grant from the University Research Institute to assist in data entry tasks at a critical stage, and Dean Ronald E. Wyllys of the Graduate School of Library and Information Science, who enabled this project to begin with the granting of the John P. Commons Teaching Fellowship for 1986–1987 and provided subsequent support to see the work through to fruition.

At Purdue University, the president and trustees provided a sabbatical leave that facilitated the early gathering of hundreds of bibliographic entries. Diane Griffin and Barbara W. Tucker assisted in examining biographical reference sources, and Barbara Tucker contributed in a major way to the development and arrangement of index entries. James K. Bracken made valuable suggestions about organization and arrangement of bibliographical citations, and Kenneth Potts assisted with proofreading. Patrick Canganelli offered essential programming assistance, and Ruth Rothenberg and the staff of Purdue's Interlibrary Loan Office demonstrated courtesy and helpfulness beyond the call of duty. At ABC-CLIO, John Graham of the production staff was most helpful in the latter stages of production. Heather Cameron, Vice President at ABC-CLIO, supported the work enthusiastically from the beginning and provided encouragement at crucial times.

Our spouses, who released us from normal pursuits and helped in many other ways, deserve our gratitude; should we attempt another work of similar scope, we shall value their counsel. Notwithstanding our debt to those mentioned above and others, the errors and imperfections in this compilation remain our own responsibility.

Donald G. Davis, Jr.
John Mark Tucker

Spring 1989

Abbreviations of Frequently Cited Reference Works

ALAWE2	ALA World Encyclopedia of Library and Information Services, Second Edition
DAB	Dictionary of American Biography
DALB	Dictionary of American Library Biography
ELIS	Encyclopedia of Library and Information Science
HBLib	Handbook of Black Librarianship
HT	Handbook of Texas
HTL	Handbook of Texas Libraries
LAAL	Leaders in American Academic Librarianship, 1925–1975
NAW	Notable American Women, 1607–1950

Abbreviations of Frequently Cited Journals

AAr	American Archivist
ABBW	AB Bookman's Weekly
AdLib	Advances in Librarianship
AHR	American Historical Review
AJE	American Journal of Education (Barnard)
AL	American Literature
ALAO	Advances in Library Administration and Organization
ALib	American Libraries
AQ	American Quarterly
ArkL	Arkansas Libraries
BALA	Bulletin of the American Library Association
BASIS	Bulletin of the American Society for Information Science
BB	Bulletin of Bibliography
BC	Book Collector
BCCQNL	Book Club of California Quarterly News Letter
BKM	Bookmark (New York)
BMLA	Bulletin of the Medical Library Association
BNYPL	Bulletin of the New York Public Library
CalL	California Librarian
CB	Current Biography
CHSQ	California Historical Society Quarterly
CLB	California Library Bulletin
CLC	Columbia Library Columns
CLW	Catholic Library World
ConnM	Connecticut Magazine
CRL	College and Research Libraries
DCL	D.C. Libraries
DCLB	Dartmouth College Library Bulletin
DLAB	Delaware Library Association Bulletin

DLQ	Drexel Library Quarterly
GL	Georgia Librarian
GPR	Government Publications Review
GranM	Granite Monthly
HB	Horn Book
HCEI	Historical Collections of the Essex Institute
HLAJ	Hawaiian Library Association Journal
HLB	Harvard Library Bulletin
HLN	Harvard Library Notes
HMPEC	Historical Magazine of the Protestant Episcopal Church
IllL	Illinois Libraries
IMH	Indiana Magazine of History
JASIS	Journal of the American Society for Information Science
JEL	Journal of Education for Librarianship
JELIS	Journal of Education for Library and Information Science
JISHS	Journal of the Illinois State Historical Society
JLH	Journal of Library History
KLAB	Kentucky Library Association Bulletin
LC	Library Chronicle
LCT	Library Chronicle of the University of Texas
LHQ	Louisiana Historical Quarterly
LHR	Library History Review
LibR	Library Review
LibT	Library Trends
LJ	Library Journal
LLAB	Louisiana Library Association Bulletin
LLJ	Law Library Journal
LQ	Library Quarterly
LRTS	Library Resources & Technical Services
LW	Library World
MAQR	Michigan Alumnus Quarterly Review
MAr	Midwestern Archivist
MHM	Maryland Historical Magazine
MHR	Missouri Historical Review
MinnL	Minnesota Libraries
MLAN	Music Library Association Notes
MoreB	More Books
NCHR	North Carolina Historical Review
NCL	North Carolina Libraries
NEM	New England Magazine
NLGPC	Norton's Literary Gazette and Publishers' Circular
NNCL	News Notes of California Libraries
NNT	News Notes (Bulletin of the Texas Library Association)
OLAB	Ohio Library Association Bulletin
PAAS	Proceedings of the American Antiquarian Society
PAPS	Proceedings of the American Philosophical Society
PBSA	Papers of the Bibliographical Society of America

PCSM	Publications of the Colonial Society of Massachusetts
PL	Public Libraries (1896-1925)
PLN	Pennsylvania Library Notes
PMHB	Pennsylvania Magazine of History and Biography
PMHS	Proceedings of the Massachusetts Historical Society
PNLAQ	PNLA Quarterly
PW	Publishers Weekly
QJLC	Quarterly Journal of the Library of Congress
RCHS	Records of the Columbia Historical Society of Washington, D.C.
SchLJ	School Library Journal
SCHM	South Carolina Historical Magazine
SEL	Southeastern Librarian
SerL	Serials Librarian
SHQ	Southwestern Historical Quarterly
SL	Special Libraries
SLAGMDB	Special Libraries Association Geography Map Division
THQ	Tennessee Historical Quarterly
TL	Texas Libraries
TLJ	Texas Library Journal
TN	Top of the News
VMHB	Virginia Magazine of History and Biography
WisLB	Wisconsin Library Bulletin
WLB	Wilson Library Bulletin
WMH	Wisconsin Magazine of History
WMQ	William and Mary Quarterly
WPHM	Western Pennsylvania Historical Magazine
YULG	Yale University Library Gazette

American Library History

1.

Historiography and Sources

Publications devoted to the writing of library history in the United States date from the 1950s but did not begin to appear with regularity until the latter stages of the 1970s. Articles on the "value of library history" have been produced by Jesse H. Shera (1952, **1.12**), Haynes McMullen (1952, **1.11**), Raymond Irwin (1958, **1.17**), Louis Shores (1961, **1.26**), and John C. Colson (1969, **1.44**) and collectively constitute a genre in their own right.

More traditional contributions reviewing and evaluating the literature stem from classic essays by Felix Reichmann ("Historical Research and Library Science," 1964, **1.29**) and Sidney L. Jackson ("Materials for Teaching Library History in the U.S.A.," 1972, **1.76**). These were followed by two fine articles on public library historiography by Sidney Ditzion and Francis Miksa, respectively (1973, **1.82**; 1982, **1.139**); overviews of the literature encompassing academic, public, and private libraries as well as key individuals and landmark publications by Shera (1973, **1.87**) and Colson (1976, **1.100**); general analyses of recent scholarship by David Kaser (1978, **1.121**) and Lee Shiflett (1984, **1.145**); and a statistical and analytical study of the historical monograph from 1975 to 1985 by Laurel A. Grotzinger (1986, **1.155**). Thematic and methodological issues came under the scrutiny of Michael H. Harris (1975, **1.97**; 1976, **1.105**; 1986, **1.157**), Elaine Fain (1979, **1.128**), Wayne A. Wiegand (1983, **1.143**), and Robert V. Williams (1984, **1.147**). Interpretive concerns, in particular, dominated the writings of Harris, an avowed revisionist, and were featured with rejoinders in two issues of the *Journal of Library History* (vol. 10, no. 2 [1975]; vol. 13, no. 1 [1978]). Harris's interpretations are discussed below and, later, in Chapter 5, "Public Libraries." Fain compared library history with the history of education (engaging some of the issues raised by Harris); Wiegand proposed the use of psychohistorical methods that have been applied to both popular and scholarly biography for the past three decades; and Williams analyzed theoretical constructs that may be applied to historical perspectives on library growth and development.

The literature of library history depends heavily on papers presented at formal programs, conferences that often reap the benefits of cross-fertilization involving not only librarians and the library history community but also scholars from the fields of intellectual and cultural history and the history of books and printing. The resulting interdisciplinary dialogue has become increasingly influential at the Library History Seminars, seven of which were conducted between 1961 and 1985.

Other meetings contributed substantially to a discussion of historiographical issues. For example, the Conference on Historical and Bibliographical Methods in Library Research, held in 1970 at the University of Illinois, featured papers by Haynes McMullen on primary source materials in library research (1971, **1.62**) and Edward G. Holley on textual criticism in library history (1971, **1.60**). The American Library Association's (ALA) American Library History Round Table meeting of 1977 included papers by Holley on historiography and questions of evidence (1977, **1.113**); Harris, who examined the interpretive approaches of library historians (1978, **1.119**); and Phyllis Dain, who responded to Harris, deriving observations from her research into the history of the New York Public Library (1978, **1.116**). The 1978 meeting of the Association of American Library Schools's Research Interest Group featured McMullen on matters of writing style and interpretation (1978, **1.123**) with responses by Betty Milum (1978, **1.124**), Joe W. Kraus (1978, **1.122**), and Donald C. Dickinson (1978, **1.118**). Library History Seminar VI opened with Neil Harris's observations on the historiography of cultural institutions and the theme of modernization (1981, **1.134**) and David W. Davies's comparison of mass culture with the culture of those devoted to intellectual pursuits (1981, **1.133**). Robert V. Williams examined variables for analysis used by public library historians (1981, **1.135**). At the 1980 meeting of the Association of College and Research Libraries Rare Books and Manuscripts Section, Paul Raabe urged librarians to research the related areas of library history and the history of the book (1984, **1.144**). The 1984 ALA Library History Round Table meeting featured presentations by Francis Miksa (1985, **1.149**), W. Boyd Rayward (1985, **1.150**), and H. Curtis Wright (1985, **1.151**) on historical relationships between librarianship and information science, while Library History Seminar VII resulted in essays by John P. Feather (1986, **1.154**) and David D. Hall (1986, **1.156**), who, to some extent echoing Paul Raabe, underscored book history as essential to an understanding of social and cultural history.

Only occasionally are publications in library historiography issued as monographs. They include the work of James G. Ollé, whose *Library History: An Examination Guidebook* (2d ed., 1971, **1.63**) was intended primarily for students but whose *Library History* (1979, **1.129**) stands as a state-of-the-art critique. Ollé aims for a British audience but includes a number of examples from the United States.

Among the most useful publications, both for their evaluative comments and suggestions for further research, are bibliographic essays reviewing recent books and articles. Michael H. Harris wrote the first of these in 1968 in the *Journal of Library History*, recounting the historical output for the previous year. He continued the series, typically on a biennial basis, working with Donald G. Davis, Jr. as co-author. The Harris-Davis articles ceased in the mid-1970s, after which they were produced by Wayne A. Wiegand, who continues to publish them in *Libraries & Culture*. Bibliographic essays treating specialized topics include those by Nathaniel Stewart on college library history (1943, **1.8**), Harry Bach on scholarly libraries (1959, **1.19**), Donald E. Oehlerts on the history of American library architecture (1976, **1.109**), and David S. Zubatsky on the history of American colleges and their libraries in the seventeenth and eighteenth centuries (1979, **1.131**).

Due to their nature as reference works, guides to the published writings and manuscript sources on library history are much less abundant than are essays on historiography. Still, their value to the profession is widely recognized, they have appeared with some consistency in the past decade, and they have emerged as essential sources for ongoing research. Perhaps the most significant work in recent years is the *Dictionary of American Library Biography* (*DALB*), edited by Bohdan S. Wynar, assited by George Bobinski and Jesse Shera (1978, **1.125**). This collection of biographical sketches of 302 deceased librarians, library educators, association officers, publishers, and benefactors provides critical essays, bibliographies of writings by and about the subjects, and the location of major primary source material for each individual. The *DALB* offers a wealth of historical information and serves as an admirable model for other professions and disciplines. Wayne A. Wiegand edited the *DALB* supplement, scheduled for publication by Libraries Unlimited in 1989. Additional sources of retrospective biographical articles and of historical perspectives on a wide range of topics are the two editions of the *ALA World Encyclopedia of Library and Information Services* (1980; 2d ed., 1986, **1.159**).

Library historians and the library community in general appreciate the practical and scholarly value of solid bibliographical sources. *American Library History: A Bibliography*, identifying more than 3,000 articles, books, theses, and dissertations, compiled by Michael H. Harris and Donald G. Davis, Jr., quickly became a first source to consult before embarking on a research project (1978, **1.120**). *Libraries & Culture* publishes Wiegand's biennial bibliographical essays as well as numerous articles on sources and methodology. Its predecessor, the *Journal of Library History*, sponsored a series of bibliographies on state library history, fourteen of which have appeared to date, while a more recent book-length publication, Aubrey E. Skinner's *Texas Library History: A Bibliography* (1983, **1.142**), serves as a model for future publications in this genre. *Libraries in American Periodicals before 1876: A Bibliography with Abstracts and an Index*, compiled by Larry J. Barr, Haynes McMullen, and Steven G. Leach, resulted from tedious spadework among thousands of periodicals scattered throughout research libraries and deserves the accolade of "classic" (1983, **1.141**). This book identifies more than 1,400 abstracted or annotated entries; it is as useful to students, researchers, and historians as H. G. T. Cannons's *Bibliography of Library Economy, 1876 to 1920* (1927, **1.4**) was to previous generations and, much later, *Cannons' Bibliography of Library Economy, 1876–1920: An Author Index with Citations,* compiled by Anne Harwell Jordan and Melbourne Jordan (1976, **1.106**).

Michael H. Harris's *Guide to Research in American Library History* (1968; 2d ed., 1974, **1.93**) consists of an annotated bibliography of theses and dissertations and introductory essays on the state of the art in library historiography and on philosophical and methodological issues in historical research. Arthur P. Young's *American Library History: A Bibliography of Dissertations and Theses* (Metuchen, N.J.: Scarecrow Press, 1988) capably supersedes the Harris guide. Young differs from Harris in excluding the introductory essays, but his work demonstrates a major effort in identifying nearly 1,200 theses, dissertations, and unpublished research papers and reports.

The library historian has long suffered from an absence of sources that identify and describe manuscript collections, a circumstance partially remedied by the appearance of *The National Catalog of Sources for the History of Librarianship,* a list of archive collections described on three sheets of microfiche with an introductory essay by Marion Casey on the use of primary materials in historical research (1982, **1.137**). Publication of the *National Catalog* grew naturally from the experiences of Maynard Brichford and the staff of the University of Illinois Archives which, in 1973, acquired and began making accessible the extensive archival records of the American Library Association. Brichford and Anne Gilliland describe the ALA record groups and how scholars may obtain access to them in *Guide to the American Library Association Archives* (2d ed., Chicago: American Library Association, 1987), a micropublication revised from the first edition issued in 1979 (**1.127**). Finally, Doris Cruger Dale has compiled a list of more than 200 oral history interviews in *A Directory of Oral History Tapes of Librarians in the United States and Canada* (1986, **1.153**), while Richard J. Cox and Anne S. K. Turkos presented compelling arguments favoring the establishment of public library archives (1986, **1.152**).

1876–1919

1.1 Texas Library Association. *Handbook of Texas Libraries*, edited by the Secretary. Austin: [Texas Library Association], 1904.

1.2 Texas Library Association. *Handbook of Texas Libraries*, No. 2, edited by J. B. Ideson. Houston: [Texas Library Association], 1908.

1.3 Texas Library Association. *Handbook of Texas Libraries*, No. 3, edited by the Publicity Committee, Texas Library Association. [Austin: A.C. Baldwin and Sons, 1915–1916].

1920–1949

1.4 Cannons, H. G. T. *Bibliography of Library Economy . . . 1876–1920*. Chicago: American Library Association, 1927.

1.5 Ideson, J. B. "Texas Libraries: Bibliography." *HTL* 4 (1935): 147–51.

1.6 Texas Library Association. *Handbook of Texas Libraries*, No. 4, edited by J. B. Ideson. Houston: [Texas Library Association], 1935.

1.7 Sills, R. M. "The 'Trumbull Manuscript Collections' and Early Connecticut Libraries." In *Papers in Honor of Andrew Keogh, Librarian of Yale University*, edited by M. C. Withington. New Haven, Conn.: Privately printed, 1938. Pp. 325–42.

1.8 Stewart, N. "Sources for the Study of American College Library History, 1800–1876." *LQ* 13 (1943): 227–31.

1.9 Butler, P. "The Intellectual Content of Librarianship." *LQ* 15 (1945): 349–50.

1.10 Pearlove, S. *A Guide to Manuscript Materials Relating to the History of the Library of Congress*. Washington, D.C.: Government Printing Office, 1949.

1950–1971

1.11 McMullen, H. "Why Read and Write Library History." *WLB* 26 (1952): 385–86.

1.12 Shera, J. H. "On the Value of Library History." *LQ* 22 (1952): 240–51.

1.13 Webb, W. P., Carroll, H. B., and Brenda, E. S., eds. *Handbook of Texas*, 3 vols. Austin: Texas State Historical Association, 1952–1976.

1.14 Bronson, B. *Bibliographical Guides to the History of American Libraries*. Urbana: University of Illinois Graduate School of Library Science, Occasional Paper no. 32, 1953.

1.15 McMullen, H. "Research in Backgrounds of Librarianship." *LibT* 6 (1957): 110–19.

1.16 Wagner, M. K. "Music Librarianship in the United States, 1876–1955: An Annotated, Classified Bibliography." Master's thesis, Catholic University of America, 1957.

1.17 Irwin, R. "Does Library History Matter?" *LibR* 128 (1958): 510–13.

1.18 Vleeschauwer, H. J. "Library History in Library Science." *Mousaion* no. 29 (1958): 4–34; no.30 (1959): 35–87.

1.19 Bach, H. *Bibliographical Essay on the History of Scholarly Libraries in the United States, 1800 to the Present*. Urbana: University of Illinois Graduate School of Library Science, Occasional Paper no. 54, 1959.

1.20 Beck, E. R. "Critiques of Representative Library Histories." In *In Pursuit of Library History*, edited by J. D. Marshall. Tallahassee: Florida State University Library School, 1961. Pp. 8–18.

1.21 Mead, C. D. "Popular Education and Cultural Agencies." In *Research Opportunities in American Cultural History*, edited by J. F. McDermott. Lexington: University of Kentucky Press, 1961. Pp. 155–67.

1.22 Mishoff, W. O. "Academic and School Library History." In *In Pursuit of Library History*, edited by J. D. Marshall. Tallahassee: Florida State University School of Library Science, 1961. Pp. 23–32.

1.23 Mishoff, W. O. "Sources for Library History." In *In Pursuit of Library History*, edited by J.D. Marshall. Tallahassee: Florida State University Library School, 1961. Pp. 33–42.

1.24 Rush, N. O. "Biographical Sources for Library History." In *In Pursuit of Library History*, edited by J. D. Marshall. Tallahassee: Florida State University Library School, 1961. Pp. 43–50.

1.25 Sessa, F. B. "Public Library History." In *In Pursuit of Library History*, edited by J. D. Marshall. Tallahassee: Florida State University School of Library Science, 1961. Pp. 19–22.

1.26 Shores, L. "The Importance of Library History." In *American Library History Reader*, edited by J. D. Marshall. Hamden, Conn.: Shoe String Press, 1961. Pp. 3–7.

1.27 Shores, L. "The Importance of Library History." In *In Pursuit of Library History*, edited by J. D. Marshall. Tallahassee: Florida State University Library School, 1961. Pp. 1–4.

1.28 Downs, R. B. "Resources for Research in Librarianship." *LibT* 13 (1964): 6–14.

1.29 Reichmann, F. "Historical Research and Library Science." *LibT* 13 (1964): 31–41.

1.30 McMullen, H. "How Should We Tell Librarians of the Future about Libraries of the Past?" *JEL* 6 (1965): 65–68.

1.31 Shera, J. H. "A Renaissance in Library History." *WLB* 40 (1965): 281.

1.32 Bartlett, R. A. "The State of the Library History Art." In *Approaches to Library History*, edited by J. D. Marshall. Tallahassee: JLH, 1966. Pp. 13–23.

1.33 Dixon, E. I. "The Implications of Oral History in Library History." *JLH* 1 (1966): 59–62.

1.34 McMullen, H. "Through History with Punch and Needle: Edge Notched Cards for Data on Early American Libraries." In *Approaches to Library History*, edited by J. D. Marshall. Tallahassee: JLH, 1966. Pp. 81–90.

1.35 Williams, R. V. "Document Sources for the History of Federal Government Libraries." In *Approaches to Library History*, edited by J. D. Marshall. Tallahassee: JLH, 1966. Pp. 61–80.

1.36 Woodford, F. B. "Second Thoughts on Writing Library History." *JLH* 1 (1966): 34–42.

1.37 Woods, B. M. "Library Association Archives and Library History." In *Approaches to Library History*, edited by J. D. Marshall. Tallahassee: JLH, 1966. Pp. 49–60.

1.38 Cutliffe, M. R. "The Value of Library History." *LibR* 21 (1967): 193–96.

1.39 Dixon, E. I. *Writing Your Library History*. Menlo Park, Calif.: Ritchie Press, 1967.

1.40 Harris, M. H. "Library History: A Critical Essay on the In-print Literature." *JLH* 2 (1967): 117–25.

1.41 Harris, M. H. *Fugitive Literature in Library Science: American Library History as a Test Case*. Albany: State University of New York, School of Library Science, 1968.

1.42 Harris, M. H. "The Year's Work in American Library History, 1967." *JLH* 3 (1968): 342–52.

1.43 Shores, L. "Place of Library History in Library Schools." *JLH* 3 (1968): 291–95.

1.44 Colson, J. C. "Speculations on the Uses of Library History." *JLH* 4 (1969): 65–71.

1.45 Shirley, S. "An Annotated Bibliography for Medical Librarianship, 1940–1968." *BMLA* 57 (1969): 391–98.

1.46 Shores, L. "The School Librarian as Historian." *School Libraries* 18 (1969): 9–15.

1.47 Stevens, N. D. "A Plea for the Librarian as Collector." *JLH* 4 (1969): 173–75.

1.48 Thompson, D. E. "A History of Library Architecture: A Bibliographic Essay." *JLH* 4 (1969): 133–41.

1.49 Zachert, M. J. "Personal Records as Historical Sources." *JLH* 4 (1969): 337–40.

1.50 Bergquist, C. C. "A Bibliography of Florida Library History." *JLH* 5 (1970): 48–65.

1.51 Brichford, M. J. "Original Source Materials for the History of Librarianship." *JLH* 5 (1970): 177–81.

1.52 Harris, M. H. "Pennsylvania Library History: A Bibliography." *Pennsylvania Library Association Bulletin* 25 (1970): 19–28.

1.53 Harris, M. H. "The Year's Work in American Library History, 1968." *JLH* 5 (1970): 133–45.

1.54 Kittelson, D. "A Bibliography of Hawaii Library History." *JLH* 5 (1970): 341–55.

1.55 Murdock, J. L. "Church Libraries: A Bibliography on Sources of Information from 1876 through 1969." *CLW* 41 (1970): 377–79, 466–71.

1.56 Zachert, M. J. "Oral History Interviews." *JLH* 5 (1970): 80–87.

1.57 Carpenter, R., Bruce, B., and Oliver, M. "A Bibliography of North Carolina Library History." *JLH* 6 (1971): 212–64.

1.58 Gillespie, D., and Harris, M. H. "A Bibliography of Virginia Library History." *JLH* 6 (1971): 72–90.

1.59 Hagler, R. "Needed Research in Library History." In *Research Methods in Librarianship: Historical and Bibliographical Methods in Library Research,* edited by R. E. Stevens. Urbana: University of Illinois Graduate School of Library Science, 1971. Pp. 128–38.

1.60 Holley, E. G. "Textual Criticism in Library History." In *Research Methods in Librarianship: Historical and Bibliographical Methods in Library Research,* edited by R. E. Stevens. Urbana: University of Illinois Graduate School of Library Science, 1971. Pp. 95–105.

1.61 Lopez, M. D. "Bibliography of the History of Libraries in New York State." *JLH* Supplemental issue, Fall (1971): 1–140.

1.62 McMullen, H. "Primary Sources in Library Research." In *Research Methods in Librarianship: Historical and Bibliographical Methods in Library Research,* edited by R. E. Stevens. Urbana: University of Illinois Graduate School of Library Science, 1971. Pp. 23–41.

1.63 Ollé, J. G. *Library History: An Examination Guidebook,* 2d ed. London: Clive Bingley, 1971.

1.64 Stevens, R. E., ed. *Research Methods in Librarianship: Historical and Bibliographical Methods in Library Research.* Urbana: University of Illinois Graduate School of Library Science, 1971.

1972–1986

1.65 Agriesti, P. A. "A Bibliography of Ohio Library History." *JLH* 7 (1972): 157–88.

1.66 Coleman, G. P. "Documenting Librarianship via Oral History." In *Library History Seminar No. 4, Proceedings, 1971,* edited by H. Goldstein and J. Goudeau. Tallahassee: Florida State University School of Library Science, 1972. Pp. 30–32.

1.67 Coleman, G. P. "Making Library History." *JLH* 7 (1972): 130–40.

1.68 Conmy, P. T. "CLA's Library History Chapter: Why History?" *CalL* 33 (1972): 205–09.

1.69 Correll, L. "American Theatre Libraries: Sources of Information." *JLH* 7 (1972): 197–207.

1.70 Drazan, J. "Alaskan Libraries in Print, 1905–1971." *JLH* 7 (1972): 50–60.

1.71 Goldhor, H. *An Introduction to Scientific Research in Librarianship.* Urbana: University of Illinois Graduate School of Library Science, 1972.

1.72 Goodwin, J. "A Preliminary Survey of Materials Available for the Study of American Library History in Washington, D.C." In *Library History Seminar No. 4, Proceedings, 1971,* edited by H. Goldstein and J. Goudeau. Tallahassee: Florida State University School of Library Science, 1972. Pp. 23–29.

1.73 Harris, M. H. "County Probate Records as a Source of American Library History." In *Library History Seminar No. 4, Proceedings, 1971,* edited by H. Goldstein and J. Goudeau. Tallahassee: Florida State University School of Library Science, 1972. Pp. 140–49.

1.74 Harris, M. H. "Two Years' Work in American Library History, 1969–70." *JLH* 7 (1972): 33–49.

1.75 Hart, M. L. "A Bibliography of Connecticut Library History." *JLH* 7 (1972): 251–74.

1.76 Jackson, S. L. "Materials for Teaching Library History in the U.S.A." *JEL* 12 (1972): 178–92.

1.77 Menan, N. V. "Library History Resources in New York City." In *Library History Seminar No. 4, Proceedings, 1971,* edited by H. Goldstein and J. Goudeau. Tallahassee: Florida State University School of Library Science, 1972. Pp. 12–22.

1.78 Winger, H. W., and Miksa, F. L. "Historical Records of the American Library Association." In *Library History Seminar No. 4, Proceedings, 1971,* edited by H. Goldstein and J. Goudeau. Tallahassee: Florida State University School of Library Science, 1972. Pp. 1–11.

1.79 Zachert, M. J. "Sources: A 'Modern' Letter, by Sally Huckaby." *JLH* 7 (1972): 189–91.

1.80 Andrews, F. E. "A Handguide to Writing Your Library's History—The Time Is Now." *WLB* 48 (1973): 324–28.

1.81 Blazek, R. "The State of Historical Research; or Please Save the Bloody Beast." *JLH* 8 (1973): 50–51.

1.82 Ditzion, S. H. "The Research and Writing of American Library History." In *Toward a Theory of Librarianship: Papers in Honor of Jesse Hauk Shera,* edited by C. Rawski. Metuchen, N.J.: Scarecrow Press, 1973. Pp. 55–69.

1.83 Halsell, W. D. "A Bibliography of Mississippi Library History." *JLH* Supplemental issue, Fall (1973): 27–50.

1.84 Harris, M. H. "American Librarians as Authors: A Bibliography of Bibliographies." *BB* 30 (1973): 143–46.

1.85 Harris, M. H. "Historians Assess the Impact of Print on the Course of American History: The Revolution as a Test Case." *LibT* 22 (1973): 127–47.

1.86 Keller, J. D. "A Bibliography of Minnesota Library History." *JLH* Supplemental issue, Fall (1973): 51–85.

1.87 Shera, J. H. "The Literature of American Library History." In *Knowing Books and Men, Knowing Computers, Too.* Littleton, Colo.: Libraries Unlimited, 1973. Pp. 124–61.

1.88 Shores, L. "The Library and Society." *JLH* 8 (1973): 143–49.

1.89 Wilkins, B. "A Bibliography of South Carolina Library History." *JLH* Supplemental issue, Fall (1973): 1–25.

1.90 Yates, B. "The Joseph L. Wheeler Papers." *JLH* 8 (1973): 96–98.

1.91 Davis, D. G., and Harris, M. H. "Three Years' Work in American Library History, 1971–1973." *JLH* 9 (1974): 296–317.

1.92 Gormley, D. M. "A Bibliographic Essay on Western Library Architecture to the Mid-Twentieth Century." *JLH* 9 (1974): 4–24.

1.93 Harris, M. H. *A Guide to Research in American Library History,* 2d ed. Metuchen, N.J.: Scarecrow Press, 1974.

1.94 Schlachter, G. A., and Thomison, D. *Library Science Dissertations, 1925–1972.* Littleton, Colo.: Libraries Unlimited, 1974.

1.95 "Bibliography: Women in Librarianship, 1920–1973." In *Women in Librarianship: Melvil's Rib Symposium,* edited by M. Myers and M. Scarborough. New Brunswick: Rutgers University Graduate School of Library Service, Bureau of Library and Information Science Research, 1975. Pp. 91–112.

1.96 Fain, E. "Manners and Morals in the Public Library: A Glance at Some New History." *JLH* 10 (1975): 99–105.

1.97 Harris, M. H. "Externalist or Internalist Frameworks for the Interpretation of American Library History—The Continuing Debate." *JLH* 10 (1975): 106–10.

1.98 Heaney, H. J. "Bibliographical Scholarship in the United States, 1949–1974: A Review." *CRL* 36 (1975): 493–510.

1.99 Krzys, R. "Library Historiography." *ELIS* 15 (1975): 294–330.

1.100 Colson, J. C. "The Writing of American Library History, 1876–1976." *LibT* 25 (1976): 7–22.

1.101 Cummings, C. S., comp. *A Biographical-Bibliographical Directory of Women Librarians.* Madison: University of Wisconsin-Madison Library School Women's Group, 1976.

1.102 Dale, D. C. *Bibliography of Illinois Library History,* State Library History Bibliography Series no. 14. Tallahasee: JLH, 1976.

1.103 Davis, D. G., and Harris, M. H. "Two Years' Work in American Library History: 1974–1975." *JLH* 11 (1976): 276–96.

1.104 Ellsworth, D. J., and Stevens, N. D. *Landmarks of Library Literature, 1876–1976.* Metuchen, N.J.: Scarecrow Press, 1976.

1.105 Harris, M. H. "'The Priest Who Slew the Slayer and Shall Himself be Slain': Revisionism in American Library History." *JEL* 16 (1976): 229–31.

1.106 Jordan, A. H., and Jordan, M. *"Cannons' Bibliography of Library Economy, 1876–1920:" An Author Index with Citations.* Metuchen, N.J.: Scarecrow Press, 1976.

1.107 Kunkle, H. J. *Bibliography of the History of Libraries in California.* Tallahassee: JLH, 1976.

1.108 Ladd, J. "Cornerstones and Landmarks in Ohio Library History." *OLAB* 46 (1976): 19–32.

1.109 Oehlerts, D. E. "Sources for the Study of American Library Architecture." *JLH* 11 (1976): 68–78.

1.110 Schwartz, P. J. "A Bibliography of Wisconsin Library History." *JLH* 11 (1976): 87–166.

1.111 Brichford, M. J. "Current Status of the American Library Association Archives: A Preliminary Report." *JLH* 12 (1977): 64–69.

1.112 "The Early History of Reference Service through 1920." In *Reference Service: An Annotated Bibliographic Guide,* compiled by M. E. Murfin and L. R. Wynar. Littleton, Colo.: Libraries Unlimited, 1977. Pp. 13–22.

1.113 Holley, E. G. "The Past as Prologue: The Work of the Library Historian." *JLH* 12 (1977): 110–27.

1.114 Starr, L. M. "Oral History." *ELIS* 20 (1977): 440–63.

1.115 Brichford, M. J. "ALA Archives." *ALA Yearbook* 3 (1978): 30–31.

1.116 Dain, P. "A Response to Issues Raised by the ALHRT Program, 'The Nature and Uses of Library History.' " *JLH* 13 (1978): 44–47.

1.117 Davis, D. G. "The Year's Work in American Library History—1976." *JLH* 13 (1978): 187–203.

1.118 Dickinson, D. C. "[The State of the Art of Writing Library History] Comment." *JLH* 13 (1978): 448–50.

1.119 Harris, M. H. "Antiquarianism, Professional Piety, and Critical Scholarship in Recent American Library Historiography." *JLH* 13 (1978): 37–43.

1.120 Harris, M. H., and Davis, D. G. *American Library History: A Bibliography.* Austin: University of Texas Press, 1978.

1.121 Kaser, D. "Advances in American Library History." *AdLib* 8 (1978): 181–99.

1.122 Kraus, J. W. "[The State of the Art of Writing Library History] Comment." *JLH* 13 (1978): 445–47.

1.123 McMullen, H. "The State of the Art of Writing Library History." *JLH* 13 (1978): 432–40.

1.124 Milum, B. L. "[The State of the Art of Writing Library History] Comment." *JLH* 13 (1978): 441–44.

1.125 Wynar, B. S., ed. *Dictionary of American Library Biography*. Littleton, Colo.: Libraries Unlimited, 1978.

1.126 "Bibliography [On the Role of Women in Librarianship]." In *The Role of Women in Librarianship 1876–1976: The Entry, Advancement, and Struggle for Equalization in One Profession,* edited by K. Weibel, K. M. Heim, and D. J. Ellsworth. Phoenix, Ariz.: Oryx Press, 1979. Pp. 295–441.

1.127 Brichford, M. J., comp. *Guide to the American Library Association Archives,* microfiche. Chicago: American Library Association, 1979.

1.128 Fain, E. "The Library and American Education." *LibT* 27 (1979): 327–52.

1.129 Ollé, J. G. *Library History*. London and New York: K.G. Saur, 1979.

1.130 Winckler, P. A. *History of Books and Printing: A Guide to Information Sources*. Detroit: Gale Research Press, 1979.

1.131 Zubatsky, D. S. *The History of American Colleges and Their Libraries in the Seventeenth and Eighteenth Centuries: A Bibliographical Essay*. Urbana: University of Illinois Graduate School of Library Science, Occasional Paper no. 140, 1979.

1.132 Hudson, P. L. "Library Development in Tennessee before the Civil War." *Tennessee Librarian* 32 (1980): 31–39.

1.133 Davies, D. W. "Libraries and the Two Cultures." *JLH* 16 (1981): 16–27.

1.134 Harris, N. "Cultural Institutions and American Modernization." *JLH* 16 (1981): 28–47.

1.135 Williams, R. V. "The Public Library as the Dependent Variable: Historically Oriented Theories and Hypotheses of Public Library Development." *JLH* 16 (1981): 329–41.

1.136 Brichford, M. J., comp. *National Catalog of Sources for the History of Librarian-*

ship, microfiche. Chicago: American Library Association, 1982.

1.137 Casey, M. "On the Use of Primary Sources in Writing Library History." In *National Catalog of Sources for the History of Librarianship,* compiled by M. Brichford. Chicago: American Library Association, 1982. Pp. 3–7.

1.138 Gambee, B. L. "Selected Books on Library History in the 1970's." *Bookmark [North Carolina]* 51 & 52 (1982): 113–27.

1.139 Miksa, F. L. "The Interpretation of American Public Library History." In *Public Librarianship: A Reader,* edited by J. Robbins-Carter. Littleton, Colo.: Libraries Unlimited, 1982. Pp. 73–90.

1.140 Wiegand, W. A. "The Literature of American Library History, 1979–1980." *JLH* 17 (1982): 292–327.

1.141 Barr, L. J., McMullen, H., and Leach, S. G., eds. *Libraries in American Periodicals before 1876: A Bibliography with Abstracts and an Index*. Jefferson, N.C.: McFarland, 1983.

1.142 Skinner, A. E., ed. *Texas Library History: A Bibliography*. Phoenix, Ariz.: Oryx Press, 1983.

1.143 Wiegand, W. A. "Psychohistory: A New Frontier for Library Historians?" *JLH* 18 (1983): 464–72.

1.144 Raabe, P. "Library History and the History of Books: Two Fields of Research for Librarians." *JLH* 19 (1984): 282–97.

1.145 Shiflett, O. L. "Clio's Claim: The Role of Historical Research in Library and Information Science." *LibT* 32 (1984): 385–406.

1.146 Wiegand, W. A. "The Literature of American Library History, 1981–1982." *JLH* 19 (1984): 390–425.

1.147 Williams, R. V. "Theoretical Issues and Constructs Underlying the Study of Library Development." *Libri* 34 (1984): 1–16.

1.148 Hayes, R. M. "The History of Library and Information Science: A Commentary." *JLH* 20 (1985): 173–78.

1.149 Miksa, F. L. "Machlup's Categories of Knowledge as a Framework for Viewing Library and Information Science History." *JLH* 20 (1985): 157–72.

1.150 Rayward, W. B. "Library and Information Science: An Historical Perspective." *JLH* 20 (1985): 120–36.

1.151 Wright, H. C. "Shera as a Bridge Between Librarianship and Information Science." *JLH* 20 (1985): 137–56.

1.152 Cox, R. J., and Turkos, A. S. K. "Establishing Public Library Archives." *JLH* 21 (1986): 574–84.

1.153 Dale, D. C., comp. *A Directory of Oral History Tapes of Librarians in the United States and Canada.* Chicago: American Library Association, 1986.

1.154 Feather, J. P. "The Book in History and the History of the Book." *JLH* 21 (1986): 12–26.

1.155 Grotzinger, L. A. "Ten Years Work in Library History: The Monograph from 1975 to 1985." *Library Science Annual* 2 (1986): 56–69.

1.156 Hall, D. D. "The History of the Book: New Questions? New Answers?" In *Libraries, Books & Culture: Proceedings of Library History Seminar VII, 6–8 March 1985, Chapel Hill, North Carolina,* edited by D. G. Davis. Austin: Graduate School of Library and Information Science, University of Texas at Austin, 1986. Pp. 27–38.

1.157 Harris, M. H. "State, Class and Cultural Reproduction: Toward a Theory of Library Service in the United States." *AdLib* 14 (1986): 211–52.

1.158 Kraus, J. W. "The History of Publishing as a Field of Research for Librarians and Others." *ALAO* 5 (1986): 33–65.

1.159 Wedgeworth, R., ed. *ALA World Encyclopedia of Library and Information Services,* 2d ed. Chicago: American Library Association, 1986.

2.

General Studies

Library historiography could benefit substantially from a much broader range of interpretive monographs of both a generalized and specialized nature, although a number of general surveys have appeared that encompass the American experience but are not limited to it. Among the earliest of these is Albert Predeek's *A History of Libraries in Great Britain and North America* (1947, **2.39**). More than twenty-five years later, Elmer D. Johnson published the fourth edition of *Communication: An Introduction to the History of Writing, Printing, Books, and Libraries* (1973, **2.162**), while his *History of Libraries in the Western World* (2d ed., 1970, **2.134**) combined with Sidney L. Jackson's *Libraries and Librarianship in the West: A Brief History* (1974, **2.173**) to form a thorough general introduction. Johnson's *History of Libraries* was revised with Michael H. Harris in 1976 and, again, by Harris alone eight years later (1984, **2.333**). Meanwhile, the distilled wisdom of James Thompson appeared in *A History of the Principles of Librarianship* (1977, **2.240e**) which has a British orientation but includes a number of references to American developments especially in the closing observations.

Since systematic surveys of U. S. library history remain scarce, several editors have attempted to fill the gap with collected works, largely successful efforts that appeared, for the most part, in the 1960s and 1970s. Three excellent collections are those by John David Marshall (*An American Library History Reader*, 1961, **2.86**), Thelma Eaton (*Contributions to American Library History*, 1964, **2.93**), and Michael H. Harris (*Reader in American Library History*, 1971, **2.144**). More recent collections were timed to coincide with the American Library Association centennial: Sidney L. Jackson's *A Century of Service: Librarianship in the United States and Canada* with Eleanor B. Herling and E. J. Josey (1976, **2.209**) and Howard Winger's *American Library History, 1876–1976* (1976, **2.224**), published as the July 1976 issue of *Library Trends* and as a separate anthology. The most important collected works issued since 1976 have been the proceedings of the Library History Seminars edited by Harold Goldstein (*Milestones to the Present*, 1978, **2.252**) and Donald G.

15

Davis, Jr. (*Libraries & Culture*, 1981, **2.299**; *Libraries, Books, & Culture*, 1986, **2.358**).

Another response to the lack of monographic surveys has been the production of scholarly essays and book chapters that treat general library historical issues. Roger Michener regards the library as an intellectual institution and urged that it be viewed through the lens of intellectual history (1978, **2.257**); John Y. Cole surveyed libraries and the uses of knowledge for the period from 1860 to 1920 (1979, **2.264**); Mark Midbon scrutinized the relationship between library development and capitalism (1980, **2.284**); Cole examined the scholarly traditions of librarians and publishers (1981, **2.297**); Michael F. Winter sought to place librarianship within sociological frameworks (1983, **2.326**); A. Robert Rogers and Kathryn McChesney included three essays (libraries as social agencies, philosophies of librarianship, and libraries and library education history) in their solid introductory text, *The Library in Society* (1984, **2.337**); George S. Bobinski interpreted the history of libraries for the years 1945 to 1970, a period he described as a "Golden Age" (1984, **2.329**); while Rosalee McReynolds contrasted the librarian's image in popular literature with the librarian's image in professional literature produced in the late nineteenth and early twentieth centuries (1985, **2.350**).

Survey histories comprise a small body of literature produced in the 1980s; the major contributions include David Kaser's definitive study, *A Book for a Sixpence: The Circulating Library in America* (1980, **4.350**; listed in Chapter 4, "Predecessors of the Public Library"); Stephen Karetzky's perceptive *Reading Research and Librarianship: A History and Analysis* (1982, **2.310**); Kathleen Molz's well-written, *National Planning for Library Service, 1935–1975* (1984, **2.335**); and Kaser's carefully researched *Books and Libraries in Camp and Battle: The Civil War Experience* (1984, **3.399**; listed in Chapter 3, "Private Libraries and Reading Tastes"). Finally, Paul Dickson's *The Library in America: A Celebration in Words and Pictures* (1986, **2.360**), emphasizing public libraries, offers an impressive photographic record. Scholarly monographs on selected issues, particular periods, or individual institutions are considerably more plentiful than the general surveys; the former have a stronger historiographic tradition, have appeared consistently throughout the past decade and, being more specialized, are cited in other chapters as well as being mentioned in the introductory essays.

Of special use to students are three chronologies, well-designed sources of practical ready-reference value: Josephine M. Smith's *A Chronology of Librarianship* (1968, **2.117**); Elizabeth W. Stone's *American Library Development, 1600–1899* (1977, **2.239**), revised and expanded from an earlier work published in 1967; and a list of significant events in black American librarianship compiled by Casper LeRoy Jordan and E. J. Josey (1977, **2.230**).

Statistically based studies have found a place in librarianship, thus reflecting their popularity in social history generally. Charles Coffin Jewett compiled the earliest major work, *Notices of Public Libraries in the United States of America* (1851, **2.2**). Various older statistical compilations, including Jewett's, came under scrutiny in recent studies such as Elmer D. Johnson's "Southern Public Libraries in the 1850s: Correcting an Error" (1969, **2.122**),

Frank Schick's "Library Statistics: A Century Plus" (1971, **2.148**), Haynes McMullen's "The Prevalence of Libraries in the United States before 1876: Some Regional Differences" (1972, **2.155**), and Kenneth G. Peterson's "Library Statistics and Libraries of the Southeast before 1876" (1972, **2.158**). In a similar vein, J. Periam Danton made effective use of statistical compilations in his comprehensive review essay on the *Dictionary of American Library Biography* (1978, **2.249**); Wayne A. Wiegand studied American Library Association (ALA) leaders from 1876 to 1917 alone and with Geri Greenway (1981, **12.364**; 1981, **12.365**; both listed in Chapter 12, "Library Associations"); and Haynes McMullen and Larry J. Barr offered a descriptive analysis of statistics resulting from their bibliography on libraries in American periodicals (1986, **2.362**).

Some issues touch on many facets of librarianship but have not produced large enough bodies of historical literature to merit separate chapters. A few examples of recent scholarship are provided for each of the following subjects: censorship and intellectual freedom, copyright, services for the handicapped, information science, library architecture, library literature, library management, microform collections and services, preservation of library materials, and racial and minority issues.

Current historical assessments of intellectual freedom in libraries begin with David K. Berninghausen, who emerged in the 1970s as one of librarianship's most articulate spokesmen on behalf of the freedom to read, as his collection, *The Flight from Reason: Essays on Intellectual Freedom in the Academy, the Press, and the Library* (1975, **2.179**) clearly demonstrated. He and Judith Krug both published articles on the history of the Library Bill of Rights (Berninghausen, 1970, **2.130**; Krug, 1972, **2.153**); Chandler B. Grannis revised Anne Haight's authoritative historical bibliography, *Banned Books* (4th ed., 1978, **2.253**); and L. B. Woods examined censorship, primarily in school and public libraries, for the period 1966 to 1975 in a monograph (1979, **2.276**) and in several essays. In the 1980s various facets of the history of censorship were explored in articles by Kenneth L. Donelson (1981, **7.118**; listed and discussed in Chapter 7, "School Libraries"), Frederick J. Stielow (1983, **2.324**), and Lou Willett Stanek (1985, **2.354**); and Evelyn Geller published her thorough analysis, *Forbidden Books in American Public Libraries, 1876–1939* (1984, **2.332**), which made effective use of sociological research in addition to literary and historical backgrounds.

Issues pertaining to copyright continue to attract attention, due partially to the federal copyright revision law of 1976. Julius J. Marke (1977, **2.233**) and John J. Holland (1978, **2.254**) both provided brief histories of American copyright law soon after the revisions went into effect. Juri Stratford examined the portion of the 1976 revision that directly affected library photocopying practices (1984, **2.340**).

Library services to the handicapped were discussed in articles by Genevieve M. Casey (1971, **2.142**; 1978, **2.246**) and with some historical perspective by Gerald Bramley (1978, **2.245**). A Library of Congress publication, *That All May Read: Library Service for Blind and Physically Handicapped People* (1983, **2.319**), contains separate essays by Eunice Lovejoy on state and federal legislation and Irvin P. Schloss on the role of the Library of Congress in providing national leadership.

In the field of information science two fine essays by Jesse H. Shera and Donald B. Cleveland (1977, **2.237**) and Saul Herner (1984, **2.334**) should be considered in the context of papers presented at the 1984 ALA Library History Round Table program (discussed in Chapter 1, "Historiography and Sources").

Historians of library architecture rely on the authoritative writings of Donald E. Oehlerts (1975, **2.190**; 1978, **2.259**), Walter C. Allen (1976, **2.196**), and David Kaser (1984, **6.135**; 1986, **6.145**; listed in Chapter 6, "Academic Libraries") to place their analyses in the context of library collections and services. Sharon C. Bonk discussed the influence of architect Henry Hobson Richardson on small public library buildings from 1865 to 1890 (1978, **2.243**); Paul Kruty surveyed the designs of nineteen Iowa public libraries constructed by the Chicago firm of Patton and Miller from 1901 to 1909 (1983, **2.318**); while Leland M. Roth (1983, **2.323**) and Richard Guy Wilson (1983, **2.325**) both issued monographs on McKim, Mead, and White, the architectural firm that designed such major library buildings as the Boston Public Library, the Low Library at Columbia University, and the J. Pierpont Morgan Library in New York.

Various writers have delved into the literature of librarianship and offered cogent insights. Notable essays have been produced by Donald W. Krummel (1966, **2.101**), Guy R. Lyle (1967, **2.105**), Francis Miksa (1973, **2.164**), J. Periam Danton (1976, **2.199**), David Kaser (1976, **6.89**; listed in Chapter 6, "Academic Libraries"), Arthur P. Young (1977, **2.241**), and F. William Summers (1985, **2.355**).

Two recent essays dealt with the history of library management. Adrian Mole surveyed major issues in his study of the years from 1870 to 1950 (1980, **2.286**). Wayne A. Wiegand analyzed cataloging and standardization for the years from 1891 to 1901 (1984, **2.341**).

Microforms have become essential if unimposing fixtures in libraries and, consequently, are the subject of occasional historical overviews. Allen B. Veaner and Alan Meckler produced the major works, *Studies in Micropublishing, 1853–1976: Documentary Sources* (1976, **2.223**) and *Micropublishing: A History of Scholarly Micropublishing in America, 1938–1980* (1982, **2.312**), respectively; these books should be supplemented with essays by Veaner (1975, **2.194**), David S. Zubatsky and Donald W. Krummel (1983, **2.328**), Mark and Rhoda Yerbergh (1984, **2.343**), Jean W. Barrington (1985, **2.344**), and Clifton Dale Foster (1985, **10.144**; listed in Chapter 10, "Archival Enterprise").

An issue closely related to microforms, the need to preserve library materials, attracted considerable attention in the 1980s. Brief overviews have been written by Pamela W. Darling and Sherelyn Ogden on the 1956 to 1980 period (1981, **2.298**) and by Rutherford D. Rogers (1985, **2.353**).

The broad outlines of library programs for blacks and the racial integration of library services are treated in essays published in the *Encyclopedia of Library and Information Science* by Joseph H. Reason (1975, **2.191**) and Doris H. Clack (1979, **2.262**). Specialized studies include two that are listed in Chapter 6, "Academic Libraries": Herman L. Tottens's essay on the Wiley College Library, the first library for blacks west of the Mississippi River (1969, **6.680**), and Jessie Carney Smith's comprehensive *Black Academic Libraries and Research Collections: An Historical Survey,* which begins with a chapter on the "Historical Perspective of the Black College" and includes a table, "Black Academic Libraries Founded Prior to 1900" (1977, **6.102**).

The *Handbook of Black Librarianship,* edited by E. J. Josey and Ann Allen Shockley (1977, **2.231**), begins with the Jordan-Josey chronology mentioned earlier. The *Handbook* includes Lucy B. Campbell's essay on the history of the Hampton Institute Library School which identifies a number of important graduates (1977, **11.139**; listed in Chapter 11, "Education for Librarianship"), various historical articles on black library associations (listed separately in Chapter 12, "Library Associations"), and biographical entries for key black librarians (listed separately in Chapter 15, "Biographies"). Four doctoral dissertations merit special mention, beginning with Lelia G. Rhodes's "A Critical Analysis of the Career Backgrounds of Selected Black Female Librarians" (1975, **2.192**), an examination of fifteen individuals including Augusta Baker, Clara Stanton Jones, Virginia Lacy Jones, Annette Phinazee, and Jessie Carney Smith. Elinor D. Sinnette produced a solid study of Arthur Schomburg and his work with black collections at Fisk University and the New York Public Library, among other topics, and Maxine M. Merriman analyzed Augusta Baker's storytelling style (1977, **15.1574**; and 1983, **15.64**; both listed in Chapter 15, "Biographies of Individual Librarians and Library Benefactors"), while Arthur C. Gunn wrote a brief analysis of the closing of the Hampton Institute Library School and the subsequent establishment of the Atlanta University Library School (1986, **11.205**; listed in Chapter 11, "Education for Librarianship"). In the 1980s Sandra Roff examined services to blacks in Brooklyn, New York in the nineteenth century (1981, **2.307**), and Rosemary R. DuMont discussed the education of black librarians in the twentieth century (1986, **11.203**; listed in Chapter 11, "Education for Librarianship"). DuMont's more comprehensive "Race in American Librarianship: Attitudes of the Library Profession" on the integration of southern public library facilities, appeared the same year (1986, **2.361**).

Finally, most monographs on the major urban public libraries that were published since the 1960s refer to services to blacks, other minorities, and the disadvantaged; and blacks are represented in studies of library education in the South. The most poignant work on blacks in American library history remains E. J. Josey's *The Black Librarian in America* (1970, **2.135**), a collection of autobiographical essays, each of which is cited separately in Chapter 15, "Biographies of Individual Librarians and Library Benefactors."

Before 1876

2.1 Bradford, G. "[Extract of a Lecture by Daniel Webster and 1793 Statistics of American Libraries]." *North American Miscellany and Dollar Magazine* 2 (19 July 1851): 575.

2.2 Jewett, C. C. *Notices of Public Libraries in the United States of America*. Washington, D.C.: Printed for the House of Representatives, 1851.

2.3 Rhees, W. J. *Manual of Public Libraries, Institutions, and Societies in the United States and British Provinces of North America*. Philadelphia: J.B. Lippincott, 1859.

1876–1919

2.4 Sumner, J. S. "Theological Libraries in the United States." In *Public Libraries in the United States of America: Their History, Condition and Management; Special Report, Part I*, U.S. Bureau of Education. Washington, D.C.: Government Printing Office, 1876. Pp. 127–60.

2.5 U. S. Bureau of Education. *Public Libraries in the United States of America: Their History, Condition and Management; Special Report, Part I*, U.S. Bureau of Education. Washington, D.C.: Government Printing Office, 1876.

2.6 Scudder, S. H. *The Entomological Libraries of the United States*. Cambridge, Mass.: University Press, J. Wilson and Sons, 1880.

2.7 Fletcher, W. I. "The Great Libraries of the United States." *Book Buyer* 11 (1894): 343–46.

2.8 Dana, J. C. "Library Movement in the Far West." *The Library* 8 (1896): 446–50.

2.9 "Outline of the Modern Library Movement in America with Most Important Foreign Events." *LJ* 26 (1901): 73–75.

2.10 Meyer, A. B. *Amerikanische Bibliotheken und Ihre Bestrebungen*. Berlin: R. Friedlander & Sohn, 1906.

2.11 Sharp, K. "Illinois Libraries [Part I, General Statement]." *University Studies [University of Illinois]* 2, no. 1 (1906): 1–84.

2.12 Wallace, A. "The Library Movement in the South Since 1899." *LJ* 32 (1907): 253–58.

2.13 [Pearson, E.L.] *The Old Librarian's Almanac* .... Woodstock, Vt.: Elm Tree Press, 1909.

2.14 Bolton, C. K. *American Library History*. Chicago: American Library Association, 1911.

2.15 "Library Progress since 1908." *HTL* 3 (1915–1916): 11–16.

2.16 Ferguson, M. J. "California Libraries: A Short Review and a Look Ahead." *NNCL* 13 (1918): 1–5.

1920–1949

2.17 Wilson, L. R. "Library Development in North Carolina." *LJ* 48 (1923): 21–26.

2.18 *Pacific Northwest Libraries: History of Their Early Development in Washington, Oregon, and British Columbia*. Seattle: University of Washington Press, 1926.

2.19 Beddie, J. S. "Libraries in the Twentieth Century." Doctoral dissertation, Harvard University, 1928.

2.20 Borden, A. K. "Sociological Beginnings of the Library Movement." *LQ* 1 (1931): 278–82.

2.21 Tripp, G. H. *New Bedford Libraries—Then and Now*. New Bedford, Mass.: N.p., 1934.

2.22 Connerly, D. H. "Texas Library Legislation, 1909–1935." *HTL* 4 (1935): 31–34.

2.23 Godet, M. *Bibliothèques Américaines: Impressions et Réflexions*. Berne: N.p., 1935.

2.24 Goree, E. S. "The Field in Texas: A Review of Recent Activities and Principal Developments since the Publication of the Handbook of 1915." *HTL* 4 (1935): 39–47.

2.25 Barker, T. D. *Libraries of the South: A Report on Developments, 1930–1935*. Chicago: American Library Association, 1936.

2.26 Munn, R. "Library Objectives." *BALA* 30 (1936): 583–86.

2.27 Sharp, H. A. *Libraries and Librarianship in America: A British Commentary and Comparison.* London: Grafton and Co., 1936.

2.28 Columbia Civic Library Association, comp. *A Directory of Negro Graduates of Accredited Library Schools 1900–1936.* Washington, D.C.: Columbia Civic Library Association, 1937.

2.29 Curry, A. R. "W.P.A. Library Work in Texas." *NNT* 13 (October 1937): 3–4.

2.30 Oklahoma Library Commission. *Oklahoma Libraries 1900–1937.* Oklahoma City, Okla.: Oklahoma Library Commission, 1937.

2.31 Munthe, W. *American Librarianship from a European Angle: An Attempt at an Evaluation of Policies and Activities.* Chicago: American Library Association, 1939.

2.32 Barker, T. D. "Library Progress in the South, 1936–1942." *LQ* 12 (1942): 353–62.

2.33 Stanford, E. B. "Library Extension under the WPA: An Appraisal of an Early Experiment in Federal Aid." Doctoral dissertation, University of Chicago, 1942.

2.34 Beaver, F. E. "A Survey of Texas Libraries." Master's thesis, University of Texas, 1943.

2.35 Wilson, L. R. "The Role of the Library in the Southeast in Peace and War." *Journal of Social Forces* 21 (1943): 463–68.

2.36 Barker, T. D. "Libraries in the Southeastern States, 1942–1946." In *Twelfth Biennial Conference, Papers and Proceedings.* Asheville, N.C.: Southeastern Library Association, 1946. Pp. 13–29.

2.37 Sawyer, R. A. "Success Story: The Public Affairs Information Service, 1910–1945." *LJ* 71 (1946): 98–100.

2.38 Brian, L. G. *"Bulletin of Bibliography, 1897–1947." BB* 19 (1947): 57–58.

2.39 Predeek, A. *A History of Libraries in Great Britain and North America,* translated by L. Thompson. Chicago: American Library Association, 1947.

2.40 Hoffman, C. *Libraries in the United States, 1940–1947.* Chicago: American Library Association, 1948.

2.41 Pafford, J. H. *American and Canadian Libraries: Some Notes on a Visit in the Summer of 1947.* London: Library Association, 1949.

2.42 Rathbone, J. A. "Pioneers of the Library Profession." *WLB* 23 (1949): 775–79.

1950–1971

2.43 Bontemps, A. "Buried Treasures of Negro Art." *Negro Digest* 9 (December 1950): 17–21.

2.44 Lawler, J. *The H.W. Wilson Company: Half a Century of Bibliographic Publishing.* Minneapolis: University of Minnesota Press, 1950.

2.45 Rairigh, W. N. "Judicial Opinion Concerning Censorship of Library Materials, 1926–1950." Master's thesis, Drexel Institute of Technology, 1950.

2.46 Ranganathan, S. R. *Library Tour 1948, Europe and America: Impressions and Reflections.* Delhi: Indian Library Association, 1950.

2.47 Smith, S. L. Nashville: Tennessee Book Company, 1950.

2.48 Clopine, J. "A History of Library Unions in the United States." Master's thesis, Catholic University of America, 1951, ACRL Microcard no. 43.

2.49 Hankins, F. D. "The Treatment of Basic Problems in the *Library Journal,* 1900–1930." Master's thesis, University of Texas, 1951.

2.50 Hohman, A. C. "An Analysis of the Literature on the Outstanding Issues and Opinions on Censorship, 1940–1950." Master's thesis, Catholic University of America, 1951.

2.51 Landram, C. O. "A Study of the Changing Concept of American Librarians as Reflected in the Novels of the Twentieth Century." Master's thesis, Texas State College, 1951.

2.52 Peirce, P. "A Study of the Philosophy of Librarianship: A Review of the Relevant Literature, 1930–1950." Master's thesis, Drexel Institute of Technology, 1951.

2.53 Bennett, W. C. "The Library in Literature of Sociology." Master's thesis, University of Texas, 1952.

2.54 Fleming, E. M. "The *Publishers Weekly* and the Library Movement, 1882–1900." In *R.R. Bowker, Militant Liberal.* Norman: University of Oklahoma, 1952. Pp. 175–95.

2.55 Shores, L. "Library Cooperation in the Southwest [1939–52]." *LQ* 22 (1952): 335–41.

2.56 Danton, E. M., ed. *Pioneering Leaders in Librarianship.* Chicago: American Library Association, 1953.

2.57 Lacy, D. M. "War Measures: Past and Present." *LQ* 23 (1953): 238–51.

2.58 Wilson, E. C. "A Study of Articles on Librarianship in Non-Library Periodicals from 1947 through 1951." Master's thesis, Atlanta University, 1953.

2.59 Wyer, M. G. *Bibliographical Center for Research: Its Origin and Organization.* Denver: Bibliographical Center, 1953.

2.60 Collins, L. M. "Foundations for Standards in Librarianship, 1876–1886." *WLB* 29 (1954): 64–65, 70.

2.61 Hesseltine, W. B., and Gara, L. "Sherman Burns the Libraries." *SCHM* 55 (1954): 137–42.

2.62 Manley, M. C. "Personalities behind the Development of *PAIS*." *CRL* 15 (1954): 263–70, 276.

2.63 Nation, M. A. "The Librarian in the Short Story: An Analysis and Appraisal." Master's thesis, Florida State University, 1954, ACRL Microcard no. 52.

2.64 Smith, P. C. "The Tennessee Valley Authority and Its Influence in the Development of Regional Libraries in the South." Master's thesis, University of North Carolina, 1954.

2.65 Blackshear, E. C. "*Wisconsin Library Bulletin* Fifty Years Ago." *WisLB* 51 (1955): 3–6.

2.66 Blough, N. L. "Histories of Some Major Library Periodicals." Master's thesis, Western Reserve University, 1955.

2.67 Maddox, J. "A Hardy and Intelligent Perennial: The *Book Review Digest:* 1905–1955." *WLB* 29 (1955): 439–45.

2.68 "*Subscription Books Bulletin* Twenty-Fifth Anniversary." *Subscription Books Bulletin* 26 (1955): 1–2.

2.69 Conduitte, G. G. "The Changing Character of Southern Libraries." *LJ* 81 (1956): 1112–18.

2.70 "Libraries in Austin." *TLJ* 32 (1956): 20–24.

2.71 McCoy, R. E. "Banned in Boston: The Development of Literary Censorship in Massachusetts." Doctoral dissertation, University of Illinois, 1956.

2.72 Smith, G. W. "Northern Libraries and the Confederacy, 1861–1865." *Virginia Librarian* 3 (1956): 7–8.

2.73 Curry, W. L. "Comstockery: A Study in the Rise of Censorship with Attention Particularly to the Reports of the New York Society for the Suppression of Vice, to Magazine Articles and to News Items and Editorials in the *New York Times*, Supplementing Other Standard Studies on Comstock and Censorship." Doctoral dissertation, Columbia University, 1957.

2.74 Long, L. E. "The Stereotyped Librarian as Portrayed in Modern American Belles-Lettres." Master's thesis, Kent State University, 1957.

2.75 Giles, F. "Texas Librarians: A Study Based on *Who's Who in Library Service, Third*

Edition, 1955." Master's thesis, University of Texas, 1958, ACRL Microcard no. 113.

2.76 Kuehn, C. "Catholic Library Practice in the United States, 1930–1949: An Annotated and Classified Bibliography." Master's thesis, Catholic University of America, 1958.

2.77 Nelson, M. N. B. "Analysis of the *Texas Library Journal* and Its Predecessor, *News Notes.*" Master's thesis, University of Texas, 1958.

2.78 Wasserman, P. "Development of Administration in Library Service." *CRL* 19 (1958): 283–94.

2.79 Ducsay, W. J. "A Translation of the *History of Libraries in the United States of America* from the Milkau Collection." Master's thesis, Western Reserve University, 1959.

2.80 Fiske, M. *Book Selection and Censorship: A Study of School and Public Libraries in California.* Berkeley: University of California Press, 1959.

2.81 Thomson, R. D. "Utah—Its Libraries and Library Problems." *Utah Libraries* 3 (1959): 5–19.

2.82 Born, L. K. "History of Microform Activity." *LibT* 8 (1960): 348–58.

2.83 Schmidt, V. L. "The Development of Personnel Selection Procedures and Placement Services in the Professional Staffing of the Library, 1935–1959." Master's thesis, University of North Carolina, 1960, ACRL Microcard no. 128.

2.84 Williams, M. L. "History and Description of the Baltimore Archdiocesan Library Council." Master's thesis, Catholic University of America, 1960.

2.85 Graham, C. A. "Trends in Library Cooperation, 1921–1955: An Analysis Based on Library Literature." Master's thesis, University of Texas, 1961.

2.86 Marshall, J. D., comp. *An American Library History Reader: Contributions to Library Literature.* Hamden, Conn.: Shoe String Press, 1961.

2.87 Marshall, J. D., ed. *In Pursuit of Library History [Library History Seminar No. 1, Proceedings, 1961].* Tallahassee: Florida State University Library School, 1961.

2.88 Speiden, V. M. "The Image of the Librarian as Seen in Eight Library Career Novels." Master's thesis, University of North Carolina, 1961, ACRL Microcard no. 134.

2.89 Nixon, L. "Books for Farm People." In *After a Hundred Years,* U.S. Department of Agriculture Yearbook 1962. Washington, D.C.: Government Printing Office, 1962. Pp. 638–45.

2.90 Radtke, L. S. "Librarians Turn Publishers: A Study of the Shoe String Press." Master's thesis, Florida State University, 1962.

2.91 Jackson, C. S. "A History of Censorship Attempts in American Libraries during 1955–1960, Based on Cases Reported in the *New York Times* during This Period." Research Paper, Emory University, 1963.

2.92 Nitecki, J. Z. "The Concept of Public Interest in the Philosophy of Librarianship: The Implications of a Multiple Approach." Master's thesis, University of Chicago, 1963.

2.93 Eaton, T., ed. *Contributions to American Library History.* Champaign, Ill.: Illini Union Bookstore, 1964.

2.94 Eaton, T., ed. *Contributions to Mid-West Library History.* Champaign, Ill.: Illini Union Bookstore, 1964.

2.95 Fall, J. "*PAIS,* Fiftieth Anniversary." *LRTS* 9 (1965): 231–34.

2.96 Gardner, R. K. "*CHOICE: Books for College Libraries;* Its Origin, Development, and Future Plans." *SEL* 15 (1965): 69–75.

2.97 Line, B. W. "A Study of Incidents and Trends in the Censorship of Books Affecting Public and School Libraries in the United States 1954–1964." Master's thesis, Catholic University of America, 1965.

2.98 Wheeler, S. B. "Directory of Early Texas Librarians, 1853–1919." Master's thesis, University of Texas, 1965.

2.99 Wiederkehr, M. A. "Bibliography and Librarianship: An Historical Survey of Their Relationship." Master's thesis, University of North Carolina, 1965.

2.100 Harris, H. J. "A History of Joseph Ruzicka, Inc., Library Bookbinders, 1758–1966." Master's thesis, University of North Carolina, 1966.

2.101 Krummel, D. W. "The Library World of *Norton's Literary Gazette.*" In *Books in America's Past: Essays Honoring Rudolph H. Gjelsness,* edited by D. Kaser. Charlottesville: University Press of Virginia, 1966. Pp. 238–65.

2.102 Marshall, J. D., ed. *Approaches to Library History [Library History Seminar No. 2, Proceedings, 1965].* Tallahassee: JLH, 1966.

2.103 Newell, M. M. "The Development of Library Services to the Blind in the United States." Master's thesis, Southern Connecticut State College, 1966.

2.104 Allanson, V. L. "A Comparative and Historical Study of the *Wilson Library Bulletin.*" Master's thesis, Kent State University, 1967.

2.105 Lyle, G. R. "An Exploration into the Origins and Evolution of the Library Survey." In *Library Surveys,* edited by M. F. Tauber and I. R. Stephens. New York: Columbia University Press, 1967. Pp. 3–22.

2.106 Powell, L. C. *Bibliographers of the Golden State.* Berkeley: University of California School of Librarianship, 1967.

2.107 Rehfus, R. O., and Skearns, E. I. "The *Library Quarterly,* 1931–1966: An Index with Commentary." Master's thesis, Kent State University, 1967.

2.108 Blanchard, J. R. "Agricultural Libraries and Collections." *ELIS* 1 (1968): 126–34.

2.109 Boyer, P. S. *Purity in Print: The Vice Society Movement and Book Censorship in America.* New York: Charles Scribner's Sons, 1968.

2.110 Burns, R. K. "The White House National Advisory Commission on Libraries: A Background Report." *DCL* 39 (1968): 28–36.

2.111 Elliot, C. A. "The U.S. Bureau of Education: Its Role in Library History, 1876." In *Library History Seminar No. 3, Proceedings, 1968,* edited by M. J. Zachert. Tallahassee: JLH, 1968. Pp. 98–111.

2.112 Hansen, E. "History of Libraries." *Journal of Hospital Dental Practice* 11 (1968): 46–48.

2.113 Havlik, R. J. "The Library Services Branch of the U.S. Office of Education: Its Creation, Growth, and Transformation." In *Library History Seminar No. 3, Proceedings, 1968,* edited by M. J. Zachert. Tallahassee: JLH, 1968. Pp. 112–23.

2.114 Leary, W. M. "Books, Soldiers, and Censorship during the Second World War." *AQ* 20 (1968): 237–45.

2.115 Pettengill, G. E. "Architectural Libraries and Collections." *ELIS* 1 (1968): 464–69.

2.116 Smith, H. B. "The Development of Automation in the Library: 1936–1966." Research Paper, Long Island University, 1968.

2.117 Smith, J. M. *A Chronology of Librarianship.* Metuchen, N.J.: Scarecrow Press, 1968.

2.118 Zachert, M. J., ed. *Library History Seminar No. 3, Proceedings, 1968.* Tallahassee: JLH, 1968.

2.119 Berninghausen, D. K. "Bill of Rights, Library." *ELIS* 2 (1969): 458–64.

2.120 Downs, M. W. "The Emergence of a Philosophy of Librarianship in the United States." Research Paper, Long Island University, 1969.

2.121 Hayes, P. F. "Bibliographical Center for Research, Rocky Mountain Region, Inc." *ELIS* 2 (1969): 391–95.

2.122 Johnson, E. D. "Southern Public Libraries in the 1850s: Correcting an Error." *JLH* 4 (1969): 268–70.

2.123 Lippman, M. "Background and Organization of the *American Library Directory.*" Research Paper, Long Island University, 1969.

2.124 Malamud, S. "Reviews of the Newbery Award Winners 1955–1965: A Statistical Analysis." Research Paper, Long Island University, 1969.

2.125 Patterson, L. R. *Copyright in Historical Perspective.* Nashville: Vanderbilt University Press, 1969.

2.126 Pazar, C. H. "Judicial Decisions in Censorship Cases of the New York Court of Appeals, 1933–1967." Research Paper, Long Island University, 1969.

2.127 Wright, W. E. "A Regimental Library in the Confederate Army." *JLH* 4 (1969): 347–52.

2.128 Allanson, V. L. *Profile of a Library Magazine: Fifty Years of the Wilson Library Bulletin.* Kent, Ohio: Kent State University School of Library Science, 1970.

2.129 Anderson, F. "Carnegie Corporation of New York." *ELIS* 4 (1970): 200–207.

2.130 Berninghausen, D. K. "The Librarian's Commitment to the Library Bill of Rights." *LibT* 19 (1970): 19–38.

2.131 Berry, J. "Bowker, R.R., Company." *ELIS* 3 (1970): 133–48.

2.132 Butler, F. W. "Children's Libraries and Librarianship." *ELIS* 4 (1970): 559–66.

2.133 Doiron, P. M. "*Choice.*" *ELIS* 4 (1970): 658–59.

2.134 Johnson, E. D. *History of Libraries in the Western World*, 2d ed. Metuchen, N.J.: Scarecrow Press, 1970.

2.135 Josey, E. J. *The Black Librarian in America.* Metuchen, N.J.: Scarecrow Press, 1970.

2.136 Kilgour, F. G. "History of Library Computerization." *Journal of Library Automation* 3 (1970): 218–29.

2.137 Pennell, L. G. "Bookmobiles." *ELIS* 3 (1970): 1–57.

2.138 Schell, H. B. "Buildings, Library." *ELIS* 3 (1970): 441–71.

2.139 Swarthout, A. W. "The Church Library Movement in Historical Perspective." *DLQ* 6 (1970): 115–18.

2.140 Batchelder, M. L. "*Top of the News:* 25 Volumes." *TN* 27 (1971): 156–76.

2.141 Beagle, A. M. "Typewriters in Libraries: A Short History of Mechanization." *LJ* 96 (1971): 46–47.

2.142 Casey, G. M. "Library Service to the Handicapped and Institutionalized: An Historical Perspective." *LibT* 20 (1971): 350–66.

2.143 Clapp, V. W. "Council on Library Resources." *ELIS* 6 (1971): 219–27.

2.144 Harris, M. H., comp. *Reader in American Library History.* Washington, D.C.: NCR Microcard Editions, 1971.

2.145 Hertz, R. S. "Libraries and the Civil War." Master's thesis, University of Minnesota, 1971.

2.146 May, R. H. "Chronicle of Notable Library Facts and Events as Seen by *Library Journal*, 1895–1933." Research Paper, Kent State University, 1971.

2.147 Pendell, L. "Deaf, Library Service to the." *ELIS* 6 (1971): 444–67.

2.148 Schick, F. L. "Library Statistics: A Century Plus." *ALib* 2 (1971): 727–31.

2.149 Wooster, H. "Current Research and Development in Scientific Documentation." *ELIS* 6 (1971): 336–65.

1972–1986

2.150 Forman, S. "Education Libraries." *ELIS* 7 (1972): 409–14.

2.151 Goldstein, H., and Goudeau, J., eds. *Library History Seminar No. 4, Proceedings,*

1971. Tallahassee: Florida State University School of Library Science, 1972.

2.152 Kanner, E. E. "The Impact of Gerontological Concepts on Principles of Librarianship." Doctoral dissertation, University of Wisconsin, 1972.

2.153 Krug, J. "History of the Library Bill of Rights." *ALib* 3 (1972): 80–82, 183–84.

2.154 Lehnus, D. J. "*JEL,* 1969–1970: An Analytical Study." *JEL* 12 (1972): 71–83.

2.155 McMullen, H. "The Prevalence of Libraries in the United States Before 1876: Some Regional Differences." In *Library History Seminar No. 4, Proceedings, 1971,* edited by H. Goldstein and J. Goudeau. Tallahassee: Florida State University School of Library Science, 1972. Pp. 115–39.

2.156 Mayer, R. A. "Ford Foundation." *ELIS* 8 (1972): 592–600.

2.157 Perlman, M. "Economics Libraries and Collections." *ELIS* 7 (1972): 345–63.

2.158 Peterson, K. G. "Library Statistics and Libraries of the Southeast before 1876." *SEL* 22 (1972): 67–73.

2.159 West Virginia Library Commission. *History of Library Service in West Virginia.* Charleston, W.Va.: West Virginia Library Commission, 1972.

2.160 Bird, O. A., and Musial, T. J. "Great Books Programs." *ELIS* 10 (1973): 159–79.

2.161 Jackson, W.V. "Funding Library Endowments in the United States." *ELIS* 9 (1973): 138–86.

2.162 Johnson, E. D. *Communication: An Introduction to the History of Writing, Printing, Books and Libraries,* 4th ed. Metuchen, N.J.: Scarecrow Press, 1973.

2.163 Kaplan, L. "Library Cooperation in the United States." *International Review* 5 (1973): 139–45.

2.164 Miksa, F. L. "The Making of the 1876 Special Report on Public Libraries." *JLH* 8 (1973): 30–40.

2.165 Plotnik, A. "H.W. Wilson." *ELIS* 10 (1973): 250–72.

2.166 Roberts, C. "Quiet Heroes Dedicated to Preserving Black Culture." *Sepia* 22 (September 1973): 58–62.

2.167 Walch, D. B. "Toward Professionalization in the Media Field." Doctoral dissertation, University of Utah, 1973.

2.168 White, J. L. "Church Libraries." *ELIS* 9 (1973): 662–73.

2.169 Altick, R. D. *Librarianship and the Pursuit of Truth,* Second Annual Richard L. Shoemaker Lecture. New Brunswick: Rutgers University Graduate School of Library Service, 1974.

2.170 Chang, H. C. "Library Goals as Responses to Structural and Mileu Requirements: A Comparative Study." Doctoral dissertation, University of Minnesota, 1974.

2.171 Fulcino, S. A. "'The Right to Know' and the Library: A Case History in the Popularization of a Slogan." Master's thesis, University of Chicago, 1974.

2.172 Geller, E. "Intellectual Freedom: Eternal Principle or Unanticipated Consequence." *LJ* 99 (1974): 1364–67.

2.173 Jackson, S. L. *Libraries and Librarianship in the West: A Brief History.* New York: McGraw-Hill, 1974.

2.174 Johnson, E. *"Horn Book Magazine." ELIS* 11 (1974): 5–8.

2.175 Lazerow, S. "Institute for Scientific Information." *ELIS* 12 (1974): 89–97.

2.176 McMullen, H. "More Statistics of Libraries in the Southeast Before 1876." *SEL* 24 (1974): 18–29.

2.177 Moore, E. T. "The Intellectual Freedom Saga in California: The Experience of Four Decades." *CalL* 35 (1974): 48–57.

2.178 Oboler, E. M. *The Fear of the Word: Censorship and Sex.* Metuchen, N.J.: Scarecrow Press, 1974.

2.179 Berninghausen, D. K. *The Flight from Reason: Essays on Intellectual Freedom in the Academy, the Press, and the Library.* Chicago: American Library Association, 1975.

2.180 Case, R. N. "Knapp Foundation of North Carolina, Inc." *ELIS* 13 (1975): 436–43.

2.181 Casey, G. M., ed. "Federal Aid to Libraries: Its History, Impact, Future." *LibT* 24 (1975): 3–153.

2.182 Collison, R. "Public Affairs Information, 1915–1975." *IFLA Journal* 1 (1975): 198–209.

2.183 Detlefsen, E. G. "*Library Journal.*" *ELIS* 15 (1975): 334–36.

2.184 Fry, J. W. "LSA and LSCA, 1956–1973: A Legislative History." *LibT* 24 (1975): 7–26.

2.185 Gecas, J. G. "The Depository Library Act of 1962: A Legislative History and Survey of Implementation." Master's thesis, University of Chicago Graduate Library School, 1975.

2.186 Goldstein, H. "*Journal of Library History, Philosophy, and Comparative Librarianship.*" *ELIS* 13 (1975): 324–25.

2.187 Horrocks, N. "*Journal of Education for Librarianship.*" *ELIS* 13 (1975): 320–23.

2.188 Kraus, J. W. "Prologue to Library Cooperation." *LibT* 24 (1975): 169–82.

2.189 Lane, N. D. "Characteristics Related to Productivity among Doctoral Graduates in Librarianship." Doctoral dissertation, University of California, Berkeley, 1975.

2.190 Oehlerts, D. E. "The Development of American Public Library Architecture from 1850 to 1940." Doctoral dissertation, Indiana University, 1975.

2.191 Reason, J. H. "Library and Segregation." *ELIS* 16 (1975): 22–26.

2.192 Rhodes, L. G. "A Critical Analysis of the Career Backgrounds of Selected Black Female Librarians." Doctoral dissertation, Florida State University, 1975.

2.193 Stuart-Stubbs, B. "An Historical Look at Resource Sharing." *LibT* 23 (1975): 649–64.

2.194 Veaner, A. B. "Microfilm and the Library: A Retrospective." *DLQ* 11 (1975): 3–16.

2.195 Winger, H. W. "*Library Quarterly.*" *ELIS* 15 (1975): 390–96.

2.196 Allen, W. C. "Library Buildings." *LibT* 25 (1976): 89–112.

2.197 Beasley, K. E. "Librarians' Continued Efforts to Understand and Adapt to Community Politics." *LibT* 24 (1976): 569–81.

2.198 Coil, N. *American Librarianship, 1876–1976: An Attempt at Identifying Some Bench Marks Useful in Measuring Achievement, and a Selective Bibliography,* Third in the 1975–76 Faculty Lecture Series. Muncie, Ind.: Ball State University, 1976.

2.199 Danton, J. P. "The Library Press." *LibT* 25 (1976): 153–76.

2.200 Edgar, N. L. "Image of Librarianship in the Media." In *A Century of Service: Librarianship in the United States and Canada,* edited by S. L. Jackson, E. B. Herling, and E. J. Josey. Chicago: American Library Association, 1976. Pp. 303–20.

2.201 Evans, C. "A History of Community Analysis in American Librarianship." *LibT* 24 (1976): 441–58.

2.202 Geller, E. "The Librarian as Censor." *LJ* 101 (1976): 1255–58.

2.203 Harris, M. H. "Portrait in Paradox: Commitment and Ambivalence in American

Librarianship, 1876–1976." *Libri* 26 (1976): 311–31.

2.204 Hepworth, B. M. "Heritage." In *Utah Libraries: Heritage and Horizons.* N.p.: Utah Library Association, 1976. Pp. 1–86.

2.205 Holley, E. G. "Librarians, 1876–1976." *LibT* 25 (1976): 177–208.

2.206 Holley, E. G. "Who We Were: Profiles of the American Librarian at the Birth of the Professional Association, 1876." *ALib* 7 (1976): 323–26.

2.207 Irvine, S. L. "U.S. Library Unionism: An Historical Outline and an Analysis Employing Industrial Relations Models and Techniques." Master's thesis, University of Chicago, 1976.

2.208 Jackson, R. L. M. "Origin and Development of Selected Personnel Management Functions in the Field of American Librarianship, 1876–1969." Doctoral dissertation, Indiana University, 1976.

2.209 Jackson, S. L. "Research." In *A Century of Service: Librarianship in the United States and Canada,* edited by S. L. Jackson, E. B. Herling, and E. J. Josey. Chicago: American Library Association, 1976. Pp. 341–54.

2.210 Jackson, S. L., Herling, E. B., and Josey, E. J., eds. *A Century of Service: Librarianship in the United States and Canada.* Chicago: American Library Association, 1976.

2.211 Kaser, D., and Jackson, R. "A Century of Personnel Concerns in Libraries." In *A Century of Service: Librarianship in the United States and Canada,* edited by S. L. Jackson, E. B. Herling, and E. J. Josey. Chicago: American Library Association, 1976. Pp. 129–45.

2.212 Killian, K. A. "An Analysis of the Depiction of Libraries and Librarians in Novels Published Between 1965 and 1972." Master's thesis, Southern Connecticut State College, 1976.

2.213 McMullen, H. "The Distribution of Libraries throughout the United States." *LibT* 25 (1976): 23–53.

2.214 Metcalfe, J. *Information Retrieval: British and American, 1876–1976.* Metuchen, N.J.: Scarecrow Press, 1976.

2.215 Molz, R. K. *Federal Policy and Library Support.* Cambridge: M.I.T. Press, 1976.

2.216 Rogers, A. R. "Library Buildings." In *A Century of Service: Librarianship in the United States and Canada,* edited by S. L. Jackson, E. B. Herling, and E. J. Josey. Chicago: American Library Association, 1976. Pp. 221–42.

2.217 Rogers, J. W. "WPA Professional and Service Projects in Texas." Master's thesis, University of Texas, 1976.

2.218 Ruffe, B. L. "Dissemination of Information in the American Library, 1900–1925." Research Paper, Brigham Young University, 1976.

2.219 Schick, F. L. "Statistical Reporting of American Library Developments by the Federal Government." *LibT* 25 (1976): 81–88.

2.220 Serebnick, J. "The Relationship between Book Reviewing and the Inclusion of Controversial Books in Public Libraries." Doctoral dissertation, Rutgers University, 1976.

2.221 Shera, J. H. "Failure and Success: Assessing a Century." *LJ* 101 (1976): 281–87.

2.222 Texas Library Association. Bicentennial Committee. "Texas Public Library Firsts." *TLJ* 52 (1976): 55.

2.223 Veaner, A. B. *Studies in Micropublishing, 1853–1976: Documentary Sources.* Westport, Conn.: Microform Review, 1976.

2.224 Winger, H. W., ed. "American Library History, 1876–1976." *LibT* 25 (1976): 3–416.

2.225 American Library Association. *Libraries and the Life of the Mind in America: Addresses Delivered at the Centennial Celebration of the American Library Association.* Chicago: American Library Association, 1977.

2.226 Andrews, T. "Pharmaceutical Libraries and Literature." *ELIS* 22 (1977): 158–78.

2.227 Bartlett, L. E. "Censorship in the McCarthy Era." Master's thesis, University of Chicago, 1977.

2.228 Benemann, W. E. "Tears and Ivory Towers: California Libraries during the McCarthy Era." *ALib* 8 (1977): 305–09.

2.229 Glogoff, S. J. "Cannons' *Bibliography of Library Economy* and Its Role in the Development of Bibliographic Tools in Librarianship." *JLH* 12 (1977): 57–63.

2.230 Jordan, C. L., and Josey, E. J. "A Chronology of Events in Black Librarianship." *HBLib*: 1977 15–24.

2.231 Josey, E. J., and Shockley, A. A., eds. *Handbook of Black Librarianship*. Littleton, Colo.: Libraries Unlimited, 1977.

2.232 Manzer, B. M. *The Abstract Journal, 1790–1920: Origin, Development and Diffusion*. Metuchen, N.J.: Scarecrow Press, 1977.

2.233 Marke, J. J. "United States Copyright Revision and Its Legislative History." *LLJ* 70 (1977): 121–52.

2.234 Otness, H. M. "Baedeker's One-Star American Libraries." *JLH* 12 (1977): 222–34.

2.235 Peritz, B. C. "Research in Library Science as Reflected in the Core Journals of the Profession: A Quantitative Analysis (1950–1975)." Doctoral dissertation, University of California, Berkeley, 1977.

2.236 Rovelstad, M. V. "The Changing Dimensions of Library Science." *Libri* 27 (1977): 9–21.

2.237 Shera, J. H., and Cleveland, D. B. "History and Foundations of Information Science." *Annual Review of Information Science and Technology* 12 (1977): 249–75.

2.238 Starr, K. D. "Educational Philosophies of Early American Librarianship—The Causes for the Lack of Intellectualism." Research Paper, Brigham Young University, 1977.

2.239 Stone, E. W. *American Library Development, 1600–1899*. New York: H.W. Wilson, 1977.

2.240 Thompson, J. *A History of the Principles of Librarianship*. London: Clive Bingley; Hamden, Conn.: Linnet Books, 1977.

2.241 Young, A. P. "Reception of the 1876 Report on Public Libraries." *JLH* 12 (1977): 50–56.

2.242 Bartenbach, W. "Public Affairs Information Service (PAIS)." *ELIS* 24 (1978): 257–67.

2.243 Bonk, S. C. "Temples of Knowledge: A Study of H.H. Richardson and His Times and Small Public Library Architecture in Massachusetts, 1865–1890." In *Milestones to the Present: Papers from Library History Seminar V*, edited by H. Goldstein. Syracuse, N.Y.: Gaylord Professional Publications, 1978. Pp. 53–69.

2.244 Bradley, C. J. "The Genesis of American Music Librarianship, 1902–1942." Doctoral dissertation, Florida State University, 1978.

2.245 Bramley, G. London: Clive Bingley, 1978.

2.246 Casey, G. M. "Library Service to the Handicapped and Institutionalized: An Historical Perspective." *Information Reports and Bibliographies* 7, no. 2 (1978): 13–17.

2.247 Close, V. L. "Buildings and Books." *DCLB* 18 (1978): 55–61.

2.248 "Contemporary Black Librarians." *ALib* 9 (1978): 81–86.

2.249 Danton, J. P. " 'The Essence of Innumerable Biographies': A Review Essay on the *Dictionary of American Library Biography*." *JLH* 13 (1978): 451–63.

2.250 Edgar, N. L. "Library Periodical Literature: A Centennial Assessment." *SerL* 2 (1978): 341–50.

2.251 Goldstein, H. "Radio-TV and the Library." *ELIS* 25 (1978): 51–57.

2.252 Goldstein, H., ed. *Milestones to the Present: Papers from Library History Seminar V*. Syracuse, N.Y.: Gaylord Professional Publications, 1978.

2.253 Haight, A. L. *Banned Books, 387 B.C. to 1978 A.D,* 4th ed., updated and enlarged by C. B. Grannis. New York: R.R. Bowker, 1978.

2.254 Holland, J. J. "Brief History of American Copyright Law." In *The Copyright Dilemma: Proceedings of a Conference Held at Indiana University: April 14–15, 1977,* edited by H. S. White. Chicago: American Library Association, 1978. Pp. 3–18.

2.255 Holley, E. G. "Scholars, Gentle Ladies, and Entrepreneurs: American Library Leaders, 1876–1976." In *Milestones to the Present: Papers from Library History Seminar V,* edited by H. Goldstein. Syracuse, N.Y.: Gaylord Professional Publications, 1978. Pp. 80–108.

2.256 Lacy, D. M. "Liberty and Knowledge—Then and Now: 1776–1876–1976." In *Milestones to the Present: Papers from Library History Seminar V,* edited by H. Goldstein. Syracuse, N.Y.: Gaylord Professional Publications, 1978. Pp. 7–52.

2.257 Michener, R. "The Contemplation of the Library in America." In *Milestones to the Present: Papers from Library History Seminar V,* edited by H. Goldstein. Syracuse, N.Y.: Gaylord Professional Publications, 1978. Pp. 216–31.

2.258 O'Connor, M. A. "Dissemination and Use of Library Science Dissertations in the Periodicals Indexed in the *Social Sciences Citation Index.*" Doctoral dissertation, Florida State University, 1978.

2.259 Oehlerts, D. E. "American Library Architecture and the World's Columbian Exposition." In *Milestones to the Present: Papers from Library History Seminar V,* edited by H. Goldstein. Syracuse, N.Y.: Gaylord Professional Publications, 1978. Pp. 73–79.

2.260 Palmer, R. C. "Contributor Affiliation and Nature of Contribution Content in U.S. Journal Articles from the Fields of Law, Library Science, and Social Work, 1965–1974." Doctoral dissertation, University of Michigan, 1978.

2.261 Wright, L. B. "Libraries—Repositories of Wisdom: An Address Given upon the Dedication of the E.H. Little Library at Davidson College." *NCL* 35 (1978): 42–47.

2.262 Clack, D. H. "Segregation and the Library." *ELIS* 27 (1979): 184–204.

2.263 Cline, G. S. "A Bibliometric Study of Two Selected Journals in Library Science, 1940–1974." Doctoral dissertation, University of Southern California, 1979.

2.264 Cole, J. Y. "Storehouses and Workshops: American Libraries and the Uses of Knowledge." In *The Organization of Knowledge in Modern America, 1860–1920,* edited by A. Oleson and J. Voss. Baltimore: Johns Hopkins University Press, 1979. Pp. 361–85.

2.265 Dain, P. "[The Democratic Vision: The Public Libraries and the Urban University] Comments." In *The Role of the Humanities in the Public Library: Proceedings of a Conference Sponsored by the School of Library Science, University of North Carolina at Chapel Hill, 1978,* edited by R. N. Broadus and B. Nielson. Chicago: American Library Association, 1979. Pp. 185–94.

2.266 Fenster, V. R. "Wisconsin Library History, 1905–1979, as Reflected in the *Wisconsin Library Bulletin,* Celebrating Its 75th Anniversary Year in 1979." *WisLB* 75 (1979): 291–95.

2.267 Holley, E. G. "Library Issues in the Seventies." In *As Much to Learn as to Teach: Essays in Honor of Lester Asheim,* edited by J. M. Lee and B. A. Hamilton. Hamden, Conn.: Shoe String Press, 1979. Pp. 25–37.

2.268 Ogden, S. "A Study of the Impact of the Florence Flood on the Development of Library Conservation in the United States: 1966–1976." *Restaurator* 3 (1979): 1–36.

2.269 Oleson, A., and Voss, J. eds. *The Organization of Knowledge in Modern America, 1860–1920.* Baltimore: Johns Hopkins University Press, 1979.

2.270 Otness, H. M. "Passenger Ship Libraries." *JLH* 14 (1979): 486–95.

2.271 Rock, R. Z. "A History of Libraries in New Mexico—Spanish Origins to Statehood." *JLH* 14 (1979): 253–73.

2.272 Smith, V. J. "The Freedom of Information Act of 1966: A Legislative History." Master's thesis, University of Chicago, 1979.

2.273 Taylor, N. B. "[The Democratic Vision: The Public Libraries and the Urban Universities] Comments." In *The Role of the Humanities in the Public Library: Proceedings of a Conference Sponsored by the School of Library Science, University of North Carolina at Chapel Hill, 1978,* edited by R. N. Broadus and B. Nielsen. Chicago: American Library Association, 1979. Pp. 195–98.

2.274 Wiegand, W. A. *The History of a Hoax: Edmund Lester Pearson, John Cotton Dana, and "The Old Librarian's Almanack".* Pittsburgh: Beta Phi Mu, 1979.

2.275 Williams, R. "The Democratic Vision: The Public Libraries and the Urban Universities." In *The Role of the Humanities in the Public Library: Proceedings of a Conference Sponsored by the School of Library Science, University of North Carolina at Chapel Hill, 1978,* edited by R. N. Broadus and B. Nielsen. Chicago: American Library Association, 1979. Pp. 168–84.

2.276 Woods, L. B. *A Decade of Censorship in America: The Threat to Classrooms and Libraries, 1966–1975.* Metuchen, N.J.: Scarecrow Press, 1979.

2.277 Woods, L. B. "Giving Lip Service to Intellectual Freedom in Wisconsin." *WisLB* 75 (1979): 163–67.

2.278 Woods, L. B. "Status of Intellectual Freedom in Georgia." *GL* 16 (1979): 6–7.

2.279 Woods, L. B. "Surveying Minnesota's Record on Intellectual Freedom." *MinnL* 26 (1979): 484–88.

2.280 Corbin, J. B. "Networking in Texas: Achievements of the Ad-Hoc Committee on Networks, 1977–1980." *TLJ* 56 (1980): 198–99.

2.281 Ferguson, R. D. "Information Science: A Bibliometric Evaluation of the Information Analysis Concept." Doctoral dissertation, Boston University, 1980.

2.282 Hammond, M. " 'Remembrances of Things Past': The Protection and Preservation of Monuments, Works of Art, Libraries, and Archives during and after World War II." *PMHS* 92 (1980): 84–99.

2.283 Line, M. B. "Storage and Deposit Libraries." *ELIS* 29 (1980): 101–11.

2.284 Midbon, M. "Capitalism, Liberty, and the Development of the Library." *JLH* 15 (1980): 188–98.

2.285 Mika, J. J. "Staff Associations." *ELIS* 28 (1980): 452–69.

2.286 Mole, A. "The Development of Library Management Concerns, 1870–1950." In *Studies in Library Management,* vol. 6, edited by A. Vaughan. London: K.G. Saur/Clive Bingley, 1980. Pp. 73–110.

2.287 Phinazee, A. L., ed. *The Black Librarian in the Southeast: Reminiscences, Activities, Challenges.* Durham, N.C.: North Carolina Central University School of Library Science, 1980.

2.288 Qureshi, N. "Standards for Libraries." *ELIS* 28 (1980): 470–99.

2.289 Stevens, N. D. "Library Networks and Resource Sharing in the United States: An Historical and Philosophical Overview." *JASIS* 31 (1980): 405–12.

2.290 Stevens, N. D. "Oscar Gustafsen: A Tragic Minor Figure of American Librarianship." *JLH* 15 (1980): 183–87.

2.291 Strable, E. G. "The Way It Was." In *The Special Library Role in Networks,* edited by R. W. Gibson, Jr. New York: Special Libraries Association, 1980. Pp. 1–16.

2.292 Thomison, D. "The Private Wars of Chicago's Big Bill Thompson." *JLH* 15 (1980): 261–80.

2.293 Velleman, R. A. "Special Education and Rehabilitation Librarianship." *ELIS* 28 (1980): 360–86.

2.294 Woods, L. B. "Assaults on Intellectual Freedom in Florida, 1966–1975." *Florida Media Quarterly* 5 (1980): 8–11.

2.295 Woods, L. B. "Censorship in Connecticut, 1966–1975." *Connecticut Libraries* 22 (1980): 22–25.

2.296 Casey, M. "Efficiency, Taylorism, and Libraries in Progressive America." *JLH* 16 (1981): 265–79.

2.297 Cole, J. Y. "Books, Libraries and Scholarly Traditions." *Scholarly Publishing* 13 (1981): 31–43.

2.298 Darling, P. W., and Ogden, S. "From Problems Perceived to Programs in Practice: The Preservation of Library Resources in the U.S.A., 1956–1980." *LRTS* 25 (1981): 9–29.

2.299 Davis, D. G., ed. *Libraries and Culture: Proceedings of Library History Seminar VI, 19–22 March, 1980, Austin, Texas.* Austin: University of Texas Press, 1981.

2.300 Dick, A. L. "A Study of a Model of Society's Knowledge System and Its Implications for Librarianship." Master's thesis, University of Washington, 1981.

2.301 Engelbarts, R. *Librarian Authors: A Biobibliography.* Jefferson, N.C.: McFarland, 1981.

2.302 Heron, D. W., ed. *A Unifying Influence: Essays of Raynard Coe Swank.* Metuchen, N.J.: Scarecrow Press, 1981.

2.303 Johns, C. J. "Union Activities in U.S. Libraries." *ELIS* 31 (1981): 356–90.

2.304 Knutson, G. S. "Content Analysis of Obituaries of Prominent Librarians Recorded in the *New York Times,* 1884–1976." Master's thesis, University of Chicago, 1981.

2.305 Martin, L. A. "Library Planning and Library Standards: Historical Perspective." *BKM* 39 (1981): 253–60.

2.306 Mills, T. F. "Preserving Yesterday's News for Today's Historian: A Brief History of Newspaper Preservation, Bibliography, and Indexing." *JLH* 16 (1981): 463–87.

2.307 Roff, S. "The Accessibility of Libraries to Blacks in Nineteenth Century Brooklyn, New York." *Afro-Americans in New York Life and History* 5 (1981): 7–12.

2.308 Winans, R. B. *A Descriptive Checklist of Book Catalogues Separately Printed in America, 1693–1800.* Worcester, Mass.: American Antiquarian Society, 1981.

2.309 Baggett, C. "Happy Birthday, *TON!* A Brief Look at Its First Forty Years." *TN* 39 (1982): 114–17.

2.310 Karetzky, S. *Reading Research and Librarianship: A History and Analysis.* Westport, Conn.: Greenwood Press, 1982.

2.311 Kilton, T. D. "The American Railroad as Publisher, Bookseller, and Librarian." *JLH* 17 (1982): 39–64.

2.312 Meckler, A. M. *Micropublishing: A History of Scholarly Micropublishing in America, 1938–1980.* Westport, Conn.: Greenwood Press, 1982.

2.313 Rayman, R. "Taking Stock: Financing Libraries in the 19th Century." *LJ* 107 (1982): 2144–45.

2.314 Wilson, P. *Stereotype and Status: Librarians in the United States.* Westport, Conn.: Greenwood Press, 1982.

2.315 Afolabi, M. "The Literature of a Bibliographical Classification: A Citation Study to Determine the Core Literature." Doctoral dissertation, Indiana University, 1983.

2.316 Joyce, W. L., Hall, D. D., Brown, R. D., and Hench, J. B. *Printing and Society in Early America.* Worcester, Mass.: American Antiquarian Society, 1983.

2.317 Kaser, D. "The Dewey Era in American Librarianship." In *Melvil Dewey: The Man and the Classification,* edited by G. Stevenson and J. Kramer-Greene. Albany, N.Y.: Forest Press, 1983. Pp. 9–24.

2.318 Kruty, P. "Patton and Miller: Designers of Carnegie Libraries." *Palimpsest* 64 (1983): 110–22.

2.319 National Library Service for the Blind and Physically Handicapped. Washington,

D.C.: Library of Congress, National Library Service for the Blind and Physically Handicapped, 1983.

2.320 O'Brien, N. "The Recruitment of Men into Librarianship Following World War II." In *The Status of Women in Librarianship: Historical, Sociological, and Economic Issues*, edited by K. M. Heim. New York: Neal-Schuman, 1983. Pp. 51–66.

2.321 Peritz, B. C. "The Role of Research in Librarianship—The View of the Early Thirties in the United States." *Libri* 33 (1983): 83–91.

2.322 Perry-Holmes, C. "Censorship and Librarians: A Look Back at the Fifties." *Newsletter on Intellectual Freedom* 32 (1983): 67–68.

2.323 Roth, L. M. *McKim, Mead & White, Architects.* New York: Harper and Row, 1983.

2.324 Stielow, F. J. "Censorship in the Early Professionalization of American Libraries, 1876 to 1929." *JLH* 18 (1983): 37–64.

2.325 Wilson, R. G. *McKim, Mead & White, Architects.* New York: Rizzalli International, 1983.

2.326 Winter, M. F. *The Professionalization of Librarianship.* Urbana: University of Illinois Graduate School of Library and Information Science, Occasional Paper no. 160, 1983.

2.327 Woods, L. B., and Schmidt, A. M. "First in Freedom? Censorship in North Carolina, 1966–1980." *NCL* 41 (1983): 23–27.

2.328 Zubatsky, D., and Krummel, D. W. "Micropublishing History—A Review Essay." *JLH* 18 (1983): 317–21.

2.329 Bobinski, G. S. "The Golden Age of American Librarianship." *WLB* 58 (1984): 338–44.

2.330 Campbell, F. D. "Numismatic Bibliography and Libraries." *ELIS* 37 (1984): 272–310.

2.331 Chong, N. S. "Panama Canal Area, Libraries In." *ELIS* 37 (1984): 310–44.

2.332 Geller, E. *Forbidden Books in American Public Libraries, 1876–1939.* Westport, Conn.: Greenwood Press, 1984.

2.333 Harris, M. H. *History of Libraries in the Western World,* 4th ed. Metuchen, N.J.: Scarecrow Press, 1984.

2.334 Herner, S. "A Brief History of Information Science." *JASIS* 35 (1984): 157–63.

2.335 Molz, R. K. *National Planning for Library Service, 1935–1975.* Chicago: American Library Association, 1984.

2.336 Nash, N. F. "The North American Hotel as Publisher, Bookseller, and Librarian." *Library History* 6 (1984): 129–52.

2.337 Rogers, A. R., and McChesney, K. *The Library in Society.* Littleton, Colo.: Libraries Unlimited, 1984.

2.338 Shields, G. R. "The Regents and the Professional Librarian." *BKM* 42 (1984): 172–75.

2.339 Stielow, F. J. "Censorship and the Dilemma of Moral Culture." *ABBW* 74 (1984): 363–64.

2.340 Stratford, J. "Library Photocopying: A Legislative History of Section 108 of the Copyright Law Revision of 1976." *GPR* 11 (1984): 91–100.

2.341 Wiegand, W. A. "View from the Top: The Library Administrator's Changing Perspective on Standardization Schemes and Cataloging Practices in American Libraries, 1891–1901." In *Reference Services and Technical Services: Interaction in Library Practice,* edited by G. Stevenson and S. Stevenson. New York: Haworth Press, 1984. Pp. 11–27.

2.342 Wright, H. K. "*Reference Books Bulletin* Editorial Review Board—ALA." *ELIS* 37 (1984): 346–52.

2.343 Yerbergh, M., and Yerbergh, R. "Where Have All the Ultras Gone? The Rise and Demise of the Ultrafiche Library Collection, 1968–1973." *Microform Review* 13 (1984): 254–61.

2.344 Barrington, J. W. "The Use of Microforms in Libraries: Concerns of the Last Ten Years." *SerL* 10 (1985): 195–99.

2.345 Gleaves, E. S. "A Watch and Chain and a Jeweled Sword: The *Festschrift* and Librarianship." *RQ* 24 (1985): 466–73.

2.346 Halsey, R. S. "*Booklist.*" *ELIS* 38 (1985): 53–67.

2.347 Hertzel, D. H. "Bibliographical Approach to the History of Idea Development in Bibliometrics." Doctoral dissertation, Case Western Reserve University, 1985.

2.348 "Library Binding Institute, 1935–1985: Focus on People in LBI's 50 Years." *New Library Scene* 4 (1985): 9–12.

2.349 McClary, A. "Beware the Deadly Books: A Forgotten Episode in Library History." *JLH* 20 (1985): 427–33.

2.350 McReynolds, R. "A Heritage Dismissed." *LJ* 110 (1985): 25–31.

2.351 Molz, R. K. "From the Territorial Frontier to the Frontier of Science: Library Service in the United States of America." *IFLA Journal* 11 (1985): 91–105.

2.352 Overmier, J. A. "Scientific Rare Book Collections in Academic and Research Libraries in Twentieth Century America." Doctoral dissertation, University of Minnesota, 1985.

2.353 Rogers, R. D. "Library Preservation: Its Scope, History, and Importance." In *The Library Preservation Program: Models, Priorities, Possibilities,* edited by J. Merrell-Oldham and M. Smith. Chicago: American Library Association, 1985. Pp. 7–18.

2.354 Stanek, L. W. "Huck Finn: 100 Years of Durn Fool Problems." *SchLJ* 31 (1985): 19–22.

2.355 Summers, F. W. "History and Development of the Survey Model for Planning." *DLQ* 21 (1985): 33–44.

2.356 Wood, J. L. "The National Information Standards Organization (Z39)." *ELIS* 39 (1985): 291–332.

2.357 Bradley, C. J. "Notes of Some Pioneers: America's First Music Librarians." *Notes* 43 (1986): 272–91.

2.358 Davis, D. G., ed. *Libraries, Books & Culture: Proceedings of Library History Seminar VII, 6–8 March 1985, Chapel Hill, North Carolina.* Austin: Graduate School of Library and Information Science, University of Texas at Austin, 1986.

2.359 Dickinson, D. C., ed. *Dictionary of American Book Collectors.* Westport, Conn.: Greenwood Press, 1986.

2.360 Dickson, P. *The Library in America: A Celebration in Words and Pictures.* New York: Facts on File, 1986.

2.361 DuMont, R. R. "Race in American Librarianship: Attitudes of the Library Profession." *JLH* 21 (1986): 488–509.

2.362 McMullen, H., and Barr, L. J. "The Treatment of Libraries in Periodicals Published in the United States before 1876." *JLH* 21 (1986): 641–72.

2.363 Wan, W. "From Railroads to Libraries—an Historical Sketch of Texas-Chinese Librarians." *TLJ* 62 (1986): 82–83.

2.364 Webreck, S. J. "National Periodicals Center." *ELIS* 40 (1986): 321–38.

3.

Private Libraries and Reading Tastes

Having dealt with general and historiographical works, most bibliographers of American library history divide their material into types of libraries and topics that correspond generally to the chronological way in which they have come to occupy places of scholarly significance. Although these divisions vary somewhat, they usually begin with works that deal with personal libraries and with the reading tastes that influenced their creation. Historians and literary scholars have tended to link these two topics and have focused much of their study on the eighteenth and early nineteenth centuries. Perhaps this is because, before the widespread establishment of social and academic libraries that were accessible to the general public, private libraries served as the principal source of reading matter for large segments of literate society. After the founding of a greater number of institutional libraries, the number of significant private collections tended to decline by comparision, and some collections were absorbed in one way or another into larger institutions. When private collections became themselves institutionalized, they frequently formed the basis of research libraries. These receive coverage in Chapter 9, "Special Libraries—Private Research Libraries."

The two sections of this chapter reflect the themes suggested above. The section on reading tastes is very selective and includes primarily those items directly related to reading and book collecting. Citations to the book trade and publishing have been omitted from this chapter. Readers should consult such standard works as G. Thomas Tanselle's still definitive *Guide to the Study of United States Imprints* (2 vols.; Cambridge, Mass.: Harvard University Press, 1971), John Tebbel's comprehensive *A History of Book Publishing in the United States* (4 vols.; New York: R. R. Bowker, 1971–1980), and Paul A. Winckler's

35

History of Books and Printing: A Guide to Information Sources (Detroit: Gale, 1979). In any case, the distinction between studies of private libraries and reading tastes is not clear. Thus, the sections that follow should be used together.

Private Libraries

Michael H. Harris and Donald G. Davis, Jr., writing in the first edition of this bibliography, stated that "there is a strange tendency among historians to consider the nature of private book ownership a significant aspect of American intellectual history prior to the Civil War, while ignoring this subject when it comes to exploring the social or intellectual history of the late nineteenth and twentieth centuries." With few exceptions, this situation still prevails. An important example of this pattern is Daniel Boorstin's award-winning trilogy *The Americans,* the first volume of which (1958, **3.96**) devotes one of four sections, "Language and the Printed Word," to the study of reading tastes, private libraries, and the book trade. The second volume contains only scattered references to the subject, and the final volume omits this aspect of intellectual history altogether.

The colonial and early national periods are now well covered. Louis B. Wright's *Cultural Life of the American Colonies* (1957, **3.95**) surveys private libraries and reading tastes broadly. New England has attracted the attention of several scholars, among them Thomas G. Wright (*Literary Culture in Early New England, 1620–1730,* 1920, **3.18**) and Samuel Eliot Morison (*Intellectual Life of Colonial New England,* 1965, **3.118**). The South has received its full treatment in Richard Beale Davis's three-volume work, *Intellectual Life in the Colonial South,* (1978, **3.389**) of which volume two is devoted to libraries. A type of research that has declined in popularity but that still holds promise is the study of private libraries in various cities and states. Many of these efforts have concentrated on the South and include the early work of E. V. Lamberton on colonial Pennsylvania (1918, **3.15**), William Houlette's study of plantation libraries in the Old South (1933, **3.24**), John McDermott's *Private Libraries in Creole St. Louis* (1938, **3.44**), George Smart's analysis of libraries in colonial Virginia (1938, **3.45**), Joseph T. Wheeler's work on private libraries in colonial Maryland (1940, **3.50**), and John Goudeau's research on Louisiana (1965, **3.117**). Walter Edgar has done continuing study of libraries in colonial South Carolina (1969, **3.131** ; 1971, **3.139** ; 1977, **3.387**). Some of this material overlaps that found in the following section, devoted to reading tastes.

A final major category of studies dealing with private libraries consists of those devoted to the collecting interests of individuals. These works range from books dealing with the development of major collections to catalogs of individual libraries and brief descriptive articles on such collections. Although Benjamin Franklin has received much attention by scholars such as Edwin Wolf (1962, **3.110**) and Margaret Korty (1967, **3.125**), others have also undergone study, as exemplified by Walter Harding's *Emerson's Library* (1967, **3.122**), Daniel Meador's *Mr. Justice Black and His Books* (1974, **3.155**), Marie

Private Libraries

Before 1876

3.1 Winne, J. *Private Libraries of New York.* New York: E. French, 1860.

1876–1919

3.2 Rodgers, H. *Private Libraries of Providence.* Providence, R.I.: Sidney S. Rider, 1878.

3.3 Blake, M. "Books Taken from Dr. Franklin's Library by Major Andre." *PMHB* 8 (1884): 430.

3.4 Pene du Bois, H. *Four Private Libraries of New York: A Contribution of the History of Bibliophilism in America,* First Series. Preface by O. Uzanne. New York: Duprat & Co., 1892.

3.5 Weeks, S. B. "Libraries and Literature in North Carolina in the Eighteenth Century." In *Annual Report for the Year 1895,* American History Association. Washington, D.C.: Government Printing Office, 1896. Pp. 169–77.

3.6 "A Catalogue of Books in the Library at Westover . . . ." In *The Writings of Colonel William Byrd,* edited by J. S. Bassett. New York: Doubleday, Page & Co., 1901. Pp. 413–33.

3.7 Williams, J. R. "A Catalogue of Books in the Library of Councillor Robert Carter." *WMQ* 10 (1902): 232–41.

3.8 Dexter, F. B. "Early Private Libraries in New England." *PAAS* 18 (1907): 135–47.

3.9 Bruce, P. A. *Institutional History of Virginia in the Seventeenth Century.* New York: G.P. Putnam's Sons, 1910.

3.10 Tuttle, J. H. "[Catalogue of Increase Mathers' Library]." *PAAS* 20 (1910): 280–90.

3.11 Tuttle, J. H. "The Libraries of the Mathers." *PAAS* 20 (1910): 312–50.

3.12 Tuttle, J. H. "Early Libraries in New England." *PCSM* 13 (1911): 288–92.

3.13 Morrison, H. A. "Alaskana: Description of the Library of Judge Wickersham, Delegate in Congress from Alaska." *SL* 4 (1913): 183–84.

3.14 Tuttle, J. H. "The Library of Dr. William Ames." *PCSM* 14 (1913): 63–66.

3.15 Lamberton, E. V. "Colonial Libraries of Pennsylvania." *PMHB* 42 (1918): 193–234.

3.16 Potter, A. C. "Catalogue of John Harvard's Library." *PCSM* 21 (1919): 190–230.

1920–1949

3.17 Hall, H. J. "Two Book-lists: 1668 and 1728." *PCSM* 24 (1920): 64–71.

3.18 Wright, T. G. *Literary Culture in Early New England, 1620–1730.* New Haven: Yale University Press, 1920.

3.19 "The Ticknor Library." *MoreB* 3 (1921): 301–06.

3.20 Eddy, G. S. "Dr. Benjamin Franklin's Library." *PAAS* 34 (1924): 206–26.

3.21 Browne, C. A. "John Winthrop's Library." *Isis* 11 (1928): 328–41.

3.22 Yarmolinsky, A. "A Russian Library in Alaska." *BNYPL* 34 (1930): 643–46.

3.23 Borden, A. K. "Seventeenth-Century American Libraries." *LQ* 2 (1932): 138–47.

3.24 Houlette, W. D. "Plantation and Parish Libraries in the Old South." Doctoral dissertation, State University of Iowa, 1933.

3.25 Cadbury, H. J. "Anthony Benezet's Library." *Bulletin of Friends' Historical Association* 23 (1934): 63–75.

3.26 Hamill, R. F. "A Plain Farmer's Library of 1814." *American Book Collector* 5 (1934): 223–25.

3.27 Keys, T. E. "Private and Semi-Private Libraries of the American Colonies." Master's thesis, University of Chicago, 1934.

3.28 Oliphant, J. O. "The Library of Archibald McKinley, Oregon Fur Trader." *Washington Historical Quarterly* 25 (1934): 23–36.

3.29 Rosenbach, A. S. W. "The Libraries of the Presidents of the United States." *PAAS* 44 (1934): 337–64.

3.30 Brayton, S. S. "The Library of an Eighteenth-Century Gentleman of Rhode Island." *New England Quarterly* 8 (1935): 277–83.

3.31 McDermott, J. F. "The Library of Father Gibault." *Mid-America* 27 (1935): 273–75.

3.32 Robinson, C. F., and Robinson, R. "Three Early Massachusetts Libraries." *PCSM* 28 (1935): 107–75.

3.33 Spruill, J. C. "The Southern Lady's Library, 1700–1776." *South Atlantic Quarterly* 34 (1935): 23–41.

3.34 Cadbury, H. J. "More of Benezet's Library." *Bulletin of Friends' Historical Association* 25 (1936): 83–85.

3.35 McDermott, J. F. "The Library of Barthelemi Tardiveau." *JISHS* 29 (1936): 89–91.

3.36 Patterson, J. M. "Private Libraries in Virginia in the Eighteenth Century." Master's thesis, University of Virginia, 1936.

3.37 Greenberg, H. "The Authenticity of the Library of John Winthrop the Younger." *AL* 8 (1937): 448–52.

3.38 Patrick, W. R. "Literature in the Louisiana Plantation Home Prior to 1861: A Study in Literary Culture." Doctoral dissertation, Louisiana State University, 1937.

3.39 Wright, L. B. "The Gentleman's Library in Early Virginia: The Literary Interests of the First Carters." *Huntington Library Quarterly* 1 (1937): 3–61.

3.40 Andrews, C. "The Historical Russian Library of Alaska." *Pacific Northwest Quarterly* 3 (1938): 201–04.

3.41 Baym, M. E. "The 1858 Catalogue of Henry Adams' Library." *Colophon* 3 (1938): 483–89.

3.42 Cannon, C. L. "William Byrd II of Westover." *Colophon* (1938): 291–302.

3.43 Keys, T. E. "The Colonial Library and the Development of Sectional Differences in American Colonies." *LQ* 8 (1938): 373–90.

3.44 McDermott, J. F. *Private Libraries in Creole St. Louis.* Baltimore: Johns Hopkins Press, 1938.

3.45 Smart, G. K. "Private Libraries in Colonial Virginia." *AL* 10 (1938): 24–52.

3.46 Baker, C. M. "Books in a Pioneer Household." *JISHS* 32 (1939): 261–87.

3.47 Keys, T. E. "The Medical Books of Dr. Charles N. Hewitt." *Minnesota History* 21 (1940): 357–71.

3.48 Keys, T. E. "Popular Authors in the Colonial Library." *WLB* 14 (1940): 726–27.

3.49 McDermott, J. F. "The Library of Henry Shaw." *Missouri Botanical Gardens Bulletin* 28 (1940): 49–53.

3.50 Wheeler, J. T. "Books Owned by Marylanders, 1700–1776." *MHM* 35 (1940): 337–53.

3.51 Wright, L. B. *The First Gentlemen of Virginia: Intellectual Qualities of the Early Colonial Ruling Class.* San Moreno, Calif.: Huntington Library, 1940.

3.52 Cannon, C. L. *American Book Collectors and Collecting from Colonial Times to the Present.* New York: H.W. Wilson, 1941.

3.53 Adams, E. B., and Scholes, F. V. "Books in New Mexico, 1598–1680." *New Mexico Historical Review* 17 (1942): 1–45.

3.54 Bay, J. C. "Private Book Collectors in the Chicago Area: A Brief Review." *LQ* 12 (1942): 363–74.

3.55 Bondurant, A. M. "Libraries and Books." In *Poe's Richmond* . . . . Richmond, Va.: Garrett & Massie, 1942. Pp. 91–121.

3.56 Peden, W. H. "Thomas Jefferson: Book Collector." Doctoral dissertation, University of Virginia, 1942.

3.57 Tolles, F. B. "John Woolman's List of 'Books Lent.'" *Bulletin of Friends' Historical Association* 31 (1942): 72–83.

3.58 Yost, G. "The Reconstruction of the Library of Norborne Berkeley, Baron de Botetourt, Governor of Virginia, 1768–1770." *PBSA* 36 (1942): 97–123.

3.59 Keys, T. E. "The Medical Books of William Worral Mayo, Pioneer Surgeon of the American Northwest." *BMLA* 31 (1943): 119–27.

3.60 Leonard, I. A. "A Frontier Library, 1799." *Hispanic American Historical Review* 23 (1943): 21–51.

3.61 Upshur, A. F., and Whitelaw, R. T. "Library of the Rev. Thomas Teackle [1696]." *WMQ* 23, ser. 2 (1943): 298–308.

3.62 Wright, L. B. "Jefferson and the Classics." *PAPS* 87 (1943): 223–33.

3.63 Adams, E. B. "Two Colonial New Mexico Libraries, 1704, 1776." *New Mexico Historical Review* 19 (1944): 135–67.

3.64 Evans, W. A. "The Library at Beauvoir." *Journal of Mississippi History* 6 (1944): 51–54, 119–21, 174–76.

3.65 Kaplan, L. "Peter Force, Collector." *LQ* 14 (1944): 234–38.

3.66 Peden, W. H. "Some Notes Concerning Thomas Jefferson's Libraries." *WMQ* 1 (1944): 265–72.

3.67 Metcalf, J. C. "Virginia Libraries in Retrospect." *Madison Quarterly* 6 (1946): 154–62.

3.68 Boyd, J. P. *The Scheide Library: A Summary View of Its History and Its Outstanding Books Together with an Account of Its Two Founders: William Taylor Scheide and John Hinsdale Scheide.* N.p.: Privately printed, 1947.

3.69 Irrman, R. H. "The Library of an Early Ohio Farmer." *Publications of Ohio State Archives and Historical Society* 42 (1948): 185–93.

3.70 Patrick, W. R. "A Louisiana French Plantation Library." *French-American Review* 1 (1948): 47–67.

3.71 Seeber, E. D. "The Brute Library in Vincennes." *Indiana Quarterly for Bookmen* 4 (1948): 81–86.

3.72 Sioussat, S. L. "The Philosophical Transactions of the Royal Society in Libraries of William Byrd of Westover, Benjamin Franklin, and the American Philosophical Society." *PAPS* 93 (1949): 99–107.

3.73 Stern, M. B. "Anton Roman: Argonaut of Books." *CHSQ* 28 (1949): 1–18.

1950–1971

3.74 Bradley, R. "Books in the California Missions." Master's thesis, Columbia University, 1950.

3.75 Geiger, M. J. "The Old Mission Libraries of California." *CLB* 11 (1950): 143–44, 147.

3.76 Maurer, M. "The Library of a Colonial Musician, 1755 [Cuthbert Ogle]." *WMQ* 7 (1950): 39–52.

3.77 Dumbauld, E. "A Manuscript from Monticello: Jefferson's Library in Legal History." *American Bar Association Journal* 38 (1952): 389–92, 446–47.

3.78 Parks, E. W. "Jefferson as a Man of Letters." *Georgia Review* 6 (1952): 450–59.

3.79 Schullian, D. M. "Unfolded Out of the Folds." *BMLA* 40 (1952): 135–43.

3.80 Sowerby, E. M., comp. *Catalogue of the Library of Thomas Jefferson,* 5 vols. Washington, D.C.: Library of Congress, 1952–1959.

3.81 McDermott, J. F. "The Library of John Hay of Cahokia and Belleville." *Missouri Historical Society Bulletin* 9 (1953): 183–86.

3.82 Houlette, W. D. "Books of the Virginia Dynasty." *LQ* 24 (1954): 226–39.

3.83 Keys, T. E. "Libraries of Some Twentieth-Century American Bibliophilic Physicians." *LQ* 24 (1954): 21–34.

3.84 Kann, P. J. "A Brief History of the Library of the Rowfant Club in Cleveland." Master's thesis, Western Reserve University, 1955.

3.85 Flanagan, J. T. "The Destruction of an Early Illinois Library." *JISHS* 49 (1956): 387–93.

3.86 Shaffer, E. "Portrait of a Philadelphia Collector: William McIntire Elkins [1882–1947]." *PBSA* 50 (1956): 115–29.

3.87 Shipley, J. B. "Franklin Attends a Book Auction." *PMHB* 80 (1956): 37–45.

3.88 Sowerby, E. M. "Thomas Jefferson and His Library." *PBSA* 50 (1956): 213–28.

3.89 Wolf, E. "B. Franklin, Bookman." *BALA* 50 (1956): 13–16.

3.90 Wolf, E. "A Key to Identification of Franklin's Books." *Manuscripts* 8 (1956): 211–14.

3.91 Wolf, E. "The Romance of James Logan's Books." *WMQ* 13 (1956): 342–53.

3.92 Ames, S. M. *Reading, Writing and Arithmetic in Virginia, 1607–1699.* Williamsburg, Va.: Virginia 350th Anniversary Celebration Corporation, 1957.

3.93 Clemons, H. *Home Library of the Garnetts of "Elmwood".* Charlottesville: University of Virginia, 1957.

3.94 Johnson, R. D. "Books in the Life of John Quincy Adams." Master's thesis, University of Chicago, 1957.

3.95 Wright, L. B. "Books, Libraries and Learning." In *The Cultural Life of the American Colonies, 1607–1763 . . . .* New York: Harper, 1957. Pp. 126–53.

3.96 Boorstin, D. J. *The Americans: The Colonial Experience.* New York: Random House, 1958.

3.97 Commager, H. S. "Jefferson and the Book Burners." *American Heritage* 9 (1958): 65–68.

3.98 Keys, T. E. "The Development of Private Medical Libraries." In *Applied Medical Library Practice.* Springfield, Ill.: Charles C. Thomas, 1958. Pp. 148–89.

3.99 McDermott, J. F. "A Frontier Library: The Books of Isaac McCoy." *PBSA* 52 (1958): 140–43.

3.100 Wolf, E. "The Dispersal of the Library of William Byrd of Westover." *PAAS* 68 (1958): 19–106.

3.101 Jackson, W. A. "Henry Stevens and Washington's Library." *PBSA* 53 (1959): 79–80.

3.102 Savin, M. B., and Abrahams, J. J. "The Botanical Library of Thomas Jefferson." *Journal of Elisha Mitchell Scientific Society* 75 (1959): 44–52.

3.103 Street, T. W. "Thomas Smyth: Presbyterian Bookman." *Journal of Presbyterian History* 37 (1959): 1–14.

3.104 Wolf, E. "The Library of a Philadelphia Judge [John Guest], 1708." *PMHB* 83 (1959): 180–91.

3.105 Abrahams, A. J. "Chemical Library of Thomas Jefferson." *Journal of Chemical Education* 37 (1960): 357–60.

3.106 Fields, J. E. "A Signer and His Signatures; or the Library of Thomas Lynch, Jr." *HLB* 14 (1960): 210–52.

3.107 Haffner, G. O., ed. "The Medical Inventory of a Pioneer Doctor." *IMH* 56 (1960): 37–63.

3.108 Davis, R. B. "Jefferson as Collector of Virginiana." *Studies in Bibliography* 19 (1961): 117–44.

3.109 Hoskin, B. *A History of the Santa Clara Mission Library*, California Heritage no. 48. Oakland, Calif.: Biobooks, 1961.

3.110 Wolf, E. "The Reconstruction of Benjamin Franklin's Library: An Unorthodox Jigsaw Puzzle." *PBSA* 56 (1962): 1–16.

3.111 Bestor, A. "Thomas Jefferson and the Freedom of Books." In *Three Presidents and Their Books*. Urbana: University of Illinois Press, 1963. Pp. 1–44.

3.112 Talbert, N. J. "Books and Libraries of the Carolina Charter Colonists, 1663–1763." *NCL* 21 (1963): 68–69.

3.113 Goff, F. R. "T.R.'s Big Game Library." *QJLC* 21 (1964): 167–71.

3.114 Jones, G. W. "A Virginia-Owned Shelf of Early Medical Imprints." *PBSA* 58 (1964): 281–90.

3.115 Wolf, E. "The Library of Ralph Ashton: The Book Background of a Colonial Philadelphia Lawyer." *PBSA* 58 (1964): 345–79.

3.116 Clower, G. W. "An Early Nineteenth Century Library: Books of Rev. William Quillin." *Georgia Historical Quarterly* 49 (1965): 193–99.

3.117 Goudeau, J. M. "Early Libraries in Louisiana: A Study of Creole Influence." Doctoral dissertation, Western Reserve University, 1965.

3.118 Morison, S. E. *The Intellectual Life of Colonial New England*. New York: New York University Press, 1965.

3.119 Wolf, E. "A Parcel of Books for the Province in 1700." *PMHB* 89 (1965): 428–46.

3.120 Rogers, A. E. "Swante Palm: With Notes on the Library of a Nineteenth Century Texas Book Collector." Master's thesis, University of Texas, 1966.

3.121 Adams, H. D. "A Note on Jefferson's Knowledge of Economics." *VMHB* 75 (1967): 69–74.

3.122 Harding, W., comp. *Emerson's Library*. Charlottesville: University Press of Virginia for the Bibliographical Society of the University of Virginia, 1967.

3.123 Harris, M. H. "A Methodist Minister's Working Library in Mid-Nineteenth Century Illinois." *Wesleyan Quarterly Review* 4 (1967): 210–19.

3.124 Jones, G. W., comp. *The Library of James Monroe (1758–1831), 5th President (1816–1824) of the United States*. Charlottesville: Bibliographical Society of the University of Virginia, 1967.

3.125 Korty, M. B. "Franklin's World of Books." *JLH* 2 (1967): 271–328.

3.126 Wolf, E. "James Logan's Correspondence with William Reading, Librarian of Sion College." In *Homage to a Bookman: Essays ... Written for Hans P. Krause ...*, edited by H. Lehmann-Haupt. Berlin: Gebr. Mann Verlag, 1967. Pp. 209–20.

3.127 Adams, E. B., and Algier, K. W. "A Frontier Book List—1800." *New Mexico Historical Review* 43 (1968): 49–59.

3.128 Jones, G. W. "The Library of Dr. John Mitchell of Urbana." *VMHB* 76 (1968): 441–43.

3.129 Reese, G. H. "Books in the Palace: The Libraries of Three Virginia Governors [Fauquier, Berkeley, Murray]." *Virginia Cavalcade* (1968): 20–31.

3.130 Zachert, M. J. "The Peter Early Estate: Inventory and Appraisement." *JLH* 3 (1968): 266–70.

3.131 Edgar, W. B. "The Libraries of Colonial South Carolina." Doctoral dissertation, University of South Carolina, 1969.

3.132 Gordon, D. "The Book-Collecting Ishams of Northamptonshire and Their Bookish Virginia Cousins." *VMHB* 77 (1969): 174–79.

3.133 Quinn, D. B. "A List of Books Purchased for the Virginia Company." *VMHB* 77 (1969): 347–60.

3.134 Waterman, J. S. "Thomas Jefferson and Blackstone's Commentaries." In *Essays in the History of Early American Law,* edited by D. H. Flaherty. Chapel Hill: University of North Carolina Press, 1969. Pp. 451–88.

3.135 Wolf, E. "The Library of Edward Lloyd IV of Wye House." *Winterthur Portfolio* 5 (1969): 87–121.

3.136 Briggs, R. T. "Books of the Pilgrims as Recorded in Their Inventories and Preserved in Pilgrim Hall." *Old-Time New England* 61 (1970–71): 41–46.

3.137 Gordon, D. "The Book-Collecting Ishams of Northamptonshire and Their Bookloving Virginia and Massachusetts Cousins." *HLB* 18 (1970): 282–97.

3.138 Read, K. T. "The Library of Robert Carter of Nomini Hall." Master's thesis, College of William and Mary, 1970.

3.139 Edgar, W. B. "Notable Libraries of Colonial South Carolina." *SCHM* 72 (1971): 105–10, 174–78.

3.140 *Library of an Early Virginia Scientist: Dr. John Mitchell, F.R.S. (1711–1763),* Occasional Paper No. 4. Fredericksburg, Va.: Lee Tinkle Library, Mary Washington College of the University of Virginia, 1971.

3.141 Watson, H. R. "The Books They Left: Some 'Liberies' in Edgecombe County, 1733–1783." *NCHR* 48 (1971): 245–57.

3.142 Wolf, E. "Great American Book Collectors to 1800." *Gazette of the Grolier Club* n.s., no. 16 (1971): 1–25.

3.143 Wolf, E. *James Logan, 1674–1751, Bookman Extraordinary.* Philadelphia: Library Company of Philadelphia, 1971.

1972–1986

3.144 Evans, E. G., ed. *Inventory of the Library of William Nelson, Jr., of Yorktown, Virginia.* Williamsburg, Va.: Botetourt Bibliographical Society, College of William and Mary, 1972.

3.145 Goff, F. R. "Jefferson the Book Collector." *QJLC* 29 (1972): 32–47.

3.146 Goudeau, J. M., and Goudeau, L. "The Canonage Library." *JLH* 7 (1972): 64–79.

3.147 Harris, M. H. "Books on the Frontier: The Extent and Nature of Book Ownership in Southern Indiana, 1800–1850." *LQ* 42 (1972): 416–30.

3.148 Harris, M. H. "The Lawyer's Library on the Frontier: Southern Indiana, 1800–1850, as a Test Case." *American Journal of Legal History* 16 (1972): 239–51.

3.149 Ketcham, J. "The Bibliomania of the Reverend William Bentley, D.D." *HCEI* 108 (1972): 275–303.

3.150 McCorison, M. A. "Donald McKay—A Collector of Western Americana." *Western Historical Quarterly* 3 (1972): 67–76.

3.151 Coghlan, J. M. "The Library of St. George Tucker." Master's thesis, College of William and Mary, 1973.

3.152 Edelstein, J. M. "The Poet as Reader: Wallace Stevens and His Books." *BC* 23 (1974): 53–68.

3.153 Gribben, A. D. "The Library and Reading of Samuel L. Clemens." Doctoral dissertation, University of California, 1974.

3.154 Kraus, J. W. "Private Libraries in Colonial America." *JLH* 9 (1974): 31–53.

3.155 Meador, D. J. *Mr. Justice Black and His Books.* Charlottesville: University Press of Virginia, 1974.

3.156 Morris, W. J. "John Quincy Adams's German Library with a Catalog of His German Books." *PAPS* 118 (1974): 321–33.

3.157 Simpson, W. S. "A Comparison of the Libraries of Seven Colonial Virginians, 1754–1789." *JLH* 9 (1974): 54–65.

3.158 Skallerup, H. R. "For His Excellency, Thomas Jefferson, Esq.: The Tale of a Wandering Book." *QJLC* 31 (1974): 116–21.

3.159 Beck, L. N. "The Library of Susan B. Anthony." *QJLC* 32 (1975): 325–35.

3.160 Goudeau, J. M., and Goudeau, L. "A Nineteenth Century Louisiana Library: The LaRue Library." *JLH* 10 (1975): 162–68.

3.161 Wolf, E. *The Library of James Logan of Philadelphia*. Philadelphia: Library Company of Philadelphia, 1975.

3.162 Korey, M. E. *The Books of Isaac Norris, 1701–1766, at Dickinson College*. Carlisle, Pa.: Dickinson College, 1976.

3.163 Berger, M. L. "Reading, Roadsters, and Rural America." *JLH* 12 (1977): 42–49.

3.164 Carroll, F. L., and Meacham, M. *The Library at Mount Vernon*. Pittsburgh: Beta Phi Mu, 1977.

3.165 Farren, D. "The Book Trades in Early America." *ABBW* 59 (1977): 1874–98.

3.166 Freeman, A. "Harry Widener's Last Books Corrigenda to A.E. Newton." *BC* 26 (1977): 173–85.

3.167 Sanford, C. B. *Thomas Jefferson and His Library: A Study of His Literary Interests and of Religious Attitudes Revealed by Relevant Titles in His Library*. Hamden, Conn.: Archon Books, 1977.

3.168 Wolf, E. "More Books from the Library of the Byrds of Westover." *PAAS* 88 (1978): 51–82.

3.169 Gilliam, F. "The Case of the Vanished Victorians." In *Book Selling and Book Buying: Aspects of the Nineteenth Century British and North American Book Trade*, edited by R. G. Landon. Chicago: American Library Association, 1979. Pp. 87–98.

3.170 Gribben, A. D. *Mark Twain's Library: A Reconstruction*, 2 vols. Boston: G.K. Hall, 1980.

3.171 Gribben, A. D. "Reconstructing Mark Twain's Library." *ABBW* 66 (1980): 755–56.

3.172 Hilliard, C. "The Thomas Wise Forgeries: The Case of the Wrenn Library." *Chicago History* 9 (1980/81): 212–18.

3.173 Hunt, P. "Mark Twain's Library: A Postscript." *ABBW* 66 (1980): 2376–86.

3.174 Bakker, J. "Summer Reading at Woodlands: A Juvenile Library of the Old South." *Children's Literature* 9 (1981): 221–32.

3.175 Vuilleumier, M. "The Sturgis Library: The Literary Legacy of the Lothrop Homestead." *Cape Cod Life* (1981–84): 127–34.

3.176 Boylston, J., comp. *John Dewey's Personal and Professional Library: A Checklist*. Carbondale, Ill.: Southern Illinois University Press, 1982.

3.177 McKee, J. L. "Professor Fitzpatrick's Amazing Library: A Bibliomaniac in Nebraska." *Nebraska Library Association Quarterly* 13 (1982): 5–7.

3.178 Abraham, M. K. "The Library of Lady Jean Skipwith: A Book Collection from the Age of Jefferson." *VMHB* 91 (1983): 296–347.

3.179 Crist, L. L. "A Bibliographical Note: Jefferson Davis's Personal Library: All Lost, Some Found." *Journal of Mississippi History* 45 (1983): 186–93.

3.180 Harding, W. "A New Checklist of the Books in Henry David Thoreau's Library." *Studies in the American Renaissance* (1983): 151–86.

3.181 Stanley, C. V. "The Library of William Byrd II of Westover." Master's thesis, University of Chicago, 1984.

3.182 Wilson, D. L. "Sowerby Revisited: The Unfinished Catalogue of Thomas Jefferson's Library." *WMQ* 41 (1984): 615–28.

3.183 Coombs, L. A., and Blouin, F. X., eds. *Intellectual Life on the Michigan Frontier: The Libraries of Gabriel Richard and John Montieth*. Ann Arbor: Bentley Historical Library, University of Michigan, 1985.

3.184 Kinney, A. F., ed. *Flannery O'Connor's Library: Resources of Being*. Athens: University of Georgia Press, 1985.

3.185 Linton, R. C. "A Heritage of Books: Selections from the Nemours Library." *Delaware History* 21 (1985): 197–216.

3.186 Anthony, R. G. "Restoring a Historic Early 19th Century Library [David Stone of Hope Plantation]." *ABBW* 77 (1986): 2938–42.

3.187 Gribben, A. D. "Private Libraries of American Authors: Dispersal, Custody, and Description." *JLH* 21 (1986): 300–314.

3.188 Miller, S. J. "Government Publications in the Private Collections of Nineteenth Century America: A Century-Long Source of Federal Document Holdings in Libraries." *GPR* 13 (1986): 355–70.

3.189 Powell, J. "My Father's Library." *WLB* 60 (1986): 35–37.

3.190 Stephens, B. M. "Icons of Learning: William Bentley's Library and Allegheny College." *WPHM* 69 (1986): 138–51.

3.191 Wolf, E. "Frustration and Benjamin Franklin's Medical Books." In *Science and Society in Early America: Essays in Honor of Whitfield J. Bell*, edited by R. S. Klein. Philadelphia: American Philosophical Society, 1986. Pp. 57–91.

Reading Tastes

1876–1919

3.192 Ford, P. L. *The New England Primer: A History of Its Origin and the Development with a Reprint of the Unique Copy of the Earliest Known Edition and Many Fac-Simile Illustrations and Reproductions.* New York: Dodd, Mead and Company, 1897.

3.193 Johnson, C. *Old Time Schools and School Books.* New York: Macmillan, 1904.

3.194 Littlefield, G. E. *Early Schools and School-Books of New England.* Boston: The Club of Odd Volumes, 1904.

3.195 Matthews, A. "Knowledge of Milton in Early New England." *Nation* 87 (1908): 624–25, 650.

3.196 Howe, D. W. "Browsing among Old Books." *IMH* 11 (1915): 187–210.

3.197 Dienst, A. "Contemporary Poetry of the Texas Revolution." *SHQ* 21 (1917): 156–84.

3.198 Herrick, C. A. "The Early New-Englanders: What Did They Read?" *The Library* 9 (1918): 1–17.

1920–1949

3.199 Campbell, K. "Poe's Reading." *University of Texas Studies in English* 5 (1925): 166–96; 7 (1927): 175–80.

3.200 Morgan, P. "Literary Trends as Indicated in Texas Newspapers, 1836–1846." Master's thesis, University of Texas, 1926.

3.201 Chinard, G., ed. *The Literary Bible of Thomas Jefferson: His Commonplace Book of Philosophers and Poets.* Baltimore: Johns Hopkins Press, 1928.

3.202 Juniger, M. "Texas Verse in Texas Newspapers, 1846–1861." Master's thesis, University of Texas, 1928.

3.203 Orians, G. H. *The Influence of Walter Scott on America and American Literature Before 1860.* Urbana: University of Illinois, 1929.

3.204 Raunick, S. M. "A Survey of German Literature in Texas." *SHQ* 33 (1929): 134–59.

3.205 Skeel, E. E. F., ed. *Mason Locke Weems: His Work and Ways*, 3 vols. New York: Plimpton Press, 1929.

3.206 Tope, M. *A Biography of William Holmes McGuffey.* Bowerston, Ohio: N.p., 1929.

3.207 Brennan, M. A. "History and Influence of the Catholic Reading Circle Movement." Master's thesis, University of Delaware, 1930.

3.208 Cross, W. O. "Ralph Waldo Emerson's Reading in the Boston Athenaeum." Master's thesis, Columbia University, 1930.

3.209 Johnson, T. H. "Jonathan Edwards' Background of Reading." *PCSM* 28 (1930–33): 193–222.

3.210 Ingraham, C. A. "Mason Locke Weems: A Great American Author and Distributor of Books." *Americana* 25 (1931): 469–85.

3.211 Landrum, G. W. "Notes on the Reading of the Old South." *AL* 3 (1931): 60–71.

3.212 Shaw, R. R. "Engineering Books Available in America Prior to 1830." Master's thesis, Columbia University, 1931.

3.213 Mullett, C. F. "Coke and the American Revolution." *Economica* 12 (1932): 457–71.

3.214 Simon, H. W. *The Reading of Shakespeare in American Schools and Colleges: An Historical Survey.* New York: Simon and Schuster, 1932.

3.215 Jones, H. M. "The Importation of French Books in Philadelphia, 1750–1800." *Modern Philology* 32 (1934): 157–77.

3.216 Kimball, L. E. "An Account of Hocquet Caritat, 18th Century New York Circulating Librarian, Bookseller, and Publisher . . . ." *Colophon* 18 (1934): 1–12.

3.217 McDermott, J. F. "Scientific Books in the Early West." *School and Society* 40 (1934): 812–13.

3.218 Wroth, L. C. *An American Bookshelf, 1755.* Philadelphia: University of Pennsylvania Press, 1934.

3.219 Greenough, C. N. "Defoe in Boston." *PCSM* 28 (1935): 461–93.

3.220 Howard, L. "Early American Copies of Milton." *Huntington Library Bulletin* 7 (1935): 169–79.

3.221 Kittredge, G. L. "A Harvard Salutatory Oration of 1662." *PCSM* 28 (1935): 1–24.

3.222 McDermott, J. F. "Books on Natural History in Early Saint Louis." *Missouri Botanical Gardens Bulletin* 23 (1935): 55–62.

3.223 Starke, A. "Books in the Wilderness." *JISHS* 28 (1935): 258–70.

3.224 Warren, A. "Hawthorne's Reading." *New England Quarterly* 8 (1935): 480–97.

3.225 Hedrick, U. P. "What Farmers Read in Western New York, 1800–1850." *New York History* 17 (1936): 281–89.

3.226 McDermott, J. F. "Voltaire and the Freethinkers in Early Saint Louis." *Revue de Littérature Comparée* 16 (1936): 720–31.

3.227 Minnich, H. C. *William Holmes McGuffey and His Readers.* New York: American Book Company, 1936.

3.228 Shoemaker, E. C. *Noah Webster.* New York: Columbia University Press, 1936.

3.229 Warfel, H. R. *Noah Webster: Schoolmaster to America.* New York: Macmillan, 1936.

3.230 McCutcheon, R. P. "Books and Booksellers in New Orleans, 1730–1830." *LHQ* 20 (1937): 606–18.

3.231 McKay, G. L. *American Book Auction Catalogues, 1713–1934: A Union List....* New York: New York Public Library, 1937.

3.232 Orians, G. H. "Censure of Fiction in American Romances and Magazines, 1789–1810." *Publications of the Modern Language Association of America* 52 (1937): 195–224.

3.233 Reitzel, W. "The Purchasing of English Books in Philadelphia, 1790–1800." *Modern Philology* 35 (1937): 159–71.

3.234 Willoughby, E. E. "The Reading of Shakespeare in Colonial America." *PBSA* 31 (1937): 45–56.

3.235 Wright, L. B. "The Purposeful Reading of Our Colonial Ancestors." *Journal of English Literary History* 4 (1937): 85–111.

3.236 Blanck, J. *Peter Parley to Penrod: A Bibliographical Description of the Best-Loved*

American Juvenile Books. New York: R.R. Bowker, 1938.

3.237 Boquer, H. F. "Sir Walter Scott in New Orleans, 1818–1832." *LHQ* 21 (1938): 420–517.

3.238 Lancaster, E. R. "Books Read in Early Nineteenth Century Virginia, 1806–1822." *VMHB* 46 (1938): 56–59.

3.239 McDermott, J. F. "Best Sellers in Early Saint Louis." *School and Society* 47 (1938): 673–75.

3.240 Waples, D. *People and Print: Social Aspects of Reading in the Depression.* Chicago: University of Chicago Press, 1938.

3.241 Davis, R. B. *Francis Walker Gilmer; Life and Learning in Jefferson's Virginia. A Study in Virginia Literary Culture in the First Quarter of the Nineteenth Century.* Richmond, Va.: Dietz Press, 1939.

3.242 Davis, R. B. "Literary Tastes in Virginia before Poe." *WMQ* 19, ser. 2 (1939): 55–68.

3.243 Dunn, E. C. *Shakespeare in America.* New York: Macmillan, 1939.

3.244 Mullett, C. F. "Classical Influences on the American Revolution." *Classical Journal* 35 (1939): 92–104.

3.245 Wheeler, J. T. "Booksellers and Circulating Libraries in Colonial Maryland." *MHM* 34 (1939): 111–37.

3.246 Wright, L. B. "Classical Tradition in Colonial Virginia." *PBSA* 33 (1939): 85–97.

3.247 Baldwin, S. "Book-Learning and Learning Books." *CRL* 1 (1940): 257–61.

3.248 Manning, J. W. "Literacy on the Oregon Trail: Books Across the Plains." *Oregon Historical Quarterly* 61 (1940): 189–94.

3.249 Patrick, W. R. "Reading Tastes in Louisiana, 1830–60." In *Studies for William A. Read...*, edited by N. M. Coffee and T. A. Kirby. Baton Rouge: Louisiana State University Press, 1940. Pp. 288–300.

3.250 Spurlin, P. M. *Montesquieu in America, 1760–1801.* Baton Rouge: Louisiana State University Press, 1940.

3.251 Wright, L. B. "Pious Reading in Colonial America." *Journal of Southern History* 6 (1940): 383–93.

3.252 Barr, M. M. *Voltaire in America, 1774–1800.* Baltimore: Johns Hopkins Press, 1941.

3.253 Fell, M. L. *The Foundations of Nativism in American Textbooks, 1783–1860.* Washington, D.C.: Catholic University of America Press, 1941.

3.254 Wheeler, J. T. "Reading Interests of the Professional Classes in Colonial Maryland, 1700–1776." *MHM* 36 (1941): 184–201, 281–301.

3.255 Bowes, F. P. *The Culture of Early Charleston.* Chapel Hill: University of North Carolina Press, 1942.

3.256 Eskridge, C. S. "Selected Newspaper Verse Published in Texas, 1836–1846." Master's thesis, University of Texas, 1942.

3.257 Jantz, H. S. "German Thought and Literature in New England, 1620–1820." *Journal of English & German Philology* 41 (1942): 1–45.

3.258 Mayfield, S. N. "Reading Interests in New Orleans, 1848–1942." Master's thesis, Tulane University, 1942.

3.259 Ransom, H. H. "The Booklore of Swante Palm." *LCT* 4 (1942): 103–11.

3.260 Wheeler, J. T. "Reading Interests of Maryland Planters and Merchants, 1700–1776." *MHM* 37 (1942): 26–41, 291–310.

3.261 Wheeler, J. T. "Literary Culture and Eighteenth Century Maryland: Summary of Findings." *MHM* 38 (1943): 273–76.

3.262 Wheeler, J. T. "Reading and Other Recreations of Marylanders, 1700–1776." *MHM* 38 (1943): 37–55, 167–80.

3.263 Lillard, R. D. "A Literate Woman in the Mines: The Diary of Rachel Haskell."

Mississippi Valley Historical Review 31 (1944): 81–98.

3.264 Dale, E. E. "Culture on the American Frontier." *Nebraska History* 26 (1945): 75–90.

3.265 Dykes, J. C. "Dime Novel Texas: Or, the Sub-Literature of the Lone Star State." *SHQ* 49 (1946): 327–40.

3.266 Hemphill, W. E., ed. "The Constitution of the Charlottesville Lyceum, 1837–1840." *Papers of Albemarle County Historical Society* 8 (1946–47): 47–64.

3.267 Hogan, W. R. *The Texas Republic: A Social and Economic History.* Norman: University of Oklahoma Press, 1946.

3.268 Minnick, N. F. "A Cultural History of Central City, Colorado, from 1859 to 1880, in Terms of Books and Libraries." Master's thesis, University of Chicago, 1946.

3.269 Power, F. M. "American Private Book Clubs." Master's thesis, Columbia University, 1946.

3.270 Robathan, D. M. "John Adams and the Classics." *New England Quarterly* 19 (1946): 91–98.

3.271 Schlesinger, A. M. *Learning How to Behave: A Historical Study of American Etiquette Books.* New York: Macmillan, 1946.

3.272 Blegen, T. C. "Frontier Bookshelves." In *Grassroots History.* Minneapolis: University of Minnesota, 1947. Pp. 175–86.

3.273 Mosier, R. D. *Making the American Mind: Social and Moral Ideas in the McGuffey Readers.* New York: King's Crown Press, 1947.

3.274 Mott, F. L. *Golden Multitudes: The Story of Best Sellers in the United States.* New York: Macmillan, 1947.

3.275 Davis, C. C. *An Early Novelist Goes to the Library: William Caruthers and His Readings, 1823–29.* New York: New York Public Library, 1948.

3.276 Powell, W. S. "Books in the Virginia Colony before 1624." *WMQ* 5 (1948): 177–84.

3.277 Spurlin, P. M. "Rousseau in America, 1760–1809." *French-American Review* 1 (1948): 8–16.

3.278 Fletcher, M. P. "Arkansas Pioneers: What They Were Reading a Century Ago." *Arkansas Historical Quarterly* 8 (1949): 211–14.

3.279 Keifer, M. *American Children through Their Books, 1700–1835.* Philadelphia: University of Pennsylvania Press, 1949.

3.280 Kesselring, M. L. *Hawthorne's Reading, 1828–1850.* New York: New York Public Library, 1949.

3.281 Peden, W. H. "A Book Peddler [Samuel Whitcomb, Jr.] Invades Monticello [1792]." *WMQ* 6 (1949): 631–36.

3.282 Sibley, A. M. *Alexander Pope's Prestige in America, 1725–1835.* New York: Columbia University Press, 1949.

1950–1971

3.283 Barker, G. E. "What Crown Pointers Were Reading One Hundred Years Ago." *New York History* 31 (1950): 31–40.

3.284 Dale, E. E. "The Frontier Society." *Nebraska History* 31 (1950): 167–82.

3.285 Hart, J. D. *The Popular Book: A History of America's Literary Taste.* New York: Oxford University Press, 1950.

3.286 Hurley, G. "Reading in the Gold Rush." *BCCQNL* 15 (1950): 85–91.

3.287 Mills, R. V. "Books in Oregon: The First Decade." *BCCQNL* 15 (1950): 51–57.

3.288 Baker, H. S. "Reading Tastes in California, 1849–1859." Doctoral dissertation, Stanford University, 1951.

3.289 Dedmond, F. B. "Emerson and the Concord Libraries." *MoreB* 3 (1951): 318–19.

3.290 Dugger, H. H. "Reading Interests and the Book Trade in Frontier Missouri." Doctoral dissertation, University of Missouri, 1951.

3.291 Quenzel, C. H. "Books for the Boys in Blue [Civil War]." *JISHS* 44 (1951): 218–30.

3.292 Winterich, J. T. "What a New Englander Was Likely to Read in 1711." *PW* 159 (1951): 759–61.

3.293 Wright, C. C. "Reading Interests in Texas from the 1830's to the Civil War." *SHQ* 54 (1951): 301–15.

3.294 Haraszti, Z. *John Adams and the Prophets of Progress.* Cambridge: Harvard University Press, 1952.

3.295 Parks, E. W. "Jefferson's Attitude toward History." *Georgia Historical Quarterly* (1952): 336–52.

3.296 Purcell, J. S. "A Book Pedlar's Progress in North Carolina." *NCHR* 29 (1952): 8–23.

3.297 Clive, J., and Bailyn, B. "England's Cultural Provinces: Scotland and America." *WMQ* 11 (1954): 200–213.

3.298 Garfinkle, N. "Conservatism in American Textbooks, 1800–1860." *New York History* 35 (1954): 49–63.

3.299 Little, E. N. "The Early Reading of Oliver Wendell Holmes." *HLB* 8 (1954): 163–203.

3.300 Noel, M. *Villains Galore: The Heyday of the Popular Story Weekly.* New York: Macmillan, 1954.

3.301 Stovall, F. "Notes on Whitman's Reading." *AL* 26 (1954): 337–62.

3.302 Baker, H. S. "Gold Rush Miners and Their Books." *Quarterly Newsletter* 10 (1955): 51–60.

3.303 McMullen, H. "Ralph Waldo Emerson and Libraries." *LQ* 25 (1955): 152–62.

3.304 Wright, L. B. *Culture on the Moving Frontier.* Bloomington: Indiana University Press, 1955.

3.305 Wright, N. "Horatio Greenough's Borrowings from the Harvard College Library." *HLB* 9 (1955): 406–10.

3.306 McDermott, J. F. "Culture and the Missouri Frontier." *MHR* 50 (1956): 355–70.

3.307 Agard, W. "Classics on the Midwest Frontier." In *The Frontier in Perspective,* edited by W. D. Wyman and C. B. Kroeber. Madison: University of Wisconsin Press, 1957. Pp. 165–83.

3.308 Esarey, L. "Elements of Culture in the Old Northwest." *IMH* 53 (1957): 257–64.

3.309 Powell, J. H. *The Books of a New Nation: United States Government Publications, 1774–1814.* Philadelphia: University of Pennsylvania Press, 1957.

3.310 Barnes, J. C. "A Bibliography of Wordsworth in American Periodicals through 1825." *PBSA* 52 (1958): 205–19.

3.311 Colbourn, H. T. "Thomas Jefferson's Use of the Past." *WMQ* 15 (1958): 56–70.

3.312 Houlette, W. D. "Sources of Books for the Old South." *LQ* 28 (1958): 194–201.

3.313 Peckham, H. "Books and Reading on the Ohio Valley Frontier." *Mississippi Valley Historical Review* 44 (1958): 649–63.

3.314 Schick, F. L. *The Paperbound Book in America: The History of Paperbacks and Their European Backgrounds.* New York: R.R. Bowker, 1958.

3.315 Bode, C. *The Anatomy of American Popular Culture, 1840–1861.* Berkeley: University of California Press, 1959.

3.316 Muir, A. F. "The Intellectual Climate of Houston during the Period of the Republic." *SHQ* 62 (1959): 312–21.

3.317 Nichols, C. H. "Who Read the Slave Narratives?" *Phylon: The Atlanta University Review of Race and Culture* 20 (1959): 149–62.

3.318 Robbins, C. *The Eighteenth Century Commonwealthman: Studies in the Transmission, Development, and Circumstances of English Liberal Thought from the Restoration of Charles II until the War with the Thirteen Colonies.* Cambridge: Harvard University Press, 1959.

3.319 Cantrell, C. H. "The Reading Habits of Antebellum Southerners." Doctoral dissertation, University of Illinois, 1960.

3.320 Colbourn, H. T. "The Reading of Joseph Carrington Cabell: A List of Books on Various Subjects Recommended to a Young Man . . . ." *Studies in Bibliography* 3 (1960): 179–88.

3.321 Walker, D. D. "Reading on the Range: The Literary Habits of the American Cowboys." *Arizona and the West* 11 (1960): 307–18.

3.322 Wilson, J. S. "Best Sellers in Jefferson's Day." *Virginia Quarterly Review* 36 (1960): 222–37.

3.323 Nietz, J. *Old Textbooks...from Colonial Days to 1900.* Pittsburgh: University of Pittsburgh Press, 1961.

3.324 Baer, E. A. "Books, Newspapers and Libraries in Pioneer St. Louis, 1808–1842." *MHR* 56 (1962): 347–60.

3.325 Bailyn, B. "Political Experience and Enlightenment Ideas in Eighteenth-Century America." *AHR* 67 (1962): 339–51.

3.326 Carpenter, C. *History of American Schoolbooks.* Philadelphia: University of Pennsylvania Press, 1963.

3.327 England, J. M. "The Democratic Faith in American Schoolbooks, 1783–1860." *AQ* 15 (1963): 191–99.

3.328 Gummere, R. M. *The American Colonial Mind and the Classical Tradition.* Cambridge: Harvard University Press, 1963.

3.329 Davis, R. B. *Intellectual Life in Jefferson's Virginia, 1790–1830.* Chapel Hill: University of North Carolina Press, 1964.

3.330 Elson, R. M. *Guardians of Tradition: American School Books of the Nineteenth Century.* Lincoln: University of Nebraska, 1964.

3.331 Nunis, D. B. *Books in Their Sea Chests: Reading Along the Early California Coast.* N.p.: California Library Association, 1964.

3.332 Seigel, J. P. "Puritan Light Reading." *New England Quarterly* 37 (1964): 185–99.

3.333 Sensabaugh, G. F. *Milton in Early America.* Princeton: Princeton University Press, 1964.

3.334 Wade, R. C. *The Urban Frontier: Pioneer Life in Early Pittsburgh, Cincinnati, Lexington, Louisville, and St. Louis.* Chicago: University of Chicago Press, 1964.

3.335 Colbourn, H. T. *The Lamp of Experience: Whig History and the Intellectual Origins of the American Revolution.* Chapel Hill: University of North Carolina Press, 1965.

3.336 Joyaux, G. J. "French Fiction in American Magazines, 1800–1848." *Arizona Quarterly* 21 (1965): 29–40.

3.337 Capps, J. L. *Emily Dickinson's Reading, 1836–1886.* Cambridge: Harvard University Press, 1966.

3.338 Dale, E. E. *The Cross Timbers: Memories of a North Texas Boyhood.* Austin: University of Texas Press, 1966.

3.339 Litto, F. M. "Addison's *Cato* in the Colonies." *WMQ* 23 (1966): 431–49.

3.340 McMullen, H. "The Use of Books in the Ohio Valley Before 1850." *JLH* 1 (1966): 43–56, 73.

3.341 Sealts, M. M. *Melville's Reading: A Checklist of Books Owned and Borrowed.* Madison: University of Wisconsin Press, 1966.

3.342 Shaffer, E. "The Children's Books of the American Sunday-School Union." *American Book Collector* 17 (1966): 21–28.

3.343 Bailyn, B. *The Ideological Origins of the American Revolution.* Cambridge: Harvard University Press, 1967.

3.344 Black, H. *The American Schoolbook.* New York: Morrow, 1967.

3.345 Grade, A. E. "A Chronicle of Robert Frost's Early Reading, 1874–1899." *BNYPL* 72 (1968): 611–28.

3.346 Cohen, H., ed. *Landmarks of American Writing.* New York: Basic Books, 1969.

3.347 Crandall, J. C. "Patriotism and Humanitarian Reform in Children's Literature, 1825–1860." *AQ* 21 (1969): 3–22.

3.348 Ensor, A. *Mark Twain and the Bible.* Lexington: University of Kentucky Press, 1969.

3.349 Kniker, C. R. "The Chautauqua Literary and Scientific Circle, 1878–1914: An Historical Interpretation of an Educational Piety in Industrial America." Doctoral dissertation, Columbia University, 1969.

3.350 Ribbens, D. N. "The Reading Interests of Thoreau, Hawthorne, and Lanier." Doctoral dissertation, University of Wisconsin, 1969.

3.351 Bethke, R. D. "Chapbook 'Gallows Literature' in Nineteenth-Century Pennsylvania." *Pennsylvania Folklife* 20 (1970): 2–15.

3.352 Downs, R. B. *Books That Changed America.* New York: Macmillan, 1970.

3.353 Roth, M. "Lawrence Sterne in America." *BNYPL* 74 (1970): 428–36.

3.354 Commager, H. S. "The American Enlightenment and the Ancient World: A Study of Paradox." *PMHS* 83 (1971): 3–15.

3.355 Downs, R. B. *Famous American Books.* New York: McGraw-Hill, 1971.

3.356 Edgar, W. B. "Some Popular Books in Colonial South Carolina." *SCHM* 72 (1971): 174–78.

3.357 Harris, M. H. "The Availability of Books and the Nature of Book Ownership on the Southern Indiana Frontier, 1800–1850." Doctoral dissertation, Indiana University, 1971.

3.358 Harris, M. H. "Books for Sale on the Illinois Frontier." *American Book Collector* 21 (1971): 15–17.

3.359 Miles, E. A. "The Old South and the Classical World." *NCHR* 48 (1971): 258–75.

1972–1986

3.360 Fiering, N. S. "Solomon Stoddard's Library at Harvard in 1664." *HLB* 20 (1972): 255–69.

3.361 Hubbell, J. B. *Who Are the Major American Writers? A Study of Changing Literary Canon.* Durham: Duke University Press, 1972.

3.362 Stobridge, W. "Book Smuggling in Mexican California." *American Neptune* 32 (1972): 117–22.

3.363 Werner, J. M. "David Hume and America." *Journal of the History of Ideas* 33 (1972): 439–56.

3.364 Woolf, H. "Science for the People: Copernicanism and Newtonianism in the Almanacs of Early America." In *The Reception of Copernicus' Heliocentric Theory...,* edited by J. Dobrzycki. Boston: D. Reidel Publishing Co., 1972. Pp. 293–309.

3.365 Cazden, R. E. "The Provision of German Books in America during the Eighteenth Century." *Libri* 23 (1973): 81–108.

3.366 Harris, M. H. "Bookstores on the Southern Indiana Frontier, 1833–1850." *American Book Collector* 23 (1973): 30–32.

3.367 Harris, M. H. "The General Store as an Outlet for Books on the Southern [Indiana] Frontier, 1800–1850." *JLH* 8 (1973): 124–32.

3.368 Liebman, S. W. "The Origins of Emerson's Early Poetics: His Reading in the Scottish Common Sense Critics." *American Literature* 45 (1973): 23–33.

3.369 Sears, D. A. "Libraries and Reading Habits in Early Portland (1763–1836)." *Maine Historical Society Newsletter* 12 (Spring 1973): 151–65.

3.370 Weyant, R. G. "Helvetius and Jefferson: Studies of Human Nature and Government in the Eighteenth Century." *Journal of History of Behavioral Science* 9 (1973): 29–41.

3.371 Harris, M. H. "Books Stocked by Six Indiana General Stores." *JLH* 9 (1974): 66–72.

3.372 Van Orman, R. A. "The Bard in the West." *Washington Historical Quarterly* 5 (1974): 29–38.

3.373 Cazden, R. E. "The German Book Trade in Ohio before 1848." *Ohio History* 84 (1975): 57–77.

3.374 Skinner, A. E. "Books and Libraries in Early Texas." *TL* 37 (1975): 169–76.

3.375 Spurlin, P. M. "Readership in the American Enlightenment." In *Literature and History in the Age of Ideas,* edited by C. G. S. Williams. Columbus: Ohio State University Press, 1975. Pp. 359–74.

3.376 Stiverson, G. A. "Books Both Useful and Entertaining: Reading Habits in Mid-Eighteenth Century Virginia." *SEL* 24 (Winter 1975): 52–58.

3.377 Tourtellot, A. B. "The Early Reading of Benjamin Franklin." *HLB* 23 (1975): 5–41.

3.378 Winans, R. B. "The Growth of a Novel-Reading Public in Late Eighteenth Century America." *Early American Literature* 9 (1975): 267–75.

3.379 Geary, S. "The Domestic Novel as a Commercial Commodity: Making a Best Seller in the 1850s." *PBSA* 70 (1976): 365–93.

3.380 Haney, R., Harris, M. H., and Tipton, L. "The Impact of Reading on Human Behavior: The Implications of Communications Research." *AdLib* 6 (1976): 139–216.

3.381 Harlan, R. D. "Colonial Printer as Bookseller in Eighteenth-Century Philadelphia: the Case of David Hall." *Studies in Eighteenth-Century Culture* 5 (1976): 355–69.

3.382 Lundberg, D., and May, H. F. "The Enlightened Reader in America." *AQ* 28 (1976): 262–93.

3.383 Simmons, M. "Authors and Books of Colonial New Mexico." In *Voices from the Southwest: A Gathering in Honor of Lawrence Clark Powell,* edited by D. C. Dickinson, W. D.

Laird, and M. F. Maxwell. Flagstaff, Ariz.: Northland Press, 1976. Pp. 13–32.

3.384 Skelley, G. T. "The Library World and the Book Trade." In *A Century of Service: Librarianship in the United States and Canada,* edited by S. L. Jackson, E. B. Herling, and E. J. Josey. Chicago: American Library Association, 1976. Pp. 281–302.

3.385 Avi. "Children's Literature: The American Revolution." *TN* 33 (1977): 149–61.

3.386 Beck, N. R. "The Use of Library and Educational Facilities by Russian-Jewish Immigrants in New York City, 1880–1914: The Impact of Culture." *JLH* 12 (1977): 128–49.

3.387 Edgar, W. B. "Reading Tastes in 18th Century South Carolina." *SEL* 27 (1977): 227–33.

3.388 Hackett, A. P., and Burke, J. H. *Eighty Years of Best Sellers, 1895–1975.* New York: R.R. Bowker, 1977.

3.389 Davis, R. B. *Intellectual Life in the Colonial South, 1585–1763,* 3 vols. Knoxville: University of Tennessee Press, 1978.

3.390 Molnar, J. E. "Publication and Retail Book Advertisements in the Virginia Gazette, *1736–1780." Doctoral dissertation, University of Michigan, 1978.*

3.391 Davis, R. B. *A Colonial Southern Bookshelf: Reading in the Eighteenth Century.* Athens: University of Georgia Press, 1979.

3.392 Stevens, E. "Books and Wealth on the Frontier: Athens County and Washington County, Ohio, 1790–1859." *Social Science History* 5 (1981): 417–43.

3.393 Sullivan, L. E. "The Reading Habits of the Nineteenth-Century Baltimore Bourgeoisie: A Cross-Cultural Analysis." *JLH* 16 (1981): 227–40.

3.394 Wolf, E., and Korey, M. E. *Quarter of a Millenium: The Library Company of Philadelphia, 1731–1981: A Selection of Books, Manuscripts, Maps, Prints, Drawings and Paintings.* Philadelphia: Library Company of Philadelphia, 1981.

3.395 Korey, M. E. "The Library Company: A Phoenix Reborn." *WLB* 56 (1982): 745–48.

3.396 Ducker, D. C. "The Ebenezer S. Lane Library: A Study in Nineteenth-Century Reading Tastes." Master's thesis, University of Chicago, 1983.

3.397 Hall, D. D. "The Uses of Literacy in New England, 1600–1850." In *Printing and Society in Early America,* edited by W. L. Joyce et al. Worcester, Mass.: American Antiquarian Society, 1983. Pp. 1–47.

3.398 Isaac, R. "Books and the Social Authority of Learning: The Case of Mid-Eighteenth Century Virginia." In *Printing and Society in Early America,* edited by W. L. Joyce et al. Worcester, Mass.: American Antiquarian Society, 1983. Pp. 228–49.

3.399 Kaser, D. *Books and Libraries in Camp and Battle: The Civil War Experience.* Westport, Conn.: Greenwood Press, 1984.

3.400 Korey, M. E. *The Wolf Years: The Renascence of the Library Company of Philadelphia.* Philadelphia: Library Company of Philadelphia, 1984.

3.401 Leary, L. *The Book-Peddling Parson: An Account of the Life and Works of Mason Locke Weems—Patriot, Pitchman, Author and Purveyor of Morality to the Citizenry of the Early United States of America.* Chapel Hill, N.C.: Algonquin Books, 1984.

3.402 Neavill, G. B. "The Modern Library Series." Doctoral dissertation, University of Chicago, 1984.

3.403 Clark, T. D. "Travel Accounts, Guides, and Gazeteers." *ELIS* 38 (1985): 387–89.

3.404 Chipley, L. "The Enlightenment Library of William Bentley." *Essex Institute. Historical Collections* 122 (1986): 2–29.

3.405 McKelvey, B. "Rochester's Library and Book Clubs: Their Origins, Programs and Accomplishments." *Rochester History* 48 (1986): 3–19.

3.406 Nance, E. H. "Wheelock, Texas, Center of Culture." *TLJ* 62 (1986): 20–22.

4.
Predecessors of the Public Library

Before considering the public library movement that emerged in the middle of the nineteenth century, a movement that defined the nature of librarianship in America, an orderly and chronological treatment of sources requires attention to those types of libraries that in some way led to the acceptance of general access to books and in many instances merged into tax-supported public libraries. These libraries were of three main types: (1) the parochial libraries of Thomas Bray, (2) social libraries, and (3) libraries devoted to specific groups of people or specific purposes.

Parochial Libraries of Thomas Bray

Thomas Bray (1658–1730) was an Anglican clergyman who, through the auspices of the Society for the Propagation of Christian Knowledge, established libraries throughout England and Wales. During a brief span as commissary to Maryland, he established parish libraries on the eastern seaboard in the early eighteenth century. Charles T. Laugher's *Thomas Bray's Grand Design* (1973, **4.31**) is the most definitive overview. However, a number of other studies treat various aspects of Bray's efforts to plant libraries in the colonies, and they deserve examination as well. Among the more important are Bernard C. Steiner's early but basic essay (1896, **4.3**), William Houlette's general article (1934, **4.8**), and Joseph T. Wheeler's studies of Bray's work in Maryland (1939, **4.13**; 1940, **4.14**). Herbert Searcy's dissertation (1963, **4.27**) is one of the few devoted to this subject. More recently, John Van Horne has edited the American correspondence of the Bray Associates from the mid-eighteenth century in *Religious Philanthropy and Colonial Slavery* (1985, **4.34**).

Social Libraries

The term *social library* has come to signify the kind of library that generally provided a circulating collection of materials and frequently a reading room for the use of any person meeting the established criteria, which usually involved a fee or subscription, or a payment to become a joint owner or stockholder, of the library. In the nineteenth century, many of these libraries were known as "public libraries," a term that gradually came to describe tax-supported, publicly administered libraries open to all freely on an equal basis. Social libraries in their many forms reached the peak of their significance by the mid-nineteenth century and have been the subject of a considerable body of research.

The standard treatment of the rise of social libraries in the United States is Jesse Shera's *Foundations of the Public Library: The Origins of the Public Library Movement in New England, 1629–1855* (1949, **4.176**). Recently, Haynes McMullen has provided complementary treatment about "The Very Slow Decline of the American Social Library" (1985, **4.310**). In a related general essay, David Kaser has provided an overview of the history of the reading room to the early twentieth century (1978, **4.297**).

While Shera's work was a landmark treatise, it also stimulated new work on the subject of social library development in various states and cities. Several efforts deserve mention here. Haynes McMullen has probably done more work in this area than anyone else and has published essays on Ohio, Illinois, and Indiana (1958, **4.228**); Kentucky (1960, **4.236**); and Pennsylvania (1965, **4.255**). Other important work has been done by John Francis McDermott on Missouri (1944, **4.161**), Frances L. Spain on South Carolina (1947, **4.168**), Ruth W. Robinson on social libraries in four Pennsylvania communities (1952, **4.197**), and Elizabeth Welborn, again on South Carolina (1956, **4.221**; 1959, **4.234**). Jane Flener has studied developments in Tennessee (1963, **4.241**), Ray Held the early period in California (1963, **4.242**), and Harry R. Skallerup the libraries and reading rooms among early American seamen (1974, **4.284**). Edward Stevens has analyzed early social libraries in Ohio (1981, **4.304**); Victoria Musmann has studied "Women and the Founding of Social Libraries in California, 1859–1910" (1982, **4.307**); and Joseph Yeatman analyzed Baltimore libraries from 1815 to 1840 (1985, **4.311**).

Many individual social libraries have attracted the attention of library historians. The earlier and more famous institutions are subjects of classic studies. America's first and perhaps most important social library—the Library Company of Philadelphia—has been explored in detail by George Abbot (1913, **4.97**), Austin Gray (1937, **4.139**), Edwin Wolf (1954, **4.207**; 1955, **4.214**; 1956, **4.222**; 1960, **4.237**; 1976, **4.292**), Dorothy F. Grimm (1955, **4.209**), and Margaret Korty (1965, **4.253**). Arthur S. Roberts (1948, **4.173**), Sister M. V. O'Connor (1956, **4.219**), and Marcus McCorison (1965, **4.254**) have examined the Redwood Library Company of Newport.

Other examples of significance include the work of Austin B. Keep (1908, **4.88**) and Marion King (1954, **4.205**) on the New York Society Library; Sarah Cutler (1917, **4.105**), J. B. Nicholson (1955, **4.211**), and Wayne A. Wiegand

(1977, **4.294**) on the "Coonskin Library" in Cincinnati; Harry M. Lydenberg on the Berkshire Republican Library at Stockbridge (1940, **4.148**); Russell Bidlack's history of the City Library of Detroit (1955, **4.208**); Charles W. David's study of the Longwood Library (1957, **4.223**); Edgar Reinke on the Charleston Library Society (1967, **4.265**); and William Van Beynum on the Book Company of Durham (1968, **4.269**). A recent addition to this literature is Barbara W. Stanley's centennial history of the Rye (New York) Free Reading Room (1984, **4.309**).

Several other types of social libraries deserve mention here. The athenaeum, an aristocratic mutation of the social library idea, is also covered in this section. Among the more important studies of this type of library are Charles K. Bolton (1909, **4.90**; 1927, **4.118**), William I. Fletcher (1914, **4.101**), Mary Regan (1927, **4.121**), Walter Whitehill (1973, **4.281**), and Ronald Story (1975, **4.287**) on the Boston Athenaeum. Joseph L. Harrison (1911, **4.94**) and Grace Leonard and Chesley Worthington (1940, **4.147**) have written on the Providence Athenaeum and Cynthia B. Wiggin has studied the Salem Athenaeum (1966, **4.262**; 1968, **4.270**).

An additional type of social library has received considerable attention— the mechanics' and mercantile library. William Boyd's dissertation (1975, **4.286**) is the definitive treatment of the subject, but a standard survey of an earlier period remains Sidney Ditzion's summary article (1940, **4.146**). Individual libraries that have received serious study include the Apprentices' Library of Philadelphia by John F. Lewis (1924, **4.112**), the San Francisco Mercantile Library by Joyce Backus (1931, **4.128**), the Mercantile Library Association of Boston by Gordon Gaskill (1949, **4.175**), and the Young Men's Mercantile Library Association of Cincinnati by Merle Carter (1951, **4.184**).

Circulating, Sunday School, School District, and YMCA Libraries

A final group of social libraries oriented toward a special purpose or a specific clientele deserves mention here. These libraries have generally lacked the level of attention that other social libraries have received, and there has been comparatively little research done in recent years. Circulating libraries, those endeavors designed for commercial profit, have been studied more thoroughly than the other specialized social libraries. While Jesse Shera's *Foundations of the Public Library* (1949, **4.176**) contains much useful material, the most significant overview is now David Kaser's *A Book for a Sixpence: The Circulating Library in America* (1980, **4.350**). Circulating libraries in the Southeast have been studied by Mary V. Moore (1958, **4.340**), while Philip Metzger has offered a more recent case study of a single such library in post–Civil War Austin, Texas (1986, **4.352**). Philip B. Eppard has studied the demise of the modern rental library (1986, **4.351**).

Although Sunday school libraries have been a popular topic for some historians, substantive work remains to be done. General studies of particular interest include the work of Frank K. Walter (1942, **4.329**), M. E. Hand (1950,

4.331), Maxine B. Fedder (1951, **4.333**), Alice B. Cushman (1957, **4.338**), F. A. Briggs (1961, **4.343**), and Ellen Shaffer (1966, **3.342**; listed in Chapter 3, "Private Libraries and Reading Tastes").

School district libraries are covered in Sidney Ditzion's classic article (1940, **4.325**). More specialized studies include Helen M. Wilcox on the early development of this type of library (1953, **4.336**) and state treatments of the early periods in New York by Alice C. Dodge (1944, **4.330**) and in California by Ray Held (1959, **4.341**).

YMCA libraries that emerged just before the Civil War and flourished afterward have not received detailed attention. However, several useful essays on the subject have appeared, including those by Doris Fletcher (1957, **4.339**) and Joe W. Kraus (1975, **4.349**). Since the precursors to the modern public library are such a diverse group of libraries, users of this bibliography would do well to examine the entries in the preceding chapter, especially those dealing with reading tastes and private book collections. Many articles in the following chapter, which deals with public libraries, will have relevant information that relates to the predecessors of individual libraries and to groups of social libraries that merged with the new tax-supported institutions. Finally, Chapter 9, "Special Libraries," contains a subdivision on historical society, museum, and institute libraries that includes relevant material, since some social libraries developed into these types of libaries as they matured or changed direction.

Parochial Libraries of Thomas Bray

4.1 Foote, H. "Remarks on King's Chapel Library, Boston, Mass." *PMHS* 18, 1st ser. (1881): 423–30.

4.2 Hurst, J. F. "Parochial Libraries [of Maryland] of the Colonial Period." *Papers of the American Society of Church History* 2 (1890): 46–49.

4.3 Steiner, B. C. "Reverend Thomas Bray and His American Libraries." *AHR* 2 (October 1896): 59–75.

4.4 Steiner, B. C. *Rev. Thomas Bray: His Life and Selected Works Relating to Maryland.* Baltimore: Maryland Historical Society, 1901.

4.5 Smith, G. "Dr. Thomas Bray." *Library Association Record* 12 (1910): 242–60.

4.6 Merritt, E. P. *The Parochial Library of the Eighteenth Century in Christ Church, Boston.* Boston: Merrymount Press, 1917.

4.7 Houlette, W. D. "Plantation and Parish Libraries in the Old South." Doctoral dissertation, State University of Iowa, 1933.

4.8 Houlette, W. D. "Parish Libraries and the Work of the Rev. Thomas Bray." *LQ* 4 (1934): 588–609.

4.9 Pennington, E. L. *The Reverend Thomas Bray.* Philadelphia: Church Historical Society, 1934.

4.10 Pennington, E. L. "The Work of the Bray Associates in Pennsylvania." *PMHB* 58 (1934): 1–25.

4.11 Wroth, L. C. "Dr. Bray's 'Proposals for the Encouragement of Religion and Learning in the Foreign Plantations': A Bibliographical Note." *PMHS* 65 (1936): 518–34.

4.12 Pennington, E. L. "Thomas Bray's Associates and Their Work among the Negroes." *PAAS* 48 (1938): 311–403.

4.13 Wheeler, J. T. "Thomas Bray and the American Parochial Libraries." *MHM* 34 (1939): 246–65.

4.14 Wheeler, J. T. "The Layman's Libraries and the Provincial Library." *MHM* 35 (1940): 60–73.

4.15 Lydekker, J. W. "Thomas Bray (1658–1730): Founder of Missionary Enterprise." *HMPEC* 12 (1943): 186–224.

4.16 Livingston, H. E. "Early American Schoolbooks and Libraries as Revealed in the Records of Thomas Bray and the Society for the Propagation of the Gospel in Foreign Parts." Master's thesis, University of California, Los Angeles, 1945.

4.17 McCulloch, S. C. "Dr. Thomas Bray's Commissary Work in London." *WMQ* 2 (1945): 333–48.

4.18 McCulloch, S. C. "The Importance of Dr. Thomas Bray's *Bibliotheca Parochialis*." *HMPEC* 15 (1946): 50–59.

4.19 Whitehill, W. M. "The King's Chapel Library." *PCSM* 38 (1949): 274–89.

4.20 Molz, J. B. "The Reverend Thomas Bray, Planner of Libraries: A Study of an Early Benefactor of Maryland Libraries." Master's thesis, Drexel Institute of Technology, 1950.

4.21 Thompson, H. P. *Into All Lands: The History of the Society for the Propagation of the Gospel in Foreign Parts, 1790–1950.* London: Society for Promoting Christian Knowledge, 1951.

4.22 Sahli, M. S. "Thomas Bray and the Founding of Libraries in Maryland." Master's thesis, Western Reserve University, 1952.

4.23 Hirsch, C. B. "The Experiences of the SPG in Eighteenth-Century North Carolina." Doctoral dissertation, Indiana University, 1953.

4.24 Fletcher, C. "The Reverend Thomas Bray, M. Alexander Vattemare, and Library Science." *LQ* 27 (1957): 95–99.

4.25 Gordon, N. S. "Thomas Bray: A Study in Early Eighteenth-Century Librarianship." Master's thesis, Catholic University of America, 1961.

4.26 Nelso, J. K. "Anglican Missions in America, 1701–1725: A Study of the Society for the Propagation of the Gospel in Foreign Parts." Doctoral dissertation, Northwestern University, 1962.

4.27 Searcy, H. L. "Parochial Libraries in the American Colonies." Doctoral dissertation, University of Illinois, 1963.

4.28 Bultmann, W. A., and Bultmann, P. W. "The Roots of American Humanitarianism: A Study of the SPCK and the APG, 1699–1720." *HMPEC* 33 (1964): 3–48.

4.29 Bray, T. *An Essay towards Promoting All Necessary and Useful Knowledge, Both Divine and Human.* Boston: G.K. Hall, 1967.

4.30 *America's First Public Library: The Provincial Library in Charlestown in Carolina, 1698.* Columbia, S.C.: South Carolina State Library, 1970.

4.31 Laugher, C. T. *Thomas Bray's Grand Design.* Chicago: American Library Association, 1973.

4.32 Boorstin, D. J. "The Indivisible Community." In *Libraries and the Life of the Mind in America: Addresses Delivered at the Centennial Celebration of the American Library Association,* edited by the American Library Association. Chicago: American Library Association, 1977.

4.33 Thompson, L. S. "Memoirs of a Backwoods Collector." *ABBW* 71 (1983): 4855–56.

4.34 Van Horne, J. C., ed. *Religious Philanthropy and Colonial Slavery: The American Correspondence of the Associates of Dr. Bray, 1717–1777.* Urbana: University of Illinois Press, 1985.

Social Libraries

Before 1876

4.35 "Public Library in Philadelphia." *American Magazine of Useful and Entertaining Knowledge* 2 (November 1835): 91.

4.36 Smith, J. J. "Notes for a History of the Library Company of Philadelphia." *Hazard's Register of Pennsylvania* 16 (26 September 1835): 201–08.

4.37 Wigglesworth, E. "Sketch of the Boston Athenaeum." *Congregational Education Society. Quarterly Journal* 12 (November 1839): 149–53.

4.38 Quincy, J. *History of the Boston Athenaeum, with Biographical Notices of Its Deceased Founders.* Cambridge, Mass.: Metcalf & Co., 1851.

4.39 "Astor Library of New York." *NLGPC* 2 (15 March 1852): 43.

4.40 "The Library Company of Philadelphia, and the Loganian Library." *NLGPC* 2 (15 July 1852): 127.

4.41 "Mercantile Library Associations." *Merchants' Magazine and Commercial Review* 29 (October 1853): 437–38.

4.42 "New York Mercantile Library Association." *Literary World [New York]* 13 (17 September 1853): 126–27.

4.43 "[New York Mercantile Library Association]." *NLGPC* ns 1 (15 June 1854): 308–09.

4.44 "The Astor Library and Its Founder." *Emerson's Magazine and Putnam's Monthly* 2 (October 1855): 137–45.

4.45 "Catalogue of the Mercantile Library of Boston [Review]." *NLGPC* ns 2 (15 January 1855): 25–26.

4.46 *Catalogue of Books in the Newton Athenaeum with a Sketch of the Origin and Object of the Institution.* Boston: Bazin & Chandler, 1856.

4.47 *A Catalogue of the Library of the Salem Athenaeum in Salem, Massachusetts: To Which is Prefixed a Brief Historical Account of the Institution, with Its Charter & Bylaws.* Boston: J. Wilson & Son, 1858.

4.48 Philadelphia. Mercantile Library Company. *Essay on the History and Growth of the Mercantile Company of Philadelphia and Its Capabilities for Future Usefulness.* Philadelphia: Jas. B. Rogers, 1867.

4.49 Read, J. M. "The Old Philadelphia Library." *American Historical Magazine* 21 (March 1868): 299–312.

4.50 Norton, F. H. "The Astor Library." *Galaxy* 7 (April 1869): 527–37.

4.51 Norton, F. H. "Ten Years in a Public Library." *Galaxy* 8 (October 1869): 528–37.

4.52 Calkins, F. W., comp. *Catalogue of Books Contained in the Odd Fellows' Library, with a Short History of the Library, Regulations, etc., etc.* Boston: Board of Trustees, 1875.

1876–1919

4.53 Perkins, F. B. "Young Men's Mercantile Libraries." In *Public Libraries in the United States of America: Their History, Condition and Management; Special Report, Part I*, U.S. Bureau of Education. Washington, D.C.: Government Printing Office, 1876. Pp. 378–85.

4.54 Buxton, P. M. "N. Yarmouth & Falmouth Social Library." *Old Times* 3 (1879): 427–29.

4.55 Athens Co., Ohio. Pioneer Association. *Memorial and History of the Western Library Association of Ames Township, Athens County, Ohio.* N.p.: Published by the Pioneer Association of Athens County, Ohio, 1882.

4.56 Ward, T. "The German-Town Road and Its Associations; Part Sixth." *PMHB* 6 (1882): 129–55.

4.57 Youngman, D. "The Winchester Library." *Winchester Record* 1 (1885): 200–202.

4.58 Cooke, G. "Winchester Library Association." *Winchester Record* 2 (1886): 483–87.

4.59 Ballard, H. H. "The History, Methods, and Purposes of the Berkshire Athenaeum." *Berkshire Historical and Scientific Society. Collections* 1 (1891): 293–306.

4.60 Mason, G. C. *Annals of the Redwood Library and Athenaeum.* Newport, R.I.: Redwood Library, 1891.

4.61 Weeks, S. B. "First Libraries in North Carolina." *Trinity Archive* 5 (October 1891): 10–20.

4.62 "Historical Sketches and Notes on Library Progress." In *New Hampshire. Board of Library Commissioners Biennial Report* 2. N.p.: 1892–1894. Pp. 25–55.

4.63 Mason, A. P. "The Fitchburg Athenaeum (1852–1859)." *Fitchburg Historical Society Proceedings* 1 (1892–94): 202–19.

4.64 "Historical Sketches and Notes on Library Progress." In *New Hampshire. Board of Library Commissioners Biennial Report* 3. N.p.: 1894–1896. Pp. 31–52.

4.65 Shaw, S. S. *The Boston Library Society: Historical Sketch.* Boston: G.H. Ellis, 1895.

4.66 Winslow, E. "The Boston Athenaeum." *Bostonian* 3 (1895): 227–36.

4.67 Annett, A. "[History of Jaffrey's Social Library]." In *Dedication of the Clay Library Building at East Jaffrey, New Hampshire, Saturday, July 4, 1896*. Concord, N.H.: Republican Press, 1896.

4.68 Hayes, J. S. *Souvenir: Our Public Library*. Somerville, Mass.: N.p., 1896.

4.69 "Historical Sketches and Notes on Library Progress." In *New Hampshire. Board of Library Commissioners Biennial Report 4*. N.p.: 1896–1898. Pp. 28–40.

4.70 Denio, H. W. "A Historical Sketch of Library Legislation in New Hampshire." In *New Hampshire State Library, Report of the Trustees, (1897–1898)*. Concord, N.H.: New Hampshire State Library, 1898. Pp. 65–173.

4.71 Palmer, H. R. "The Libraries of Rhode Island." *NEM* 22 (1900): 478–500.

4.72 Larned, J. N. "An Historical Sketch of the Buffalo Library, Prior to the Free Library Movement." *Publications of the Buffalo Historical Society* 3 (1902): 361–84.

4.73 "Boston Athenaeum." *Public Library Monthly* 1 (1903): 35–39.

4.74 Gay, J. *An Historical Address Delivered at the Annual Meeting of the Village Library Company of Farmington, Connecticut*. Hartford, Conn.: Hartford Press, 1903.

4.75 Haddonfield, N. J., Library Company. *Papers Read at the Hundredth Anniversary of the Founding of the Haddonfield Library Company*. Haddonfield, N.J.: The Library, 1903.

4.76 Kellogg, A. W. "The Boston Athenaeum." *NEM* 25 (1903): 167–85.

4.77 Ridpath, J. W. *History of Abington Library Society of Jenkintown, Pennsylvania, Prepared and Read by J.W. Ridpath at the One Hundredth Anniversary June 12, 1903*. Jenkintown, Pa.: Times-Chronicle Print, 1903.

4.78 Crawford, M. C. "The Boston Athenaeum." *National Magazine* 20 (1904): 272–77.

4.79 Johnston, W. D. "Early History of the Washington Library Company and Other Local Libraries." *RCHS* 7 (1904): 20–38.

4.80 Ellis, H. "The First Library in Indiana." *PL* 10 (1905): 509–12.

4.81 Haverstick, D. C. "History of the Mechanics' Library." *Proceedings of the Lancaster Historical Society* 9 (1905): 334–51.

4.82 Edmunds, A. J. "The First Books Imported by America's First Great Library [Library Company of Philadelphia]: 1732." *PMHB* 30 (1906): 300–308.

4.83 Fletcher, W. I. "Proprietary Library in Relation to the Public Library Movement." *LJ* 31 (1906): 268–72.

4.84 Harris, W. S. "What Our Grandparents Read—A Sketch of the Windham Social Library." *GranM* 38 (March 1906): 85–89.

4.85 *The Athenaeum Centenary: The Influence and History of the Boston Athenaeum*. Boston: The Athenaeum, 1907.

4.86 Hooker, M. W. "Book Lovers of 1738—One of the First Libraries in America." *Journal of American History* 1 (1907): 177–85.

4.87 Canavan, M. J. "The Old Boston Public Library, 1656–1747." *PCSM* 12 (1908): 116–33.

4.88 Keep, A. B. *History of the New York Society Library, with an Introductory Chapter on Libraries in Colonial New York*. New York: De Vinne Press, 1908.

4.89 "Proposals for a Public Library at Albany in 1758." *BNYPL* 12 (1908): 575–76.

4.90 Bolton, C. K. "Social Libraries in Boston." *PCSM* 12 (1909): 332–38.

4.91 Fitch, A. W. "Ashtabula Social Library." *Old Northwest Genealogical Quarterly* 12 (1909): 146–47.

4.92 Sanborn, F. B. "Two New Hampshire Libraries in Hampton Falls, 1785." *PMHS* 43 (1910): 33–45.

4.93 Goodwin, D. "Some Early Rhode Island Libraries." *Magazine of History* 14 (1911): 182–95.

4.94 Harrison, J. L. *The Providence Athenaeum, 1753–1911.* [Providence, R.I.]: N.p., 1911.

4.95 Bolton, C. K. "Proprietary and Subscription Libraries." In *Manual of Library Economy.* Chicago: ALA Publishing Board, 1912. Pp. 1–10.

4.96 Williams, S. R. "The Libraries of Paddy's Run." *Publications of Ohio State Archives and Historical Society* 21 (1912): 462–65.

4.97 Abbot, G. M. *A Short History of the Library Company of Philadelphia; Compiled from the Minutes, Together with Some Personal Reminiscences.* Philadelphia: Published by order of the Board of Directors, 1913.

4.98 Fowler, S. P. "The New Mills Social Library." *Danvers Historical Society Collections* 1 (1913): 95–96.

4.99 Norton, W. T. "Early Libraries in Illinios." *JISHS* 6 (1913): 246–51.

4.100 Serrill, K. W. "A Sketch of the Darby Library Company." *PLN* 6 (1913): 63–65.

4.101 Fletcher, W. I. "Some Recollections of the Boston Athenaeum, 1861–1866." *LJ* 39 (1914): 579–83.

4.102 "Early Documents of the Library Company of Philadelphia, 1733–1734." *PMHB* 39 (1915): 450–53.

4.103 Edwards, A. "The Boston Athenaeum." *Massachusetts Magazine* 9 (1916): 115–26.

4.104 Ashton, J. N. *The Salem Athenaeum, 1810–1910.* Salem, Mass.: Berkeley Press, 1917.

4.105 Cutler, S. B. "The Coonskin Library." *Publications of Ohio State Archives and Historical Society* 26 (1917): 58–77.

4.106 "The Library Company of Baltimore [1795–]." *MHM* 12 (1917): 297–310.

4.107 Rosenberg Library, Galveston, Texas. *Henry Rosenberg, 1824–1893: To Commemorate the Gifts of Henry Rosenberg to Galveston, This Volume Is Issued by the Rosenberg Library.* Galveston, Tex.: [The Rosenberg Library; New York: DeVinne Press], 1918.

4.108 Rowell, J. C. "The First Public Library in California: Monterey Library Association, 1850." *NNCL* 13 (1918): 39–40.

1920–1949

4.109 Woodberry, G. E. "The Salem Athenaeum." In *The Torch and Other Lectures and Addresses.* New York: Harcourt, Brace, and Howe, 1920. Pp. 351–57.

4.110 "Original Rules and Members of the Charleston Library Society [1750]." *SCHM* 23 (1922): 163–70.

4.111 Lonn, E. "The History of an Unusual Library." *IMH* 19 (1923): 209–25.

4.112 Lewis, J. F. *History of the Apprentices' Library of Philadelphia 1820–1920, the Oldest Free Circulating Library in America.* Philadelphia: N.p., 1924.

4.113 Webber, M. L. "The Georgetown Library Society." *SCHM* 25 (1924): 94–100.

4.114 Ingram, E. F. *The Lucius Beebe Memorial Library: An Historical Sketch.* Wakefield, Mass.: Item Press, 1925.

4.115 Blait, M. G. "Some Early Libraries of Oregon." *Washington Historical Quarterly* 17 (1926): 259–70.

4.116 Paltsits, V. H. "Petitioners for Founding the Albany Library in 1792." *BNYPL* 30 (1926): 649–50.

4.117 Smith, C. W. "Early Library Development in Washington." *Washington Historical Quarterly* 17 (1926): 246–58.

4.118 Bolton, C. K. *The Boston Athenaeum, 1807–1927: A Sketch.* Boston: The Athenaeum, 1927.

4.119 Burbank, M. "Story of the Honolulu Library and Reading Room Association."

Annual Report of the Hawaiian Historical Society 36 (1927): 14–27.

4.120 Cole, G. W. *Early Library Development in New York State (1800–1900).* New York: New York Public Library, 1927.

4.121 Regan, M. J. *Echoes from the Past: Reminiscences of the Boston Athenaeum.* Boston: The Athenaeum, 1927.

4.122 Tapley, H. S. "Libraries." In *Salem Imprints, 1768–1825,* edited by H. S. Tapley. Salem, Mass.: Essex Institute, 1927.

4.123 Bowker, R. R. *The Stockbridge Library (1904–1928), Address by R.R. Bowker, President of the (Stockbridge Library) Association at the Annual Meeting, September 29, 1928.* Pittsfield, Mass.: Sun Printing Co., 1928.

4.124 Jordan, B. C. "History of Atlas Ladies' Library." *Michigan Library Bulletin* 19 (1928): 201–04.

4.125 Warfel, H. R. "The Phoenix Library." *WPHM* 11 (1928): 69–75.

4.126 Warren, E. L., comp. *Townsend Public Library 1858–1928.* N.p.: 1929?.

4.127 Cadbury, H. J. "The Passing of Friends' Library." *The Friend* 103 (1930): 459–61.

4.128 Backus, J. "A History of the San Francisco Mercantile Library Association." Master's thesis, University of California, 1931.

4.129 Jackson, J., ed. "Carpenter's Hall." *Encyclopedia of Philadelphia* 2 (1931): 376–79.

4.130 Pugh, J. F. "The History of the Library of North Carolina." *University of North Carolina Magazine* 31 (1931): 207–13.

4.131 Hallenbeck. C. T., ed. "A Colonial Reading List: From the Union Library of Hatboro, Pennsylvania (1762–1787)." *PMHB* 56 (1932): 289–340.

4.132 Kitchell, J. "The Old Vincennes Library." *IMH* 28 (1932): 240–46.

4.133 Livingood, J. W. "A History of Libraries in Pennsylvania before 1832." *PLN* 13 (1932): 152–55.

4.134 Pennington, E. L. "The Beginnings of the Library in Charles Town, South Carolina." *PAAS* 44 (1934): 159–87.

4.135 Cincinnati Young Men's Mercantile Library Association. *History of the Young Men's Mercantile Library Association of Cincinnati, 1835–1935.* Cincinnati: Ebbert and Richards Co., 1935.

4.136 Gregorie, A. K. "The First Decade of the Charleston Library Society." *Proceedings of the South Carolina Historical Association* (1935): 3–10.

4.137 Martin, D. V. "A History of the Library Movement in Ohio to 1850 with a Special Study of Cincinnati's Library Development." Master's thesis, Ohio State University, 1935.

4.138 Robinson, O. "A Frontier Library— 1806." *Americana* 32 (1935): 461–69.

4.139 Gray, A. K. *Benjamin Franklin's Library: A Short Account of the Library Company of Philadelphia, 1731–1931,* Foreword by Owen Wister. New York: Macmillan, 1937.

4.140 McCutcheon, R. P. "Libraries in New Orleans, 1771–1833." *LHQ* 20 (1937): 152–58.

4.141 Wyatt, E. A. "Schools and Libraries in Petersburg, Virginia, Prior to 1861." *Tyler's Quarterly Historical and Genealogical Magazine* 19 (1937): 65–86.

4.142 Gambrell, H. P. "The Founding of the Philosophical Society of Texas." *Chronicles of Oklahoma* 16 (1938): 197–213.

4.143 McDaniel, C. E. "Educational and Social Interests of the Grange in Texas, 1873–1905." Master's thesis, University of Texas, 1938.

4.144 Dalphin, M. "Library Beginnings in Westchester County." *Westchester County Historical Society Bulletin* 15 (1939): 73–80.

4.145 Jones, L. R. "The Howard Library Association." *WMH* 23 (1939–40): 304–08.

4.146 Ditzion, S. H. "Mechanics' and Mercantile Libraries." *LQ* 10 (1940): 192–219.

4.147 Leonard, G., and Worthington, C. *The Providence Athenaeum: A History, 1753–1939.* Providence, R.I.: The Athenaeum, 1940.

4.148 Lydenberg, H. M. "The Berkshire Republican Library at Stockbridge, 1794–1818." *PAAS* 50 (1940): 4–38.

4.149 Manning, J. W. "Books in Early Oregon: 1821–1883." Master's thesis, University of Oregon, 1940.

4.150 Swan, M. M. *The Athenaeum Gallery, 1827–1873: The Boston Athenaeum as an Early Patron of Art . . . .* [Boston]: Boston Athenaeum, 1940.

4.151 Gustafson, R. E. "The Average Man's Library, 1830–1860." Master's thesis, Drake University, 1941.

4.152 Jarrell, L. "The Austin Lyceum, 1839–1841." Master's thesis, University of Texas, 1941.

4.153 Harris, D. G. "History of the Friends' Meeting Libraries." *Bulletin of Friends' Historical Association* 31 (1942): 42–62.

4.154 Packard, F. R. *Charter Members of the Library Company.* Philadelphia: Library Company of Philadelphia, 1942.

4.155 Palmer-Poroner, B. J. "The Library Movement in Reading, 1820–1860." *Historical Review of Berks County* 7 (1942): 70–74.

4.156 Rugheimer, V. C., and Cardwell, G. A. "The Charleston Library Society: Source Materials for the Study of Southern Literary Culture, III." *South Atlantic Bulletin* 8 (1942): 4–5.

4.157 Day, N. J. "History and Administration of the Social Library of Bedford, New Hampshire." Master's thesis, University of Michigan, 1943.

4.158 Maestri, H. L. "A History of the New Orleans Commercial Library Society, 1831–1842." Master's thesis, Tulane University, 1943.

4.159 Thompson, C. S. "The Darby Library in 1743." *LC* 11 (1943): 15–22.

4.160 Kieffer, E. C. "Libraries in Lancaster." *Proceedings of the Lancaster Historical Society* 48 (1944): 71–80.

4.161 McDermott, J. F. "Public Libraries in St. Louis, 1811–39." *LQ* 14 (1944): 9–27.

4.162 Marta, O. V. "The Truth about Cincinnati's First Library." *Ohio Archaeological and Historical Quarterly* 53 (1944): 193–208.

4.163 Sherman, S. C. "The Library Company of Baltimore, 1795–1854." *MHM* 39 (1944): 6–24.

4.164 Sabine, J. E. "Antecedents of the Newark Public Library." Doctoral dissertation, University of Chicago, 1946.

4.165 Berkshire Athenaeum and Museum. *1872–1947: 75 Years of Library Service.* Pittsfield, Mass.: N.p., 1947.

4.166 Mershon, G. L. "The Kingston, New Jersey, Library of 1812." *Proceedings of the New Jersey Historical Society* 65 (1947): 100–103.

4.167 Miller, C. E. "St. Louis Mercantile Library: An Old Library and Its Civic Background." *Missouri Library Association Quarterly* 8 (1947): 23–31.

4.168 Spain, F. L. "Libraries of South Carolina: Their Origins and Early History, 1700–1830." *LQ* 17 (1947): 28–42.

4.169 Wecter, D. "Instruments of Culture on the Frontier." *Yale Review* 36 (1947): 242–56.

4.170 Wroth, L. C., and Lewis, W. S. *Redwood Library and Athenaeum: Addresses Commemorating Its 200th Anniversary, 1747–1947.* Newport, R.I.: Redwood Library, 1947.

4.171 Goodfellow, D. M. "Centenary of a Pittsburgh Library." *WPHM* 31 (1948): 21–25.

4.172 Gray, V. G. "The Friend's Free Library, 1848–1948: Some Notes in Retrospect." *The Friend* 122 (1948): 6–9.

4.173 Roberts, A. S. *The Redwood Library and Athenaeum, Newport, Rhode Island (1747–1948)*. Providence, R.I.: N.p., 1948.

4.174 Romberg, A. "A Texas Literary Society of Pioneer Days." *SHQ* 52 (1948): 60–65.

4.175 Gaskill, G. A. "The Cultural Significance of the Mercantile Library Association of Boston." Master's thesis, Brown University, 1949.

4.176 Shera, J. H. *Foundations of the Public Library: The Origins of the Public Library Movement in New England, 1629–1855*. Chicago: University of Chicago Press, 1949.

4.177 Silver, R. J. "The Boston Lads Were Undaunted [Boston Mechanics' Library]." *LJ* 74 (1949): 995–97.

4.178 Spain, F. L. "Early Libraries in Pendleton." *SCHM* 50 (1949): 115–26.

4.179 Travous, R. L. "Pioneer Illinois Library." *JISHS* 42 (1949): 446–53.

1950–1971

4.180 Ball, P. "The First Hundred Years: Foundations of a University Library." *Arizona Librarian* 7 (1950): 5–9.

4.181 "The Library Association of Portland [Oregon, 1864–1950]." *PNLAQ* 14 (1950): 126–28.

4.182 Pulling, H. A. "Libraries in Gold Rush California." *CLB* 11 (1950): 145–46, 178.

4.183 Williams, D. A. "The New Harmony Working Man's Institute." *LQ* 20 (1950): 109–18.

4.184 Carter, M. "The Young Men's Mercantile Library Association of Cincinnati." Master's thesis, Western Reserve University, 1951.

4.185 Culp, B. A. "The History of the Gainesville XLI Club and Its Relation to the General Women's Club Movement." Master's thesis, North Texas State University, 1951.

4.186 Davis, E. G. "John Bradford's Contributions to Printing and Libraries in Lexington, Kentucky, 1787–1800." Master's thesis, University of Kentucky, 1951.

4.187 Mead, C. D. *Yankee Eloquence in the Middle West: The Ohio Lyceum, 1850–1870*. East Lansing, Mich.: Michigan State College Press, 1951.

4.188 Peterson, C. E. "The Library Hall: Home of the Library Company of Philadelphia, 1790–1880." *PAPS* 95 (1951): 266–85.

4.189 Reilly, P. G. "Some Nineteenth-Century Predecessors of the Free Library of Philadelphia." Master's thesis, Drexel Institute of Technology, 1951.

4.190 "Austin Lyceum." *HT* 1 (1952): 87.

4.191 Gambrell, H. P. "Philosophical Society of Texas." *HT* 2 (1952): 373–74.

4.192 Hedbavny, L. "Some Leisure-Time Organizations in New York City, 1830–1870: Clubs, Lyceums, and Libraries." Master's thesis, New York University, 1952.

4.193 Lovett, R. W. "From Social Library to Public Library: A Century of Library Development in Beverly, Massachusetts [1802–1902]." *HCEI* 88 (1952): 219–53.

4.194 Maestri, H. L. "New Orleans Public Library in the Nineteenth Century." *LLAB* 15 (1952): 35–43.

4.195 Markwell, D. "Liberty and Intelligence Hand in Hand." *Settler* 1 (1952): 4–9.

4.196 Mayer, V. J. "The Coonskin Library." *WLB* 26 (1952): 43–49.

4.197 Robinson, R. W. "Four Community Subscription Libraries in Colonial Pennsylvania: Darby, Hatboro, Lancaster, and Newtown, 1743–1790." Doctoral dissertation, University of Pennsylvania, 1952.

4.198 Turrell, G. H. "The Evolution of a Library." *Long Island Forum* 15 (1952): 23–25, 33, 38, 47, 54–57.

4.199 Baroco, J. V. "The Library Association of Penascola, 1885–1933." Master's thesis, Florida State University, 1953.

4.200 Flanders, F. V. "History of the Ouachita Parish Library [1951–53]." *LLAB* 16 (1953): 137–40.

4.201 Kelso, J. G. "The Lyceum and the Mechanics' Institutes: Pre-Civil War Ventures in Adult Education." Doctoral dissertation, Harvard University, 1953.

4.202 Kennedy, A. M. "The Athenaeum: Some Account of Its History from 1814–1850." *Transactions of the American Philosophical Society* 43 (1953): 260–65.

4.203 Sabine, J. E. "Books and Libraries in Newark (from 1765) to 1847." *Proceedings of the New Jersey Historical Society* 71 (1953): 254–78.

4.204 Wolcott, M. D. "The History and Development of the Sandusky Library Association, Sandusky, Ohio." Master's thesis, Kent State University, 1953.

4.205 King, M. *Books and People: Five Decades of New York's Oldest Library.* New York: Macmillan, 1954.

4.206 Kirkpatrick, L. H. "Gathering Books for the Saints: A History of Libraries in Territorial Utah." *BMLA* 42 (1954): 1–2.

4.207 Wolf, E. "The First Books and Printed Catalogues of the Library Company of Philadelphia." *PMHB* 78 (1954): 45–70.

4.208 Bidlack, R. E. *The City Library of Detroit, 1817–1837: Michigan's First Public Library.* Ann Arbor: University of Michigan, Department of Library Science, 1955.

4.209 Grimm, D. F. "A History of the Library Company of Philadelphia, 1731–1835." Doctoral dissertation, University of Pennsylvania, 1955.

4.210 Low, J. F. "A History of Cuyahoga Falls Library Association and the Taylor Memorial Association." Master's thesis, Western Reserve University, 1955.

4.211 Nicholson, J. B. *"Coonskin Library": A Legend of Books in the Wilderness,* Aspects of Librarianship, No. 9. Kent, Ohio: Kent State University Library Science Department, 1955.

4.212 Ross, R. R. *Union Library Company of Hatboro: An Account of the First Two Hundred Years Done out of the Original Records.* Hatboro, Pa.: Union Library Company, 1955.

4.213 Rugheimer, V. C. "Charleston Library Society." *SEL* 5 (1955): 137–40.

4.214 Wolf, E. "The Early Buying Policy of the Library Company of Philadelphia [1735–70]." *WLB* 30 (1955): 316–18.

4.215 Bald, F. C. "Beginnings of Libraries in Michigan." *Michigan Librarian* 20 (1956): 3–5.

4.216 Engebretson, B. L. "Books for Pioneers: The Minneapolis Athenaeum." *Minnesota History* 35 (1956–57): 222–32.

4.217 Grimm, D. F. "Franklin's Scientific Institution." *Pennsylvania History* 23 (1956): 437–62.

4.218 Library Company of Philadelphia. *A Catalogue of Books Belonging to the Library Company of Philadelphia: A Facsimile of the Edition of 1741 Printed by Benjamin Franklin, with an Introduction by Edwin Wolf, 2nd.* Philadelphia: Library Company of Philadelphia, 1956.

4.219 O'Conner, M. V. "History of the Redwood Library and Athenaeum of Newport, Rhode Island." Master's thesis, Catholic University of America, 1956.

4.220 Teeter, L. W. "A Brief History of the Growth and Development of the Youngstown Library Association, Youngstown, Ohio." Master's thesis, Kent State University, 1956.

4.221 Welborn, E. C. "The Development of Libraries in South Carolina, 1830–1860." Master's thesis, George Peabody College for Teachers, 1956.

4.222 Wolf, E. "Franklin and His Friends Choose Their Books." *PMHB* 80 (1956): 1–36.

4.223 David, C. W. "The Longwood Library." *PBSA* 51 (1957): 183–202.

4.224 Stiffler, S. A. "The Antecedents of the Public Library in the Western Reserve, 1800–1860." Master's thesis, Western Reserve University, 1957.

4.225 Chase, V. "Village Library." *Downeast* 5 (March 1958): 28, 53–56.

4.226 Donze, S. L. "A History of the Dr. Sloan Library." Master's thesis, Western Reserve University, 1958.

4.227 Freeman, J. "Early Libraries in North Carolina." *NCL* 16 (1958): 125–27.

4.228 McMullen, H. *The Founding of Social and Public Libraries in Ohio, Indiana, and Illinois Through 1850.* Urbana: University of Illinois Graduate School of Library Science, Occasional Paper no. 51, 1958.

4.229 Thomas, E. F. "The Origin and Development of the Society of the Four Arts Library, Palm Beach, Florida." Master's thesis, Florida State University, 1958.

4.230 Baker, H. S. " 'Rational Amusement in Our Midst,' Public Libraries in California, 1849–1859." *CHSQ* 38 (1959): 295–320.

4.231 Burke, B. L. "The Development of Libraries in Guilford, Connecticut." Master's thesis, Southern Connecticut State College, 1959.

4.232 "North Carolina Library Rules: 1817." *NCL* 17 (1959): 118.

4.233 Oldham, E. M. "A Much-Traveled Book Returns to Boston." *Boston Public Library Quarterly* 11 (1959): 149–50.

4.234 Welborn, E. C. "Libraries of South Carolina, 1830–1860." *SEL* 9 (1959): 171–76.

4.235 Crook, M. R. "Collections of Books and the Beginnings of Libraries in the Oregon Territory from the Great Migration to the End of the Frontier Period." Master's thesis, University of Washington, 1960.

4.236 McMullen, H. "Social Libraries in Antebellum Kentucky." *Register of the Kentucky State Historical Society* 58 (1960): 97–128.

4.237 Wolf, E. "Some Books of Early English Provenance in the Library Company of Philadelphia." *BC* 9 (1960): 275–84.

4.238 Bowman, J. N. "Libraries in Provincial California." *Historical Society of Southern California Quarterly* 43 (1961): 426–39.

4.239 Bradsher, E. L. "A Model American Library in 1793 [Thaddeus Harris' Selected Catalogue of Some of the Most Esteemed Publications in the English Language Proper to Form a Social Library 272 Titles]." *Sewanee Review* 24 (1961): 458–75.

4.240 Held, R. "The Odd Fellows' Library Associations of California." *LQ* 32 (1962): 148–63.

4.241 Flener, J. G. "A History of Libraries in Tennessee Before the Civil War." Doctoral dissertation, Indiana University, 1963.

4.242 Held, R. *Public Libraries in California, 1849–1878.* Berkeley: University of California Press, 1963.

4.243 Lowrey, S. G. R. "A History of Libraries in Madison [East Guilford], Connecticut." Master's thesis, Southern Connecticut State College, 1963.

4.244 Anderson, K. E. *Historical Sketch of the Library Association of Portland, 1864–1964.* Portland, Ore.: Library Association of Portland, 1964.

4.245 Bailey, A. H. "The Antecedents of the Peoria Public Library." In *Contributions to Mid-West Library History,* edited by T. Eaton. Champaign, Ill.: Illini Union Bookstore, 1964. Pp. 54–105.

4.246 Geiger, M. J. "The Story of California's First Libraries." *Southern California Quarterly* 46 (1964): 109–24.

4.247 Parker, W. W. "The Jarvis Library." *Serif* 1 (July 1964): 5–18.

4.248 Wiggin, C. B. *Salem Athenaeum: A Short History.* Salem, Mass.: Salem Athenaeum, 1964.

4.249 Constantine, J. R. "The Vincennes Library Company: A Cultural Institution in Pioneer Indiana." *IMH* 61 (1965): 305–89; 62 (1966): 121–54, 305–44; 63 (1967): 125–54.

4.250 Gross, S. C. "Tumblin' Creek's Cabin Library." *Senior Scholastic* 87 (Suppl. 1965): 17–19.

4.251 Habekotte, B. H. "The Old Chapell Hill Library." *TL* 27 (1965): 147–49.

4.252 Hatch, O. W. *Lyceum to Library: A Chapter in the Cultural History of Houston.* Houston: Texas Gulf Coast Historical Association, 1965.

4.253 Korty, M. B. "Benjamin Franklin and Eighteenth Century American Libraries." *Transactions of the American Philosophical Society* 55 (1965): 1–83.

4.254 McCorison, M. A., ed. *The 1764 Catalogue of the Redwood Library Company at Newport, Rhode Island.* New Haven: Yale University Press, 1965.

4.255 McMullen, H. "The Founding of Social Libraries in Pennsylvania, 1731–1876." *Pennsylvania History* 32 (1965): 130–52.

4.256 Mumford, R. L., and Mumford, R. F. "The New Castle Library Company: The Founding and Early History of a Subscription Library, 1811 to 1850." *Delaware History* 11 (1965): 282–300.

4.257 Anderson, M. T. "History of Colonial American Libraries, 1607–1776." Master's thesis, University of Missouri, 1966.

4.258 Castegnetti, N. R. "The History of Russell Library Company, Middletown, Connecticut." Master's thesis, Southern Connecticut State College, 1966.

4.259 Goulder, G. "Some Early Ohio Libraries." *Serif* 3 (March 1966): 3–8.

4.260 Wallace, D. H. "Reconstruction of Four Philadelphia Eighteenth Century Libraries." *JLH* 1 (1966): 63–65.

4.261 Wellman, T. B. "The First Library Society." *Historical Lynnfield* 12 (1966): 2.

4.262 Wiggin, C. B. "The Kirwan Collection at the Salem Athenaeum with a Biographical Sketch of Richard Kirwan and the History of Acquisition of the Collection." *HCEI* 102 (1966): 26–36.

4.263 Held, R. "Libraries in California before the Deluge." *CalL* 28 (1967): 83–93.

4.264 Nunmeker, F. G. "The Unique Ohioana Library." *Wonderful World of Ohio* 31 (January 1967): 13–15.

4.265 Reinke, E. C. "A Classical Debate of the Charleston, South Carolina, Library Society." *PBSA* 61 (1967): 83–99.

4.266 Conmy, P. T. *Oakland Library Association, 1868–1878.* Oakland, Calif.: Oakland Public Library, 1968.

4.267 Kaser, D. "Tom Brown's Library at Rugby." In *Library History Seminar No. 3, Proceedings, 1968,* edited by M. J. Zachert. Tallahassee: JLH, 1968. Pp. 124–36.

4.268 Rogers, T. W. "Libraries in the Ante-Bellum South." *Alabama Historical Quarterly* 30 (1968): 15–26.

4.269 Van Beynum, W. J. "The Book Company of Durham." In *Library History Seminar No. 3, Proceedings, 1968,* edited by M. J. Zachert. Tallahassee: JLH, 1968. Pp. 73–97.

4.270 Wiggin, C. B. "Salem Athenaeum." *JLH* 3 (1968): 257–60.

4.271 Harrell, L. "The Development of the Lyceum Movement in Mississippi." *Journal of Mississippi History* 31 (1969): 187–201.

4.272 Wiggin, C. B. "History of the Salem Book Club." *HCEI* 105 (1969): 137–41.

4.273 Chadbourne, E. H. "Early Social Libraries in Maine." *Maine Library Bulletin* 31 (1970): 3–12.

4.274 Gower, C. W. "Lectures, Lyceums and Libraries in Early Kansas, 1854–1864." *Kansas Historical Quarterly* 36 (1970): 175–82.

4.275 Jackson, S. "Seldom, Snug, and Gave No Scandal; or, the Junto and After." *Stechert-*

Hafner Book News 24 (1970): 133–36; 25 (1970): 1–3.

4.276 Clark, T. D. "Building Libraries in the Early Ohio Valley." *JLH* 6 (1971): 101–19.

4.277 Kalisch, P. A. "High Culture on the Frontier: The Omaha Library Association." *Nebraska History* 52 (1971): 411–17.

4.278 Kelly, E. D. "Berkshire Athenaeum." *Berkshire Athenaeum* 1 (1971): 15–20.

4.279 McCauley, E. B. "The New England Mill Girls: Feminine Influence in the Development of Public Libraries in New England, 1820–1860." Doctoral dissertation, Columbia University, 1971.

1972–1986

4.280 McCauley, E. B. "The Manufacturers' and Village Library in Somersworth, New Hampshire." *Historic New Hampshire* 27 (1972): 89–107.

4.281 Whitehill, W. M. *A Boston Athenaeum Anthology: 1807–1972. Selected From His Annual Reports.* Boston: Boston Athenaeum, 1973.

4.282 Whitehill, W. M. "Portrait Busts in the Library of the Boston Athenaeum." *Antiques* 105 (1973): 1141–56.

4.283 Morrison, T. *Chautauqua: A Center for Education, Religion and the Arts in America.* Chicago: University of Chicago Press, 1974.

4.284 Skallerup, H. R. *Books Afloat and Ashore: A History of Books, Libraries, and Reading Among Seamen During the Age of Sail.* Hamden, Conn.: Archon Books, 1974.

4.285 Albrecht, T. J. "The Music Libraries of the German Singing Societies in Texas, 1850–1855." *MLAN* 31 (1975): 517–29.

4.286 Boyd, W. D. "Books for Young Businessmen: Mercantile Libraries in the United States, 1820–1865." Doctoral dissertation, Indiana University, 1975.

4.287 Story, R. "Class and Culture in Boston: The Athenaeum, 1807–1860." *AQ* 27 (1975): 178–99.

4.288 Wolf, E. "Library Company of Philadelphia." *ELIS* 15 (1975): 1–19.

4.289 Gambrell, H. P. "Philosophical Society of Texas." *HT* 3 (1976): 729–30.

4.290 Neyman, M. "By the Light of Pine Knots . . . The First Library in Ohio." *OLAB* 46 (1976): 4–7.

4.291 Tolzmann, D. H. "The St. Louis Free Congregation Library: A Study of German-American Reading Interests." *MHR* 70 (1976): 142–61.

4.292 Wolf, E. "At the Instance of Benjamin Franklin"—A Brief History of The Library Company of Philadelphia, 1731–1976. Philadelphia: Library Company of Philadelphia, 1976.

4.293 Stark, B. "Libraries, Education and Culture in Eighteenth Century Lebanon, Connecticut." Master's thesis, Southern Connecticut State College, 1977.

4.294 Wiegand, W. A. "The 'Great' Debate: Who Had the First 'Public' Library in the Northwest Territory?" *Cincinnati Historical Society Bulletin* 35 (1977): 248–57.

4.295 Cazden, R. E. "Libraries in the German American Community and the Rise of the Public Library Movement." In *Milestones to the Present: Papers from Library History Seminar V*, edited by H. Goldstein. Syracuse, N.Y.: Gaylord Professional Publications, 1978. Pp. 193–211.

4.296 Fain, E. "Commentary [Libraries in the German-American Community and the Rise of the Public Library Movement]." In *Milestones to the Present: Papers from Library History Seminar V*, edited by H. Goldstein. Syracuse, N.Y.: Gaylord Professional Publications, 1978. Pp. 212–15.

4.297 Kaser, D. "Coffee House to Stock Exchange: A Natural History of the Reading Room." In *Milestones to the Present: Papers from Library History Seminar V*, edited by H. Goldstein. Syracuse, N.Y.: Gaylord Professional Publications, 1978. Pp. 238–54.

4.298 Blazek, R. "The Development of Library Service in the Nation's Oldest City: The St. Augustine Library Association, 1874–1880." *JLH* 14 (1979): 160–82.

4.299 Gordon, D. *The Hughes Free Public Library: Rugby, Tennessee, 1880–1895.* Rugby, Tenn.: Rugby Restoration Press, 1979.

4.300 Winkelman, J. H. "The Wadsworth Library (1869–1955) in Genesee Valley: A Study of an Aspect of the Intellectual Development of New York State." *Journal of Library and Information Science* 5 (1979): 189–220.

4.301 Greenburg, A. M. "Splendid Establishment . . . Charmingly Arranged: Eighteenth and Nineteenth Century Observers of the Charleston Library Society." *South Carolina Librarian* 24 (1980): 5–10.

4.302 Fishman, J., ed. "The Pittsburgh Law LIbrary Association, 1837–1841: A Manuscript Minute Book." *WPHM* 64 (1981): 189–208.

4.303 Moore, M. C. *The Edwardsville Library of 1819: Its Founders, Catalog, Subsequent History and Importance.* Edwardsville, Ill.: Friends of the Lovejoy Library, Southern Illinois University, and Madison County Historical Society, 1981.

4.304 Stevens, E. "Relationships of Social Library Membership, Wealth, and Literary Culture in Early Ohio." *JLH* 16 (1981): 574–94.

4.305 Wolf, E. "The Library Company of Philadelphia, America's First Museum." *Antiques [U.S.A.]* 120 (1981): 348–60.

4.306 Kennan, G. F., and Bell, W. J. "Views from Another East Berlin." *PAPS* 126 (1982): 472–80.

4.307 Musmann, V. K. "Women and the Founding of Social Libraries in California, 1859–1910." Doctoral dissertation, University of Southern California, 1982.

4.308 Paul, R. "Joseph Smith and the Manchester [New York] Library." *Brigham Young University Studies* 22 (1982): 333–56.

4.309 Stanley, B. W. *Century One: A Centennial History of the Rye Free Reading Room, 1884–1984.* Rye, N.Y.: Rye Free Reading Room, 1984.

4.310 McMullen, H. "The Very Slow Decline of the American Social Library." *LQ* 55 (1985): 207–25.

4.311 Yeatman, J. L. "Literary Culture and the Role of Libraries in Democratic America: Baltimore, 1815–1840." *JLH* 20 (1985): 345–67.

4.312 Aveney, B. "The Mechanic's Institute Library: A San Francisco Treat." *WLB* 61 (1986): 23–25.

4.313 Baughman, J. C. "Sense is Preferable to Sound." *LJ* 111 (1986): 42–44.

4.314 Colson, J. C. "The Fire Company Library Associations of Baltimore, 1838–1858." *JLH* 21 (1986): 158–76.

4.315 Copp, R. V. H. "South Carolina Library Societies, 1800–1900: The Foundation of South Carolina's Public Library System." *South Carolina Librarian* 30 (1986): 17–25.

4.316 Greene, J. P. *The Intellectual Heritage of the Constitutional Era: The Delegates' Library.* Philadelphia: Library Company of Philadelphia, 1986.

4.317 Schorsch, A. A. "A Library in America, 1758 to 1858 [Burlington, N.J.]." Doctoral dissertation, Princeton University, 1986.

Circulating, Sunday School, School District, and YMCA Libraries

4.318 Brainerd, C. "The Libraries of Young Men's Christian Associations." In *Public Libraries in the United States of America: Their History, Condition and Management; Special Report, Part I,* U.S. Bureau of Education. Washington, D.C.: Government Printing Office, 1876. Pp. 386–88.

4.319 Dunning, A. E. *The Sunday School Library*. Boston: Congregational Sunday School & Publishing Society, 1883.

4.320 Bolton, C. K. "Circulating Libraries in Boston, 1765–1865." *PCSM* 11 (1907): 196–208.

4.321 Keep, A. B. "Booksellers and Circulating Libraries, 1763–1776." In *History of the New York Society Library, with an Introductory Chapter on Libraries in Colonial New York*. New York: De Vinne Press, 1908. Pp. 101–11.

4.322 Gray, G. "A History of the Franklin Society and Library Company of Lexington, Virginia." Master's thesis, Washington and Lee University, 1922.

4.323 Kennedy, I. W. "The History of the Pennsylvania Home Teaching Society and Free Circulating Library for the Blind." *Outlook for the Blind* 22 (1923): 29–31.

4.324 Sullivan, M. D. "Boys Reading Club Inception of Library." *NNT* 11 (April 1935): 17.

4.325 Ditzion, S. H. "The District School Library, 1835–55." *LQ* 10 (1940): 545–77.

4.326 Patrick, W. R. "A Circulating Library of Antebellum Louisiana." *LHQ* 23 (1940): 131–40.

4.327 Raddin, G. G. *An Early New York Library of Fiction, with a Checklist of the Fiction in H. Caritat's Circulating Library No.1, City Hotel, Broadway, New York, 1804*. New York: H.W. Wilson, 1940.

4.328 Rush, O. W. "Maine's First Circulating Library." *Maine Library Bulletin* 3 (1942): 13–14.

4.329 Walter, F. K. "A Poor but Respectable Relation—The Sunday School Library." *LQ* 12 (1942): 731–39.

4.330 Dodge, A. C. "Origins of the School District Library Movement in New York State." Master's thesis, University of Chicago, 1944.

4.331 Hand, M. E. "American Sunday School Library." Master's thesis, Carnegie Institute of Technology, 1950.

4.332 Adams, L. G. "Sunday School Libraries." *Antiques Journal* 6 (1951): 24–26.

4.333 Fedder, M. B. "The Origin and Development of the Sunday School Library in America." Master's thesis, University of Chicago, 1951.

4.334 Meirose, L. H. "St. Elizabeth Parish Library: A History and Survey." Master's thesis, Western Reserve University, 1951.

4.335 Raddin, G. G. *Hocquet Caritat and the Early New York Literary Scene*. Dover, N.J.: Dover Advance Press, 1953.

4.336 Wilcox, H. M. "School District Public Libraries— A Step in Popular Education in the Nineteenth Century with Emphasis on the Period from 1820–1850." Master's thesis, Drexel Institute of Technology, 1953.

4.337 O'Rourke, M. M. "History of the Cathedral Free Circulating Library of New York City (1887–1905)." *Catholic Literary World* 25 (1954): 115–19.

4.338 Cushman, A. B. "A Nineteenth Century Plan for Reading: The American Sunday School Movement." *HB* 33 (1957): 61–71, 159–66.

4.339 Fletcher, D. M. "Read a Book and Sin No More: The Early YMCA Libraries." *WLB* 31 (1957): 521–22, 528.

4.340 Moore, M. V. "Circulating Libraries in the Southeastern United States, 1762–1842: A Selected Study." Master's thesis, University of North Carolina, 1958, University of Kentucky Press Microcard Series B, no. 22.

4.341 Held, R. "The Early School-District Library in California." *LQ* 29 (1959): 79–93.

4.342 Cushing, J. D. "The Lancaster Circulating Library." *BNYPL* 64 (1960): 432–36.

4.343 Briggs, F. A. "Sunday School Libraries in the 19th Century." *LQ* 31 (1961): 166–77.

4.344 McDonald, M. F. "An Analysis of the American Sunday School Union Publications in the Old Juvenile Collection in the Brooklyn Public Library." Master's thesis, University of North Carolina, 1963.

4.345 Richie, J. F. "Railroad Reading Rooms and Libraries in Ohio, 1865–1900." Master's thesis, Kent State University, 1965, ACRL Microcard no. 149.

4.346 Young, R. L. "A History of the Young Men's Christian Association Historical Library, New York, N.Y." Research Paper, Long Island University, 1967.

4.347 "Benton Library." *Belmont [Massachusetts] Historical Society Newsletter* 7 (1973): 1–4.

4.348 Halsell, W. D. "Sunday School Libraries." *Mississippi Library News* 37 (1973): 151–53.

4.349 Kraus, J. W. "Libraries of the Young Men's Christian Association in the Nineteenth Century." *JLH* 10 (1975): 3–21.

4.350 Kaser, D. *A Book for a Sixpence: The Circulating Library in America.* Pittsburgh: Beta Phi Mu, 1980.

4.351 Eppard, P. B. "The Rental Library in Twentieth-Century America." *JLH* 21 (1986): 240–52.

4.352 Metzger, P. A. "A Circulating Library in the Southwest: J.S. Penn in Austin, Texas." *JLH* 21 (1986): 228–39.

5.

Public Libraries

Public libraries have drawn more attention from historians than any other single aspect of American library history. Jesse Shera's essay, "Literature of American Library History" (1973, **1.87**; listed and discussed in Chapter 1, "Historiography and Sources"), treats the development of this literature from its antiquarian beginnings to the early 1970s. David Kaser has suggested in his survey, "Advances in American Library History" (1978, **1.121**; listed in Chapter 1, "Historiography and Sources"), that, especially from the mid–1960s to the mid–1970s, "the rise of the public library has fired the curiosity of American Library historians perhaps because it is more uniquely American, ... its once-vaunted social significance gives it greater romantic appeal, ... [and] the inscrutable vagaries of its motivation are more subject to interpretation." Among the other various treatments of public library history literature found in Chapter 1 the recent compilation of annotated dissertations and theses by Arthur P. Young (Metuchen, N.J.: Scarecrow Press, 1988) deserves special mention.

Early studies of public library history, such as the reminiscences of Samuel S. Green (1913, **5.26**), although valuable for contemporary assessments, tended to be antiquarian in nature and more inclined to description and applause than critical analysis. However, in the 1930s scholars began to call for the application of the critical standards of historical research to public library history. An important stimulus to this new perspective was Arnold Borden's brief essay, "Sociological Beginnings of the Library Movement" (1931, **2.20**; listed in Chapter 2, "General Studies"). Influenced by Borden's persuasive insistence that libraries must be studied in the context of their coeval culture, a number of classic and still valuable studies of the public library were completed by doctoral students at Chicago and Columbia. Most notable of these were Sidney Ditzion's *Arsenals of a Democratic Culture* (1947, **5.66**) and Jesse Shera's *Foundations of the Public Library* (1949, **4.176**; listed and discussed in Chapter 4, "Predecessors of the Public Library") which together

75

cover the period to 1900. Gladys Spencer's *The Chicago Public Library* (1943, **5.359**) represents an institutional history of this genre.

The fact that these works were such *tours de force* seemed to have preempted further substantive work on the subject for nearly twenty years. However, beginning in the late 1950s and continuing into the 1960s, a number of new studies, focusing on special aspects of public library history, provided a basis for the reconsideration of previous findings. These new efforts approached the subject from a variety of specialized angles; taken together, they represent a significant portion of the more recent historical writing in the field. For instance, two excellent monographs analyzed Andrew Carnegie on the development of the American public library—a general study by George Bobinski (1969, **5.127**) and one on Wisconsin by David McLeod (1968, **5.1079**). David T. Javersak's more recent case study of Wheeling, West Virginia (1979, **5.1069**) has served as a fruitful model for further research. Another example of a new interpretation was Robert Lee's *Continuing Education for Adults through the American Public Library, 1833–1964* (1966, **5.116**), which, read with Margaret Monroe's pioneering work on this subject (1963, **5.106**), revises earlier treatments.

Other scholars began to investigate public library development in individual states and regions as well as particular issues faced by public librarians. The most impressive of the monographs in this genre is Ray Held's history of the public movement in California in two volumes (1963, **4.242**; listed and discussed in Chapter 4, "Predecessors of the Public Library"; and 1973, **5.263**) which carries the story to 1917. Important state studies in dissertation form include John Colson's study of Wisconsin, 1836–1900 (1973, **5.1080**) and Chieko Tachihata's work on Hawaii and the Hawaii State Library, 1913–1971 (1981, **5.349**). Donald G. Davis, Jr.'s paper on "The Rise of the Public Library in Texas, 1876–1920" (1978, **5.1032**) exemplifies an initial effort at statewide analysis.

Numerous studies have focused on the services of libraries to different groups in the community or the relationship of the public library to other types of libraries. Examples of this research include the studies of Harriet Long (1969, **7.93**) and Budd Gambee (1973, **7.97**) both listed in Chapter 7, "School Libraries," and Miriam Braverman (1979, **5.190**) which deal with the tension between the public library and service to youth and school libraries. Elfrieda B. McCauley's study, "The New England Mill Girls: Feminine Influence in the Development of Public Libraries in New England, 1820–1860" (1971, **4.279**; listed in Chapter 4, "Predecessors of the Public Library"), Rosemary DuMont's work on big city public libraries from 1890 to 1915 (1977, **5.175**), and Nelson Beck's articles on service to New York immigrant groups (1977, **3.386**; listed in Chapter 3, "Private Libraries and Reading Tastes"; and 1978, **5.773**) are but a sample of the research conducted on various constituencies. These studies supplement studies on service to minorities by Haynes McMullen (1976, **5.170**) and A. P. Marshall (1976, **5.171**). Esther J. Carrier's surveys of fiction in public libraries from 1876 to 1950 (1965, **5.113**; 1985, **5.214**) and Evelyn Geller's *Forbidden Books in American Public Libraries, 1876–1939* (1984, **2.332**; listed and discussed in Chapter 2, "General Studies") concentrate on yet another aspect of library history.

Institutional histories of individual public libraries have been a continuing feature of public library history that has provided impetus for comparative studies as well as local history. Although they vary somewhat in sophistication, classic works include Walter Whitehill, *Boston Public Library: A Centennial History* (1956, **5.526**); Frank Woodford, *Parnassus on Main Street: A History of the Detroit Public Library* (1965, **5.563**); Philip Kalisch, *The Enoch Pratt Free Library: A Social History* (1969, **5.468**); Phyllis Dain, *The New York Public Library: A History of Its Founding and Early Years* (1972, **5.765**); Clarence Cramer, *Open Shelves and Open Minds: A History of the Cleveland Public Library* (1972, **5.897**); Bruce Benidt, *The Library Book: Centennial History of the Minneapolis Public Library* (1984, **5.577**); and Joseph B. Rounds, *The Time Was Right: A History of the Buffalo and Erie County Public Library, 1940–1975* (1985, **5.790**).

Many major studies of large public libraries and good case studies of smaller libraries remain only in dissertation and thesis format or have appeared as journal articles. Among these are Jerry F. Cao's "The Los Angeles Public Library: Origins and Development, 1872–1910" (1977, **5.265**), Stanley Rubinstein's "The Role of the Trustees and the Librarians in the Development of the Enoch Pratt Free Library and the Free Library of Philadelphia, 1880–1914" (1978, **5.472**), and the fine articles of Ron Blazek on Florida libraries, among them, St. Augustine (1979, **4.298**, listed in Chapter 4, "Predecessors of the Public Library").

Students of public library history will want to read these and similar studies in conjunction with the publications about prominent public librarians and biographical sketches of lesser-known figures that appear in Chapter 15, "Biographies of Individual Librarians and Library Benefactors." Studies of particular importance are those by Joseph A. Boromé on Justin Winsor (1950, **15.1963**), Edward G. Holley on Charles Evans (1963, **15.607**), and William L. Williamson on William Frederick Poole (1963, **15.1400**).

One of the obvious results of the increasingly solid research conducted before 1970 has been the more recent growth of studies that have sought to analyze, clarify, and explain aspects of public library history and to integrate that phenomenon into the mainstream of historical thought. Some efforts seem to have been ideologically oriented, while others have drawn primarily on new approaches and methods. Insofar as they differ from the more traditional treatments, they may deserve status as revisionist. Among those who stimulated new thinking about the role of public libraries in society were Dee Garrison whose dissertation on public library leaders, 1876–1910 (1973, **5.145**) and accompanying articles (1971, **5.134**; 1973, **5.146**) excited broad appeal, and Michael H. Harris whose "The Purpose of the American Public Library: A Revisionist Interpretation of History" (1973, **5.147**) and a more complete treatment, *The Role of the Public Library in American Life: A Speculative Essay* (1975, **5.158**), struck a more historiographic chord. Garrison's widely cited *Apostles of Culture: The Public Librarian and American Society, 1876–1920* (1979, **5.191**) synthesized much of growing literature on the debate that had ensued in the mid–1970s and made a persuasive case for the new study of motivations and perceptions. The "Harris-Dain Debate" brought other scholars into the discussion, such as Evelyn Geller ("Intellectual Freedom: Eternal Principle or Unanticipated Consequence," 1974, **5.151**) and Phyllis Dain ("Ambivalence and Paradox: The Social Bonds of the Public Library," 1975, **5.156**. This scholarly argument carried on in more popular as well as academic journals. Two issues of the *Journal of Library History* (vol. 10, no. 2 [1975]; vol. 13, no. 1 [1978]) capture the flavor and vigor of the dialogue.

The outcome of this intellectual ferment was a much broader, stronger, and better integrated pattern of research in the past decade. Among the various approaches, the books and articles of Wayne A. Wiegand are significant, and they are scattered throughout this chapter as well as Chapter 12, "Library Associations," and Chapter 15, "Biographies of Individual Librarians and Library Benefactors." One example is his "British Propaganda in American Public Libraries, 1914–1917" (1983, **5.210**). Other scholars who are finding new approaches include Daniel F. Ring who employed socio-biographical methods to study the Cleveland Public Library during World War I (1983, **5.910**), and Robert V. Williams with his statistical study of the 1850–1870 period (1986, **5.219**). The opening of new research fronts has also yielded fresh insight into women's roles in libraries as demonstrated in Chapter 14 "Women in Librarianship."

Interest in public library history continues, and the past fifteen years demonstrate that, as a phenomenon with a peculiarly American stamp, the subject retains its hold on the professional imagination.

General Studies

Before 1876

5.1 Edwards, E. "The Libraries of the United States of America." In *Memoirs of Libraries . . .*, vol. 2, edited by E. Edwards. London: 1859. Pp. 163–242.

5.2 Spofford, A. R. "The Public Libraries of the United States." *Journal of Social Science* 2 (1870): 92–114.

1876–1919

5.3 "Free Town Libraries." In *Public Libraries in the United States of America: Their History, Condition and Management; Special Report, Part I*, U.S. Bureau of Education. Washington, D.C.: Government Printing Office, 1876. Pp. 445–59.

5.4 "Public Libraries of Ten Principal Cities." In *Public Libraries in the United States of America: Their History, Condition and Management; Special Report, Part I*, U.S. Bureau of Education. Washington, D.C.: Government Printing Office, 1876. Pp. 837–1009.

5.5 Quincy, J. P. "Free Libraries." In *Public Libraries in the United States of America: Their History, Condition and Management; Special Report, Part I*, U.S. Bureau of Education. Washington, D.C.: Government Printing Office, 1876. Pp. 389–402.

5.6 Scudder, H. E. "Public Libraries a Hundred Years Ago." In *Public Libraries in the United States of America: Their History, Condition and Management; Special Report, Part I*, U.S. Bureau of Education. Washington, D.C.: Government Printing Office, 1876. Pp. 2–37.

5.7 U. S. Bureau of Education. *Public Libraries in the United States of America: Their History, Condition and Management; Special Report, Part I*, U.S. Bureau of Education. Washington, D.C.: Government Printing Office, 1876.

5.8 Winsor, J. "The Beginnings of Our Public Library System." *LW* 10 (1879): 121–22.

5.9 Winsor, J. "The Library Movement Thirty Years Ago." *LW* 10 (1879): 330–31.

5.10 Jevons, S. W. "The Rationale of Free Public Libraries." *Contemporary Review* 39 (1881): 18–23.

5.11 Tyler, M. C. "The Historic Evolution of the Free Public Library in America and Its Functions." *LJ* 9 (1884): 40–47.

5.12 Poole, W. F. "[The Public Library of Our Time] Address of the President." *LJ* 12 (1887): 311–20.

5.13 Gilman, D. C. *Development of the Public Library in America: An Address Delivered at the Opening of the Cornell University Library . . . 1891*. Ithaca: Cornell University, 1891.

5.14 Fletcher, W. I. "The Public Library Movement." *Cosmopolitan* 18 (1894): 99–106.

5.15 Harrison, J. L. "Movement for Public Libraries in the United States." *NEM* 10 (1894): 709–22.

5.16 Bolton, S. K. "Andrew Carnegie and His Libraries." In *Famous Givers and Their Gifts*, edited by S. K. Bolton. New York: Crowell, 1896.

5.17 "Reading Rooms for Children." *PL* 2 (1897): 125–31.

5.18 Adams, H. B. *Public Libraries and Popular Education*. Albany: University of the State of New York, 1900.

5.19 Keogh, A. "English and American Libraries: A Comparison." *PL* 6 (1901): 388–95.

5.20 Goodknight, J. L. *The Evolution of American Libraries: An Address Delivered at the Dedication of the Carnegie Library Building, Lincoln, Illinois, April 29, 1903*. Lincoln, Ill.: News-Herald Print, 1903.

5.21 Haines, H. E. "The Rapid Growth of Public Libraries." *World's Work* 5 (1903): 3086–90.

5.22 Fletcher, W. I. *Public Libraries in America,* Columbian Knowledge Series, no. 2. Boston: Roberts Brothers, 1904.

5.23 Wood, M. E. "Libraries as Cultural Centers." *Outlook* 80 (1905): 859–61.

5.24 Wallace, A. "The Southern Library Movement." *BALA* 1 (1907): 62–68.

5.25 Rathbone, J. A. "Modern Library Movement." *PL* 13 (1908): 197–201.

5.26 Green, S. S. *The Public Library Movement in the United States, 1853–1893: From 1876, Reminiscences of the Writer.* Boston: Boston Book Co., 1913.

5.27 Crenshaw, M. V. "Public Libraries in the South." *LJ* 42 (1917): 163–74.

5.28 Koch, T. W. *A Book of Carnegie Libraries.* White Plains, N.Y.: H.W. Wilson, 1917.

5.29 Koch, T. W. *Books in the War: The Romance of Library War Service.* Boston: Houghton Mifflin, 1919.

1920–1949

5.30 Williamson, C. C. *Andrew Carnegie: His Contribution to the Public Library Movement. A Commemorative Address.* Cleveland: Privately printed, 1920.

5.31 Learned, W. S. *The American Public Library and the Diffusion of Knowledge.* New York: Harcourt, 1924.

5.32 Rees, G. "United States of America." In *Libraries for Children.* London: Grafton, 1924. Pp. 83–138.

5.33 Long, H. C. "Development of Rural Library Service." In *County Library Service.* Chicago: American Library Association, 1925. Pp. 15–23.

5.34 Black, D. M. "The Influence of Public Libraries as Revealed through Biography and Autobiography." Master's thesis, University of Illinois, 1928.

5.35 Bostwick, A. E. *The American Public Library,* 4th ed. New York: Appleton, 1929.

5.36 Conner, M. *Outline of the History of the Development of the American Public Library.* Chicago: American Library Association, 1931.

5.37 Waples, D. "The Public Library in the Depression." *LQ* 2 (1932): 321–43.

5.38 Duffus, R. L. *Books, Their Place in a Democracy.* Boston: Houghton Mifflin, 1933.

5.39 Duffus, R. L. *Our Starving Libraries: Studies in Ten American Communities During Depression Years.* Boston: Houghton Mifflin, 1933.

5.40 Wachtel, L. "State Provisions for the Support of Municipal Public Libraries and Some Comparisons with State Provisions for the Support of Public Schools." *LQ* 3 (1933): 373–89.

5.41 Byrnes, H. W. "The Library Movement in the United States: Social and Economic Trends Indicating the Purpose and Growth of the Library in a Democracy." *Franklin Lectures* 1 (1935): 48–68.

5.42 Wellard, J. H. "Popular Reading and the Origin of the Public Library in America." *LJ* 60 (1935): 185–87.

5.43 Chancellor, J. *The Library in the TVA Adult Education Program.* Chicago: American Library Association, 1937.

5.44 Wellard, J. H. "The Historical Background of the Public Library." In *Book Selection.* London: Grafton and Co., 1937. Pp. 3–68.

5.45 Wellard, J. H. "Trends in the American Public Library Movement During the Nineteenth Century." In *Book Selection.* London: Grafton and Co., 1937. Pp. 47–58.

5.46 Ditzion, S. H. "The Public Library Movement in the United States as It Was Influenced by the Needs of the Wage Earner, 1850–1900." Master's thesis, College of the City of New York, 1938.

5.47 Johnson, A. S *The Public Library: A People's University.* New York: American Association for Adult Education, 1938.

5.48 Ditzion, S. H. "Social Reform, Education, and the Library, 1850–1900." *LQ* 9 (1939): 156–84.

5.49 Predeek, A. "The Idea of the American Library." *LQ* 9 (1939): 445–76.

5.50 Atkins, E. "The Government and Administration of Public Library Service to Negroes in the South." Doctoral dissertation, University of Chicago, 1940.

5.51 Johnson, M. I. "The Development of Separate Service for Young People in the Public Libraries of the United States, and Its Implications for Library Schools." Master's thesis, Columbia University, 1940.

5.52 Wellard, J. H. *The Public Library Comes of Age.* London: Grafton and Co., 1940.

5.53 Esterquest, R. T. "War Attitudes and Activities of American Libraries, 1914–1918." *WLB* 15 (1941): 621–36.

5.54 Gleason, E. V. A. "Historical Background." In *The Southern Negro and the Public Library: A Study of the Government and Administration of Public Library Service to Negroes in the South.* Chicago: University of Chicago, 1941. Pp. 8–29.

5.55 Levy, R. G. "Certain Aspects of the Library Movement in the Southern Association of Colleges and Secondary Schools from 1929 to 1941." Master's thesis, University of Alabama, 1941.

5.56 Sandoe, M. W. "Library Service to Rural People." In *County Library Primer.* New York: H.W. Wilson, 1942. Pp. 14–20.

5.57 Herdman, M. M. "The Public Library in Depression." *LQ* 13 (1943): 310–34.

5.58 Lester, R. M. *Carnegie Grants for Library Buildings, 1890–1917.* New York: Carnegie Corporation, 1943.

5.59 Power, E. L. "The Rise of Children's Libraries." In *Work with Children in Public Libraries.* Chicago: American Library Association, 1943. Pp. 9–20.

5.60 Rossel, B. S. *Public Libraries in the Life of the Nation.* Chicago: American Library Association, 1943.

5.61 Wadsworth, R. W. "Notes on the Development of Music Collections in American Public Libraries." Master's thesis, University of Chicago, 1943.

5.62 Bontemps, A. "Special Collections of Negroana." *LQ* 14 (1944): 187–206.

5.63 Ulveling, R. A. "The Public Library in the Large Community." In *The Library in the Community,* edited by L. Carnovsky and L. Martin. Chicago: University of Chicago Press, 1944. Pp. 23–37.

5.64 Ditzion, S. H. "The Anglo-American Library Scene: A Contribution to the Social History of the Library Movement." *LQ* 16 (1946): 281–302.

5.65 Root, M. E. S. "An American Past in Children'sWork." *LJ* 71(1946):547–51,1422–24.

5.66 Ditzion, S. H. *Arsenals of a Democratic Culture: A Social History of the American Public Library Movement in New England and the Middle Atlantic States from 1850 to 1900.* Chicago: American Library Association, 1947.

5.67 Joeckel, C., and Winslow, A. *A National Plan for Public Library Service.* Chicago: American Library Association, 1948.

5.68 Kaiser, W. H. "Statistical Trends of Large Public Libraries, 1900–1946." *LQ* 18 (1948): 278–79.

5.69 Schick, F. L. "Board-Librarian Relationships in American Public Libraries." Master's thesis, University of Chicago, 1948.

5.70 Berelson, B., and Asheim, L. E. *The Library's Public: A Report of the Public Library Inquiry.* New York: Columbia University Press, 1949.

5.71 Ditzion, S. H. "Opening the People's Library on the Lord's Day." *School and Society* 70 (1949): 49–53.

5.72 Garceau, O. *The Public Library in the Political Process.* New York: Columbia University Press, 1949.

5.73 Stibitz, M. T. "Relation of the Public Library to Workers' Education, 1918 to 1939." Master's thesis, Columbia University, 1949.

1950–1971

5.74 Anders, M. E. "The Contributions of the Carnegie Corporation and the General Education Board to Library Development in the Southeast." Master's thesis, University of North Carolina, 1950.

5.75 Leigh, R. D. *The Public Library in the United States: The General Report of the Public Library Inquiry.* New York: Columbia University Press, 1950.

5.76 Stevenson, G. M. "The Changing Concepts in Public Library Service as Evidenced by the Three Major Surveys: 1876, 1926, and 1950." Master's thesis, Kent State University, 1950.

5.77 Dix, W. S. "The Library and the American Tradition [since 1741]." *TLJ* 27 (1951): 60–66.

5.78 Eberhart, L. "Concepts of the (American) Library's Role in Adult Education, 1926–1951." Master's thesis, University of Wisconsin, 1951.

5.79 Munn, R. "Hindsight on the Gifts of Carnegie." *LJ* 76 (1951): 1967–70.

5.80 Borthwick, H. H. "Trends in Post-War Public Library Architecture." Master's thesis, Carnegie Institute of Technology, 1952.

5.81 Purdy, B. A. "Famous Children's Libraries: A Survey of Five Libraries Devoted Exclusively to Work with Children." Master's thesis, Pratt Institute, 1952.

5.82 Thompson, C. S. *Evolution of the American Public Library, 1653–1876.* Washington, D.C.: Scarecrow Press, 1952.

5.83 Batchelder, M. L. "Public Library Influence on School Libraries." *LibT* 1 (1953): 271–85.

5.84 Collier, F. G. "A History of the American Public Library Movement through 1880." Doctoral dissertation, Harvard University, 1953.

5.85 Conmy, P. T. "The Diamond Jubilee of California Public Libraries." *CalL* 15 (1953): 48, 61.

5.86 Poll, B. "Working People and Their Relationship to the American Public Library: History and Analysis." Master's thesis, University of Washington, 1953.

5.87 Thompson, L. B. "Book Selection Policies and Practices in Public Libraries, 1876–1900." Master's thesis, Catholic University of America, 1953.

5.88 Zimmerman, C. R. "The Public Library and the Political Process." *WLB* 28 (1953): 70–76.

5.89 Rose, E. *The Public Library in American Life.* New York: Columbia University Press, 1954.

5.90 Klopenstein, M. J. "The American Library and Some of Its Benefactors." Master's thesis, Western Reserve University, 1955.

5.91 Boyd, C. "A Survey of Literature on Adult Book-Selection Theory in American Public Libraries, 1900–1950." Master's thesis, Catholic University of America, 1956.

5.92 Lester, R. M. "The Carnegie Corporation and the Library Renaissance in the South." *WLB* 31 (1956): 244–49.

5.93 Lester, E. L. "An Analysis of Post-War Trends in the Planning and Design of Public Library Buildings, 1945–1955." Master's thesis, Atlanta University, 1957.

5.94 Sloan, R. M. "The History of the Phonograph Record in the American Public

Library: Its Origins and Growth through 1949." Master's thesis, Western Reserve University, 1957.

5.95 Speirs, C. H. "The Effects of Political Censorship in the United States on Public Libraries and Librarians from 1945–1955." Master's thesis, Western Reserve University, 1957.

5.96 Anders, M. E. "The Development of Public Library Services in the Southeastern States, 1895–1950." Doctoral dissertation, Columbia University, 1958.

5.97 Tracy, W. F. "The Public Library and the Courts." Doctoral dissertation, University of Chicago, 1958.

5.98 Boyd, M. R. "The Effect of Censorship Attempts by Private Pressure Groups on Public Libraries, 1945–1957." Master's thesis, Kent State University, 1959.

5.99 Davis, F. C. "The Development of the Traveling Library." Master's thesis, East Texas State College, 1959.

5.100 Shockley, A. A. *A History of Public Library Services to Negroes in the South, 1900–1955.* Dover, Del.: Delaware State College, 1959.

5.101 Daniel, H. *Public Libraries for Everyone: The Growth and Development of Library Services in the United States, Especially since the Passage of the Library Services Act.* Garden City, N.Y.: Doubleday, 1961.

5.102 Kittle, A. T. "Management Theories in Public Library Adminstration in the United States, 1925–1955." Doctoral dissertation, Columbia University, 1961.

5.103 Anderson, F., comp. *Carnegie Corporation Library Program, 1911–1961.* New York: Carnegie Corporation, 1963.

5.104 Bell, B. L. "Integration in Public Library Service in Thirteen Southern States, 1954–1962." Master's thesis, Atlanta University, 1963.

5.105 Bell, B. L. "Public Library Integration in Thirteen Southern States, 1954–1962." *LJ* 88 (1963): 4713–15.

5.106 Monroe, M. E. *The Library Adult Education: Biography of an Idea.* New York: Scarecrow Press, 1963.

5.107 Oko, D. K., and Downey, B. F. "Historical Relationship Between Public Libraries and Trade Unions." In *Library Service to Labor.* New York: Scarecrow Press, 1963. Pp. 62–68.

5.108 Oko, D. K., and Downey, B. F. "Library Service to Labor: Historical Roots and Current Needs." In *Library Service to Labor.* New York: Scarecrow Press, 1963. Pp. 51–61.

5.109 Handlin, O. "Libraries and Learning." *Atlantic Monthly* 213 (1964): 103–05.

5.110 Molz, R. K. "The Public Library: The People's University?" *American Scholar* 34 (1964): 95–102.

5.111 Morsch, L. M. "Foundations of the American Public Library." In *Bases of Modern Librarianship,* edited by C. M. White. New York: Macmillan, 1964. Pp. 29–41.

5.112 Binkowski, M. "An Evaluative Survey of the Literature on Public Library Service to Business, 1925–1962." Master's thesis, Catholic University of America, 1965.

5.113 Carrier, E. J. *Fiction in Public Libraries, 1876–1900.* New York: Scarecrow Press, 1965.

5.114 Conant, R. W., ed. *The Public Library and the City.* Cambridge: M.I.T. Press, 1965.

5.115 Frantz, R. W. "A Re-examination of the Influence of Literary Nationalism on the Public Library." *JLH* 1 (1966): 182–86.

5.116 Lee, R. E. *Continuing Education for Adults through the American Public Library, 1833–1964.* Chicago: American Library Association, 1966.

5.117 Mitchell, M. W. "An Historical Study of the Silas Bronson Library of Waterbury, Connecticut." Master's thesis, Southern Connecticut State College, 1966.

5.118 Benson, E. C. "An Analysis of the Periodical Literature Relative to Book Selection in Public Libraries, 1926–1963." Master's thesis, Atlanta University, 1967.

5.119 Brown, E. F. *Bookmobiles and Book-mobile Service.* Metuchen, N.J.: Scarecrow Press, 1967.

5.120 Green, C. S. "Library Services to the Blind in the United States: Origins and Development to 1931." Master's thesis, University of Chicago, 1967.

5.121 Hassenforder, J. *Développement comparé des Bibliothèques Publiques en France, en Grand-Bretagne et aux Etats-Unis dans la Seconde Moitié du XIXe siècle (1850–1914).* Paris: Cercle de la Librairie, 1967.

5.122 Jackson, B. "An Evaluative Guide to the Literature about Bookmobiles, 1905–1965." Master's thesis, Catholic University of America, 1967.

5.123 Olech, J. "Public Library Service to Business, 1904–1964." Master's thesis, Southern Connecticut State College, 1967.

5.124 Wannarka, M. B. "Medical Collections in Public Libraries of the United States: A Historical Study." Master's thesis, University of Minnesota, 1967.

5.125 Hassenforder, J. "Development of Public Libraries in France, the United Kingdom and the United States." *UNESCO Bulletin for Libraries* 22 (1968): 13–19.

5.126 Moss, J. R. "A Historical Survey of Ultra-Right Pressure Groups: Their Effect on Public Library Policy, 1950–1967." Master's thesis, East Texas State University, 1968.

5.127 Bobinski, G. S. *Carnegie Libraries: Their History and Impact on American Public Library Development.* Chicago: American Library Association, 1969.

5.128 Knight, D. M., and Nourse, E. S., eds. *Libraries at Large.* New York: R.R. Bowker, 1969.

5.129 Prentis, G. "The Evolution of the Library System." *LQ* 39 (1969): 78–79.

5.130 Wight, E. A. "Precursors of Current Public Library Systems." *LQ* 39 (1969): 23–40.

5.131 Duane, F. P. "The Carnegie Libraries." *JLH* 5 (1970): 165–70.

5.132 Werkley, C. E. *Mister Carnegie's Lib'ary.* New York: American Heritage Press, 1970.

5.133 Brown, E.F. "Factors Behind the Increasing Involvement of Libraries." In *Library Service to the Disadvantaged.* Metuchen, N.J.: Scarecrow Press, 1971. Pp. 13–26.

5.134 Garrison, D. "Cultural Custodians of the Gilded Age: The Public Librarian and Horatio Alger." *JLH* 6 (1971): 327–36.

5.135 Henderson, J. D. "County Libraries." *ELIS* 6 (1971): 254–68.

5.136 Murison, W. J. *The Public Library: Its Origins, Purpose, and Significance,* 2d ed. London: George G. Harrap, 1971.

5.137 Ulrich, C. "The Role of the Library in Public Opinion Formation during World War I." *Minnesota University Bulletin* 2 (1971): 91–104.

1972–1986

5.138 Conant, R. W., and Molz, R. K., eds. *The Metropolitan Library.* Cambridge: M.I.T. Press, 1972.

5.139 Epstein, J. S. "History of Urban Main Library Service ." *LibT* 20 (1972): 598–624.

5.140 Guyton, T. L. "Unionization of Public Librarians: A Theoretical Interpretation." Doctoral dissertation, University of California, Los Angeles, 1972.

5.141 Jackson, S. "Tax-Supported Library Service to the People: Why was 1876–1877 the Nodal Point?" *International Library Review* 4 (1972): 417–21.

5.142 Potter, D. C. "Extension Work, Public Library." *ELIS* 8 (1972): 330–37.

5.143 Shera, J. H. "The Public Library in Perspective." In *The Metropolitan Library,* edited by R. W. Conant and K. Molz. Cambridge: M.I.T. Press, 1972. Pp. 101–22.

5.144 Campbell, H. C. *Public Libraries in the Urban Metropolitan Setting.* London: Clive Bingley, 1973.

5.145 Garrison, D. "Cultural Missionaries: A Study of American Public Library Leaders, 1876–1910." Doctoral dissertation, University of California, Irvine, 1973.

5.146 Garrison, D. "The Tender Technicians: The Feminization of Public Librarianship, 1876–1905." *Journal of Social History* 6 (1973): 131–59.

5.147 Harris, M. H. "The Purpose of the American Public Library: A Revisionist Interpretation of History." *LJ* 98 (1973): 2509–14.

5.148 Prentice, A. E. *The Public Library Trustee: Image and Performance on Funding.* Metuchen, N.J.: Scarecrow Press, 1973.

5.149 Betancourt, J. A. "Library Service to Puerto Ricans: An Overview." In *Puerto Rican Perspectives*, edited by E. Mapp. Metuchen, N.J.: Scarecrow Press, 1974. Pp. 97–103.

5.150 Davies, D. W. *Public Libraries as Culture and Social Centers: The Origin of the Concept.* Metuchen, N.J.: Scarecrow Press, 1974.

5.151 Geller, E. "Intellectual Freedom: Eternal Principle or Unanticipated Consequence." *LJ* 99 (1974): 1364–67.

5.152 Harwell, R., and Michener, R. "As Public as the Town Pump." *LJ* 99 (1974): 959–63.

5.153 Hurwitz, J. D. "Public Library as 'People's University': An Analytical History of the Concept as Part of the American Public Library Movement in the Late Nineteenth and Early Twentieth Centuries." Master's thesis, University of Chicago, 1974.

5.154 Wellisch, J. B., Patrick, R. J., Black, D. V., and Cuadra, C. A. *The Public Library and Federal Policy.* Westport, Conn.: Greenwood Press, 1974.

5.155 Bertrand, C. "The Americanization of the Immigrant: The Role of the Public Library, 1900–1920." Research Paper, Queens College, 1975.

5.156 Dain, P. "Ambivalence and Paradox: The Social Bonds of the Public Library." *LJ* 100 (1975): 261–66.

5.157 Garrison, D. "Rejoinder [to Elaine Fain's critique of her work]." *JLH* 10 (1975): 111–16.

5.158 Harris, M. H. *The Role of the Public Library in American Life: A Speculative Essay.* Urbana: University of Illinois Graduate School of Library Science, Occasional paper no. 117, 1975.

5.159 Johns, E. A. "The Development of Automation in the Catalogue Department of Public Libraries in the United States." Research Paper, Texas Woman's University, 1975.

5.160 Kramp, R. S. "The Great Depression: Its Impact on Forty-six Large Public Libraries; An Inquiry Based on Content Analysis of the Published Writings of Their Directors." Doctoral dissertation, University of Michigan, 1975.

5.161 LaFleur, L. B. "Librarian's Response to Adverse Economic Conditions: A Study of Public Libraries in the Great Depression (1929–1938) and the Current Recession (1970–1975)." Research Paper, University of Missouri-Columbia, 1975.

5.162 Mickelson, P. "American Society and the Public Library in the Thought of Andrew Carnegie." *JLH* 10 (1975): 117–38.

5.163 Unger, C. P. "The School-housed Public Library Revisited." Master's thesis, University of Chicago, 1975.

5.164 Bloom, H. "Adult Services: 'The Book That Leads You On.' " *LibT* 25 (1976): 379–98.

5.165 Cole, E. D. H. "A History of Public Library Services to Blacks in the South, 1900–1975." Research Paper, Texas Woman's University, 1976.

5.166 Franklin, H. R. "Service to the Urban Rank and File." In *A Century of Service: Librarianship in the United States and Canada*, edited by S. L. Jackson, E. B. Herling, and E. J. Josey. Chicago: American Library Association, 1976. Pp. 1–19.

5.167 Garrison, D. "Immoral Fiction in the Late Victorian Library." *AQ* 28 (1976): 71–89.

5.168 Harris, M. H. "Public Libraries and the Decline of the Democratic Dogma." *LJ* 101 (1976): 2225–30.

5.169 Harris, M. H. "The Gamin's Lament." *ALib* 7 (1976): 87.

5.170 McMullen, H. "Service to Ethnic Minorities Other than Afro-Americans and American Indians." In *A Century of Service: Librarianship in the United States and Canada*, edited by S. L. Jackson, E. B. Herling, and E. J. Josey. Chicago: American Library Association, 1976. Pp. 42–61.

5.171 Marshall, A. P. "Service to Afro-Americans." In *A Century of Service: Librarianship in the United States and Canada*, edited by S. L. Jackson, E. B. Herling, and E. J. Josey. Chicago: American Library Association, 1976. Pp. 62–78.

5.172 Rothstein, S. "Service to Academia." In *A Century of Service: Librarianship in the United States and Canada*, edited by S. L. Jackson, E. B. Herling, and E. J. Josey. Chicago: American Library Association, 1976. Pp. 79–109.

5.173 Smith, T. E. "Municipal Reference Libraries." *ELIS* 18 (1976): 299–301.

5.174 Blayney, M. S. " 'Libraries for the Millions': Adult Public Library Services and the New Deal." *JLH* 12 (1977): 235–49.

5.175 DuMont, R. R. *Reform and Reaction: The Big City Public Library in American Life.* Westport, Conn.: Greenwood Press, 1977.

5.176 Palmer, J. W. "Contributions of the Carnegie Corporation to the Development of Public Library Film Service." *JLH* 12 (1977): 325–41.

5.177 Freestone, R. "The Geography of Urban Public Library Development." *MinnL* 25 (1978): 299–310.

5.178 Harris, M. H. "The Intellectual History of American Public Librarianship." In *Milestones to the Present: Papers from Library History Seminar V*, edited by H. Goldstein. Syracuse, N.Y.: Gaylord Professional Publications, 1978. Pp. 232–37.

5.179 Harris, M. H. "The Purpose of the American Public Library: A Revisionist Interpretation of History." In *Public Library Purpose: A Reader*, compiled by B. Totterdell. London: Clive Bingley; Hamden, Conn.: Linnet Books, 1978. Pp. 39–53.

5.180 Hilton, R. C. "Public Support for Library Service: Revolutionary Democracy in Action." *LJ* 103 (1978): 1223–38.

5.181 Holowell, L. S. "Benjamin Franklin and the Subscription Library: The Foundations." Research Paper, Texas Woman's University, 1978.

5.182 Keller, L. E. "The History of Contributions of Blacks to Public Librarianship from 1903–1976." Research Paper, Texas Woman's University, 1978.

5.183 Molz, R. K. "The Historical Role and Function of the Main Urban Library." In *Future of the Main Urban Library*, edited by P. P. Price. Las Cruces, N.M.: Urban Libraries Council, 1978. Pp. 5–22.

5.184 Rayward, W. B. "Introduction: The Public Library—A Perspective and Some Questions." *LQ* 48 (1978): 383–92.

5.185 Savage, A. L. "Access to Information: The Development of the American Public Library as a Social Institution." Doctoral dissertation, State University of New York at Buffalo, 1978.

5.186 Schmidt, S. "A History of ABE Services in Public Libraries." *DLQ* 14 (1978): 5–13.

5.187 Sessa, F. B. "Public Libraries, International: History of the Public Library." *ELIS* 24 (1978): 267–91.

5.188 Sigler, R. F. "Rationale for the Film as a Public Library Resource and Service." *LibT* 27 (1978): 9–26.

5.189 "[The American Public Library: Its Historic Concern for the Humanities] Discussion." In *The Role of the Humanities in the Public Library: Proceedings of a Conference Sponsored by the School of Library Science, University of North Carolina at Chapel Hill,*

1978, edited by R. N. Broadus and B. Nielsen. Chicago: American Library Association, 1979. Pp. 48–69.

5.190 Braverman, M. *Youth, Society, and the Public Library.* Chicago: American Library Association, 1979.

5.191 Garrison, D. *Apostles of Culture: The Public Librarian and American Society, 1876–1920.* New York: Free Press, 1979.

5.192 Molz, R. K. "[The American Public Library: Its Historic Concern for the Humanities] Discussion." In *The Role of the Humanities in the Public Library: Proceedings of a Conference Sponsored by the School of Library Science, University of North Carolina at Chapel Hill, 1978 University of North Carolina at Chapel Hill, 1978*, edited by R. N. Broadus and B. Nielsen. Chicago: American Library Association, 1979. Pp. 30–47.

5.193 Williams, R. V. "Sources of the Variability in the Level of Public Library Development in the United States: A Comparative Analysis." *Library Research* 2 (1980): 157–76.

5.194 deGruyter, L. "The History and Development of Rural Public Libraries." *LibT* 28 (1980): 513–23.

5.195 Birge, L. E. *Serving Adult Learners: A Public Library Tradition.* Chicago: American Library Association, 1981.

5.196 Harris, M. H., and Sodt, J. "Libraries, Users, and Librarians: Continuing Efforts to Define the Nature and Extent of Public Library Use." *AdLib* 11 (1981): 109–33.

5.197 Breish, K. A. "Small Public Libraries in America, 1850–1890: The Invention and Evolution of a Building Type." Doctoral dissertation, University of Michigan, 1982.

5.198 Davies, D. W. "Libraries as Centers of Culture." In *Public Librarianship: A Reader,* edited by J. Robbins-Carter. Littleton, Colo.: Libraries Unlimited, 1982. Pp. 98–109.

5.199 Davies, D. W. "Libraries as Social and Entertainment Centers." In *Public Librarianship: A Reader,* edited by J. Robbins-Carter.

Littleton, Colo.: Libraries Unlimited, 1982. Pp. 109–27.

5.200 Ditzion, S. H. "Democratic Strivings." In *Public Librarianship: A Reader,* edited by J. Robbins-Carter. Littleton, Colo.: Libraries Unlimited, 1982. Pp. 42–62.

5.201 Goudy, F. W. "Funding Local Public Libraries, FY 1966 to FY 1980." *Public Libraries [1970–]* 21 (1982): 52–54.

5.202 Harris, M. H. "The Purpose of the American Public Library: A Revisionist Interpretation of History." In *Public Librarianship: A Reader,* edited by J. Robbins-Carter. Littleton, Colo.: Libraries Unlimited, 1982. Pp. 63–72.

5.203 Lee, R. E. "Educational Objective of the Public Library." In *Public Librarianship: A Reader,* edited by J. Robbins-Carter. Littleton, Colo.: Libraries Unlimited, 1982. Pp. 93–98.

5.204 Shera, J. H. "Causal Factors in Public Library Development." In *Public Librarianship: A Reader,* edited by J. Robbins-Carter. Littleton, Colo.: Libraries Unlimited, 1982. Pp. 12–41.

5.205 Shontz, M. L. "Selected Research Related to Children's and Young Adult Services in Public Libraries." *TN* 38 (1982): 152–42.

5.206 Weibel, K. *The Evolution of Library Outreach 1960–75 and Its Effect on Reader Services: Some Considerations.* Urbana: University of Illinois Graduate School of Library and Information Science Occasional Paper Series No. 156, December 1982.

5.207 Colson, J. C. "Form against Function: The American Public Library and Contemporary Society." *JLH* 18 (1983): 111–42.

5.208 Fain, E. "Books for New Citizens: Public Libraries and Americanization Programs, 1900–1925." In *The Quest for Social Justice: The Morris Franklin Memorial Lectures, 1970–1980,* edited by R. M. Aderman. Madison: University of Wisconsin Press, 1983. Pp. 255–76.

5.209 Steinfirst, S. "Programming for Young Adults." In *Reaching Young People through*

Media, edited by N. B. Pillon. Littleton, Colo.: Libraries Unlimited, 1983. Pp. 123–50.

5.210 Wiegand, W. A. "British Propaganda in American Public Libraries, 1914–1917." *JLH* 18 (1983): 237–54.

5.211 Rouzer, S. M. "The Great Books Movement in the American Public Library." Master's thesis, University of Chicago, 1984.

5.212 Soltow, M. J. "Public Libraries' Services to Organized Labor: An Overview." *RQ* 24 (1984): 163–68.

5.213 Birdsall, W. F. "Community, Individualism, and the American Public Library." *LJ* 110 (1985): 21–24.

5.214 Carrier, E. J. *Fiction in Public Libraries, 1900–1950.* Littleton, Colo.: Libraries Unlimited, 1985.

5.215 James, S. E. "The Relationship between Local Economic Conditions and the Use of Public Libraries." *LQ* 55 (1985): 255–72.

5.216 Schuchat, T. *The Library Book.* Seattle: Madrona Publishers, 1985.

5.217 Atkinson, J. "Pioneers in Public Library Service to Young Adults." *TN* 43 (1986): 27–44.

5.218 Monroe, M. E. "The Evolution of Literacy Programs in the Context of Library Adult Education." *LibT* 35 (1986): 197–205.

5.219 Williams, R. V. "Public Library Development in the United States, 1850–1870: An Empirical Analysis." *JLH* 21 (1986): 177–201.

Special Studies Arranged by State

Alabama

5.220 Fonville, E. R. "A History of Pubic Library Service to Negroes in Bessemer, Alabama." Master's thesis, Atlanta University, 1962.

5.221 Grayson, B. R. "The History of Public Library Service for Negroes in Montgomery, Alabama." Master's thesis, Atlanta University, 1965.

5.222 Johnson, K. R. "The Early Library Movement in Alabama." *JLH* 6 (1971): 120–32.

5.223 Miller, W. T. "Library Service for Negroes in the New South: Birmingham, Alabama, 1871–1918." *Alabama Librarian* 27 (1975): 6–8.

Alaska

5.224 Brady, J. G. "Libraries of Alaska: Historical Library at Sitka." *LJ* 30 (1905): 141–43.

5.225 Anderson, R. "Alaskan Libraries in 1945." *PNLAQ* 9 (1945): 147–49.

5.226 Mauseth, B. J. "A Brief History of the Ketchikan, Alaska, Public Library, 1901–1956." Master's thesis, University of Washington, 1956.

5.227 Stewart, J. "Library Service in Alaska: A Historical Study." Master's thesis, University of Washington, 1957.

Arizona

5.228 "Public Library Histories." *Arizona Librarian* 7 (1950): 1–15.

Arkansas

5.229 Gates, J. K. "Library Progress in Tax-Supported Institutions in Arkansas, 1924–1949." Master's thesis, Catholic University of America, 1951.

5.230 Tillman, R. H. "The History of Public Library Service to Negroes in Little Rock, Arkansas, 1917–1951." Master's thesis, Atlanta University, 1953.

5.231 McNeil, G. "History of the Library in Arkansas." Master's thesis, University of Mississippi, 1957.

5.232 Roberts, B. "Arkansas' Carnegie Libraries." *ArkL* 35 (December 1978): 17–19.

California

5.233 Lichtenstein, J. "San Francisco's Public Library." *Sunset Magazine* 13 (1904): 163–70.

5.234 Kendall, H. A. "The Eureka Free Library." In *History of Humboldt County,* edited by L. H. Irvine. Los Angeles: Historic Record Co., 1915. Pp. 166–70.

5.235 Los Angeles County Free Library. *History of the Los Angeles County Free Library, 1912–1927.* Los Angeles: The Library, 1927.

5.236 Miller, G. C. *The Palo Alto Public Library: Its History and Development.* Palo Alto, Calif.: N.p., 1929.

5.237 Nourse, L. M. "A Comparison of the Establishment and Growth of County Libraries in California and New Jersey As Influenced by Their Respective Legal, Geographical, and Administrative Differences." Master's thesis, Columbia University, 1931.

5.238 Hyers, F. H. "Brief History of the Los Angeles Public Library." In *Forty-Eighth Annual Report of the Los Angeles Public Library.* Los Angeles: The Public Library, 1936. Pp. 25–78.

5.239 Cooley, L. C. "The Los Angeles Public Library." *Historical Society of Southern California Quarterly* 23 (1941): 5–23.

5.240 Conmy, P. T. "The San Francisco Earthquake and Fire of 1906 and Its Effect upon Libraries." *CalL* 12 (1950): 87–90.

5.241 Lichtenstein, J. "Recollections of the Early San Francisco Public Library." *CLB* 11 (1950): 165–68.

5.242 Warren, A. "The Public Library Movement in California." *CLB* 11 (1950): 147–48, 179–80.

5.243 Steig, L. F. "Notes on the Origins of Public Libraries in California, 1850–1900." *LQ* 22 (1952): 263–69.

5.244 Mackenzie, A. D. "The Beginnings of a Library Tradition." *CalL* 14 (1953): 216–18.

5.245 Wheeler, J. L. "Ideas behind the San Diego Public Library." *CalL* 15 (1954): 224–26.

5.246 Eddy, H. G. *County Free Library Organizing in California, 1909–1918: Personal Recollections of Harriet G. Eddy, County Library Organizer, Calif. State Library.* Berkeley: Committee on Callifornia Library History, Bibliography and Archives, California Library Association, 1955.

5.247 Hensley, H. C. "The Public Reading Room." *San Diego Historical Society Quarterly* 7 (1955): 10.

5.248 Hensley, H. C. "Early Days of the Public Library." *San Diego Historical Society Quarterly* 4 (1958): 37–39.

5.249 Bailey, B. "The Library Comes to Antelope Valley." *CalL* 27 (1966): 236a–d.

5.250 Kirkwood, H. W., Kountz, J. C., and Wetherell, E. *Orange County Free Library, 1921–1965.* Orange, Calif.: Orange County Free Library, 1966.

5.251 Sugg, E. "The San Francisco Public Library, 1917–1929." Master's thesis, University of California, 1966.

5.252 Blanford, L. *A History of the Kern County Library.* [Bakersfield, Calif.]: Kern County Historical Society, 1967.

5.253 Davis, D. G. "In Fair and Foul: Early Fresno Libraries." *CalL* 28 (1967): 232a–d.

5.254 Conmy, P. T. "Centennial of Oakland Public Library." *CalL* 30 (1969): 42–47.

5.255 Conmy, P. T. *The Dismissal of Ina Coolbrith as Head Librarian of Oakland Free Public Library and a Discussion of the Tenure Status of Head Librarians.* Oakland, Calif.: Oakland Public Library, 1969.

5.256 Conmy, P. T. *The Organic Structure of the Oakland Public Library: Its History and Development.* Oakland, Calif.: Oakland Public Library, 1969.

5.257 Irshay, P. C. "The A.K. Smiley Public Library and How It Grew." *CalL* 30 (1969): 166–72.

5.258 Benedetti, L. S. "A History of Public Library Service in Menlo Park, California, 1889–1969." Master's thesis, California State University, San Jose, 1970.

5.259 Conmy, P. T. "California Libraries in the 1870s." *CalL* 31 (1970): 37–45.

5.260 Souza, M. A. "The History of the Santa Cruz Public Library System." Master's thesis, San Jose State College, 1970.

5.261 James, B. L. "History of the Redwood City Public Library, Redwood City, California, 1865–1939." Master's thesis, San Jose State College, 1971.

5.262 Mahoney, B. L. "The History of the Marin County Free Library System." Master's thesis, California State University, San Jose, 1972.

5.263 Held, R. *The Rise of the Public Library in California.* Chicago: American Library Association, 1973.

5.264 Siegel, E., and Bruckman, J. D. "Los Angeles Public Library." *ELIS* 16 (1975): 337–43.

5.265 Cao, J. F. "The Los Angeles Public Library: Origins and Development, 1872–1910." Doctoral dissertation, University of Southern California, 1977.

5.266 Sigler, R. F. "The Film Censorship Controversy at Los Angeles Public Library—1971: A Case Study." Doctoral dissertation, Florida State University, 1977.

5.267 Henderson, J. D. "The Rise of the County Public Library—A Personal View." *CalL* 39 (1978): 16–23.

5.268 Reid, T. "The Development of Public Library Service to Children and Young People in California: Random Personal Comments, Observations, and Opinion." *CalL* 39 (1978): 24–30.

5.269 Wood, R. F. "Public Libraries in California, 1850–1920." In *Milestones to the Present: Papers from Library History Seminar V,* edited by H. Goldstein. Syracuse, N.Y.: Gaylord Professional Publications, 1978. Pp. 155–65.

5.270 Ramirez, W., and Gumina, D. "The San Francisco Public Library: A History." *ELIS* 26 (1979): 299–307.

5.271 Thorne, M. "San Diego Public Library." *ELIS* 26 (1979): 296–98.

5.272 Blake, F. M. "The W.P.A. and the San Francisco Public Library." In *Studies in Creative Partnership: Federal Aid to Public Libraries during the New Deal,* edited by D. F. Ring. Metuchen, N.J.: Scarecrow Press, 1980. Pp. 124–40.

5.273 Struhsaker, V. "Hazelton's Marble Library, Stockton's Pride." *Pacific Historian* 24 (1980): 168–81.

5.274 Struhsaker, V. "The Stewart Library: A Dream Realized." *Pacific Historian* 24 (1980): 8–20.

5.275 Struhsaker, V. "The Stockton Public Library Today and Its County Branches." *Pacific Historian* 24 (1980): 456–71.

5.276 Struhsaker, V. "The Stockton-San Joaquin County Public Library Built 'With Stubborn Patience and Triple Steel'." *Pacific Historian* 24 (1980): 256–83.

5.277 Breed, C. E. " 'Two Reading Rooms—One for Each Sex': Public Library Buildings." *Journal of San Diego History* 28 (1982): 162–71.

5.278 Breed, C. E., and McPhail, E. C. *Turning the Pages: San Diego Public Library History, 1882–1982.* San Diego: Friends of the San Diego Public Library, 1983.

Colorado

5.279 Colorado State Library. *Colorado's Century of Public Libraries.* Denver: The Library, 1959.

5.280 Eastlick, J. T. "Denver Public Library." *ELIS* 6 (1971): 588–92.

Connecticut

5.281 New Haven. Free Public Library. *The Free Public Library of New Haven, Conn., Containing a Brief History* .... New Haven, Conn.: The Library, 1893.

5.282 Dexter, F. B. "The First Public Library in New Haven." *Papers of the New Haven Colony Historical Society* 6 (1900): 301–13.

5.283 Hewins, C. M. "The Development of the Public Library in Connecticut." *ConnM* 9 (1905): 161–84.

5.284 Miller, M. M. "Public Libraries in Connecticut: Founding and Development of the Public Library at Greenwich, Connecticut." *ConnM* 10 (1906): 490–93.

5.285 Stetson, W. "Development of the Free Public Library in New Haven." *ConnM* 10 (1906): 129–38.

5.286 Trumbull, J. "Public Libraries in Connecticut: A Presentation of the Founding and Development of the Otis Library at Norwich." *ConnM* 10 (1906): 345–49.

5.287 Norton, C. B., comp. *History of the Scoville Memorial Library.* Salisbury, Conn.: Lakeview Journal Press, 1941.

5.288 Agard, R. M. "The Development of Public Libraries in Connecticut, 1875–1900." Master's thesis, Brown University, 1944.

5.289 Wead, K. H. *Public and School Libraries and the State Board of Education: History [1893–1950], Statistics.* Hartford, Conn.: Connecticut State Department of Education, 1951.

5.290 Bryan, B. D. "Fairfield Public Library: Antecedents and Development." Master's thesis, Southern Connecticut State College, 1964.

5.291 Giddings, R. L. "The West Hartford Public Library: Its History, Development, and Present Status." Master's thesis, Southern Connecticut State College, 1965.

5.292 Waggoner, L. B. "The Development of the Cheshire Public Library." Master's thesis, Southern Connecticut State College, 1965.

5.293 DeAngelis, P. "A History of Library Service in Kensington, Connecticut." Master's thesis, Southern Connecticut State College, 1967.

5.294 Hausmann, A. F. "Origin and Development of the New Haven Free Public Library, 1886–1911." Master's thesis, Southern Connecticut State College, 1968.

5.295 Bergen, E. "History of the Bridgeport Public Library and Reading Room." Master's thesis, Southern Connecticut State College, 1969.

5.296 Early, S. E. "The History of Public Library Service in Milford, Connecticut, 1639–1970." Master's thesis, Southern Connecticut State College, 1971.

5.297 Semmler, E. A. "A History of the Public Library in Plainsville, Connecticut, 1785–1973." Master's thesis, Southern Connecticut State College, 1973.

5.298 Via, N. S. "The History, Development, and Growth of the Clark Memorial Library, Bethany, Connecticut." Master's thesis, Southern Connecticut State College, 1973.

5.299 Brophy, E. D. "The History of the Libraries of Windsor, Connecticut." Master's thesis, Southern Connecticut State College, 1975.

Delaware

5.300 Nields, J. P. *The Wilmington Public Library and the New Castle County Free Library: A Historical Sketch.* Wilmington, Del.: Wilmington Institute, 1943.

5.301 "Historical Views and News [Public Libraries in Delaware]." *DLAB* 20 (Spring 1966): 13–31.

5.302 Baumgartner, B. "The New Castle County Free Library, 1927–1933." *Delaware History* 13 (1968): 45–56.

District of Columbia

5.303 Johnston, W. D. "Earliest Free Public Library Movement in Washington, 1849–1874." *RCHS* 9 (1906): 9–13.

5.304 De Caindry, W. "The Washington City Free Library." *RCHS* 16 (1913): 64–95.

5.305 Noble, A. D. "Short Survey of the Libraries in the District of Columbia." *DCL* 4 (1933): 70–87.

5.306 Cook, V. R. "A History and Evaluation of the Music Division of the District of Columbia Public Library." Master's thesis, Catholic University of America, 1952.

5.307 Maples, H. L. "The Peabody Library of Georgetown, District of Columbia: A History and Evaluation." Master's thesis, Drexel Institute of Technology, 1952.

5.308 King, M. L. "Beginnings and Early History of the Public Library of the District of Columbia, 1896–1904." Master's thesis, Catholic University of America, 1953.

5.309 Shibley, F. W. *Washington Public Library—1899.* Washington, D.C.: Public Library of the District of Columbia, 1953.

5.310 Williams, M. D. "The Peabody Room in the Georgetown Branch of the D.C. Public Library." *DCL* 24 (1953): 11–16.

5.311 Mason, D. D. "The Public Library of the District of Columbia: An Historical Perspective, 1895–1948." *DCL* 20 (1954): 2–5.

5.312 Hecht, A. "The Takoma Park Public Library." *RCHS* (1966–1968): 318–35.

5.313 Franklin, H. R. "Washington. District of Columbia Public Library." *ELIS* 32 (1981): 386–401.

Florida

5.314 "The Carnegie Library at Ocala, Florida." *LJ* 42 (1917): 379–81.

5.315 U. S. Works Progress Administration, Florida. *Florida Libraries.* Jacksonville, Fla.: Works Progress Administration, 1939.

5.316 McCullough, M. W. "The Davis S. Walker Library [Tallahassee]." *Apalachee* (1946): 13–18.

5.317 Carruth, E., and Monro, I. "Hannibal Square Library [Winter Park, Fla., 1936–52]." *WLB* 26 (1952): 463–65.

5.318 Gill, S. "The History of the Miami Public Library System, Miami, Florida." Master's thesis, Western Reserve University, 1954.

5.319 Neuman, R. "Business Library Service Moves South [to Miami Public]." *LJ* 79 (1954): 2143–45.

5.320 Curry, J. L. "History of Public Library Service to Negroes in Jacksonville, Florida." Master's thesis, Atlanta University, 1957.

5.321 Barfield, I. R. "A History of the Miami Public Library, Miami, Florida." Master's thesis, Atlanta University, 1958.

5.322 Patane, J. S. "A History of the Public Library in St. Petersburg, Florida." Master's thesis, Florida State University, 1960.

5.323 Worley, M. M. "Tampa, Florida, Public Library." Master's thesis, University of Mississippi, 1961.

5.324 Obenaus, K. M. "Private Subscription Built the Indian River County Library." *LJ* 87 (1962): 4353–54.

5.325 Perres, M. J. "History and Development of Public Library Service for Negroes in Pensacola, Florida, 1947–1961." Master's thesis, Atlanta University, 1963.

5.326 Mason, P. R. "A History of Public Library Development in Florida." Master's thesis, University of Chicago, 1968.

5.327 Sessa, F. B. "Miami-Dade Public Library." *ELIS* 18 (1976): 44–49.

5.328 Blazek, R. "Florida's First Public Library." *SEL* 27 (1977): 167–73.

5.329 Blazek, R. "Library in a Pioneer Community: Lemon City, Florida." *Tequesta: Journal of the Historical Association of Southern Florida* 42 (1982): 39–55.

Georgia

5.330 Jamison, A. H. "Development of the Library in Atlanta." *Atlanta Historical Bulletin* 4 (1939): 96–111.

5.331 Daniel, E. C. "Books in Brooks." *Georgia Review* 1 (1947): 242–51.

5.332 Fleming, J. B. *199 Years of Augusta's Library: A Chronology (1732–1949).* Athens: University of Georgia Press, 1949.

5.333 Harris, S. M. "Regional Library Development and Service in Georgia." *Georgia Review* 3 (1949): 298–310.

5.334 Adkins, B. M. "A History of Public Library Service to Negroes in Atlanta, Georgia." Master's thesis, Atlanta University, 1951.

5.335 Cooper, N. W. "The History of Public Library Service to Negroes in Savannah, Georgia." Master's thesis, Atlanta University, 1960.

5.336 Crittenden, J. L. J. "A History of Public Library Service to Negroes in Columbia, Georgia, 1831–1959." Master's thesis, Atlanta University, 1960.

5.337 Satterfield, H. C. "History of Highland County District Library." Master's thesis, Kent State University, 1960.

5.338 Redd, G. L. "A History of Public Library Service to Negroes in Macon, Georgia." Master's thesis, Atlanta University, 1961.

5.339 Williams, B. C. "A History of the Cairo, Georgia, Public Library." Master's thesis, Florida State University, 1961.

5.340 Hutzler, H. C. "History of the Rome, Georgia, Carnegie Library (1911–1961)." Master's thesis, Catholic University of America, 1963.

5.341 Howard, L. "The Statesboro Regional Library: History, Development and Services." Master's thesis, Florida State University, 1964.

5.342 Johnston, R. P. "The Development of the Decatur-deKalb Regional Library." Research Paper, Emory University, 1964.

5.343 Moore, M. G. "A Study of the History and Development of the Troup-Harris-Coweta Regional Library." Research Paper, Emory University, 1964.

5.344 Odom, E. P. *History of the Public Library of Moultrie, Georgia, 1906–1965.* Moultrie, Ga.: Moultrie-Colquitt County Library, 1966.

Guam

5.345 Caldwell, M. S. "A History of the Guam Public Library System, 1947–1975." Doctoral dissertation, Western Michigan University, 1977.

Hawaii

5.346 Okubo, S. "The Development of Public Library Service in the County of Maui, Territory of Hawaii." Master's thesis, University of Hawaii, 1941.

5.347 Matsushige, H. "The Library of Hawaii, 1913–1949: A Brief Historical

Description." Master's thesis, Pratt Institute, 1951.

5.348 Ramachandran, R. "Origins of the Carnegie Grant to the Library of Hawaii (1901–1909)." *CalL* 34 (1973): 44–50.

5.349 Tachihata, C. "The History and Development of Hawaii Public Libraries: The Library of Hawaii and the Hawaii State Library, 1913–1971." Doctoral dissertation, University of Southern California, 1981.

Idaho

5.350 Miller, H. M. "The Library Services Act in Idaho, Together with a History of the Idaho Public Library Development since 1901." *Idaho Librarian* 14 (July 1962): 67–73.

Illinois

5.351 "The Chicago Public Library: History of Its Origin and Formation." *Chicago Librarian* 1 (January 1873): 3–17.

5.352 Hoyne, T. *Historical Sketch of the Origin and Foundation of the Chicago Public Library: Compiled From the Original Documents and Correspondence and Contemporary Publications . . . .* Chicago: Beach, Bernard & Co., 1877.

5.353 Kimball, C. F. "History of Withers Public Library [Bloomington, Ill.]." *Transactions of the McLean County Historical Society* 2 (1903): 224–40.

5.354 Sharp, K. "Illinois Libraries: [Part II] Public Libraries (Excepting Chicago)." *University Studies [University of Illinois]* 2, no. 3 (1907): 137–284.

5.355 *The Chicago Public Library, 1873–1923: Proceedings of the Celebration of the Fiftieth Anniversary of the Opening of the Library, January First, Fourth, and Sixth, 1923.* Chicago: The Public Library, 1923.

5.356 Kratz, E. A. *History of the Champaign Public Library and Reading Room.* Champaign, Ill.: The Library, 1926.

5.357 Prichard, L. G. "A History of the Chicago Public Library." Master's thesis, University of Illinois, 1928.

5.358 Steuernagel, B. *The Belleville Public Library, 1836–1936: An Historical Sketch.* Belleville, Ill.: News Democrat Journal, 1936.

5.359 Spencer, G. S. *The Chicago Public Library: Origins and Backgrounds.* Chicago: University of Chicago Press, 1943.

5.360 Berg, V. A. "History of the Urbana Free Library, 1874–1894." Master's thesis, University of Illinois, 1948.

5.361 Perry, M. E. "Decatur Public Library, 1901–1951." *IllL* 33 (1951): 350–54.

5.362 Bruder, M. "The Chicago Public Library (1873–1952)." *Chicago Schools Journal* 33 (1952): 159–62.

5.363 Burrell, M. R. "A Short History of the Galesburg Ladies' Library Association." In *Contributions to Mid-West Library History,* edited by T. Eaton. Champaign, Ill.: Illini Union Bookstore, 1964. Pp. 130–53.

5.364 Bullock, E. V. "A History of the Geneva Public Library." Master's thesis, Northern Illinois University, 1965.

5.365 Mills, F. L., and Hurley, L. J. "A History of Racine Public Library Lectures: 1927–1966." *IllL* 48 (1966): 540–43.

5.366 Beasley, R. "O'Fallon Public Library." *IllL* 50 (1968): 662–63.

5.367 Bell, E. "Jerseyville Free Library." *IllL* 50 (1968): 642.

5.368 Bostian, I., ed. "Histories of Public Libraries." *IllL* 50 (1968): 597–722.

5.369 Breen, T. V. N. "Withers Public Library, Bloomington." *IllL* 50 (1968): 614–18.

5.370 Burster, M. G. "El Paso Public Library." *IllL* 50 (1968): 632–35.

5.371 Carter, K. E. "Manteno Township Library." *IllL* 50 (1968): 659–60.

5.372 Chandler, A. "Kankakee Public Library." *IllL* 50 (1968): 645–47.

5.373 Chitwood, J. R. "Rockford Public Library." *IllL* 50 (1968): 665–67.

5.374 Davenport, N. "Vespasian Warner Public Library, Clinton." *IllL* 50 (1968): 620–21.

5.375 Federici, Y. D. "History of Public Library Service to Children in Illinois." *IllL* 50 (1968): 962–70.

5.376 Fisher, M. "Illiopolis Public Library." *IllL* 50 (1968): 640–41.

5.377 Gillespie, E. "Vienna Carnegie Public Library." *IllL* 50 (1968): 678–79.

5.378 Gregory, R. W. "Waukegan Public Library." *IllL* 50 (1968): 683–85.

5.379 Heck, R. S. "Mercer Township Free Public Library, Aledo." *IllL* 50 (1968): 604–07.

5.380 Henderson, T. B. "Columbia Public Library." *IllL* 50 (1968): 621–23.

5.381 Herrick, C. C. "Helen M. Plum Memorial Library, Lombard." *IllL* 50 (1968): 656–59.

5.382 Ladenson, A. "Bringing Books to People in Illinois, 1818–1968." *IllL* 50 (1968): 597–604.

5.383 Larson, E. M. "DeKalb Public Library." *IllL* 50 (1968): 623–26.

5.384 Lathrop, M, and Clute, M. "Gail Borden Public Library, Elgin." *IllL* 50 (1968): 629–32.

5.385 Lengelsen, R. "Mt. Carmel Carnegie Library." *IllL* 50 (1968): 660–62.

5.386 Lindquist, V. "Glen Ellyn Public Library." *IllL* 50 (1968): 635–38.

5.387 McCarthy, P. "Walnut Township Memorial Library." *IllL* 50 (1968): 680–82.

5.388 McClendon, M. "Benton Public Library." *IllL* 50 (1968): 612–14.

5.389 McDonald, O. "East Alton Public Library." *IllL* 50 (1968): 627–29.

5.390 Marchi, M. M. "Woodstock Public Library." *IllL* 50 (1968): 691–93.

5.391 O'Neill, H. "Hinsdale Public Library." *IllL* 50 (1968): 638–39.

5.392 Ohrman, M. A. "Villa Park Public Library." *IllL* 50 (1968): 679–80.

5.393 Pohl, R. K. "Joliet Public Library." *IllL* 50 (1968): 643–45.

5.394 Preiss, V. D. "River Forest Public Library." *IllL* 50 (1968): 663–65.

5.395 Sheffield, F. C. "Lincoln Library, Springfield." *IllL* 50 (1968): 667–78.

5.396 Siniff, H. J. "Wilmette Public Library." *IllL* 50 (1968): 686–90.

5.397 Snyder, E. J. "Cairo Public Library." *IllL* 50 (1968): 619–20.

5.398 Steuernagel, B. "Bellville Public Library, 1836–1936." *IllL* 50 (1968): 607–12.

5.399 Uschold, M. E. "Lacon Public Library." *IllL* 50 (1968): 652–56.

5.400 Woolsey, M. L. "Knoxville Public Library." *IllL* 50 (1968): 647–52.

5.401 "Histories of Public Libraries." *IllL* 51 (1969): 357–452.

5.402 Kram, R. I. "The Foreign Language Collections of the Chicago Public Library, 1872–1947." Master's thesis, University of Chicago, 1970.

5.403 Ladenson, A. "Chicago Public Library." *ELIS* 4 (1970): 530–39.

5.404 "Chicago Public Library 100th Anniversary." *IllL* 54 (1972): 250–306.

5.405 *The Treasures of All Knowledge: The Official Centennial Publication.* Chicago: Chicago Public Library, 1972.

5.406 Ladenson, A. "The Chicago Public Library W.P.A. Omnibus Project." In *Studies in Creative Partnership: Federal Aid to Public Libraries during the New Deal*, edited by D. F. Ring. Metuchen, N.J.: Scarecrow Press, 1980. Pp. 47–65.

5.407 Clayton, S. A. H. "A Public Library's History and Development; East Saint Louis, Illinois' Public Library." Doctoral dissertation, Southern Illinois University, Carbondale, 1981.

5.408 Hess, J. D. "Childhood Memories of Books, Libraries and Librarians." *TN* 43 (1986): 87–96.

Indiana

5.409 Henry, W. E. *Municipal and Institutional Libraries of Indiana: History, Condition, and Management*. Indianapolis: 1904.

5.410 Peters, O. M. *The Gary Public Library, 1907–1944*. Gary, Ind.: Public Library of Gary, 1945.

5.411 Middleton, E. H., comp. *The First Seventy-Five Years: A Sketch of the Muncie Public Library, 1874–1949*. Muncie, Ind.: Muncie Public Library, 1949.

5.412 Feaster, D. M. "History of Story Telling in the Indianapolis Public Library." Master's thesis, Western Reserve University, 1951.

5.413 Taylor, M. V. "Public Library Commission of Indiana, 1899–1925." Master's thesis, University of Kentucky, 1953, University of Kentucky Press Microcard Series B, no. 3.

5.414 Lewis, D. F. "History of the Marion County, Indiana, Library, 1844–1930." Master's thesis, Indiana University, 1954.

5.415 Hull, T. V. "The Origin and Development of the Indianapolis Public Library, 1873–1899." Master's thesis, University of Kentucky, 1956, University of Kentucky Press Microcard Series B, no. 2.

5.416 McFadden, M. *The Indianapolis Public Library: A Portrait Against the Background of the Past Decade, 1945–1955*. Indianapolis: N.p., 1956.

5.417 Walther, L. A. "Legal and Governmental Aspects of Public Library Development in Indiana, 1816–1953." Doctoral dissertation, Indiana University, 1957.

5.418 Beamon, M. "The Origin and Development of the School Services Department of the Indianapolis Public Library." Master's thesis, Indiana University, 1962.

5.419 Zimmerman, M. "A History of the South Bend Public Library from 1888–1961." Master's thesis, Catholic University of America, 1962.

5.420 Curless, M. "Library Development in Lagrange County, Indiana." In *Contributions to Mid-West Library History*, edited by T. Eaton. Champaign, Ill.: Illini Union Bookstore, 1964. Pp. 164–80.

5.421 Boyd, F. *A History of Public Library Service in Terre Haute and Vigo County, Indiana, from 1823 to 1966*. Terre Haute, Ind.: Fairbanks-Vigo County Public Library, 1966.

5.422 Constantine, J. R. *The Role of Libraries in the Cultural History of Indiana*. Bloomington, Ind.: Indiana Library Studies, 1970.

5.423 *A Century of Service, 1873–1973: Historical Highlights of the Indianapolis-Marion County Public Library*. Indianapolis: The Library, 1973.

5.424 Edson, H. "Thanksgiving Day Sermon [at the Indianapolis Public Library 26 November 1868]." In *Indianapolis in the World of Books*. Indianapolis: Indianapolis-Marion County Public Library, 1974. Pp. 1–12.

5.425 Holley, E. G. "The Indianapolis Public Library: A Live Thing in the Whole Town." In *Indianapolis in the World of Books*. Indianapolis: Indianapolis-Marion County Public Library, 1974. Pp. 13–29.

5.426 McDonough, I. R. *History of the Public Library in Vigo County, 1816–1975*. Terre Haute, Ind.: Vigo County Public Library, 1977.

5.427 Ashton, R. J. "A Commitment to Excellence in Genealogy: How the Public Library Became the Only Tourist Attraction in Fort Wayne, Indiana." *LibT* 32 (1983): 89–96.

Iowa

5.428 McGuire, L. P. "A Study of the Public Library Movement in Iowa." *Iowa Journal of History and Politics* 35 (1937): 22–72.

5.429 Coughlin, B. "History of the Davenport Public Library." Master's thesis, Western Reserve University, 1952.

5.430 Snyder, E. B. "The History and Development of the Music Collection and Department of the Public Library of Des Moines." Master's thesis, Western Reserve University, 1958.

5.431 Blanks, E. W. "The Public Library of Des Moines, Iowa: A History of the First Fifty Years, 1866–1916." Master's thesis, University of Texas, 1967.

5.432 Pease, K. R. "Iowa Public Library Service in Recent History." Master's thesis, University of Chicago, 1968.

Kansas

5.433 Crumpacker, G. F. "Library Legislation and the Library Movement in Kansas." Master's thesis, University of Illinois, 1932.

5.434 Gibson, H. B. C. "Wichita and Her Public Libraries." *Kansas Historical Quarterly* 6 (1937): 387–93.

5.435 Biby, W. A. "History of the Topeka Free Public Library (1870–1948)." *Bulletin of the Shawnee County Historical Society* 2 (1948): 67–78.

5.436 Gaiser, B. F. "A History of the Public Library of Leavenworth, Kansas." Master's thesis, Kansas State Teachers College of Emporia, 1959.

5.437 Hoffman, W. H. "Kansas City Public Library." *ELIS* 13 (1975): 393–99.

Kentucky

5.438 Ridgway, F. H. *Developments in Library Service in Kentucky: A Review.* Berea, Ky.: Berea College Press, 1940.

5.439 Works Progress Administration. *Libraries and Lotteries: A History of the Louisville Free Public Library.* Cynthiana, Ky.: Hobson Book Press, 1944.

5.440 Wilkins, J. "Blue's 'Colored' Branch: A 'Second Plan' That Became a First in Librarianship." *AL* 7 (1976): 256–57.

5.441 Chandley, J. T. "From Saddlebags to Shelves: A History of the Clinton County Public Library." *KLAB* 41 (1977): 9–16.

5.442 Bolte, B. "It Is an Ill-Wind That Blows Some Good! The Beginnings of the Bowling Green Public Library." *KLAB* 42 (1978): 9–14.

Louisiana

5.443 Manint, H. R. "A History of the New Orleans Public Library and the Howard Memorial Library." Master's thesis, Tulane University, 1939.

5.444 Schultz, F. A. "New Orleans Public Library in the Twentieth Century (1897–1951)." *LLAB* 15 (1952): 78–83.

5.445 Vaughan, B. "The Shreve Memorial Library [Shreveport, 1923–53]." *LLAB* 16 (1953): 123–25.

5.446 Culver, E. M., and Gittinger, N. M. "A History of the Citizens' Library Movement [1937–53]." *LLAB* 17 (1954): 18–23.

5.447 Howell, D. B. "The Historical Development and Foreclosure of a Public Library in Alexandria, Louisiana." Research Paper, University of Mississippi, 1960.

5.448 Rush, S. C. "History of Public Library Service to Negroes in Ouachita Parish, Monroe, Louisiana, 1949–1965." Master's thesis, Atlanta University, 1967.

5.449 Smith, R. C. "A Historical Study of Selected Effects of Federal Funding upon Public Libraries in Louisiana, 1956–1973." Doctoral dissertation, Louisiana State University, 1975.

Maine

5.450 "History of the Vassalboro Free Public Library." *Maine Library Association Bulletin* 20 (1959): 13–14.

5.451 Hemmer, P. B. "History of the Lewiston Public Library: Lewiston, Maine." Master's thesis, Catholic University of America, 1965.

5.452 O'Connor, W. "A History of the Portland (Maine) Public Library, 1763–1969." Research Paper, Long Island University, 1971.

5.453 Scott, K. J. "The Origins of the Public Library in Portland, Maine." Master's thesis, University of Chicago Graduate Library School, 1974.

Maryland

5.454 Enoch Pratt Free Library. Baltimore, Md. *The Enoch Pratt Free Library of Baltimore City: Letters and Documents Relating to Its Foundation and Organization, with the Dedicatory Addresses and Exercises, January 4, 1886.* Baltimore: N.p., 1886.

5.455 Uhler, P. R. "A Sketch of the History of the Public Libraries in Baltimore." *LJ* 15 (1890): 334–37.

5.456 Wheeler, J. L. "Origin of the Enoch Pratt Library Central Building." *LJ* 71 (1946): 815–16.

5.457 McMurty, B. B. "The County Public Library: With Special Reference to Maryland and to Prince George's County in Maryland." Master's thesis, Western Maryland College (Westminster), 1947.

5.458 Koch, J. V. "The Enoch Pratt Free Library: Its History, Organization, and Service to Readers." Master's thesis, Western

Reserve University, 1951.

5.459 Titcomb, M. L., and Holzapfel, M. L. *The Washington County Free Library, 1901–1951.* Hagerstown, Md.: N.p., 1951.

5.460 Kahn, R. A. "A History of the Peabody Institute Library, Baltimore, Maryland, 1857–1916." Master's thesis, Catholic University of America, 1953, ACRL Microcard no. 16.

5.461 Morison, N. H. *The Peabody Library [1871].* Baltimore: Peabody Institute Library, 1954.

5.462 Darby, M. R. "A History of the Prince George's County, Maryland Memorial Library." Master's thesis, Catholic University of America, 1961.

5.463 Rice, D. M. "A History of the Silver Springs, Maryland, Public Library from 1931 to 1951." Master's thesis, Catholic University of America, 1961.

5.464 Blinkhorn, M. E. "A History of the Bethesda, Maryland, Public Library." Master's thesis, Catholic University of America, 1963.

5.465 *The Enoch Pratt Free Library at Seventy-Five, 1886–1961: A Retrospective Report.* Baltimore: The Library, 1963.

5.466 Moltenberry, F. "History of Peabody Institute Library: University of the People." In *Approaches to Library History,* edited by J. D. Marshall. Tallahassee: JLH, 1966. Pp. 151–64.

5.467 Powell, N. L. "A History of the Washington County, Maryland, Free Library, 1952–65." Master's thesis, Catholic University of America, 1966.

5.468 Kalisch, P. A. *The Enoch Pratt Free Library: A Social History.* Metuchen, N.J.: Scarecrow Press, 1969.

5.469 Castagna, E. "Enoch Pratt Free Library." *ELIS* 8 (1972): 117–26.

5.470 Jackl, W. E. "Station Number Eleven of the Enoch Pratt Free Library." *JLH* 7 (1972): 141–56.

5.471 Kalisch, P. A. "A Parable of Three Branch Libraries: A Social and Historical Analysis of the Waterfront Branches of the Enoch Pratt Free Library, Baltimore, Maryland." In *Library History Seminar No. 4, Proceedings, 1971,* edited by H. Goldstein and J. Goudeau. Tallahassee: Florida State University School of Library Science, 1972. Pp. 85–108.

5.472 Rubinstein, S. "The Role of the Trustees and the Librarians in the Development of the Enoch Pratt Free Library and the Free Library of Philadelphia, 1880–1914." Doctoral dissertation, George Washington University, 1978.

5.473 Colson, J. C. " 'Almost a Boon . . .' Federal Relief Programs and the Enoch Pratt Free Library, 1933–1943." In *Studies in Creative Partnership: Federal Aid to Public Libraries during the New Deal,* edited by D. F. Ring. Metuchen, N.J.: Scarecrow Press, 1980. Pp. 1–31.

5.474 Rubinstein, S., and Farley, J. "The Enoch Pratt Free Library and Black Patrons: Equality in Library Services, 1882–1915." *JLH* 15 (1980): 445–53.

Massachusetts

5.475 Hillard, G. S. "History of the Boston Public Library." *AJE* 2 (1856): 203–04.

5.476 Hillard, G. S. "The Public Library of the City of Boston." *AJE* 2 (1856): 203–09.

5.477 "The Public Library of Boston." *AJE* 7 (1859): 253–69.

5.478 Heard, J. M. *Origins of the Free Public Library System of Massachusetts.* Clinton, Mass.: Office of the Saturday Courant, 1860.

5.479 Smith, C. C. "Index to the Catalogue of Books in the Upper Hall of the Public Library of the City of Boston [Review]." *North American Review* 93 (1861): 567–70.

5.480 "John Green and the Free Public Library." *AJE* os 13, ns 3 (1863): 606–09.

5.481 Davis, L. C. "The Public Library of Boston." *McBride's Magazine* 3 (1869): 278–93.

5.482 Plumley, G. S. "George Ticknor's Spanish Collection." *Harper's Magazine* 43 (1871): 893–96.

5.483 Winser, F. "The Boston Public Library." *Century, a Popular Quarterly* 3 (December 1871): 150–56.

5.484 Winsor, J. "The Boston Public Library." *Scribner's Monthly* 3 (1871): 150–56.

5.485 "The Prince World [Boston Public Library]." *Literary World [Boston]* 5 (1875): 169.

5.486 Newton, Mass. Free Library. *Historical Statement of [the] Origin and Growth, Adopted by the Board of Managers, Nov. 24, 1875.* Boston: Rockwell and Churchill Press, 1876.

5.487 Winsor, J. "Libraries in Boston." In *Memorial History of Boston, Including Suffolk County, Massachusetts, 1630–1880,* vol. 4. Boston: James Osgood and Co., 1880. Pp. 279–94.

5.488 *Catalogue of the Norwood Public Library, Together with a Brief History of the Library . . . .* Boston: T.O. Metcalf, 1886.

5.489 Green, S. S. "Public Libraries." In *History of Worcester County, Massachusetts,* edited by D. H. Hurd. Philadelphia: J.W. Lewis & Co., 1889. Pp. 1491–1509.

5.490 Raymond, J. M. *Address of the Hon. John M. Raymond, at the Opening of the Salem Public Library, June 26, 1889, with . . . a Brief Historical Sketch of the Movement for the Establishment of Such Library in Salem and a Notice of the Libraries Now in Existence in the City.* Salem, Mass.: Salem Press, 1889.

5.491 Tillinghast, C. B. *The Free Public Libraries of Massachusetts.* Boston: N.p., 1891.

5.492 Carpenter, E. J. "The Story of the Boston Public Library." *NEM* 12 (1895): 737–56.

5.493 Wilson, F. A. *The Nahant Public Library: Containing a Brief Sketch of the Public Library Movement, a History of the Nahant Public Library and a Description of the New Library Building.* Linn [sic], Mass.: Macfarlane Press, 1895.

5.494 Nourse, H. S., comp. "The Free Public Libraries of Massachusetts." In *Ninth Report of the Free Public Library Commission of Massachusetts, 1899.* Boston: N.p., 1899.

5.495 Sargent, M. E. F. "The Evolution of the Medford Public Library." *Medford Historical Register* 2 (1899): 76–91.

5.496 Whitney, J. L. "Incidents in the History of the Boston Public Library." *LJ* 27 (1902): 16–24.

5.497 Shumway, M. T. *The Groton Public Library: A Paper Read Before the Groton Historical Society in 1898, Rev. 1905.* Boston: Sparrell Print, 1905.

5.498 Tarbell, M. A. *A Village Library.* Boston: N.p., 1905.

5.499 Oxford Mass. Free Public Library. *Souvenir of the Charles Learned Memorial and the Free Public Library, Oxford, Massachusetts, 1906.* Boston: Geo. H. Ellis, 1906.

5.500 Rice, C. B., ed. *The Field Memorial Library, Comway, Mass.* Boston: Arakelyan Press, 1907.

5.501 Rolfe, W. J., and Ayer, C. W., comps. *1858–1908: History of the Cambridge Public Library, with the Addresses at the Celebration of Its Fiftieth Anniversary, List of Officers, etc.* Cambridge, Mass.: Public Library, 1908.

5.502 Benton, J. H. *The Working of the Boston Public Library: An Address Before the Beacon Society of Boston, January 2, 1909.* Boston: Rockwell and Churchill Press, 1909.

5.503 Jenks, G. A. "The Newton Library." *Bucks County Historical Society Papers* 3 (1909): 316–31.

5.504 Wright, H. P. *Fobes Memorial Library, Oakham Mass . . . .* Oakham, Mass.: 1909.

5.505 Bacon, J. W. "Natick Public Libraries and Their Origins." *Historical, Natural History and Library Society of South Natick Historical Collections* 2 (1910): 41–45.

5.506 Worcester, Mass. Free Public Library. *The Fiftieth Anniversary of the Founding of the Worcester Free Public Library, to Dec. 23, 1909.* Worcester, Mass.: Press of F.S. Blanchard and Co., 1910.

5.507 *History of the Peabody Institute, Danvers, Mass. 1852–1911.* Boston: Thomas Todd, 1911.

5.508 Wadlin, H. G. *The Public Library of the City of Boston: A History.* Boston: The Trustees, 1911.

5.509 Green, C. R. "The Jones Library in Amherst." *Amherst Graduates Quarterly* 18 (February 1929): 87–93.

5.510 Gloucester Lyceum and Sawyer Free Library. *Gloucester Lyceum and Sawyer Free Library, Inc., 1830–1930: The Record of a Century.* Gloucester, Mass.: N.p., 1930.

5.511 Pearl, E. E. "History of the [West Boxford Public] Library from January 14, 1881." *Ingalls Memorial Public Library Bulletin* (September 1931): [4–5].

5.512 Kidder, N. T. *The First Sixty Years of the Milton Public Library, 1870–1931.* Milton, Mass.: Privately printed [Plimpton Press, Norwood, Mass.], 1932.

5.513 *History of the Orange Public Library Covering the Period from Its Inception in 1847 to 1933.* Orange, Mass.: Enterprise and Journal, 1933.

5.514 Turner, B. M. "Our Library and How it Grew [Littlefield Library]." *V.I.A. Annual* 40 (1935): 1, 4–5.

5.515 Harrison, J. L. *Forbes Library: The Half Century, 1894–1944.* Northampton, Mass.: Printed for the Board of Trustees, 1945.

5.516 Nash, R. "The Society of Printers and the [Boston] Public Library." *MoreB* 20 (1945): 221–26.

5.517 Haraszti, Z. "A Hundred Years Ago." *MoreB* 23 (1948): 83–89.

5.518 Weis, F. L. *Historical Sketch of the Lancaster Town Library, 1790–1862–1950.* Lancaster, Mass.: N.p., 1950.

5.519 Gifford, G. E. *Biography of Charles L. Flint [and] History of Flint Public Library.* N.p.: 1952?

5.520 Siebens, C. R. *A Historical Sketch of the Libraries of Cape Cod and Martha's Vineyard and Nantucket.* Hyannis, Mass.: Patriot Press, 1952.

5.521 *Building a Great Future upon a Glorious Past.* Boston: Boston Public Library Centennial Commission, 1953.

5.522 McCord, D. T. W. *As Built with Second Thoughts, Reforming What Was Old: Reflections on the Centennial Anniversary of the Boston Public Library.* Boston: Centennial Commission of Boston Public Library, 1953.

5.523 Gillis, F. J. "Boston Public Library: A Centennial of Service, 1854–1954." *School and Society* 79 (1954): 49–53.

5.524 Haraszti, Z. "Twenty-five Years of the Treasure Room (of the Boston Public Library, 1930–55)." *Boston Public Library Quarterly* 7 (1955): 115–27.

5.525 MacDonald, H., and MacDonald, M. *A History of the Lenox Library, Written for Its 100th Anniversary.* Lenox, Mass.: N.p., 1956.

5.526 Whitehill, W. M. *Boston Public Library: A Centennial History, 1854–1954.* Cambridge: Harvard University Press, 1956.

5.527 Woodwell, R. H. *Amesbury Public Library, 1856–1956.* Amesbury, Mass.: N.p., 1956.

5.528 Hodges, E. J. *A History of the Leominster Public Library. From the Report of the Librarian for 1955: Revised and Amended.* Leominster, Mass.: The Library, 1957.

5.529 Ripley, E. F. *Weston Town Library History, 1857–1957.* Weston, Mass.: N.p., 1957.

5.530 Buchanan, J. B. "Early Directions of the Boston Public Library and the Genesis of an American Public Library Psychology." Master's thesis, Southern Connecticut State College, 1962.

5.531 Hill, L. D. *The Crane Library.* Quincy, Mass.: Published by the Trustees of the Thomas Crane Public Library, 1962.

5.532 Clark, R. B. "History of the Talbot County Free Library, Easton, Massachusetts, 1925–1962." Master's thesis, Catholic University of America, 1963.

5.533 Galick, V. G. "History, Structure and Government of Public Libraries in Massachusetts." *Bay State Librarian* 54 (July 1964): 7.

5.534 McGowan, O. T. P. "A Centennial History of the Fall River Public Library, 1861–1961." Master's thesis, Catholic University of America, 1964.

5.535 Baron, M. S. "Evolution of the Springfield, Massachusetts, Public Library, 1796–1912." Master's thesis, Catholic University of America, 1966.

5.536 Whitehill, W. M. *Boston in the Age of John Fitzgerald Kennedy.* Norman: University of Oklahoma Press, 1966.

5.537 Bush-Brown, A. *Books, Bass, Barnstable: An Address Delivered at the Centennial Celebration of the Sturgis Library, Barnstable, Massachusetts, August 26, 1967.* Barnstable, Mass.: Great Marshes Press, 1967.

5.538 Conyngham, M. H. "Forbes Library, Northampton, Massachusetts, 1881–1903." Master's thesis, University of Maryland, 1967.

5.539 Cary Memorial Library, Lexington, Mass. *A Century of Service: 1868–1968.* [Lexington, Mass.: Cary Memorial Library, 1968].

5.540 Rand, F. P. *The Jones Library in Amherst, 1919–1969.* Amherst, Mass.: Jones Library, 1969.

5.541 "The Rowe Town Library." *Rowe Historical Society Bulletin* 6 (1969): 3–10.

5.542 Salfas, S. G. "History of the Springfield City Library, 1912–1948." Master's thesis, Southern Connecticut State College, 1969.

5.543 Steves, N. E. *A History of the Sandwich Public Library.* [Bourne, Mass.]: Horace C. Pearsons, 1969.

5.544 Colodny, S. "A Centennial History of an Association Library, Lenox, Massachusetts, 1856–1956." Research Paper, Long Island University, 1970.

5.545 Lord, M. E. "Boston Public Library." *ELIS* 3 (1970): 100–104.

5.546 Whitehill, W. M. "The Making of an Architectural Masterpiece—The Boston Public Library." *American Art Journal* 2 (1970): 13–35.

5.547 *One Hundred Years A-Growing, 1871–1971 [Milton Public Library].* Milton, Mass.: N.p., 1972.

5.548 Wikander, L. E. *Disposed to Learn: The First Seventy-five Years of the Forbes Library.* Northampton, Mass.: Trustees of the Forbes Library, 1972.

5.549 Fund, C. K. "Boston Public Library Building of 1895." Master's thesis, University of Chicago, 1973.

5.550 Harris, M. H., and Spiegler, G. "Everett, Ticknor and the Common Man: The Fear of Societal Instability as the Motivation for the Founding of the Boston Public Library." *Libri* 24 (1974): 249–75.

5.551 Talcott, M. T. *Athol Public Library, 1882–1972: 90 Years of Service.* [Athol, Mass.: Transcript Press, 1974].

5.552 Woodward, D. M., Hughes, D. E., and Canavan, B. *Stoughton Public Library: 100 Years, 1874–1974.* [Stoughton, Mass.: Stoughton Public Library, 1974].

5.553 Tietjen, L. M. "A History of the Libraries in Old Saybrook." Master's thesis, Southern Connecticut State College, 1975.

5.554 Boston Public Library. *Evolution of a Catalogue: From Film to Fiche; Report on the Research Library Catalog Project.* Boston: Boston Public Library, 1981.

Michigan

5.555 Bixby, Mrs. A. F. *Historical Sketches of the Ladies' Library Associations of the State of Michigan,* compiled and arranged by Mrs. A. F. Bixby and Mrs. A. Howell. Adrian, Mich.: Times and Expositor Steam Print, 1876.

5.556 Michigan. Board of Library Commissioners. *Legislative History of Township Libraries in the State of Michigan from 1835 to 1901,* compiled by L. M. Miller and printed by the order of the Board of Library Commissioners. Lansing, Mich.: R. Smith Printing Co., 1902.

5.557 Walton, G. M. *Libraries in Michigan: An Historical Sketch in the Year of the Golden Jubilee of the American Library Association, 1876–1926.* Lansing: Michigan State Library, 1926.

5.558 "When Culture Came to Kalamazoo." *Inside Michigan* 2 (1952): 24–27.

5.559 Hamner, P. N. "The Ladies' Library Association of Michigan: A Curious Byway in Library History." Master's thesis, Western Reserve University, 1954.

5.560 Hoesch, M. J. "A History of the Grosse Pointe Public Library." Master's thesis, Western Reserve University, 1955.

5.561 Helms, C. E. "The Development of Library Services in Allegan County, Michigan." In *Contributions to Mid-West Library History,* edited by T. Eaton. Champaign, Ill.: Illini Union Bookstore, 1964. Pp. 106–29.

5.562 Lonie, C. A. "The Ladies' Library Association of Niles Michigan, as Reported in a Contemporary Newspaper." In *Contributions to Mid-West Library History,* edited by T. Eaton. Champaign, Ill.: Illini Union Bookstore, 1964. Pp. 154–63.

5.563 Woodford, F. B. *Parnassus on Main Street: A History of the Detroit Public Library.* Detroit: Wayne State University Press, 1965.

5.564 Burich, N. J. "Years of Consolidation and Expansion: A History of the Lansing Public Library from 1930 to 1967." Master's thesis, Kent State University, 1968.

5.565 Ulveling, R. A. "Detroit Public Library." *ELIS* 7 (1972): 121–28.

5.566 Thurner, A. W. "How a Library Came to Copper Country [Calumet, Mich.]." *WLB* 50 (1976): 608–12.

Minnesota

5.567 Longhway, M. W. *The History of the Library in Wabasha, Minnesota.* [Minneapolis: Division of Library Instruction of the University of Minnesota], 1938.

5.568 *Minneapolis Public Library: Fifty Years of Service, 1889–1939.* Minneapolis: The Library, 1939.

5.569 Baldwin, C. F. "The Public Library Movement in Minnesota, 1900–1936." *MinnL* 14 (1945): 384–98.

5.570 Carlstadt, E. "Public Library Movement in Minnesota, 1849–1900." *MinnL* 14 (1945): 351–63.

5.571 Gibson, F. E. "The Effects of the Activities of the Unions in the Minneapolis Public Library on Library Functions and Administrative Processes, and Upon Union Members." Master's thesis, University of Minnesota, 1952.

5.572 Lincoln, M. E. "Cultural Significance of the Minneapolis Public Library in Its Origins and Development: A Study in the Relations of the Public Library and American Society." Doctoral dissertation, University of Minnesota, 1958.

5.573 Nylander, E. P. "A History of the Duluth Public Library System." Master's thesis, University of Minnesota, 1962.

5.574 Gaines, E. J. "Minneapolis Public Library." *ELIS* 18 (1976): 141–43.

5.575 Wagner, E. "The Saint Paul Public Library: 1857–1978." *ELIS* 26 (1979): 279–86.

5.576 White, J. F. "The Minneapolis Public Library and the W.P.A. Experience: Collaboration for Community Need." In *Studies in Creative Partnership: Federal Aid to Public Libraries during the New Deal*, edited by D. F. Ring. Metuchen, N.J.: Scarecrow Press, 1980. Pp. 105–23.

5.577 Benidt, B. W. *The Library Book: Centennial History of the Minneapolis Public Library.* Minneapolis: Minneapolis Public Library and Information Center, 1984.

5.578 Ostendorf, P. J. "The History of the Public Library Movement in Minnesota from 1849 to 1916." Doctoral dissertation, University of Minnesota, 1984.

Mississippi

5.579 Snedeker, C. D. "Gulf-Coast Library." *HB* 25 (1949): 4–5.

5.580 Dickey, P. W. "A History of Public Library Service for Negroes in Jackson, Mississippi, 1950–1957." Master's thesis, Atlanta University, 1960.

5.581 Morse, D. B. "The Historical Development and Foreclosure of a Public Library." Master's thesis, University of Mississippi, 1960.

5.582 Green, E. B. "The History and Growth of Lee County Library." Master's thesis, University of Mississippi, 1961.

5.583 Sparks, E. C. "People with Books: The Services of Northeast Regional Library." Master's thesis, University of Mississippi, 1962.

5.584 Gunn, M. H. "History of Jackson Municipal Library, Jackson, Mississippi." Master's thesis, Texas Woman's University, 1965.

5.585 Peebles, M., and Howell, J. B., eds. *A History of Mississippi Libraries.* N.p.: Mississippi Library Association, 1975.

Missouri

5.586 Greenwood, J. M. *A History of the Kansas City Public Library from 1873 to 1893.* Kansas City, Mo.: Rigby-Ramsey, 1893.

5.587 Compton, C. H. *Fifty Years of Progress of the St. Louis Public Library, 1876–1926.* St. Louis: St. Louis Public Library, 1926.

5.588 Wright, P. B. *Historical Sketch of the Kansas City Public Library, 1911–1936, with Extracts from Annual Reports of Librarian, 1911–1920.* Kansas City, Mo.: N.p., 1937.

5.589 Compton, C. H. "An Unfinished Chapter in Missouri Library Legislation." *LQ* 12 (1942): 412–21.

5.590 Brinton, E. H. "History of Public Libraries in Missouri to 1920." *Missouri Library Association Quarterly* 11 (1950): 5–7.

5.591 Compton, C. H. *Twenty-five Crucial Years of the St. Louis Public Library, 1927–1952.* St. Louis: The Public Library, 1953.

5.592 Swartz, R. G. "The Ozark Regional Library: Its Background and Development, 1947–1965." Master's thesis, University of Chicago, 1968.

5.593 Browning, L. A. "History of the Public Library Movement in Columbia, Missouri." Research Paper, University of Missouri, 1969.

5.594 Jennings, K. L. "Kansas City Public Library, 1873 to 1898: Its Historical Growth as Related to the Development of the Public School System of Kansas City." Research Paper, University of Missouri, 1971.

5.595 Pittman, C. K. "History of the Two Attempts to Establish a Tax-Supported Public Library in Adair County, 1948 and 1967." Research Paper, University of Missouri, 1971.

5.596 Hoffman, W. H., ed. *Kansas City, Missouri Public Library, 1873–1973: An Illustrated History.* Kansas City, Mo.: Kansas City Public Library, 1973.

5.597 Jones, A. H. "State Aid to Public Libraries in Missouri, 1945–1955." Research Paper, University of Missouri, 1973.

5.598 O'Driscoll, P. D. "History of the Mid-City Branch of the St. Louis (City) Public Library." Research Paper, University of Missouri, 1973.

5.599 Showalter, G. W. "History of Public Libraries in Washington County, Missouri."

Research Paper, University of Missouri, 1973.

5.600 Boeckman, L. "History of the Scotland County Library in Memphis, Missouri." Research Paper, University of Missouri, 1974.

5.601 Sommer, J. M. "History of the Genealogical Collection of the St. Louis Public Library." Research Paper, University of Missouri, 1974.

5.602 Strunk, A. L. "History of the Lucy Wortham James Memorial Library, 1930–1953." Research Paper, University of Missouri, 1974.

5.603 Doering, N. "History of the Missouri Library Commission, 1907–1946." Research Paper, University of Missouri-Columbia, 1975.

5.604 Price, P. P. "Saint Louis Public Library." *ELIS* 26 (1979): 268–79.

5.605 Page, H. C. *Early Library Development in Missouri, 1938–1943: An Outline of the Contributions Made by a Federal Agency to Public Library Service, Consisting of a Collection of Reports, Pictures, and My Recollections of More than Forty Years.* Kansas City, Mo.: Hazel C. Page, 1981.

5.606 Casey, P. A. "Memories of the Cabanne Branch Library, 1916–1929." *Show-Me Libraries* 33 (1982): 37–39.

Montana

5.607 Longworth, R. O. "Glacier County Library [Cut Bank, Mont.]: An Example of Cooperation." *WLB* 29 (1954): 73–74.

Nebraska

5.608 Lenfest, G. E. "The Development and Present Status of the Library Movement in Nebraska." Master's thesis, University of Illinois, 1931.

5.609 Kalisch, P. A. "The Early History of the Omaha Public Library." Master's thesis, University of Omaha, 1964.

New Hampshire

5.610 Fitz, L. "The Library Movement in New Hampshire." *GranM* 15 (November 1893): 349–55.

5.611 Brennan, J. F. "Peterborough Town Library: The Pioneer Public Library." *GranM* 28 (1900): 281–91.

5.612 "Histories of Public Libraries." *New Hampshire State Library. Report* 8 (1906): 363–497.

5.613 *The Amherst Town Library, Amherst, New Hampshire: Its Birth and Rebirth.* Amherst, N.H.: The Trustees, 1911.

5.614 *Old Dover and Its Library.* Dover, N.H.: 1914.

5.615 Lewis, W. P. "New Hampshire Libraries." *GranM* 59 (March 1927): 88–90.

5.616 Mason, E. R. "North Conway Public Library." *GranM* 59 (1927): 51–53.

5.617 Irwin, F. T. "The Peterborough Library." *GranM* 60 (May 1928): 213–16.

5.618 Manchester, New Hampshire. City Library. *Seventy-Five Years of the City Library.* Manchester, N.H.: N.p., 1929.

5.619 Wilber, C. C. "Library Beginnings in Keene." *Old Timer* 8 (22 November 1939): 4–5.

5.620 Ford, C. E. "Fifty Years A-Growing: The Howe Library at Hanover." *New Hampshire Troubadour* 20 (1950): 10–13.

5.621 Richardson, L. B. *The Howe Library of Hanover, New Hampshire, Fiftieth Anniversary, April 7, 1950.* Hanover: The Library, 1950.

5.622 McKay, M. P., and Allen, E. W. "Extension Service in New Hampshire." *North County Libraries* 1 (1958): 5–9.

5.623 Fox, K. *Significant Dates in the History of the Keene Public Library.* Keene, N.H.: N.p., 1967.

5.624 Yates, E. "Bradford's Brown Memorial Library." *New Hampshire Echoes* 1 (1970): 29–31.

5.625 Lord, C. M. *Diary of a Village Library.* Somersworth, N.H.: New Hampshire Publishing Co., 1971.

5.626 Bissell, P. "Jackson Public Library." *Granite State Libraries* 14 (1978): 9–10.

5.627 Warntz, C. "Some Promises Kept: The Peterborough Town Library." *WLB* 56 (1982): 342–46.

New Jersey

5.628 Curtis, C. M. "The Development of the Public Library in New Jersey." Master's thesis, Columbia University, 1935.

5.629 [Winser, B.] *Fifty Years [Newark Public Library]: 1889–1939.* [Newark, N.J.: Public Library of Newark, 1939].

5.630 Gallant, E. F. "The History of the Free Library of Teaneck, New Jersey." Master's thesis, Pratt Institute, 1954.

5.631 Newark Public Library. *A Half-Century of Power for Business, 1904–1954.* Newark, N.J.: Newark Public Library, Business Library, 1954.

5.632 Lum, L. *As I Remember: A Story of Chatham's Libraries.* Chatham, N.J.: Chatham Free Public Library, 1955.

5.633 Hughes, H. L., comp. *Public Libraries in New Jersey, 1750–1850.* N.p.: New Jersey Library Association, 1956.

5.634 Clark, E. S. *The Orange Public Library: A History of the First Seventy-Five Years, 1883–1958.* [Orange, N.J.: Orange Free Library, 1958].

5.635 Newark Public Library. *This Is to Be a People's Library: Newark Public Library, 1888–1963.* Newark, N.J.: The Library, 1963.

5.636 O'Brien, M. B. "The History of the Development of a Library Plan for Clark, New Jersey." Master's thesis, Catholic University of America, 1965.

5.637 Doyle, M. A. "A History of the Trenton Free Public Library." Master's thesis, Catholic University of America, 1968.

5.638 Andrews, F. E. *The Tenafly Public Library: A History, 1891–1970.* Tenafly, N.J.: The Public Library, 1970.

5.639 Curley, A. "Montclair [N.J.] Free Public Library." *ELIS* 18 (1976): 268–71.

5.640 Sabine, J. E. "Newark Public Library." *ELIS* 19 (1976): 446–50.

New York

5.641 Cutter, C. A. "Buffalo Public Library in 1893: An Excursion in the Land of Dreams." *LJ* 8 (1883): 211–17.

5.642 New York Public Library. Board of Trustees. "Progress of the New York Public Library, 1896–1906." *BNYPL* 10 (1906): 343–57.

5.643 Utica, New York. Public Library. *Utica Public Library, 1893–1908.* Utica, N.Y.: The Library, 1909.

5.644 Billings, J. S. "New York's Public Library." *LJ* 36 (1911): 233–43.

5.645 Garnett, R. "New York and Its Three Libraries." *North American Review* 193 (1911): 850–60.

5.646 New York Public Library. "Proceedings at the New Building of the New York Public Library, Astor, Lenox and Tilden Foundation, Tuesday, May 23, 1911." *BNYPL* 15 (1911): 327–48.

5.647 New York Public Library. "Dedication of the New York Public Library Building, May 23, 1911." *Report of the American Scenic and Historical Preservation Society* 17 (1912): 317–42.

5.648 Lydenberg, H. M. *History of the New York Public Library: Astor, Lenox and Tilden Foundation.* New York: New York Public Library, 1923.

5.649 Cole, G. W. "Early Library Development in New York State (1809–1900)." *BNYPL* 30 (1926): 849–57, 917–25.

5.650 *Seventeen Years of Service of the Rochester Public Library, 1912–1928.* Rochester, N.Y.: Rochester Public Library, 1929.

5.651 Howard, J. G. "Portfolio of Plans for the New York Public Library: Placed Second in a Competition 1897." *Architecture & English* 113 (1933): 33–37.

5.652 Goldberg, A. *The Buffalo Public Library: Commemorating Its First Century of Service to the Citizens of Buffalo, 1836–1936.* Buffalo, N.Y.: The Library, 1937.

5.653 McKelvey, B., ed. *The History of Rochester Libraries.* New York: Rochester Historical Society, 1937.

5.654 Haygood, W. C. *Who Uses the Public Library: A Survey of the Patrons of the Circulation and Reference Departments of the New York Public Library.* Chicago: University of Chicago Press, 1938.

5.655 Mamaroneck, N. Y. Free Library. *The Story of the Mamaroneck Free Library, 1922–1947.* Mamaroneck, N.Y.: N.p., 1947.

5.656 New York Public Library. *After One Hundred Years: An Account of the Partnership Which Has Built and Sustained the New York Public Library, 1848–1948.* [New York: The Library, 1948].

5.657 Armstrong, C. M., McDiarmid, E. W., Schenk, G. K., Van Dusen, N. C., and Vedder, A. B. *Development of Library Services in New York State,* Bulletin no. 1376. Albany: State University of New York, Division of Research, 1949.

5.658 Overton, J. M. "The Children's Library of Westbury (Long Island): Its First Twenty-five Years [1924–49]." *HB* 25 (1949): 451–66.

5.659 Lydenberg, H. M. "New York Libraries (1848–1950): The Long View." *SL* 41 (1950): 169–71, 242–45.

5.660 Breen, M. H. "The Traveling Library Service of the New York Public Library in Richmond and the Bronx: A Descriptive History." Master's thesis, Pratt Institute, 1951.

5.661 Campbell, V. M. "A History of the Lackawanna Public Library." Master's thesis, Canisius College, 1953.

5.662 Goldstein, D. "The Library for the Blind of the New York Public Library." Master's thesis, Drexel Institute of Technology, 1953.

5.663 Davis, J. M. "Chemung County Library: Past, Present, and Future." Master's thesis, Pratt Institute, 1954.

5.664 Wong, R. "A History of the Chatham Square Branch of the New York Public Library." Master's thesis, Pratt Institute, 1955.

5.665 Fess, M. R. *The Grosvenor Library and Its Times.* Buffalo, N.Y.: Grosvenor Reference Division of the Buffalo and Erie County Public Library, 1956.

5.666 Fannin, G. M. "A Resume of the History, Growth and Development of the Story Hour in the New York Public Library." Master's thesis, Atlanta University, 1958.

5.667 McVee, M. F. "Public Library Contributions to Formal Adult Education Programs in Small Cities of New York State." Master's thesis, State University of New York at Albany, 1958.

5.668 Alexander, G. L. "Some Notes toward a History of the New York Public Library Map Room for the Years 1923–1941." *SLAGMDB* 35 (1959): 4–7.

5.669 Milliken, M. C. "A History of the Rochester Public Library from 1912 to 1936." Master's thesis, Catholic University of America, 1959.

5.670 Rollins, O. H. "The Hepburn Libraries of the St. Lawrence Valley." Master's thesis, Western Reserve University, 1960, University of Kentucky Press Microcard Series B, no. 44.

5.671 Eisner, J. "Development of Public Libraries and Library Legislation in New York State." *New York Library Association Newsletter* 9 (1961): 13–17.

5.672 McKelvey, B. "The Semi-Centennial of the Rochester Public Library." *Rochester History* 23 (1961): 1–24.

5.673 Bullock, J. Y. "A Resume of the History, Growth, and Development of Library Service to Hospital Patients by the Queens Borough (New York) Public Library." Master's thesis, Atlanta University, 1962.

5.674 Gore, D. J. "The Schomberg Collection and Its Catalog: A Historical Sketch." Master's thesis, University of North Carolina, 1963.

5.675 Hutson, J. B. "The Schomburg Collection." *Freedomways* 3 (1963): 430–35.

5.676 New York Public Library. *Municipal Reference Library: 50th Anniversary, 1913–1963.* New York: New York Public Library, 1963.

5.677 Shirley, N. "A Survey of Library Development in Hudson, N.Y." Master's thesis, State University of New York at Albany, 1963.

5.678 Buxton, K. "The Emma S. Clark Memorial Library in Setauket, Long Island, New York: A History." Research Paper, Long Island University, 1965.

5.679 Flick, H. M. "Milestones in Library Development in New York State." *BKM* 24 (1965): 201–03.

5.680 Franklin, W. D. "A Historical Study of Library Development in New York State Compared with That in Catskill, N.Y." Master's thesis, State University of New York at Albany, 1965.

5.681 Halpin, J. R. "A History of the Farmingdale Public Library, Including Background on the Town of Farmingdale." Research Paper, Long island University, 1965.

5.682 O'Brian, A. "A History of the Mineola (New York) Memorial Library." Research Paper, Long Island University, 1965.

5.683 Seryneck, W. P. "The First Fifty Years: A History of the Amityville Free Library,

1907–1957." Research Paper, Long Island University, 1965.

5.684 Bennett, H. E. "The Jamaica Library Service: Its Foundations and Development." Master's thesis, Southern Connecticut State College, 1966.

5.685 Chapin, V. J. "A Historical Study of the Origins of the Library in Huntington, Long Island, New York, 1759–1929." Research Paper, Long Island University, 1966.

5.686 Chichester, M. "Library Service for a Growing Population: A History of the Massapequa Public Library, 1953–1965." Research Paper, Long Island University, 1966.

5.687 Dziewiatkowski, N. "History of the Jesse Merrit Memorial Library at Salisbury Park, L.I." Research Paper, Long Island University, 1966.

5.688 Gold, E. "A History of the West Islip (New York) Public Library." Research Paper, Long Island University, 1966.

5.689 Goldberg, J. "The History of the Northport-East Northport Public Libraries." Research Paper, Long Island University, 1966.

5.690 Haase, L. "History of the Manhasset (New York) Public Library, 1945–1965." Research Paper, Long Island University, 1966.

5.691 Kavasch, D. "History of the Cold Spring Harbor (New York) Library." Research Paper, Long Island University, 1966.

5.692 Maxian, M. B. "A History of the Morton Penny-packer Library, Long Island, Collection." Research Paper, Long Island University, 1966.

5.693 Seaton, E. "Origins of the Shelter Rock (New York) Public Library." Research Paper, Long Island University, 1966.

5.694 Wensley, D. D. "The Children's Library, Robert Bacon Memorial, Westbury, Long Island, 1924–1965; Five Owls and the Winds of Change." Research Paper, Long Island University, 1966.

5.695 Berkowitz, S. "Historical Study of the Elmont (New York) Public Library, 1939–1965." Research Paper, Long Island University, 1967.

5.696 Bleier, M. "A History of the Hewlett-Woodmere (New York) Public Library." Research Paper, Long Island University, 1967.

5.697 Coogan, I. M. "The Lynbrook (New York) Public Library, 1913–1964: An Historical Study." Research Paper, Long Island University, 1967.

5.698 Ellison, V. N. "The History of the Nassau County Law Library." Research Paper, Long Island University, 1967.

5.699 Gillie, M. H. "The History of the Port Jefferson, Long Island, New York, Library, 1908–1966." Research Paper, Long Island University, 1967.

5.700 Gould, L. P. "Historical Study of the East Meadow (New York) Public Library, 1954–1965." Research Paper, Long Island University, 1967.

5.701 Jespersen, H. "A History of the Garden City (New York) Public Library." Research Paper, Long Island University, 1967.

5.702 Katz, L. F. "A History of the Great Neck (New York) Public Library." Research Paper, Long Island University, 1967.

5.703 Kirsch, S. "A History of the Rockville Centre Public Library, Long Island, New York." Research Paper, Long Island University, 1967.

5.704 Page, J. S. "A History of the Oceanside (New York) Free Library." Research Paper, Long Island University, 1967.

5.705 Robertson, M. P. "History of the Westbury Memorial Public Library, Westbury, New York." Research Paper, Long Island University, 1967.

5.706 Seabury, J. B. "A History of the Hampton Library in Bridge Hampton, N.Y." Research Paper, Long Island University, 1967.

5.707 Siegel, H. "A History of the Plainview-Old Bethpage Public Library from Its Beginning to 1965." Research Paper, Long Island University, 1967.

5.708 Sisson, L. K. "A History of the Riverhead (New York) Free Library, Including a Brief History of the Town of Riverhead." Research Paper, Long Island University, 1967.

5.709 Sokol, E. "Conflicting Community Interests: The Establishment of the South Huntington (New York) Public Library." Research Paper, Long Island University, 1967.

5.710 Timlin, D. S. "A History of the Bay Shore Public Library." Research Paper, Long Island University, 1967.

5.711 Bailey, M. "An Early History of the Stenson Memorial Library, Sea Cliff, New York." Research Paper, Long Island University, 1968.

5.712 Barnes, H. C. "The Valley Stream Public Library, Valley Stream, Long Island, New York: A History." Research Paper, Long Island University, 1968.

5.713 Bloomgarden, C. B. "History of the Port Washington (New York) Public Library, 1892–1967." Research Paper, Long Island University, 1968.

5.714 Brown, E. T. "An Historical Study of the East Rockaway (New York) Free Library." Research Paper, Long Island University, 1968.

5.715 Erichsen, R. H. "History of the Smithtown Library, Smithtown, Long Island, New York, from 1907 to 1967." Research Paper, Long Island University, 1968.

5.716 Groves, M. N. "The History of the Freport Memorial Library, 1884–1938." Research Paper, Long Island University, 1968.

5.717 Hyman, T. A. "A History of the Walter Hampden Memorial Library." Research Paper, Long Island University, 1968.

5.718 Jacobson, S. "A Study of the Growth and Development of the Hicksville Public Library, Hicksville, New York." Research Paper, Long Island University, 1968.

5.719 Lapidus, B. "A Historical Study of the North Bellmore (New York) Public Library." Research Paper, Long Island University, 1968.

5.720 Licandro, M. L. "History of the Bryant Library, Roslyn, N.Y. (1878–1953)." Research Paper, Long Island University, 1968.

5.721 Lukoski, L. L. "History of the Sayville (New York) Library from 1914–1967." Research Paper, Long Island University, 1968.

5.722 Lusak, R. "A History of the Islip Public Library from 1923 to 1965." Research Paper, Long Island University, 1968.

5.723 Malino, E. "A History of the Bethpage (New York) Public Library from 1927–1966." Research Paper, Long Island University, 1968.

5.724 Provenzano, L. "Study of the Growth and Development of the Library in Huntington, Long Island (New York) 1929–1967." Research Paper, Long Island University, 1968.

5.725 Rigali, D. L. "History of the Seaford Public Library, Seaford, New York." Research Paper, Long Island University, 1968.

5.726 Silver, C. K. "An Historical Study of the Peninsula Public Library in Lawrence, New York, 1950–1967." Research Paper, Long Island University, 1968.

5.727 Weber, H. "A History of the Merrick (New York) Library, 1891–1965." Research Paper, Long Island University, 1968.

5.728 Anhalt, L. "The History, Development, and Organization of the Record Collection of the Great Neck (New York) Library." Research Paper, Long Island University, 1969.

5.729 Appleget, N. M. "The Grand Old Lady of Grand Street: A History of the White Plains (New York) Public Library, 1812 to 1969." Research Paper, Long Island University, 1969.

5.730 Brown, G. "History of the Long Beach (New York) Public Library." Research Paper, Long Island University, 1969.

5.731 Connally, E. "A History of the Mount Vernon (New York) Public Library from 1948 through 1968." Research Paper, Long Island University, 1969.

5.732 Corsaro, J. "History of the Albany Library with an Examination of Reading Vogues in Albany, 1824–1829." Research Paper, State University of New York, Albany, 1969.

5.733 Freund, E. "A History of the Malverne (New York) Public Library, 1929–1968." Research Paper, Long Island University, 1969.

5.734 Gordon, H. S. "A History of the Crestwood Branch of the Yonkers (New York) Public Library." Research Paper, Long Island University, 1969.

5.735 Hisz, E. "History of the Theatre Collection, New York Public Library at Lincoln Center." Master's thesis, Long Island University, 1969.

5.736 Keenan, B. M. "A History of the Newspaper Division of the New York Public Library, 1911–1968." Research Paper, Long Island University, 1969.

5.737 Nichols, B. B. "Westchester Library System: The History and Evaluation of a Program of Service." Master's thesis, Southern Connecticut State College, 1969.

5.738 Normandeau, C. "History of the Brentwood (New York) Public Library." Research Paper, Long Island University, 1969.

5.739 Peer, S. *The First Hundred Years: A History of the Cornell Public Library, Ithaca, New York, and the Cornell Library Association, 1864–1964.* Ithaca, N.Y.: The Library, 1969.

5.740 Quain, M. "A History and Descriptive Study of the Music Division of the Library and Museum of the Performing Arts, The New York Public Library at Lincoln Center, New York, N.Y." Research Paper, Long Island University, 1969.

5.741 Scanlon, R. "A History of the Delancey Floyd-Jones Free Library, Massapequa, New York, from Its Origin, 1896, to the Establishment of the Massapequa Public Library, 1953." Research Paper, Long Island University, 1969.

5.742 Young, B. A. "A Historical Study of the Countee Cullen Regional Branch Library of the New York Public Library System: Its Inception, Trends, Developments." Master's thesis, Southern Connecticut State College, 1969.

5.743 Carbino, N. "History of the Plainedge Public Library, Massapequa, New York." Research Paper, Long Island University, 1970.

5.744 Clark, C. "An Historical Study of the Various Controversies in Which the Farmingdale Public Library Has Been Engaged since 1963." Research Paper, Long Island University, 1970.

5.745 Holzer, S. "A History of the Sarah Hull Hallock Free Library, Milton, New York." Research Paper, Long Island University, 1970.

5.746 Karro, T. "Harborfields, New York: A Community without a Public Library." Research Paper, Long Island University, 1970.

5.747 Lo, H. "History of the Flushing Branch of The Queens Burough Public Library." Research Paper, Long Island University, 1970.

5.748 Lutrin, D. B. "History of the Establishment of the North Merrick (New York) Public Library, 1951–1969." Research Paper, Long Island University, 1970.

5.749 Sayle, S. "A History of the Mamaroneck (New York) Free Library, Inc. from 1951 through 1969." Research Paper, Long Island University, 1970.

5.750 True, P. "A History of the New City Free Library, New York City, New York, from 1936 to 1968." Research Paper, Long Island University, 1970.

5.751 Williamson, L. "History of the Syosset (New York) Public Library." Research Paper, Long Island University, 1970.

5.752 Berde, M. "History of the Williston Park (New York) Public Library from the Founding in 1937 to the Present Day." Research Paper, Long Island University, 1971.

5.753 Davidoff, D. "History and Development of the Bellmore (New York) Memorial Library from Its Establishment in 1948 to 1970." Research Paper, Long Island University, 1971.

5.754 Gerard, H. L. "A History of the Westhampton Free Library, Westhampton Beach, N.Y." Research Paper, Long Island University, 1971.

5.755 Iber, E. "History of the Founding of the Deer Park (New York) Public Library." Research Paper, Long Island University, 1971.

5.756 Jacobson, B. "History of the New York Library for the Blind and Physically Handicapped, 1895–1969." Master's thesis, Long Island University, 1971.

5.757 Jawitz, M. "History of the Babylon (New York) Public Library, 1895–1970." Research Paper, Long Island University, 1971.

5.758 King, D. "History of the East Hampton Free Library, 1897–1970." Research Paper, Long Island University, 1971.

5.759 Morris, R. "Finkelstein Memorial Library, Spring Valley, New York: An Oral History of the Early Years, 1917–1940." Research Paper, Long Island University, 1971.

5.760 O'Connor, S. "A History of the John Jermain Memorial Library, Sag Harbor, New York." Research Paper, Long Island University, 1971.

5.761 Resnick, S. "A History and Descriptive Study of the Greenpoint Branch of the Brooklyn (New York) Public Library." Research Paper, Long Island University, 1971.

5.762 Rubin, P. "History of the Jewish Division of the New York Public Library, 1897–1970." Research Paper, Long Island University, 1971.

5.763 Schneberg, B. "The History of the Lindenhurst (New York) Memorial Library, 1945–1970." Research Paper, Long island University, 1971.

5.764 Vinicombe, M. "A History of the Baldwin (New York) Public Library from Its Founding in 1919 to the Present Day." Research Paper, Long Island University, 1971.

5.765 Dain, P. *The New York Public Library: A History of Its Founding and Early Years.* New York: New York Public Library, 1972.

5.766 Gavurin, E. A. "Guide to the Archival Collections in the Public Libraries of Nassau County, New York." Research Paper, Long Island University, 1972.

5.767 Folcarelli, R. J. "A History and Description of Audiovisual Services and Programs of the Public Library Systems of New York State, 1950–1970." Doctoral dissertation, New York University, 1973.

5.768 Barnes, J. W., and Barnes, R. W. "From Books to Multimedia: A History of the Reynolds Library and the Reynolds Audio-Visual Department of the Rochester Public Library." *Rochester History* 36 (1974): 1–38.

5.769 Moran, I. S. "Brooklyn Public Library—75 Years Young." *LHR* 1 (March 1974): 55–82.

5.770 Rogers, F. *The Story of a Small Town Library: The Development of the Woodstock, N.Y., Library.* Woodstock, N.Y.: Overlook Press, 1974.

5.771 Bell, C. M. "Grinnell Library Association of Wappingers Falls, New York, 1867–1940." Research Paper, Long Island University, 1975.

5.772 Hedges, H. A. "A History of the Mattituck Free Library in Mattituck, New York." Research Paper, Long Island University, 1975.

5.773 Beck, N. R. "The Board of Directors of the Aguilar Free Library Society, 1886–1903: A Prosopographical Study." *Libri* 28 (1978): 141–64.

5.774 Biddle, S. F. "Partnership in Progress—The Schomburg Center for

Research in Black Culture." *Crisis* 85 (1978): 330–37.

5.775 Dain, P. "Outreach Programs in Public Libraries—How New? With Specific Reference to the New York Public Library." In *Milestones to the Present: Papers from Library History Seminar V,* edited by H. Goldstein. Syracuse, N.Y.: Gaylord Professional Publications, 1978. Pp. 255–80.

5.776 Harvey, D. I. "The Process of Metropolitan Political Integration: A Case Study of the Formation of the Onondaga County Public Library." Doctoral dissertation, Syracuse University, 1978.

5.777 Hutson, J. B. "The Schomburg Center for Research in Black Culture." *ELIS* 26 (1979): 355–60.

5.778 Miller, P. L., and Campbell, F. C. "How the Music Division of the New York Public Library Grew: A Memoir." *MLAN* 35 (1979): 537–55.

5.779 Gayle, S. "The Home That Schomburg Built." *Black Enterprise* 2 (December 1980): 21.

5.780 Karp, M., and Garoogian, R. "The W.P.A. and the New York Public Library." In *Studies in Creative Partnership: Federal Aid to Public Libraries during the New Deal,* edited by D. F. Ring. Metuchen, N.J.: Scarecrow Press, 1980. Pp. 67–88.

5.781 Baker, J. P. "Preservation Programs of the New York Public Library, Part One: The Early Years." *Microform Review* 10 (1981): 25–28.

5.782 Baker, J. P. "Preservation Programs of the New York Public Library, Part Two: From the 1930s to the 60s." *Microform Review* 11 (1981): 22–30.

5.783 Barr, D. J. "A Profile of the Buffalo and Erie County Public Library." *BKM* 40 (1982): 80–84.

5.784 Menna, E. B. "The New York Public Library." *BKM* 40 (1982): 89–92.

5.785 Nyren, D. "The Brooklyn Public Library." *BKM* 40 (1982): 109–11.

5.786 Ryan, N. D., and Chase, E. H. "The Rochester Public Library." *BKM* 40 (1982): 97–101.

5.787 Salaam, Y. A. "The Schomburg Library Then and Now." *Freedomways* 23 (1983): 29–36.

5.788 Gregory, R. G. "The Development of the Eastern African Collection at Syracuse University." *Courier* 19 (1984): 29–59.

5.789 Hueting, G. P. "Alvaro-Agustin de Liano and His Books in Leopold von Ranke's Library." *Courier* 20 (1985): 31–48.

5.790 Rounds, J. B. *The Time Was Right: A History of the Buffalo and Erie County Public Library, 1940–1975,* edited by M. C. Mahaney. Buffalo, N.Y.: Grosvenor Society, 1985.

5.791 Szladits, L. *Brothers: The Origins of the Henry W. and the Albert A. Berg Collections of English and American Literature.* New York: New York Public Library, Astor, Lenox and Tilden Foundations, 1985.

5.792 Reed, H. H. *The New York Public Library; Its Architecture and Decoration.* New York: W.W. Norton, 1986.

5.793 Rosenberg-Naparsteck, R. "The Role of the Library—Public Service." *Rochester History* 48 (1986): 20–31.

North Carolina

5.794 Gardner, O. M. *The Significance of the Citizen's Library Movement.* Raleigh, N.C.: North Carolina Library Association, 1929.

5.795 Eury, W. "The Citizen's Library Movement in North Carolina." Master's thesis, George Peabody College for Teachers, 1951.

5.796 von Oesen, E. "Public Library Service in North Carolina and the W.P.A." Master's thesis, University of North Carolina, 1951.

5.797 Flournoy, M. W. *A Short History of the Public Library of Charlotte and Mecklenburg County, Charlotte, North Carolina.* Charlotte, N.C.: Public Library of Charlotte and Mecklenburg County, 1952.

5.798 von Oesen, E. "Public Library Extension in North Carolina and the WPA [1932–42]." *NCHR* 29 (1952): 379–99.

5.799 Murphy, S. B. "The History of the Rockingham County Library, 1930–1955." Master's thesis, University of North Carolina, 1956.

5.800 Ballance, P. S., comp. *The First Fifty Years of Public Library Service in Winston-Salem, 1906–1956.* Winston-Salem, N.C.: Public Library of Winston-Salem and Forsyth County, North Carolina, n.d.

5.801 Taylor, J. "Public Library Legislation in the State of North Carolina, 1897–June 30, 1956." Master's thesis, University of North Carolina, 1958, University of Kentucky Press Microcard Series B, no. 29.

5.802 Batten, S. S. "The History of the Johnson County Public Library System, 1941–1951." Master's thesis, University of North Carolina, 1960.

5.803 Moore, B. L. "A History of Public Library Service to Negroes in Winston-Salem, North Carolina, 1927–1951." Master's thesis, Atlanta University, 1961.

5.804 Cooke, A. M. "A History of the Public Library in Murphy, North Carolina." Master's thesis, Florida State University, 1962.

5.805 Whedbee, M. M. "A History of the Development and Expansion of Bookmobile Service in North Carolina, 1923–1960." Master's thesis, University of North Carolina, 1962.

5.806 Stewart, W. L. "A History of the High Point, North Carolina, Public Library." Master's thesis, University of North Carolina, 1963.

5.807 Aldrich, W. L. B. "The History of Public Library Service to Negroes in Salisbury, North Carolina, 1937–1963." Master's thesis, Atlanta University, 1964.

5.808 Hunter, C. P. "A History of the Olivia Raney Library, 1899–1959." Master's thesis, University of North Carolina, 1964.

5.809 Garrison, B. S. "A History of the Concord Public Library of Concord, North Carolina." Master's thesis, University of North Carolina, 1965.

5.810 Scoggin, R. B. "The Development of Public Library Services in Chowan, Tyrrell and Washington Counties." Master's thesis, University of North Carolina, 1967.

5.811 Hoover, A. R. "History of the Carnegie Library of Charlotte and Mecklenburg County, North Carolina, 1903–1920." Master's thesis, University of North Carolina, 1968.

5.812 Memory, M. W. "A History of the Randolph Public Library, 1935–1967." Master's thesis, University of North Carolina, 1968.

5.813 High, W. M. "A History of the Durham Public Library, 1895–1940." *NCL* 34 (1977): 35–48.

5.814 Sawyer, M. H. "Most Worthy Child: The Williamsburg Free Public Library, 1909 to 1933." Research Paper, University of North Carolina-Chapel Hill, 1981.

North Dakota

5.815 Brudvig, G. L. "Public Libraries in North Dakota: The Formative Years, 1880–1920." Master's thesis, University of Minnesota, 1962.

5.816 Brudvig, G. L. "Development of Public Library Service in North Dakota." *North Dakota Historical Quarterly* 31 (1963): 61–66.

Ohio

5.817 Moss, Mrs. F. C. B. "The Evolution of the Sandusky Free Library." *Firelands Pioneer* 13 (1900): 658–67.

5.818 Porter, W. T. "First County Library in Ohio." *PL* 6 (1901): 208–09.

5.819 Galbreath, C. B., comp. *Sketches of Ohio Libraries.* Columbus, Ohio: F.J. Heer, 1902.

5.820 Galbreath, C. B. *The Library Movement in Ohio.* Columbus, Ohio: Progress and Ohio Magazine, 1909.

5.821 Clarke, J. H. "Cleveland Public Library." In *A History of Cleveland, Ohio,* vol. 1, edited by S. P. Orth. Chicago: S.J. Clarke Publishing Co., 1910. Pp. 577–88.

5.822 Metz, C. A. "The Brumback Library of Van Wert County." *Ohio Education Monthly* 61 (1912): 202–05.

5.823 Antrim, Mrs. S. *The County Library: The Pioneer County Library (the Brumback Library of Van Wert County, Ohio) and the County Library Movement in the United States . . . .* Van Wert, Ohio: Pioneer Press, 1914.

5.824 Battles, F. M. "An Account of the Development of the Public Library Movement in Ohio, with Special Reference to Some Outstanding Libraries." Master's thesis, University of Illinois, 1928.

5.825 Toledo Public Library. *The Toledo Public Library: A Century of Progress, 1838–1938.* Toledo, Ohio: Toledo Public Library, 1938.

5.826 Cincinnati. Public Library. *A Decade of Service, 1930–1940.* Cincinnati: Public Library of Cincinnati and Hamilton County, 1941.

5.827 Pardee, H. L. *A Story of the Akron Public Library, 1834–1942.* Akron, Ohio: Published by the Library, 1943.

5.828 Thayer, G. W. "Cleveland's Public Library—1869–1944." *Cleveland Plain Dealer* (11–14, 16–17 October 1944): .

5.829 Meshot, G. V. "A History of the Hubbard Public Library." Master's thesis, Western Reserve University, 1949.

5.830 Nolan, C. "The History of the County Library in Ohio." Master's thesis, Western Reserve University, 1949.

5.831 Yockey, R. "The Winged Bequest: An Account of the Cleveland Public Library's Service to the Incapacitated." Master's thesis, Western Reserve University, 1949.

5.832 Crammer, J. C. "History and Development of Library Services in the Township of Hudson, Summit County, Ohio." Master's thesis, Kent State University, 1950.

5.833 Hazeltine, R. E. "The History of Birchard Library, Freemont, Ohio, 1847–1950." Master's thesis, Western Reserve University, 1950.

5.834 Lewis, M. E. "A History of the Mount Vernon, Ohio, Public Library, 1888–1949." Master's thesis, Western Reserve University, 1950.

5.835 MacCampbell, B. B. "History of the Kent, Ohio, Free Library." Master's thesis, Western Reserve University, 1950.

5.836 Schryver, N. E. "A History of the Business Information Bureau of the Cleveland Public Library." Master's thesis, Western Reserve University, 1950.

5.837 Spaulding, V. A. "A History of the Two Public Libraries in Mentor, Ohio." Master's thesis, Western Reserve University, 1950.

5.838 Bradley, N. B. "The Development of Service to Children in the Cleveland Public Library, with Special Reference to Perkins Library." Master's thesis, Western Reserve University, 1951.

5.839 Collins, L. T. "A History of the East Cleveland Public Library." Master's thesis, Western Reserve University, 1951.

5.840 Goodale, G. "History of the Portage County Library, Ohio." Master's thesis, Western Reserve University, 1951.

5.841 Murray, K. "History of the Development of Bookmobile Service, Hamilton County, Ohio." Master's thesis, Western Reserve University, 1951.

5.842 Murray, M. E. "The Branch Library: A Mirror of Its Community, with Case Histories of Several Branches of the Cleveland Public Library." Master's thesis, Western Reserve University, 1951.

5.843 Sheffield, H. G. "A Report on the History and Development of the Library for the

Blind of the Cleveland Public Library." Master's thesis, Western Reserve University, 1951.

5.844 Weis, L. A. "The History of Children's Work at Akron Public Library in Akron, Ohio." Master's thesis, Western Reserve University, 1951.

5.845 Burton, A. S. "The Cuyahoga County (Ohio) Library System: A History." Master's thesis, Western Reserve University, 1952.

5.846 Mutschler, H. F. "The Ohio Public Library and State Aid." Master's thesis, Western Reserve University, 1952.

5.847 Nagy, M. C. "History and Relationship of the Rice Branch Library to Its Hungarian Patrons." Master's thesis, Western Reserve University, 1952.

5.848 Buzzard, R. A. "History of Bookmobile Service, Dayton Public Library, Dayton, Ohio." Master's thesis, Western Reserve University, 1953.

5.849 Shewmaker, J. D. "History of the Willoughby Public Library, Willoughby, Ohio." Master's thesis, Western Reserve University, 1953.

5.850 Silver, R. A. "A Description and History of the Foreign Literature Division of the Cleveland Public Library." Master's thesis, Western Reserve University, 1953.

5.851 Baughman, R. O. "Fifty-three Years of Progress: Public Libraries in Lima, Ohio, 1855–1908." Master's thesis, Western Reserve University, 1954.

5.852 Copeland, E. F. "A History of the Carnegie West Branch of the Cleveland Public Library." Master's thesis, Western Reserve University, 1954.

5.853 Fleischer, M. L. "A History of the Rocky River Public Library." Master's thesis, Western Reserve University, 1954.

5.854 Forney, D. J. "The History of the East Palestine Public Library." Master's thesis, Western Reserve University, 1954.

5.855 Greene, J. T. "A History and Description of the Literature Division of the Cleveland Public Library." Master's thesis, Western Reserve University, 1954.

5.856 Ingalls, M. E. "The History and Description of the Philosophy and Religion Division of the Cleveland Public Library." Master's thesis, Western Reserve University, 1954.

5.857 Shamp, B. K. "The Music Section of the Cleveland Public Library." Master's thesis, Western Reserve University, 1954.

5.858 Szkudlarek, M. E. "Historical Development of Work with Children in the Toledo Public Library." Master's thesis, Western Reserve University, 1954.

5.859 Young, S. S. "History of the Norwalk Public Library from 1853–1927." Master's thesis, Western Reserve University, 1954.

5.860 Arthur, A. W. "A History of the Warder Public Library, Springfield, Ohio." Master's thesis, Kent State University, 1955.

5.861 Bowden, C. N. "The History of Lane Public Library, Hamilton, Ohio." Master's thesis, Western Reserve University, 1955.

5.862 Eckert, C. J. "A History of the New Philadelphia—Tuscarawas County (Ohio) District Library." Master's thesis, Western Reserve University, 1955.

5.863 Harshe, C. E. "Lima Public Library Extension Services: History and Development." Master's thesis, Western Reserve University, 1955.

5.864 Nestleroad, R. "A History of Fifty Years of Library Service: Napoleon Public Library, Napoleon, Ohio." Master's thesis, Western Reserve University, 1956.

5.865 Brookover, B. "A History of the Leonard Case Library, Cleveland, Ohio, 1846–1941." Master's thesis, Western Reserve University, 1957.

5.866 Gooch, R. E. "History of the Birchard Public Library and the Sandusky County Extension Service." Master's thesis, Western Reserve University, 1957.

5.867 Harshfield, L. "The Wagnall's Memorial." Master's thesis, Western Reserve University, 1957.

5.868 Hopkins, L. "The Development of the Local History and Genealogy Division of the Toledo Public Library." Master's thesis, Western Reserve University, 1957.

5.869 Jones, G. "Materials Relating to the Development of a History of Public Libraries in the Western Reserve." Master's thesis, Kent State University, 1957.

5.870 Phillips, V. "Fifty-six Years of Service to the Foreign-born by the Cleveland Public Library." Master's thesis, Western Reserve University, 1957.

5.871 Ryberg, H. T. "Warren Public Library: A History." Master's thesis, Western Reserve University, 1957.

5.872 Wine, E. "The Development of the Dayton Public Library, Dayton, Ohio, 1900–1957." Master's thesis, Western Reserve University, 1958.

5.873 Young, M. J. "The Akron Public Library, 1942–1957." Master's thesis, Western Reserve University, 1958.

5.874 Reed, M. M. "History of the Lakewood Public Library, Lakewood, Ohio: The First Twenty-five Years, 1913–1938." Master's thesis, Western Reserve University, 1959.

5.875 Elias, W. D. "History of the Reed Memorial Library, Ravenna, Ohio." Master's thesis, Kent State University, 1961.

5.876 Faries, E. "History of Libraries in Ohio." *OLAB* 31 (1961): 3–6.

5.877 Boone, H. H. "A History of the Salem (Ohio) Public Library." Master's thesis, Kent State University, 1962, University of Kentucky Press Microcard Series B, no. 53.

5.878 Somerville, S. A. "A Brief History of the Public Libraries of Mentor, Ohio." Master's thesis, Kent State University, 1962, University of Kentucky Press Microcard Series B, no. 59.

5.879 Thomas, M. E. "History of Public Library Service in Jackson County, Ohio." Master's thesis, Kent State University, 1963.

5.880 Weller, J. M. "160 Years of Library Service to Cincinnati and Hamilton County." In *Contributions to Mid-West Library History*, edited by T. Eaton. Champaign, Ill.: Illini Union Bookstore, 1964. Pp. 1–53.

5.881 Heim, H. R. "A History of the Lepper Library of Lisbon, Ohio." Master's thesis, Kent State University, 1965.

5.882 Dax, E. R. "Land Public Library's First 100 Years." *OLAB* 36 (1966): 6–10.

5.883 Gankoski, I. F. "History of the Massillon, Ohio, Public Library from 1899 to 1920." Research Paper, Kent State University, 1969.

5.884 Havron, H. J. "A History of Library Service in Crawford County, Ohio." Master's thesis, Kent State University, 1969.

5.885 Lane, M. S. "Development of the Public Library in Troy, Ohio." Research Paper, Kent State University, 1969.

5.886 McQuade, J. W. "History of the Mansfield, Ohio, Public Library." Research Paper, Kent State University, 1969.

5.887 Seabrook, J. H. "History of the Worthington, Ohio, Public Library, 1803–1967." Research Paper, Kent State University, 1969.

5.888 Vandemark, P. "The Cleveland Public Library: 1869–1969." *WLB* 43 (1969): 728–33.

5.889 Bollenbacher, B., and Long, F. *The Proud Years, 1869–1969: A Pictorial History of the Cleveland Public Library.* Cleveland: The Library, 1970.

5.890 Carter, B. "Taylor Memorial Library, Cuyahoga Falls, Ohio, 1955–1970." Research Paper, Long Island University, 1970.

5.891 Lewis, R. A. "History of the Colburn Library, 1904–1968." Research Paper, Kent State University, 1970.

5.892 McKnight, J. A. "History of the Wayne County Public Library." Research Paper, Kent State University, 1970.

5.893 Bollenbacher, B. "Cleveland Public Library." *ELIS* 5 (1971): 197–205.

5.894 Cool, D. "History of the Warren Public Library, 1950–1970." Research Paper, Kent State University, 1971.

5.895 Pikovnik, R. "History of the Lorain Public Library to the Year 1926." Research Paper, Kent State University, 1971.

5.896 Rodstein, F. M. "The East 79th Street Branch of the Cleveland Public Library: An Historical Overview, 1909–1970." Master's thesis, Kent State University, 1971.

5.897 Cramer, C. H. *Open Shelves and Open Minds: A History of the Cleveland Public Library.* Cleveland: Western Reserve University Press, 1972.

5.898 Stratton, G. W. "History of Public Library Service in Solon." Master's thesis, Kent State University, 1972.

5.899 Waters, J. K. "History of the Canal Fulton (Ohio) Public Library." Research Paper, Kent State University, 1972.

5.900 Lawson, L. G. "History of the Books/Jobs Project: Akron Public Library, July 1, 1968–June 30, 1972." Research Paper, Kent State University, 1973.

5.901 Tucker, C. "Development of Guernsey County District Public Library (Ohio) from 1898 to 1972, with Particular Consideration of the Professional Staff, Physical Facility, and the Library Services to the Community." Research Paper, Kent State University, 1973.

5.902 Barnett, L. F. "A History of the Akron Public Library, 1874–1942." Master's thesis, Kent State University School of Library Science, 1974.

5.903 Blair, J. *Akron Public Library—One Hundred Years of Service, 1874–1974.* Akron, Ohio: Friends of Akron-Summit County Public Library, 1974.

5.904 Butrick, M. W. "History of the Foreign Literature Department of the Cleveland Public Library, 1925–1972." Master's thesis, Kent State University, 1974.

5.905 Hibbs, J. E. "A History of the Toledo Public Library." *Northwest Ohio Quarterly* 46 (1974): 72–116.

5.906 Ring, D. F. "The Cleveland Public Library and the WPA: A Study in Creative Partnership." *Ohio History* 84 (1975): 158–64.

5.907 Woodward, P. K. "History of the Stow Public Library, 1924–1974." Research Paper, Kent State University, 1975.

5.908 Agnoni, L. V. "Public Library Service in Alliance, Ohio: 1885 to 1956." Research Paper, Kent State University, 1976.

5.909 Ring, D. F. "The Cleveland Public Library and the W.P.A.: A Study in Creative Partnership." In *Studies in Creative Partnership: Federal Aid to Public Libraries during the New Deal,* edited by D. F. Ring. Metuchen, N.J.: Scarecrow Press, 1980. Pp. 33–46.

5.910 Ring, D. F. "Fighting for Their Hearts and Minds: William Howard Brett, the Cleveland Public Library, and World War I." *JLH* 18 (1983): 1–20.

Oklahoma

5.911 Henke, E. M. "The History of Public Libraries in Oklahoma." Master's thesis, University of Oklahoma, 1954.

Oregon

5.912 Barrett, M. "History of Oregon Public Libraries." Master's thesis, University of Oregon, 1940.

5.913 Kirchem, C. E. "Library Development in Clackamas County, Oregon." Master's thesis, University of Washington, 1952.

5.914 Kembel, D. "The Development and Activities of the Library Association of Portland." Master's thesis, University of Portland, 1954.

5.915 *Public Library Buildings in Oregon, 1905–1955.* Portland: Oregon State Library, 1955.

5.916 McGuire, M. P. "The Albina Branch Library, Portland (Oregon); Its First Half Century." Research Paper, Portland State University, 1962.

5.917 Carver, R. V. "Portland Public Library (Oregon)." *ELIS* 23 (1978): 130–36.

Pennsylvania

5.918 Montgomery, T. L. "A Survey of Pennsylvania Libraries." *PLN* 6 (1913): 45–59.

5.919 Mathews, E. L. "Public Libraries of Pennsylvania." *PLN* 14 (1934): 402–07.

5.920 Martin Memorial Library, York, Pennsylvania. *The Founding and the Establishment of the Martin Memorial Library of York, Pennsylvania, and Its Founder, Wilton Daniel Martin, with the Program of Presentation of the Library to the Public of York and York County.* York, Pa.: N.p., 1935.

5.921 Lingfelter, M. R. *Books on Wheels.* New York: Funk and Wagnalls, 1938.

5.922 Munn, R. "Books Alive since '95: Celebrating Fifty Years of Library Service to the People of Pittsburgh." *Carnegie Magazine* 19 (1945): 99–103.

5.923 Smith, M. H. "Three Rural Libraries of Chester County, Pennsylvania: A Historical Survey of Their Development and Services to the Community." Master's thesis, Drexel Institute of Technology, 1950.

5.924 Di Pietro, L. N. "The Free Library of Philadelphia: Its Formation and Early Physical Growth from 1891 to 1917." Master's thesis, Drexel Institute of Technology, 1952.

5.925 Keim, A. "The History of Cambria Free Library, Johnstown, Pennsylvania, 1925–1951." Master's thesis, Drexel Institute of Technology, 1952.

5.926 Philadelphia City Institute. *The One Hundredth Anniversary of the Philadelphia City Institute: A Branch of the Free Library of Philadelphia.* [Philadelphia: N.p., 1952].

5.927 Barker, J. W. "The History and Development of the Monessen Public Library, Monessen, Pennsylvania." Master's thesis, Western Reserve University, 1953.

5.928 Klugiewicz, E. "Short History of the Erie (Penn.) Public Library." Master's thesis, Western Reserve University, 1953.

5.929 Meyer, W. P. "A History of the Reading, Pennsylvania, Public Library, and Its Services to the Community, 1898–1952." Master's thesis, Drexel Institute of Technology, 1953.

5.930 Girvin, C. M. "The Allentown Free Library: A History of Its Growth and Services." Master's thesis, Drexel Institute of Technology, 1954.

5.931 Tuck, R. S. "Evolution of the Chester County Library: A History." Master's thesis, Drexel Institute of Technology, 1954.

5.932 Winger, A. K. "History of the Huntingdon County Library, Huntingdon, Pennsylvania, 1935–1953." Master's thesis, Drexel Institute of Technology, 1954.

5.933 Egolf, J. L. "A History of the Bethlehem Public Library, Bethlehem, Pennsylvania, 1901 to 1954." Master's thesis, Drexel Institute of Technology, 1955.

5.934 Whitney, E. M. "History of the Morristown (Penn.) Public Library." Master's thesis, Drexel Institute of Technology, 1955.

5.935 Ambler, B. H. "History of the Children's Department of the Free Library of Philadelphia, 1898–1953." Master's thesis, Drexel Institute of Technology, 1956.

5.936 Diana, J. P. "History of the Osterhout Free Library, 1889–1961." Master's thesis, Marywood College (Scranton, Pa.), 1961.

5.937 Philadelphia Free Library. *Decade of Growth, 1951–1960: The Free Library of Philadelphia.* Philadelphia: Philadelphia Free Library, 1961.

5.938 Munn, R. *Carnegie Library of Pittsburgh: A Brief History and Description.* Pittsburgh: Carnegie Library of Pittsburgh, 1968.

5.939 Potera, E. J. "History of the Back Mountain Memorial Library, Dallas, Pennsylvania." Master's thesis, Marywood College (Scranton, Pa.), 1969.

5.940 Munn, R. "Carnegie Library of Pittsburgh." *ELIS* 4 (1970): 207–11.

5.941 Shaffer, E. "The Rare Book Department, Free Library of Philadelphia." *PBSA* 64 (1970): 1–11.

5.942 Heizmann, L. J. *The Library That Would Not Die: The Turbulent History of the Reading Public Library.* Reading, Pa.: Reading Eagle Press, 1971.

5.943 Doms, K. "Free Library of Philadelphia." *ELIS* 9 (1973): 105–11.

Rhode Island

5.944 "Redwood Library, Newport, R.I." *NLGPC* 2 (15 December 1852): 235–36.

5.945 Koopman, H. L. "Library Progress in Rhode Island." *LJ* 31 (1906): 10–17.

5.946 [Gardner, H. B.] *The History and Present Need of the Providence Public Library.* Providence, R.I.: Livermore and Knight Co., 1926.

5.947 Foster, W. E. *The First Fifty Years at the Providence Public Library, 1878–1928.* Providence, R.I.: Providence Public Library, 1928.

5.948 Harding, M. F. "A History of the Providence Public Library, Providence, Rhode Island, from 1878 to 1960." Master's thesis, Catholic University of America, 1964.

5.949 Sherman, S. C. *The First Ninety Years of the Providence Public Library, 1878–1968.* Providence, R.I.: N.p., 1968.

South Carolina

5.950 Bowers, C. W. "The History and Development of the Newberry County (South Carolina) Library." Master's thesis, University of South Carolina, 1942.

5.951 Jarrell, P. H. "The Development of the County Library System in South Carolina from 1929 to 1943." Master's thesis, University of North Carolina, 1955.

5.952 Orlando, P. "The Rocky Bottom, South Carolina, Transient Camp Library." Master's thesis, Southern Connecticut State College, 1960.

5.953 Stringfellow, K. "History of Chester County Library." *South Carolina Librarian* 5 (1960): 19–21.

5.954 Walker, E. P. *The Public Library in South Carolina, 1698–1980.* Columbia, S.C.: South Carolina State Library, 1981.

5.955 Walker, E. P. "The Public Library in South Carolina, 1698–1980." *SEL* 31 (1981): 147–52.

5.956 Crouch, M. L. "The Library Movement in South Dakota with Special Reference to Some Outstanding Libraries." Master's thesis, University of Illinois, 1930.

5.957 "Histories of South Dakota Libraries by Their Librarians." *South Dakota Library Bulletin* 49 (1963): 5–95.

Tennessee

5.958 Moore, Mrs. J. T. "The First Century of Library History in Tennessee, 1813–1913." *Publications of East Tennessee Historical Society* 16 (1944): 3–21.

5.959 Govan, J. F. "The History of the Chattanooga Public Library, 1905–1950." Master's thesis, Emory University, 1955.

5.960 Hoffman, R. P. "A History of Public Library Services to Negroes in Memphis, Tennessee." Master's thesis, Atlanta University, 1955.

5.961 Davant, M. *Cossitt Library, 1888–1959*. Memphis: Toof, 1959.

5.962 Hansbrough, I. C. "Public Library Service to Negroes in Knoxville, Tennessee." Master's thesis, Atlanta University, 1959.

5.963 McCrary, M. E. "A History of Public Library Service to Negroes in Nashville, Tennessee, 1916–1958." Master's thesis, Atlanta University, 1959.

5.964 Buck, J. P. "A History of the Library Resources of Putnam County." Master's thesis, Tennessee Polytechnic Institute, 1961.

5.965 Ogletree, M. B. "The History of the Nashville and Davidson County Public Library." Research Paper, George Peabody College for Teachers, School of Library Science, 1971.

5.966 Memphis Public Library. *The First 80 Years: Cossitt Library—Memphis Public Library and Information Center*. Memphis: Memphis Public Library, 1973.

5.967 Deaderick, L. "Knoxville-Knox County Public Library." *ELIS* 13 (1975): 445–49.

5.968 Stewart, D. M. "Nashville Public Libraries." *ELIS* 19 (1976): 16–26.

5.969 Wallis, C. L. "Memphis and Shelby County Public Library and Information Center." *ELIS* 17 (1976): 439–48.

5.970 McNamara, S. G. "Early Public Library Work with Children." *TN* 43 (1986): 59–72.

Texas

5.971 Wyche, B. "Free Public Libraries in Texas." *TL* 1 (1909): 6–7.

5.972 "Historical Sketches: Additions to the Historical Sketches in the Handbook for 1908." *HTL* 3 (1915–1916): 17–34.

5.973 "Special Features in the Larger [Public] Libraries." *HTL* 3 (1915–1916): 35–54.

5.974 *The History of the Texas Federation of Women's Clubs*, edited by S. L. Christian. Houston: Published by the Authority of the Texas Federation of Women's Clubs, [1919].

5.975 McCracken, P. C. "History and Present Status of the County Library in Texas." Master's thesis, Southern Methodist University, 1927.

5.976 El Paso, Texas. Public Library. *El Paso Public Library Progress Report, 1894–1929*. El Paso, Tex.: Ellis Brothers Printing Co., 1929.

5.977 Dickson, H. "Work with Children in the Public Libraries of Texas: Historical Sketch and Survey." *HTL* 4 (1935): 139–41.

5.978 Searcy, K. A. "History of the Brenham Public Library." *NNT* 11 (April 1935): 9, 19.

5.979 Toler, V. P. "Educational Activities of the Texas Federation of Women's Clubs—1897–1937." Master's thesis, University of Texas, 1938.

5.980 Peterson, H. N. "Fort Worth's New Public Library, Including a Brief History from Its Beginnings." *LJ* 64 (1939): 965–69.

5.981 Stoneham, F. M. "History of the County Library Movement of Texas." Master's thesis, Sam Houston State Teachers College, 1939.

5.982 Agnew, E. "The Texas Collection in the Houston Public Library, 1791–1871." Master's thesis, University of Texas, 1941.

5.983 West, E. H. "Libraries Look Forward in Texas." *NNT* 17 (July 1941): 7–11.

5.984 Grothaus, J. "People's Library Movement for Texas." *NNT* 18 (July 1942): 20–22.

5.985 Davis-Randall, B. "Public Library Service for Negroes." *NNT* 19 (April 1943): 13–14.

5.986 "Book Lanes through Texas." *NNT* 21 (July 1945): 5–13.

5.987 Self, H. "A History of the Cooke County Library, Gainsville, Texas." Master's thesis, North Texas State University, 1945.

5.988 Antilley, W. M. "The Taylor County Rural Circulating Library." *NNT* 25 (April 1949): 68–69.

5.989 Greene, A. C. "The Carnegie Public Library of Abilene." *NNT* 25 (April 1949): 37–41.

5.990 Mason, L. G. "The Founding of the Beaumont, Texas, Public Library, 1850–1926." Master's thesis, Texas State College, 1951.

5.991 Morgan, W. M. "Rosenberg Library." *HT* 2 (1952): 505–06.

5.992 Gillespie, R. C. "La Retama Public Library: Its Origin and Development, 1909–1952." Master's thesis, University of Texas, 1953.

5.993 San Antonio, Texas. Public Library. *The First Fifty Years: News of the San Antonio Public Library.* [San Antonio, Tex.: The Library], 1953.

5.994 Woodman, J. "The Fort Worth Public Library [1892–1952]." *Junior History* 3 (1953): 29–30.

5.995 Wales, B. "Through Many Generations . . . Rosenburg Library's First 50 Years [Galveston, 1900–1954]." *TLJ* 30 (1954): 200–202.

5.996 Dulaney, M., and Scott, W. H. O. "Waco Public Library." *TL* 17 (1955): 202–07.

5.997 Ganey, M. M. *History of the Abilene Carnegie Library, 1899–1955.* Abilene, Tex.: The Library, 1956.

5.998 Hanke, K. G "The Austin Public Library." *TL* 18 (1956): 119–23.

5.999 Barnes, G. S. "A History of Public Library Service to Negroes in Galveston, Texas, 1904–1955." Master's thesis, Atlanta University, 1957.

5.1000 Pepper, E. "The County-City Library of Sweetwater." *TL* 19 (1957): 11–13.

5.1001 Santy, A. B. "Waco Public Library." Master's thesis, Texas Woman's University, 1958.

5.1002 Cody, N. B. "Historical Development of Public Libraries in Gregg County, Texas." Master's thesis, East Texas State College, 1959.

5.1003 Lee, R. E. "Texas Library Development: Its Relation to the Carnegie Movement, 1898–1915." Master's thesis, University of Texas, 1959.

5.1004 Suhler, S. A. "The Austin Public Library, 1926–1956." Master's thesis, University of Texas, 1959.

5.1005 Dallas, Texas. Public Library. *Five Years Forward: The Dallas Public Library, 1955–1960.* Dallas: [Friends of the Library, 1961?].

5.1006 Marburger, H. J. "Success of Four Texas Cities Should Spur Building Program." *TL* 24 (1962): 15–23.

5.1007 Taylor, B. A. "The Taylor Public Library: A Case Study of Community Cooperation." Master's thesis, University of Texas, 1962.

5.1008 Smith, M. H. K. "A History of the Libraries of Bonham, Texas." Master's thesis, East Texas State College, 1963.

5.1009 Mays, F. N. "A History of Public Library Service to Negroes in Houston, Texas, 1907–1962." Master's thesis, Atlanta University, 1964.

5.1010 Allen, D. L. "The Kemp Public Library: A History, 1896–1963." Master's thesis, University of Texas, 1965.

5.1011 Downing, M. L. "The P.W.A. and the Acquisition of the Fort Worth Public Library Building, 1933–1939." *TL* 27 (1965): 126–32, 142.

5.1012 Hunt, J. E. "The Denison Public Library." *TL* 27 (1965): 113–17.

5.1013 Jeffress, I. P. "The Friends of the Seguin-Guadalupe County Public Library: History and Analysis, 1954–66." Master's thesis, University of Texas, 1967.

5.1014 Swogetinsky, B. A. "A Study of Censorial Demands on Texas Libraries,

1952–1957." Master's thesis, University of Texas, 1967.

5.1015 Teague, A. H. "Carnegie Library Building Grants to Texas Communities: A Brief Account and a Comparison." Master's thesis, University of Texas, 1967.

5.1016 Varner, J. "Austin Public Library—Dramatic Past, Exciting Future." *TL* 29 (1967): 49–58.

5.1017 Teague, A. H. "Carnegie Building Grants to Texas Libraries." *TLJ* 44 (1968): 25–28.

5.1018 Wyche, B. "Free Public Libraries in Texas: Ten Years' Growth, 1899–1909." *TL* 31 (1969): 88–89.

5.1019 Bradshaw, L. M. "Dallas Public Library." *ELIS* 6 (1971): 407–17.

5.1020 "Waco Public Library." In *Handbook of Waco and McLennan County*, edited by D. Kelley. Waco, Tex.: Texian Press, 1972. P. 285.

5.1021 "Waco-McLennan County Library." In *Handbook of Waco and McLennan County*, edited by D. Kelley. Waco: Texian Press, 1972. Pp. 283–84.

5.1022 Fulton, S. "Waxahachie's Sims Library, One of the State's Oldest." *TL* 37 (1975): 119–28.

5.1023 Waller, H. C. "A History of the Sherman Public Library, Sherman, Texas, to 1974." Research Paper, Texas Woman's University, 1975.

5.1024 "Rosenberg Library." *HT* 3 (1976): 815–16.

5.1025 Wells, M. L. "Denton Public Library Then and Now." Research Paper, Texas Woman's University, 1976.

5.1026 Eatenson, E. "The Making of a History for the Dallas Public Library." *TL* 39 (1977): 109–12.

5.1027 Field, J. E. F. "History of Dunlap Memorial Library, Italy, Texas." Research Paper, Texas Woman's University, 1977.

5.1028 Foto, S. T. "The History of the Houston Public Library." Research Paper, Texas Woman's University, 1977.

5.1029 Grove, L. *The Dallas Public Library: The First 75 Years.* Dallas: Dallas Public Library, 1977.

5.1030 Howe, M. J. "The Public Library of Beaumont, Texas: A History." Research Paper, Texas Woman's University, 1977.

5.1031 Sanders, L. M. "Nicholson Memorial Library, Garland, Texas, 1927 to Present." Research Paper, Texas Woman's University, 1977.

5.1032 Davis, D. G. "The Rise of the Public Library in Texas: 1876–1920." In *Milestones to the Present: Papers from Library History Seminar V*, edited by H. Goldstein. Syracuse, N.Y.: Gaylord Professional Publications, 1978. Pp. 166–83.

5.1033 Ferguson, E. O. "The History and Development of Lee Public Library and John Ben Sheppard, Jr. Texana Collection Memorial—Gladewater, Texas." Research Paper, Texas Woman's University, 1978.

5.1034 Kenamore, J. "Texas History at Rosenberg Has History of Its Own." *TL* 41 (1979): 28–33.

5.1035 Culp, P. M. "Carnegie Libraries: The Past No Longer Present." *TL* 43 (1981): 132–44.

5.1036 Culp, P. M. "Carnegie Libraries of Texas: The Past Still Present." *TL* 43 (1981): 81–96.

5.1037 Hunter, L. G. "Robert J. Kleberg Public Library Building (1927–1957)." *TL* 43 (1981): 183–89.

5.1038 Sheffield, S. "Arlington Public Library System: Sixty Years of Service." *TLJ* 58 (1982): 44–45.

5.1039 Lange, P., and Saxon, G. "Dallas Public Library: A Reputation for Excellence." *WLB* 58 (1984): 703–07.

5.1040 Porte, M. R. "Four Decades of Programming: Dallas Public Library." *Film Library Quarterly* 17 (1984): 9–16.

5.1041 Perry, G. "Andrew Carnegie: Santa Claus of Texas Public Libraries." *TL* 46 (1985): 23–27.

5.1042 Aull, P. B. "A Little Library and How It Grew [Hutchinson County Library]." *TLJ* 62 (1986): 16–19.

5.1043 Bocock, L. C. "Texas Libraries and the Texas Federation of Women's Clubs." *TLJ* 62 (1986): 26.

5.1044 Gower, G. "Clark Library." *TLJ* 62 (1986): 59–60.

Utah

5.1045 Hepworth, B. M. "Carnegie Libraries in Utah." Research Paper, Brigham Young University, 1976.

5.1046 Tessman, N. "Salt Lake City Public Library." *ELIS* 26 (1979): 286–90.

Vermont

5.1047 Johnson, L. B. "The Kimball Public Library [Randolph, Vt.]." *Vermonter* 8 (1903): 300–303.

5.1048 Coolidge, Mrs. O. H. "A Golden Anniversary: The Founding and the History of the Rutland Free Library." *Vermont Library Bulletin* 31 (1936): 54–56.

5.1049 Vermont. Free Public Library Commission. "Libraries in Vermont." *Vermont Library Bulletin* 34 (1938): 4–36.

5.1050 Ellis, M. "The History of the Brookfield Library." *Vermont Quarterly* 18 (1950): 29–32.

5.1051 Latham, J. "Traumatic Birth of a Vermont Library." *WLB* 52 (1978): 479–84.

Virginia

5.1052 Hoover, F. R. "The Rockingham Public Library, 1928–1947." *Madison Quarterly* 8 (1948): 74–85.

5.1053 Brandt, B. S. "The Alexandria, Virginia, Library: Its History, Present Facilities, and Future Program." Master's thesis, Catholic University of America, 1950.

5.1054 Elliott, M. E. "The Development of Library Service in Fairfax County, Virginia, since 1939." Master's thesis, Drexel Institute of Technology, 1951.

5.1055 Moyers, J. C. "History of the Rockingham Public Library, Harrisonburg, Virginia." Master's thesis, University of North Carolina, 1959.

Washington

5.1056 Strother, J. V. "The Development and the Adequacy of the Library as an Institution in the State of Washington." Master's thesis, University of Washington, 1938.

5.1057 Johns, H. "The Founding of the Longview [Washington] Public Library." *PNLAQ* 15 (1951): 116–22.

5.1058 Pitcher, P. M. "A Historical Study of Library Development in Chelan County, Washington." Master's thesis, University of Washington, 1952.

5.1059 Hake, S. D. "A History of Library Development in Kittitas County, Washington." Master's thesis, University of Washington, 1953.

5.1060 Orr, M. F. "Development of the Walla Walla Public Library." Master's thesis, University of Washington, 1953.

5.1061 Newson, H. E. "Fort Vancouver Regional Library: A Study of the Development of Public Library Service in Clark and Skamania Counties, Washington." Master's thesis, University of Washington, 1954.

5.1062 Wallace, W. S. "Founding the Public Library in Yakima." *Pacific Northwest Quarterly* 45 (1954): 95–101.

5.1063 Ward, B. A. "A History of Public Library Development in Whitman County, Washington." Master's thesis, University of Washington, 1960.

5.1064 Brass, L. J. *Eighty Years of Service: A History of the Children's Department, Seattle Public Library.* Seattle: Seattle Public Library, 1971.

5.1065 Suzuki, A. N. "The Foundations and Development of the Yakima Valley Regional Library." Master's thesis, Southern Connecticut State College, 1973.

West Virginia

5.1066 White, A. W. "The Public Library Movement in West Virginia." Master's thesis, Columbia University, 1935.

5.1067 Wade, B. A. "History of the Waitman Barbe Public Library of Morgantown, West Virginia, 1926–1956." Master's thesis, Western Reserve University, 1957.

5.1068 Davis, W. P. "The West Virginia Library Commission and Public Library Development Since 1972." Research Paper, Texas Woman's University, 1979.

5.1069 Javersak, D. T. "One Place on This Great Green Planet Where Andrew Carnegie Can't Get a Monument with His Money." *West Virginia History* 41 (1979): 7–19.

Wisconsin

5.1070 Hutchins, F. A. "Free City Libraries." In *The Columbian History of Education in Wisconsin,* edited by J. W. Stearns. Milwaukee: State Committee on Educational Exhibit for Wisconsin, 1893. Pp. 413–21.

5.1071 West, T. "Milwaukee Public Library." In *The Columbian History of Education in Wisconsin,* edited by J. W. Stearns. Milwaukee: State Committee on Educational Exhibit for Wisconsin, 1893. Pp. 422–27.

5.1072 Stearns, L. E., ed. "Wisconsin Supplement." *LJ* 21 (1896): 171–94.

5.1073 Wisconsin Free Library Commission. *Free Traveling Libraries in Wisconsin: The Story of Their Growth, Purposes and Development; With Accounts of a Few Kindred Movements.*

Madison, Wis.: Wisconsin Free Library Commission, 1897.

5.1074 "History of the Wisconsin Library Commission." *WisLB* 5 (1909): 287–89.

5.1075 Lester, C. B. "The Library Movement in Wisconsin." In *Wisconsin: Its History and Its People,* vol. 2, edited by M. M. Quaife. Chicago: S.J. Clarke Publishing Co., 1924. Pp. 411–32.

5.1076 Saucerman, K. "A Study of the Wisconsin Library Movement, 1850–1900." Master's thesis, University of Wisconsin, 1944.

5.1077 Malone, E. G. "The Madison Free Library Since the Ulveling-Rutzen Survey of 1951." Master's thesis, University of Wisconsin, 1958.

5.1078 Vaeth, H. *Origins of the Milwaukee Public Library.* Milwaukee: Milwaukee Public Library, 1965.

5.1079 MacLeod, D. I. *Carnegie Libraries in Wisconsin.* Madison, Wis.: Published for the Department of History, University of Wisconsin, by the State Historical Society of Wisconsin, 1968.

5.1080 Colson, J. C. "The Public Library Movement in Wisconsin, 1836–1900." Doctoral dissertation, University of Chicago, 1973.

5.1081 Ela, J. *Free and Public.* Madison, Wis.: Madison Public Library, 1974.

5.1082 Colson, J. C. " 'Public Spirit' at Work: Philanthropy and Public Libraries in Nineteenth-Century Wisconsin." *WMH* 59 (1976): 192–209.

5.1083 Goren, R. "Milwaukee Public Library." *ELIS* 18 (1976): 123–38.

5.1084 Ring, D. F. "The New Deal Work Projects at the Milwaukee Public Library." *Wisconsin Academy of Sciences, Arts and Letters* 65 (1977): 28–40.

5.1085 Bates, H. E. "The Milwaukee Public Library, 1942–1980: A Pioneer in Data Processing." *Public Library Quarterly* 2 (1980): 59–70.

5.1086 Fain, E. "Going Public: The Anger Williams Cox Library, the Village of Pardeeville, and the Wisconsin Supreme Court, 1927–1929." *JLH* 15 (1980): 52–61.

5.1087 Loeh, B. B. "History of the Joseph Mann Library, Two Rivers, Wisconsin, 1890–1979." Master's thesis, University of Wisconsin-Oshkosh, 1980.

5.1088 Ring, D. F. "The New Deal Work Projects at the Milwaukee Public Library." In *Studies in Creative Partnership: Federal Aid to Public Libraries during the New Deal,* edited by D. F. Ring. Metuchen, N.J.: Scarecrow Press, 1980. Pp. 89–103.

5.1089 Evans, D. W. "The Early History of the Appleton, Wisconsin, Public Library, 1887–1900." Master's thesis, University of Wisconsin-Oshkosh, 1981.

Wyoming

5.1090 Hayden, E. C. "Teton County Library: Its Birth and Growth, Jackson, Wyoming." *Wyoming Library Roundup* 10 (1954): 2–4.

5.1091 Wilkinson, M. "Experience of a [Library] Field Worker in Platte County Early 1900s." *Wyoming Library Roundup* 51 (1986): 50–53.

6.

Academic Libraries

The major contributions to the history of academic libraries began with Louis Shores's *Origins of the American College Library, 1638–1800* (1934, **6.11**), originally written as a dissertation at George Peabody College for Teachers. Analyzing nine colonial colleges and giving particular attention to administration and collection growth, Shores established a methodological pattern still respected and utilized in library historiography, that of drawing generalizations by examining closely a selected group of institutions as they evolved during clearly defined historical periods. Later syntheses resembling the Shores model include Benjamin E. Powell's, "The Development of Libraries in Southern State Universities to 1920" on libraries at the universities of Alabama, Georgia, Mississippi, North Carolina, South Carolina, Tennessee, and Virginia as well as Louisiana State University (1946, **6.23**); an especially thoughtful study by Kenneth Brough, *Scholar's Workshop: Evolving Conceptions of Library Service* (1953, **6.31**), on Columbia, Harvard, Yale, and the University of Chicago from 1876 to 1946; and Robert E. Brundin's, "Changing Patterns of Library Service in Five California Junior Colleges, 1907–1967" (1970, **6.162**).

Additional topical studies of particular note resulted from research conducted by Thomas Harding whose *College Literary Societies: Their Contribution to Higher Education in the United States 1815–1876* (1971, **6.60**) is recognized as a comprehensive work, national in scope, and Neil A. Radford who produced *The Carnegie Corporation and the Development of American College Libraries, 1928–1941* (1984, **6.137**). Radford considers two topics underrepresented in the historical literature: college libraries (as distinguished from university libraries) and the role of private philanthrophy in library development.

Two general syntheses in the history of American academic libraries, based essentially on foundational sources, appeared almost simultaneously. Arthur T. Hamlin divided *The University Library in the United States* (1981, **6.116**) into a chronology tracing academic libraries from the Colonial era to the

127

post–World War II period and a collection of essays on governance, organization, services, architecture, cooperative efforts, collection building, technical processing, technology, and finance, interspersing his narrative with personal reminiscences. Similarly, Lee Shiflett provided a synthesis by analyzing previously printed works. His *Origins of American Academic Librarianship* (1981, **6.121**), summarizing trends from 1876 to 1923, considered the subject in the context of bureaucratic and curricular developments in higher education, arguing that librarians never enjoyed a "Golden Age" of full acceptance by the professoriate or internal consensus about priorities of service and expertise. These two monographs had been preceded by Richard D. Johnson's *Libraries for Teaching, Libraries for Research: Essays for a Century* (1977, **6.100**), a collection of historical articles on academic libraries and librarians published in 1976 in *College & Research Libraries* as part of the American Library Association's centennial celebration. Well-researched and carefully edited, essays from the Johnson anthology are listed separately in this chapter (except for those that deal exclusively with private research libraries).

Considerably less comprehensive, though quite useful for general perspectives, are articles by W. N. C. Carlton on academic libraries in the mid-nineteenth century (1907, **6.4**) and Arthur E. Bestor, Jr., "The Transformation of American Scholarship, 1875–1917" (1953, **6.30**), detailing research developments in higher education and subsequent growth in university libraries. These were complemented somewhat later by three important articles on college libraries: Howard Clayton, "The American College Library: 1800–1860" (1968, **6.53**); Richard Harwell, "College Libraries" (1971, **6.61**); and John Caldwell, "Perceptions of the Academic Library: Midwestern College Libraries as They Have Been Depicted in College Histories" (1984, **6.132**).

Most of the recent articles have tended to focus on specific aspects of academic librarianship. Edward R. Johnson studied subject divisional organization from 1939 to 1974 (1977, **6.99**); J. Periam Danton examined budgets in the selected years of 1860, 1910, and 1960 (1983, **6.128**); and David Kaser reviewed architectural style and function for the years 1960 to 1984 (1984, **6.135**) and 1870 to 1890 (1986, **6.145**). Wayne A. Wiegand's collection, *Leaders in American Academic Librarianship, 1925–1975* (1983, **6.131**), provides a variety of insights into university library management. Individual entries from this collection appear by subject, together with other entries in Chapter 15, "Biographies of Individual Librarians and Library Benefactors."

Among three major areas of library organization—collection development, public services, and technical services—the first two are discussed in this chapter. Since most of the historical writing on technical services examines developments not only in academic libraries but in other types of libraries, frequently treating issues that transcend jurisdictional and geographical boundaries, it is listed in Chapter 13, "Special Aspects of Librarianship," rather than here.

Solid studies devoted to collection development began with "Book Collections of Five Colonial College Libraries: A Subject Analysis" (1960,

6.43), a dissertation by Joe Kraus that resulted in several journal articles and established his work as a standard for subsequent research. Soon thereafter, J. Periam Danton compared book selection and collection development in the United States and Germany (1963, **6.46**). Lowell Simpson examined society libraries at Columbia, Dartmouth, Princeton, and Yale from 1783 to 1830, concluding as did his predecessors that the society libraries were superior to their college counterparts with regard to physical facilities, accessibility, and collection quality (1977, **6.101**). Charles B. Osburn discussed the post–World War II period, concentrating on library growth and patterns of research in major disciplines and concluding that growth in research collections paralleled growth in research efforts but without responding directly to those efforts (1979, **6.108**). David Kaser hypothesized the existence of five distinct periods from 1780 to 1980 in "Collection Building in American Universities" (1980, **6.110**). Michael J. Waldo challenged some of the prevalent ideas about the book collections of college libraries and literary society libraries in his comparative study of twelve midwestern campuses during the mid-nineteenth century (1985, **6.141**).

Public services in academic libraries have attracted much less attention historically than has collection development. One must rely on the broad studies of reference work by Samuel Rothstein (1953, **13.235**; 1955, **13.237**; 1977 **13.245**), still authoritative more than thirty-five years after initial publication, and Robert Wagers (1978, **13.248**). Since these writers do not treat academic libraries exclusively, their publications are cited in Chapter 13, "Special Aspects of Librarianship." Particularly in light of recent calls for reform, the development of reference work in college and university libraries merits much more research, although Richard E. Miller's study of seven liberal arts colleges from 1876 to 1976 represents an important beginning (1984, **6.136**). Miller examined Amherst, Bowdoin, Carleton, Mt. Holyoke, Smith, Trinity in Connecticut, and Williams. Bibliographic instruction has also been subjected to historical scrutiny, most recently by John Mark Tucker (1979, **6.109**; 1980, **6.115**; 1984, **6.138**), Frances L. Hopkins (1981, **6.117**; 1982, **6.124**), and Peter Hernon (1982, **6.123**).

As generally illustrated by studies mentioned in this essay, doctoral programs produced the lion's share of the substantial research during the past fifty years. Thus, graduate work in history, librarianship, and, to a lesser extent, education has produced a large number of histories of academic libraries. Many of these works, whose interpretive quality varies widely, discuss selected time periods, which are often determined by the tenure of chief administrators. Most of the studies of liberal arts and teachers college libraries tend to be treated in master's theses, while research university libraries tend to be treated in doctoral dissertations. Thus, libraries at large universities have become the focus of the most extensive inquiry. The major studies, several of which have subsequently appeared as journal articles, include Haynes McMullen on the University of Chicago (1952 and 1953, **6.239**), Russell Bidlack on the University of Michigan (1962, **6.415**), Wayne Yenawine on the University of Illinois (1955, **6.241**), Mildred Lowell on Indiana University (1961, **6.261**), Winifred Linderman on Columbia

University (1959, **6.475**), James Skipper on Ohio State University (1960, **6.568**), Roscoe Rouse on Baylor University (1962, **6.672**), Robert Munn on the University of West Virginia (1962, **6.738**), Kenneth Peterson on the University of California at Berkeley (1970, **6.163**), Louis Moloney on the University of Texas (1970, **6.682**), and Clarence C. Gorchels on Washington State University (1971, **6.734**). These were followed—after a hiatus of more than a decade—by Thomas F. O'Connor on Yale University (1984, **6.197**), Christine Desjarlais-Leuth on Brown University (1985, **6.630**), and Francis X. Roberts on the University of Buffalo (now the State University of New York at Buffalo; 1986, **6.522**).

Occasionally, a university takes an active role in publishing the history of its library. See, for example, Harry Clemons's *The University of Virginia Library* (1954, **6.718**), J. Orin Oliphant's *The Library of Bucknell University* (1962, **6.610**), John Jennings's *The Library of the College of William and Mary in Virginia, 1693–1793* (1968, **6.724**), and Kenneth Peterson's previously mentioned study of the University of California (1970, **6.163**).

Finally, more recent research has yielded library histories that are less lengthy but of equal interpretive value. William S. Dix on Princeton University (1978, **6.452**), Charles R. Schultz on Texas A&M University (1979, **6.695**), and Merrily E. Taylor on Yale University (1982, **6.196**) merit special mention.

General Studies

1876–1919

6.1 Warren, S. R., and Clark, S. N. "College Libraries." In *Public Libraries in the United States of America: Their History, Condition and Management; Special Report, Part I,* U.S. Bureau of Education. Washington, D.C.: Government Printing Office, 1876. Pp. 60–126.

6.2 Guild, R. A. "The College Library." *LJ* 10 (1885): 216–21.

6.3 Winsor, J. "The Development of the Library." *LJ* 19 (1894): 370–75.

6.4 Carlton, W. N. C. "College Libraries in the Mid-Nineteenth Century." *LJ* 32 (1907): 479–86.

1920–1949

6.5 Gilchrist, D. B. "The Evolution of College and University Libraries." *BALA* 20 (1926): 293–99.

6.6 Shafer, H. "College Libraries in the United States from 1790–1830." Master's thesis, Columbia University, 1927.

6.7 Thurber, E. "The Library of the Land-Grant College, 1862–1900: A Preliminary Study." Master's thesis, Columbia University, 1928.

6.8 Knoer, M. M. A. "A Historical Survey of the Libraries of Certain Catholic Institutions of Learning in the United States." Master's thesis, University of Illinois, 1930.

6.9 Church, F. E. "A Historical Survey of the Libraries in a Group of State Normal Schools Prior to 1900." Master's thesis, Columbia University, 1931.

6.10 Wilson, L. R. *The Emergence of the College Library: An Address by Dr. Louis R. Wilson.* New York: Carnegie Corporation, 1931.

6.11 Shores, L. *Origins of the American College Library, 1638–1800.* New York: Barnes and Noble, 1934.

6.12 Bishop, W. W. *Carnegie Corporation and College Libraries, 1929–1938.* New York: Carnegie Corporation, 1938.

6.13 Lowell, M. H. "College and University Library Consolidations." Master's thesis, University of Chicago, 1939.

6.14 Strauss, L. H. "The Liberal Arts College Library, 1929–1940: A Comparative Interpretation of Financial Statistics of Sixty-Eight Representative and Twenty Selected Liberal Arts College Libraries." Master's thesis, University of Chicago, 1942.

6.15 Thompson, L. S. "The Historical Background of Departmental and Collegiate Libraries." *LQ* 12 (1942): 49–74.

6.16 Barous, T. R. *Carnegie Corporation and College Libraries, 1938–1943.* New York: Carnegie Corporation, 1943.

6.17 Holbert, J. A. "The Negro College Library." *Journal of Negro Education* 12 (1943): 623–29.

6.18 Buchanan, L. B. "Library Buildings of Teacher's Colleges, 1932–1942." Master's thesis, Columbia University, 1944.

6.19 Henry, E. A. *"Doctoral Dissertations Accepted—Ten Years of History."* CRL 5 (1944): 309–14.

6.20 Andrews, T. "Trends in College Library Buildings." Master's thesis, University of Chicago, 1945.

6.21 Storie, C. P. "The American College Society Library and the College Library." *CRL* 6 (1945): 240–48.

6.22 Thurber, E. "American Agricultural College Libraries, 1862–1900." *CRL* 6 (1945): 346–52.

6.23 Powell, B. E. "The Development of Libraries in Southern State Universities to 1920." Doctoral dissertation, University of Chicago, 1946.

131

6.24 Buchanan, R. E. "The Development and Function of a Research Library, 1922–46." *CRL* 8 (1947): 294–97.

6.25 Evans, L. H. "Research Libraries in the War Period, 1939–45." *LQ* 17 (1947): 241–62.

6.26 Doherty, F. X. "The New England Deposit Library History and Development." *LQ* 18 (1948): 245–54.

1950–1971

6.27 Armour, A. W., ed. "College Library Routine a Century Ago." *Autograph Collectors' Journal* 3 (January 1951): 26–29.

6.28 Muller, R. H. "College and University Library Buildings, 1929–1949." *CRL* 12 (1951): 261–65.

6.29 Thompson, L. S. "University Libraries and the Future of Scholarship in the South [1920–50]." *South Atlantic Quarterly* 50 (1951): 192–98.

6.30 Bestor, A. E. "The Transformation of American Scholarship, 1875–1917." *LQ* 23 (1953): 164–79.

6.31 Brough, K. J. *Scholar's Workshop: Evolving Conceptions of Library Service.* Urbana: University of Illinois Press, 1953.

6.32 Brumbaugh, W. D. "Developmental Aspects of Film Library Centers in Selected Colleges and Universities from 1942–1951." *Studies in Education* 4 (1953): 65–69.

6.33 Kulp, A. C. "The Historical Development of Storage Libraries in America." Master's thesis, University of Illinois, 1953, ACRL Microcard no. 12.

6.34 Reynolds, H. M. "University Library Buildings in the United States, 1890–1939." *CRL* 14 (1953): 149–57.

6.35 Metcalf, K. D. "The New England Deposit Library after Thirteen Years." *HLB* 8 (1954): 313–22.

6.36 Powell, B. E. "Southern University Libraries during the Civil War." *WLB* 31 (1956): 250–54, 259.

6.37 Martens, A. "A Study of the History and Development of the Protestant Theological Seminary Library Movement in the United States." Master's thesis, Southern Connecticut State College, 1958.

6.38 Scott, R. P. "A Survey of the Literature on the Financial Aspects of Libraries in the Institutions of Higher Education in the United States, 1926–1956." Master's thesis, Catholic University of America, 1958.

6.39 Allen, H. B. "The Old Library, 1764–January 24, 1939." *Harvard Alumni Bulletin* 41 (1959): 543–47.

6.40 Harding, T. S. "College Literary Societies: Their Contribution to the Development of Academic Libraries, 1815–76." *LQ* 29 (1959): 1–26, 94–112.

6.41 Orr, R. S. "Financing and Philanthropy in the Building of Academic Libraries Constructed between 1919 and 1958." Master's thesis, Western Reserve University, 1959.

6.42 Gelfand, M. A. "A Historical Study of the Evaluation of Libraries in Higher Institutions by the Middle States Association of Colleges and Secondary Schools." Doctoral dissertation, New York University, 1960.

6.43 Kraus, J. W. "Book Collections of Five Colonial College Libraries: A Subject Analysis." Doctoral dissertation, University of Illinois, 1960.

6.44 Boll, J. J. "Library Architecture 1800–1875: A Comparison of Theory and Buildings with Emphasis on New England College Libraries." Doctoral dissertation, University of Illinois, 1961.

6.45 Erickson, E. W. *College and University Library Surveys, 1938–1952.* Chicago: American Library Association, 1961.

6.46 Danton, J. P. *Book Selection and Collections: A Comparison of German and American*

University Libraries. New York: Columbia University Press, 1963.

6.47 Jones, H. D. *The Development of Reference Services in Colleges for Teacher Education, 1929–1958*. Rochester, N.Y.: Association of College and Research Libraries, 1963, Microcard no. 139.

6.48 Jones, V. H. "The Influence of the American College Fraternity on Chapter House Library Development." Research Paper, Emory University, 1964.

6.49 Smith, J. C. "Patterns of Growth in Library Resources in Certain Land-Grant Universities." Doctoral dissertation, University of Illinois, 1964.

6.50 Almy, P. "Background and Development of the Junior College Library." *LibT* 14 (1965): 123–31.

6.51 Liu, N. "A History of the New England Deposit Library (1942–1962)." Master's thesis, Long Island University, 1966.

6.52 Rouse, R. "The Libraries of Nineteenth-Century College Societies." In *Books in America's Past: Essays Honoring Rudolph H. Gjelsness*, edited by D. Kaser. Charlottesville: University Press of Virginia, 1966. Pp. 26–42.

6.53 Clayton, H. "The American College Library: 1800–1860." *JLH* 3 (1968): 129–37.

6.54 Houze, R. A. "CORAL: San Antonio's Success Story in Library Cooperation." *TLJ* 44 (1968): 151–52, 185–88.

6.55 Back, H. "The Snows of Yesteryear." *CRL* 30 (1969): 301–06.

6.56 Stevens, N. D. "Three Early Academic Library Surveys." *CRL* 30 (1969): 498–505.

6.57 Braden, I. A. *The Undergraduate Library.* Chicago: American Library Association, 1970.

6.58 Downs, R. B. "Status of Academic Librarians in Retrospect." In *A Case for Faculty Status for Academic Librarians*, edited by L. C. Branscomb. Chicago: American Library Association, 1970. Pp. 111–18.

6.59 Kansfield, N. J. "The Origins of Protestant Theological Seminary Libraries in the United States." Master's thesis, University of Chicago, 1970.

6.60 Harding, T. S. *College Literary Societies: Their Contribution to Higher Education in the United States, 1815–1876*. Brooklyn: Pageant-Poseidon, 1971.

6.61 Harwell, R. "College Libraries." *ELIS* 5 (1971): 269–81.

6.62 Miller, L. A. "Changing Patterns of Circulation Services in University Libraries." Doctoral dissertation, Florida State University, 1971.

6.63 Nelson, C. A. "University and Public Libraries." In *Portraits of the American University 1890–1910,* compiled by J. C. Stone et al. San Francisco: Jossey-Bass, 1971. Pp. 346–56.

1972–1986

6.64 Massman, V. F. *Faculty Status for Librarians.* Metuchen, N.J.: Scarecrow Press, 1972.

6.65 Moore, J. "Bibliographic Control of American Doctoral Dissertations: A History." *SL* 63 (1972): 227–30.

6.66 Rothstein, S. "From Reaction to Interaction: The Development of the North American University Library." *Canadian Library Journal* 29 (1972): 111–15.

6.67 Kraus, J. W. "The Book Collections of Early American College Libraries." *LQ* 43 (1973): 142–59.

6.68 Radford, N. A. "Academic Library Surveys Prior to 1930." *JLH* 8 (1973): 150–58.

6.69 Bryant, D. W. "The Changing Research Library." *HLB* 22 (1974): 365–73.

6.70 Johnson, E. R. "The Development of the Subject-Divisional Plan in American University Libraries." Doctoral dissertation, University of Wisconsin, 1974.

6.71 Stanford, E. B. "Federal Aid for Academic Library Construction." *LJ* 99 (1974): 112–15.

6.72 Yueh, N. N. "The Development of Library Collections at Former State Teacher Education Institutions: 1920–1970, with Special Consideration of Six New Jersey State Colleges." Doctoral dissertation, Columbia University, 1974.

6.73 Gossage, W. "The American Library College Movement to 1968: The Library as Curriculum and Teaching with Books." *Education Libraries Bulletin* 18 (1975): 1–21.

6.74 Kaplan, L. "The Midwest Inter-Library Center, 1949–1964." *JLH* 10 (1975): 291–310.

6.75 Kindlin, J., and Engle, J. "Library School Libraries." *ELIS* 16 (1975): 1–22.

6.76 Lemke, D. H. "Origins, Structures and Activities of Five Academic Library Consortia." Doctoral dissertation, Indiana University, 1975.

6.77 Powell, B. E. "Collection Development in Southeastern Libraries since 1948." *SEL* 24 (Winter 1975): 59–67.

6.78 Schorr, A. E. "Library-College and Its Critics since 1965: A Bibliographic Essay." *PNLAQ* 40 (1975): 4–11.

6.79 Shores, L. "Library-College: Prototype for a Universal Higher Education." *ELIS* 14 (1975): 464–84.

6.80 Skelley, G. T. "Characteristics of Collections Added to American Research Libraries, 1940–1970: A Preliminary Investigation." *CRL* 36 (1975): 52–60.

6.81 Terwilliger, G. H. P. "The Library-College; A Movement for Experimental and Innovative Learning Concepts; Applications and Implications for Higher Education." Doctoral dissertation, University of Maryland, 1975.

6.82 Bradley, C. J. "Music Libraries in the United States." *ELIS* 18 (1976): 358–62.

6.83 Downs, R. B. "The Growth of Research Collections." *LibT* 25 (1976): 55–80.

6.84 Downs, R. B. "The Role of the Academic Librarian, 1876–1976." *CRL* 37 (1976): 491–502.

6.85 Dunlap, C. R. "Organizational Patterns in Academic Libraries, 1876–1976." *CRL* 37 (1976): 395–407.

6.86 Edelman, H., and Tatum, G. M. "The Development of Collections in American University Libraries." *CRL* 37 (1976): 222–45.

6.87 Flanagan, C. C. "Sound Recordings, Private Collectors, and Academic Research Libraries." Doctoral dissertation, University of Illinois, 1976.

6.88 Holley, E. G. "Academic Libraries in 1876." *CRL* 37 (1976): 15–47.

6.89 Kaser, D. "A Century of Academic Librarianship as Reflected in the Literature." *CRL* 37 (1976): 110–27.

6.90 Leach, S. "The Growth Rates of Major Academic Libraries: Rider and Purdue Reviewed." *CRL* 37 (1976): 531–42.

6.91 McElderry, S. "Readers and Resources: Public Services in Academic and Research Libraries, 1876–1976." *CRL* 37 (1976): 408–20.

6.92 Orne, J. "Academic Library Buildings: A Century in Review." *CRL* 37 (1976): 316–31.

6.93 Tuttle, H. W. "From Cutter to Computer: Technical Services in Academic and Research Libraries, 1876–1976." *CRL* 37 (1976): 421–51.

6.94 Veit, F. "Library Service to College Students." *LibT* 25 (1976): 361–78.

6.95 Wallace, J. O. "Newcomer to the Academic Scene: The Two-Year College Library/Learning Center." *CRL* 37 (1976): 503–13.

6.96 Weber, D. C. "A Century of Cooperative Programs Among Academic Librarians." *CRL* 37 (1976): 205–21.

6.97 Hintz, C. W. "Oregon State System of Higher Education." *ELIS* 21 (1977): 1–6.

6.98 Holley, E. G. *The Land-Grant Movement and the Development of Academic Libraries: Some Tentative Explorations*, Texas A&M University Libraries Miscellaneous Publication, 15. College Station: Texas A&M University Libraries, 1977.

6.99 Johnson, E. R. "Subject-Divisional Organization in American University Libraries, 1939–1974." *LQ* 47 (1977): 23–42.

6.100 Johnson, R. D., ed. *Libraries for Teaching, Libraries for Research: Essays for a Century.* Chicago: American Library Association, 1977.

6.101 Simpson, L. "The Development and Scope of Undergraduate Literary Society Libraries at Columbia, Dartmouth, Princeton, and Yale, 1783–1830." *JLH* 12 (1977): 209–21.

6.102 Smith, J. C. *Black Academic Libraries and Research Collections: An Historical Survey.* Westport, Conn.: Greenwood Press, 1977.

6.103 Smith-Burnett, G. C. K. "The Development of the College Library." In *The College Library: A Collection of Essays*, edited by G. Jefferson and G. C. K. Smith-Burnett. Hamden, Conn.: Linnet Books, 1978. Pp. 17–59.

6.104 Childress, B. "Library History and College Catalogs." *SEL* 29 (1979): 210–17.

6.105 Hadidian, D. Y. "Seminary Libraries." *ELIS* 27 (1979): 215–41.

6.106 Hamlin, A. T. "A Backward Glance into the Future of University Library Support." In *New Horizons for Academic Libraries: Papers Presented at the First National Conference of the Association of College and Research Libraries, Boston, Massachusetts, November 8–11, 1978*, edited by R. D. Stueart and R. D. Johnson. New York: K.G. Saur, 1979. Pp. 324–29.

6.107 Hardin, W. "An Analysis of the Growth Patterns in Select Black Land-Grant Colleges and Universities: Five Case Studies." Doctoral dissertation, Simmons College, 1979.

6.108 Osburn, C. B. *Academic Research and Library Resources: Changing Patterns in America.* Westport, Conn.: Greenwood Press, 1979.

6.109 Tucker, J. M. "The Origins of Bibliographic Instruction in Academic Libraries, 1876–1914." In *New Horizons for Academic Libraries: Papers Presented at the First National Conference of the Association of College and Research Libraries, Boston, Massachusetts, November 8–11, 1978*, edited by R. D. Stueart and R. D. Johnson. New York: K.G. Saur, 1979. Pp. 268–76.

6.110 Kaser, D. "Collection Building in American Universities." In *University Library History: An International Review*, edited by J. Thompson. New York: K.G. Saur, 1980. Pp. 33–55.

6.111 Orne, J. "The Evolution of the Academic Library Staff in the United States." In *University Library History: An International Review*, edited by J. Thompson. New York: K.G. Saur, 1980. Pp. 77–91.

6.112 Smith, R. S. "The History of Academic Library Buildings." In *University Library History: An International Review*, edited by J. Thompson. New York: K.G. Saur, 1980. Pp. 128–46.

6.113 Thompson, J., ed. *University Library History: An International Review.* New York: K.G. Saur, 1980.

6.114 Tucker, J. M. *Articles on Library Instruction in Colleges and Universities, 1876–1932.* Urbana: University of Illinois Graduate School of Library Science, Occasional Paper no. 143, 1980.

6.115 Tucker, J. M. "User Education in Academic Libraries: A Century in Retrospect." *LibT* 29 (1980): 9–27.

6.116 Hamlin, A. T. *The University Library in the United States.* Philadelphia: University of Pennsylvania Press, 1981.

6.117 Hopkins, F. L. "User Instruction in the College Library: Origins, Prospects, and a Practical Program." In *College Librarianship*, edited by W. Miller and D. S. Rockwood. Metuchen, N.J.: Scarecrow Press, 1981. Pp. 173–204.

6.118 Kansfield, N. J. " 'Study the Most Approved Authors': The Role of the Seminary Library in Nineteenth-Century American Protestant Ministerial Education." Doctoral dissertation, University of Chicago, 1981.

6.119 Rebman, E. H. "Undergraduate Libraries." *ELIS* 31 (1981): 329–41.

6.120 Schad, J. G. "The Evolution of College and University Standards." In *Libraries and Accreditation in Institutions of Higher Education*. Chicago: Association of College and Research Libraries, 1981. Pp. 9–17.

6.121 Shiflett, O. L. *Origins of American Academic Librarianship*. Norwood, N.J.: Ablex Publishing Corp., 1981.

6.122 Cline, G. S. "*College and Research Libraries*: Its First Forty Years." *CRL* 43 (1982): 208–32.

6.123 Hernon, P. "Instruction in the Use of Academic Libraries: A Preliminary Study of the Early Years as Based on Selective Extant Materials." *JLH* 17 (1982): 16–38.

6.124 Hopkins, F. L. "A Century of Bibliographic Instruction: The Historical Claim to Professional and Academic Legitimacy." *CRL* 43 (1982): 192–98.

6.125 Reboul, J. *Les cathèdrales du savoir ou les bibliothèques universitaires de recherche aux Etats-Unis*. Paris: Publications de la Sorbonne, 1982.

6.126 Stueart, R. D., ed. *Academic Librarianship: Yesterday, Today and Tomorrow*. New York: Neal-Schuman, 1982.

6.127 Wells, M. B. "Requirements and Benefits for Academic Librarians: 1959–1979." *CRL* 43 (1982): 450–58.

6.128 Danton, J. P. "University Library Book Budgets—1860, 1910, and 1960: Introduction to an Inquiry." *LQ* 53 (1983): 384–93.

6.129 Thompson, L. S. *The University Libraries and the Antiquarian Book Trade: Fragments of Library History*. Lexington: University of Kentucky Libraries, Occasional Paper no. 4, 1983.

6.130 Ward, J. E. "Trends in the Growth of Bibliographic Instruction in Twentieth Century American Academic Libraries." In *Reference Services and Library Education: Essays in Honor of Frances Neel Cheney*, edited by E. S. Gleaves and J. M. Tucker. Lexington, Mass.: Lexington Books, 1983. Pp. 75–94.

6.131 Wiegand, W. A., ed. *Leaders in American Academic Librarianship, 1925–1975*. Pittsburgh: Beta Phi Mu, 1983.

6.132 Caldwell, J. "Perceptions of the Academic Library: Midwestern College Libraries as They Have Been Depicted in College Histories." In *Academic Libraries: Myths and Realities: Proceedings of the Third National Conference of the Association of College and Research Libraries*, edited by S. C. Dodson and G. L. Menges. Chicago: American Library Association, 1984. Pp. 301–07.

6.133 Carr, R. D. "Changing Profiles of University Library Directors, 1966–1981." *CRL* 45 (1984): 282–86.

6.134 Haskell, J. D. "Subject Bibliographers in Academic Libraries: An Historical and Descriptive Overview." *ALAO* 3 (1984): 73–84.

6.135 Kaser, D. "Twenty-Five Years of Academic Library Building Planning." *CRL* 45 (1984): 268–81.

6.136 Miller, R. E. "Development of Reference Services in the American Liberal Arts College, 1876–1976." Doctoral dissertation, University of Minnesota, 1984.

6.137 Radford, N. A. *The Carnegie Corporation and the Development of American College Libraries, 1928–1941*. Chicago: American Library Association, 1984.

6.138 Tucker, J. M. "Emerson's Library Legacy: Concepts of Bibliographic Instruction." In *Increasing the Teaching Role of Academic Libraries*, edited by T. G. Kirk. San Francisco: Jossey-Bass, 1984. Pp. 15–24.

6.139 Jarred, A. D. "Patterns of Growth in Academic Libraries of Four-Year, State-Supported Institutions of Louisiana and South Carolina, 1960–1979: A Comparative Study." Doctoral dissertation, Texas Woman's University, 1985.

6.140 Murray, M. B. "An Evaluative Survey of the Journal Literature on Community/Junior College Libraries and Learning Resources Centers: 1965–1983." Doctoral dissertation, Southern Illinois University, Carbondale, 1985.

6.141 Waldo, M. J. "A Comparative Analysis of Nineteenth-Century Academic and Literary Society Library Collections in the Midwest." Doctoral dissertation, Indiana University, 1985.

6.142 DeVinney, G. "Academic Librarians and Academic Freedom in the United States: A History and Analysis." *Libri* 36 (1986): 24–39.

6.143 Hardesty, L. L., Schmitt, J. P., and Tucker, J. M., comps. *User Instruction in Academic Libraries: A Century of Selected Readings.* Metuchen, N.J.: Scarecrow Press, 1986.

6.144 Hubbard, T. E., ed. *Research Libraries: The Past 25 Years, the Next 25 Years: Papers for a Festschrift Honoring L.W. Anderson, Director of Libraries, Colorado State University.* Boulder: Colorado Associated University Press, 1986.

6.145 Kaser, D. "The American Academic Library Building, 1870–1890." *JLH* 21 (1986): 60–71.

6.146 Molyneux, R. E., and Gerould, J. T. *The Gerould Statistics, 1907/08–1961/62.* Washington, D.C.: Association of Research Libraries, 1986.

Special Studies Arranged by State

Alabama

6.147 Sellers, J. B. "The Library." In *History of the University of Alabama*, vol. 1, 1818–1902.

University, Ala.: University of Alabama Press, 1953. Pp. 404–15.

6.148 King, A. G. "The Tuskegee Institute Libraries." *ELIS* 38 (1985): 391–97.

Alaska

6.149 Sandler, M. "Workers Must Read: The Commonwealth College Library, 1925–1940." *JLH* 20 (1985): 46–69.

Arizona

6.150 Heisser, W. A. "A Historical Survey of the Phoenix College Library: Phoenix, Arizona, 1925–1957." Master's thesis, Arizona State College, 1958.

Arkansas

6.151 Reynolds, J. H., and Thomas, D. Y. "The Library, Museum, and Laboratories." In *History of the University of Arkansas.* Fayetteville, Ark.: University of Arkansas, 1910. Pp. 313–22.

6.152 Vaulx, J. R. "The Library." In *University of Arkansas 1871–1948*, by H. Hale. Fayetteville, Ark.: University of Arkansas Alumni Association, 1948. Pp. 206–10.

California

6.153 Rowell, J. C. "Red Letter Annals of the Library." *California University Chronicle* 14 (1912): 341–50.

6.154 Smith, D. "History of the University of California Library to 1900." Master's thesis, University of California, 1930, ACRL Microcard no. 21.

6.155 Elliott, O. L. "The Library." In *Stanford University: The First Twenty-Five Years.* Stanford: Stanford University Press, 1937. Pp. 127–32.

6.156 Coulter, E. M. "Collecting Californiana at the University of California." *CLB* 11 (1950): 149, 181.

6.157   Powell, L. C. "From Private Collection to Public Institution: the William Andrews Clark Memorial Library." *LQ* 20 (1950): 101–08.

6.158   Laudine, M. "The Honnold Library of Claremont College: Its History and Services, 1952–1961." Master's thesis, Immaculate Heart College, 1961.

6.159   Coney, D., and Michel, J. G. "The Berkeley Library of the University of California: Some Notes on Its Formation." *LibT* 15 (1966): 286–302.

6.160   Hansen, R. W. "The Library That Never Was [Stanford University]." *CalL* 27 (1966): 164a–d.

6.161   Halmos, D. M. "The Building of a Library." *Coranto: Journal of the Friends of Libraries of the University of Southern California* 5 (1967): 3–12; 5 (1968): 27–33; 6 (1969): 13–18.

6.162   Brundin, R. E. "Changing Patterns of Library Service in Five California Junior Colleges, 1907–1967." Doctoral dissertation, Stanford University, 1970.

6.163   Peterson, K. G. *The University of California Library at Berkeley, 1900–1945.* Berkeley: University of California Press, 1970.

6.164   Voigt, M. J. "California. University of California Libraries." *ELIS* 3 (1970): 659–68.

6.165   Hansen, R. W. "The Stanford University Library: Genesis 1891–1906." *JLH* 9 (1974): 138–58.

6.166   Paul, G. N. "The Development of the Hoover Institution on War, Revolution and Peace Library, 1919–1944." Doctoral dissertation, University of California, 1974.

6.167   Lyon, E. W. "A Central Library Building." In *The History of Pomona College, 1887–1969.* Claremont, Calif.: Pomona College, 1977. Pp. 441–46.

6.168   Reynolds, F. E. "Albert Bender and the Mills College Library." *CalL* 38 (1977): 6–16.

6.169   Hansen, R. W. "Stanford University Libraries." *ELIS* 29 (1980): 1–32.

6.170   Peterson, K. G. "Joseph C. Rowell and California's Bacon Library." *JLH* 17 (1982): 278–90.

6.171   McClung, P. "Still Growing Strong: UCLA Library." *WLB* 57 (1983): 822–27.

Colorado

6.172   Wilson, E. H. "A Century with Friends of the [University of Colorado] Libraries." *Occasional Notes* 16 (1976): 1–8.

Connecticut

6.173   "Yale College Library." *NLGPC* 2 (15 October 1852): 187.

6.174   Gilman, D. C. "The Library of Yale College." *University Quarterly: Conducted by an Association of Collegiate and Professional Students, in the U.S. and Europe* 2 (October 1860): 244–61.

6.175   Gilman, D. C. "Bishop Berkeley's Gifts to Yale College [1733]." *Papers of the New Haven Colony Historical Society* 1 (1865): 147–70.

6.176   Bassett, J. S. "The Trinity College Library." *Trinity Archive* 16 (1905): 273–79.

6.177   Keogh, A. "Bishop Berkeley's Gift of Books in 1733." *YULG* 8 (1933): 1–26.

6.178   Bryant, L. M., and Patterson, M., comps. "The List of Books Sent by Jeremiah Dummer." In *Papers in Honor of Andrew Keogh, Librarian of Yale University*, edited by M. C. Withington. New Haven, Conn.: Privately printed, 1938. Pp. 423–92.

6.179   Powers, Z. J. "A Yale Bibliophile in European Book Shops." In *Papers in Honor of Andrew Keogh, Librarian of Yale University*, edited by M. C. Withington. New Haven, Conn.: Privately printed, 1938. Pp. 373–422.

6.180   Pratt, A. S. "The Books Sent from England by Jeremiah Dummer to Yale College." In *Papers in Honor of Andrew Keogh, Librarian of Yale University*, edited by M. C.

Withington. New Haven, Conn.: Privately printed, 1938. Pp. 7–44.

6.181 Pratt, A. S. *Isaac Watts and His Gift of Books to Yale College*, Yale University Library Miscellanies, II. New Haven: Yale University Library, 1938.

6.182 Troxell, G. M. "Bookplates of the Yale Libraries, 1780–1846." In *Papers in Honor of Andrew Keogh, Librarian of Yale University*, edited by M. C. Withington. New Haven, Conn.: Privately printed, 1938. Pp. 145–56.

6.183 Wing, D. G., and Johnson, M. L. "The Books Given by Elihu Yale in 1718." *YULG* 13 (1939): 46–47.

6.184 Pratt, A. S., and Keogh, A. "The Yale Library of 1742." *YULG* 15 (1940): 29–40.

6.185 Rider, F. "The Growth of American College and University Libraries . . . and Wesleyan's." *About Books* 11 (September 1940): 1–11.

6.186 Bontemps, A. "The James Weldon Johnson Memorial Collection of Negro Arts and Letters." *YULG* 18 (1943): 19–26.

6.187 Fuller, H. M. "Bishop Berkeley as a Benefactor of Yale." *YULG* 28 (1953): 1–18.

6.188 Stephens, F. J. "History of the Babylonian Collection." *YULG* 36 (1962): 126–32.

6.189 Colla, M. B. "A History of the Pope Pius XII Library, St. Joseph College, West Hartford, Connecticut, 1932–1962." Master's thesis, Catholic University of America, 1964.

6.190 Clarke, M. G. M. *David Watkinson's Library: One Hundred Years in Hartford, Connecticut, 1866–1966*. Hartford, Conn.: Trinity College Press, 1966.

6.191 Hegel, R. "Some Libraries of Yale's Old Campus." *Journal of the New Haven Colony Historical Society* 17 (1968): 117–52.

6.192 Kennett, M. E. "Annhurst College Library, South Woodstock, Connecticut, 1941–1967." Master's thesis, Southern Connecticut State College, 1968.

6.193 Kelly, T. A. "The History, Growth, and Development of the Albertus Magnus College Library, New Haven, Connecticut 1925–1970." Master's thesis, Southern Connecticut State College, 1972.

6.194 Lewis, L. L. "The History and Use of the Bookplate in College Libraries in Connecticut." Master's thesis, Southern Connecticut State College, 1972.

6.195 Straka, K. M. U. "The Linonian Society Library of Yale College: The First Years (1768–1790)." *YULG* 54 (1980): 183–92.

6.196 Taylor, M. E. "The Yale University Library 1701–1978: Its History, Collections, and Present Organization." *ELIS* 33 (1982): 265–365.

6.197 O'Connor, T. F. "The Yale University Library, 1865–1931." Doctoral dissertation, Columbia University, 1984.

6.198 Gallup, D. "The Ezra Pound Archives at Yale." *YULG* 60 (1986): 161–77.

6.199 Parks, S., comp. *The Elizabethan Club of Yale University and Its Library*. New Haven: Yale University Press, 1986.

Delaware

6.200 Able, A. H., and Lewis, W. D. "The Library Story (1833–1953) [Newark College]." *Delaware Notes* 26 (1953): 77–91.

6.201 "Colleges and Universities." *DLAB* 20 (Spring 1966): 49–50.

6.202 Bauersfeld, S. H. "The Growth and Development of the University of Delaware Library, Newark, Delaware, 1833–1965." Master's thesis, Catholic University of America, 1967.

6.203 Dawson, J. M. "Delaware. University of Delaware Library." *ELIS* 6 (1971): 546–47.

District of Columbia

6.204 Beach, F. M. "A History of the Library of Trinity College, Washington, D.C."

Master's thesis, Catholic University of America, 1951, ACRL Microcard no. 41.

6.205 Duncan, A. M. "History of Howard University Library, 1867–1929." Master's thesis, Catholic University of America, 1951, ACRL Microcard no. 42.

6.206 Reason, J. H. "The Howard University Libraries (1867–1953)." *DCL* 24 (1953): 8–12.

6.207 Terrell, D. "History of the Dumbarton Oaks Research Library of Harvard University, 1940–1950." Master's thesis, Catholic University of America, 1954.

6.208 Pendell, L. "Gallaudet College Library [since 1876]." *DCL* 28 (1957): 4–8.

6.209 Chamberlain, L. C. "Georgetown University Library, 1789–1937." Master's thesis, Catholic University of America, 1962.

6.210 Kortendick, J. J. *The Library in the Catholic Theological Seminary in the United States.* Washington, D.C.: Catholic University of America Press, 1963.

6.211 Conmy, P. T. "Bishop Turner and Joseph Schneider and the Development of Catholic University's Library." *CLW* 56 (1984): 164–67.

Florida

6.212 Shaw, B. "University of Florida's Chinsegut Hill Library." *LJ* 81 (1956): 1118–20.

6.213 Adams, K. B. "The Growth and Development of the University of Florida Libraries, 1940–1958." Master's thesis, Catholic University of America, 1959.

6.214 Hansen, A. M. "Rollins College Library." In *In Pursuit of Library History*, edited by J. D. Marshall. Tallahassee: Florida State University School of Library Science, 1961. Pp. 63–64.

6.215 Smith, C. A. "Stetson University Library." In *In Pursuit of Library History*, edited by J. D. Marshall. Tallahassee: Florida

State University School of Library Science, 1961. P. 65.

6.216 Husselbee, M. V. "History of the University of Miami Libraries, 1928–1960." Master's thesis, University of North Carolina, 1962.

6.217 Quinn, C. "A History of the St. Vincent DePaul Seminary Library, Boynton Beach, Florida." Research Paper, Long Island University, 1971.

6.218 Axford, H. W. "Florida Atlantic University Library." *ELIS* 8 (1972): 545–57.

Georgia

6.219 Satterfield, V. "The History of College Libraries in Georgia as Interpreted from the Study of Seven Selected Libraries." Master's thesis, Columbia University, 1936.

6.220 Satterfield, V. "College Libraries in Georgia." *Georgia Historical Quarterly* 25 (1941): 16–38.

6.221 LaBoone, E. "A History of the University of Georgia Library." Master's thesis, University of Georgia, 1954.

6.222 "The Ilah Dunlap Little Library." In *The University of Georgia under Sixteen Administrations 1785–1955.* Athens: University of Georgia Press, 1956. Pp. 215–17.

6.223 English, T. H. "The Libraries." In *Emory University 1915–1965: A Semicentennial History.* Atlanta: Emory University, 1966. Pp. 185–93.

6.224 English, T. H. "Emory University Library." *ELIS* 8 (1972): 34–43.

6.225 Fennell, J. C. "Libraries Are Not Made, They Grow: An Historical Perspective on the Georgia College Library." *GL* 22 (1985): 62–64.

6.226 Price, J., Kinman, V., and Vidor, A. "A History of the Georgia Tech Library." *GL* 23 (1986): 98–102.

Hawaii

6.227 Kittelson, D. "University of Hawaii Library, 1920–1941." *HLAJ* 30 (1973): 16–26.

6.228 West, S. "Hawaii. University of Hawaii Libraries." *ELIS* 10 (1973): 385–90.

6.229 Kittelson, D. "The University of Hawaii Library, 1941–1961." *HLAJ* 40 (1983): 53–65.

6.230 Kittelson, D. "The University of Hawaii Library, 1960–1983." *HLAJ* 41 (1984): 59–70.

Illinois

6.231 Willcox, L. B. E. "History and Description of the Theological Seminary Libraries of Chicago and Vicinity." Research Paper, University of Illinois, 1900.

6.232 Ambrose, L. "The Library." In *Northwestern University, A History: 1855–1905*, by A. H. Wilde. New York: University Publishing Society, 1905. Pp. 191–215.

6.233 James, E. J. "Libraries and Museums." In *Sixteen Years at the University of Illinois*. Urbana: University of Illinois Press, 1920. Pp. 100–127.

6.234 Sexton, M. M. "The Cavagna Library at the University of Illinois." *PBSA* 19 (1925): 66–72.

6.235 Wilcox, L. E. "History of the University of Illinois Library, 1868–1897." Master's thesis, University of Illinois, 1931.

6.236 Dorf, A. T. "The University of Chicago Libraries [and J.C.M. Hanson]: A Historical Note." *LQ* 4 (1934): 185–97.

6.237 Ratcliffe, T. E. "Development of the Buildings, Policy, Collections of the University of Illinois Library in Urbana, 1895–1940." Master's thesis, University of Illinois, 1949.

6.238 Maxfield, D. K., ed. "College and University Libraries in Illinois." *IllL* 33 (1951): 175–79, 208–10, 264–67, 373–75, 418–21, 462–64.

6.239 McMullen, C.H. "Administration of the University of Chicago Libraries, 1892–1928." *LQ* 22 (1952): 325–34; 23 (1953): 23–32.

6.240 Archer, H. R. "Some Aspects of the Acquisition Program at the University of Chicago: 1892–1928." Doctoral dissertation, University of Chicago, 1954.

6.241 Yenawine, W. S. "The Influence of Scholars on Research Library Development at the University of Illinois." Doctoral dissertation, University of Illinois, 1955.

6.242 Jackson, W. *The Development of Library Resources at Northwestern University [1920–49]*. Urbana: University of Illinois Graduate School of Library Science, Occasional Paper no. 26, 1957.

6.243 Johnson, E. C. "A History of the Theological Book Collection in the Library of Augustana College and Theological Seminary." Master's thesis, University of Chicago, 1957.

6.244 Plochmann, G. K. "The University Libraries." In *The Ordeal of Southern Illinois University*. Carbondale, Ill.: SouthernIllinois University Press, 1959. Pp. 198–203.

6.245 Heckman, M. L. "A History of the Library of Bethany Biblical Seminary, Chicago, Illinois." Master's thesis, University of Chicago, 1963.

6.246 Clancy, M. M. "An Historical Survey of the Rosary College Library." Master's thesis, Rosary College, 1964.

6.247 Lundean, J. W. "History of the Library of the Chicago Lutheran Theological Seminary of Maywood, Illinois." Master's thesis, University of Chicago, 1967.

6.248 Miller, A. H. "The Harriet Monroe Modern Poetry Library: Origins and Growth to 1960." Master's thesis, University of Chicago, 1968.

6.249 Malik, A. "A History of the Center for Research Libraries (1949–1965)." Research Paper, Long Island University, 1969.

6.250 Gwynn, S. E. "University of Chicago Library." *ELIS* 4 (1970): 542–59.

6.251 White, L. C. "Illinois. University of Illinois Library." *ELIS* 11 (1974): 183–96.

6.252 Erickson, R. H. "Northwestern University Libraries." *ELIS* 20 (1977): 200–242.

6.253 McGregor, J. W. "Northeastern Illinois University Library." *ELIS* 20 (1977): 192–93.

6.254 Smith, L. K. "Northern Illinois University Libraries." *ELIS* 20 (1977): 193–96.

Indiana

6.255 "The Lemonnier Library." In *A Brief History of the University of Notre Dame du Lac Indiana from 1842 to 1892*. Chicago: Werner, 1895. Pp. 199–201.

6.256 Lind, L. R. "Early Literary Societies at Wabash College." *IMH* 42 (1946): 173–76.

6.257 Stanley, E. L. "The Earlham College Library: A History of Its Relation to the College, 1847–1947." Master's thesis, University of Illinois, 1947.

6.258 Springer, N. P. "The Mennonite Historical Library at Goshen College." *Mennonite Quarterly Review* 25 (1951): 296–319.

6.259 Alexander, W. A. "The Indiana University Library." In *History of Indiana University, 1902–1937, The Bryan Administration*, vol. 2, edited by B. D. Meyers. Bloomington: Indiana University, 1952. Pp. 597–611.

6.260 *The Roy O. West Library, Dedicated October 20, 1956*. Greencastle, Ind.: DePauw University, 1956.

6.261 Lowell, M. H. "Indiana University Libraries, 1829–1942." *CRL* 22 (1961): 423–29, 462–64.

6.262 Manhart, G. M. "The Library." In *DePauw through the Years*. Greencastle, Ind.: DePauw University, 1962. Pp. 451–53.

6.263 Boardman, N. S. "Indiana University Libraries." *ELIS* 11 (1974): 474–76.

6.264 Miller, R. C. "Notre Dame. University of Notre Dame Libraries." *ELIS* 36 (1983): 385–95.

Iowa

6.265 Throne, M. "The History of the State University of Iowa: The University Libraries." Master's thesis, University of Iowa, 1943.

6.266 Friley, C. E., and Orr, R. W. "A Decade of Book Storage at Iowa State College." *CRL* 12 (1951): 7–19.

6.267 Fullerton, M. G. "The Library." In *Grinnell College*, by J. S. Nollen. Iowa City, Iowa: State Historical Society of Iowa, 1953. Pp. 184–89.

6.268 Slavens, T. P. "A History of the Drake University Libraries." Master's thesis, University of Minnesota, 1962.

6.269 Monson, M. "The Library Fire of 1897." *Palimpsest* 61 (1980): 118–23.

Kansas

6.270 Watson, C. M. "History of the Library." In *Quarter-Centennial History of the University of Kansas 1866–1891*, edited by W. Sterling. Topeka, Kans.: George W. Crane, 1891. Pp. 103–28.

6.271 Stephens, H. H. "A Study of the Growth and Development of the Library of Kansas State Teachers College, Emporia, 1875–1930." Master's thesis, Kansas State Teachers College, 1935.

6.272 Kansas State Teachers College. Emporia. *A Memorial to a Great American [William Allen White Library]*. Emporia, Kans.: [1952?].

6.273 Williams, M. G. "The William Allen White Memorial Library of Kansas State Teachers College, Emporia, 1930–1959." Master's thesis, Kansas State Teachers College, 1959.

6.274 Heron, D. W. "Kansas. University of Kansas Libraries." *ELIS* 13 (1975): 402–07.

Kentucky

6.275 Scott, E. "The History and Influence of the Old Library of Transylvania University." Master's thesis, University of Kentucky, 1929.

6.276 Transylvania University. *The Transylvania Library.* Lexington, Ky.: The University, 1948.

6.277 Bull, J. "The Samuel M. Wilson Library." *Register of the Kentucky State Historical Society* 47 (1949): 52–54.

6.278 Thompson, L. W. "Books at the University of Kentucky." *Filson Club History Quarterly* 24 (1950): 58–65.

6.279 Bruner, J. E. "The History of the University of Louisville Libraries." Master's thesis, University of North Carolina, 1953, ACRL Microcard no. 60.

6.280 McMullen, H. "College Libraries in Ante-Bellum Kentucky." *Register of the Kentucky State Historical Society* 60 (1962): 106–33.

6.281 Stevenson, D. E. "Front and Center— The Library." In *Lexington Theological Seminary, 1865–1965.* St. Louis: Bethany Press, 1964. Pp. 306–14.

6.282 Forth, S. "Kentucky. University of Kentucky Libraries." *ELIS* 13 (1975): 430–32.

6.283 Brown, M. R. "Kentucky. University of Kentucky Libraries." *ELIS* 37 (1984): 186–95.

Louisiana

6.284 Knighten, L. "A History of the Library of Southwestern Louisiana Institute, 1900–1948." Master's thesis, Columbia University, 1949.

6.285 Green, C. W. "History of the Louisiana State University Libraries [1860–1952]." *LLAB* 15 (1952): 110–15.

6.286 Greenwood, R. W. "The Tulane University Library: An Informal History." *ELIS* 31 (1981): 152–204.

Maine

6.287 Fernald, M. C., and Jones, R. K. "The Library." In *History of the Maine State College and the University of Maine.* Orono, Maine: University of Maine, 1916. Pp. 226–43.

6.288 Herrick, M. D., and Rush, N. O. "Early Literary Societies and Their Libraries in Colby College, 1824–78." *CRL* 6 (1944): 58–63.

6.289 Rush, N. O. *The History of College Libraries in Maine.* Worcester, Mass.: Clark University Library, 1946.

6.290 Michener, R. "The Bowdoin College Library: From Its Beginning to the Present Day." Master's thesis, University of Chicago, 1972.

6.291 Michener, R. "Rivals and Partners: Early Literary Societies at Bowdoin College." *JLH* 10 (1975): 214–30.

Maryland

6.292 Falley, E. W. "Goucher College Library, 1919–1929." *Goucher Alumnae Quarterly* 7 (1929): 30–34.

6.293 Barnes, G. "Our Library History." *Maryland Alumni News* 8, no. 8 (1937): 7.

6.294 Brisco, R. "A History of the Library of the University of Maryland, 1813–1938." *University of Maryland School of Medicine Bulletin* 23 (1938): 44–57.

6.295 French, J. C. "The University's Libraries." In *A History of the University Founded by Johns Hopkins.* Baltimore: Johns Hopkins Press, 1946. Pp. 206–18.

6.296 Goodwillie, M. C. "The Friends of the Library, 1931–1949." *Johns Hopkins Alumni Magazine* 37 (1949): 126–29.

6.297 "Age of Discovery." *Johns Hopkins Alumni Magazine* 2 (1950): 17–23.

6.298 Kirby, M. B. "A History of the Goucher College Library, Baltimore, Maryland, 1885–1949." Master's thesis, Catholic University of America, 1952, ACRL Microcard no. 26.

6.299 Klein, S. J. "The History and Present Status of the Library of St. John's College, Annapolis." Master's thesis, Catholic University of America, 1952.

6.300 Ownings, V. B. "A History of the Library of Morgan State College from 1867 to 1939." Master's thesis, Catholic University of America, 1952.

6.301 Hoff, A. "A History of the Library of Western Maryland College." Master's thesis, Drexel Institute of Technology, 1954.

6.302 Roddy, R. "A History of Saint Joseph College Library, 1902–1955." Master's thesis, Catholic University of America, 1956.

6.303 Greer, J. J. "A History of the Library of Woodstock College of Baltimore County, Maryland, from 1869 to 1957." Master's thesis, Drexel Institute of Technology, 1957.

6.304 Nichols, M. E. "Historical Survey of the Library of the College of Notre Dame of Maryland." Master's thesis, Catholic University of America, 1957.

6.305 Hawkins, H. "Books Ordered by the Trustees in 1874." In *Pioneer: A History of the Johns Hopkins University, 1874–1889*. Ithaca: Cornell University Press, 1960. Pp. 329–31.

6.306 Dutrow, K. E., ed. "Histories of the College Libraries in Maryland." *Maryland Libraries* 27 (1961): 4–16.

6.307 Griswold, A. M. "A History of the Columbia Union College Library, Takoma Park, Maryland, 1904–1954." Master's thesis, Catholic University of America, 1964.

6.308 Williams, R. V. "George Whitefield's Bethesda: The Orphanage, the College and the Library." In *Library History Seminar No. 3, Proceedings, 1968*, edited by M. J. Zachert. Tallahassee: JLH, 1968. Pp. 47–72.

6.309 Brown, A. W. "The Phoenix: A History of the St. John's College Library." *MHM* 65 (1970): 413–29.

6.310 Rovelstad, H. "Maryland. University of Maryland Libraries." *ELIS* 17 (1976): 205–24.

6.311 Reid, M. T. "Exchange History as Found in the Johns Hopkins University Library Correspondence." *Library Acquisitions: Practice and Theory* 8 (1984): 99–103.

Massachusetts

6.312 "Harvard College." *NLGPC* 2 (15 June 1852): 107.

6.313 "Williams College Library." *NLGPC* 3 (15 March 1853): 37.

6.314 Cutter, C. A. "Harvard College Library." *North American Review* 107 (1868): 568–93.

6.315 Winthrop, R. C. "Reminiscences of a Night Passed in the Library of Harvard College." *Missouri Historical Society Publications* 2 ser., 3 (1886–87): 216–18.

6.316 Bolton, C. K. "Harvard University Library: A Sketch of Its History and Its Benefactors." *NEM* 9 (1892): 433–49.

6.317 Lane, W. C. "Justin Winsor's Administration of the Harvard Library, 1877–1897." *Harvard Graduate Magazine* 6 (1897): 182–88.

6.318 Potter, A. C., and Bolton, C. K. *The Librarians of Harvard College, 1667–1877*. Cambridge: Library of Harvard University, 1897.

6.319 Wilson, L. N. "The Library." In *Clark University 1889–1899*. Worcester, Mass.: Norwood Press, 1899. Pp. 187–97.

6.320 Gardiner, J. H. "Equipment for Research." In *Harvard*. New York: Oxford University Press, 1914. Pp. 233–55.

6.321 Coolidge, A. C. "The Harvard College Library." *Harvard Graduate Magazine* 24 (1915): 23–31.

6.322 *Gore Hall, the Library of Harvard College, 1838–1913.* Cambridge: Harvard University Press, 1917.

6.323 Lane, W. C. "New Hampshire's Part in Restoring the Library and Apparatus of Harvard College after the Fire of 1764." *PCSM* 25 (1922–24): 24–33.

6.324 Potter, A. C. "The Harvard College Library, 1726–1735." *PCSM* 25 (1922–1924): 1–13.

6.325 Lane, W. C. "The Sojourn of the Harvard Library in Concord, Massachusetts, 1775–1776." In *Essays Offered to Herbert Putnam by His Colleagues and Friends on His Thirtieth Anniversary as Librarian of Congress, 5 April 1929,* edited by W. W. Bishop and A. Keogh. New Haven: Yale University Press, 1929. Pp. 275–87.

6.326 Lane, W. C. "The Harvard College Library, 1877–1928." In *The Development of Harvard University Since the Inauguration of President Eliot, 1869–1929,* edited by S. E. Morison. Cambridge: Harvard University Press, 1930. Pp. 608–31.

6.327 Seybolt, R. F. "Student Libraries at Harvard, 1763–1764." *PCSM* 28 (1930–33): 449–61.

6.328 Potter, A. C. *Descriptive and Historical Notes on the Library of Harvard University,* 4th ed. Cambridge: Library of Harvard University, 1934.

6.329 Morison, S. E. "'A Prity Library Begune,' 1638–1650." In *The Founding of Harvard College.* Cambridge: Harvard University Press, 1935. Pp. 263–70.

6.330 Morison, S. E. "The College Library, 1655–1723." In *Harvard College in the Seventeenth Century.* Cambridge: Harvard University Press, 1936. Pp. 284–97.

6.331 Roberts, E. D. *A Brief History of the Wellesley College Library.* Wellesley, Mass.: N.p., 1936.

6.332 Goodhue, A. "The Reading of Harvard Students, 1770–1781, as Shown by the Records of the Speaking Club." *HCEI* 63 (1937): 107–29.

6.333 "Harvard College Library, 1638–1938." *HLN* 29 (1939): 207–90.

6.334 Walton, C. E. *The Three-Hundredth Anniversary of the Harvard University Library.* Cambridge: Harvard College Library, 1939.

6.335 Cadbury, H. J. "Harvard College Library and the Libraries of the Mathers." *PAAS* 50 (1940): 20–48.

6.336 Briggs, W. B. "Sundry Observations upon Four Decades of Harvard College Library." *Cambridge Historical Society Publications* 27 (1941): 29–41.

6.337 Grieder, E. M. "The Littauer Center Library: A Few Notes on Its Origins." *HLN* 32 (1942): 97–104.

6.338 Cadbury, H. J. "John Harvard's Library." *PCSM* 34 (1943): 353–77.

6.339 Smith, M. B. "The Founding of the Memorial Hall Library, Andover." *HCEI* 79 (1943): 246–55.

6.340 Engley, D. B. "The Emergence of the Amherst College Library, 1821–1911." Master's thesis, University of Chicago, 1947.

6.341 Lovett, R. W. "The Undergraduate and the Harvard Library, 1877–1937." *HLB* 1 (1947): 221–37.

6.342 Metcalf, K. D. "Spatial Growth in University Libraries." *HLB* 1 (1947): 133–54.

6.343 Metcalf, K. D. "The Undergraduate and the Harvard Library, 1765–1877." *HLB* 1 (1947): 29–51.

6.344 Metcalf, K. D. "The Undergraduate and the Harvard Library, 1937–1947." *HLB* 1 (1947): 288–305.

6.345 Robinson, F. N. "Celtic Books at Harvard: The History of a Departmental Collection." *HLB* 1 (1947): 52–65.

6.346 Jones, F. N. "The Libraries of the Harvard Houses." *HLB* 2 (1948): 362–77.

6.347 Lovett, R. W. "Harvard Union Library, 1901–1948." *HLB* 2 (1948): 230–37.

6.348 Lovett, R. W. "The Hasty Pudding Club Library, 1808–1948." *HLB* 2 (1948): 393–401.

6.349 Metcalf, K. D. "Spatial Growth in the Harvard Library, 1638–1947." *HLB* 2 (1948): 98–115.

6.350 Lovett, R. W. "Pecuniary Mulets and the Harvard Library [1650–1949]." *HLB* 3 (1949): 288–94.

6.351 Shepley, H., and Metcalf, K. D. "The Lamont Library." *HLB* 3 (1949): 5–30.

6.352 Lovett, R. W. "Harvard College and the Supply of Textbooks." *HLB* 4 (1950): 114–22.

6.353 Metcalf, K. D. "Problems of Acquisition Policy in a University Library." *HLB* 4 (1950): 98–115.

6.354 Swan, M. W. S. "Professor Longfellow, Scandinavian Book Buyer." *HLB* 4 (1950): 359–73.

6.355 Cadbury, H. J. "Religious Books at Harvard." *HLB* 5 (1951): 159–80.

6.356 Hoffleit, D. "The [Phillips] Library of the Harvard College Observatory [1845–1950]." *HLB* 5 (1951): 102–11.

6.357 McNiff, P. J. "A Century of College Libraries in Massachusetts." *Massachusetts Library Association Bulletin* 41 (1951): 24–26.

6.358 Metcalf, K. D. "Harvard's Book Collections." *HLB* 5 (1951): 51–62, 209–20.

6.359 Robbins, C. "Library of Liberty—Assembled for Harvard College by Thomas Hollis of Lincoln's Inn." *HLB* 5 (1951): 5–23, 181–96.

6.360 Cook, R. U. "The Library of the Department of Architecture [Harvard University, 1893–1952]." *HLB* 6 (1952): 263–69.

6.361 Davison, A. T. "The Isham Memorial Library [Harvard University Library, 1932–52]." *HLB* 6 (1952): 376–80.

6.362 Elkins, K. C. "The Harvard Library and the Northeastern Boundary Dispute [1828–52]." *HLB* 6 (1952): 255–63.

6.363 Munn, J. B. "The Child Memorial Library [Harvard University 1892–1951]." *HLB* 6 (1952): 110–18.

6.364 Work, R. L. "Ninety Years of Professor Agassiz's Natural History Library." *HLB* 6 (1952): 202–18.

6.365 Cadbury, H. J. "Bishop Berkeley's Gifts to the Harvard Library." *HLB* 7 (1953): 73–87, 196–207.

6.366 Metcalf, K. D. "Administrative Structure of the Harvard University Library." *HLB* 7 (1953): 5–18.

6.367 Metcalf, K. D. "The Finances of the Harvard University Library." *HLB* 7 (1953): 333–48.

6.368 Elkins, K. C. "President Eliot and the Storage of 'Dead' Books." *HLB* 8 (1954): 299–312.

6.369 Elkins, K. C., ed. "Foreshadowings of Lamont: Proposals in the Nineteenth Century." *HLB* 8 (1954): 41–53.

6.370 Sweeney, J. L. "A Place for Poetry: The Woodberry Poetry Room in Widener and Lamont [1931–53]." *HLB* 8 (1954): 65–73.

6.371 Birkhoff, G. "The George David Birkhoff Mathematical Library (1888–1954)." *HLB* 9 (1955): 282–84.

6.372 Broderick, J. H. "The Robbins Library of Philosophy (1906–55)." *HLB* 9 (1955): 415–17.

6.373 Porritt, R. K. "The Radcliffe College Library After Seventy-Five Years." *HLB* 9 (1955): 335–49.

6.374 Coleman, E. E. "Copyright Deposit at Harvard (1783–90)." *HLB* 10 (1956): 135–40.

6.375 Hickman, R. W. "The Physics Libraries of Harvard University (1884–1956)." *HLB* 10 (1956): 356–66.

6.376 Metcalf, K. D. "Vital Statistics of the Harvard University Library, 1937–1955." *HLB* 10 (1956): 119–29.

6.377 [Adams, T. R.] *A Brief Account of the Origins and Purpose of the Chapin Library at Williams College.* Williamstown, Mass.: 1956.

6.378 Copeland, M. T. "The Business School Library." In *And Mark an Era: The Story of the Harvard Business School.* Boston: Little, Brown, 1958. Pp. 311–23.

6.379 Williamson, G. B. "When the Students Owned the Library." *DCLB* n.s. 2 (1958–1959): 7–13.

6.380 Brown, H. M. "Wellesley College Library: An Historical Sketch." *Bay State Librarian* 49 (1959): 1–5.

6.381 Kraus, J. W. "The Harvard Undergraduate Library of 1773." *CRL* 22 (1961): 247–52.

6.382 Buck, P. H. *Libraries and Universities.* Cambridge: Harvard University Press, 1964.

6.383 Bryant, D. W., and Williams, E. E. "The Harvard Library in the 1960's." *HLB* 15 (1967): 82–98.

6.384 Wang, S. Y. "Harvard-Yenching Library: Harvard University, History and Development." Master's thesis, Southern Connecticut State College, 1967.

6.385 James, J. W. "History and Women at Harvard: The Schlesinger Library." *HLB* 16 (1968): 385–99.

6.386 *The Library of Mount Holyoke College: 1837–1968.* [South Hadley, Mass.: Mount Holyoke College Library, 1968].

6.387 Bryant, R. K. *Harvard University Library, 1638–1968.* Cambridge, Mass.: N.p., 1969.

6.388 Williams, E. E. "Harvard University Library." *ELIS* 10 (1973): 317–73.

6.389 Greever, M. F. C. "The Harvard Library in Colonial America." Research Paper, Texas Woman's University, 1975.

6.390 Bentinck-Smith, W. *Building a Great Library: The Coolidge Years at Harvard.* Cambridge: Harvard University Press, 1976.

6.391 Nicholson, N. N. "The Massachusetts Institute of Technology Libraries." *ELIS* 17 (1976): 239–59.

6.392 Altman, E. C. "A History of the Baker Library at the Harvard University Graduate School of Business Administration." *HLB* 29 (1981): 169–96.

6.393 Gold, R. "A Room of One's Own: Radcliffe's Schlesinger Library." *WLB* 55 (1981): 750–55.

6.394 Seaburg, A. "An Enlightened Ministry: Andover-Harvard Theological Library, 1950–1980." *HLB* 29 (1981): 307–20.

6.395 Brown, H. M. "The Wellesley College Library." *ELIS* 33 (1982): 1–4.

6.396 Williams, E. E. "The Harvard University Library: A Century of Changes in Administrative Structure." *LQ* 53 (1983): 359–70.

6.397 Hammond, M. "The Library of Kirkland House—The John Hicks House." *HLB* 32 (1984): 149–75.

6.398 Kilgour, F. G. "The First Century of Scientific Books in the Harvard College Library." In *Collected Papers of Frederick G. Kilgour: Early Years.* Dublin, Ohio: OCLC, 1984. Pp. 11–14.

6.399 Bartoshesky, F. "Business Records at the Harvard Business School." *Business History Review* 59 (1985): 475–83.

6.400 Carpenter, K. E. *The First 350 Years of the Harvard University Library: Description of an Exhibition.* Cambridge: Harvard University Library, 1986.

6.401 King, P. M. "Forty Years of Collecting on Women: The Arthur and Elizabeth Schlesinger Library on the History of Women in America, Radcliffe College." In *Women's Collections: Libraries, Archives, and Consciousness*, edited by S. Hildenbrand. New York: Haworth Press, 1986. Pp. 75–100.

6.402 Rogers, R. R. "The Kress Library of Business and Economics." *Business History Review* 60 (1986): 281–88.

Michigan

6.403 Hinsdale, B. A. "The Libraries." In *History of the University of Michigan*. Ann Arbor: University of Michigan, 1906. Pp. 118–23.

6.404 *University of Michigan Library, 1905–1912: A Brief Review by the Librarian*. Ann Arbor, Mich.: Ann Arbor Press, 1912.

6.405 Oddon, Y. "Une Bibliothèque Universitaire aux États-Unis; la Bibliothèque de l'Université de Michigan." *Revue des Bibliothèques* 38 (1928): 129–55.

6.406 Adams, R. G. *The Whys and Wherefores of the William L. Clements Library: A Brief Essay on Book Collecting as a Fine Art*. Ann Arbor: University of Michigan Press, 1931.

6.407 Bishop, W. W. "The University [of Michigan] Library's Bookplates [1915–30]." *MAQR* 57 (1951): 348–50.

6.408 Abbott, J. C. "Raymond Cazallis Davis and the University of Michigan General Library, 1877–1905." Doctoral dissertation, University of Michigan, 1957.

6.409 Bidlack, R. E. "Book Collection of the Old University of Michigan." *MAQR* 64 (1958): 100–113.

6.410 Bidlack, R. E. "Four Early Donors of Books to the University of Michigan." *MAQR* 65 (1958): 110–22.

6.411 Bishop, W. W. "The University Library to 1941." In *The University of Michigan, An Encyclopedic Survey*. Ann Arbor: University of Michigan Press, 1958. Pp. 1369–84.

6.412 Peckham, H. "The William L. Clements Library of American History." In *The University of Michigan, An Encyclopedic Survey*. Ann Arbor: University of Michigan Press, 1958. Pp. 1402–10.

6.413 Rice, W. G. "The University Library, 1941–53." In *The University of Michigan, An Encyclopedic Survey*. Ann Arbor: University of Michigan Press, 1958. Pp. 1384–97.

6.414 Towne, J. E. *A History of the Michigan State University Library, 1855–1959*. Rochester, N.Y.: Association of College and Research Libraries, 1961, Microcard no. 132.

6.415 Bidlack, R. E. *Nucleus of a Library: A Study of the Book Collection of the University of Michigan and the Personalities Involved in Its Acquisition, 1837–1845*. Ann Arbor: University of Michigan Department of Library Science, 1962.

6.416 Bidlack, R. E. "Early Handling of Books at the University of Michigan." In *Books in America's Past: Essays Honoring Rudolph H. Gjelsness*, edited by D. Kaser. Charlottesville: University Press of Virginia, 1966. Pp. 150–64.

6.417 Hanawalt, L. L. "The Libraries (1923–)." In *A Place of Light: The History of Wayne State University, A Centennial Publication*. Detroit: Wayne State University Press, 1968. Pp. 257–68.

6.418 Koch, H. C. "Michigan State University Libraries." *ELIS* 18 (1976): 53–55.

6.419 Peckham, H. "Michigan. The University of Michigan Library: Clements (William L.) Library." *ELIS* 18 (1976): 65–66.

6.420 Stewart, R. C. "Michigan. The University of Michigan Library." *ELIS* 18 (1976): 56–64.

6.421 Bosler, G. F., and Doyle, J. M. "Academic Interlibrary Loan Networks in Michigan: History and Present Status." *Michigan Academician* 14 (1981): 141–57.

6.422 Pings, V. M. "Wayne State University Libraries." *ELIS* 32 (1981): 459–69.

Minnesota

6.423 Walter, F. K. "Notes on the Beginning of a Midwest University Library." In *Essays Offered to Herbert Putnam by His Colleagues and Friends on His Thirtieth Anniversary as Librarian of Congress, 5 April 1929*, edited by W. W. Bishop and A. Keogh. New Haven: Yale University Press, 1929. Pp. 510–19.

6.424 Fortin, C. C. "A History of the St. Thomas College Library." Master's thesis, University of Minnesota, 1951.

6.425 Gray, J. "Dispensary of the Soul." In *The University of Minnesota 1851–1951*. Minneapolis: University of Minnesota Press, 1951. Pp. 527–39.

6.426 Roloff, R. W. "St. John's University Library: A Historical Evaluation." Master's thesis, University of Minnesota, 1953, ACRL Microcard no. 34.

6.427 Miller, V. P. "A History of the Library of Gustavus Adolphus College, St. Peter, Minnesota." Master's thesis, University of Minnesota, 1961.

6.428 Nelson, K. "The Kerlan Collection, 1949 to 1971." *Minnesota University Bulletin* 3 (1972): 41–53.

6.429 Genaway, D. C. "Quasi-Departmental Libraries: Their Origin, Function and Relationship to the University Library System—A Case Study of the University of Minnesota Twin Cities Campus." Doctoral dissertation, University of Minnesota, 1975.

6.430 Stanford, E. B. "Minnesota. University of Minnesota Libraries." *ELIS* 18 (1976): 155–75.

Mississippi

6.431 Nichols, M. E. "Early Development of the University of Mississippi Library." Master's thesis, University of Mississippi, 1957, ACRL Microcard no. 111.

Missouri

6.432 Severance, H. O. "The Columbia Library, 1866–1892." *MHR* 7 (July 1913): 232–36.

6.433 Severance, H. O. *History of the Library of the University of Missouri*. Columbia: University of Missouri, 1928.

6.434 Severance, H. O. "University of Missouri Library." In *Richard Henry Jesse, President of the University of Missouri, 1891–1908*. Columbia, Mo.: Henry O. Severance, 1937. Pp. 88–91.

6.435 Carlin, O. R. *History of William Jewell College Library, 1854–1939*. Liberty, Mo.: William Jewell College Press, 1940.

6.436 Hoyer, M. "The History of Automation in the University of Missouri Library, 1947–1963." Master's thesis, Indiana University, 1965, ACRL Microcard no. 166.

6.437 Carroll, C. E. "Missouri. University of Missouri Libraries." *ELIS* 19 (1976): 212–28.

6.438 Deweese, B. J. *The History of the Library, University of Missouri-Columbia, 1928–1946*. Columbia, Mo.: Elmer Ellis Library, 1980.

6.439 Eaton, A. J. "Washington University Libraries (Saint Louis)." *ELIS* 32 (1981): 413–16.

6.440 Atherton, L. E. "The Western Historical Collection of the University of Missouri, 1943–1983." *MHR* 78 (1983): 1–13.

6.441 LaBudde, K. J. "Missouri Academic Libraries—Looking Back." *Show-Me Libraries* 36 (1984): 5–7.

Nebraska

6.442 Johnson, E. M. "Nebraska. University of Nebraska Libraries." *ELIS* 19 (1976): 219–29.

Nevada

6.443 Hulse, J. H. "The Libraries." In *The University of Nevada: A Centennial History.* Reno: University of Nevada Press, 1974. Pp. 172–74.

New Hampshire

6.444 Stone, E. P. "The Durham Library." *[New Hampshire State College Monthly] Enaichsee* 1 (1894): 72–73.

6.445 *The Isaiah Thomas Donation [to the Library of Dartmouth College].* Hanover, N.H.: Dartmouth College Library, 1949.

6.446 Morin, R. W. "Dartmouth College Libraries." *ELIS* 6 (1971): 428–34.

6.447 Stinehour, R. D. "Testimonial to a Library." *DCLB* 19 (1978): 2–7.

6.448 Wilson, M. T., and Wilson, A. M. "Symbol of a Seat of Learning: Dartmouth's Baker Library." *DCLB* 19 (1978): 8–14.

New Jersey

6.449 Princeton University Library. *College and University Library Statistics, 1919/20 to 1943/44.* Princeton: Princeton University Library, 1947.

6.450 Gapp, K. S. "The Theological Seminary Library [Princeton 1811–1953]." *Princeton University Library Chronicle* 15 (1954): 90–100.

6.451 Dix, W. S. *The Princeton University Library in the Eighteenth Century.* Princeton: Princeton University Library, 1978.

6.452 Dix, W. S. "The Princeton University Library in the Eighteenth Century." *Princeton University Library Chronicle* 40 (1978): 1–102.

6.453 Dix, W. S. "Princeton University Library." *ELIS* 23 (1978): 264–75.

6.454 Whitney, V. P., and Montanaro, A. "Rutgers University Libraries." *ELIS* 26 (1979): 251–66.

6.455 Berberian, K. R. *Princeton University Library, 1746–1860.* Roselle, N.J.: Creative Graphic Art Service, 1980.

6.456 Dykeman, A. "To Look a Gift Horse in the Mouth: The History of the Theodore Stanton Collection." *JLH* 17 (1982): 468–73.

New Mexico

6.457 Bandy, C. N. L. "The First Fifty Years of the New Mexico State University Library, 1889–1939." Master's thesis, University of Oklahoma, 1971.

6.458 Horgan, P. "An Amateur Librarian [New Mexico Military Institute]." In *Voices from the Southwest: A Gathering in Honor of Lawrence Clark Powell,* edited by D. C. Dickinson, W. D. Laird, and M. F. Maxwell. Flagstaff, Ariz.: Northland Press, 1976. Pp. 65–75.

New York

6.459 Harris, G. W. *Twenty-Five Years of the Annals of the Cornell University Library, 1868–1893.* Ithaca: Cornell University Library, 1893.

6.460 Gillett, C. R. "The Library, General Catalogue and the Alumni." In *The Union Theological Seminary in the City of New York: Its Design and Another Decade of Its History,* by G. L. Prentiss. Asbury Park, N.J.: M.W. and C. Pennypacker, 1899. Pp. 352–62.

6.461 Canfield, J. H. "The Library." In *A History of Columbia University, 1754–1904: Published in Commemoration of the One Hundred and Fiftieth Anniversary of the Founding of King's College.* New York: Columbia University Press, 1904. Pp. 427–42.

6.462 Hewett, W. T. "The University Library." In *Cornell University: A History.* New York: University Publishing Society, 1905. Pp. 357–76.

6.463 Keep, A. B. "The Library of King's College." *Columbia University Quarterly* 13 (1911): 275–84.

6.464 Gilchrist, D. B. "The Rush Rhees Library at the University of Rochester." *LJ* 56 (1931): 343–46.

6.465 Butler, N. M. "The Libraries of Columbia." *Columbia University Quarterly* 27 (1935): 1–5.

6.466 Stewart, N. J. "A History of the Library of the College of the City of New York." Master's thesis, College of the City of New York, 1935.

6.467 Gilchrist, D. B. "A History of the University of Rochester Libraries." *Rochester Historical Society Publications* 16 (1937): 101–34.

6.468 Bogart, R. E. "College Library Development in New York State During the 19th Century." Master's thesis, Columbia University, 1948.

6.469 Berthel, J. "Their Wine Will Warm: An Appreciation of the Bancroft Bequest." *CLC* 1 (1952): 12–16.

6.470 Galpin, W. F. "The Ranke Library." In *Syracuse University: The Pioneer Days, Volume One*. Syracuse, N.Y.: Syracuse University Press, 1952. Pp. 88–101.

6.471 Hamlin, T. F. "The Avery Architectural Library of Columbia University [1890]." *American Society Legion of Honor Magazine* 24 (1953): 261–81.

6.472 Coffin, H. S. "The Libraries." In *A Half Century of Union Theological Seminary 1896–1945: An Informal History*. New York: Scribner's, 1954. Pp. 202–06.

6.473 Jones, R. "A History of the Library of Teachers College, Columbia University, 1887–1952." Master's thesis, Drexel Institute of Technology, 1958, ACRL Microcard no. 39.

6.474 Kato, A. "A History of Brady Memorial Library, Manhattanville College of the Sacred Heart: Purchase, New York, 1841–1957." Master's thesis, Catholic University of America, 1959.

6.475 Linderman, W. B. "History of the Columbia University Library, 1876–1926."

Doctoral dissertation, Columbia University, 1959.

6.476 Galpin, W. F. "The Carnegie Library." In *Syracuse University: The Pioneer Days, Volume Two*. Syracuse, N.Y.: Syracuse University Press, 1960. Pp. 126–50.

6.477 Elliott, E. C. B. "President White in His Library." In *History of Cornell*, by M. Bishop. Ithaca: Cornell University Press, 1962. Pp. 617–20.

6.478 Slavens, T. P. "The Library of Union Theological Seminary in the City of New York, 1836 to the Present." Doctoral dissertation, University of Michigan, 1965.

6.479 Beasley, C. W. "Syracuse University Library: Its History from 1922 to 1942." Master's thesis, Syracuse University, 1966.

6.480 Morris, R. "Case History of the Library of the Nassau Community College." Research Paper, Long Island University, 1967.

6.481 Schwartz, M. "History of the Library of the Jewish Theological Seminary of America." Research Paper, Long Island University, 1967.

6.482 Sussman, D. "History of the Brooklyn (New York) College Library from 1930 to 1966." Research Paper, Long Island University, 1967.

6.483 Allan, J. M. "The Library of Hamilton College, Clinton, New York from January, 1793 to January, 1963: The Development of an American Liberal Arts College-Library." Master's thesis, The Library Association [U.K.], 1968.

6.484 O'Shea, J. M. "History of the Library of the Suffolk County (New York) Community College." Research Paper, Long Island University, 1968.

6.485 Parsons, K. C. "'Here the Great Library Will Stand.'" In *The Cornell Campus: A History of Its Planning and Development*. Ithaca: Cornell University Press, 1968. Pp. 152–75.

6.486 Slavens, T. P. "The Acquisition of the Van Ess Collection by Union Theological Seminary." In *Library History Seminar No. 3, Proceedings, 1968,* edited by M. J. Zachert. Tallahassee: JLH, 1968. Pp. 26–34.

6.487 Imberman, A. "The History of the Vassar College Library, 1861–1968." Master's thesis, University of Chicago, 1969.

6.488 Oh, S. J. "A Study of the Edwin Markham Collection of the Horman Library of Wagner College, Staten Island, New York, 1940–1969." Research Paper, Long Island University, 1969.

6.489 Sun, D. "History of the Chinese Section of the East Asian Library, Columbia University, New York, New York." Research Paper, Long Island University, 1969.

6.490 Hayes, C. D. "The History of the University of Rochester Libraries—120 Years." *University of Rochester Library Bulletin* 25 (1970): 59–112.

6.491 Bonnell, A. H. "Columbia University Libraries." *ELIS* 5 (1971): 362–70.

6.492 Ross, N. "History of the Hofstra University Library, 1935–1970." Research Paper, Long Island University, 1971.

6.493 Shepherd, G. F. "Cornell University Libraries." *ELIS* 6 (1971): 167–81.

6.494 Brassel, D. "Syracuse University Library, 1871–1972." *The Courier* 9:4 and 10:1 (1972): 16–26.

6.495 Jones, H. D. "Brooklyn College Library: A Profile." *LACUNY Journal* 1 (1972): 24–28.

6.496 Thorpe, J. "Pioneering in the Pre-Olin Day." *Cornell University Library Bulletin* 183 (1973): 13–17.

6.497 Slavens, T. P. "The Development of the Library of Union Theological Seminary in the City of New York." *LHR* 1 (June 1974): 84–93.

6.498 Cook, D. C. "New York. State University of New York at Stony Brook Libraries." *ELIS* 19 (1976): 407–13.

6.499 Rochell, C. C. "New York University Libraries." *ELIS* 19 (1976): 418–20.

6.500 Passanti, F. "The Design of Columbia in the 1890s, McKim and His Client." *Journal of the Society of Architectural Historians* 36 (1977): 69–84.

6.501 Strassberg, R., and Harper, S. F. "The Martin P. Catherwood Library." *Bulletin of the Cornell University Libraries* 206 (1977): 9–14.

6.502 Watanabe, R. "The Sibley Music Library of the Eastman School of Music, University of Rochester." *Notes* 33 (1977): 783–802.

6.503 Hayes, C. D. "Rochester, University of Rochester Library." *ELIS* 25 (1978): 445–70.

6.504 Muller, R. H. "Queens College Library." *ELIS* 25 (1978): 38–50.

6.505 Bradley, C. J., and Coover, J. B. "Vassar's Music Library: The First Hundred Years." *MLAN* 35 (1979): 819–46.

6.506 Murphy, H. T. "The Albert R. Mann Library: A Brief History." *Bulletin of the Cornell University Libraries* 202 (1979): 1–3.

6.507 Doherty, A. S. "Syracuse University Libraries." *ELIS* 29 (1980): 381–90.

6.508 Evans, G. T. "State University of New York Libraries." *ELIS* 29 (1980): 55–77.

6.509 Dykeman, A. "To Look a Gift Horse in the Mouth: The History of the Theodore Stanton Collection." *JLH* 17 (1982): 468–73.

6.510 Kranich, N. "New York University Libraries, 1831–1981." *BKM* 40 (1982): 85–88.

6.511 Kreh, D. H. "Faculty Status and Collective Bargaining: SUNY Librarians 1965–1982." *BKM* 40 (1982): 195–99.

6.512 Pitschmann, L. A. "Cornell University Libraries 1981: A Profile of a NYSILL Referral Library." *BKM* 40 (1982): 75–79.

6.513 Spoor, R. D. "Union Theological Seminary Library." *BKM* 40 (1982): 112–14.

6.514 Taylor, M. E. "The Columbia University Libraries." *BKM* 40 (1982): 105–08.

6.515 Watstein, S. "Teachers College Library." *BKM* 40 (1982): 117–22.

6.516 Tutt, C. "Library Service to the Columbia University School of Social Work, 1898–1979." Doctoral dissertation, Columbia University, 1983.

6.517 Braverman, M. "A Review of the Board of Regents and State Education Department's Reports and Recommendations, 1956–1983." *BKM* 42 (1984): 153–56.

6.518 Corsaro, J. "The Regents and Libraries in Nineteenth Century New York." *BKM* 42 (1984): 141–46.

6.519 Coville, B. "Treasure in the Library Attic: Von Ranke at Syracuse." *WLB* 59 (1984): 98–102.

6.520 *The Rare Book and Manuscript Library of Columbia University: Collections and Treasures.* New York: Columbia University Libraries, 1985.

6.521 Norton, A. A. *A History of the United States Military Academy Library.* Wayne, N.J.: Avery Publishing Group, 1986.

6.522 Roberts, F. X. "The Growth and Development of the Libraries of the University of Buffalo, 1846–1960." Doctoral dissertation, State University of New York at Buffalo, 1986.

6.523 Slavens, T. P. *A Great Library through Gifts.* New York: K.G. Saur, 1986.

North Carolina

6.524 Pugh, J. F. "The History of the Library of the University of North Carolina." *University of North Carolina Magazine* 44 (1914): 207–13.

6.525 Adams, C. M. "Woman's College Library, the University of North Carolina." *CRL* 14 (1953): 135–39.

6.526 Halmos, D. M. "The Hancock Library of Biology and Oceanography." *CRL* 15 (1954): 29–32.

6.527 Nicholson, J. M. "A History of the Wake Forest College Library, 1878–1946." Master's thesis, University of North Carolina, 1954, ACRL Microcard no. 78.

6.528 Breedlove, J. P. "Duke University Library, 1840–1940: A Brief Account with Reminiscences." *Library Notes: A Bulletin Issued by the Friends of the Duke University Library* 30 (1955): 1–81.

6.529 Holder, E. J. "A History of the Library of the Woman's College of the University of North Carolina, 1892–1945." Master's thesis, University of North Carolina, 1955, ACRL Microcard no. 86.

6.530 Pearsall, T. F. "History of the North Carolina Agricultural and Technical College Library." Master's thesis, Western Reserve University, 1955.

6.531 Diaz, A. J. "A History of the Latin American Collection of the University of North Carolina Library." Master's thesis, University of North Carolina, 1956.

6.532 Eaton, J. D. "A History and Evaluation of the Hanes Collection in the Louis R. Wilson Library, University of North Carolina." Master's thesis, University of North Carolina, 1957.

6.533 Wilson, L. R. "The Library Begins to Grow." In *The University of North Carolina, 1900–1930: The Making of a Modern University,* vol. 1. Chapel Hill: University of North Carolina Press, 1957. Pp. 128–37.

6.534 Wilson, L. R. "A Library for a Real University." In *The University of North Carolina, 1900–1930: The Making of a Modern University,* vol. 2. Chapel Hill: University of North Carolina Press, 1957. Pp. 472–82.

6.535 Moore, G. G. "The Southern Historical Collection in the Louis Round Wilson Library of the University of North Carolina from the Beginning of the Collection Through 1948." Master's thesis, University of North Carolina, 1958.

6.536 Orr, A. P. "A History and Analysis of the Freshman Library Instruction Program Presented at the University of North Carolina."

Master's thesis, University of North Carolina, 1958, ACRL Microcard no. 125.

6.537 Bahnsen, J. C. "Collections in the University of North Carolina Library Before 1830." *CRL* 20 (1959): 125–29.

6.538 Farrow, M. H. "The History of Guilford College Library, 1837–1955." Master's thesis, University of North Carolina, 1959, ACRL Microcard no. 120.

6.539 Battle, M. E. "A History of the Carnegie Library at Johnson C. Smith University." Master's thesis, University of North Carolina, 1960.

6.540 Wilson, L. R. *The Library of the First State University: A Review of Its Past and a Look at Its Future.* Chapel Hill: University of North Carolina Library, 1960.

6.541 Wilson, L. R. "First Book in the Library of the First State University." *CRL* 22 (1961): 35–39.

6.542 Perkins, T. E. "The History of Elon College Library, 1890–1957." Master's thesis, University of North Carolina, 1962.

6.543 Cranford, J. P. "The Documents Collection of the University of North Carolina Library from Its Beginning Through 1963." Master's thesis, University of North Carolina, 1965.

6.544 Heindel, S. W. "A History of the Institute of Government Library of the University of North Carolina." Master's thesis, University of North Carolina, 1965.

6.545 List, B. T. "The Friends of the University of North Carolina Library, 1932–1962." Master's thesis, University of North Carolina, 1965.

6.546 Tarlton, S. M. "The Development of the Library of Charlotte College, 1946–July 1, 1965." Master's thesis, University of North Carolina, 1966.

6.547 Powell, B. E. "Duke University Library." *ELIS* 7 (1972): 314–23.

6.548 Leonard, H. V. "The Divinity School Library: The Historical Background Since 1850." *Library Notes of Duke University Library* 45 (1973): 19–42.

6.549 Govan, J. F. "North Carolina. University of North Carolina Library." *ELIS* 20 (1977): 167–75.

6.550 Young, B. I. *The Library of the Women's College, Duke University, 1930–1972.* Durham, N.C.: Regulator Press, 1978.

6.551 York, M. C. "The Dialectic and Philanthropic Societies' Contributions to the Library of the University of North Carolina, 1886–1906." *NCHR* 59 (1982): 327–53.

Ohio

6.552 Hopper, O. C. "History of the Ohio State University Library, 1910–1925." In *History of the Ohio State University*, vol. 2. Columbus: Ohio State University Press, 1926.

6.553 Mendenhall, T. C. "The Library, Its Humble Beginnings and Growth [to 1910]." In *History of the Ohio State University*, vol. 1. Columbus: Ohio State University Press, 1926. Pp. 122–28.

6.554 Beach, A. G. "The Library." In *A Pioneer College: The Story of Marietta.* n.p.: Privately printed, 1935. Pp. 300–302.

6.555 Irwin, M. "History of the Ohio Wesleyan University Library, 1844–1940." Master's thesis, University of California, 1941.

6.556 Adam, C. "Kent State University Library." Master's thesis, Kent State University, 1950.

6.557 Stein, J. H. "The Development of the Hiram College Library from the Literary Societies Which Formed Its Nucleus." Master's thesis, Kent State University, 1950.

6.558 Bobinski, G. S. "A Brief History of the Libraries of Western Reserve University, 1826–1952." Master's thesis, Western Reserve University, 1952, ACRL Microcard no. 50.

6.559 Mathews, S. G. "Marian Library of the University of Dayton: Origin and Development." Master's thesis, Western Reserve University, 1952.

6.560 Tucker, J. S. "Oberlin College Library, 1833–1885." Master's thesis, Western Reserve University, 1953, ACRL Microcard no. 45.

6.561 Vermilya, N. C. "A History of the Otterbein College Library." Master's thesis, Western Reserve University, 1955, ACRL Microcard no. 58, as Baughman, N. C.

6.562 Clinefeller, R. W. "A History of Bierce Library of the University of Akron." Master's thesis, Kent State University, 1956.

6.563 Mount Union College. *The History of the Mount Union College Library, 1854–1955: With Summary Reports of the Library for the Years 1920–1955, by Robert E. Stauffer, Librarian, 1920–1955.* Alliance, Ohio: Mount Union College, 1956.

6.564 Schink, R. J. "A History of the Youngstown University and Its Library." Master's thesis, Western Reserve University, 1956.

6.565 Zafren, H. C. "The Hebrew Union College Library." *SL* 47 (1956): 314–17.

6.566 Saviers, S. H. "The Literary Societies and Their Libraries at Hiram College." Master's thesis, Kent State University, 1958.

6.567 Silva, M. F. C. "A History of the Ursuline College Library, Cleveland, Ohio, 1922–1957." Master's thesis, Western Reserve University, 1958, ACRL Microcard no. 108.

6.568 Skipper, J. E. "The Ohio State University Library, 1873–1913." Doctoral dissertation, University of Michigan, 1960.

6.569 Meyers, J. K. "A History of the Antioch College Library, 1850–1929." Master's thesis, Kent State University, 1963, ACRL Microcard no. 150.

6.570 Musser, A. "A History of Muskingum College Library." Master's thesis, Kent State University, 1963.

6.571 Wilhelmi, I. *History and Development of the Departmental Libraries at Ohio State University from 1931–1965.* Columbus: Ohio State University, 1966.

6.572 Barnett, M. F. "A History of the Baldwin-Wallace College Library, 1913–1964." Master's thesis, Kent State University, 1967.

6.573 Harper, J. R. "A History of Mount Union College Library." Master's thesis, Kent State University, 1968.

6.574 Schoyer, G. *History of the Ohio State University Libraries: 1870–1970.* Columbus: Ohio State University Libraries, 1970.

6.575 Fry, J. W. *The Ohio State University Library, 1913–1928.* Columbus: Ohio State University Library, 1972.

6.576 Metcalf, K. D. *Personal Reminiscences on the History of the Oberlin College Library System.* Oberlin, Ohio: Oberlin College, 1974.

6.577 Belanger, M. D. "The Library that Letters Built." *OLAB* 46 (1976): 10–12.

6.578 Schloyer, G., and Atkinson, H. C. "Ohio State University Libraries." *ELIS* 20 (1977): 362–78.

6.579 Weis, I. J. "The Historical Development of the University of Toledo Libraries." *Northwest Ohio Quarterly* 53 (1981): 3–81.

Oregon

6.580 Sheldon, H. D. *The University of Oregon Library, 1882–1942.* [Eugene]: University of Oregon Library, [1943?].

6.581 Carlson, W. H. "History and the Present Status of the Centralization of the Libraries of the Oregon State System of Higher Education (1931–53)." *CRL* 14 (1953): 414–17.

6.582 Carlson, W. H. "Oregon State University Library." *ELIS* 20 (1977): 468–512.

6.583 Hintz, C. W. "Oregon. University of Oregon Library." *ELIS* 21 (1977): 6–12.

Pennsylvania

6.584 Skillman, D. B. "The Origin and Growth of the Library." In *The Biography of a College: Being the History of the First Century of the Life of Lafayette College.* Easton, Pa.: Lafayette College, 1932. Pp. 324–29.

6.585 Cheney, E. P. "The Henry C. Lea Library." *LC* 1 (1933): 4–5.

6.586 Tauber, M. F. "A Brief History of the Library of Temple University." *Temple University News* 14 (1934): 5.

6.587 Thompson, C. S. "The Gift of Louis XVI." *LC* 2 (1934): 37–48, 60–67.

6.588 Armstrong, E. V. *The Story of the Edgar Fahs Smith Memorial Collection in the History of Chemistry.* Philadelphia: University of Pennsylvania, 1937.

6.589 Swathmore College Faculty. "Honors Work and the Library." In *An Adventure in Education: Swathmore College under Frank Aydolette.* New York: Macmillan, 1941. Pp. 136–46.

6.590 Dunaway, W. F. "Library." In *History of the Pennsylvania State College.* State College, Pa.: Pennsylvania State College, 1946. Pp. 356–62.

6.591 Phillips, J. W. "The Sources of the Original Dickinson College Library." *Pennsylvania History* 14 (1947): 108–17.

6.592 Jones, S. B. "The Early Years of the University Library." *Library Chronicle: Bicentennial Issue Published in Memory of the Founding of the University of Pennsylvania Library, 1750* 17 (1950): 8–22.

6.593 Shinn, M. E. "Sine Quibus Non: The University of Pennsylvania Librarians." *LC* 17 (1950): 23–29.

6.594 Wagner, L. F. "A Descriptive History of the Library Facilities of Lafayette College, Easton, Pennsylvania, 1826–1941." Master's

thesis, Catholic University of America, 1951, ACRL Microcard no. 27.

6.595 David, C. W. "The University Library in 1886." *LC* 18 (1952): 72–76.

6.596 Nehlig, M. E. "The History and Development of the Drexel Institution Library, 1892–1914." Master's thesis, Drexel Institute of Technology, 1952.

6.597 Williams, C. W. "A History of the Krauth Memorial Library and Staff of the Lutheran Theological Seminary at Philadelphia, from 1864 to 1951." Master's thesis, Drexel Institute of Technology, 1952.

6.598 Richardson, E. R. "The La Salle College Library, Philadelphia, 1930–1953." Master's thesis, Drexel Institute of Technology, 1953.

6.599 Smith, D. J. "The Early History of the Library of Allegheny College, Meadville, Pennsylvania." Master's thesis, Western Reserve University, 1953, ACRL Microcard no. 61.

6.600 Girvin, A. G. "The Albright Alumni Memorial Library." Master's thesis, Drexel Institute of Technology, 1954.

6.601 McTaggart, J. B. "The History of the Eastern Baptist Theological Seminary Library, 1925–1953." Master's thesis, Drexel Institute of Technology, 1954.

6.602 Osborne, J. T. "The Ursinus College Library, 1869–1953." Master's thesis, Drexel Institute of Technology, 1954.

6.603 Davidson, J. S. "Literary Society Libraries at Muhlenberg College [1867–1912]." *CRL* 16 (1955): 183–86.

6.604 Earnshaw, J. "A History of the Henry Lea Library at the University of Pennsylvania." Master's thesis, Drexel Institute of Technology, 1955.

6.605 McFarland, M. M. "History of the Development of Bucknell University Library, Lewisburg, Pennsylvania." Master's thesis, Drexel Institute of Technology, 1955.

6.606 Meyerend, M. H. "A History and Survey of the Fine Arts Library of the University of Pennsylvania from Its Founding to 1953." Master's thesis, Drexel Institute of Technology, 1955.

6.607 Valentine, M. "Holy Family College Library: The First Decade." Master's thesis, Marywood College (Scranton, Pa.), 1956.

6.608 Smith, D. J. "Early Libraries in Crawford County." *WPHM* 40 (1957): 251–76.

6.609 Schuetz, A. R. "A History of the St. Vincent Archabbey-College Libraries." Master's thesis, Catholic University of America, 1959.

6.610 Oliphant, J. O. *The Library of Bucknell University.* Lewisburg, Pa.: Bucknell University Press, 1962.

6.611 Wolf, E. "Some Books of Early English Provenance in the 1823 Library of Allegheny College." *PAAS* 73 (1963): 13–44.

6.612 Shellem, J. J. "The Archbishop Ryan Memorial Library of St. Charles Borromeo Seminary, Overbrook, Pennsylvania." *American Catholic Historical Society* 75 (1964): 53–55.

6.613 Kraft, M. I. "A History of the Library of Chestnut Hill College: Philadelphia, Pennsylvania, 1890–1965." Master's thesis, Catholic University of America, 1967.

6.614 Jewkes, P. M. "The Growth and Development of the Pennsylvania State University Libraries." Research Paper, University of Pittsburgh Graduate School of Library and Information Science, 1969.

6.615 Forth, S. "Pennsylvania State University Libraries." *ELIS* 21 (1977): 497–505.

6.616 Heidtmann, T. "Pennsylvania. University of Pennsylvania Libraries." *ELIS* 22 (1977): 1–4.

6.617 Jamison, L. W. "Pittsburgh. University of Pittsburgh Libraries." *ELIS* 22 (1977): 291–303.

6.618 Hamlin, A. T. "Temple University Library." *ELIS* 30 (1980): 276–82.

Rhode Island

6.619 "Library of Brown University, Providence, R.I." *NLGPC* 2 (15 August 1852): 147.

6.620 Guild, R. A. "The Library of Brown University." *University Quarterly: Conducted by an Association of Collegiate and Professional Students, in the U.S. and Europe* 3 (1 April 1861): 253–72.

6.621 Winship, G. P. *The John Carter Brown Library: A History.* Providence, R.I.: N.p., 1914.

6.622 Graniss, R. "The John Carter Brown Library and Its Catalogue." *LJ* 45 (1920): 67–69.

6.623 Wroth, L. C. *The John Carter Brown Library in Brown University, Providence, Rhode Island.* Providence, R.I.: Privately printed, 1936.

6.624 Van Hoesen, H. B. *Brown University Library: The Library of the College or University in the English Colony of Rhode Island and Providence Plantations in New England in America [1767–1782].* Providence, R.I.: Privately printed, 1938.

6.625 Chase, E. *The Library: Rhode Island School of Design.* Providence, R.I.: N.p., 1942.

6.626 Everhart, M. "A Historical Survey of the Annmary Brown Memorial, Providence, Rhode Island." Master's thesis, Catholic University of America, 1957.

6.627 *A Collection's Progress: Two Retrospective Exhibitions.* Providence, R.I.: Associates of the John Carter Brown Library, 1968.

6.628 Adams, T. R. "John Carter Brown Library." *ELIS* 3 (1970): 378–82.

6.629 Jonah, D. A. "Brown University Library." *ELIS* 3 (1970): 382–408.

6.630 Desjarlais-Leuth, C. "Brown University and Its Library: A Study of the Beginnings of an Academic Library." Doctoral dissertation, University of Illinois, Urbana-Champaign, 1985.

South Carolina

6.631 "South Carolina College Library." *NLGPC* 3 (15 December 1853): 213.

6.632 Green, E. L. "The Library of the University of South Carolina." *University of South Carolina Bulletin* 7 (1906): 1–22.

6.633 Everhart, F. B. "The South Carolina College Library: Background and Beginning." *JLH* 3 (1968): 221–41.

6.634 Hahn, S. S. "A History of the Lutheran Theological Southern Seminary and Its Library, 1830–1934." Master's thesis, University of Chicago, 1977.

6.635 Hahn, S. S. "Lexington's Theological Library, 1832–1859." *SCHM* 80 (1979): 36–49.

6.636 Toombs, K. E. "South Carolina. University of South Carolina Libraries." *ELIS* 28 (1980): 267–76.

6.637 "History of College and University Libraries." *South Dakota Library Bulletin* 49 (1963): 97–114.

Tennessee

6.638 Atkins, E. "A History of Fisk University Library and Its Standing in Relation to the Libraries of Other Comparable Institutions." Master's thesis, University of California, 1936.

6.639 Duncan, R. B. "A History of the George Peabody College Library, 1785–1910." Master's thesis, George Peabody College for Teachers, 1940.

6.640 Mims, E. "The Joint University Libraries." In *History of Vanderbilt University*. Nashville: Vanderbilt University Press, 1946. Pp. 439–47.

6.641 McClary, B. H., ed. "Not for the Moment Only: Edward Berts to Mary Percival, February 18, 1886." *THQ* 24 (1965): 54–62.

6.642 Kuhlman, A. F. "Joint University Libraries, Nashville, Tennessee." *ELIS* 13 (1975): 289–99.

6.643 Abel, G. M., and Townsend, D. H. "Tennessee. University of Tennessee/Knoxville Library." *ELIS* 30 (1980): 292–97.

6.644 Childress, B. "The East Tennessee University Library: The Civil War and Reconstruction Years." *Tennessee Librarian* 32 (1980): 40–46.

6.645 Tusculum College Library. *The Charles Coffin Collection at Tusculum College: The Original Library of Greenville College, 1794–1827*. Greenville, Tenn.: Tusculum College Library, 1981.

Texas

6.646 "College and University Libraries." *HTL* 3 (1915–1916): 66–75.

6.647 "The People's Loan Library." *HTL* 3 (1915–1916): 80–81.

6.648 Ralston, H. E. "History of the San Antonio Junior College." Master's thesis, University of Texas, 1933.

6.649 Baker, O. J. "Senior College Library Facilities for Negroes in Texas." Master's thesis, Columbia University, 1936.

6.650 Castañeda, C. E. "The Human Side of a Great Collection [Latin American Collection, University of Texas]." *Books Abroad* 14 (1940): 116–21.

6.651 Hamer, M. L. "Texas Collection of U.T. Library." *NNT* 18 (April 1942): 7–9.

6.652 Baker, O. J. "Library Services in Negro Colleges." *NNT* 19 (April 1943): 3–10.

6.653 Bailey, L. "The Cooperative Program of the North Texas Regional Libraries." *NNT* 22 (July 1946): 7–9.

6.654 Baker, O. J. "Selected Activities of the W.B. Banks Library during 1945–1947." *NNT* 23 (October 1947): 131–32.

6.655 Walker, M. B. "An Analysis of the Development of the Public and Private Junior Colleges in Texas from 1934–1935 to 1944–1945, Inclusive." Master's thesis, University of Texas, 1947.

6.656 Andrews, T. "Hardin-Simmons University Library." *NNT* 25 (April 1949): 42–48.

6.657 Allen, W., and Hunnicutt, H. "A New Center for Southwestern Historical Studies. IV. The Archives Collection." *LCT* 4 (Fall 1950): 11–18.

6.658 Barker, E. C. "To Whom Credit Is Due." *SHQ* 54 (1950): 6–12.

6.659 Carroll, H. G. "A New Center for Southwestern Historical Studies. V. The Texas State Historical Association." *LCT* 4 (Fall 1950): 18–24.

6.660 Friend, L. B. "A New Center for Southwestern Historical Studies. I. The Eugene C. Barker History Center." *LCT* 4 (Fall 1950): 3–5.

6.661 Gambrell, H. P. "The Eugene C. Barker Texas History Center." *SHQ* 54 (1950): 1–5.

6.662 Hamer, M. L. "A New Center for Southwestern Historical Studies. III. The Texas Collection: Growth." *LCT* 4 (Fall 1950): 8–11.

6.663 Winkler, E. W. "A New Center for Southwestern Historical Studies. II. The Texas Collection: Inauguration and Benefactors." *LCT* 4 (Fall 1950): 5–8.

6.664 Benson, N. L. "Latin American Collection [University of Texas]." *HT* 2 (1952): 35.

6.665 "Eugene C. Barker Texas History Center." *HT* 2 (1952): 574.

6.666 Ratchford, F. E. "Rare Book Collections." *HT* 2 (1952): 441.

6.667 Ratchford, F. E. "The Rare Book Collection of the University of Texas." *TLJ* 28 (1952): 28–29.

6.668 Sampley, A. M. "North Texas Regional Union List of Periodicals." *HT* 2 (1952): 287.

6.669 Cochran, M. A. "The University of Texas Package Loan Library, 1914–1954." Master's thesis, University of Texas, 1956.

6.670 Lee, J. B. "A History of the Library of Texas College of Arts and Industries, 1925–1955." Master's thesis, University of Texas, 1958.

6.671 Parks, E. G. B. "Study of the Extramural Loans of the University of Texas Library, 1957–1958." Master's thesis, University of Texas, 1960.

6.672 Rouse, R. "A History of the Baylor University Library, 1845–1919." Doctoral dissertation, University of Michigan, 1962.

6.673 Amyett, P. D. W. "A History of Literary Societies at Baylor University." Master's thesis, Baylor University, 1963.

6.674 Schmaus, F. T. "Engineering Library." In *Men of Ingenuity: From Beneath the Orange Tower, 1884–1964; the College of Engineering of the University of Texas*, edited by W. R. Woolrich. Austin: Engineering Foundation of the College of Engineering, 1964. Pp. 209–15.

6.675 Thorne, B. B. "The History of the Sam Houston State Teachers College as Reflected in the Library and the Library Science Department." Master's thesis, Texas Woman's University, 1964.

6.676 Hawkins, J. A. W. "The University of Texas Audio Library." Master's thesis, University of Texas, 1966.

6.677 Rouse, R. "The Two Libraries of Baylor University." In *Approaches to Library History*, edited by J. D. Marshall. Tallahassee: JLH, 1966. Pp. 128–40.

6.678 Sitter, C. L. "The History and Development of the Rare Books Collections of the University of Texas Based on Recollections of Miss Fannie Ratchford." Master's thesis, University of Texas, 1966.

6.679 Napier, S. "History of the Everett De-Golyer Book Collection." Master's thesis, Southern Methodist University, 1967.

6.680 Totten, H. L. "The Wiley College Library, The First Library for Negroes West of the Mississippi." *Negro History Bulletin* 32 (January 1969): 6–10.

6.681 Clark, J. B. "The Odyssey of a University Library, 1869–1968 [Trinity University]." *JLH* 5 (1970): 119–32.

6.682 Moloney, L. C. "A History of the University Library at the University of Texas, 1833–1934." Doctoral dissertation, Columbia University, 1970.

6.683 Herring, J. "Armstrong Browning Library." In *Handbook of Waco and McLennan County*, edited by D. Kelley. Waco, Tex.: Texian Press, 1972. P. 10.

6.684 "Texas Collection." In *Handbook of Waco and McLennan County*, edited by D. Kelley. Waco, Tex.: Texian Press, 1972. P. 263.

6.685 Southern Methodist University, Dallas, Texas. Library. *Special Collections in the Libraries at Southern Methodist University.* Dallas: SMU Printing Office, 1973.

6.686 Jones, C. L., and Carter, B. R. "The Moody Medical Library and Its Historical Relevance." *BMLA* 62 (1974): 25–33.

6.687 Benson, N. L. "Latin American Collection [University of Texas]." *HT* 3 (1976): 508.

6.688 DeGolyer, E. L. "DeGolyer Foundation." *HT* 3 (1976): 235.

6.689 "Eugene C. Barker Texas History Center." *HT* 3 (1976): 285.

6.690 Moll, J. "Rare Book Collections." *HT* 3 (1976): 779.

6.691 Murray, L. "Armstrong Browning Library." *HT* 3 (1976): 39–40.

6.692 Dyess, S. W. "A History and Analysis of Library Formula Funding in Texas Public

Higher Education." Doctoral dissertation, Texas Tech University, 1977.

6.693 Griffin, B. C. "The History and Development of The Criswell Center for Biblical Studies Library." Research Paper, Texas Woman's University, 1978.

6.694 O'Keefe, R. L. "Rice University Libraries." *ELIS* 25 (1978): 438–40.

6.695 Schultz, C. R. *Making Something Happen: Texas A&M University Libraries, 1876–1976.* College Station: Texas A&M University Libraries, 1979.

6.696 Bucknall, C. "Texas. University of Texas Libraries." *ELIS* 30 (1980): 356–80.

6.697 Schultz, C. R. "Texas A&M University Libraries." *ELIS* 30 (1980): 331–41.

6.698 Almaraz, F. D. "Carlos E. Castañeda's Rendezvous with a Library: The Latin American Collection, 1920–1927—The First Phase." *JLH* 16 (1981): 315–28.

6.699 Holland, R. "Southern History in Texas: The Littlefield Collection." *TL* 43 (1981): 119–24.

6.700 Carleton, D. E., and Adams, K. J. " 'A Work Peculiarly Our Own': The Origins of the Barker Texas History Center, 1883–1950." *SHQ* 86 (1982): 197–230.

6.701 Moloney, L. C. "A History of the University of Texas Library." *TL* 44 (1983): 109–18.

6.702 Bigley, J. "Early Library Development at Southwestern University." *TL* 45 (1984): 90–94.

6.703 Lentz, L. "The Parsons Collection Revisited." *LCT* 30 (1985): 72–81.

6.704 Conrad, J. "Gretchen Howell Colehour at East Texas State University." *TLJ* 62 (1986): 58.

6.705 Conrad, J. H. "A History of the James G. Gee Library." *TL* 47 (1986): 80–86.

6.706 Loyd, R. L. "Theological Libraries in Texas." *TLJ* 62 (1986): 78–81.

6.707 Olbrich, W. L. " 'An Adjunct, Necessary and Proper . . .': The Black Academic Library in Texas, 1876–1986." *TLJ* 62 (1986): 94–103.

6.708 Roberts, W. "D.H. Lawrence at Texas: A Memoir." *LCT* 34 (1986): 22–37.

6.709 Schultz, C. R. " 'A Good Library is an Invitation to Learning': The Texas A&M University Library." *TLJ* 62 (1986): 40–47, 50.

6.710 Snapp, E. "The Woman's Collection, the Texas Woman's University Library." *Special Collections* no. 3 (1986): 101–14.

Vermont

6.711 Winslow, W. C. "The Library of Vermont University." *University Quarterly: Conducted by an Association of Collegiate and Professional Students, in the U.S. and Europe* 4 (July 1861): 30–48.

6.712 White, R. A. "The Library That Saved a University [of Vermont]." *JLH* 1 (1966): 66–69.

Virginia

6.713 Tyler, L. G. "Library of the College of William and Mary." *WMQ* 19 (1910): 48–51.

6.714 *1928 Catalogue of the Library of the University of Virginia*, reproduced in facsimile with an introduction by W. H. Peden. Charlottesville: Printed for the Alderman Library of the University of Virginia, 1945.

6.715 Jennings, J. M. "Notes on the Original Library of the College of William and Mary in Virginia, 1693–1705." *PBSA* 41 (1947): 239–67.

6.716 Byrd, R. E. "The Tracy W. McGregor Library (University of Virginia, 1936–48)." *Antiquarian Bookman* 2 (1948): 973–74.

6.717 Cometti, E., ed. *Jefferson's Ideas on a University Library: Letters from the Founder of the University of Virginia to a Boston Bookseller*. Charlottesville: Tracy W. McGregor Library, University of Virginia, 1950.

6.718 Clemons, H. *The University of Virginia Library*. Charlottesville: University of Virginia Library, 1954.

6.719 Orr, H. A. "The History of the Emory and Henry College Library, 1839–1954." Master's thesis, East Tennessee State College, 1954.

6.720 Edsall, M. H. "History of the Library of the Protestant Episcopal Theological Seminary in Virginia, 1823–1955." Master's thesis, Catholic University of America, 1955.

6.721 O'Neal, W. B. *Jefferson's Fine Arts Library for the University of Virginia, with Additional Notes on Architectural Volumes Known to Have Been Owned by Jefferson*. Charlottesville: University Press of Virginia, 1956.

6.722 Servies, J. A. "Notes on William and Mary Library History." In *In Pursuit of Library History*, edited by J. D. Marshall. Tallahassee: Florida State University School of Library Science, 1961. Pp. 60–62.

6.723 Hudson, J. P. "A History of the Roanoke College Library, 1842–1959." Master's thesis, University of North Carolina, 1963.

6.724 Jennings, J. M. *The Library of the College of William and Mary in Virginia, 1693–1793*. Charlottesville: Published for the Earl Swenn Library by the University Press of Virginia, 1968.

6.725 Alvey, E. "The Library." In *History of Mary Washington College 1908–1972*. Charlottesville: University Press of Virginia, 1974. Pp. 621–51.

6.726 O'Neal, W. B. *Jefferson's Fine Arts Library: His Selections for the University of Virginia Together with His Own Architectural Books*. Charlottesville: University Press of Virginia, 1976.

6.727 Kondayan, B. R. "The Library of Liberty Hall Academy." *VMHB* 86 (1978): 433–46.

6.728 Childress, B. "The Nature of Library Use: The University of Virginia, 1878/79." *JLH* 15 (1980): 454–64.

6.729 Kondayan, B. R. *A Historical Sketch of the Library of Washington and Lee University from the Beginnings in 1776 through 1937*, University Library Publication no. 7. Lexington, Va.: Washington and Lee University, 1980.

6.730 Kondayan, B. R. *The Library of Liberty Hall Academy*, University Library Publication no. 5. Lexington, Va.: Washington and Lee University, 1980.

Washington

6.731 Bauer, H. C. "Books at the University of Washington." *Pacific Spectator* 3 (1949): 63–72.

6.732 Potter, J. C. "The History of the University of Washington Library." Master's thesis, University of Washington, 1954, ACRL Microcard no. 56.

6.733 Golicz, L. J. "A History of Washington State University Libraries from 1946 to 1949." Master's thesis, Washington State University, 1968.

6.734 Gorchels, C. C. "A Land-Grant University Library: The History of the Library of the Washington State University, 1892–1946." Doctoral dissertation, Columbia University, 1971.

6.735 Milczewski, M. A. "Washington. University of Washington Libraries, Seattle." *ELIS* 32 (1981): 426–38.

West Virginia

6.736 Harris, V. "Library Development in Five Denominational Colleges in West Virginia." Master's thesis, Western Reserve University, 1952.

6.737 Amos, A. "A History of Robert F. Kidd Library." Master's thesis, Western Reserve University, 1953.

6.738 Munn, R. F. "West Virginia University Library, 1867–1917." Doctoral dissertation, University of Michigan, 1962.

6.739 Powell, R. A. "A History of the Fairmont State College Library, 1867–1967." Master's thesis, Kent State University, 1967.

6.740 Munn, R. F. "West Virginia University Library." *ELIS* 33 (1982): 107–09.

Wisconsin

6.741 Krueger, H. E. "History of the Carroll College Library." Master's thesis, University of Chicago, 1943.

6.742 Towne, J. E. "President [Charles Kendall] Adams and the University [of Wisconsin] Library [1893–1902]." *WMH* 35 (1952): 257–61.

6.743 Fansler, E. A. *The University of Wisconsin Library: A History (1848–1953)*. Madison: University of Wisconsin Library School, 1953.

6.744 Hubbard, C. L. "History of Wisconsin State College, Oshkosh, Library: September 1871–August 1953." Master's thesis, Drexel Institute of Technology, 1954.

6.745 Fansler, E. A., and Patch, W. H. "The University of Wisconsin Library: A History." *University of Wisconsin Library News* 5 (May 1965): 1–8; 6 (June 1965): 6–14; 7 (September 1965): 9–12; 8 (October 1965): 9–12; 9 (November 1965): 4–8; 10 (December 1965): 6–11; 11 (January 1966): 1–5.

6.746 Cain, S. M. *History of Harold G. Andersen Library at Wisconsin State University—Whitewater*. Whitewater, Wis.: N.p., 1968.

6.747 Daniels, J. P., Johnson, S. F., Nelson, J. A., Roselle, W. C., and Treyz, J. H. "Wisconsin. University of Wisconsin System Libraries." *ELIS* 33 (1982): 194–239.

6.748 Roselle, W. C. "Wisconsin. The American Geographical Society Collection of the University of Wisconsin—Milwaukee." *ELIS* 33 (1982): 176–85.

Wyoming

6.749 Chisum, E. D. "Notes on the Development of the University of Wyoming Libraries and Special Collections." *Annals of Wyoming* 54 (1982): 26–35.

6.750 Chisum, E. D. "Wyoming. University of Wyoming Library." *ELIS* 33 (1982): 260–65.

7.
School Libraries

Broadly conceived interpretive studies of the history of school libraries have yet to be written. This gap in the literature is remarkable given the abundance and depth of the historiography of elementary and secondary education in the United States. The work of historians such as Bernard Bailyn, John Hardin Best, Robert L. Church, Lawrence Cremin, Diane Ravitch, Alexander Rippa, and others as well as revisionists Michael Apple and Michael B. Katz offers substantial background and a variety of intellectual frameworks for potentially fruitful research.

Despite the existence of a number of foundational studies with their ability to support general works that would synthesize trends and ideas, no recent writing has been produced that proposes a major synthesis or hypothesis. Since the early 1970s, the production rate of even the "building block" studies has declined. The surveys began with Stella McClenahan (1932, **7.12**) and Azile Wofford (1940, **7.25**) and continued with H. L. Cecil and W. A. Heaps whose monograph, *School Library Service in the United States: An Interpretive Survey* (1940, **7.24**), remains an essential source. These were followed in the 1950s with contributions by Rosemae W. Campbell (1953, **7.43**), Carolyn I. Whitenack (1956, **7.54**), and T. J. Cole (1959, **7.58**) and, later, by Mabel Smith (1967, **7.75**), C. A. Stolt (1971, **7.96**), Sarah Fenwick who produced an especially well-documented overview, "Library Service to Children and Young People" (1976, **7.104**), and Mary Jane Anderson (1977, **7.110**).

A number of historical works on school libraries have appeared in the form of monographs, theses, or dissertations dealing with growth and development in states or regions of the country. The more significant studies include those by Margaret I. Rufsvold on the South (1934, **7.14**); Margaret Lane on New Jersey (1938, **7.21**); Margaret I. Briggs on Minnesota (1945, **7.29**); Frances E. Hammitt on Illinois, Indiana, and Wisconsin (1948, **7.34**); M. Louise Galloway, whose thesis on Kentucky includes comparisons of school library programs for both blacks and whites (1952, **7.41**); Frederic D. Aldrich on Ohio (1959, **7.57**); M. Constance Melvin on Pennsylvania (1966, **7.71**); James S.

165

Cookston on Louisiana (1971, **7.95**); Ann E. Hall on California (1974, **7.101**); Betty J. Buckingham on Iowa (1978, **7.113**); and Phillip H. Tucker on Missouri (1986, **7.128**). Master's theses or doctoral dissertations have been completed on school libraries in twenty-three states that, when combined with Rufsvold's study on the South and the November 1968 issue of *Illinois Libraries*, containing histories of individual school libraries in the state of Illinois, should provide enterprising historians with a solid foundation for interpretive monographs on American school librarianship.

Not surprisingly, issues pertaining to intellectual freedom and censorship have become essential to an understanding of school libraries and media centers in the twentieth century. Historical insights have been offered by W. Boyd Rayward (1976, **7.109**), Margaret Coughlan (1977, **7.111**), and L. B. Woods, whose statistically oriented analysis deals largely, though not exclusively, with school libraries from 1966 to 1975 (1979, **2.276**; listed in Chapter 2, "General Studies"). Finally, Kenneth L. Donelson surveyed literary and moral censorship and their impact on youth (1981, **7.118**), while Gail P. Sorenson examined the removal of books from school libraries during the period 1972 to 1982 (1983, **7.122**).

Perhaps the most promising studies from a historiographical viewpoint, beginning in the 1940s and continuing into the 1980s, focus on special aspects of school librarianship such as administrative policies, change and growth during selected periods, particular programs or services, and the relationship between school libraries and other types of libraries. Studies in this genre began with Dawson E. Lemley's dissertation on administrative policies in school libraries from 1907 to 1947 (1949, **7.36**). Two decades passed before major studies began to appear with some frequency—the newer contributions include Julia W. Lord's work on the ideology of the school librarian as it evolved from 1900 to 1965 (1968, **7.83**); Gene D. Lanier's dissertation on modern school libraries (1968, **7.82**); Harriet Long's book on children's services in public libraries, one of several studies of similar scope that has clear implications for school libraries (1969, **7.93**); Budd L. Gambee's papers on standards for school media centers (1970, **7.94**) and on the early tension between school and public libraries (1973, **7.97**); Brenda Branyan's overview of women who promoted unified school library and audiovisual programs from 1950 to 1975 (1981, **14.34**; listed in Chapter 14, "Women in Librarianship"); and Rhonda J. Vinson's examination of school media services for the handicapped from 1950 to 1980 (1983, **7.123**). Finally, Robert S. Martin's study of Louis Round Wilson's work on behalf of the 1927 school library standards of the Southern Association serves as a model of scholarship in the history of school libraries (1984, **7.125**).

Before 1876

7.1 "Mr. Divoll and the Public School Library at St. Louis." *American Journal of Education [St. Louis]* 1 (September 1868): 1–2.

1876–1919

7.2 Hutchins, F. A. "School Libraries in Wisconsin." In *The Columbian History of Education in Wisconsin*, edited by J. W. Stearns. Milwaukee: State Committee on Educational Exhibit for Wisconsin, 1893. Pp. 410–12.

7.3 Scudder, H. E. "School Libraries." *Atlantic Monthly* 72 (1893): 678–81.

7.4 Rathbone, J. A. "Co-operation between Libraries and Schools: An Historical Sketch." *LJ* 26 (1901): 187–91.

7.5 Sharp, K. "Illinois Libraries: [Part III] College, Institutional and Special Libraries (Excepting Chicago); Public School Libraries by Counties." *University Studies [University of Illinois]* 2, no. 6 (1907): 369–491.

7.6 Greenman, E. D. "The Development of Secondary School Libraries." *LJ* 38 (1913): 183–89.

7.7 Powell, S. "Early Libraries for Children." In *The Children's Library: A Dynamic Factor in Education.* New York: H.W. Wilson, 1917. Pp. 33–46.

1920–1949

7.8 Williams, M. R. "The Academy Library, 1795–1927." *Phillips Exeter Academy Bulletin* 24 (1928): 5–16.

7.9 Carroll, F. C. "School Library Development in Indiana." Master's thesis, University of Illinois, 1929.

7.10 Huggins, M. A. "High School Libraries in North Carolina: A Study of their Origin, Development, and Present Status." Master's thesis, University of North Carolina, 1929.

7.11 Wesson, J. J. "The High School Library in Mississippi." Master's thesis, University of Mississippi, 1931.

7.12 McClenahan, S. "Growth of School Libraries in America." Master's thesis, Colorado State Teachers College, 1932.

7.13 Abraham, M. L. "Development of Public School Libraries in Pennsylvania." *Pennsylvania Library and Museum Notes* 14 (1934): 411–13.

7.14 Rufsvold, M. I. *History of School Libraries in the South*, Peabody Contributions to Librarianship Number 1. N.p.: George Peabody College for Teachers, 1934.

7.15 Hodnett, V. C. "History of Rural Education in Texas, 1900–1935." Master's thesis, University of Texas, 1935.

7.16 West, E. H. "Texas School Libraries." *HTL* 4 (1935): 97–105.

7.17 Davidge, I. B. "Development of the Public School Library." *LJ* 62 (1937): 680–82.

7.18 Hembree, M. M. "The Growth and Development of Libraries in the Elementary Schools of Texas." Master's thesis, Southern Methodist University, 1937.

7.19 Tinklepaugh, D. K. "School Libraries in New York State: Their History from 1890 to 1930." Master's thesis, Columbia University, 1937.

7.20 Hoyle, N. E. "A Study of the Development of Library Service in the Public Schools of Virginia." Master's thesis, Columbia University, 1938.

7.21 Lane, M. "The Development of Library Service to Public Schools in New Jersey." Master's thesis, Columbia University, 1938.

7.22 Skaar, M. O. "Public School Libraries in Wisconsin: A Historical Survey of School Libraries under the Supervision of the State

167

Department of Public Instruction." Master's thesis, Columbia University, 1938.

7.23 Wofford, A. "The History and Present Status of School Libraries in South Carolina, 1868–1938." Master's thesis, Columbia University, 1938.

7.24 Cecil, H. L., and Heaps, W. A. *School Library Service in the United States: An Interpretive Survey.* New York: H.W. Wilson, 1940.

7.25 Wofford, A. "School Library Evolution." *Phi Delta Kappan* 22 (1940): 283–88.

7.26 Hall, E. "Wisconsin High School Library Housing, 1935–1940." Master's thesis, Columbia University, 1941.

7.27 Gillespie, R. C. "The Development of the High School Library in Texas." Master's thesis, University of Texas, 1942.

7.28 Richardson, O. S. "Library Service in Negro Schools." *NNT* 19 (April 1943): 11–13.

7.29 Briggs, M. I. "The Development of Public School Libraries in Minnesota, 1861–1938." Master's thesis, University of Chicago, 1945.

7.30 Spain, F. L. "High School Libraries in the South." In *Secondary Education in the South,* edited by W. C. Ryan, J. M. Gwynn, and A. K. King. Chapel Hill: University of North Carolina Press, 1946. Pp. 95–114.

7.31 Floyd, G. H. "Library Service in the Public Elementary Schools of Texas." Doctoral dissertation, University of Texas, 1947.

7.32 Taylor, I. M. "Development of School Library Service in Tennessee, 1796 to 1947." Master's thesis, George Peabody College for Teachers, 1947.

7.33 Burge, N. T. "Development of Public School Libraries in North Carolina, 1900–1947." Master's thesis, George Peabody College for Teachers, 1948.

7.34 Hammitt, F. E. "School Library Legislation in Indiana, Illinois, and Wisconsin: A Historical Study." Doctoral dissertation, University of Chicago, 1948.

7.35 Lynch, D. N. *Libraries and Library Service for Children in Brooklyn to 1914.* Brooklyn: N.p., 1948.

7.36 Lemley, D. E. "The Development and Evaluation of Administrative Policies and Practices in Public School Library Service as Evidenced in City School Surveys, 1907–1947." Doctoral dissertation, University of Pittsburgh, 1949.

7.37 Murray, N. L., Jennings, G., and Weathersby, D. B. "Libraries of Abilene City Schools." *NNT* 25 (April 1949): 62–64.

1950–1971

7.38 Piscitello, C. M. "High School Library Standards, 1918–1949: A Critical Summary of Changes and Developments in the United States." Research Paper, University of Illinois, 1950.

7.39 Williams, M. R. "The Academy Library, Then and Now." *Phillips Exeter Academy Bulletin* 46 (1950): 8–12.

7.40 Adams, N. E. "A Study of Regional Library Services for Children in Rural Vermont, 1930–1950." Master's thesis, Drexel Institute of Technology, 1952.

7.41 Galloway, M. L. "The Historical Development and Present Status of Public High School Libraries in Kentucky: 1908 to 1950." *[University of Kentucky Department of Education] Education Bulletin* 20 (1952): 5–121.

7.42 Loyola, M. "School Library: A History." *Catholic School Journal* 53 (1952): 43–45.

7.43 Campbell, R. W. "The Development of Public School Librarianship in the United States." Master's thesis, Colorado College, 1953.

7.44 Noonan, M. Z. "The Development of Libraries in the Chicago Public Elementary Schools." Master's thesis, DePaul University, 1953.

7.45 Rothberger, F. A. "The Provision of Reading Materials, Other than Textbooks, by the Public Schools of New Braunfels, Texas." Master's thesis, University of Texas, 1953.

7.46 Wenger, E. M. "The Development of Brooklyn School Library, 1940–1950, in Relation to Other Cuyahoga County Library Standards." Master's thesis, Western Reserve University, 1953.

7.47 Daughtrey, J. A. "A Content Analysis of Periodical Literature Relating to the Certification of Librarians, 1906–1952." Master's thesis, Atlanta University, 1954.

7.48 Donaldson, L. L. "A Decade and a Half with the School Libraries of Texas." Master's thesis, Texas State College for Women, 1954.

7.49 Donaldson, L. L. "Decade and a Half with Texas School Libraries." *TLJ* 30 (1954): 203–06.

7.50 Feeney, R. B. "The History and Development of the Library in the Public Schools of Houston, Texas." Master's thesis, Texas State College for Women, 1954.

7.51 Henne, F. "The Basic Need in Library Service for Youth and Children." *LQ* 25 (1955): 37–46.

7.52 Songer, F. H. "Development of Public School Libraries in Georgia, 1890–1950." Master's thesis, University of North Carolina, 1955.

7.53 Reifel, L. E. R. "The Texas Congress of Parents and Teachers and the Public School Libraries of Texas." Master's thesis, University of Texas, 1956.

7.54 Whitenack, C. I. "Historical Development of the Elementary School Library." *IllL* 38 (1956): 143–49.

7.55 Redding, B. N. "The Developmental History of the Elementary School Libraries in Guilford County, North Carolina." Master's thesis, University of North Carolina, 1957.

7.56 Van Allen, S. J. "A History of the Elementary School Library in New York State." Master's thesis, State University of New York at Albany, 1958.

7.57 Aldrich, F. D. *The School Library in Ohio with Special Emphasis on Its Legislative History.* New York: Scarecrow Press, 1959.

7.58 Cole, T. J. "Origin and Development of School Libraries." *Peabody Journal of Education* 37 (1959): 87–92.

7.59 Foster, P. M. "An Historical and Descriptive Study of the Bellevue Public School Library System and of Its Administrative Pattern with Implications for the Future." Master's thesis, University of Washington, 1959.

7.60 White, M. "Early Days of the School Library in California." *Bulletin of the School Library Association of California* 31 (1960): 3–5.

7.61 Pratt, S. M. "The Library of St. Stephen's Episcopal School, Austin, Texas, 1950–60." Master's thesis, University of Texas, 1961.

7.62 Seth, O. C. "Development of School Library Standards in Texas." Master's thesis, University of Texas, 1961.

7.63 Vaughan, J. E. "Grammar School Library in the Late Seventeenth Century." *School Libraries* 10 (1961): 511–12.

7.64 Holden, O. "The History of Library Service in Austin Public Schools." Master's thesis, University of Texas, 1962.

7.65 Bell, D. "History of School Libraries in Connecticut, 1839–1860." Master's thesis, Southern Connecticut State College, 1964.

7.66 Gates, E. S. "The Library-School Council of Wethersfield, Connecticut." Master's thesis, Southern Connecticut State College, 1964.

7.67 Bowman, D. J. D. "Case Study of the Office of the School Library Supervisor in the Public Schools of Austin, Texas, 1963." Master's thesis, University of Texas, 1965.

7.68 Dunkley, G. C. "Development of Public School Libraries in Virginia with Emphasis on the Period 1958–1959 through 1963–1964." Master's thesis, University of North Carolina, 1965.

7.69 Lunnon, B. S. "Dade's Libraries: The Nation's Best." *Florida Education* 42 (1965): 19–21.

7.70 Bennett, H. H. "School Libraries in Delaware." *DLAB* 20 (Spring 1966): 9.

7.71 Melvin, M. C. "A History of State Administration and Public School Libraries in Pennsylvania." In *Approaches to Library History,* edited by J. D. Marshall. Tallahassee: JLH, 1966. Pp. 106–18.

7.72 "Public School Library News." *DLAB* 20 (Spring 1966): 31–43.

7.73 Singer, A. R. "History of School Libraries in Connecticut, 1871–1916." Master's thesis, Southern Connecticut State College, 1966.

7.74 Dengler, T. P. "The Public Library in School Library Service, Madison, Wisconsin, 1902–1953." Master's thesis, University of Chicago, 1967.

7.75 Smith, M. "Development of the Elementary School Library." Master's thesis, University of Mississippi, 1967.

7.76 Adams, R. T. "A History of School Libraries in Connecticut, 1948–1967." Master's thesis, Southern Connecticut State College, 1968.

7.77 Brown, T. M. "Some Comments on the Growth of Library Service at the New Trier High Schools, Northfield-Winnetka." *IllL* 50 (1968): 925–30.

7.78 Crawford, L. "Those Things That Are Best, Library Services at Oak Park-River Forest High School." *IllL* 50 (1968): 931–37.

7.79 "The Development of Evanston Elementary School Library Service." *IllL* 50 (1968): 958–61.

7.80 Donahue, R. "Elementary School Libraries Grow in Decatur." *IllL* 50 (1968): 944–48.

7.81 Karloski, R. "History of the Carlinville Community Unit School Libraries." *IllL* 50 (1968): 891–94.

7.82 Lanier, G. D. "The Transformation of School Libraries into Instructional Materials Centers." Doctoral dissertation, University of North Carolina, 1968.

7.83 Lord, J. W. "The Cosmic World of Childhood: The Ideology of the Children's Librarians, 1900–1965." Doctoral dissertation, Emory University, 1968.

7.84 Miller, M. "The Development of an IMC." *IllL* 50 (1968): 938–43.

7.85 Peterson, M., and Vogenthaler, E. "Incandescence: The History of School Library Service in the Chicago Public Schools." *IllL* 50 (1968): 895–906.

7.86 Putnam, V. "The History and Development of School Library Service in the Elementary Schools of Oak Park Elementary School No. 97." *IllL* 50 (1968): 949–57.

7.87 Rukus, A. T. "History of School Libraries in Connecticut, 1917–1947." Master's thesis, Southern Connecticut State College, 1968.

7.88 Stevenson, M. "From Wastepaper to Plenty." *IllL* 50 (1968): 888–90.

7.89 Taylor, L. K. "A Tradition of Innovation: A History of Evanston Township High School's Library." *IllL* 50 (1968): 907–24.

7.90 Thomassen, C., ed. "History of [Illinois] School Libraries." *IllL* 50 (1968): 853–970.

7.91 Van Oord, J. E. I. "Illinois School Libraries: An Historical Survey." *IllL* 50 (1968): 855–59.

7.92 Johnson, M. H. "The History and Development of Instructional Materials Centers in School Libraries." Master's thesis, Atlanta University, 1969.

7.93 Long, H. G. *Public Library Service to Children: Foundation and Development.* Metuchen, N.J.: Scarecrow Press, 1969.

7.94 Gambee, B. L. "Standards for School Media Programs, 1920: A Lesson from History." *AL* 1 (1970): 483–85.

7.95 Cookston, J. S. "Development of Louisiana Public School Libraries, 1929–1965." Doctoral dissertation, Louisiana State University, 1971.

7.96 Stolt, C. A. "Schools and School Libraries over Two Centuries: The Presidential Address at the Annual Conference of the School Library Association on 30th December, 1970." *School Libraries* 19 (1971): 15–23, 101–07.

1972–1986

7.97 Gambee, B. L. "'An Alien Body': Relationships Between the Public Library and the Public Schools, 1876–1920." In *Ball State University Library Science Lectures*, First Series. Muncie, Ind.: Ball State University, Department of Library Science, 1973. Pp. 1–23.

7.98 Gaston, M. "Greenville High School: Mississippi's Oldest School Library." *Mississippi Library News* 37 (1973): 29–30.

7.99 Sassé, M. "Invisible Women: The Children's Librarian in America." *LJ* 98 (1973): 213–17.

7.100 Alvey, R. G. "The Historical Development of Organized Story-Telling to Children in the United States." Doctoral dissertation, University of Pennsylvania, 1974.

7.101 Hall, A. E. "Public Elementary and Secondary School Library Development in California, 1850–1966." Doctoral dissertation, Columbia University, 1974.

7.102 Hill, M. E. "The Philosophical Aspects of the Newbery Medal Award Books, 1922–1971." Doctoral dissertation, Arizona State University, 1974.

7.103 Barr, J. L. C. "The Immigrant in Children's Fictional Books Recommended for American Libraries, 1883–1939." Doctoral dissertation, Indiana University, 1976.

7.104 Fenwick, S. I. "Library Service to Children and Young People." *LibT* 25 (1976): 329–60.

7.105 Geller, E. "Somewhat Free: Post-Civil War Writing for Children." *WLB* 51 (1976): 172–76.

7.106 Jackson, C. O. "Service to Urban Children." In *A Century of Service: Librarianship in the United States and Canada*, edited by S. L. Jackson, E. B. Herling, and E. J. Josey. Chicago: American Library Association, 1976. Pp. 20–41.

7.107 Lopez, M. D. "Children's Libraries: Nineteenth Century American Origins." *JLH* 11 (1976): 316–42.

7.108 Pratt, C. "San Jacinto Unified School and Library: A History." *California School Libraries* 47 (1976): 11–16.

7.109 Rayward, W. B. "What Shall They Read? A Historical Perspective." *WLB* 51 (1976): 146–53.

7.110 Anderson, M. J. "Trends in Library Service for Children: Past, Present, and Where Do We Go from Here?" *NCL* 34 (1977): 49–54.

7.111 Coughlan, M. "Guardians of the Young . . . Why There Has Never Been—and Probably Never Will Be—Intellectual Freedom for Children." *TN* 33 (1977): 137–48.

7.112 Hawks, G. P. "A Nineteenth-Century School Library: Early Years in Milwaukee." *JLH* 12 (1977): 359–63.

7.113 Buckingham, B. J. "The Role of Professional Associations in the Development of School Librarians in Iowa." Doctoral dissertation, University of Minnesota, 1978.

7.114 Davies, R. A. "School Libraries." *ELIS* 26 (1979): 360–71.

7.115 Herrin, B. R. "A History and Analysis of the William Allen White Children's Book Award." Doctoral dissertation, Kansas State University, 1979.

7.116 Miller, M. "How Long, Oh Lord, Do We Roam in the Wilderness?" *SchLJ* 26 (1979): 5–11.

7.117 Morrison, L. "Fifty Years of 'Books for the Teenage.' " *SchLJ* 26 (1979): 44–50.

7.118 Donelson, K. L. "Shoddy and Pernicious Books and Youthful Purity: Literary and Moral Censorship, Then and Now." *LQ* 51 (1981): 4–19.

7.119 Vance, K. E. "Then and Now: A Personal View of School Libraries in Michigan, 1950–1980." *Media Spectrum* 8 (1981): 3–4.

7.120 Pentlin, F. C. "The Evolution of Public School Libraries in Missouri and the 1901 Library Law." Master's thesis, Central Missouri State University, 1982.

7.121 Thomas, F. H. "The Genesis of Children's Services in the American Public Library: 1875–1906." Doctoral dissertation, University of Wisconsin, 1982.

7.122 Sorenson, G. P. "Removal of Books from School Libraries, 1972–1982: Board of Education v. Pico and Its Antecedents." *Journal of Law and Education* 12 (1983): 17–41.

7.123 Vinson, R. J. "School Library Media Service for Handicapped Students, 1950–1980." Doctoral dissertation, Southern Illinois University, 1983.

7.124 Griggs, B. "School Libraries in New York State: Their Roots." *BKM* 42 (1984): 166–71.

7.125 Martin, R. S. "Louis Round Wilson and the Library Standards of the Southern Association, 1926–1929." *JLH* 19 (1984): 259–81.

7.126 McCracken, A. "Concord: Chronology of a Crisis." *ArkL* 42 (March 1985): 6–10.

7.127 Rodenberger, L. "It All Depended on the Teacher: Learning Resources in Texas Rural Schools." *TLJ* 62 (1986): 87–92.

7.128 Tucker, P. H. "Public Elementary and Secondary School Library Development in Missouri, 1945–1980." Doctoral dissertation, Southern Illinois University, Carbondale, 1986.

8.
State Libraries

The historiography of state libraries resembles that of school libraries in one important respect—although a number of the foundation studies are in place, the broad interpretive monographs have not been written. Background information is readily available in the form of state statutes, archival records, and narrative histories. Cultural geographers Wilbur Zelinsky and Raymond D. Gastil in *The Cultural Geography of the United States* (Englewood Cliffs, N.J.: Prentice-Hall, 1973) and *Cultural Regions of the United States* (Seattle: University of Washington Press, 1975), respectively, offer insight into state and regional characteristics and habits of mind that may affect library services and collections. Impressionistic works such as John Gunther's *Inside U.S.A.* (New York: Harper, 1947) and *The Book of America: Inside 50 States Today* by Neal R. Peirce and Jerry Hagstrom (New York: Norton, 1983) help further to capture something of a "spirit of place."

Unlike local history, state history has long been the preserve of academic and professional historians. The number of recent scholarly monographs, available for all fifty states and offering a wide array of viewpoints for retrospective analysis, grew significantly with the publication in the 1970s of the States and the Nation Series, consisting of brief studies for each state issued jointly by W. W. Norton and the American Association for State and Local History. It bears mention that many state histories are applicable either to more general or to more specialized studies and may add considerably to an understanding of economic, social, or cultural developments in a state or region, including those relating to librarianship.

Perhaps the absence of a general history of state libraries in the United States is due, in part, to the difficulties in making broad statements about a wide array of organizational structures and institutional objectives as well as statutory and financial support systems. (To use one example, sixteen state libraries are under a department of education, twenty report to an independent board or commission, twelve belong to a unit of the executive branch, and two are under the legislative branch.)

The more comprehensive and thoroughly researched studies should become the foundation for future regional or national histories of state library development. One can only single out a few works of major importance from among the several useful, but generally limited, studies about individual state libraries or library commissions that are listed here. Of special note are works by Eugenia R. Babylon on the North Carolina Library Commission (1954, **8.39**), Harriet Stephenson on the Louisiana State Library (1957, **8.47**), John C. Larsen on the Michigan State Library (1967, **8.63**), Cecil R. Roseberry on the New York State Library (1970, **8.71**), M. M. Vannorsdall on state library services in Ohio (1974, **8.76**), Larry J. Barr on the Indiana State Library (1976, **8.79**), and Jeannine L. Laughlin on the Mississippi Library Commission (1983, **8.87**).

The profession can hope that state library services will be subjected to serious research in the form of scholarly articles such as those by Richard Logsdon and M. J. Smith whose careful study of the librarians of the state of Indiana appeared in the final two issues of *Library Occurrent* (1980, **8.83**; 1980, **8.84**). Wayne A. Wiegand's "The Historical Development of State Library Agencies" offers the most possibilities in terms of its potential for further analysis (1986, **8.90**). Wiegand hypothesized the existence of four distinct periods of development: before 1890, when libraries grew largely by gifts and exchange; 1890 to 1920, when literacy movements undergirded the creation of library commissions; 1920 to 1956, when a number of states consolidated library services in order to reduce duplication; and 1956 to 1986, when federal support assisted state agencies in strengthening uniform services on a statewide basis. Writings of similar scope and purpose, whether in the form of articles or monographs, would add substantially to an understanding of state librarianship.

Before 1876

8.1 "New York State Library." *NLGPC* 2 (15 December 1852): 235.

1876–1919

8.2 Homes, H. A. "State and Territorial Libraries." In *Public Libraries in the United States of America: Their History, Condition and Management; Special Report, Part I,* U.S. Bureau of Education. Washington, D.C.: Government Printing Office, 1876. Pp. 292–311.

8.3 Galbreath, C. B. "The State Library and the Public Schools." *Ohio Education Monthly* 46 (1897): 468–72.

8.4 Winkler, E. W. "Some Historical Activities of the Texas Library and Historical Commission." *[Texas State Historical Association] Quarterly* 14 (1911): 294–304.

8.5 "Texas Library and Historical Commission." *HTL* 3 (1915–1916): 76–80.

8.6 New York State Library. *New York State Library, 1818–1918: A Souvenir of the Visit of the ALA July 6, 1918, Commemorating the 100th Anniversary of the Founding of the Library.* Albany, N.Y.: The Library, 1918.

8.7 Ryan, D. T. "The State Library and Its Founder." *Publications of Ohio State Archives and Historical Society* 38 (1919): 98–114.

1920–1949

8.8 Tennessee Historical Committee. *Tennessee Department of Library, Archives, and History.* Nashville: Tennessee Industrial School Printing Department, 1922.

8.9 "A Century of the Massachusetts State Library." *LJ* 51 (1926): 229–30.

8.10 Godard, G. S. "Development of the State Library." *Connecticut Bar Journal* 1 (1927): 319–29.

8.11 Suess, G. M. "Library Legislation in Nebraska." Master's thesis, University of Illinois, 1927.

8.12 Michigan State Library. *Michigan State Library, 1828–1928, One Hundred Years.* Lansing: Michigan State Library, 1928.

8.13 Godard, G. S. "A Brief Summary of the Activities of the Connecticut State Library." In *Essays Offered to Herbert Putnam by His Colleagues and Friends on His Thirtieth Anniversary as Librarian of Congress, 5 April 1929,* edited by W. W. Bishop and A. Keogh. New Haven: Yale University Press, 1929. Pp. 172–77.

8.14 McNitt, E. U. "Short History of the Indiana State Library." *Library Occurrent* 10 (1931): 21–30.

8.15 Young, C. "The History of the Texas State Library." Master's thesis, University of Texas, 1932.

8.16 MacKinney, G. "A Century of Library Development of the Pennsylvania State Library." *PLN* 14 (1934): 407–11.

8.17 Wilcox, F. M. "The Texas Library and Historical Commission; State Library." *HTL* 4 (1935): 135–38.

8.18 Smith, C. E. "The Growth of the Service of the Ohio State Traveling Library." Master's thesis, University of Cincinnati, 1936.

8.19 Thornton, E. M. *The Georgia State Library, 1926–1935.* Atlanta: Stein Printing Co., State Printers, 1936.

8.20 Bliss, R. P. *A History of the Pennsylvania State Library.* Harrisburg, Pa.: Printed for the Pennsylvania Library Association by the Telegraph Press, 1937.

8.21 Rowe, W. D. "The Development of the Oregon State Library and Its Contributions to the Public Schools." Master's thesis, University of Oregon, 1939.

8.22 Cheney, F. N. "Historical and Bibliographical Study of the Administrative

Departments of the State of Tennessee." Master's thesis, Columbia University, 1940.

8.23 VanMale, J. E. "A History of Library Extension in Colorado, 1890–1930." Master's thesis, University of Denver, 1940.

8.24 Wright, L. M. "Iowa's Oldest Library." *Iowa Journal of History and Politics* 38 (1940): 408–28.

8.25 Flack, H. E. "History and Growth of Legislative Reference Libraries." *SL* 32 (1941): 294–97.

8.26 Gillis, M. R. "California State Library: Its Hundred Years (1850–1950)." *CLB* 11 (1949): 55–57.

8.27 Wilson, L. R. "North Carolina Library Commission, 1909–1949." *NCL* 8 (1949): 7–10.

1950–1971

8.28 Dixon, M., and Gittinger, N. M. *The First Twenty-five Years of the Louisiana State Library, 1925–1950.* Baton Rouge: The Library, 1950.

8.29 Chalker, W. J. "The Historical Development of the Florida State Library, 1845–1959." Master's thesis, George Peabody College for Teachers, 1951.

8.30 Richards, E. S. "Fifty Years with the Library Commission for the State of Delaware." Master's thesis, Drexel Institute of Technology, 1951.

8.31 Settlemire, C. L. "The Tennessee State Library, 1854–1923." Master's thesis, George Peabody College for Teachers, 1951.

8.32 Smith, D. "Texas State Library and Historical Commission." *HT* 2 (1951): 763.

8.33 Bird, M. F. "History of the Demonstration Program of the Illinois State Library." Master's thesis, University of Chicago, 1952.

8.34 Gibson, T. J. "The Texas State Library [since 1839]." *TLJ* 28 (1952): 84–91.

8.35 Johnston, M. E. "New Jersey State Library: A History of the Development in Public Library Service." Master's thesis, Kent State University, 1952.

8.36 Smither, H. W. "Texas State Library." *HT* 2 (1952): 762–63.

8.37 Culver, E. M. "Louisiana State Library [and Its Predecessors, 1909–53]." *LLAB* 16 (1953): 18–20, 41–48.

8.38 Moore, M. D. "The Tennessee State Library in the Capitol (1853–1953)." *THQ* 12 (1953): 3–22.

8.39 Babylon, E. R. "History of the North Carolina Library Commission." Master's thesis, University of North Carolina, 1954.

8.40 *A Gift From the State to Oregonians: A Half Century of Reading in Oregon, 1905–1955.* Salem, Ore.: Oregon State Library, 1955.

8.41 Hintz, C. W. "Oregon State Library: Its First Fifty Years." *PNLAQ* 20 (1955): 15–19.

8.42 Coover, R. W. "A History of the Maryland State Library, 1827–1939 (with a Summary of Events from 1939 to 1959)." Master's thesis, Catholic University of America, 1956, ACRL Microcard no. 88.

8.43 "John M. Bernhisel and the Territorial Library." *Utah Historical Quarterly* 24 (1956): 359–62.

8.44 Rose, K. "The Story of a Music Collection." *THQ* 15 (1956): 356–63.

8.45 Vloebergh, H. E. "A History of the New York State Library from 1818 to 1905." Master's thesis, Catholic University of America, 1956, ACRL Microcard no. 83.

8.46 Byrnes, H. W. "State Library Commission Observes Its Fiftieth Anniversary, 1907–1957." *North Dakota Library Notes and News* 39 (Winter 1957): 1–3.

8.47 Stephenson, H. S. "History of the Louisiana State Library, Formerly Louisiana Library Commission." Doctoral dissertation, Louisiana State University, 1957.

8.48 Barrett, M. A. "Development of Library Extension in New Mexico." Master's thesis, Western Reserve University, 1958, ACRL Microcard no. 97.

8.49 Swint, H. L. "The Historical Activities of the State of Tennessee." *THQ* 17 (1958): 291–300.

8.50 Currier, L. G. "The Lengthened Shadow: Essae M. Culver and the Louisiana State Library [1925–58]." *BALA* 53 (1959): 35–37.

8.51 Peace, W. K. "A History of the Texas State Library with Emphasis on the Period from 1930 to 1958." Master's thesis, University of Texas, 1959.

8.52 Phelps, D. J. "Organization and Development of the Alaska Department of Library Service, 1955–1959." Master's thesis, University of Utah, 1960.

8.53 MacKay, M. B. "South Dakota State Library Commission." *South Dakota Library Bulletin* 49 (1963): 5–9.

8.54 Burnett, P. M. "The Development of State Libraries and Library Extension Service in Arizona and New Mexico." *LQ* 35 (1965): 31–51.

8.55 Cahill, A. M. "19th Century Library Innovation: The Division of Library Extension from 1890 to 1940." *Bay State Librarian* 55 (1965): 7–12.

8.56 Drury, J. W. *The Kansas Traveling Library Commission: An Administrative History.* Lawrence: University of Kansas, Governmental Research Center, 1965.

8.57 Handy, C. H. "The Connecticut State Library, 1851–1936." Master's thesis, Southern Connecticut State College, 1965.

8.58 "Massachusetts Division of Library Extension, Executive Staff, 1890–1965." *Bay State Librarian* 55 (1965): 15–16.

8.59 Capozzi, M. R. "A History of Maryland State Library Agencies, 1902–1945." Master's thesis, Catholic University of America, 1966.

8.60 Jamsen, E. "Michigan State Library: Its First Hundred Years." *Michigan Librarian* 32 (1966): 8–11.

8.61 "Sixty-Five Years of Progress: The State Library Commission, 1901–1966." *DLAB* 20 (Spring 1966): 10–12.

8.62 Winfrey, D. H. "The Texas State Library: Its History and Service to the People of Texas." *TL* 28 (1966): 12–22.

8.63 Larsen, J. C. "A Study in Service: The Historical Development of the Michigan State Library and Its Territorial Predecessor, the Legislative Council Library, 1828–1941." Doctoral dissertation, University of Michigan, 1967.

8.64 Levine, L. E. "The Assembly Legislative Reference Service: A Short History." *CalL* 28 (1967): 107–11.

8.65 Simmons, B. S. "In Retrospect: Audiovisual Services in the Illinois State Library." *IllL* 49 (1967): 106–17.

8.66 Smith, C. "Books for People, 1817–1967." *Wonderful World of Ohio* 31 (December 1967): 22–27.

8.67 Smith, C. "The State Library—150 Years." *OLAB* 38 (1968): 4–7.

8.68 Brown, C. C. "History of the New Hampshire State Library." Master's thesis, Southern Connecticut State College, 1969.

8.69 Kunkle, H. J. "A Historical Survey of the Extension Activities of the California State Library with Particular Emphasis on Its Role in Rural Library Development, 1850–1966." Doctoral dissertation, Florida State University, 1969.

8.70 Larsen, J. C. "The Ventriloquist and the State Library: The Vattemare Correspondence." *Michigan Librarian* 36 (1970): 6–7.

8.71 Roseberry, C. R. *A History of the New York State Library.* Albany: New York State Library, 1970.

1972–1986

8.72 Friend, L. B. "Herbert Eugene Bolton and the Texas State Library." *TL* 35 (1973): 49–65.

8.73 Clack, C. Y. "The State Library: 1835–1883." *TL* 36 (1974): 99–113.

8.74 Conmy, P. T. "California's Ex-Officio State Librarians, 1850–1861." *NNCL* 69 (1974): 247–57.

8.75 Friend, L. B. "The Texas State Library: A Seed Bed for the Study of Texas History and Government." *TL* 36 (1974): 147–65.

8.76 Vannorsdall, M. M. "The Development of Library Services at the State Level in Ohio, 1817–1896." Doctoral dissertation, University of Michigan, 1974.

8.77 Esbin, M. "Old Capitol Library: Its History, Contents, and Restoration." *Annals of Iowa* 42 (1975): 523–40.

8.78 Rogers, J. W. "The Texas State Library, 1918–1928." *TL* 37 (1975): 23–47.

8.79 Barr, L. J. "The Indiana State Library, 1825–1925." Doctoral dissertation, Indiana University, 1976.

8.80 Winfrey, D. H. "Texas State Library." *HT* 3 (1976): 995–96.

8.81 "Chronology of the Illinois State Library." *IllL* 59 (1977): 388–404.

8.82 York, M. C. "A History of the North Carolina State Library, 1812–1888." Master's thesis, University of North Carolina, 1978.

8.83 Logsdon, R. L., and Smith, M. J. "The Foundation is Laid: The Indiana Librarians from 1851–1875." *Library Occurrent* 26 (1980): 423–37.

8.84 Logsdon, R. L., and Smith, M. J. "Indiana State Library (1825–1851) and the Men Who Ran It." *Library Occurrent* 26 (1980): 379–90.

8.85 [Huff, M.] "Commission Members Included Distinguished Men and Women." *TL* 42 (1980): 187–96.

8.86 Schultz, M. "The Changing Role of the Texas State Library: Alternate Models for Coordination of Statewide Library Service." Doctoral dissertation, University of Texas, 1981.

8.87 Laughlin, J. L. "The Mississippi Library Commission: A Force for Library Development." Doctoral dissertation, Indiana University, 1983.

8.88 Josey, E. J. "The Regents and the Development of a Statewide Library Policy and Program, 1905–1950." *BKM* 42 (1984): 147–52.

8.89 Noe, K. "The Vision and the Reality: A History of the KDLA." *Kentucky Libraries* 49 (1985): 2–8.

8.90 Wiegand, W. A. "The Historical Development of State Library Agencies." In *State Library Services and Issues: Facing Future Challenges,* edited by C. R. McClure. Norwood, N.J.: Ablex Publishing Corp., 1986. Pp. 1–16.

9.

Special Libraries

A special library has always been difficult for librarians to define. Usually the term refers to a library that provides information for institutions whose subject focus is limited in scope. Given the organization of this bibliography, this chapter includes, in addition to a section on general studies, citations to six kinds of special libraries: private research libraries; historical society, museum, and institute libraries; business and industrial libraries; law libraries; medical libraries; and government libraries and programs. In order to keep citations from appearing in more than one chapter and to fit the entries of this chapter into the bibliography as a whole, several decisions became necessary. Departmental libraries of academic and public libraries are treated in relevant previous chapters rather than here, with the exception of law and medical libraries, which appear here, since they have strong bonds across institutional lines. State libraries, certainly government libraries, receive their own chapter. Early society libraries that ceased before the mid-nineteenth century will be found in Chapter 4, "Predecessors of the Public Library." Items relating to special library associations will be found in Chapter 12, "Library Associations."

General Studies

A general overview of special library development is A. W. John's book on the subject (1968, 9.20) which provides a useful historical summary. Two later interpretations have appeared in the contributions of Elin B. Christianson (1976, 9.32) and Angelina Martinez (1976, 9.34). The definitive historical study of special libraries in America has not yet been written.

179

Private Research Libraries

One of the best places to begin for an overview of this type of library, the kind that would include members of the Independent Research Libraries Association, is *Research Institutions and Learned Societies*, edited by Joseph C. Kiger (1982, **9.130**). Extending coverage to types of libraries found in the following sections of this essay, it provides good historical summaries for dozens of private research libraries.

Individual libraries have received treatment in a variety of publications. The more significant of these include William E. Lingelbach (1946, **9.62**; 1953, **9.83**) and Murphy D. Smith (1976, **9.122**) on the American Philosophical Society; Clifford K. Shipton (1949, **9.68**), Clarence S. Brigham (1958, **9.90**), and William Joyce (1981, **9.129**) on the American Antiquarian Society; Guy Marco (1966, **9.95**) and Lawrence Towner (1970, **9.108**) on the Newberry Library; J. Christian Bay (1945, **9.60**) on the Crerar Library; Robert O. Schad (1931, **9.56**) and John E. Pomfret (1969, **9.106**) on the Huntington Library; and Giles E. Dawson (1949, **9.65**), Stanley King (1950, **9.71**), Louis B. Wright (1968, **9.102**), and Dorothy Mason with others (1969–70, **9.105**) on the Folger Library. One should also consult Chapter 3, "Private Libraries and Reading Tastes," and Chapter 15, "Biographies of Individual Librarians and Library Benefactors," for a number of relevant references that deal with the origins of some of these institutions. Presidential libraries, bearing the names of the persons they honor, are included in the section on government libraries.

Historical Society, Museum, and Institute Libraries

Only a few of the nation's many historical society and museum libraries have received adequate treatment by historians, even though they have made great use of these libraries in research. However, several informative studies are available, mostly articles and master's theses. In recent years these libraries have attracted renewed interest. Examples include Lawrence Reed's dissertation on the manuscript collection of the State Historical Society of Wisconsin (1983, **9.261**) and John Colson's paper on the relation of the Society with the American Bureau of Industrial Research in the early twentieth century (1983, **9.258**). Pamela Spence Richards has brought the history of the New York Historical Society up to date with her monograph (1984, **9.264**).

A number of citations to the history and development of historical societies have been included since they treat, to a large extent, the libraries and the manuscript and book collecting habits of the societies and because such sources were discovered in the systematic examination of various reference tools. A comprehensive list of the histories of state and local historical societies is beyond the scope of this compilation even though a work of this nature could conceivably result in a number of historical references to libraries. Definitional issues involving the closely related terms of "library," "history," and "archives" are discussed in Chapter 10, "Archival Enterprise."

Business and Industrial Libraries

This type of special library is ripe for substantive scholarship. The standard work on the subject is still Anthony T. Kruzas's excellent book, *Business and Industrial Libraries in the United States, 1820–1940* (1965, **9.299**), but much has happened since the war years. Some serious work is underway and renewed interest in business archives may encourage more effort. Two examples of more recent work are Victor Jelin's controversial study of the intellectual origins of the modern industrial library (1970, **9.306**) and Ellis Mount's history of the Engineering Societies Library (1982, **9.311**).

Law Libraries

Law libraries have become the focus of a substantial number of studies. Especially important in providing general interpretive frameworks for the study of law libraries are such works as Christine A. Brock's "Law Libraries and Librarians: A Revisionist History" (1974, **9.360**). Other studies deal with specific aspects of libraries concerned with legal materials, such as Maurice L. Cohen and others on the historical development of the lawyer's library (1968, **9.351**); Michael H. Harris on the lawyer's library on the frontier (1972, **3.148**; listed in Chapter 3, "Private Libraries and Reading Tastes"); and James L. Mullins on law school libraries, 1932–1976 (1984, **9.375**). Still other works deal with individual law libraries. Citations to libraries in correctional institutions are represented by the work of Ruth E. Johnson (1959, **9.343**) and Austin H. MacCormick (1970, **9.356**).

Medical Libraries

Medical library history has enjoyed steady growth. Although most studies deal with individual collections, several general and broader treatments exist. One such work is Virginia Donley's chronology of medical library development (1957, **9.433**). Others dealing with more limited topics include Albert Huntington's survey of the early development of medical libraries (1904, **9.385**); Thomas Keys's essay on private medical libraries (1958, **3.98**; listed in Chapter 3, "Private Libraries and Reading Tastes"); and Marjorie Wannarka's history of medical library collections in public libraries (1968, **9.464**). The nation's leading medical library—the National Library of Medicine, founded as the library of the Army Surgeon General—has attracted considerable attention from historians. E. E. Hume contributed a number of articles on this library, the most extensive being an essay in *Isis* (1937, **9.398**). The landmark work now is Wyndham D. Miles's volume, *A History of the National Library of Medicine: The Nation's Treasury of Medical Knowledge* (1982, **9.487**).

Government Libraries and Programs

This section includes the Library of Congress, federal and state departmental and agency libraries, presidential libraries, military service libraries, and government library programs deriving from legislative initiatives. Medical, law, prison, state, and other types of libraries, as well as archival repositories, receive treatment in other sections and chapters as previously indicated. Although many major and minor government libraries have been studied historically by librarians and others, the Library of Congress has attracted the most sustained attention. An important survey and still a standard overview is David Mearns's book (1947, **9.533**). The leading authority on Library of Congress history is John Y. Cole, who has written extensively about the library, its development, and its leaders. His book-length chronological history (1979, **9.646**) is a valuable contribution, as are his more than a dozen articles on special aspects of the Library's history, many of them appearing in the now defunct *Quarterly Journal of the Library of Congress*. Another volume that presents an updated historical overview is by Charles A. Goodrum and Helen W. Dalrymple (1982, **9.672**). For librarians of Congress one should consult the extensive material in Chapter 15, "Biographies of Individual Librarians and Library Benefactors." The Smithsonian Institution library has had a checkered history; a basic work for the early years, which has several chapters on the library, is *The Smithsonian Institution, 1846–1896: The History of Its First Half Century* (1897, **9.502**). A comprehensive history has yet to be written. A final example of extensive historical treatment of a government library is *That All May Read: Library Service for Blind and Physically Handicapped People* (1983, **2.319**; listed and discussed in Chapter 2, "General Studies.")

In recent decades federal initiatives, in cooperation with state and local governments, significantly affected library development and thus library history. Some important works that evaluate these programs have begun to appear. Among the more noteworthy of these are *The Library Services and Construction Act: An Historical Overview from the Viewpoint of Major Participants* (1983, **9.682**), edited by Edward G. Holley and Robert F. Schremser, and Kathleen Molz's survey, *National Planning for Library Service, 1935–1975* (1984, **2.335**; listed in Chapter 2, "General Studies.") More works such as these may be anticipated.

General Studies

9.1 Moss, L. *Annals of the United States Christian Commission.* Philadelphia: Lippincott, 1868.

9.2 Dana, J. C. "The Evolution of the Special Library." *SL* 5 (1914): 70–76.

9.3 Usher, R. J. "The Place of the Endowed Reference Library in the Community." In *Essays Offered to Herbert Putnam by His Colleagues and Friends on His Thirtieth Anniversary as Librarian of Congress, 5 April 1929,* edited by W. W. Bishop and A. Keogh. New Haven: Yale University Press, 1929. Pp. 467–73.

9.4 Kahn, F. "The Alex W. Spence Memorial Library of the Civic Federation of Dallas." *NNT* 11 (April 1935): 3–4.

9.5 Coman, E. T. "Special Librarianship in California." *CLB* 11 (1950): 174–76.

9.6 Varner, C. "The Development of Special Libraries in St. Paul and Minneapolis, Minnesota, 1849–1949." Master's thesis, University of Chicago, 1950.

9.7 Brown, R. E. "History of Special Libraries in Denver, Colorado, 1861–1953." Master's thesis, University of Chicago, 1955.

9.8 Irwin, R. B. "Libraries for the Blind." In *As I Saw It.* New York: American Foundation for the Blind, 1955. Pp. 67–81.

9.9 Irwin, R. B. "Periodicals for the Blind." In *As I Saw It.* New York: American Federation for the Blind, 1955. Pp. 109–23.

9.10 Irwin, R. B. "The Talking Book." In *As I Saw It.* New York: American Foundation for the Blind, 1955. Pp. 83–07.

9.11 Thomas, R. D. "An Evaluation and Analysis of the Literature on the Newspaper Library, 1900–1957." Master's thesis, Catholic University of America, 1959.

9.12 McMullen, H. "Special Libraries in Antebellum Kentucky." *Register of the Kentucky State Historical Society* 59 (1961): 29–46.

9.13 Stevens, E. L. "One Hundred and Ten Years of Special Library Service in Honolulu." *SL* 52 (1961): 143–47.

9.14 Brodman, E. "The Special Library, Mirror of Its Society: Keynote Address." In *Approaches to Library History,* edited by J. D. Marshall. Tallahassee: JLH, 1966. Pp. 32–48.

9.15 Hartos, M. A. C. "The Provision of Libraries in Protestant Churches in the United States of America, with Examples of Current Practice Drawn from Libraries in Houston, Texas." Master's thesis, University of Texas, 1966.

9.16 Mullins, L. S. "The Rise of Map Libraries in America during the Nineteenth Century." *SLAGMDB* 63 (1966): 2–11.

9.17 "Special Libraries." *DLAB* 20 (Spring 1966): 43–48.

9.18 Zachert, M. J. "American Special Libraries: Eighteenth Century Ancestors." In *Approaches to Library History,* edited by J. D. Marshall. Tallahassee: JLH, 1966. Pp. 141–50.

9.19 Ristow, W. W. "The Emergence of Maps in Libraries." *SL* 58 (1967): 400–419.

9.20 Johns, A. W. *Special Libraries: Development of the Concept, Their Organization, and Their Services.* Metuchen, N.J.: Scarecrow Press, 1968.

9.21 Schultz, C. K., and Garwig, P. L. "History of the American Documentation Institute—A Sketch." *American Documentation* 20 (1969): 152–60.

9.22 McLoughlin, E. C. "History of the Joseph Conrad Memorial Library of the Seaman's Church Institute of New York." Research Paper, Long Island University, 1970.

9.23 West, E. K. "A History of the Bibliographic Center for Research: Rocky Mountain Region, 1942–1966." Master's thesis, Long Island University, 1970.

9.24 Brodman, E. "Scientists as Librarians: A Historical Review." *Library and Information Science [Mita Society]* 9 (1971): 105–13.

9.25 Cavitt, L. C. "History of the Civic Federation of Dallas." Master's thesis, Southern Methodist University, 1971.

9.26 Higgins, M. H. "A History of the Submarine Force Library and Museum in New London, Connecticut." Research Paper, Long Island University, 1971.

9.27 Yanchisin, D. A. "For Carolina's Sake—A Case History in Special Librarianship." *JLH* 6 (1971): 41–71.

9.28 Smith, M. J. "American Battleship Libraries." *Library Occurrent* 24 (1973): 335–38.

9.29 Langner, M. C. "User and User Services in Science Libraries, 1945–1965." *LibT* 23 (1974): 7–30.

9.30 Adkinson, B. W. "Federal Government's Support of Information Activities." *BASIS* 2 (1976): 24–26.

9.31 Becker, J. "The Rich Heritage of Information Science." *BASIS* 2 (1976): 9–13.

9.32 Christianson, E. B. "Special Libraries: Putting Knowledge to Work." *LibT* 25 (1976): 399–416.

9.33 Emard, J. P. "An Information Science Chronology in Perspective." *BASIS* 2 (1976): 51–56.

9.34 Martinez, A. "Services to Special Clienteles." In *A Century of Service: Librarianship in the United States and Canada,* edited by S. L. Jackson, E. B. Herling, and E. J. Josey. Chicago: American Library Association, 1976. Pp. 110–28.

9.35 Salton, G. "Computers and Information Science." *BASIS* 2 (1976): 19–21.

9.36 Shera, J. H. "Two Centuries of American Librarianship." *BASIS* 2 (1976): 39–40.

9.37 Patri, D. "An Annotated, Classified, and Selected Bibliography of American Theatre Libraries and American Theatre Librarians: 1902–1976." Research Paper, Queens College, 1978.

9.38 Wong, W. S. "Alfred Kaiming Chiu and Chinese American Librarianship." *CRL* 39 (1978): 384–88.

9.39 Butler, E. "Social Welfare Libraries and Collections." *ELIS* 28 (1980): 95–103.

9.40 Christianson, E. B. *Daniel Nash Handy and the Special Library Movement.* New York: Special Libraries Association, Insurance Division, 1980.

9.41 Griffen, M. "A Pioneer in Retrospect." In *Special Librarianship: A New Reader,* edited by E. B. Jackson. Metuchen, N.J.: Scarecrow Press, 1980. Pp. 562–71.

9.42 Ristow, W. W. *The Emergence of Maps in Libraries.* Hamden, Conn.: Linnet Books, 1980.

9.43 Sidel, P. S. "Social Science Data Archives." *ELIS* 28 (1980): 45–60.

9.44 Cooper, M. A. "United States Secondary Information Services in Physical Science and Engineering: Evolution and Trends from Sputnik to Nixon." Doctoral dissertation, Catholic University of America, 1981.

9.45 Boylan, R. "The Center for Research Libraries." *ELIS* 36 (1983): 156–67.

9.46 Ferguson, E., and Mobley, E. R. *Special Libraries at Work.* Hamden, Conn.: Library Professional Publications, 1984. Pp. 22–30.

9.47 Peterson, L. "The Intellectual World of the IWW: An American Worker's Library in the First Half of the 20th Century." *History Workshop Journal* 22 (Autumn 1986): 153–72.

Private Research Libraries

Before 1876

9.48 Franklin Typographical Society, Boston. *A Sketch of the History of the Franklin Typographical Society, and of Its Library, Read before the Society at Its April Meeting, by the Librarian.* Boston: H.W. Dutton & Son, 1860.

9.49 Wheatland, H. "Historical Sketch of the Philosophical Library at Salem, with Notes." *HCEI* 4 (1862): 175–81, 271–82.

1876–1919

9.50 Bierstadt, O. A. *The Library of Robert Hoe; A Contribution to the History of Bibliophilism in America.* New York: Duprat, 1895.

9.51 Camp, D. N. "Institute Libraries of New Britain, Connecticut." *ConnM* 9 (1905): 781–94.

9.52 Edwards, A. "The Library of the American Antiquarian Society." *Massachusetts Magazine* 9 (1916): 3–17.

1920–1949

9.53 Law, R. A. "Two Texas Libraries." *Texas Review* 5 (1920): 349–57.

9.54 "The Pierpont Morgan Library." *LJ* 49 (1924): 215–20.

9.55 Mackall, L. L. "Goethe's Letter to Joseph Green Cogswell." In *Essays Offered to Herbert Putnam by His Colleagues and Friends on His Thirtieth Anniversary as Librarian of Congress, 5 April 1929,* edited by W. W. Bishop and A. Keogh. New Haven: Yale University Press, 1929. Pp. 315–26.

9.56 Schad, R. O. *Henry Edwards Huntington, the Founder and the Library.* Cambridge: Harvard University Press, 1931.

9.57 Adams, J. Q., and Cret, P. P. *The Folger Shakespeare Library, Washington.* Washington, D.C.: Trustees of Amherst College, 1933.

9.58 Wright, L. B. "More Than a Library [Huntington Library]." *American Scholar* 2 (1933): 366–70.

9.59 Fisher, H. H. "The Hoover Library on War, Revolution and Peace." *PBSA* 33 (1939): 107–15.

9.60 Bay, J. C. *The John Crerar Library, 1895–1944: An Historical Report....* Chicago: John Crerar Library, 1945.

9.61 Hill, W. C. *A Century of Genealogical Progress, Being a History of the New England Historic Genealogical Society, 1845–1945.* Boston: New England Historic Genealogical Society, 1945.

9.62 Lingelbach, W. E. "The Library of the American Philosophical Society [1743]." *WMQ* 3 (1946): 48–69.

9.63 Fulton, J. F. "The Library of a Scholar: Arnold C. Klebs." *YULG* 22 (1947): 1–6.

9.64 Baker, C. H. C. "Our Founder's Foresight." *Huntington Library Quarterly* 12 (1949): 331–38.

9.65 Dawson, G. E. "The Resources and Policies of the Folger Shakespeare Library [1885–1949]." *LQ* 19 (1949): 178–85.

9.66 McLean, P. T. "The Hoover Institute and Library (1914–19)." *LQ* 19 (1949): 235–49.

9.67 Pierpont Morgan Library. New York. *The First Quarter Century of the Pierpont Morgan Library (1924–48): A Retrospective Exhibition in Honor of Belle da Costa Greene....* New York: N.p., 1949.

9.68 Shipton, C. K. "America's First Research Library." *LJ* 74 (1949): 89–90.

9.69 Spell, L. M. "The Sutro Library." *Hispanic American Historical Review* 29 (1949): 452–54.

1950–1971

9.70 Bliss, C. S. "The Huntington Library." *Antiquarian Bookman* 5 (1950): 697–98.

9.71 King, S. *Recollections of the Folger Shakespeare Library*. [Ithaca, N.Y.]: Published for the Trustees of Amherst College by the Cornell University Press, 1950.

9.72 Pierpont Morgan Library. New York. *The Pierpont Morgan Library: Review of the Activities and Major Acquisitions of the Library, 1941–1948; With a Memoir of John Peirpont Morgan and the Pierpont Morgan Library, 1913–1943.* New York: 1950.

9.73 Cowles, L. H. "The First Century of the Library of the New Britain Institute." Master's thesis, Western Reserve University, 1951.

9.74 Foster, J. T. "Folger: Biggest Little Library in the World." *National Geographic Magazine* 100 (1951): 411–24.

9.75 Schad, R. O. "A Quarter Century at the Huntington Library." *BCCQNL* 17 (1951): 75–80.

9.76 Boyce, G. K. "The Pierpont Morgan Library, 1883–1951." *LQ* 22 (1952): 21–35.

9.77 Chinard, G. "Adventures in a Library." *Newberry Library Bulletin* 2 (1952): 223–28.

9.78 Dillon, R. "A Peek at Sutro Library." *BCCQNL* 17 (1952): 27–32.

9.79 Sahlin, N. G. "Our Institute's Library 1929–51." *American Swedish Institute Bulletin* 7 (1952): 24–29.

9.80 Wright, L. B. "The Folger Library as a Research Institute [1932–51]." *CRL* 13 (1952): 14–17.

9.81 Carpenter, E. H. "Three Rare Book Libraries in Southern California." *CalL* 14 (1953): 224–26, 255.

9.82 Gladeck, A. A. "The Library of the Franklin Institute." Master's thesis, Drexel Institute of Technology, 1953, ACRL Microcard no. 37.

9.83 Lingelbach, W. E. "The American Philosophical Society Library from 1942 to 1952, with a Survey of Its Historical Background [since 1743]." *PAPS* 97 (1953): 471–92.

9.84 Stoneman, R. E. "The Libraries of the Art Institute of Chicago." *IllL* 35 (1953): 348–50.

9.85 Lydenberg, H. M. "The Ecology of the Pierpont Morgan Library and Its First Director." In *Studies in Art and Literature for Belle da Costa Greene*, edited by D. E. Miner. Princeton: Princeton University Press, 1954. Pp. 6–9.

9.86 Lydenberg, H. M. "Footnotes on the Astor Library's History from George Templeton Strong's Diary." *BNYPL* 58 (1954): 167–73.

9.87 Pomfret, J. E. "Publishing at the Huntington Library, 1928–54." *CRL* 15 (1954): 388–92.

9.88 Scheide, W. H. "Love for the Printed Word as Espressed in the Scheide Library." *PBSA* 51 (1957): 214–26.

9.89 Waldeck, F. "Adolph Sutro's Lost Library." *CRL* 18 (1957): 19–22.

9.90 Brigham, C. B. *50 Years of Collecting Americana for the Library of the American Antiquarian Society, 1908–1958.* Worcester, Mass.: Antiquarian Society, 1958.

9.91 "John Hinsdale Scheide 1875–1942." In *Grolier 75: A Biographical Retrospective to Celebrate the Seventy-Fifth Anniversary of the Grolier Club in New York.* New York: Grolier Club, 1959. Pp. 191–93.

9.92 Burstyn, H. L. "The Salem Philosophical Library: Its History and Importance for American Science." *HCEI* 96 (1960): 169–206.

9.93 Adams, F. B. *An Introduction to the Pierpont Morgan Library.* New York: In conjunction with New York Times Foundation, 1964.

9.94 Davidson, H. L. "The Lilly Library—76 Years." *SL* 57 (1966): 391–94.

9.95 Marco, G. "Beginnings of the Newberry Library Music Collection: Background and Personal Influences." In *Approaches to Library History*, edited by J. D. Marshall. Tallahassee: JLH, 1966. Pp. 165–81.

9.96 Pomfret, J. E. "The Huntington Library: Fifteen Years of Growth, 1951–1966." *CHSQ* 45 (1966): 241–57.

9.97 Couch, C. R. "The DeGolyer Foundation Library." Master's thesis, University of Texas, 1967.

9.98 Dillon, R. "Adolph Sutro Finds a Librarian." *JLH* 2 (1967): 225–34.

9.99 Hilker, E. W. "The Franklin Institute Library." *Pennsylvania Library Association Bulletin* 23 (1967): 98–104.

9.100 Myers, A. "Washington Irving and the Astor Library." *BNYPL* 72 (1968): 378–99.

9.101 Towner, L. W. "The Newberry Library: A Research Opportunity in Library History." In *Library History Seminar No. 3, Proceedings, 1968*, edited by M. J. Zachert. Tallahassee: JLH, 1968. Pp. 1–16.

9.102 Wright, L. B. *The Folger Library: Two Decades of Growth, an Informal Account.* Charlottesville: University Press of Virginia, 1968.

9.103 Faigel, M. "Berenson Library (Biblioteca Berenson)." *ELIS* 2 (1969): 335–43.

9.104 Huntington Library. *The Founding of the Henry E. Huntington Library and Art Gallery: Four Essays.* San Marino, Calif.: Huntington Library, 1969.

9.105 Mason, D. E., Flower, E., and Knachel, P. A. "The Folger Shakespeare Library in Washington, D.C.: A Brief History." *RCHS* (1969–1970): 346–70.

9.106 Pomfret, J. E. *The Henry E. Huntington Library and Art Gallery: From Its Beginnings to 1969.* San Marino, Calif.: Huntington Library, 1969.

9.107 Towner, L. W. "Every Silver Lining Has a Cloud: The Recent Shaping of the Newberry Library's Collections." In *The Flow of Books and Manuscripts*, edited by A. N. L. Munby and L. W. Towner. Los Angeles: William Andrews Clark Library, 1969. Pp. 35–50.

9.108 Towner, L. W. *An Uncommon Collection of Uncommon Collections: The Newberry Library.* Chicago: Newberry Library, 1970.

9.109 Tu, S. "History of the Library of the Grolier Club." Research Paper, Long Island University, 1970.

9.110 Henkle, H. H. "Crerar, John, Library." *ELIS* 6 (1971): 268–71.

9.111 Towner, L. W. "The Library and the Collector: The Newberry Library." *Louisiana State Library Lectures* Nos. 9–16 (1971): 14–23.

1972–1986

9.112 Knachel, P. A. "Folger Shakespeare Library." *ELIS* 8 (1972): 582–91.

9.113 Dougan, R. O. "Henry E. Huntington Library and Art Gallery." *ELIS* 10 (1973): 390–98.

9.114 Hilker, E. W. "Franklin Institute Library." *ELIS* 9 (1973): 96–103.

9.115 Stinson, D. "The Winston Churchill Memorial and Library in the United States." *JLH* 8 (1973): 70–77.

9.116 William L. Clements Library. *History of the William L. Clements Library, 1923–1973: Its Development and Its Collections.* Ann Arbor: University of Michigan, 1973.

9.117 Pierpont Morgan Library. New York. *Major Acquisitions of the Pierpont Morgan Library, 1924–1974,* 4 vols. New York: Pierpont Morgan Library, 1974.

9.118 Snowden, E. "Women's History Library–1968 until Today." *LHR* 1 (September 1974): 51–63.

9.119 Finkelman, P. "Class and Culture in Late Nineteenth-Century Chicago: The Founding of the Newberry Library." *American Studies* 16 (1975): 5–22.

9.120 Shipman, J. C. "Linda Hall Library." *ELIS* 16 (1975): 186–89.

9.121 Budington, W. S. " 'To Enlarge the Sphere of Human Knowledge': The Role of the Independent Research Library." *CRL* 37 (1976): 299–315.

9.122 Smith, M. D. *Oak from an Acorn: A History of the American Philosophical Society Library, 1770–1803.* Wilmington, Del.: Scholarly Resources, 1976.

9.123 Towner, L. W. "The Newberry Library." *ELIS* 19 (1976): 450–56.

9.124 Adams, F. B. "Pierpont Morgan Library." *ELIS* 22 (1977): 250–62.

9.125 Ashton, R. J. "Curators, Hobbyists, and Historians: Ninety Years of Genealogy at the Newberry Library." *LQ* 47 (1977): 149–62.

9.126 Drazniowsky, R. "The American Geographical Society's Collection." In *The Map Librarian in the Modern World: Essays in Honor of Walter W. Ristow,* edited by H. Wallis and L. Zögner. New York: K.G. Saur, 1979. Pp. 127–42.

9.127 Knox, K. M. *The Story of the Frick Art Reference Library: The Early Years.* New York: Frick Art Reference Library, 1979.

9.128 Ball, W., and Martin, T. *Rare Afro-Americana: A Reconstruction of the Adger Library.* Boston: G.K. Hall, 1981.

9.129 Joyce, W. L. "Antiquarians and Archaeologists: The American Antiquarian Society 1812–1912." *PAAS* 91 (1981): 301–17.

9.130 Kiger, J. C., ed. *Research Institutions and Learned Societies.* Westport, Conn.: Greenwood Press, 1982.

9.131 Milner, A. "The Franklin Institute: As Diverse as Its Namesake." *WLB* 56 (1982): 735–39.

9.132 Pike, K. J. "Western Reserve Historical Society." *ELIS* 33 (1982): 131–36.

9.133 Trimble, W. F. "Western Pennsylvania, Historical Society Of." *ELIS* 33 (1982): 129–31.

9.134 Pomeroy, E. "Paradise Found: The Huntington Library." *WLB* 57 (1983): 833–37.

9.135 Reilly, R. *A Promise Kept: The Story of the James S. Copley Library.* La Jolla, Calif.: Copley Press, 1983.

9.136 Byrd, C. K., and DeFord, C., eds. *The Lilly Library: The First Quarter Century, 1960–1985.* Bloomington: Indiana University Library, 1985.

9.137 Duignan, P., ed. *The Library of the Hoover Institution on War, Revolution and Peace.* Stanford: Hoover Institution, Stanford University, 1985.

9.138 Cohen, P. "Columbia I: Castles, Skyscrapers, and the Charles V. Paterno Library." *Italian American* 8 (1986): 9–14.

9.139 Gottlieb, J. S. "History of Science at the Newberry Library: A Hidden Treasure Revealed." *SL* 77 (1986): 36–43.

9.140 McKinley, C. D. "A National Resource: The New England Legacy of Isaiah Thomas." *ABBW* 78 (1986): 1860–71.

9.141 Van Zanten, D. "The Lenox Library: What Hunt Did and Did Not Learn in France." In *The Architecture of Richard Morris Hunt*, edited by S. R. Stein. Chicago: University of Chicago Press, 1986. Pp. 90–106.

Historical Society, Museum, and Institute Libraries

Before 1876

9.142 "Account of the Books and Manuscripts, Lately Deposited by the Old South Church and Society in the Library of the Massachusetts Historical Society." *Massachusetts Historical Society, Boston. Collections* 2nd ser. 7 (1826): 179–85.

9.143 *Statutes of the Naval Library & Institute, Navy Yard, Charlestown, Mass., Adopted December 31, 1866, with an Account of Its Origin and Purpose, and a List of the Officers & Members Past and Present.* Boston: J.E. Farwell, 1867.

1876–1919

9.144 Homes, H. A., and Fletcher, W. I. "Historical Society Libraries in the United States." In *Public Libraries in the United States of America: Their History, Condition and Management; Special Report, Part I*, U.S. Bureau of Education. Washington, D.C.: Government Printing Office, 1876. Pp. 312–77.

9.145 Thwaites, R. G. "Wisconsin State Historical Society Library." *LJ* 16 (1891): 203–07.

9.146 Green, S. A. "Formation and Growth of the Society's Library." *PMHS* 8 (1892–94): 312–44.

9.147 Thwaites, R. G. "The State Historical Society." In *The Columbian History of Education in Wisconsin*, edited by J. W. Stearns.

Milwaukee: State Committee on Educational Exhibit for Wisconsin, 1893. Pp. 395–405.

9.148 Hess, H., comp. *A Catalogue of the Library of the Insurance Library Association of Boston; To Which Is Added a Sketch of the History and Work of the Association Together with Other Information.* Boston: F. Wood, 1899.

9.149 Lea, J. "History of the Tennessee Historical Society." *American Historical Magazine* 6 (1901): 354–56.

9.150 Shambaugh, B. F. "A Brief History of the State Historical Society of Iowa." *Iowa Journal of History and Politics* 1 (1903): 139–52.

9.151 Kelby, R. H. *The New-York Historical Society, 1804–1904.* New York: New-York Historical Society, 1905.

9.152 Cheney, A. P. "The First Fourteen Years of the Historical, Natural History and Library Society of South Natick." *Historical, Natural History and Library Society of South Natick Historical Collections* 2 (1910): 11–26.

9.153 Dennis, A. W. "The Library of Massachusetts Historical Society." *Massachusetts Magazine* 3 (1910): 225–39.

1920–1949

9.154 Rothert, O. A. *The Filson Club and Its Activities, 1884–1922.* Louisville, Ky.: Filson Club, 1922.

9.155 Rothert, O. A. "The Filson Club, 1884–1934." *Filson Club History Quarterly* 8 (1934): 139–47.

9.156 Mitchell, A. M. "Massachusetts Diocesan Library and the Parish Historian." *HMPEC* 7 (1938): 277–86.

9.157 Duniway, D. C. "The Administration of Six Selected State Historical Society Libraries: A Historical Study." Master's thesis, University of California, 1939.

9.158 Carson, H. L. *A History of the Historical Society of Pennsylvania*, 2 vols. Philadelphia: Historical Society of Pennsylvania, 1940.

9.159 Benton, E. J. *A Short History of the Western Reserve Historical Society, 1867–1942.* Cleveland: Western Reserve Historical Society, 1942.

9.160 Miller, R. C. "The California Academy of Sciences and the Early History of Science in the West." *CHSQ* 21 (1942): 363–71.

9.161 Jillson, W. R. *A Sketch and Bibliography of the Kentucky Historical Society, 1836–1943.* Frankfort, Ky.: Kentucky Historical Society, 1943.

9.162 Dunlap, L. W. *American Historical Societies, 1790–1860.* Madison, Wis.: Cantwell, 1944.

9.163 Moore, Mrs. J. T. "The Tennessee State Historical Society, 1849–1918." *THQ* 3 (1944): 195–225.

9.164 "Wyoming State Historical Department: A Sketch of the Development." *Annals of Wyoming* 19 (January 1947): 55–59.

9.165 Libbey, D. C. "The Library of the Chicago Historical Society: A Study." Master's thesis, University of Chicago, 1948.

9.166 Shoemaker, F. C. *The State Historical Society of Missouri: A Semi-centennial History.* Columbia, Mo.: State Historical Society of Missouri, 1948.

9.167 Berthel, M. W., and Cater, H. D. "The Minnesota Historical Society: Highlights of a Century." *Minnesota History* 30 (1949): 293–330.

9.168 Currier, M. "The Peabody Museum Library." *HLB* 3 (1949): 94–101.

1950–1971

9.169 Hitcham, J. S. "Memorial Genealogical Library (Oklahoma) Daughters of the American Revolution (1925–50)." *Chronicles of Oklahoma* 28 (1950): 292–98.

9.170 Waldron, R. K. "A History of the Library of the State Historical Society of Colorado, 1879–1940." Master's thesis, University of Denver, 1950.

9.171 Heskin, M. K. "The Philadelphia Commercial Museum Library, 1896–1952." Master's thesis, Drexel Institute of Technology, 1952.

9.172 Sims, E. E. "The Allen Memorial Art Museum Library, Oberlin, Ohio: A Study." Master's thesis, Western Reserve University, 1952.

9.173 Walker, M. H. "The Library of the Western Reserve Historical Society." Master's thesis, Kent State University, 1952.

9.174 Hafen, L. R. "History of the State Historical Society: 1900–1925." *Colorado Magazine* 30 (1953): 283–310.

9.175 Hafen, L. R. "History of the State Historical Society of Colorado: The First Twenty Years." *Colorado Magazine* 30 (1953): 162–85.

9.176 Kane, L. M. "Collecting Policies of the Minnesota Historical Society: 1849–1952." *AAr* 16 (1953): 127–36.

9.177 King, D. M. "Minnesota Historical Society Library, a Treasure House of Information." *MinnL* 17 (1953): 227–30.

9.178 Scriven, M. "Chicago Historical Society." *IllL* 35 (1953): 158–60.

9.179 Whitehill, W. M. "The Centenary of the Dowse Library." *Massachusetts Historical Society. Proceedings* 71 (1953–1957): 167–78.

9.180 Wolf, N. E. "The Library of the Genealogical Society of Pennsylvania, 1892–1952." Master's thesis, Drexel Institute of Technology, 1953.

9.181 Coats, N. M. "The Academy's John Shepard Wright Memorial Library." *Proceedings of the Indiana Academy of Science* 63 (1954): 248–52.

9.182 Hafen, L. R. "History of the State Historical Society of Colorado: 1925–1950." *Colorado Magazine* 31 (1954): 37–68.

9.183 Hudson, Ohio, Library and Historical Society. *"Open the Books If You Wish to be Free": A Commemorative Book Published...on the Occasion of the Opening of the Enlarged Historical House.* Hudson, Ohio: Hudson Library and Historical Society, 1954.

9.184 Pease, M. E. "The Illinois Historical Survey Library, University of Illinois [1909–54]." *IllL* 36 (1954): 298–301.

9.185 Pressing, K. L. "The Library of the Historical Society of Delaware." Master's thesis, Drexel Institute of Technology, 1954.

9.186 Vail, R. W. G. *Knickerbocker Birthday: A Sesqui-Centennial History of the New-York Historical Society, 1804–1954.* New York: New York Historical Society, 1954.

9.187 Anderson, R. H. *The Rowfant Club.* Cleveland: The Rowfant Club, 1955.

9.188 Smail, H. A. "A History of the Eleanor Squire Memorial Library of the Garden Center of Greater Cleveland." Master's thesis, Western Reserve University, 1955.

9.189 Bishop, C. "The Museum of Modern Art Film Library, 1935–55." In *Educational Film Society Primer,* edited by C. Starr. Forest Hills, N.Y.: American Federation of Film Societies, 1956. Pp. 56–61.

9.190 Hook, A. "Resources of the Library of the Historical and Philosophical Society of Ohio." *Bulletin of the Historical & Philosophical Society of Ohio* 14 (1956): 105–21.

9.191 Jerabek, E. "Library of the Minnesota Historical Society." *MinnL* 18 (1956): 204–07.

9.192 Towne, J. E. "The Inception of the Library Building for the State Historical Society of Wisconsin, 1893–1900." *WMH* 39 (1956): 73–75.

9.193 Lenhart, J. M. "The Historical Library at the Central Bureau of the Catholic Central Verein in St. Louis, Mo., Founded in 1913 by F.P. Kenkel." *Social Justice Review* 49 (1957): 348–52, 384–87; 50 (1957): 24–27.

9.194 "Utah Historical Society: Sixty Years of Organized History." *Utah Historical Quarterly* 25 (1957): 191–220.

9.195 Welch, E. W. "A Library Grows Up." *JISHS* 50 (1957): 176–89.

9.196 Wells, I. S. "A History of the D.A.R. Genealogical Library: Its Objectives, Policies, and Services as a Library of Americana." Master's thesis, Catholic University of America, 1958.

9.197 Brennan, P. M. "A History of the Library of the Rhode Island Historical Society of Providence, R.I." Doctoral dissertation, Catholic University of America, 1959.

9.198 Chenery, F. L. "The Library of the Church Historical Society." *HMPEC* 28 (1959): 187–90.

9.199 Coolidge, J. "American Art Museum Libraries: Past, Problems, and Potentials." *SL* 50 (1959): 119–22.

9.200 Cooper, M. K. "The Founding of the Martha Kinney Cooper Ohioana Library." *Ohioana* 2 (1959): 75–76, 114.

9.201 Hill R. H. "The Filson Club's Seventy-Fifth Anniversary 1884–1959. Brief Sketches of the Founders, Benefactors, Builders, and Accomplishments of the Filson Club." *Filson Club History Quarterly* 33 (1959): 187–94.

9.202 Riley, S. T. *The Massachusetts Historical Society, 1791–1959.* Boston: Massachusetts Historical Society, 1959.

9.203 Harris, A. W. "Cass Gilbert's Old Library Building: The Eugene C. Barker Texas History Center, 1910–1960." *SHQ* 64 (1960): 1–13.

9.204 Petersen, W. J. "The State Historical Society of Iowa." *Palimpsest* 41 (1960): 357–404.

9.205 Perry, C. C. "Daughters of the Republic of Texas Library." *TLJ* 39 (1963): 7–8.

9.206 Manakee, H. R. "A Quarter-Century of Growth at the Maryland Historical Society." *MHM* 60 (1965): 56–92.

9.207 Hupp, J. L. "The Movement for the Formation of the West Virginia Department of Archives and History." *West Virginia History* 28 (1967): 249–55.

9.208 Skidmore, S. "History of the Library of The Huntington Historical Society." Research Paper, Long Island University, 1967.

9.209 Skidmore, W. L. "A History of the Peninsula (Ohio) Library and Historical Society, 1941–1967." Master's thesis, Kent State University, 1967.

9.210 Knowles, M. K. *The First Hundred Years, 1867–1967: The Western Reserve Historical Society.* Cleveland: Western Reserve Historical Society, 1968.

9.211 Bettie, P. M. "Growth and Development of the Library Collection at the Marine Historical Association, Incorporated, Mystic, Connecticut." Master's thesis, Southern Connecticut State College, 1969.

9.212 Peabody Museum of Salem. *Brief History of the Peabody Museum of Salem.* Salem, Mass.: N.p., 1969.

9.213 Schnitzler, N. L. "The Mennonite Historical Society and the Reconstruction of Mennonite History Library and Publishing Program at Goshen, Indiana." Master's thesis, University of Chicago, 1969.

9.214 Fabian, S. "History of the New York Institute Library." Research Paper, Long Island University, 1970.

9.215 Putnam, L. A. "The Library of the Field Museum of Natural History." Master's thesis, University of Chicago, 1971.

9.216 Rundell, W. *The State Historical Society of Iowa: An Analysis.* Ames, Iowa: Privately printed, 1971.

1972–1986

9.217 Leonard, G. M. "The Utah State Historical Society, 1897–1972." *Utah Historical Quarterly* 40 (1972): 300–334.

9.218 Thompson, L. S. "The Filson Club." *ELIS* 8 (1972): 457–59.

9.219 Zaremba, M. "An Historical-Descriptive Study of the Library Archives of the Leo Baeck Institute." Research Paper, Long Island University, 1972.

9.220 Gilreath, J. W. "The Formation of the Western Reserve Historical Society's Shaker Collection." *JLH* 8 (1973): 133–42.

9.221 Hinds, C. F. "Historical Society Libraries in the United States." *ELIS* 10 (1973): 435–45.

9.222 Niles, A. "The Historical Society of Western Pennsylvania: An Updated History." *WPHM* 57 (1974): 1–14.

9.223 Wainwright, N. B. *One Hundred and Fifty Years of Collecting by the Historical Society of Pennsylvania, 1824–1974.* Philadelphia: Historical Society of Pennsylvania, 1974.

9.224 Thompson, L. S. "Kentucky Historical Society." *ELIS* 13 (1975): 417–20.

9.225 Nolan, M. P., and Papert, E. N. "The Photograph and Slide Library [Metropolitan Museum of Art]." *ELIS* 17 (1976): 483–91.

9.226 Thompson, L. S. "The Massachusetts Historical Society." *ELIS* 17 (1976): 237–39.

9.227 Thompson, L. S. "Minnesota Historical Society." *ELIS* 18 (1976): 143–45.

9.228 Thompson, L. S. "Missouri Historical Society." *ELIS* 18 (1976): 201–03.

9.229 Thompson, L. S. "New England Historic Genealogical Society." *ELIS* 19 (1976): 326–27.

9.230 Thompson, L. S. "New-York Historical Society." *ELIS* 19 (1976): 361–65.

9.231 Usher, E. R. "The Metropolitan Museum of Art Library (Research and Reference) (Memorial Name: The Thomas J. Watson Library)." *ELIS* 17 (1976): 473–81.

9.232 Thompson, L. S. "Ohio Historical Society." *ELIS* 20 (1977): 348–49.

9.233 Thompson, L. S. "Oregon Historical Society." *ELIS* 20 (1977): 463–64.

9.234 Thompson, L. S. "Peabody Museum of Salem." *ELIS* 21 (1977): 474–76.

9.235 Thompson, L. S. "Pennsylvania. The Historical Society of Pennsylvania." *ELIS* 21 (1977): 482–85.

9.236 Brubaker, R. L. "Chicago History: The Development of a Major Research Center." *ABBW* 61 (1978): 4396–4407.

9.237 Chudacoff, N. F. "The Rhode Island Historical Society." *ELIS* 25 (1978): 380–84.

9.238 Alexander, E. P. *Museums in Motion: An Introduction to the History and Functions of Museums.* Nashville: American Association of State and Local History, 1979.

9.239 Cox, J. W. "The Origin of the Maryland Historical Society: A Case Study in Cultural Philanthropy." *MHM* 74 (1979): 103–16.

9.240 Moss, J. E. "The San Diego Historical Society." *ELIS* 26 (1979): 291–96.

9.241 Sweeney, A. P. "Some Contributions of a Librarian to the American Museum Movement: Henry Watson Kent at the Metropolitan Museum of Art." *NCL* 37 (1979): 5–8.

9.242 Woodward, D. "The Herman Dunlap Smith Center for the History of Cartography: A Review of Its Early Development." In *The Map Librarian in the Modern World: Essays in Honor of Walter W. Ristow,* edited by H. Wallis and L. Zögner. New York: K.G. Saur, 1979. Pp. 143–60.

9.243 Benson, M. "The State Historical Society of Colorado." *ELIS* 29 (1980): 32–36.

9.244 Canaday, O. W. "South Dakota State Historical Society." *ELIS* 28 (1980): 298–300.

9.245 Giaquinta, J. "The State Historical Society of Iowa." *ELIS* 29 (1980): 36–42.

9.246 McBride, R. M. "Tennessee Historical Society." *ELIS* 30 (1980): 282–84.

9.247 Ruegamer, L. "The Library." In *A History of the Indiana Historical Society 1830–1980.* Indianapolis: Indiana Historical Society, 1980. Pp. 240–52.

9.248 Waddell, G. "South Carolina Historical Society." *ELIS* 28 (1980): 259–61.

9.249 Howell, J. B. "Winyah Indigo Society Library." *SEL* 31 (1981): 115–16.

9.250 Nuquist, R. D. "Vermont Historical Society." *ELIS* 32 (1981): 351–56.

9.251 Thatcher, L. "Utah State Historical Society Library." *ELIS* 32 (1981): 314–16.

9.252 Draz, P. "Wisconsin, State Historical Society Of." *ELIS* 33 (1982): 173–76.

9.253 Holland, J. "Glorious Anachronism: The American Philosophical Society." *WLB* 56 (1982): 740–44.

9.254 Jenkins, M. M. "West Virginia Department of Culture and History." *ELIS* 33 (1982): 101–04.

9.255 Kirkpatrick, N. "Major Issues of the Past Ten Years in Visual Resource Curatorship." *Art Libraries Journal* 7 (1982): 30–35.

9.256 Prosser, J. "The Wyoming Archives, Museums, and Historical Department." *ELIS* 33 (1982): 254–59.

9.257 Root, N. J. "The Library of the American Museum of Natural History." *BKM* 40 (1982): 93–96.

9.258 Colson, J. C. *Academic Ambitions and Library Development: The American Bureau of Industrial Research and the State Historical Society of Wisconsin, 1904–1918.* Urbana: University of Illinois Graduate School of Library and Information Science, Occasional Paper no. 159, 1983.

9.259 Gwyn, A. "Changing Hands: Johns Hopkins Aquires [sic] Peabody Library." *WLB* 57 (1983): 401–04.

9.260 McCrank, L. J. *Mt. Angel Abbey: A Centennial History of a Benedictine Community and Its Library, 1882–1984.* Wilmington, Del.: Scholarly Resources, 1983.

9.261 Reed, L. L. "The Development of the Manuscript Collections at the State Historical Society of Wisconsin Through 1969." Doctoral dissertation, University of Wisconsin, 1983.

9.262 Cornwall, A. W. "The Tower Room of St. Paul's Church, Winston-Salem, N.C." *HMPEC* 53 (1984): 335–38.

9.263 Kubicek, E. C. "New Mexico, Historical Society Of: A Brief History." *ELIS* 37 (1984): 265–67.

9.264 Richards, P. S. *Scholars and Gentlemen: The Library of the New York Historical Society, 1804–1982.* Hamden, Conn.: Archon Books, 1984.

9.265 Anderson, R. J. "Building a Multi-Ethnic Collection: The Research Library of the Balch Institute for Ethnic Studies." *Ethnic Forum* 5 (1985): 7–19.

9.266 Arnold, E. "The American Geographical Society Library, Map and Photographic Collection: A History, 1951–1978." Doctoral dissertation, University of Pittsburgh, 1985.

9.267 Bigelow, M. M. "Michigan. Bureau of History, Michigan Department of State." *ELIS* 39 (1985): 278–81.

9.268 Clark, R. M. "The Montana Historical Society." *ELIS* 39 (1985): 281–91.

9.269 DeMuth, P. J. "The Alaska Historical Library." *ELIS* 39 (1985): 36–38.

9.270 Earl, P. I. "The Nevada Historical Society." *ELIS* 39 (1985): 336–38.

9.271 Graham, T. "St. Augustine Historical Society, 1883–1983." *Florida Historical Quarterly* 64 (1985): 1–31.

9.272 Jochims, L. "Kansas State Historical Society." *ELIS* 39 (1985): 249–56.

9.273 Johnson, D. D. "The Hawaiian Historical Society." *ELIS* 39 (1985): 199–202.

9.274 Lawrence, D. E. "A History of the Brooklyn Museum Libraries." *BKM* 43 (1985): 92–93.

9.275 Lemieux, D. J. "The Louisiana Historical Association." *ELIS* 39 (1985): 268–73.

9.276 McCain, D. R. "The Connecticut Historical Society." *ELIS* 38 (1985): 129–37.

9.277 Shera, J. H. "The Rowfant Club." *ELIS* 39 (1985): 387–94.

9.278 Skemer, D. C. "The New Jersey Historical Society." *ELIS* 39 (1985): 339–40.

9.279 Sullivan, L. E. "Maryland Historical Society." *ELIS* 38 (1985): 266–76.

9.280 Collier-Thomas, B. "Towards Black Feminism: The Creation of the Bethune Museum-Archives." In *Women's Collections: Libraries, Archives, and Consciousness*, edited by S. Hildenbrand. New York: Haworth Press, 1986. Pp. 43–66.

9.281 Kriauciunas, J. "ALKA Preserves Material of Lithuanian Culture." *Lituanus* 32 (1986): 67–74.

Business and Industrial Libraries

9.282 Joannes, E. "A Fifty-Year-Old Technical Library." *SL* 30 (1939): 254–57.

9.283 Handy, D. N. *The First Sixty Years: The Story of the Insurance Library Association of Boston, Incorporated December 28, 1887; an Historical Sketch.* Boston: N.p., 1947.

9.284 Wilkerson, M. "The Library of the Federal Reserve Bank of Dallas." *NNT* 25 (October 1949): 161–63.

9.285 Skeen, J. R. "The Origin and Influence of Major Technical Libraries in Philadelphia." *Journal of the Franklin Institute* 250 (1950): 381–90.

9.286 Laubach, H. "Library Service to Business, Labor and Industry: Its Development in Libraries at Princeton, Akron, and Pittsburgh." Master's thesis, Carnegie Institute, 1952.

9.287 Tessman, E. M. "Thirty-four Years of Library Service [First Wisconsin National Bank of Milwaukee]." *Bankers Monthly* 69 (April 1952): 44–45.

9.288 Archer, H. R. "The Lakeside Press Library." *BCCQNL* 20 (1954): 12–19.

9.289 Benjamin, H. C. "The Library of the Industrial Relations Sections [of the Department of Economic and Social Institutions]." *Princeton University Library Chronicle* 15 (1954): 151–55.

9.290 Leasure, M. F. "A History of the Libraries of the Baltimore and Ohio Railroad Company." Master's thesis, Drexel Institute of Technology, 1954.

9.291 Schmutz, C. A. "Standard and Poor's Corporation Library [New York]." *SL* 45 (1954): 147–50.

9.292 Strable, E. G. "The Origin, Development and Present Status of Advertising Agency Libraries in the United States." Master's thesis, University of Chicago, 1954.

9.293 Buckley, A. K. "The Keeneland Association Library." Master's thesis, University of Kentucky, 1957.

9.294 Brown, J. V. "History of the Industrial Relations Research Libraries." Master's thesis, Western Reserve University, 1958.

9.295 Harris, J. F. "The Newspaper Library: Its History, Function, and Value with Special Reference to the *New York Herald Tribune.*" Master's thesis, Southern Connecticut State College, 1959.

9.296 Tilghman, G. "Seaboard Air Line Railway Free Traveling Library System." *SEL* 10 (1960): 126–29.

9.297 Mechanic, S. "Brooklyn's Business Library—20 Years Old." *SL* 54 (1963): 339–44.

9.298 Axelrod, H. B. "The History, Development, and Organization of the *New York Times* Library and Contributions of the *Times* to Scholarship." Master's thesis, Southern Connecticut State College, 1965.

9.299 Kruzas, A. T. *Business and Industrial Libraries in the United States, 1820–1940.* New York: Special Libraries Association, 1965.

9.300 Young, E. J., and Williams, A. S. *Historical Development and Present Status—Douglas Aircraft Company Computerized Library Program.* Santa Monica, Calif.: Douglas Aircraft Company, 1965.

9.301 Turnow, W. H. "The Engineering Societies Library: A History of Its Origins and Early Development, 1852–1928." Research Paper, Long Island University, 1967.

9.302 Albright, H. "History of the Research Library of Brookhaven National Laboratory." Research Paper, Long Island University, 1968.

9.303 Synodis, E. J. "History of the Library of the Institute of Life Insurance, New York City, N.Y." Research Paper, Long Island University, 1969.

9.304 Bogardus, J. "Business Libraries and Collections." *ELIS* 3 (1970): 530–53.

9.305 Huleatt, R. S. "The Stone and Webster Library, 1900–1970." *SL* 61 (1970): 374–76.

9.306 Jelin, V. "The 'Instrumental' Use of Libraries: A Study of the Intellectual Origins of the Modern Industrial Libraries in Nineteenth Century America." *Libri* 20 (1970): 15–28.

9.307 Lopez, M. D. "Books and Beds: Libraries in Nineteenth and Twentieth Century American Hotels." *JLH* 9 (1974): 196–221.

9.308 Blanchard, J. R. "The History of Agricultural Libraries in the United States." In *Agricultural Literature: Proud Heritage Future Promise; A Bicentennial Symposium.* N.p.: 1977. Pp. 219–35.

9.309 Cabeen, S. K., and Soroka, M. "The Engineering Societies Library." *BKM* 40 (1982): 115–16.

9.310 Creek, A. B. "A Business Library for Ellwanger and Barry." *University of Rochester Library Bulletin* 35 (1982): 60–68.

9.311 Mount, E. *Ahead of Its Time: The Engineering Societies Library, 1913–1980.* Hamden, Conn.: Linnet Books, 1982.

9.312 Landau, H. B. *"Engineering Index,* 1884–1984: Its History and Its Service to Special Libraries." *SL* 75 (1984): 312–18.

9.313 Tenopir, C. "Characteristics of Corporations that Founded Libraries: 1910–1921." *SL* 76 (1985): 43–52.

9.314 Nash, M. "Business History at the Hagley Museum and Library." *Business History Review* 60 (1986): 104–20.

Law Libraries

9.315 Griswold, S. B. "Law Libraries." In *Public Libraries in the United States of America:* *Their History, Condition and Management; Special Report, Part I,* U.S. Bureau of Education. Washington, D.C.: Government Printing Office, 1876. Pp. 161–70.

9.316 Warren, S. R., and Clark, S. N. "Libraries in Prisons and Reformatories." In *Public Libraries in the United States of America: Their History, Condition and Management; Special Report, Part I,* U.S. Bureau of Education. Washington, D.C.: Government Printing Office, 1876. Pp. 218–29.

9.317 Berry, W. J. C. *Association of the Bar of the City of New York: The First Quarter-Century of Its Library.* New York: Privately printed, [1895?].

9.318 Arnold, J. H. "The Harvard Law Library." *HB* 16 (1906): 230–41.

9.319 Arnold, J. H. "The Harvard Law Library and Some Account of Its Growth." *LLJ* 5 (1912): 17–25.

9.320 Truman, L. S. *The Louisville Law Library, 1839–1912.* Louisville, Ky.: Smith and Dugan, 1912.

9.321 "Supreme Court Library." *HTL* 3 (1915–1916): 81–82.

9.322 Gholdson, E. "The Cincinnati Law Library." *LLJ* 13 (1921): 75–79.

9.323 Lathrop, O. C. "History of Michigan Law Libraries and Their Relation to General Libraries in Michigan." *LLJ* 16 (1923): 15–23.

9.324 Grinnell, F. W. "A Brief History of the Social Law Library." *Massachusetts Law Quarterly* 10 (1925): 48–53.

9.325 Williamson, R. *The Law Library in the Capitol, Washington, D.C.* Washington, D.C.: J. Byrne and Co., 1929.

9.326 U. S. Library of Congress. *Centennial of the Law Library, 1832–1932: An Exhibit of Books, Prints, and Manuscripts in Honor of the Supreme Court of the United States, and the American Bar Association on the Occasion of* *the Laying of the Cornerstone of the Supreme Court Building, October 13, 1932.* Washington, D.C.: Government Printing Office, 1932.

9.327 "The First Step Towards a Public Law Library." *IMH* 32 (1936): 274–76.

9.328 Clarke, O. "The Library of the Supreme Court of the United States." *LLJ* 31 (1938): 89–102.

9.329 Elliott, L. "History of the Law Library." In *A Century of Legal Education,* edited by R. H. Wettach. Chapel Hill: University of North Carolina Press, 1947. Pp. 96–107.

9.330 Bade, E. S. "Quo Vadimus?" *Journal of Legal Education* 2 (1949): 41–52.

9.331 Petty, W. E. "The History of the Ohio Penitentiary Library." Master's thesis, Western Reserve University, 1949.

9.332 Pulling, A. C. "The Harvard Law School Library [1817–1949]." *LLJ* 43 (1950): 1–11.

9.333 Hench, M. "The Library of the Supreme Court of the United States." Master's thesis, Drexel Institute of Technology, 1951.

9.334 Pound, R. "The Harvard Law Library (1829–1951)." *HLB* 5 (1951): 290–303.

9.335 Price, O. M. "Legal Education during the Past Fifty Years as Reflected in the Changing Character of Law Library Acquisitions." *University of Florida Law Review* 6 (1953): 221–30.

9.336 Roalfe, W. R., and Schwerin, K. "The Elbert H. Gary Law Library of Northwestern University (1859–1953)." *LLJ* 46 (1953): 219–34.

9.337 Marke, J. J. "The Mills Memorial Library of the School of Law of New York University." *SL* 45 (1954): 107–10.

9.338 Johnston, G. A. "Our Predecessors and Their Achievements." *LLJ* 49 (1956): 138–47.

9.339 Peterson, L. "Law Libraries of New England, 1946–1955." *LLJ* 49 (1956): 198–203.

9.340 Coffey, H. "The Law Library." In *The University of Michigan, An Encyclopedic Survey.* Ann Arbor: University of Michigan Press, 1958. Pp. 1397–1402.

9.341 Brown, E. G., and Blume, W. W. "The Law Library: Books, Serials, and Manuscripts." In *Legal Education at Michigan 1859–1959.* Ann Arbor: University of Michigan Law School, 1959. Pp. 359–87.

9.342 Hudon, E. G. "The Supreme Court of the United States: A History of Its Books and Library [1812–1956]." *Federal Bar Journal* 19 (1959): 185–99.

9.343 Johnson, R. E. "Libraries in Correctional Institutions." Master's thesis, Western Reserve University, 1959.

9.344 Rahl, J. E., and Schwerin, K. "The Library." In *Northwestern University School of Law—A Short History to Commemoriate Its Centennial 1859–1959.* Chicago: Northwestern University School of Law, 1960. Pp. 69–78.

9.345 Holloway, D. P. "History of the Akron Law Library, with Special Attention to Pertinent Legislation." Master's thesis, Kent State University, 1962.

9.346 Hazelton, P. A. "The New Hampshire State Law Library." *New Hampshire Bar Journal* 6 (1963–1964): 270–72.

9.347 Brooks, R. E. "The Yale University Law School Library: Its History, Organization and Development, 1824 to 1962." Master's thesis, Southern Connecticut State College, 1964.

9.348 Hudon, E. G. "U.S. Supreme Court Library: An Account of Its Development and Growth." *LLJ* 59 (1966): 166–76.

9.349 Proctor, M. M. "Historical Survey of the Law School Library of Texas Southern University, Houston, Texas." Master's thesis, Catholic University of America, 1966.

9.350 Coates, A. "Law School Library." *North Carolina Law Review* 47 (1968): 61–65.

9.351 Cohen, M. L., Wolf, E., and Jeffery, W. "Historical Development of the American Lawyer's Library." *LLJ* 61 (1968): 440–62.

9.352 Coyte, D. E. "A History of the University of Louisville School of Law Library, 1846–1966." Master's thesis, University of North Carolina, 1968.

9.353 Cropper, M. S. "An Analysis of the Literature of Law Library Administration, 1936–1968." Master's thesis, Atlanta University, 1969.

9.354 Russy, E. N. de. "The Library Company of the Baltimore Bar since 1940." *Maryland Libraries* 35 (1969): 15–17.

9.355 Taylor, R. M. *History of the North Carolina Supreme Court Library [July 1, 1969].* St. Paul, Minn.: West Publishing Co., 1969.

9.356 MacCormick, A. H. *A Brief History of Libraries in American Correctional Institutions.* [Chicago: Association of Hospital and Institutional Libraries Division, American Library Association], 1970.

9.357 Engelbarts, R. *Books in Stir: A Bibliographic Essay about Prison Libraries and about Books Written by Prisoners and Prison Employees.* Metuchen, N.J.: Scarecrow Press, 1971.

9.358 Lahey, J. "The University of Connecticut Law School Library: History, Organization, and Development, 1921–1972." Master's thesis, Southern Connecticut State College, 1972.

9.359 Reynolds, R. C. "The Role of Librarianship in Penal Institutions: A Historical Review and a Survey of Contemporary Training Programs." Master's thesis, California State University, San Jose, 1973.

9.360 Brock, C. A. "Law Libraries and Librarians: A Revisionist History, or More Than You Ever Wanted to Know." *LLJ* 67 (1974): 325–61.

9.361 Harris, M. H. "Jewett's Role in the National Library for U.S.A." *LHR* 2 (March 1975): 63–101.

9.362 Johnson, A. H. "Prison Libraries in the United States 1965–1975." Research Paper, Texas Woman's University, 1975.

9.363 Kavass, I. I. "Law Libraries in the United States: Development and Growth." *LHR* 2 (March 1975): 10–42.

9.364 "State Law Library." *HT* 3 (1976): 925.

9.365 Zabel, J. M. "Prison Libraries." *SL* 67 (1976): 1–7.

9.366 Ellsworth, F. L. "The Library: A Laboratory for Legal Education." In *Law on the Midway: The Founding of the University of Chicago Law School.* Chicago: Law School of the University of Chicago, 1977. Pp. 111–18.

9.367 Wilkins, B. "The Correctional Facility Library: History and Standards." *LibT* 26 (1977): 119–23.

9.368 Cheeseman, M. "Prison (Correctional) Libraries." *ELIS* 24 (1978): 117–24.

9.369 Ritchie, J. "The Law Library." In *The First Hundred Years: A Short History of the School of Law of the University of Virginia for the Period 1826–1926.* Charlottesville: University Press of Virginia, 1978. Pp. 106–10.

9.370 Bellefontaine, E. J. "The Social Law Library: 175 Years of Service to the Bench and Bar of Massachusetts." *Boston Bar Journal* 24 (1980): 5.

9.371 Chadbourn, E. S. "Documenting the American Legal Scene: The Manuscript Division of the Harvard Law School Library." *HLB* 30 (1982): 55–73.

9.372 Cooper, B. D. "Anglo-American Legal Citations: Historical Development and Library Implications." *LLJ* 75 (1982): 3–33.

9.373 Dyer, C. R. "A Short Look at Twenty-Five Years of the *Law Library Journal*." *LLJ* 75 (1982): 187–91.

9.374 Mersky, R. M., and Jacobstein, J. M. "An Analysis of Academic Law Library Growth since 1907." *LLJ* 75 (1982): 212–24.

9.375 Mullins, J. L. "A Study of Selected Factors Affecting Growth Rates in American Law School Libraries, 1932–1976." Doctoral dissertation, Indiana University, 1984.

9.376 Davis, G. B. "The Raison d'etre for Library Service to Institutional Populations." *BKM* 44 (1986): 94–95.

9.377 Warthen, R. L. "The Non-emergence of the Anglo-American Law Code." *Legal Reference Service Quarterly* 6 (1986): 129–61.

Medical Libraries

1876–1919

9.378 Billings, J. S. "Medical Libraries in the United States." In *Public Libraries in the United States of America: Their History, Condition and Management; Special Report, Part I*, U.S. Bureau of Education. Washington, D.C.: Government Printing Office, 1876. Pp. 171–82.

9.379 Chadwick, J. R. *The Medical Libraries of Boston: A Report Read at the First Annual Meeting of the Boston Medical Library Association, Held on Oct. 3, 1876*. Cambridge, Mass.: Riverside Press, 1876.

9.380 Purple, S. S. *An Address on the Medical Libraries of New York*. New York: New York Academy of Medicine, 1877.

9.381 Chadwick, J. R. "Medical Libraries, Their Development and Use." *Boston Medical & Surgical Journal* 134 (1896): 101–04.

9.382 Spivak, C. D. "The Medical Libraries in the U.S." *Philadelphia Medical Journal* 2 (1898): 817–58.

9.383 Fisher, C. P. "Library of the College of Physicians, Philadelphia." *BMLA* 1 (1902): 43–44.

9.384 Chadwick, J. R. "The Boston Medical Library." *Medical Library and Historical Journal* 1 (1903): 132.

9.385 Huntington, A. T. "The Medical Library Movement in the United States." *Medical Library and Historical Journal* 2 (1904): 119–28.

9.386 Dock, G. "The Medical Library of the University of Michigan." *Medical Library and Historical Journal* 3 (1905): 165–73.

9.387 Fisher, C. P. "An Account of the Library of the College of Physicians of Philadelphia." *Transcript of the College of Physicians of Philadelphia* 28 (1906): 291–302.

9.388 Farlow, J. W. *The History of the Boston Medical Library*. Norwood, Mass.: Plimpton Press, 1918.

1920–1949

9.389 Keen, W. W. "The Library of the College of Physicians of Philadelphia." *National History* 20 (1920): 283–85.

9.390 Grindon, J. "Medical Library Enterprises and Activities in St. Louis and Their Lessons." *BMLA* 12 (1922): 12–16.

9.391 Ray, F. K. "New York State Medical Library, Established Thirty-one Years Ago." *Albany Medical Annals* 43 (1922): 320–35.

9.392 *Celebration of the Fiftieth Anniversary of the Boston Medical Library, January 19, 1926.* Norwood, Mass.: Plimpton Press, 1926.

9.393 Johns Hopkins University. *The William H. Welch Medical Library of Johns Hopkins University: An Account of Its Origin and Development, Together with a Description of the Building and an Account of the Exercises Held on the Occasion of the Dedication of the Library and the Inauguration of the Chair of the History of Medicine at the Johns Hopkins University, Baltimore, Maryland, October 17 and 18, 1929.* Baltimore: Williams and Wilkins, 1929.

9.394 Malloch, A. "A Century of American Medical Libraries, 1830–1930." In *Celebration of the Centennial of the Library of the Medical & Chirugical Faculty of the State of Maryland 1830–1930.* Baltimore: Medical & Chirugical Faculty, 1931. P. 7.

9.395 Packard, F. R. "The Earliest Medical LIbrary in the United States (Pennsylvania Hospital, Philadelphia)." *Virginia Medical Monthly* 60 (1933): 139–44.

9.396 Hume, E. E. "The Celebration of the Centenary of the Army Medical Library, 1836–1936." *Johns Hopkins Alumni Magazine* 34 (1936): 107–35.

9.397 Nixon, P. I. *A Century of Medicine in San Antonio: The Story of Medicine in Bexar County.* San Antonio, Tex.: Privately printed by the author, 1936.

9.398 Hume, E. E. "The Army Medical Library of Washington, D.C.: The Largest Medical Library That Has Ever Existed." *Isis* 26 (1937): 423–47.

9.399 Hume, E. E. "Buildings for the Army Medical Library." *Military Surgeon* 80 (1937): 45–53.

9.400 Hume, E. E. "Garrison and the Army Medical Library, 1891–1930." *Bulletin of the History of Medicine* 5 (1937): 301–46.

9.401 Hume, E. E. "The History and the Work of the Army Medical Library." *Science* 85 (1937): 207–10.

9.402 Jones, H. W. "The Centenary of the Army Medical Library." *Military Surgeon* 80 (1937): 1–4.

9.403 Marshall, M. "A History of Dental Libraries in the United States: With Sketches of Important Dental Libraries in Canada and Foreign Countries." *BMLA* 26 (1937): 86–99.

9.404 Dean-Throckmorton, J. "History of the Iowa State Medical Library." *Iowa State Medical Society Journal* 29 (1939): 472–75.

9.405 Denton, G. B. "The Beginnings and Growth of Dental Libraries." *SL* 31 (1940): 403–06.

9.406 Hume, E. E. "The Army Medical Library of Washington and Its Collection of Early Kentuckiana." *Kentucky Medical Journal* 38 (1940): 258–67.

9.407 Hume, E. E. "The Story of the Army Medical Library." *Virginia Medical Monthly* 67 (1940): 261–72.

9.408 Simons, C. M. "The Lloyd Library and Museum—A Brief History of its Founders and Its Resources." *CRL* 2 (1941): 245–47.

9.409 Wilson, J. E. "An Early Baltimore Physician and His Medical Library." *Annals of Medical History* 4 (1942): 63–80.

9.410 Fulton, J. F. "History of the Yale Medical Libraries." *BMLA* 34 (1946): 184–88.

9.411 Fulton, J. F. "A Brief History of Yale's Medical Collections." *YULG* 21 (1947): 47–53.

9.412 Adams, S. "The Army Medical Library and Other Medical Libraries of the Nation (1836–1947)." *CRL* 9 (1948): 126–32.

9.413 Coffman, C. "The Dental-Pharmacy Library: A Short History." *Temple University Library Bulletin* 1 (1948): 9–10.

9.414 Holt, A. C. "The Library at the Harvard Medical School, 1847 and 1947." *HLB* 2 (1948): 32–43.

9.415 Van Ingen, P. "The Library Without a Home." *Academic Bookman* 1 (FALL 1948): 2–7.

9.416 Alessios, A. B. "Library Work with the Blind [1892–1948]." *WLB* 23 (1949): 369–75.

1950–1971

9.417 Waring, J. I. "The Library of the Medical Society of South Carolina (1791–1949)." *BMLA* 38 (1950): 253–60.

9.418 Freund, C. E. "The Library of the College of Physicians of Philadelphia." Master's thesis, Drexel Institute of Technology, 1951.

9.419 RePass, E. W. "A History of the Library of the Medical Society of the City and County of Denver (1893–1948)." *BMLA* 39 (1951): 128–34.

9.420 Webster, J. P. "The Story of a Plastic Surgery Library." *CLC* 1 (1951): 9–17.

9.421 O'Malley, C. D. "The Barkan Library of the History of Medicine and Natural Science Books: An Account of Its Development." *Stanford Medical Bulletin* 9 (1952): 145–55.

9.422 Allen, A. W. "The Doctor and His Books." *New England Journal of Medicine* 249 (1953): 320–22.

9.423 Brodman, E. *The Development of Medical Bibliography*. N.p.: Medical Library Association, 1954.

9.424 Brodman, E., MacDonald, M. R., and Rogers, F. B. "The National Medical Library: The Survey and Ten Years Progress." *BMLA* 42 (1954): 439–46.

9.425 Cunning, E. T. "A History of Jefferson Medical College Library, 1898–1953." Master's thesis, Drexel Institute of Technology, 1954.

9.426 Farr, L. M. "The History of the Buncombe County Medical Library [1935–53]." *North Carolina Medical Journal* 15 (1954): 87–89.

9.427 Simons, C. M. "Lloyd Library: Pharmacy in Cincinnati [1864–1953]." *SL* 45 (1954): 70–73.

9.428 Wilson, W. J. "Early Plans for a National Medical Library." *BMLA* 42 (1954): 426–34.

9.429 McColl, M. C. "The Evans Dental Library, University of Pennsylvania: History and Service." Master's thesis, Drexel Institute of Technology, 1955.

9.430 Sevy, B. "Temple University School of Medicine Library 1910–1954." Master's thesis, Drexel Institute of Technology, 1955.

9.431 Thomas, E. H. "A History of the National Institutes of Health Library, 1901–1954." Master's thesis, Catholic University of America, 1956.

9.432 Thompson, K. S. "America's Oldest Medical Library: The Pennsylvania Hospital (1762–1950)." *BMLA* 44 (1956): 428–30.

9.433 Donley, V. "A Chronology of Medical Libraries in the United States with Some Bibliographic Notes Pertaining to Their Early History." Master's thesis, Western Reserve University, 1957.

9.434 Draper, W. "Medical Libraries of New York State." *New York State Journal of Medicine* 57 (1957): 584–94.

9.435 Fry, A., and Adams, S. "Medical Library Architecture in the Past Fifty Years [1911–57]." *BMLA* 45 (1957): 471–79.

9.436 Lage, L. C., Miller, L. B., and Washburn, D. "Dental, Nursing, and Pharmaceutical Libraries, 1947–1957." *BMLA* 45 (1957): 371–77.

9.437 Morris, D. A. "Medical Books Used by Physicians and Medical Students in the United States, 17th–19th Centuries." Master's thesis, Western Reserve University, 1957.

9.438 Balkema, J. A. "A History of the Robert Lefevre Memorial Library at the New York University College of Medicine." Master's thesis, Drexel Institute of Technology, 1958.

9.439 Schullian, D. M., and Rogers, F. "The National Library of Medicine." *LQ* 28 (1958): 1–17, 95–121.

9.440 Clymer, B. F. "The History of the Division of Health Affairs Library of the University of North Carolina." Master's thesis, University of North Carolina, 1959.

9.441 "The Library and Its Publications." In *Northwestern University Medical School 1859–1959*. Evanston, Ill.: Northwestern University, 1959. Pp. 443–60.

9.442 *The Making of a Library: Extracts and Letters, 1934–1941, of Harvey Cushing, Arnold C. Klebs, [and] John F. Fulton,* Presented to John Fulton by His Friends on His Sixtieth Birthday, 1 November 1959. New Haven, Conn.: N.p., [1959].

9.443 Kilgour, F. G. *The Library of the Medical Institute of Yale College and Its Catalogue of 1865*. [New Haven]: Yale University Press, 1960.

9.444 *The First Catalogue of the Library of the Surgeon General's Office, Washington, 1840,* facsimile copy. Washington, D.C.: National Library of Medicine, 1961.

9.445 Keys, T. E. "Sir William Osler and the Medical Library." *BMLA* 49 (1961): 24–41, 127–48.

9.446 Kilgour, F. G. "First Century of Medical Books in the Yale College Library." *YULG* 35 (1961): 101–05.

9.447 Schullian, D. M. "Adams Jewett and John Shaw Billings, Partners in Acquisition." *BMLA* 49 (1961): 443–49.

9.448 Bernier, B. R. "A History of the Art Collection of the National Library of Medicine." Master's thesis, University of North Carolina, 1962.

9.449 Fulton, J. F., Kilgour, F. G., and Stanton, M. E. *Yale Medical Library: The Formation and Growth of Its Historical Library*. New Haven: Associates of the Yale Medical Library, 1962.

9.450 Robinson, I. M. *The Health Sciences Library, University of Maryland, A History, 1813–1960*. Baltimore: University of Maryland Health Sciences Library, 1962.

9.451 Draper, W. "Merger in Brooklyn: The Academy of Medicine and the Downstate Medical Center Libraries: History of the Academy of Medicine of Brooklyn Library." *BMLA* 51 (1963): 168–75.

9.452 Henkle, H. H. "The History of Medical Libraries of Chicago." *International College of Surgeons Journal* 40 (1963): 611–19.

9.453 Koudelka, J. B. "A History of the Johns Hopkins Medical Libraries, 1889–1935." Master's thesis, Catholic University of America, 1963.

9.454 Grandbois, M. "The *Nursing Literature Index*: Its History, Present Needs, and Future Plans." *BMLA* 52 (1964): 676–83.

9.455 "The Medical Library." In *The First Twenty Years of the University of Texas M.D. Anderson Hospital and Tumor Institute*. Houston: University of Texas, 1964. Pp. 247–51.

9.456 Simons, C. M. "Centennial of the Lloyd Library: A Century of Contribution to the Pharmaceutical, Botanical and Biological

Sciences, 1864–1964." *Lloydia, the Journal of Natural Products* 27 (1964): 141–47.

9.457 Titley, J. "The Library of the Louisville Medical Institute, 1837–1846." *BMLA* 52 (1964): 353–69.

9.458 Nonacs, M. "The Kornhauser Memorial Medical Library: Its History and Development." Master's thesis, University of Texas, 1966.

9.459 Thornton, J. L. *Medical Books, Libraries, and Collectors.* London: Deutsch, 1966.

9.460 Weakley, M. E. "The Origin and History of the Medical Library of the University of Virginia School of Medicine, 1825–1962." Master's thesis, University of North Carolina, 1966.

9.461 Wannarka, M. B. "History of a Medical Collection Housed in the Denver Public Library, 1893–1899." *Rocky Mountain Medical Journal* 64 (1967): 55–57.

9.462 Warner, H. J. "A History of the New York State Medical Library." Master's thesis, State University of New York at Albany, 1967.

9.463 Baird, V. M. "Books and the Doctor in Nineteenth-Century Texas: Some Early Attempts to Establish Medical Libraries." *BMLA* 56 (1968): 428–34.

9.464 Wannarka, M. B. "Medical Collections in Public Libraries of the United States: A Brief Historical Study." *BMLA* 56 (1968): 1–14.

9.465 Beatty, W. K. "Biomedical Libraries." *ELIS* 2 (1969): 554–62.

9.466 Opler, P. S. "The Origin and Trend of Bibliotherapy as a Device in American Mental Hospital Libraries." Master's thesis, San Jose State College, 1969.

9.467 Wortman, L. J. "A Study of the Library of The New York Academy of Medicine, 1847–1968." Research Paper, Long Island University, 1969.

9.468 Bracken, M. C. "An Analysis of the Evolution of the National Library of Medicine: Implications for the Development of Scientific and Technical Information Networks." Doctoral dissertation, American University, 1971.

1972–1986

9.469 Adams, S. "The Way of the Innovator: Notes toward a Prehistory of MEDLARS." *BMLA* 60 (1972): 523–33.

9.470 Bell, W. J. "The Old Library of the Pennsylvania Hospital." *BMLA* 60 (1972): 543–50.

9.471 Rees, A. "Medical School Libraries, 1961–1971." *BMLA* 60 Suppl (April 1972): 13–18.

9.472 Waserman, M. J. "Historical Chronology and Selected Bibliography Relating to the National Library of Medicine." *BMLA* 60 (1972): 551–58.

9.473 Waugh, E. S. "History of the Library Trust Fund [Florence A. Moore Library]." *Journal of the American Medical Women's Association* 28 (1973): 590–94.

9.474 Sanders, B. "History of the Henry L. Wolfner Memorial Library for the Blind and Physically Handicapped." Research Paper, University of Missouri-Columbia, 1974.

9.475 Lemkau, H. L. "Crossroads: The Story of the Medical Library." In *To Each His Farthest Star: University of Rochester Medical Center, 1925–1975,* edited by J. Romano. Rochester, N.Y.: University of Rochester Medical Center, 1975. Pp. 145–61.

9.476 Adams, S., and McCarn, D. B. "From Fascicules to On-Line Terminal: One Hundred Years of Medical Indexing [National Library of Medicine]." In *Communication in the Service of American Health . . . A Bicentennial Report from the National Library of Medicine.* Bethesda, Md.: N.p., 1976. Pp. 14–25.

9.477 Olson, C. A. "Librarianship in the History of Medicine." Research Paper, Brigham Young University, 1976.

9.478 Wiggins, E. V. "The National Library of Medicine." *ELIS* 19 (1976): 116–46.

9.479 Picciano, J. "Nursing Libraries and Literature." *ELIS* 20 (1977): 316–26.

9.480 Schmidt, D. A. "Certification of Medical Librarians, 1949–1977." *BMLA* 67 (1979): 31–35.

9.481 Wallis, E. "The University of Arkansas Medical Sciences Library, 1879–1979." *ArkL* 36 (March 1979): 13–19.

9.482 Brodman, E. "Education and Attitudes of Early Medical Librarians to Their Work: A Discussion Based on the Oral History Project of the Medical Library Association." *JLH* 15 (1980): 167–82.

9.483 Isetts, C. A. "Medical Libraries in Cincinnati." *Cincinnati Historical Society Bulletin* 38 (1980): 51–71.

9.484 Adams, S. *Medical Bibliography in an Age of Discontinuity.* Chicago: Medical Library Association, 1981.

9.485 Brodman, E. "Washington University School of Medicine Library (Saint Louis)." *ELIS* 32 (1981): 417–26.

9.486 Kirkpatrick, B. A. "The New York Academy of Medicine Library." *BKM* 40 (1982): 102–04.

9.487 Miles, W. D. *A History of the National Library of Medicine: The Nation's Treasury of Medical Knowledge.* Bethesda, Md.: National Library of Medicine, 1982.

9.488 Stevenson, L. G. "The Blake Era at HMD." *Bulletin of the History of Medicine* 56 (1982): 455–59.

9.489 Dunkel, L. M. "Moral and Humane: Patients' Libraries in Early Nineteenth Century American Mental Hospitals." *BMLA* 71 (1983): 274–81.

9.490 Hirsch, R., ed. *A Catalogue of the Manuscripts and Archives of the Library of the College of Physicians of Philadelphia.* Philadelphia: University of Pennsylvania Press, 1983.

9.491 Berkley, A. L. "The Library of the St. Louis Society for Medical and Scientific Education." *Show-Me Libraries* 36 (1985): 27–29.

9.492 Donato, A. K., and Greene, H. "The Waring Historical Library Manuscript Guide." *SCHM* 86 (1985): 128–52.

9.493 Atlas, A. "Half a Century of Library Service at Pilgrim Psychiatric Center, 1935–1985." *BKM* 44 (1986): 99–103.

9.494 Blake, J. B. "From Surgeon-General's Bookshelf to National Library of Medicine: A Brief History." *BMLA* 74 (1986): 318–24.

9.495 Holtz, V. H. "Measures of Excellence: The Search for the Gold Standard." *BMLA* 74 (1986): 305–14.

9.496 Ray, J. M. "The P.I. Nixon Medical Library: A Research Center for Medical Texana." *TLJ* 62 (1986): 84–86.

Government Libraries and Programs

Before 1876

9.497 Poore, B. P. "The Library of Congress." *Harper's Magazine* 46 (December 1872): 41–50.

1876–1919

9.498 Warren, S. R., and Clark, S. N. "Libraries of the General Government." In *Public Libraries in the United States of America: Their History, Condition and Management; Special Report, Part I,* U.S. Bureau of Education. Washington, D.C.: Government Printing Office, 1876. Pp. 252–78.

9.499 Adkins, M. T. "Growth of a Great National Library, 1800–1889." *Magazine of American History* 22 (1889): 229–33.

9.500 Adler, C. "The Smithsonian Library." In *The Smithsonian Institution, 1846–1896: The History of Its First Half Century*, edited by G. B. Goode. Washington, D.C.: N.p., 1897. Pp. 265–302.

9.501 Billings, J. S. "The Influence of the Smithsonian Institution Upon the Development of Libraries, the Organization and Work of Societies, and the Publication of Scientific Literature in the United States." In *The Smithsonian Institution, 1846–1896: The History of Its First Half Century*, edited by G. B. Goode. Washington, D.C.: N.p., 1897. Pp. 815–22.

9.502 Goode, G. B., ed. *The Smithsonian Institution, 1846–1896: The History of Its First Half Century.* Washington, D.C.: N.p., 1897.

9.503 Spofford, A. R. "The Relation between the Smithsonian Institution and the Library of Congress." In *The Smithsonian Institution, 1846–1896: The History of Its First Half Century*, edited by G. B. Goode. Washington, D.C.: N.p., 1897. Pp. 823–32.

9.504 Greathouse, C. H. "Development of Agricultural Libraries." In *Yearbook of the United States Department of Agriculture, 1899.* Washington, D.C.: Government Printing Office, 1900. Pp. 491–512.

9.505 Rhees, W. J. *The Smithsonian Institution: Documents Relative to Its Origin and History, 1835–1887.* Washington, D.C.: Government Printing Office, 1901.

9.506 Putnam, H. "A National Library for the United States." *Bookman* 15 (1902): 52–57.

9.507 Johnston, W. D. "The Smithsonian Institution and the Plans for a National Library." In *History of the Library of Congress, 1800–1864*, edited by W. D. Johnston. Washington, D.C.: Government Printing Office, 1904. Pp. 403–506.

9.508 Johnston, W. D., ed. *History of the Library of Congress, 1800–1864.* Washington, D.C.: Government Printing Office, 1904.

9.509 Vrooman, F. "Our National Library." *Arena* 36 (1906): 278–85.

9.510 Bishop, W. W. *Library of Congress.* Chicago: American Library Association Publishing Board, 1911.

9.511 Barnett, C. R. "Government Libraries—Old and New." *SL* 9 (1918): 214–19.

1920–1949

9.512 Lacy, M. G. "The Library of the U.S. Department of Agriculture and Its Branches." *LJ* 46 (1921): 493–95.

9.513 Schmeckebier, L. F. *The Government Printing Office: Its History, Activities, and Organization.* Baltimore: Johns Hopkins Press, 1925.

9.514 Ashley, F. W. "Three Eras in the Library of Congress." In *Essays Offered to Herbert Putnam by His Colleagues and Friends on His Thirtieth Anniversary as Librarian of Congress, 5 April 1929*, edited by W. W. Bishop and A. Keogh. New Haven: Yale University Press, 1929. Pp. 57–67.

9.515 Bishop, W. W. "Thirty Years of the Library of Congress, 1899–1929." In *Essays Offered to Herbert Putnam by His Colleagues and Friends on His Thirtieth Anniversary as Librarian of Congress, 5 April 1929*, edited by W. W. Bishop and A. Keogh. New Haven: Yale University Press, 1929. Pp. 24–34.

9.516 Bishop, W. W. "Thirty Years of the Library of Congress, 1899 to 1929." *LJ* 54 (1929): 379–87.

9.517 Ford, W. C. "A Division of Manuscripts." In *Essays Offered to Herbert Putnam by His Colleagues and Friends on His Thirtieth Anniversary as Librarian of Congress, 5 April 1929*, edited by W. W. Bishop and A. Keogh. New Haven: Yale University Press, 1929. Pp. 156–61.

9.518 Ashley, F. W. *The Collection of John Boyd Thacher in the Library of Congress.* Washington, D.C.: Government Printing Office, 1931.

9.519 Vance, J. T. "The Centennial of the Law Library of Congress." *American Bar Association Journal* 18 (1931): 597–99.

9.520 Ashley, F. W. *The Vollbehr Incunabula and the Book of Books.* Washington, D.C.: Government Printing Office, 1932.

9.521 Vought, S. W. "The Library of the Federal Office of Education." *Peabody Journal of Education* 12 (1934): 21–25.

9.522 Hill, D. *Libraries of Washington.* Chicago: American Library Association, 1936.

9.523 MacLeish, A. "The American Experience: The Hispanic Foundation in the Library of Congress." *Bulletin of the Pan-American Union* 73 (1939): 621–34.

9.524 Smith, R. C. "The Hispanic Foundation in the Library of Congress." *Bulletin of the Pan-American Union* 73 (1939): 625–34.

9.525 Solberg, T. "A Chapter in the Unwritten History of the Library of Congress from January 17–April 5, 1899." *LQ* 9 (1939): 285–98.

9.526 Colkel, M. B., and Preston, E. H. "Local History and Genealogical Reference Section, Library of Congress." *American Genealogy* 17 (1940): 65–68.

9.527 Connor, R. D. W. "The Franklin D. Roosevelt Library." *AAr* 3 (1940): 81–92.

9.528 Diamond, I. S. "The U.S. Treasury Department Library: Its Growth and Development from 1817 to the Present Time." *SL* 33 (1942): 113–15.

9.529 Salamanca, L. *Fortress of Freedom: The Story of the Library of Congress.* Philadelphia: Lippincott, 1942.

9.530 MacLeish, A. "The Reorganization of the Library of Congress, 1939–44." *LQ* 14 (1944): 277–315.

9.531 Mugridge, D. H. "Thomas Jefferson and the Library of Congress." *WLB* 18 (1944): 608–11.

9.532 Ballou, R. O. *A History of the Council on Books in Wartime, 1942–1946.* New York: Council on Books in Wartime, 1946.

9.533 Mearns, D. C. *The Story up to Now: The Library of Congress, 1800–1946.* Washington, D.C.: Library of Congress, 1947.

9.534 Clapp, V. W. "The Library of Congress and the Other Scholarly Libraries of the Nation [1800–1947]." *CRL* 9 (1948): 116–25.

9.535 Mood, F. "The Continental Congress and the Plan for a Library of Congress in 1782–1783: An Episode in American Cultural History." *PMHB* 72 (1948): 3–24.

9.536 Baatz, W. Y. "Library Service in the Veterans Administration (1921–49)." *LQ* 19 (1949): 166–77.

9.537 Stevens, M. H. "Enough Fathom-Long Swine." *LLJ* 42 (1949): 1–11.

1950–1971

9.538 Evans, L. H. "The Strength by Which We Live." *BALA* 44 (1950): 339–45.

9.539 Fry, B. M., Warheit, I. A., and Randall, G. E. "The Atomic Energy Commission Library System: Its Origin and Development (1946–49)." *CRL* 11 (1950): 5–9.

9.540 Gabriel, R. H. "The Library of Congress and American Scholarship." *BALA* 44 (1950): 349–50.

9.541 Giandonato, R. M. H. "Connecticut Agricultural Experiment Station Library, 1875–1950." *SL* 41 (1950): 352–58, 370.

9.542 Gropp, A. E. "The Library of Congress and the Hispanic-American Field." *BALA* 44 (1950): 358–59.

9.543 Irwin, R. B. "The Talking Book." In *Blindness, Modern Approaches to the Unseen Environment,* edited by P. A. Zahl. Princeton: Princeton University Press, 1950. Pp. 346–53.

9.544 Lacy, D. M. "The Library of Congress: A Sesquicentenary Review 1800–1950." *LQ* 20 (1950): 157–79, 235–58.

9.545 Lord, M. E. "The Library of Congress." *BALA* 44 (1950): 346–48.

9.546 Marchman, W. P. *The Hayes Memorial.* Columbus, Ohio: Ohio State Archaeological and Historical Society, 1950.

9.547 Marchman, W. P. "The Hayes Memorial Library [Fremont, Ohio]." *Autograph Collectors' Journal* 3 (October 1950): 8–10.

9.548 Steele, H. M. "The Library of the United States Department of Labor, Washington, D.C. [1917–50]." *SL* 41 (1950): 93–97.

9.549 U. S. Library of Congress. Rare Book Division. *The Rare Books Division: A Guide to Its Collections and Services.* Washington, D.C.: Library of Congress, 1950.

9.550 Luckett, G. R. "A History of the United States Naval Academy Library, 1845–1907." Master's thesis, Catholic University of America, 1951.

9.551 Mearns, D. C. "Virginia in the History of the Library of Congress, or Mr. Jefferson's Other Seedlings." *Vermont Library Bulletin* 16 (1951): 1–4.

9.552 U. S. Library of Congress. Map Division. *The Services and Collections of the Map Division (1897–1951).* Washington, D.C.: Library of Congress, 1951.

9.553 Brinkley, C. "Army Post Library Service: An Inquiry into Its Origin and Development, Present Organization, and Future." Master's thesis, University of Washington, 1952.

9.554 Breisacher, R. "A History and Survey of the Library of the National Bureau of Standards." Master's thesis, Catholic University of America, 1953.

9.555 Horgan, M. "Survey of Library Facilities in the Department of the Interior." Master's thesis, Catholic University of America, 1953.

9.556 Mearns, D. C. "The First White House Library (1801–11)." *DCL* 24 (1953): 2–7.

9.557 North, N. "O.A.E.S.L.: A History of the Library of the Ohio Agricultural Experiment Station at Wooster, Ohio." Master's thesis, Western Reserve University, 1953.

9.558 Stevens, R. D. *The Role of the Library of Congress in the International Exchange of Official Publications: A Brief History.* Washington, D.C.: Library of Congress, 1953.

9.559 Willis, D. E. "The History and Present Status of the Library of the United States Geological Survey." Master's thesis, Catholic University of America, 1953.

9.560 Leland, W. G. "The Creation of the Franklin D. Roosevelt Library: A Personal Narrative." *AAr* 18 (1955): 11–29.

9.561 Lloyd, D. D. "The Harry S. Truman Library." *AAr* 18 (1955): 99–110.

9.562 Scott, C. D. "The History and Present Status of the Library of the United States Tariff Commission." Master's thesis, Catholic University of America, 1955, ACRL Microcard no. 53.

9.563 Story, J. "A National Library: Mr. Justice Story Speaks. A Letter Edited by Mortimer D. Schwartz and John Hogan." *Journal of Legal Education* 8 (1955): 328–30.

9.564 Marchman, W. P. "The Rutherford B. Hayes Library." *CRL* 17 (1956): 224–27.

9.565 Burnette, P. J. "The Army Library." *LQ* 27 (1957): 23–37.

9.566 Commons. E. "The Libraries of the Department of Health, Education, and Welfare [Since 1947]." *LQ* 27 (1957): 173–86.

9.567 Diamond, I. S. "The Library of the U.S. Treasury Department." *LQ* 27 (1957): 83–87.

9.568 Gartland, H. J. "The Veterans Administration Medical Library Program, 1946–1956." *BMLA* 45 (1957): 389–98.

9.569 Howard, P. "The Department of Interior Library System." *LQ* 27 (1957): 38–46.

9.570 Junior Service League, Independence, Mo. *The Harry S. Truman Library in Historic Independence.* [Independence: N.p., 1957].

9.571 Mohrhardt, F. E. "The Library of the United States Department of Agriculture [since 1862]." *LQ* 27 (1957): 81–82.

9.572 Sturdevant, E. "The Walter Reed Army Medical Center Library [Since 1928]." *DCL* 28 (1957): 3–10.

9.573 Berthold, A. M. "The Library of the Department of State." *LQ* 28 (1958): 27–37.

9.574 Bromiley, F. "The History and Organization of the Franklin D. Roosevelt Library, Hyde Park, New York." Master's thesis, Western Reserve University, 1959, ACRL Microcard no. 117.

9.575 Goldman, S. "History of the United States Weather Bureau Library." Master's thesis, Catholic University of America, 1959.

9.576 Dutch, T. C. "The History and Present Status of the Library of the United States Department of Justice." Master's thesis, Catholic University of America, 1960.

9.577 LaMontagne, L. E. "Jefferson and the Library of Congress." In *American Library Classification: With Special Reference to the Library of Congress,* edited by L. E. LaMontagne. Hamden, Conn.: Shoe String Press, 1961. Pp. 27–62.

9.578 "Centenary of the National Agricultural Library, U.S.D.A. 1862–1962: Papers in Celebration of the Occasion." *Quarterly Bulletin of the International Association of Agricultural Librarians and Documentalists* 7 (1962): 97–137.

9.579 Childs, J. B. "The Story of the United States Senate Documents, 1st Congress, 1st Session, New York, 1789." *PBSA* 56 (1962): 175–94.

9.580 Washburn, W. E. "The Influence of the Smithsonian Institution on the Intellectual Life in Mid-Nineteenth Century Washington." *RCHS* (1963–1966): 96–121.

9.581 Childs, J. B. " 'Disappeared in the Wings of Oblivion': The Story of the United States House of Representatives Printed Documents at the First Session of the First Congress, New York, 1789." *PBSA* 58 (1964): 91–132.

9.582 Cameron, J. K. *Air University Library, 1946–1966: Twenty Years of Service.* Maxwell Air Force Base, Ala.: Maxwell Air Force Base, 1966.

9.583 Frantz, J. C., and Cohen, N. M. *The Federal Government and Public Libraries: A Ten-Year Partnership, 1957–1966.* Washington, D.C.: Government Printing Office, 1966.

9.584 Stillman, M. E. "The United States Air Force Library Service: Its History, Organization and Administration." Doctoral dissertation, University of Illinois, 1966.

9.585 McDonough, J. "Justin Smith Morrill and the Library of Congress." *Vermont History* 35 (1967): 141–50.

9.586 Mumford, L. Q. "Bibliographic Developments at the Library of Congress." *Libri* 17 (1967): 294–304.

9.587 Cook, H. F. "United States Air Force Library Service." *ELIS* 1 (1968): 561–66.

9.588 Crawford, A. "Army Library Program." *ELIS* 1 (1968): 539–48.

9.589 Deininger, D. F. "The Navy and Marine Corps System of Shipboard Libraries and General Libraries Ashore." *ELIS* 1 (1968): 557–61.

9.590 Paciorek, L. A. "The History of the United States Military Academy Library at West Point, New York." Research Paper, Long Island University, 1968.

9.591 Stansfield, G. J. "Libraries of Military Educational Institutions." *ELIS* 1 (1968): 549–57.

9.592 Goff, F. R. "Early Library of Congress Bookplates." *QJLC* 26 (1969): 55–61.

9.593 Goff, F. R. "Oldest Library in Washington: The Rare Book Division of the Library of Congress." *RCHS* (1969–1970): 332–45.

9.594 Smith, L. E. "The Library List of 1783: Being a Catalogue of Books, Composed and Arranged by James Madison, and Others, and Recommended for the Use of Congress on January 24, 1783, with Notes and an Introduction." Doctoral dissertation, Claremont Graduate School and University Center, 1969.

9.595 Stephenson, R. W., ed. *Federal Map Collecting: A Brief History.* Washington, D.C.: Special Libraries Association, 1969.

9.596 Dale, D. C. *The United Nations Library: Its Origin and Development.* Chicago: American Library Association, 1970.

9.597 Morrisey, M. "Historical Development and Organization of the Federal Library Committee." *DLQ* 6 (1970): 207–31.

9.598 Cole, J. Y. "Ainsworth Spofford and the National Library." Doctoral dissertation, George Washington University, 1971.

9.599 Cole, J. Y. "Of Copyright, Men and a National Library." *QJLC* 28 (1971): 114–36.

9.600 Marris, A. "Franklin D. Roosevelt and the Franklin D. Roosevelt Library." Research Paper, State University of New York, Albany, 1971.

1972–1986

9.601 Cole, G. L. "Presidential Libraries." *Journal of Library Automation* 4 (1972): 115–29.

9.602 Cole, J. Y. "Smithmeyer and Pelz: Embattled Architects of the Library of Congress." *QJLC* 29 (1972): 282–307.

9.603 Cylke, F. K. "Federal Libraries." *ELIS* 8 (1972): 371–87.

9.604 El-Erian, T. S. "The Public Law 480 Program in American Libraries." Doctoral dissertation, Columbia University, 1972.

9.605 Lorenz, J. G., et al. "The Library of Congress Abroad." *LibT* 20 (1972): 548–76.

9.606 Rogers, J. W. "The WPA Library Project in Texas." *TL* 34 (1972): 209–18.

9.607 Schwartz, A. E. "American Libraries Abroad: U.S. Military Libraries." *LibT* 20 (1972): 527–37.

9.608 Cole, J. Y. "L.C. and ALA, 1876–1901." *LJ* 98 (1973): 2965–70.

9.609 Cole, J. Y. "The National Monument for a National Library: Ainsworth Rand Spofford and the New Library of Congress, 1871–1897." *RCHS* (1973): 468–507.

9.610 Dennis, R. "Herbert Hoover Presidential Library." *ELIS* 10 (1973): 398–400.

9.611 Marshall, J. W. "The Franklin D. Roosevelt Library." *ELIS* 9 (1973): 93–96.

9.612 Basler, R. P. *The Muse and the Librarian.* Westport, Conn.: Greenwood Press, 1974.

9.613 Cole, J. Y. "The Library of Congress in the Nineteenth Century: An Informal Account." *JLH* 9 (1974): 222–40.

9.614 Goodrum, C. A. *The Library of Congress.* New York: Praeger Publishers, 1974.

9.615 Grefrath, R. W. "War Information Centres in the United States during World War II." *LHR* 1 (September 1974): 1–21.

9.616 U. S. National Agricultural Library. Associates. *The National Agricultural Library: A Chronology of Its Leadership and Attainments, 1839–1973.* [Beltsville, Md.]: Associates of the National Agricultural Library, [1974].

9.617 Belanger, S. E. "History of the Library of Marine Biological Laboratory, 1888–1973." *JLH* 10 (1975): 255–63.

9.618 Cole, J. Y. "For Congress and the Nation: The Dual Nature of the Library of Congress." *QJLC* 32 (1975): 118–38.

9.619 Kaula, N. "175 Years of the Library of Congress." *Herald of Library Science* 14 (1975): 244–46.

9.620 Krettek, G. "Library Legislation, Federal." *ELIS* 15 (1975): 337–54.

9.621 Lethbridge, M. C., and McClung, J. W. "Library of Congress." *ELIS* 15 (1975): 19–93.

9.622 McCoy, D. R. "The Beginnings of the Franklin D. Roosevelt Library." *Prologue* 7 (1975): 136–50.

9.623 Marley, S. B. "Newspapers and the Library of Congress." *QJLC* 32 (1975): 207–37.

9.624 Snapp, E. "The Acquisition of the Vollbehr Collection of Incunabula for the Library of Congress." *JLH* 10 (1975): 152–61.

9.625 Stocking. R. E. "John F. Kennedy Library." *ELIS* 13 (1975): 276–80.

9.626 Cole, J. Y. "The National Libraries of the United States and Canada." In *A Century of Service: Librarianship in the United States and Canada*, edited by S. L. Jackson, E. B. Herling, and E. J. Josey. Chicago: American Library Association, 1976. Pp. 243–59.

9.627 Holmes, R. R. "Microfilming Clearing House of the Library of Congress." *ELIS* 18 (1976): 72–76.

9.628 Koestler, F. A. "Books for the Blind." In *The Unseen Minority: A Social History of Blindness in the United States*. New York: David McKay, 1976. Pp. 115–29.

9.629 Koestler, F. A. "The Talking Book." In *The Unseen Minority: A Social History of Blindness in the United States*. New York: David McKay, 1976. Pp. 130–52.

9.630 Moran, L. P. "National Agricultural Library." *ELIS* 19 (1976): 27–45.

9.631 Pandiri, A. M. "A Study of the History, Growth, and Development of the Public Law 480 Program and Its Impact on American Academic Libraries with Special Reference to Yale University Library." Master's thesis, Southern Connecticut State College, 1976.

9.632 Childs, J. B. "Official Documents." *ELIS* 20 (1977): 335–38.

9.633 Klassen, R. "Office of Education (U.S.), Office of Libraries and Learning Resources." *ELIS* 20 (1977): 327–32.

9.634 Milum, B. L. "Choosing MacLeish's Successor: The Recurring Debate." *JLH* 12 (1977): 86–109.

9.635 Quarterly Journal of the Library of Congress. *Librarians of Congress, 1802–1974*. Washington, D.C.: Library of Congress, 1977.

9.636 Waldo, M. J. "An Historical Look at the Debate over How to Organize Federal Government Documents in Depository Libraries." *GPR* 4 (1977): 319–29.

9.637 Adkinson, B. K. *Two Centuries of Federal Information*. Stroudsburg, Pa.: Dowden, Hutchinson and Ross, distributed by Academic Press, 1978.

9.638 Cole, J. Y. "Herbert Putnam and the National Library." In *Milestones to the Present: Papers from Library History Seminar V*, edited by H. Goldstein. Syracuse, N.Y.: Gaylord Professional Publications, 1978. Pp. 109–22.

9.639 Cole, J. Y. "The Library of Congress, 1800–1975." In *The Library of Congress in Perspective: A Volume Based on the Reports of the 1976 Librarian's Task Force and Advisory Groups*. New York: R.R. Bowker, 1978. Pp. 1–83.

9.640 Cole, J. Y. "The Library of Congress in American Life." *AdLib* 8 (1978): 55–79.

9.641 Dennis, R. "Presidential Libraries." *ELIS* 23 (1978): 223–53.

9.642 Hernon, P. "Academic Library Reference for the Publications of Municipal, State, and Federal Government: A Historical Perspective Spanning the Years up to 1962." *GPR* 5 (1978): 31–50.

9.643 Stewart, R. A. "The Development of National Library Functions in the British Museum and the Library of Congress." Master's thesis, University of Chicago, 1978.

9.644 Thomison, D. "Trouble in Camelot: An Early Skirmish of Kennedy's New Frontier." *JLH* 13 (1978): 148–56.

9.645 Barnett, W. J. "The Depository Library Program." *WLB* 54 (1979): 31–35.

9.646 Cole, J. Y. *For Congress and the Nation: A Chronological History of the Library of Congress.* Washington, D.C.: Library of Congress, 1979.

9.647 Hedrick, L. F. "The History and Development of Presidential Libraries." Research Paper, Texas Woman's University, 1979.

9.648 Hu, S. C. *The Development of the Chinese Collection in the Library of Congress.* Boulder, Colo.: Westview Press, 1979.

9.649 Metcalf, K. D. "Librarians of Congress, 1802–1974: A Review Essay." *JLH* 14 (1979): 43–55.

9.650 Wolter, J. A., Modelski, A. M., Stephenson, R. W., and Carrington, D. K. "A Brief History of the Library of Congress Geography and Map Division, 1897–1978." In *The Map Librarian in the Modern World: Essays in Honor of Walter W. Ristow,* edited by H. Wallis and L. Zögner. New York: K.G. Saur, 1979. Pp. 47–90.

9.651 Cole, J. Y. "The Library of Congress and American Research Libraries." In *University Library History: An International Review,* edited by J. Thompson. New York: K.G. Saur, 1980. Pp. 187–207.

9.652 Cylke, F. K., Wintle, M. J., and Hagle, A. D. "Talking Books." *ELIS* 30 (1980): 70–95.

9.653 Goff, F. R. "T.I.: Mr. Jefferson's Books in Washington, D.C." *RCHS* 50 (1980): 81–94.

9.654 Herrick, D. "Toward a National Film Collection: Motion Pictures at the Library of Congress." *Film Library Quarterly* 13 (1980): 5–25.

9.655 Hilker, H. A. *Ten First Street Southeast: Congress Builds a Library 1886–1897.* Washington, D.C.: Library of Congress, 1980.

9.656 Miller, S. J. "The Depository Library System: A History of the Distribution of Federal Government Publications to Libraries of the United States from the Early Years of the Nation to 1895." Doctoral dissertation, Columbia University, 1980.

9.657 Newman, W. A. "Congress and the Public Library: Legislative Proposals and Action for Federal Assistance 1938–1956." Doctoral dissertation, Case Western Reserve University, 1980.

9.658 Ring, D. F. "The Michigan Imprints Inventory of the Historical Records Survey." *Detroit in Perspective: A Journal of Regional History* 4 (1980): 111–17.

9.659 Ring, D. F., ed. *Studies in Creative Partnership: Federal Aid to Public Libraries during the New Deal.* Metuchen, N.J.: Scarecrow Press, 1980.

9.660 Shank, R. "Smithsonian Institution Libraries." *ELIS* 28 (1980): 36–44.

9.661 Smith, T. A. "Before Hyde Park: The Rutherford B. Hayes Library." *AAr* 43 (1980): 485–88.

9.662 Williams, R. L. "The Library of Congress Can't Hold All Man's Knowledge—But It Tries." *Smithsonian Magazine* 11 (April 1980): 38–49.

9.663 Clark, H. "The Library of Congress in 1880—A User's Report." *JLH* 16 (1981): 523–30.

9.664 Elson, B. L. "The Library of Congress: A Merger of American Functionalism and Cosmopolitan Eclecticism." Doctoral dissertation, University of Maryland, 1981.

9.665 Goff, F. R. "Uncle Sam Has a Book." *QJLC* 38 (1981): 123–33.

9.666 Hausrath, D. C. "United States International Communication Agency." *ELIS* 32 (1981): 70–112.

9.667 Lane, R. B. "United States. Air University Library." *ELIS* 32 (1981): 44–55.

9.668 Matthews, J. V. "Libraries, Books, and the Nature of America: The Creation of the

Smithsonian Institution." *JLH* 16 (1981): 152–65.

9.669 Bartis, P. T. "A History of the Archive of Folk Song at the Library of Congress: The First Fifty Years." Doctoral dissertation, University of Pennsylvania, 1982.

9.670 Berninger, D. E. "Some Reflections on Federal Policy for Secondary Information Systems and Services, 1945–1981." *JASIS* 33 (1982): 162–67.

9.671 Goodrum, C. A., and Dalrymple, H. W. "Computerization at the Library of Congress: The First Twenty Years." *WLB* 57 (1982): 115–21.

9.672 Goodrum, C. A., and Dalrymple, H. W. *The Library of Congress.* Boulder, Colo.: Westview Press, 1982.

9.673 Library of Congress. "Affirmative Action at the Library of Congress: A Historical Overview, 1973–1982." *Library of Congress Information Bulletin* 41 (1982): 383–88.

9.674 Library of Congress. *The 1812 Catalogue of the Library of Congress: A Facsimilie.* Washington, D.C.: Government Printing Office, 1982.

9.675 Shiflett, O. L. "The Government as Publisher: An Historical Overview." *Library Research* 4 (1982): 115–35.

9.676 United States, National Commission on Libraries and Information Science. *Annual Report—National Commission on Library and Information Science, 1980–1981: A Decade of Accomplishment.* Washington, D.C.: Government Printing Office, 1982.

9.677 Willingham, R. M. "Bookish Bureaucracy: The Work of the American Imprints Inventory in Georgia, 1937–41." *GL* 19 (1982): 3–6.

9.678 Wolff, B. H. "History of Information Sharing in New York Government." *BKM* 40 (1982): 141–47.

9.679 Cole, J. Y. "Amassing American 'Stuff': The Library of Congress and the Federal Arts Project in the 1930s." *QJLC* 40 (1983): 356–89.

9.680 Cole, J. Y. "Cross-currents: The British Library and the Library of Congress in Historical Perspective." *Library Research* 32 (1983): 247–58.

9.681 Helicher, K. "Franklin D. Roosevelt: Reading and Public Library Legislation—A PragmaticRelationship." *BKM* 42 (1983): 52–55.

9.682 Holley, E. G., and Schremser, R. F., eds. *The Library Services and Construction Act: An Historical Overview from the Viewpoint of Major Participants.* Greenwich, Conn.: JAI Press, 1983.

9.683 Slattery, A. H. "Jose Ignacio Rodriguez and the Columbus Memorial Library." *Americas: Quarterly Review of Inter-American Cultural History* 39 (1983): 548–54.

9.684 Bohanan, R. D. "The Presidential Libraries System Study: The Carter's Project Experience." *Provenance* 2 (1984): 32–38.

9.685 Cole, J. Y. "The Library of Congress and the Presidential Parade, 1800–1984." *Library of Congress Information Bulletin* 43 (1984): 343–48.

9.686 Cole, J. Y., ed. *Books in Action: The Armed Services Editions.* Washington, D.C.: Library of Congress, 1984.

9.687 Friis, H. R. "Map Division, China Theater Research and Analysis Branch, Office of Strategic Services, World War II, 1945." *SLAGMDB* 136 (1984): 23–39.

9.688 Fung, M. C. "Safekeeping of the National Peiping Library's Rare Chinese Books at the Library of Congress, 1941–1965." *JLH* 19 (1984): 359–72.

9.689 Hafertepe, K. *America's Castle: The Evolution of the Smithsonian Building and Its Institution, 1840–1878.* Washington, D.C.: Smithsonian Institution, 1984.

9.690 Heister, C. G. "Over 125 Years of Service: The Illinois Natural History Survey Library." *IllL* 66 (1984): 194–95.

9.691 Shubert, J. F. "The Regents and Library Aid Legislation in the 1970s and 1980s." *BKM* 42 (1984): 188–96.

9.692 Wickman, J. E. "Dwight D. Eisenhower Library." *ELIS* 37 (1984): 73–79.

9.693 Goggin, J. "Carter G. Woodson and the Collection of Source Materials for Afro-American History." *AAr* 48 (1985): 261–71.

9.694 Hernon, P., McClure, C. R., and Purcell, G. R. *GPO's Depository Library Program: A Descriptive Analysis*. Norwood, N.J.: Ablex Publishing Corp., 1985.

9.695 McMahon, N. "Air Force Library Program." *ELIS* 38 (1985): 7–11.

9.696 York, M. C. "The American Imprints Inventory in North Carolina." *NCL* 43 (1985): 87–97.

9.697 Hooks, M. "The General Land Office: Custodian of Texas Land Records." *TLJ* 62 (1986): 61–63.

9.698 Kahles, W. R. "Congress, Higher Education, and the U.S. Federal Depository Program." *GPR* 13 (1986): 233–42.

9.699 Nelson, G. K., and Richardson, J. V. "Adelaide Hasse and the Early History of the U.S. Superintendent of Documents Classification Scheme." *GPR* 13 (1986): 79–96.

9.700 Olsen, D. "Military Libraries in Texas." *TLJ* 62 (1986): 14–15.

9.701 Rosenberg, J. A. "Foundation for Service: The 1896 Hearings on the Library of Congress." *JLH* 21 (1986): 107–30.

9.702 Wilson, J. "The American Imprints Inventory in Illinois." *LQ* 56 (1986): 303–15.

10.

Archival Enterprise

by Frederick J. Stielow
with James Gregory Bradsher

Archivists in the United States trace their origins to Colonial times and claim a professional organization, the Society of American Archivists (SAA), that has been active for more than fifty years. Ironically, the zeal of archivists for preserving the records of enduring value of other individuals and institutions has not extended to their own documentary history. Most astounding perhaps is that a field dominated and populated by trained historians is served by an inadequately developed historiography lacking differentiated schools of thought.

The bibliographer of archival history faces some unique semantic problems. Confusion arises naturally from the fact that archive repositories are generally part of a larger historical society or library, or from instances where the "library" should more properly be called an "archive," as with the presidential library system. Indeed, the bibliographer must exercise caution due to the ubiquity and overlap of the terms "history" and "archives." Research in collections that comprise an archival repository is almost synonymous with historical research; hence, uncertainties arise due to the difficulties inherent in isolating a purely archival history from reports about the collections themselves. Similarly, and unlike library studies, a definitional dilemma results from the tendency of archival scholars to include longitudinal factors about their own repositiories in such reports.

Although the bulk of the printed material is available in journal articles such as those cited in this chapter, bibliographies provide essential beginning points. The key background source for the pre–1942 era remains Solon Buck and Ernst Posner's *Selected References on Phases of Archival Administration* (1942, **10.17**). Staff members from the National Archives continued this work with classified yearly summaries in the *American Archivist* until 1978. P. A. Andrews and B. J. Grier followed with coverage for the years 1979 to 1982 in a volume carrying the still unfulfilled promise of renewed annual compilations (1985, **10.136**). Meanwhile, Frank B. Evans must be cited as the major bibliographer in the modern era and the producer of several volumes: in

215

particular, *Modern Archives and Manuscripts: A Select Bibliography* (1975, **10.80**) and *The History of Archives Administration: A Select Bibliography*, which is international in scope but includes some thirty pages of references to the United States (1979, **10.98**).

For library users perhaps as much as for those interested in historical issues, the best starting places for archival research are the published guides to archives and archival holdings: Philip M. Hamer's *Guide to Archives and Manuscripts in the United States* (1961, **10.45**), the Library of Congress's *National Union Catalog of Manuscript Collections* (from 1962, **10.47**), Frank G. Burke's *Directory of Archives and Manuscript Repositories in the United States* (1978, **10.92**) and its revision (2d ed., Phoenix: Oryx Press, 1988), and Mary Pease Smith's directory, *Historical Agencies in North America* (13th ed., Nashville, Tenn.: American Association for State and Local History, 1986).

Since the broader scope of American archival theory is deeply rooted in the European experience, a general study of the modern era must devolve from the classic works of Britisher Hilary Jenkinson's *A Manual of Archival Administration*, (1922 and its revision of 1937, **10.11**) and the second Dutch edition of Muller, Feith, and Fruin's manual published in 1920 and translated by Arthur H. Leavitt (1940, **10.13**). Significant contributions from the American side have been made by T. R. Schellenberg (1956, **10.34**; 1965, **10.52**), whose classic 1956 manual, *Modern Archives: Principles and Techniques*, has been joined by the writings of Kenneth W. Duckett (1975, **10.79**) and David B. Gracy (1981, **10.105**).

Unfortunately, much of the historical writing is anecdotal or celebratory, and it represents promotional accounts issued at anniversaries or upon the acquisition of individual collections. Solid historical research dates from the 1940s with Ernst Posner (1940, **10.14**), a refugee German scholar and the central figure in archival education with his program at American University and the National Archives. His *American State Archives* (1964, **10.50**); O. Lawrence Burnette's *Beneath the Footnote*, constituted of samples from *American Archivist* (1969, **10.58**); and Maygene F. Daniels and Timothy Walch's *Modern Archives Reader* (1984, **10.130**) join Schellenberg's works as beginning points in the history of the American archival enterprise. Again, however, these studies and even Richard C. Berner's *Archival Theory and Practice in the United States: A Historical Analysis* (1983, **10.118**) aim as much for current practice as for historical scholarship.

The beginning of the modern archives movement (as distinguished from historical research on archives) normally is dated from the founding of the National Archives in 1935. A convenient summary of important nineteenth-century developments that preceded the National Archives and that chronicled the growth of historical societies is provided in David Van Tassel's *Recording America's Past* (1960, **10.41**). More recent studies that capture the evolution and maturity of the National Archives as well as its gestation period include Donald McCoy's *The National Archives: America's Ministry of Documents, 1934–1968* (1978, **10.93**), Victor Gondos, Jr.'s *J. Franklin Jameson and the Birth of the National Archives, 1906–1926* (1981, **10.104**), and Timothy Walch's *Guardian of Heritage: Essays on the History of the National Archives* (1985, **10.152**).

Concurrently, the allied organizational structure provided by the American Historical Association (AHA) and its Public Archives Commission were discussed in the AHA *Annual Reports*. Of special value were reports written by J. Franklin Jameson, Reuben Thwaites, and Victor H. Paltsits, author of "An Historical Resume of the Public Archives Commission from 1899 to 1921" (1922, **10.9**).

Unfortunately, developments at the state and local levels have been slighted somewhat by the emphasis on the National Archives since the time of the Works Projects Administration's (WPA) Historical Records Surveys (themselves featured in a special issue of *American Archivist* [1974, no. 2]). The Colonial record-keeping practices in Maryland are an exception to this pattern, as is the coverage for Illinois through various special issues of *Illinois Libraries* (1970, no. 2; 1971, no. 1; 1975, no. 3; 1981, nos. 3 & 4; 1987, no. 8). Greenwood Press may partially fill the void through its Reference Guides to State History and Research Series, the first of which was on Louisiana by L. T. Cummins and Glen Jeansonne (1982, **10.112**). Ernst Posner (1964, **10.50**) and H. G. Jones (1969, **10.59**) have offered convenient overviews of the development of state and local record-keeping practices, while the World War II and later development of records management can be seen in the opening chapters of *Information and Records Management* by M. F. Robek, W. O. Maedke, and G. F. Brown (3d ed., Encino, Calif.: Glencoe Press, 1987).

Among expected historical genres, biographies remain at an inchoate level, with nothing comparable to the *Dictionary of American Library Biography*. Major exceptions to this tendency appeared in a series of articles in the *American Archivist* that included Rodney A. Ross on Posner, Jane F. Smith on Schellenberg, and Marcia D. Talley on Maryland State Archivist Morris Radoff (1981, **10.107**; 1981, **10.109**; 1981, **10.110**). Several volumes of collected works have been issued, including those by Waldo Gifford Leland (1955, **10.32**), Ernst Posner (1967, **10.56**), and Margaret Cross Norton (1975, **10.83**).

A few themes would continue to intrigue researchers. Education for archivists, the ties between archivists and historians, and the struggle between historical and library science foundations have been featured frequently in historical inquiries. Robert L. Clark's *Archives-Library Relations* (1976, **10.85**) serves as a useful introduction to these issues in the contemporary period. Gerald Ham's "The Archival Edge" (1975, **10.81**) and Frank G. Burke's questioning of the nature of archival theory (1981, **10.103**) have emerged as the most frequently cited articles in the post–1970 period. The archival enterprise itself has entered a new phase: professional consciousness was stimulated by the bicentennial and funding from the National Endowment for the Humanities and the National Historic Publications and Records Commission, plus the appointment of an executive director for the SAA and the growth of graduate education programs.

Archival history had been overshadowed by the recent push for an administrative and information science base. However, matters began to change in the 1980s with the emergence of an archival history movement. An Archival History Roundtable appeared in the SAA in 1987, flowing directly from Richard J. Cox's consciousness-raising article on the value of archival history, "American Archival History: Its Development, Needs, and Opportunities" (1983, **10.120**). Graduate education has encouraged some to consider archival history. Other venues have been opened through the Mellon Foundation-supported Archival Institute at the University of Michigan's Bentley Library, and publishing opportunities have expanded with the appearance of newer journals such as *Midwestern Archivist, Provenance,* and *Archival History Newsletter.* Thus, a "critical mass" of archival historians has emerged (including Gregory Bradsher, Richard J. Cox, and Jackie Goggin), offering a promising future, and revised versions of this chapter may be far more positive.

Before 1876

10.1 [Jewett, H. J.] "The Archive War of Texas." *DeBow's Review* 26 (1859): 513–23.

1876–1919

10.2 Barker, E. C. "Report on the Public Archives of Texas." In *Annual Report for 1901,* American Historical Association. Washington, D.C.: Government Printing Office, 1902. Pp. 353–58.

10.3 [Bugbee, L. G., and Barker, E. C.] "Report on the Bexar Archives." In *Annual Report for 1902,* American Historical Association. Washington, D.C.: Government Printing Office, 1903. Pp. 357–63.

10.4 Bolton, H. E. "Spanish Mission Records at San Antonio." *[Texas State Historical Association] Quarterly* 10 (1907): 297–307.

10.5 Jameson, J. F. "The American Historical Association, 1884–1909." *AHR* 15 (1909): 1–20.

10.6 Winkler, E. W. "Destruction of Historical Archives of Texas." *[Texas State Historical Association] Quarterly* 15 (1911): 148–55.

10.7 Paullin, C. O., comp. "History of the Movement for a National Archives Building in Washington, D.C." *Congressional Record* 53 (1916): Pt. 14, App. 1116–19.

10.8 Blegen, T. C. "Archives and Their Administration: A Study of European and American Practices." In *A Report on the Public Archives.* Madison, Wis.: State Historical Society of Wisconsin, Bulletin of Information No. 94, 1918.

1920–1949

10.9 Paltsits, V. H. "An Historical Resume of the Public Archives Commission from 1899 to 1921." *Annual Report of the American Historical Association* 1 (1922): 152–60.

10.10 Ramsdell, C. W. "The Preservation of Texas History." *NCHR* 6 (1929): 1–16.

10.11 Jenkinson, H. *A Manual of Archival Administration,* 2d ed. London: Lund, Humphries, 1937.

10.12 Yager, H. "The Archive War in Texas." Master's thesis, University of Texas, 1939.

10.13 Muller, S., Feith, J. A., and Fruin, R. *Manual for the Arrangement and Description of Archives,* translated from the second Dutch edition of 1920 by A. H. Leavitt. New York: H.W. Wilson, 1940.

10.14 Posner, E. "Some Aspects of Archival Development since the French Revolution." *AAr* 3 (1940): 159–72.

10.15 Smither, H. W. "The Archives of Texas." *AAr* 3 (1940): 187–200.

10.16 Leland, W. G. "Historians and Archivists in the First World War." *AAr* 4 (1941): 1–17.

10.17 Buck, S. J., and Posner, E. *Selected References on Phases of Archival Administration.* Washington, D.C.: National Archives, 1942.

10.18 Norton, M. C. "Some Legal Aspects of Archives." *AAr* 8 (1945): 1–11.

10.19 Wilcox, S. S. "The Spanish Archives of Laredo." *SHQ* 49 (1946): 341–60.

10.20 Brooks, P. C. "Archives in the United States During World War II, 1939–45." *LQ* 17 (1947): 263–80.

10.21 Shelley, F. "The Interest of J. Franklin Jameson in the National Archives: 1908–1934." *AAr* 12 (1949): 99–130.

1950–1971

10.22 Leland, W. G. "The First Conference of Archivists, December 1909." *AAr* 13 (1950): 109–20.

10.23 Heard, J. N. "Preservation and Publication of Texana by the Texas State Historical Association." Master's thesis, University of Texas, 1951.

10.24 Allen, W. "Nacogdoches Archives." *HT* 2 (1952): 257.

10.25 "Laredo Archives." *HT* 2 (1952): 28–29.

10.26 Smither, H. W. "Archives of Texas." *HT* 1 (1952): 65–67.

10.27 Thomas, M. A. "The Delaware State Archives: 1931–1951." Master's thesis, Drexel Institute of Technology, 1952.

10.28 Butterfield, L. H. "Archival and Editorial Enterprise in 1850 and 1950." *American Philosophical Society Proceedings* 98 (1954): 159–70.

10.29 Grover, W. C. "The National Archives at Age 20." *AAr* 17 (1954): 99–107.

10.30 Bahmer, R. H. "The National Archives after 20 Years." *AAr* 18 (1955): 195–205.

10.31 Brand, K. E. "The Place of the Register in the Manuscripts Division of the Library of Congress." *AAr* 18 (1955): 59–67.

10.32 National Archives. *Archival Principles: Selections from the Writings of Waldo Gifford Leland.* Washington, D.C.: Government Printing Office, 1955.

10.33 Taylor, V. H. *The Spanish Archives of the General Land Office of Texas.* Austin: Lone Star Press, 1955.

10.34 Schellenberg, T. R. *Modern Archives: Principles and Techniques.* Chicago: University of Chicago Press, 1956.

10.35 Taylor, V. H. "A Brief History of the Texas State Archives." *TL* 19 (1957): 13–16.

10.36 Bauer, G. P. "Public Archives in the United States." In *In Support of Clio: Essays in Memory of Herbert A. Kellar,* edited by W. B. Hesseltine and D. R. McNeil. Madison, Wis.: State Historical Society of Wisconsin, 1958. Pp. 49–76.

10.37 Hesseltine, W. B., and McNeil, D. R., eds. *In Support of Clio: Essays in Memory of Herbert Kellar.* Madison, Wis.: State Historical Society of Wisconsin, 1958.

10.38 Krauskopf, R. W. "The Hoover Commissions and Federal Recordkeeping." *AAr* 21 (1958): 371–99.

10.39 Pinkett, H. T. "Investigations of Federal Record Keeping, 1887–1906." *AAr* 21 (1958): 163–92.

10.40 Smiley, D. L. "The W.P.A. Historical Records Survey." In *In Support of Clio: Essays in Memory of Herbert A. Kellar,* edited by W. B. Hesseltine and D. R. McNeil. Madison, Wis.: State Historical Society of Wisconsin, 1958. Pp. 3–28.

10.41 Van Tassel, D. D. *Recording America's Past: An Interpretation of the Development of Historical Studies in America, 1607–1884.* Chicago: University of Chicago Press, 1960.

10.42 Winfrey, D. H. "The Archive War in Texas." *AAr* 23 (1960): 431–37.

10.43 Winfrey, D. H. "The Texan Archive War of 1842." *SHQ* 64 (1960): 171–84.

10.44 Winfrey, D. H. "The Texas State Archives." *TL* 22 (1960): 112–18.

10.45 Hamer, P. M. *A Guide to Archives and Manuscripts in the United States.* New Haven: Yale University Press, 1961.

10.46 Lane, C. "Catholic Archives of Texas: History and Preliminary Inventory." Master's thesis, University of Texas, 1961.

10.47 U. S. Library of Congress. *National Union Catalog of Manuscript Collections, 1959– .* Washington, D.C.: Library of Congress, 1962–.

10.48 Lamb, W. K. "The Archivist and the Historian." *AHR* 68 (1963): 385–91.

10.49 Lane, C. *Catholic Archives of Texas: History and Preliminary Inventory.* Houston: Sacred Heart Dominican College, 1964.

10.50 Posner, E. *American State Archives.* Chicago: University of Chicago Press, 1964.

10.51 Holmes, O. W. "History and Theory of Archival Practices." In *University Archives: Papers Presented at an Institute by the Univer-*

sity of Illinois Graduate School of Library Science, edited by R. E. Stevens. Champaign, Ill.: Illinois Union Bookstore, 1965. Pp. 1–21.

10.52 Schellenberg, T. R. The Management of Archives. New York: Columbia University, 1965.

10.53 Stevens, R. E., ed. University Archives: Papers Presented at an Institute by the University of Illinois Graduate School of Library Science. Champaign, Ill.: Illinois Union Bookstore, 1965.

10.54 Santos, R. G. "An Annotated Survey of the Spanish Archives of Laredo at Saint Mary's University of San Antonio, Texas." Texana 4 (Spring 1966): 41–46.

10.55 Santos, R. G. "A Preliminary Survey of the San Fernando Archives." TL 28 (1966): 152–72.

10.56 Posner, E. Archives and the Public Interest: Selected Essays by Ernst Posner, edited by K. W. Munden. Chicago: University of Chicago Press, 1967.

10.57 Wise, E. B. "State of West Virginia Department of Archives and History." Research Paper, Morris Harvey College, 1968.

10.58 Burnette, O. L. Beneath the Footnote: A Guide to the Use and Preservation of American Historical Sources. Madison: University of Wisconsin Press, 1969.

10.59 Jones, H. G. The Records of a Nation: Their Management, Preservation and Use. New York: Atheneum, 1969.

10.60 Kinney, J. M. "Archives of the General Convention of the Episcopal Church." AAr 32 (1969): 345–46.

10.61 Gondos, V. J., ed. Reader for Archives and Records Center Buildings. Washington, D.C.: Society of American Archivists, 1970.

10.62 Rundell, W. In Pursuit of American History: Research and Training in the United States. Norman: University of Oklahoma Press, 1970.

10.63 Shipton, C. K. "The Harvard University Archives in 1938 and in 1969." HLB 18 (1970): 205–11.

10.64 Gondos, V. J. "The Movement for a National Archives of the United States, 1906–1926." Doctoral dissertation, American University, 1971.

1972–1986

10.65 Barker, C. M., and Fox, M. H. Classified Files. New York: Twentieth Century Fund, 1972.

10.66 Evans, F. B. "Educational Needs for Work in Archival and Manuscript Depositories." Indian Archives 21 (1972): 13–30.

10.67 Birdsall, W. F. "The American Archivists' Search for Professional Identity, 1909–1936." Doctoral dissertation, University of Wisconsin, 1973.

10.68 Clausen, M. P. "Revisiting America's State Papers, 1789–1861." AAr 36 (1973): 523–36.

10.69 Kahn, H., Evans, F. B., and Hinding, A. "Documenting American Culture through Three Generations." AAr 36 (1973): 147–58.

10.70 Simpson, K. R. "Leland to Connor: An Early Survey of American State Archives." AAr 36 (1973): 513–22.

10.71 Bowie, C. "The Historical Records Survey in Wisconsin." AAr 37 (1974): 247–62.

10.72 Cox, R. J. "The Historical Development of the Manuscripts Division of the Maryland Historical Society." MHM 69 (1974): 409–17.

10.73 Cox, R. J. "Public Records in Colonial Maryland." AAr 37 (1974): 263–76.

10.74 National Archives. Guide to the National Archives of the United States. Washington, D.C.: National Archives and Records Service, 1974.

10.75 Peterson, T. H. "The Iowa Historical Records Survey, 1936–1942." *AAr* 37 (1974): 223–46.

10.76 Radoff, M. "The Maryland Records in the Revolutionary War." *AAr* 37 (1974): 277–86.

10.77 Rapport, L. "Dumped from a Wharf into Casco Bay: The Historical Records Survey Revisited." *AAr* 37 (1974): 201–10.

10.78 Birdsall, W. F. "The Two Sides of the Desk: The Archivist and the Historian, 1901–35." *AAr* 38 (1975): 159–74.

10.79 Duckett, K. W. *Modern Manuscripts: A Practical Manual for Their Management, Care and Use.* Nashville: American Association for State and Local History, 1975.

10.80 Evans, F. B. *Modern Archives and Manuscripts: A Select Bibliography.* Chicago: Society of American Archivists, 1975.

10.81 Ham, F. G. "The Archival Edge." *AAr* 38 (1975): 5–14.

10.82 Motley, A. "Chicago Historical Society." *IllL* 57 (1975): 223–26.

10.83 Norton, M. C. *Norton on Archives: The Writings of Margaret Cross Norton on Archival and Records Management,* edited by T. W. Mitchell. Carbondale, Ill.: Southern Illinois University, 1975.

10.84 Quinn, P. M. "Profile in Purple: The Northwestern University Archives." *IllL* 57 (1975): 220–23.

10.85 Clark, R. L., ed. *Archives-Library Relations.* New York: Bowker, 1976.

10.86 "Laredo Archives." *HT* 3 (1976): 506.

10.87 Rhoads, J. B. "National Archives (United States)." *ELIS* 19 (1976): 45–50.

10.88 High, W. M. "Unused Materials Await Library Historians in North Carolina State Archives." *SEL* 27 (1977): 241–44.

10.89 Pearson, M. S., and Laforte, R. S. "The Eyes of Texas: The Texas County Records Inventory Project." *AAr* 40 (1977): 179–87.

10.90 Weinberg, A. "Municipal Archives and the Philadelphia Paradigm." *DLQ* 13 (1977): 34–44.

10.91 Berner, R. C. "Arrangement and Description: Some Historical Observations." *AAr* 41 (1978): 169–82.

10.92 Burke, F. G. *Directory of Archives and Manuscript Repositories in the United States.* Washington, D.C.: National Historical Publications and Records Commission, 1978.

10.93 McCoy, D. R. *The National Archives: America's Ministry of Documents, 1934–1968.* Chapel Hill: University of North Carolina Press, 1978.

10.94 Rundell, W. "Photographs as Historical Evidence: Early Texas Oil." *AAr* 41 (1978): 373–91.

10.95 Ashdown, E. "Florida's Black Archives: A Substantial Past." *Change* 11 (1979): 48–49.

10.96 Birdsall, W. F. "Archivists, Librarians, and Issues during the Pioneering Era of the American Archival Movement." *JLH* 14 (1979): 457–79.

10.97 Cox, R. J. "The Plight of American Municipal Archives: Baltimore, 1729–1929." *AAr* 42 (1979): 281–92.

10.98 Evans, F. B. *The History of Archives Administration: A Select Bibliography.* Paris: UNESCO, 1979.

10.99 Wilsted, T. "Kiwis, Kangaroos and Bald Eagles: Archival Development in Three Countries." *MAr* 4 (1979): 35–51.

10.100 Saxine, A. "Laredo Archives Now Housed at Saint Mary's University." *TL* 42 (1980): 160–64.

10.101 Benedict, K. M. *A Selected Bibliography on Business Archives and Records Management.* Chicago: Society of American Archivists, 1981.

10.102 Berner, R. C. "Archival Education and Training in the United States, 1937 to the Present." *JEL* 22 (1981): 3–19.

10.103 Burke, F. G. "The Future Course of Archival Theory in America." *AAr* 44 (1981): 40–46.

10.104 Gondos, V. J. *J. Franklin Jameson and the Birth of the National Archives, 1906–1926*. Philadelphia: University of Pennsylvania Press, 1981.

10.105 Gracy, D. B. *Introduction to Archives and Manuscripts*. New York: Special Libraries Association, 1981.

10.106 Pratt, N. F. "Archival Resources and Writing Immigrant American History: The Bund Archives of the Jewish Labor Movement." *JLH* 16 (1981): 166–76.

10.107 Ross, R. A. "Ernst Posner: Bridge between the Old World and the New." *AAr* 44 (1981): 304–12.

10.108 Skinner, A. E. "Mrs. Eberly and That Cannon: Myth-making in Texas History." *TL* 43 (1981): 155–63.

10.109 Smith, J. F. "Theodore Schellenberg." *AAr* 44 (1981): 313–26.

10.110 Talley, M. D. "Morris Leon Radoff." *AAr* 44 (1981): 327–40.

10.111 Brichford, M. J. "The Origins of Modern European Archival Theory." *MAr* 7 (1982): 87–101.

10.112 Cummins, L. T., and Jeansonne, G. *A Guide to the History of Louisiana*. Westport, Conn.: Greenwood Press, 1982.

10.113 Ernst, J. W. "The Rockefeller Archive Center: A Reservoir of Information." *Journal of Thought* 17 (1982): 28–38.

10.114 Field, J. "The Impact of Federal Funding on Archival Management in the United States." *MAr* 7 (1982): 77–86.

10.115 Fields, J. E. "The Founding of the Manuscript Society." *Manuscripts* 34 (1982): 269–78.

10.116 Smith, D. R. "An Historical Look at Business Archives." *AAr* 45 (1982): 273–78.

10.117 Baumann, R. M. "Samuel Hazard: Editor and Archivist for the Keystone State." *PMHB* 107 (1983): 195–215.

10.118 Berner, R. C. *Archival Theory and Practice in the United States: A Historical Analysis*. Seattle: University of Washington Press, 1983.

10.119 Cook, J. F. "The Blessings of Providence on an Association of Archivists." *AAr* 46 (1983): 374–99.

10.120 Cox, R. J. "American Archival History: Its Development, Needs, and Opportunities." *AAr* 46 (1983): 31–41.

10.121 Cox, R. J. "A Century of Frustration: The Movement for a State Archives in Maryland, 1811–1935." *MHM* 78 (1983): 106–17.

10.122 Cox, R. J. "The Need for Comprehensive Records Programs in Local Government: Learning by Mistakes in Baltimore, 1945–1982." *Provenance* 1 (1983): 14–34.

10.123 Elliot, C. A., ed. *Understanding Progress as Process: Documentation of the History of Postwar Science and Technology in the United States*. Chicago: Society of American Archivists, 1983.

10.124 Ross, R. A. "Waldo Gifford Leland: Archivist by Association." *AAr* 46 (1983): 264–76.

10.125 Russell, M. U. "The Influence of Historians on the Archival Profession in the United States." *AAr* 46 (1983): 277–85.

10.126 Seltzer, R. J. "Center for History of Chemistry Inaugurated." *Chemical & Engineering News* 61 (4 April 1983): 26–29.

10.127 Smith, J. D. "Alfred Holt Stone: Mississippi Planter and Archivist/Historian of Slavery." *Journal of Mississippi History* 45 (1983): 262–70.

10.128 Stapleton, R. "Jenkinson and Schellenberg: A Comparison." *Archivaria* 17 (1983–1984): 75–85.

10.129 Stover, C. "Museum Archives: Growth and Development." *DLQ* 19 (1983): 66–77.

10.130 Daniels, M. F., and Walch, T., eds. *Modern Archives Reader: Basic Readings on Archival Theory and Practice.* Washington, D.C.: National Archives and Records Service, 1984.

10.131 Gillette, G. W. "A National Archives and the Mission of the Church." *HMPEC* 53 (1984): 307–11.

10.132 Goggin, J. "That We Shall Truly Deserve the Title of 'Profession': The Training and Education of Archivists, 1930–1960." *AAr* 47 (1984): 243–54.

10.133 Hedlin, E. "Archival Programs in the Southeast." *Provenance* 2 (1984): 1–15.

10.134 Viola, H. *The National Archives of the United States.* New York: Harry N. Abrams, 1984.

10.135 Wosh, P. J. "Keeping the Faith? Bishops, Historians, and Catholic Diocesan Archivists, 1790–1980." *MAr* 9 (1984): 15–26.

10.136 Andrews, P. A., and Grier, B. J. *Writings on Archives, Historical Manuscripts, and Current Records: 1979–1982.* Washington, D.C.: National Archives, 1985.

10.137 Barclay, M. J., ed. "North Carolina Archival Program—A Tradition of Excellence." *NCL* 43 (1985): 98–107.

10.138 Bowling, M. D. "Another New Frontier: Archives and Manuscripts in the National Park Service." *SL* 76 (1985): 164–76.

10.139 Bradsher, J. G. "An Administrative History of the Disposal of Federal Records, 1789–1949." *Provenance* 3 (1985): 1–21.

10.140 Bradsher, J. G. "Taking America's Heritage to the People: The Freedom Train Story." *Prologue* 17 (1985): 229–45.

10.141 Dearstyne, B. W. "Archival Politics in New York State, 1892–1915." *New York History* 66 (1985): 165–84.

10.142 Elliot, C. A. "Bibliographies, Reference Works, and Archives." *Osiris* 1 (1985): 295–310.

10.143 Engst, E. D. "Establishing a Vietnam War Veterans Archives." *MAr* 10 (1985): 43–52.

10.144 Foster, C. D. "Microfilming Activities of the Historical Records Survey, 1935–1942." *AAr* 48 (1985): 45–55.

10.145 Geselbracht, R. "The Four Eras in the History of the Presidential Papers." *Prologue* 15 (1985): 37–42.

10.146 Martin, G. J. "Preservation of the History of Geography." *Journal of Geography* 84 (1985): 186–88.

10.147 Miller, P. P. "National Archives' 50th Anniversary: Independence and Prospects for the Future." *GPR* 12 (1985): 411–19.

10.148 Nolte, W. M. "Walter Rundell, Jr.: The Archival Interests of a Historian." *AAr* 48 (1985): 377–87.

10.149 Proffitt, K. "The American Jewish Archives." *Ethnic Forum* 5 (1985): 20–29.

10.150 Stewart, B. "The Development of the Missouri Documents Depository System: 1971–1977." *GPR* 12 (1985): 321–44.

10.151 Stewart, V. "Archives in the Midwest: Assessments and Prospects." *MAr* 10 (1985): 5–16.

10.152 Walch, T., ed. *Guardian of Heritage: Essays on the History of the National Archives.* Washington, D.C.: National Archives and Records Service, 1985.

10.153 Warner, R. M. "The National Archives at Fifty." *MAr* 10 (1985): 25–32.

10.154 Bradsher, J. G. "A Brief History of the Growth of Federal Government Records, Archives and Information, 1789–1985." *GPR* 13 (1986): 491–505.

10.155 Cox, R. J. "Archivists and Public Historians." *Public Historian* 8 (1986): 14–34.

10.156 Geselbracht, R. "The Origins of Restrictions on Access to Personal Papers at the Library of Congress and the National Archives." *AAr* 49 (1986): 142–62.

10.157 Giunta, M. A. "The NHPRC: Its Influence on Documentary Editing, 1964–1984." *AAr* 49 (1986): 134–41.

10.158 Green, M. R. "The Archive War." *TLJ* 62 (1986): 67–71.

10.159 Hackman, L. J. "A Perspective on American Archives." *Public Historian* 8 (1986): 10–28.

10.160 Hedlin, E. "Chinatown Revisited: The Status and Prospects of Government Records in America." *Public Historian* 8 (1986): 46–59.

10.161 Jones, H. G. "Clio in the Courthouse: North Carolina's Local Records Program at Age Twenty-Five." *AAr* 49 (1986): 41–51.

10.162 Ostroff, H. "From Clay Tablets to MARC AMC: The Past, Present, and Future of Cataloging Manuscript and Archival Collections." *Provenance* 4 (1986): 1–11.

10.163 Peterson, T. H. "The National Archives and the Archival Theorist Revisited, 1954–1984." *AAr* 49 (1986): 125–33.

10.164 Peterson, T. H. "Counting and Accounting: A Speculation on Change in Record Keeping Practices." *AAr* 49 (1986): 125–33.

10.165 Rothberg, M. D. "The Brahmin as Bureaucrat: J. Franklin Jameson at the Carnegie Institution of Washington, 1905–1928." *Public Historian* 8 (1986): 47–60.

10.166 Stielow, F. J. "Toward a Theory of Sound Archives." In *The Management of Oral History Sound Archives*. Westport, Conn.: Greenwood Press, 1986. Pp. 11–33.

11.

Education for Librarianship

The historical literature of education for librarianship consists of general surveys and chronological treatments, thematic and regional analyses, classic reports and evaluations, and studies of individual schools. Although many of the major works in this field derive from doctoral dissertations, the general subject has attracted other serious scholarly research, including some inspired by anniversary commemorations. The centennial of American library education in 1986–1987 led to a special issue of *Library Trends* (1986, **11.201**) and two issues of the *Journal of Education for Library and Information Science* (1986, **11.200**).

General treatments, setting the context for more specific studies, provide a good beginning point. Louis R. Wilson's "Historical Development of Education for Librarianship in the United States" in *Education for Librarianship* (1949, **11.31**) remains one of the seminal essays. Though now dated, its insights remain provocative. The introduction of Robert B. Downs, "Education for Librarianship in the United States and Canada," to the published conference proceedings that appeared as *Library Education: An International Survey* (1968, **11.76**) followed somewhat the same summary approach. As highly respected library educators, their work is particularly significant. Carl White's brief study, *A Historical Introduction to Library Education: Problems and Progress to 1951* (1976, **11.138**), is an interpretive review of the formative period. A general survey carried to the mid–1970s is Donald G. Davis, Jr.'s "Education for Librarianship," which appeared in the *Library Trends* centennial of librarianship issue (1976, **11.133**).

The general sources for the subject have been well covered as a result of several doctoral dissertations completed between 1959 and 1969. Three are now published monographs. Sarah Vann's *Training for Librarianship before*

227

1923 (1961, **11.60**) is the most heavily documented from primary sources and provides complete coverage to the celebrated Williamson Report. Charles Churchwell continued the chronology in his *The Shaping of American Library Education* (1975, **11.124**). C. Edward Carroll's *The Professionalization of Education for Librarianship* (1970, **11.89**) deals primarily with the years 1940 to 1960. Definitive surveys of the quarter-century since 1960 have not yet emerged.

Instead, in recent years scholars have been studying trends, themes, and patterns in education for librarianship. For example, Lloyd Houser and Alvin Schrader have offered their analysis of the status of scientific professional research by reviewing the record of American library education (1978, **11.146**). Kathleen M. Heim has contributed a major study that compares the historical development of professional education in librarianship with that in several other professions (1979, **11.151**), while Wayne A. Wiegand has related librarianship to the general literature on the history of professions to reach conclusions about the development of library education (1986, **11.217**). Rosemary DuMont's "The Educating of Black Librarians: An Historical Perspective" (1986, **11.203**) exemplifies a topic that has called for fuller treatment. An example of regional studies in the history of library education is Edward G. Holley's "The Development of Library Education in the South" in the collection *Reference Services and Library Education* (1983, **11.178**) which includes two other contributions on library education history.

The general contemporary reports contain historical content in addition to being important milestones in their own right. The most significant single contemporary document remains Charles C. Williamson's *Training for Library Service* (Boston: Merrymount Press, 1923), a report for the Carnegie Corporation that has been reprinted and has received textual study and analysis by Sarah Vann as *The Williamson Reports of 1921 and 1923* (1971, **11.105**) and *The Williamson Reports: A Study* (1971, **11.104**). Although many studies of the state of library education have minimal historical introduction and have historical significance in their own right as contemporary documents, several have survived the test of time to be landmarks of their periods, such as Ernest J. Reece's *The Curriculum in Library Schools* (1936, **11.17**) and Joseph L. Wheeler's *Progress and Problems in Education for Librarianship* (1946, **11.29**). The centennial compilations referred to above may reach this status in time.

Individual schools, particularly the older and more prominent ones, have been the subjects of occasional commemorative volumes, such as those covering the school at Columbia: *School of Library Economy of Columbia College, 1887–1889: Documents for a History* (1937, **11.19**) and Ray Trautman's *History of the School of Library Service, Columbia University* (1954, **11.41**). The more recent research of Francis L. Miksa (1986, **11.211**) sheds new light on the early years. Among the major studies of other individual schools are Valmai R. Fenster's dissertation on the 1895–1921 period at Wisconsin (1977, **11.142**); C. H. Cramer's *The School of Library Science at Case Western Reserve University: Seventy-Five Years, 1904–1979* (1979, **11.150**), which, although unfootnoted, provides a critical history of a prominent school now closed; and John V.

Richardson, Jr.'s *The Spirit of Inquiry: The Graduate Library School at Chicago, 1921–1951* (1982, **11.176**) which derives from the author's doctoral dissertation and has spawned other efforts. The work of John Mark Tucker on the defunct Peabody school (1983, **11.181**) is a tribute to that school's contribution. Brief historical accounts of individual schools appear in separate entries in the *Encyclopedia of Library and Information Science.*

One will find helpful material in other sections of this work. For example, the history of the Association of American Library Schools (now Association for Library and Information Science Education) to 1968 is treated in detail by Donald G. Davis, Jr. (1974, **12.229**; and listed in Chapter 12, "Library Associations"). Biographical treatments of library educators will be found in Chapter 15, "Biographies of Individual Librarians and Library Benefactors."

1876–1919

11.1 Carnegie Library of Pittsburgh. *A Brief History of the Training School for Children's Librarians.* Pittsburgh: Carnegie Library, 1906.

11.2 Bacon, C. "Summer Session." In *The First Quarter Century of the New York State Library School 1887–1912.* Albany: New York State Library School, 1912. Pp. 27–33.

11.3 "Chronological Summary." In *The First Quarter Century of the New York State Library School 1887–1912.* Albany: New York State Library School, 1912. Pp. 24–26.

11.4 Dewey, M. "The Genesis of the Library School." In *The First Quarter Century of the New York State Library School 1887–1912.* Albany: New York State Library School, 1912. Pp. 13–23.

11.5 "The New York State Library School from the Student's Point of View." In *The First Quarter Century of the New York State Library School 1887–1912.* Albany: New York State Library School, 1912. Pp. 39–62.

11.6 Smith, B. S. "New York State Library School Association." In *The First Quarter Century of the New York State Library School 1887–1912.* Albany: New York State Library School, 1912. Pp. 34–38.

11.7 Wyer, J. I. *The First Quarter Century of the New York State Library School, 1887–1912.* Albany: New York State Library School, 1912.

11.8 Wyer, J. I. "Administrative History of the New York State Library School." In *The First Quarter Century of the New York State Library School 1887–1912.* Albany: New York State Library School, 1912. Pp. 7–12.

1920–1949

11.9 Smith, E. S. "The Carnegie Library School—A Bit of History." *LJ* 46 (1921): 791–94.

11.10 Wisconsin Library School Association. "Some Interesting History." *WisLB* 20 (1924): 53–56.

11.11 Tai, T. C. *Professional Education for Librarianship.* New York: Wilson, 1925.

11.12 Wyer, J. I. "The New York State Library School: An Historical Sketch." In *New York State Library School Register, 1887–1926.* New York: New York State Library School Association, 1928. Pp. v–viii.

11.13 Reece, E. J. "Historical Sketch of the School." In *Library School of the New York Public Library: Register 1911–1926,* edited by NYPL Editorial Committee. New York: New York Public Library, 1929. Pp. 7–10.

11.14 Incarnata, M. "Library Training in Texas and the Southwest." *Reports of Proceedings and Addresses* (1931): 189–97.

11.15 Wisconsin University Library School. *Directory of Graduates for Twenty-five Classes, 1907–1931.* Madison: Wisconsin University Library School, 1931.

11.16 Hill, A. C. "Education for Librarianship in Texas." *HTL* 4 (1935): 128–30.

11.17 Reece, E. J. *The Curriculum in Library Schools.* New York: Columbia University Press, 1936.

11.18 "Accredited Library School Histories." *LJ* 62 (1937): 24–35.

11.19 Columbia University. School of Library Service. *School of Library Economy of Columbia College, 1887–1889: Documents for a History.* New York: Columbia University School of Library Service, 1937.

11.20 Wyer, J. I. "The New York State Library School, 1887–1926." *LJ* 62 (1937): 5–10.

11.21 Howe, H. E. "Two Decades of Education for Librarianship." *LQ* 12 (1942): 447–70.

11.22 Roden, C. B. "An Essay in Retrospection [University of Chicago Graduate Library School]." *LQ* 12 (1942): 659–65.

11.23 Singleton, M. E. "Reference Teaching in the Pioneer Library Schools, 1883–1903." Master's thesis, Columbia University, 1942.

11.24 Buffum, M. S. "T.S.C.W. [Texas State College for Women] Library Science Department." *NNT* 19 (October 1943): 8–11.

11.25 Clare, F. "Our Lady of the Lake College Library Service Department." *NNT* 19 (October 1943): 4–7.

11.26 Hoole, W. S. "The Library Service Department of N.T.S.T.C. [North Texas State Teachers College]." *NNT* 19 (October 1943): 13–14.

11.27 Illinois, University. Library School. *Fifty Years of Education for Librarianship*, Papers Presented at the Celebration of the Fiftieth Anniversary of the University of Illinois Library School, 2 March 1943. Urbana: University of Illinois Press, 1943.

11.28 Lohrer, A. "The Teacher-Librarian Training Program, 1900–1944." Master's thesis, University of Chicago, 1944.

11.29 Wheeler, J. L. *Progress and Problems in Education for Librarianship*. New York: Carnegie Corporation, 1946.

11.30 Doe, J. "The Development of Education for Medical Librarianship." *BMLA* 37 (1949): 213–20.

11.31 Wilson, L. R. "Historical Development of Education for Librarianship in the United States." In *Education for Librarianship*, edited by B. Berelson. Chicago: American Library Association, 1949. Pp. 44–59.

1950–1971

11.32 Mitchell, S. B. "Education for Librarianship in California: A Preliminary Historical Sketch." *CLB* 11 (1950): 159–62.

11.33 Mitchell, S. B. "The Pioneer Library School in Middle Age." *LQ* 20 (1950): 272–88.

11.34 Cantrell, C. H. "Education for Librarianship, 1900–1925." *Alabama Librarian* 2 (1951): 7–11.

11.35 Norton, F. "Five Decades of Library Education in the South." *LLAB* 14 (1951): 5–12.

11.36 Stanbery, G. W. "History of the Carnegie Library School: Through Its First Fifty Years." Master's thesis, Carnegie Institute, 1951.

11.37 Emert, F. A. "Trends in Thought on the Training of Special Librarians from the Beginning of the Special Libraries Association in 1909 through 1950." Master's thesis, Western Reserve University, 1952.

11.38 Campion, A. L. "Education for Special Librarians in the United States and Canada in 1946 and 1952." Master's thesis, Drexel Institute of Technology, 1953.

11.39 Wicklzer, A. F. "Education for Librarianship: A Brief History, 1886–1953." Master's thesis, Western Reserve University, 1953.

11.40 Wilson, L. R. "Challenge of Library Literature to Education for Librarianship, 1923–1953." In *Challenges to Librarianship*, edited by L. Shores. Tallahassee: Florida State University, 1953. Pp. 125–40.

11.41 Trautman, R. L. *A History of the School of Library Service, Columbia University*. New York: Columbia University, 1954.

11.42 Wiesner, J. "A Brief History of Education for Librarianship [1887–1954]." *Education* 74 (1954): 173–77.

11.43 Asheim, L. E. "Education for Librarianship." *LQ* 25 (1955): 76–90.

11.44 Morton, F. F. "Twenty-Five Years in the Life of a Library School: Louisiana State University Library School." *LLAB* 18 (1955): 126–42.

11.45 Osburn, H. "A History of the Library Science Department of the Millersville State Teachers College, Millersville, Pennsylvania." Master's thesis, Drexel Institute of Technology, 1955.

11.46 Penland, P. R. "Accrediting Library Schools: A Study of the Background and Problems." Master's thesis, University of Michigan, 1955.

11.47 Davenport, F. B. "A History of the Western Reserve University Library School,

1904–1954." Master's thesis, Western Reserve University, 1956.

11.48 Doane, G. H. "Library School Heritage." *WisLB* 52 (1956): 184–86.

11.49 Nesbitt, E. "Training of Children's Librarians: History and Implications." *BNYPL* 60 (1956): 605–10.

11.50 Schenk, R. K. "Highlights in the History of the Library School of the University of Wisconsin." *WisLB* 52 (1956): 187–90.

11.51 Jordan, M. "Events in the Development of Education for Medical Librarianship in the Last Decade." *BMLA* 45 (1957): 341–60.

11.52 Luther, K. *The Teaching of Cataloging and Classification at the University of Illinois Library School [1893–1949].* Urbana: University of Illinois Library School, Occasional Paper no. 5, 1957.

11.53 Stallmann, E. L. *Library Internships: History, Purpose, and a Proposal.* Urbana: University of Illinois Graduate School of Library Science, Occasional Paper no. 37, 1957.

11.54 Wing, M. J. "A History of the School of Library Science of the University of North Carolina: The First Twenty-Five Years." Master's thesis, University of North Carolina, 1958, ACRL Microcard no. 119.

11.55 Adrian, J. M. "A History of the Library Science Department of East Texas State College." Master's thesis, East Texas State College, 1959.

11.56 Danton, J. P. "Doctoral Study in Librarianship in the United States." *CRL* 20 (1959): 435–53, 458.

11.57 *New York State Library School Register, 1887–1926.* New York: State Library School Association, 1959.

11.58 Elliott, A. W. "A History of the Division of Library Education, Kansas State Teachers College, Emporia, 1930–1959." Master's thesis, Kansas State Teachers College, 1960.

11.59 Steele, U. M. "A Study of Characteristics of Graduates of the Division of Librarianship of Emory University, 1931–1953." Research Paper, Emory University, 1960.

11.60 Vann, S. K. *Training for Librarianship before 1923: Education for Librarianship Prior to the Publication of Williamson's Report on Training for Library Service.* Chicago: American Library Association, 1961.

11.61 Dwyer, C. L. "Theses and Reports Accepted by the University of Texas Graduate School of Library Science." Master's thesis, University of Texas, 1963.

11.62 Fleischer, M. B. "Credentials Awarded through August, 1961, by Agencies Presently or Formerly Approved or Accredited by the American Library Association." Master's thesis, University of Texas, 1963.

11.63 Webb, D. A. "Local Efforts to Prepare Library Assistants and Librarians in Texas from 1900 to 1942." Doctoral dissertation, University of Chicago, 1963.

11.64 Wofford, A. "History of the Department of Library Science." Research Paper, University of Kentucky, 1963.

11.65 Donnell, J. "The History of the School of Library Science of the University of Oklahoma, 1929–1960." *Oklahoma Librarian* 14 (January 1964): 15–23.

11.66 Thorne, B. B. "The History of Sam Houston State Teachers College as Reflected in the Library and the Library Science Department." Master's thesis, Texas Woman's University, 1964.

11.67 Garvey, S. K. "Twenty-Five Years [Kansas State, Emporia, Library School]." *Library School Review [Kansas State, Emporia]* 4 (December 1965): 1–2.

11.68 English, T. H. "The Library School—Division of Librarianship." In *Emory University 1915–1965: A Semicentennial History.* Atlanta: Emory University, 1966. Pp. 170–71.

11.69 Cain, S. M. *History of the Library Science Department, Wisconsin State*

University, Whitewater. Whitewater, Wis.: Wisconsin State University, 1967.

11.70 Callaham, B. E. "The Carnegie Library School of Atlanta, 1905–1925." *LQ* 37 (1967): 149–79.

11.71 Carnovsky, L. "Changing Patterns in Librarianship: Implications for Library Education." *WLB* 41 (1967): 484–91.

11.72 Carnovsky, L. "The Evaluation and Accreditation of Library Schools." *LQ* 37 (1967): 333–47.

11.73 Grotzinger, L. A. "The University of Illinois Library School, 1893–1942." *JLH* 2 (1967): 129–41.

11.74 Vogel, C. "Carnegie Library School, Carnegie Institute of Technology to the Graduate Library School, University of Pittsburgh, a Chronology of the Transition." Research Paper, University of Pittsburgh, School of Education, 1967.

11.75 Boaz, M. "The Good Old Days [Library School of the Los Angeles Public Library]." *CalL* 29 (1968): 40a–d.

11.76 Downs, R. B. "Education for Librarianship in the United States and Canada." In *Library Education: An International Survey*, edited by L. E. Bone. Champaign: University of Illinois Graduate School of Library Science, 1968. Pp. 1–20.

11.77 Easter, M. J. "Education for Librarianship at the University of Buffalo, 1919–1945." Research Paper, State University of New York, Buffalo, School of Information and Library Studies, 1968.

11.78 Farley, J. J. "Albany, State University of New York at Albany, School of Library Science." *ELIS* 1 (1968): 147–48.

11.79 Jones, H. G. "Archival Training in American Universities, 1938–1968." *AAr* 31 (1968): 135–54.

11.80 Padgett, H. "History of the Instructional Materials Department in the Office of the State Superintendent of Public Instruction." *IllL* 50 (1968): 883–87.

11.81 Wendt, P. "History of the Instructional Materials Department at Southern Illinois University." *IllL* 50 (1968): 873–74.

11.82 Wert, L. M. "Education for School Librarianship in Illinois 1900 to the Present." *IllL* 50 (1968): 860–72.

11.83 Bramley, G. *A History of Library Education.* New York: Archon Books, 1969.

11.84 Evraiff, L. A. K. "A Survey of the Development and Emerging Patterns in the Preparation of School Librarians." Doctoral dissertation, Wayne State University, 1969.

11.85 Fyock, E. R. "A History of Instruction in Library Science at Northern Illinois University." Research Paper, Northern Illinois University, 1969.

11.86 Galvin, T. J. "The Accreditation Controversy: An Essay in Issues and Origins." *JEL* 10 (1969): 11–27.

11.87 Jones, V. L. "Atlanta University School of Library Service." *ELIS* 2 (1969): 82–87.

11.88 Carnovsky, L., and Swanson, D. R. "The University of Chicago Graduate Library School." *ELIS* 4 (1970): 540–42.

11.89 Carroll, C. E. *The Professionalization of Education for Librarianship, with Special Reference to the Years 1940–1960.* Metuchen, N.J.: Scarecrow Press, 1970.

11.90 Grotzinger, L. A., and Noble, V., eds. *Perspectives: A Library School's First Quarter Century, 1945–1970.* Kalamazoo, Mich.: Western Michigan University, School of Librarianship, 1970.

11.91 Horn, A. H. "California. University of California at Los Angeles, Graduate School of Library Service." *ELIS* 3 (1970): 670–80.

11.92 Kortendick, J. J. "Catholic University of America, Graduate Department of Library Science." *ELIS* 4 (1970): 319–22.

11.93 Rothstein, S. "Issues, Decisions, and Continuing Debate: The History of American Library Education, 1870–1970." In *Workshop* *on Education for Librarianship.* Edmonton, Alta.: University of Alberta, 1970. Pp. 3–11.

11.94 Shera, J. H. "Case Western Reserve University School of Library Science." *ELIS* 4 (1970): 220–28.

11.95 Debons, A. "Dayton. University of Dayton, Department of Information Science." *ELIS* 6 (1971): 440–44.

11.96 Dubois, P. Z. *Education for Librarianship at Kent State University.* Kent, Ohio: Kent State University, 1971.

11.97 Evans, G. E. "An Historical Note Relating to Library Degrees and the Two Year Program." *JEL* 11 (1971): 308–24.

11.98 Goggin, M. K. "University of Denver Graduate School of Librarianship." *ELIS* 6 (1971): 592–95.

11.99 Linderman, W. B. "Columbia University, School of Library Service." *ELIS* 5 (1971): 370–90.

11.100 North Carolina Central University. *Alumni Day, School of Library Science, 1941–1971; Thirty Years of Service.* Durham, N.C.: North Carolina Central University, 1971.

11.101 Reed, S. R. "The Curriculum of Library Schools Today: A Historical Overview." In *Education for Librarianship: The Design of the Curriculum for Library Schools,* edited by H. Goldhor. Urbana: University of Illinois Graduate School of Library Science, 1971. Pp. 19–45.

11.102 Reed, S. R. "Feast or Famine." *Library and Information Science [Mita Society]* 9 (1971): 61–83.

11.103 Roper, F. W. "A Comparative Analysis of Programs in Medical Library Education in the United States, 1957–1971." Doctoral dissertation, Indiana University, 1971.

11.104 Vann, S. K. *The Williamson Reports: A Study.* Metuchen, N.J.: Scarecrow Press, 1971.

11.105 Vann, S. K., ed. *The Williamson Reports of 1921 and 1923.* Metuchen, N.J.: Scarecrow Press, 1971.

1972–1986

11.106 Burgess, R. S. "Education for Librarianship—U.S. Assistance." *LibT* 20 (1972): 515–26.

11.107 Debons, A. "Education in Information Science." *ELIS* 7 (1972): 465–74.

11.108 Garrison, G. "Drexel University Graduate School of Library Science." *ELIS* 7 (1972): 302–05.

11.109 Goldstein, H. "Florida State University Graduate School of Library Science." *ELIS* 8 (1972): 561–66.

11.110 Kunkle, H. J. "The California State Library School." *JEL* 12 (1972): 232–39.

11.111 Lawson, V. "Emory University Division of Librarianship." *ELIS* 8 (1972): 28–34.

11.112 Nasri, W. Z. "Education for Librarianship." *ELIS* 7 (1972): 414–64.

11.113 Gleaves, E. S. "George Peabody College, School of Library Science." *ELIS* 9 (1973): 365–71.

11.114 Slamecka, V. "Georgia Institute of Technology, School of Information and Computer Science." *ELIS* 9 (1973): 380–83.

11.115 Stevens, R. D. "Hawaii. University of Hawaii Graduate School of Library Studies." *ELIS* 10 (1973): 381–85.

11.116 Blazek, R. "The Place of History in Library Education." *JLH* 9 (1974): 193–95.

11.117 Broadus, R. N., and Stieg, L. F. "Illinois. Northern Illinois University Department of Library Science." *ELIS* 11 (1974): 180–81.

11.118 Brown, R. E. "Illinois. University of Illinois Graduate School of Library Science." *ELIS* 11 (1974): 181–83.

11.119 Parker, M. I. "A History of the Department of Librarianship at San Jose State University, 1928–1969." Research Paper, San Jose State University, 1974.

11.120 Rufsvold, M. I. "Indiana University. Graduate Library School." *ELIS* 11 (1974): 459–74.

11.121 Allen, L. A. "Kentucky. University of Kentucky College of Library Science." *ELIS* 13 (1975): 424–30.

11.122 Bloesch, E. "Iowa. University of Iowa, School of Library Science." *ELIS* 13 (1975): 13–15.

11.123 Carroll, C. E. "History of Library Education." In *The Administrative Aspects of Education for Librarianship: A Symposium,* edited by M. B. Cassata and H. L. Totten. Metuchen, N.J.: Scarecrow Press, 1975. Pp. 2–28.

11.124 Churchwell, C. D. *The Shaping of American Library Education.* Chicago: American Library Association, 1975.

11.125 Foos, D. D. "Louisiana State University Graduate School of Library Science." *ELIS* 16 (1975): 348–60.

11.126 Gillespie, J. T. "Long Island University, Palmer Graduate Library School, C.W. Post Center." *ELIS* 16 (1975): 336–37.

11.127 "Library Education at Madison: The University of Wisconsin Library School." *WisLB* 71 (1975): 332–38.

11.128 McChesney, K. "Kent State University, School of Library Science." *ELIS* 13 (1975): 415–17.

11.129 Williams, M. G. "Kansas State Teachers College, Department of Librarianship." *ELIS* 13 (1975): 400–402.

11.130 Bidlack, R. E. "Michigan. The University of Michigan School of Library Science." *ELIS* 18 (1976): 67–71.

11.131 Bobinski, G. S. "New York. State University of New York at Buffalo, School of Information and Library Studies." *ELIS* 19 (1976): 402–07.

11.132 Chisholm, M. "Maryland. University of Maryland College of Library and Information Services." *ELIS* 17 (1976): 197–204.

11.133 Davis, D. G. "Education for Librarianship." *LibT* 25 (1976): 113–34.

11.134 Kaldor, I. L. "New York. State University College of Arts and Science, School of Library and Information Science. Geneseo." *ELIS* 19 (1976): 388–402.

11.135 Khurshid, A. "Intellectual Foundations of Library Education." *International Library Review* 8 (1976): 3–21.

11.136 Parker, R. H. "Missouri. University of Missouri School of Library and Informational Science." *ELIS* 18 (1976): 229–30.

11.137 Shove, R. H. "Minnesota. University of Minnesota Library School." *ELIS* 18 (1976): 175–87.

11.138 White, C. M. *A Historical Introduction to Library Education: Problems and Progress to 1951.* Metuchen, N.J.: Scarecrow Press, 1976.

11.139 Campbell, L. B. "The Hampton Institute Library School." *HBLib*: 1977 35–46.

11.140 Carroll, D. E. "North Texas State University—School of Library and Information Sciences." *ELIS* 20 (1977): 197–200.

11.141 Dalton, J. "Library Education in the Southeast Since World War II." In *Louis Round Wilson Centennial Day: Proceedings of Two Symposia Sponsored in Honor of Louis Round Wilson's 100th Birthday,* edited by C. Brock. Chapel Hill: University of North Carolina School of Library Science, 1977. Pp. 7–23.

11.142 Fenster, V. R. "The University of Wisconsin Library School: A History, 1895–1921." Doctoral dissertation, University of Wisconsin, 1977.

11.143 Galvin, T. J. "Pittsburgh. University of Pittsburgh Graduate School of Library and Information Sciences." *ELIS* 22 (1977): 280–91.

11.144 Holley, E. G. "North Carolina. University of North Carolina School of Library Science." *ELIS* 20 (1977): 176–91.

11.145 Totten, H. L. "Oregon. University of Oregon School of Librarianship." *ELIS* 21 (1977): 12–16.

11.146 Houser, L. J., and Schrader, A. M. *The Search for a Scientific Profession: Library Science Education in the U.S. and Canada.* Metuchen, N.J.: Scarecrow Press, 1978.

11.147 Meder, M. D. "People in Our Past and Present: The Story of the School of Library Science, Emporia State University through Its Faculty, 1902–1978." *Library School Review [Kansas State, Emporia]* 17 (1978): 23–31.

11.148 Sharify, N. "The Pratt Institute Graduate School of Library and Information Science." *ELIS* 23 (1978): 145–70.

11.149 Tryon, J. S. "Rhode Island. University of Rhode Island Graduate Library School." *ELIS* 25 (1978): 399–402.

11.150 Cramer, C. H. *The School of Library Science at Case Western Reserve University: Seventy-Five Years, 1904–1979.* Cleveland: Case Western Reserve School of Library Science, 1979.

11.151 Heim, K. M. "Professional Education: Some Comparisons." In *As Much to Learn as to Teach: Essays in Honor of Lester Asheim,* edited by J. M. Lee and B. A. Hamilton. Hamden, Conn.: Shoe String Press, 1979. Pp. 128–76.

11.152 Jones, V. L. *Reminiscences in Librarianship and Library Education: With Words of Appreciation by Friends and Colleagues in Celebration of the Conferring upon Dean Jones the Honorary Degree Doctor of Letters by the University of Michigan in Ann Arbor, August 19, 1979.* Ann Arbor: University of Michigan School of Library Science, 1979.

11.153 McCusker, L. "Rosary College Graduate School of Library Science." *ELIS* 26 (1979): 154–59.

11.154 Mott, T. H., Anselmo, E. H., and Samuels, A. R. "Rutgers—The State University of New Jersey, Graduate School of Library and Information Studies." *ELIS* 26 (1979): 245–51.

11.155 Saracevic, T. "Essay on the Past and Future of Information Science Education—I: Historical Overview." *Information Processing and Management* 15 (1979): 1–15.

11.156 Shera, J. H. " 'The Spirit Giveth Life': Louis Round Wilson and Chicago's Graduate Library School." *JLH* 14 (1979): 77–83.

11.157 Starke, R. "History of the School of Library and Information Science at the University of Missouri-Columbia." Research Paper, University of Missouri-Columbia, 1979.

11.158 Stueart, R. D. "Simmons College School of Library Science." *ELIS* 27 (1979): 402–05.

11.159 Boaz, M. "Southern California. University of Southern California School of Library Science." *ELIS* 28 (1980): 305–23.

11.160 Coburn, L. "Library Internship: A Historical Overview." In *Classroom and Field: The Internship in American Library Education.* Flushing, N.Y.: Queens College of the City University of New York, 1980. Pp. 14–29.

11.161 Douglass, R. R., and Sparks, C. G. "Texas. University of Texas at Austin, Graduate School of Library Science." *ELIS* 30 (1980): 353–56.

11.162 Koss, H. "Southern Connecticut State College. Division of Library Science and Instructional Technology." *ELIS* 28 (1980): 323–28.

11.163 Pfister, F. C. "South Florida. University of South Florida. Library, Media, and Information Studies Graduate Department." *ELIS* 28 (1980): 300–302.

11.164 Pope, E. "South Carolina. University of South Carolina, College of Librarianship." *ELIS* 28 (1980): 262–67.

11.165 Purcell, G. R. "Tennessee. University of Tennessee Graduate School of Library and Information Science." *ELIS* 30 (1980): 288–92.

11.166 Rinehart, C., and Magrill, R. M. *The More It Is the Same: Fifty Years of Library Science Graduates at the University of Michigan.* Ann Arbor: University of Michigan School of Library Science, 1980.

11.167 Taylor, R. S., and Van der Veer, B. "Syracuse University School of Information Studies." *ELIS* 29 (1980): 391–94.

11.168 Turner, F. L. "Texas Woman's University: School of Library Science." *ELIS* 30 (1980): 381–84.

11.169 Booth, R. E., and Maurstad, B. L. "Wayne State University, College of Education, Division of Library Science." *ELIS* 32 (1981): 451–58.

11.170 Fenster, V. R. "Carnegie's Secret Gift for the Establishment of the Wisconsin Library School." *JLH* 16 (1981): 595–605.

11.171 Lieberman, I. "Washington. University of Washington (Seattle) School of Librarianship." *ELIS* 32 (1981): 438–51.

11.172 Lurie, M. N. "Library History Materials at Rutgers, Including Archives Relating to the New Jersey College for Women Library School and the Founding of the Rutgers Graduate School of Library and Information Studies." *Journal of the Rutgers University Libraries* 43 (1981): 41–65.

11.173 Bartley, B. G. "Wisconsin. University of Wisconsin—Milwaukee School of Library Science." *ELIS* 33 (1982): 188–94.

11.174 Clarke, J. A. "Wisconsin. University of Wisconsin—Madison Library School." *ELIS* 33 (1982): 185–88.

11.175 Lowrie, J. E. "Western Michigan University, School of Librarianship." *ELIS* 33 (1982): 110–23.

11.176 Richardson, J. V. *The Spirit of Inquiry: The Graduate Library School at Chicago, 1921–1951.* Chicago: American Library Association, 1982.

11.177 Colson, J. C. "Learning about Libraries and Librarianship." *JELIS* 24 (1983): 71–88.

11.178 Holley, E. G. "The Development of Library Education in the South." In *Reference Services and Library Education: Essays in Honor of Frances Neel Cheney,* edited by E. S. Gleaves and J. M. Tucker. Lexington, Mass.: Lexington Books, 1983. Pp. 161–88.

11.179 Krummel, D. W. "Kinkeldy Revisited: American Music Library Education in 1937 and 1982." *Fontes Artis Musicae* 30 (1983): 56–60.

11.180 Richardson, J. V. "Theory into Practice: W.W. Charters and the Development of American Library Education." In *Reference Services and Library Education: Essays in Honor of Frances Neal Cheney,* edited by E. S. Gleaves and J. M. Tucker. Lexington, Mass.: Lexington Books, 1983. Pp. 209–23.

11.181 Tucker, J. M. "Southern School Libraries and Northern Philanthropy: The Founding of the Peabody Library School." In *Reference Services and Library Education: Essays in Honor of Frances Neel Cheney,* edited by E. S. Gleaves and J. M. Tucker. Lexington, Mass.: Lexington Books, 1983. Pp. 189–207.

11.182 Dickinson, D. C. "Arizona. University of Arizona Graduate Library School." *ELIS* 37 (1984): 8–10.

11.183 Holley, E. G. "The Influence of ARL on Academic Librarianship, Library Education, and Legislation." *ALAO* 3 (1984): 295–305.

11.184 Marchant, M. P. "Brigham Young University, School of Library and Information Sciences." *ELIS* 37 (1984): 18–20.

11.185 Norell, I. P. "San José State University, Division of Library Science." *ELIS* 37 (1984): 352–54.

11.186 Ramer, J. D. "Alabama. University of Alabama Graduate School of Library Science." *ELIS* 37 (1984): 1–2.

11.187 Rupert, E. A. "Clarion University of Pennsylvania, College of Library Science." *ELIS* 37 (1984): 43–48.

11.188 Sineath, T. W. "Kentucky. University of Kentucky College of Library and Information Science." *ELIS* 37 (1984): 179–86.

11.189 Bidlack, R. E. "Accreditation of Library Education." *ELIS* 39 (1985): 1–34.

11.190 Biggs, M. "Who/What/Why Should a Library Educator Be?" *JELIS* 25 (1985): 262–78.

11.191 Maxwell, M. F. "A Most Necessary Discipline: The Education of Technical Services Librarians." *LRTS* 29 (1985): 239–47.

11.192 Meder, M. D. "Emporia State University School of Library and Information Management." *ELIS* 39 (1985): 169–84.

11.193 Palmer, P. R. "Graduate Education of Academic Librarians." Doctoral dissertation, Memphis State University, 1985.

11.194 Phinazee, A. L., and Speller, B. F. "North Carolina Central University School of Library Science." *ELIS* 38 (1985): 286–94.

11.195 Powell, L. C. *The UCLA Graduate School of Library and Information Science: Its Origins and Founding.* Los Angeles: UCLA Graduate School of Library and Information Science, 1985.

11.196 Robinson, W. C. "Time Present and Time Past." *JELIS* 26 (1985): 79–95.

11.197 Schrader, A. M. "A Bibliometric Study of the *JEL*, 1960–1984." *JELIS* 25 (1985): 279–300.

11.198 Wendler, A. V. "The Development of Library Education in Illinois." *IllL* 67 (1985): 432–35.

11.199 Adams, K. J. "The Beginnings of Library Education in Texas." *TLJ* 62 (1986): 64–66.

11.200 "Centennial Issue—I & II." *JELIS* 26 (1986): 139–81, 211–80.

11.201 Davis, D. G., and Dain, P., eds. "History of Library and Information Science." *LibT* 34 (1986): 357–531.

11.202 Detlefsen, E. G., and Galvin, T. J. "Education for Health Sciences/Biomedical Librarianship: Past, Present, Future." *BMLA* 74 (1986): 148–53.

11.203 DuMont, R. R. "The Educating of Black Librarians: An Historical Perspective." *JELIS* 26 (1986): 233–49.

11.204 Grotzinger, L. A. "Curriculum and Teaching Styles: Evolution of Pedagogical Patterns." *LibT* 34 (1986): 451–68.

11.205 Gunn, A. C. "Early Training for Black Librarians in the U.S.: A History of the Hampton Institute Library School and the Establishment of the Atlanta University Library School." Doctoral dissertation, University of Pittsburgh, 1986.

11.206 Harris, M. H. "The Dialectic of Defeat: Antimonies in Research in Library and Information Science." *LibT* 34 (1986): 515–31.

11.207 Holley, E. G. "One Hundred Years of Progress: The Growth and Development of Library Education." *ALA Yearbook of Library and Information Services* 11 (1986): 23–28.

11.208 Maack, M. N. "Women in Library Education: Down the Up Staircase." *LibT* 34 (1986): 401–32.

11.209 McMullen, H. "Library Education: A Mini-History; What Hath Dewey's Daring Venture Wrought?" *ALib* 17 (1986): 406–08.

11.210 Metzger, P. A. "An Overview of the History of Library Science Teaching Materials." *LibT* 34 (1986): 469–88.

11.211 Miksa, F. L. "Melvil Dewey: The Professional Educator and His Heirs." *LibT* 34 (1986): 359–81.

11.212 Rayward, W. B. "Research and Education for Library and Information Science: Waples in Retrospect." *LQ* 56 (1986): 348–59.

11.213 Richardson, J. V. "Paradigmatic Shifts in the Teaching of Government Publications, 1895–1985." *JELIS* 26 (1986): 249–66.

11.214 Stone, E. W. "The Growth of Continuing Education." *LibT* 34 (1986): 489–513.

11.215 Sullivan, P. A. "ALA and Library Education: A Century of Changing Roles and Actors, Shifting Scenes and Plots." *JELIS* 26 (1986): 143–53.

11.216 Tucker, E. E. "Mississippi, University of, Graduate School of Library and Information Science." *ELIS* 40 (1986): 318–21.

11.217 Wiegand, W. A. "Perspectives on Library Education in the Context of Recently Published Literature on the History of Professions." *JELIS* 26 (1986): 267–80.

11.218 Wiegand, W. A. "The Socialization of Library and Information Science Students: Reflections on a Century of Formal Education for Librarianship." *LibT* 34 (1986): 383–99.

11.219 Williams, R. V., and Zachert, M. J. "Specialization in Library Education: A Review of the Trends and Issues." *JELIS* 26 (1986): 215–32.

11.220 Williamson, W. L. "A Century of Students." *LibT* 34 (1986): 433–49.

12.

Library Associations

The printed materials dealing with library associations have generally consisted of brief historical surveys and criticisms of library associations, and works treating individual library associations. The latter may in turn be divided into anniversary or commemorative pieces and scholarly treatises that are frequently commissioned or result from doctoral or master's research. The official journals and publications of the various organizations and the general library press serve as ready sources for historical articles and notes dealing with particular associations. For an overview one should consult the *Library Trends* issue (January 1955, **12.75**), edited by David H. Clift, "Library Associations in the United States and the British Commonwealth." The editor's contribution, "Associations in the United States," provides a fine historical survey and coverage of the early printed literature.

Among the general surveys of library associations are articles evaluating associations as a group. These include Ralph E. Ellsworth's "Critique of Library Associations in America" (1961, **12.114**), Eli M. Oboler's "Library Associatons: Their History and Influence" (1967, **12.148**), and the centennial study of Peter Conmy and Caroline M. Coughlin (1976, **12.266**). Judging from the dissertations that appear below, these essays have stimulated serious interest in the history of library associations.

Although the smaller national and the state and regional associations have attracted some notice, the American Library Association (ALA) has received most of the scholarly attention. Studies tend to cover chronological periods, individual units, or special activities of the association. Dennis V. Thomison's rather uneven overview, covering the story to 1972 (1978, **12.333**), should be supplemented with Edward G. Holley's "ALA at 100" (1976, **12.276**). Holley's *Raking the Historic Coals* (1967, **12.146**) provides documents and commentary relating to the 1876 meeting that resulted in the formation of the association; M. A. J. O'Loughlin studied the same meeting in detail (1971, **12.203**). George B. Utley's *Fifty Years of the American Library Association* (1926, **12.14**) carries the story forward in summary fashion; the more recent analysis of Wayne A. Wiegand, covering the period 1876 to 1917, employs much hitherto untouched primary material (1986, **12.413**). Arthur P. Young has treated the specific activities related to World War I in *Books for Sammies* (1981, **12.366**) and other works.

Specific groups within the American Library Association receiving extended treatment include the American Association of School Librarians, studied by Charles W. Koch (1976, **12.280**) and Patricia K. Pond (1982, **12.373**), and the Association of College and Research Libraries, studied by Charles E. Hale (1976, **12.272**)—none of which are in published form.

Particular aspects of the Association's history have received full treatment in recent years. One in published form is Gary E. Kraske's study of the Association in relation to the emergence of U.S. cultural diplomacy in the period 1938–1949 (1985, **12.394**). Examples of unpublished dissertations that treat topics within limited time periods are Eugene R. Hanson on cataloging (1974, **12.236**), Evelyn G. Clement on audiovisual concerns (1975, **12.248**), and David S. Zubatsky on resource sharing (1982, **12.375**).

Other library associations, though the subject of fewer exhaustive studies, have nevertheless attracted attention, especially at times of anniversary celebrations. Examples of this genre include *Special Libraries Association: Its First Fifty Years, 1909–1959* (1959, **12.108**), supplemented by the surveys of Robert V. Williams and Martha Jane Zachert in the seventy-fifth anniversary issues of *Special Libraries* (1983, **12.381**; 1983, **12.382**). More recent examples include Carol June Bradley's lengthy article on the Music Library Association (1981, **12.355**) and the articles by Stephen A. McCarthy and others on the fiftieth anniversary of the Association of Research Libraries (1984, **12.389**).

A number of doctoral dissertations and master's theses have focused on other library associations—national, statewide, and specialized. Most have not been published but may be the basis for journal articles. Among the organizations discussed in dissertations are the Association of Research Libraries by Frank M. McGowan (1972, **12.215**); the American Theological Library Association by Warren R. Mehl (1973, **12.224**); and the American Documentation Institute, which became the American Society for Information Science, by Irene S. Farkas-Conn (1984, **12.387**). The 1972 dissertation of Donald G. Davis, Jr., on the Association of American Library Schools, now Association for Library and Information Science Education, appeared later as a monograph (1974, **12.229**). Smaller state, local, and highly specialized organizations have tended to be the subjects of master's theses and research reports. Library associations receive minimal coverage in summary form in reference works and directories.

Before 1876

12.1 "The Congregational Library Association: Its Origins and Objects." *Congregational Quarterly* 1 (1859): 70–73.

1876–1919

12.2 Poole, W. F. "Conference of Librarians: Address of the President." *LJ* 11 (1886): 199–204.

12.3 Wyche, B. "The Texas State Library Association." *The University of Texas Record* 4 (1902): 408–14.

12.4 "History of the Wisconsin Library Association." *WisLB* 5 (1909): 76–79.

12.5 "The History of the Medical Library Association." *BMLA* 1 (1911–12): 7–9.

12.6 Marion, G. E. "Resume of the Association's Activities, 1910–1915." *SL* 6 (1915): 143–46.

12.7 Rathbone, J. A. "The Association of American Library Schools." *LJ* 40 (1915): 302–03.

12.8 Stevens, W. F. *The Keystone State Library Association, 1901–1915.* N.p.: Printed by Order of the Executive Committee, 1916.

12.9 Browning, W. "The Development of the Association of Medical Librarians." *BMLA* 9 (1919): 1–5.

1920–1949

12.10 Marion, G. E. "The Special Libraries Association." *LJ* 45 (1920): 294–304.

12.11 Stevens, W. F. *The Keystone State Library Association, 1916–1922.* N.p.: Printed by Order of the Executive Committee, 1923.

12.12 Tower, E. B. "The Story of the A.M.M.L.A." *SL* 14 (1923): 69–72.

12.13 Bowker, R. R. "Seed Time and Harvest—The Story of the ALA." *BALA* 20 (1926): 355–56.

12.14 Utley, G. B. *Fifty Years of the American Library Association.* Chicago: American Library Association, 1926.

12.15 Miltimore, C. "Later Days of the Florida Library Association." *Florida Library Bulletin* 1 (May 1, 1927): 3–9.

12.16 Utley, G. B. "Early Days of the Florida Library Association." *Florida Library Bulletin* 1 (May 1, 1927): 1–2.

12.17 West, E. H. "The Library Section, 1915–1928 [of the Texas State Teachers Association]." *Texas School Libraries Yearbook* 1 (1928): 7–8.

12.18 Brigham, H. O. "The Special Libraries Association—A Historical Sketch." *LJ* 54 (1929): 337–40.

12.19 Utley, G. B. "The Library War Service and Its General Director." In *Essays Offered to Herbert Putnam by His Colleagues and Friends on His Thirtieth Anniversary as Librarian of Congress, 5 April 1929,* edited by W. W. Bishop and A. Keogh. New Haven: Yale University Press, 1929. Pp. 474–91.

12.20 McCord, J. L. V. "History of the District of Columbia Library Association, 1894–1930." *DCL* 1 (1930): 67–74.

12.21 Brigham, H. O. "The Special Libraries Association: Personalities and Projects, 1909–1917." *SL* 23 (1932): 204–09.

12.22 Corwin, E. K. "Twenty-five Years of the Kentucky Library Association." *KLAB* 1 (January 1933): 4–8.

12.23 Power, E. S. "Forty Years of Growth: A Brief History of the Ohio Library Association." In *Handbook,* edited by Ohio Library Association. Columbus, Ohio: Ohio Library Association, 1935. Pp. 7–19.

12.24 Simmons, E. "History of the Southwestern Library Association." *HTL* 4 (1935): 131–34.

12.25 Francis, W. W. "Margaret Charleton and the Early Days of the Medical Library Association." *BMLA* 25 (1936): 58–63.

243

12.26 Shelton, W. "History of the New Mexico Library Association." *New Mexico Library Bulletin* 6 (1937): 3–6.

12.27 Dyer, J. R. "Centennial of the St. Louis Law Library Association." *Missouri Bar Journal* 9 (1938): 265–66.

12.28 Langdell, M. E. "W.L.A. through Fifty Years." *WisLB* 37 (1941): 98–101.

12.29 McDaniel, W. B. "Notes on the Association's Interests and Activities as Reflected in the *Bulletin*, 1911–1941." *BMLA* 30 (1941): 72–79.

12.30 Van Hoesen, H. B. "The Bibliographical Society of America—Its Leaders and Activities, 1904–1939." *PBSA* 35 (1941): 177–202.

12.31 Baldwin, C. F. "Minnesota Library Association, 1900–1942." *MinnL* 13 (1942): 327–30.

12.32 Countryman, G. A. "Early History of the Minnesota Library Association, 1891–1900." *MinnL* 13 (1942): 322–26.

12.33 Bowerman, G. F. "The District of Columbia Library Association: Semicentennial Notes." *DCL* 15 (1944): 9–10.

12.34 West, E. H. "The T.L.A. as an Observer Recalls It, 1902–1918." *NNT* 20 (April 1944): 1, 34–36.

12.35 Elliott, E. M. "Federal Relations of the American Library Association, 1930–1940." Master's thesis, University of Chicago, 1946.

12.36 Netter, E. "T.L.A. in Review." *NNT* 22 (July 1946): 3–5.

12.37 Utley, G. B. "American Library Institute: A Historical Sketch." *LQ* 16 (1946): 152–59.

12.38 Connecticut Library Association. *The Connecticut Library Association: Its History and Its Members.* Hartford, Conn.: [Connecticut Library Association], 1947.

12.39 Ballard, J. F. "The Past History of the Medical Library Association, Inc." *BMLA* 36 (1948): 227–41.

12.40 Dugan, H. "The Past Is Prelude: KLA's First Forty Years." *KLAB* 12 (June 1948): 3–7.

12.41 Smith, C. W. "The Early Years of the P.N.L.A." *PNLAQ* 12 (1948): 130–35; 13 (1949): 70–76, 107–13.

12.42 Baker, F. "History of the Northern Section." *Bulletin of the California School Library Association* 20 (1949): 13–14.

12.43 Brigham, H. O., and Cox, M. "Remembrance of Things Past." *SL* 40 (1949): 134–44.

12.44 Dana, J. C. "Special Libraries Association Chronology: 1909–1949." *SL* 40 (1949): 125–35.

12.45 Potter, H. "Great Beginnings—the Southern Section (1915–49)." *Bulletin of the California School Library Association* 20 (1949): 15–16.

12.46 Steinbarger, H. "What Is Past Is Prologue: Development of the Middle Atlantic States Regional Area Conference." *DCL* 21 (1949): 3–8.

1950–1971

12.47 American Library Association. *Division of Cataloging and Classification in Retrospect: A History of the Division of Cataloging and Classification of the American Library Association, 1900–1950.* Chicago: American Library Association, 1950.

12.48 Glasier, G. G. "Beginnings of the American Association of Law Libraries (1906–11)." *LLJ* 43 (1950): 147–59.

12.49 Henderson, J. D. "The C.L.A. since 1906: An Essay in Retrospection." *CLB* 11 (1950): 172–73, 186–87.

12.50 Jamieson, J. A. *Books for the Army: The Army Library Service in the Second World War.* New York: Columbia University Press, 1950.

12.51 Michelson, A. I. "The American Merchant Marine Library Association—Its History and Functions." Master's thesis, Western Reserve University, 1950.

12.52 Rowe, H. M. "The Genesis of the California Library Association." *CLB* 11 (1950): 174–76.

12.53 Butters, A. J. "Concepts of Library Purpose in the Professional Works of Seven Founders of the American Library Association." Master's thesis, Catholic University of America, 1951.

12.54 Golter, P. "The Arizona State Library Association—Twenty-five Years: 1926–1951." *Arizona Librarian* 8 (1951): 4–10.

12.55 Reynolds, H. D. "Friends of Libraries." *TLJ* 27 (1951): 146–48.

12.56 Utley, G. B. *The Librarians Conference of 1853: A Chapter in American Library History.* Chicago: American Library Association, 1951.

12.57 Wilgus, A. C. "The Interamerican Bibliographical and Library Association, 1930–1950." *Inter-American Review of Bibliography* 1 (1951): 6–11.

12.58 Abrahamson, D. "The Louisiana Library Association: Its History [1909–1952]." *LLAB* 15 (1952): 66–74.

12.59 Anders, M. E. "State Library Associations in the Southeast [nine states, 1897–1950]." *SEL* 2 (1952): 7–24.

12.60 Emert, F. A. "Trends in Thought on the Training of Special Librarians from the Beginning of the Special Libraries Association in 1909 through 1950." Master's thesis, Western Reserve University, 1952.

12.61 Gillies, M. "The Wyoming Library Association: An Historical Footnote [1913–17]." *Wyoming Library Roundup* 8 (1952): 1–7.

12.62 Goree, E. S. "Texas Library Association." *HT* 2 (1952): 746.

12.63 Mitchell, A. C. "Special Libraries Association: A Brief History [1909–50]." *SL* 43 (1952): 162–64.

12.64 Prime, L. M. "The Medical Library Association: Aims, Activities, and a Brief History." *BMLA* 40 (1952): 30–36.

12.65 Sparks, C. G. "Presidential Addresses Made to the American Library Association, 1876–1951: A Content Analysis." Master's thesis, University of Texas, 1952, ACRL Microcard no. 131.

12.66 Anderson, I. T., and Osborne, G. E. "The History of the Committee on Libraries of the American Association of Colleges of Pharmacy (1933–53)." *BMLA* 41 (1953): 414–18.

12.67 Council of National Library Associations. *The American Book Center for War Devastated Libraries, Inc., 1944–1948: A Report.* New York: [Council of National Library Associations], 1953.

12.68 Dane, C. "A Chapter in the History of ALA: The Publishing Board, 1909–1915." *IllL* 36 (1954): 186–89.

12.69 Easterly, A. "The Tennessee Library Association's First Fifty Years, 1902–1951." Master's thesis, George Peabody College for Teachers, 1954.

12.70 Folmer, F. " 'As Others See Us': The Background." *TLJ* 30 (1954): 107–13.

12.71 Neal, P. "Library Problems, 1876–1886: An Analysis of "Notes and Queries" in *Library Journal* and *Proceedings of the American Library Association.*" Master's thesis, Carnegie Institute of Technology, 1954.

12.72 Schunk, R. J. "The First National Library Conference in Minnesota." *MinnL* 17 (1954): 293–301.

12.73 Bennett, J. D. "An Anniversary." *DCL* 26 (1955): 7–10.

12.74 Clift, D. H. "Associations in the United States." *LibT* 3 (1955): 221–37.

12.75 Clift, D. H., ed. "Library Associations in the United States and British Commonwealth." *LibT* 3 (1955): 219–329.

12.76 Maggetti, M. T. "The Medical Library Association: Its History and Activities, 1898–1953." Master's thesis, Drexel Institute of Technology, 1955.

12.77 Moore, M. R. "Southern Association, State and Local Leadership for Library Service in Texas Schools." Master's thesis, University of Texas, 1955.

12.78 Oregon Library Association, Manual Committee. *History of the Oregon Library Association.* Eugene, Ore.: Oregon Library Association, 1955.

12.79 Willet, M. M. "A History and Survey of the Nassau County Library Association Union Catalog." Master's thesis, Drexel Institute of Technology, 1955.

12.80 Anders, M. E. "Southeastern Library Association, 1920–1950." *SEL* 6 (1956): 9–39, 68–81.

12.81 DiCanio, F. "The Chicago Association of Law Libraries, 1945–1955." *LLJ* 49 (1956): 204–08.

12.82 Fitzgerald, W. A. "From Birth to Maturity in a Quarter of a Century." *CLW* 27 (1956): 260–65.

12.83 Heckel, J. W. "American Association of Law Libraries: Charter Members, Officers, and Meeting Places, 1906–1956." *LLJ* 49 (1956): 225–31.

12.84 Johns, H. *Twenty-five Years of the Washington Library Association.* [Palo Alto, Calif.]: Pacific Books, [1956].

12.85 Kell, B. F. "An Analysis of Texas Library Association Membership and Officers, 1902–1956." Master's thesis, University of Texas, 1956.

12.86 Leverette, S., and Elliott, L. "History of the Carolina-South Eastern Chapter (of the American Association of Law Libraries), 1937–1955." *LLJ* 49 (1956): 180–85.

12.87 MacDonald, Z. Z. "Bexar Library Club." *TL* 18 (1956): 38–40.

12.88 Marke, J. J. "The Law Library Association of Greater New York (LLAGNY), 1938–1956." *LLJ* 49 (1956): 186–90.

12.89 Rothe, B. M. "The Law Librarians Society of Washington, D.C., 1939–1955." *LLJ* 49 (1956): 191–97.

12.90 Bennett, J. P. "The Music Library Association, 1931–1956." Master's thesis, Western Reserve University, 1957.

12.91 Carlson, W. H. "The Washington Library Association, 1931–55: A Review Article." *Pacific Northwest Quarterly* 48 (1957): 25–26.

12.92 Harris, S. L. "U.L.A.: A Brief History 1912–1957." *Utah Libraries* 1 (Fall 1957): 3–4, 19–20.

12.93 James, M., and Kalp, M. E. "The Association of American Library Schools, 1915–1924." *AALS Newsletter* 9 (1957): 8–13.

12.94 McDaniel, W. B. "A Salute to Some Milestones, Detours, and Dead-Ends in the History of the [Medical Library] Association since 1898." *BMLA* 45 (1957): 461–65.

12.95 Pound, M. E. "District Organization in the Texas Library Association." Master's thesis, University of Texas, 1957.

12.96 Pound, M. E. "District Organization in the Texas Library Association." *TLJ* 33 (1957): 129–34.

12.97 Seabrook, M. "A History of the District of Columbia Library Association, 1894–1954." Master's thesis, Catholic University of America, 1957.

12.98 Troxel, W. "The Medical Library Association, 1947–1957." *BMLA* 45 (1957): 378–85.

12.99 Allen, M. E. *History of the Connecticut School Library Association.* [Norwalk]: Connecticut School Library Association, 1958.

12.100 Maddox, L. J. "Trends and Issues in American Librarianship as Reflected in the Papers and Proceedings of the American Library Association, 1876–1885." Doctoral dissertation, University of Michigan, 1958.

12.101 Ross, M. C. "A Study of the Catholic Library Association Based on Presidential Addresses Made During the Years, 1931–1956." Master's thesis, University of Texas, 1958.

12.102 Seabrook, M. "The First Sixty Years—DCLA, 1894–1954." *DCL* 29 (1958): 46–53.

12.103 Ball, S. B. "Reminiscences of Things Past." *SL* 50 (1959): 211–12.

12.104 Foreman, C. "An Analysis of Publications Issued by the American Library Association, 1907–1957." Master's thesis, University of Texas, 1959, ACRL Microcard no. 118.

12.105 Gershevsky, R. H. *PNLA 1909–1959; a Chronological Summary of Fifty Eventful Years.* N.p.: Pacific Northwest Library Association, 1959.

12.106 Marchesseault, R. E. "A History of the Connecticut Library Association, 1891–1955." Master's thesis, Catholic University of America, 1959.

12.107 Mitchell, A. C. *Putting Knowledge to Work: Fifty Years of the Special Libraries Association, 1909–1959,* mimeographed. New York: Special Libraries Association, 1959.

12.108 Mitchell, A. C., ed. *Special Libraries Association: Its First Fifty Years, 1909–1959.* New York: Special Libraries Association, 1959.

12.109 Walker, M. J. D. "The Southwestern Library Association, 1922–1954." Master's thesis, University of Texas, 1959.

12.110 Winser, M. C. "John Cotton Dana and the Special Libraries Association, 1909–14." *SL* 50 (1959): 208–11.

12.111 Anders, M. E. *The Tennessee Valley Library Council, 1940–1949: A Regional Approach to Library Planning.* Atlanta: Southeastern Library Association, 1960.

12.112 Roper, D. F. "The American Library Association Subscription Books Committee and Its Influence on Encyclopedia Publishing, 1930–1938." Master's thesis, Florida State University, 1960.

12.113 Shove, R. H. "AALS before 1915." *JEL* 1 (1960): 81–86.

12.114 Ellsworth, R. E. "Critique of Library Associations in America." *LQ* 31 (1961): 382–400.

12.115 "History, 1896–1960." In *Illinois Library Association Organization Manual.* Urbana, Ill.: Illinois Library Association, 1961. Pp. 5–14.

12.116 Neal, E. F. "An Analysis of the Programs of the School Libraries Division of the Texas Library Association." Master's thesis, University of Texas, 1961.

12.117 Perham, M. "Reference Section, a Short History." *WisLB* 57 (1961): 160–64+.

12.118 Tuttle, M. L. "A History of the American Theological Library Association." Master's thesis, Emory University, 1961.

12.119 Archer, N. W. "The Georgia Library Association: The First Forty Years." Master's thesis, Emory University, 1962.

12.120 Hendrickson, R. M. "The Rio Grande Chapter of the Special Libraries Association." Master's thesis, University of Texas, 1962.

12.121 Hoffman, J. "The Alabama Library Association, 1904–39: A History of Its Organization, Growth and Contribution to Library Development." Master's thesis, Florida State University, 1962.

12.122 Fleischer, M. B. "Credentials Awarded through August, 1961, by Agencies Presently or Formerly Approved or Accredited by the American Library Association." Master's thesis, University of Texas, 1963.

12.123 McGregor, J. W. "History of the American Association of Law Libraries from

1906 to 1942." Master's thesis, University of Chicago, 1963.

12.124 Dunleavy, C. M. "The History of the Catholic Library Association, 1921–1961." Master's thesis, Catholic University of America, 1964.

12.125 Herold, J. V. "Friends of Library Organizations in Texas." Master's thesis, University of Texas, 1964.

12.126 McKenna, F. E. "A Genealogical Chart for SLA Divisions." *SL* 55 (1964): 357–60.

12.127 Marion, G. E. "The Founding Fathers Recalled." *SL* 55 (1964): 353–55.

12.128 Rankin, R. B. "SLA in the Early Twenties." *SL* 55 (1964): 356.

12.129 Shirley, W. "Spotlight on the Archons of Colophon and on the Melvil Dui Chowder and Marching Association." *New York Library Association Newsletter* 12 (May–June 1964): 61–63.

12.130 "Special Libraries Association Chronology, 1909–1964." *SL* 55 (1964): 361–82.

12.131 Wheeler, J. L. "SLA's Early Days and Indexing Achievements." *SL* 55 (1964): 351–52.

12.132 Woods, B. M. "The 'Impolite' Librarians." *SL* 55 (1964): 345–50.

12.133 Consolata, M. "History of the Catholic Library Association." *CLW* 36 (1965): 526–27, 611–12; 37 (1965–66): 104–08, 192–94, 257–59, 482–83, 530–31, 591–92; 38 (1966–67): 266–67, 388–89, 441–43; 39 (1967–68): 220–21, 342–53, 518–19, 591–92, 651–52; 40 (1968): 186–88, 243–44.

12.134 McCreedy, M. L. "The San Antonio Unit of the Catholic Library Association: A Glance Back." *TLJ* 41 (1965): 18–21.

12.135 Saniel, I. "A Quarter Century of the Philippine Library Association." *Bulletin of the Philippine Library Association* 1 (1965): 1–12.

12.136 Agria, J. J. "The American Library Association and the Library Services Act." Doctoral dissertation, University of Chicago, 1966.

12.137 Burns, M. "History of DLA from the Files." *DLAB* 20 (Spring 1966): 7–9.

12.138 McClaren, D. N. "The First Ten Years of the Teenage Library Association of Texas, 1949–1959." Master's thesis, University of Texas, 1966.

12.139 Mastrangelo, E. A. "A History of the American Documentation Institute, 1937–1952." Research Paper, Drexel University, 1966.

12.140 Wilcox, B. H. *The Wisconsin Library Association, 1891–1966.* Madison, Wis.: Wisconsin Library Association, 1966.

12.141 Annan, G. L. "The Medical Library Association in Retrospect, 1937–1967." *BMLA* 55 (1967): 379–89.

12.142 Brunton, D. W. "When Librarians Meet." *CalL* 28 (1967): 32a–d.

12.143 Colburn, E. B. "In Retrospect: RTSD, 1957–67." *LRTS* 11 (1967): 5–10.

12.144 Freedly, G. "The Theatre Library Association: 1937–1967." *SL* 58 (1967): 354–55.

12.145 Frost, J. "The Library Conference of '53." *JLH* 2 (1967): 154–60.

12.146 Holley, E. G., ed. *Raking the Historic Coals: The ALA Scrapbook of 1876,* Beta Phi Mu Chapbook no. 8. [Chicago: Lakeside Press], 1967.

12.147 Kaegi, M. A. "The Church Library Council: An Example of Church Library Cooperation." Master's thesis, Catholic University of America, 1967.

12.148 Oboler, E. M. "Library Associations: Their History and Influence." *DLQ* 3 (1967): 255–62.

12.149 Prassel, M. A. "Some Notes toward a History of the Texas Library Association, 1902–1909." Master's thesis, University of Texas, 1967.

12.150 Samuels, C. "The American Library Association and the Field of Reprint Publishing, 1924–1965: Some Aspects of History." *Reprint Bulletin* 12 (1967): 2–11.

12.151 Wessells, H. E. "History of the International Relations Round Table." In *Foreign Service Directory of American Librarians*, 3d ed., edited by J. C. Phillips. Pittsburgh: University of Pittsburgh Book Center, 1967. Pp. ix–xi.

12.152 Cain, S. M. *History of the College and University Section of the Wisconsin Library Association*, mimeographed. Whitewater, Wis.: Wisconsin State University, 1968.

12.153 Cameron, J. K. "Alabama Library Association." *ELIS* 1 (1968): 143–45.

12.154 Charpentier, A. A. "American Association of Law Libraries." *ELIS* 1 (1968): 224–37.

12.155 Dabagh, J. "Hawaii Library Association—And How It Grew." *HLAJ* 25 (1968): 23–24.

12.156 Donovan, M. J. "Presidential Addresses to the Medical Library Association, 1890–1965: A Thematic Analysis." Master's thesis, Catholic University of America, 1968.

12.157 Gibson, C. E. "Aerospace Division, SLA." *ELIS* 1 (1968): 110–11.

12.158 Harris, M. "Alaska State Library Association." *ELIS* 1 (1968): 145–46.

12.159 Kuney, J. H. "American Chemical Society Information Program." *ELIS* 1 (1968): 247–66.

12.160 Lohrer, A. "The Illinois Association of School Librarians: An Historical Perspective." *IllL* 50 (1968): 875–82.

12.161 *The Mississippi Library Association: A History, 1909–1968.* N.p.: Mississippi Library Association, 1968.

12.162 Mixer, C. W. "Archons of Colophon." *ELIS* 1 (1968): 519–20.

12.163 Morroni, J. R. "The Music Library Association, 1931–1961." Master's thesis, University of Chicago, 1968.

12.164 Nasri, W. Z. "Alpha Beta Alpha." *ELIS* 1 (1968): 166–69.

12.165 O'Leary, M. H. "Advertising and Marketing Division, SLA." *ELIS* 1 (1968): 99–105.

12.166 Poland, R. R. "Arizona State Library Association." *ELIS* 1 (1968): 536–38.

12.167 Shepard, M. D. "Assembly of Librarians of the Americas." *ELIS* 1 (1968): 672–75.

12.168 Shipton, C. K., and Nasri, W. Z. "American Antiquarian Society." *ELIS* 1 (1968): 219–24.

12.169 Stevenson, G. T. "American Library Association." *ELIS* 1 (1968): 267–303.

12.170 Taylor, R. S., and Borko, H. "American Society for Information Science." *ELIS* 1 (1968): 303–07.

12.171 Wilson, B. "History of AHIL." *AHIL Quarterly* 8 (1968): 48–54.

12.172 Appell, A. "Beta Phi Mu." *ELIS* 2 (1969): 347–50.

12.173 Bilinkoff, H. "A History of the Nassau-Suffolk School Library Association." Research Paper, Long Island University, 1969.

12.174 Chin, J. "A History of School Library Standards Published by the American Library Association." Research Paper, Long Island University, 1969.

12.175 Denison, B. A., and McFarland, A. "Bibliographic Systems Center. Case Western Reserve University." *ELIS* 2 (1969): 388–91.

12.176 Edelstein, J. M. "Bibliographical Society of America." *ELIS* 2 (1969): 395–401.

12.177 "A Further Remembrance of Things Past: SLA's Sixty Years, 1909/1969." *SL* 60 (1969): 535–58.

12.178 Madden, J. D., and Revens, L. "Association for Computing Machinery." *ELIS* 2 (1969): 42–46.

12.179 Massman, V. F. "From Out of a Desk Drawer: The Beginnings of ALA Headquarters." *BALA* 63 (1969): 475–81.

12.180 Rafish, E. "Biological Sciences Division of Special Libraries Association." *ELIS* 2 (1969): 351–54.

12.181 "The Reference and Subscription Books Review Committee: Its Purpose, History, and Method of Reviewing." *Booklist* 66 (1969): 65–74.

12.182 Rogers, J. W. "The Nineties Were Not Really Gay: Notes on DCLA's 75th Anniversary." *DCL* 40 (1969): 63–70.

12.183 Roxas, S. A. "Bibliographical Societies, Development of." *ELIS* 2 (1969): 384–88.

12.184 Runge, W. H. "Bibliographical Society of the University of Virginia." *ELIS* 2 (1969): 406.

12.185 Shove, R. H. "Association of American Library Schools." *ELIS* 2 (1969): 1–26.

12.186 Whalum, C. G. "A Content Analysis of American Library Association Presidential Inaugural Addresses, 1940–1964." Master's thesis, Atlanta University, 1969.

12.187 White, L. W. "Some Highlights of the ILA's Past." *IllL* 51 (1969): 190–99.

12.188 Williams, E. E. "Association of Research Libraries." *ELIS* 2 (1969): 51–55.

12.189 Beiber, D. "History of the American Association of Law Libraries, 1937–1967." Research Paper, Long Island University, 1970.

12.190 Brunton, D. W. "California Library Association." *ELIS* 3 (1970): 649–53.

12.191 Georgi, C. "Business and Finance Division, Special Libraries Association." *ELIS* 3 (1970): 526–30.

12.192 Leinoff, T. "A Study of the Long Island Library Resources Council, Inc., 1963–1969." Research Paper, Long Island University, 1970.

12.193 McKenna, J. R. "New England Library Association (NELA): A Brief History." *Vermont Libraries* 1 (July–August 1970): 9–10.

12.194 Smith, R. S. "Church and Synagogue Library Association." *ELIS* 4 (1970): 674–81.

12.195 Wells, J. M. "Caxton Club." *ELIS* 4 (1970): 322–23.

12.196 Wilt, M. R. "Catholic Library Association." *ELIS* 4 (1970): 312–17.

12.197 Wilt, M. R. "*Catholic Periodical and Literature Index.*" *ELIS* 4 (1970): 317–18.

12.198 Bennett, H. H. "Delaware Library Association." *ELIS* 6 (1971): 543–46.

12.199 Brewster, E., and Houk, J. "Colorado Library Association." *ELIS* 5 (1971): 355–56.

12.200 Dwyer, M. J. "Council of Planning Librarians." *ELIS* 6 (1971): 235–37.

12.201 Farber, K. A., and Beck, C. "Council of Social Science Data Archives (CSSDA)." *ELIS* 6 (1971): 238–39.

12.202 Ferguson, E. "Council of National Library Associations." *ELIS* 6 (1971): 229–35.

12.203 O'Loughlin, M. A. J. "The Emergence of American Librarianship: A Study of Influences Evident in 1876." Doctoral dissertation, Columbia University, 1971.

12.204 Rudnick, M. C. "Council on Library Technology." *ELIS* 6 (1971): 227–28.

1972–1986

12.205 "A Backward Glance: 1957–72." *Adult Services* 9 (1972): 30–36.

12.206 Ball, A. D. "District of Columbia Library Association." *ELIS* 7 (1972): 241–42.

12.207 Beach, R. F. "Once Over Lightly: Reminiscences of ATLA from Its Founding to the Present." In *Summary of Proceedings, Twenty-Fifth Annual Conference, American Theological Library Association,* edited by

American Theological Library Association. Philadelphia: American Theological Library Association, 1972. Pp. 141–51.

12.208 Carbone, C. "Engineering Division, SLA." *ELIS* 8 (1972): 48–49.

12.209 Chapman, M. L. "Florida Library Association." *ELIS* 8 (1972): 557–61.

12.210 Clairmont, S. A. "Coming of Age of Intellectual Freedom in the American Library Association." Research Paper, State University of New York, Albany, 1972.

12.211 Dick, E. J. "Educational Film Library Association (EFLA)." *ELIS* 7 (1972): 481–86.

12.212 Grosch, A. N. "Documentation Division, SLA." *ELIS* 8 (1972): 264–69.

12.213 Jenks, R. L. "History and Organization of the Missouri Library Association from Its Inception in 1900 to 1950." Research Paper, University of Missouri, Department of Library Science, 1972.

12.214 Kraus, J. W. "The Progressive Librarians' Council." *LJ* 97 (1972): 2551–54.

12.215 McGowan, F. M. "The Association of Research Libraries, 1932–1962." Doctoral dissertation, University of Pittsburgh, 1972.

12.216 Thomison, D. "F.D.R., the ALA, and Mr. MacLeish." *LQ* 42 (1972): 390–98.

12.217 Turner, H. M. "Conference of Eastern College Librarians." *ELIS* 7 (1972): 338–45.

12.218 Wall, J. E. "Exhibits Round Table." *ELIS* 8 (1972): 296–97.

12.219 Conmy, P. T. "Centennial and Bi-Centennial: American Library Association and the United States." *Oak Letter [Oakland, Calif.]* 2 (1973): 1–7.

12.220 Davis, D. G. "An Assessment of AALS." *JEL* 13 (1973): 155–68.

12.221 Estes, D. E. "Georgia Library Association." *ELIS* 9 (1973): 383–86.

12.222 Harris, I. W. "Hawaii Library Association." *ELIS* 10 (1973): 377–81.

12.223 Magrath, G. "Library Conventions of 1853, 1876, and 1877." *JLH* 8 (1973): 52–69.

12.224 Mehl, W. R. "The Role of the American Theological Library Association in American Protestant Theological Libraries and Librarianship, 1947–1970." Doctoral dissertation, Indiana University, 1973.

12.225 *National Federation of Abstracting and Indexing Services—History and Issues, 1958–1973.* Philadelphia: National Federation of Indexing and Abstracting Services, 1973.

12.226 Whitten, J. N. "The Melvil Dui Chowder and Marching Association." *Library Scene* 2 (Winter 1973): 19–22.

12.227 Crawford, D. R. "Black Librarians' Caucus of the American Library Association as Seen by Itself; Materials for a History." Research Paper, Kent State University, 1974.

12.228 Culbertson, D. S. "Information Science and Automation Division (ISAD), ALA." *ELIS* 11 (1974): 495–500.

12.229 Davis, D. G. *The Association of American Library Schools, 1915–1968: An Analytical History.* Metuchen, N.J.: Scarecrow Press, 1974.

12.230 Davis, D. G. *Comparative Historical Analysis of Three Associations of Professional Schools.* Urbana: University of Illinois Graduate School of Library Science, Occasional Paper no. 115, 1974.

12.231 Debagh, J. "A History of the Hawaii Library Association, 1921–1974." *HLAJ* 31 (1974): 11–13.

12.232 Ferguson, E. "Insurance Division, SLA." *ELIS* 12 (1974): 149–52.

12.233 Gelfand, M. A. "International Relations Round Table (IRRT)." *ELIS* 12 (1974): 434–35.

12.234 Greenaway, E. "International Relations Committee, ALA." *ELIS* 12 (1974): 432–34.

12.235 Gregory, R. W. "Illinois Library Association." *ELIS* 11 (1974): 173–79.

12.236 Hanson, E. R. "Cataloging and the American Library Association, 1876–1956." Doctoral dissertation, University of Pittsburgh, 1974.

12.237 Hardison, O. B. "Independent Research Libraries Association (IRLA)." *ELIS* 11 (1974): 285–86.

12.238 Howard, E. A. "Indiana Library Association." *ELIS* 11 (1974): 447–58.

12.239 Orr, R. H. "Institute for Advancement of Medical Communication (IAMC)." *ELIS* 12 (1974): 84–89.

12.240 Schwartz, B. "The Role of the American Library Association in the Selection of Archibald MacLeish as Librarian of Congress." *JLH* 9 (1974): 241–64.

12.241 Thomison, D. "The A.L.A. and Its Missing Presidents." *JLH* 9 (1974): 362–67.

12.242 Walker, M. J. D., and McGuire, L. "Pioneer Days of the New Mexico Library Association." *New Mexico Libraries Newsletter* 3 (Fall 1974): 18–20, 25–37.

12.243 White, R. A. "Idaho Library Association (ILA)." *ELIS* 11 (1974): 152–53.

12.244 Whitman, J. B. "History of the Western North Carolina Library Association." *NCL* 32 (1974): 15–17.

12.245 Wilgus, A. C. "Inter-American Bibliographical and Library Association." *ELIS* 12 (1974): 187–93.

12.246 Zurkowski, P. G. "Information Industry Association." *ELIS* 11 (1974): 438–47.

12.247 Alford, H. W. "Iowa Library Association." *ELIS* 13 (1975): 3–13.

12.248 Clement, E. G. "Audiovisual Concerns and Activities in the American Library Association, 1924–1975." Doctoral dissertation, Indiana University, 1975.

12.249 Conmy, P. T. "The Centennial of the American Library Association and Togetherness." *CLW* 46 (1975): 338–41.

12.250 Cox, D. J. "The Illinois Association of School Librarians: A History." Doctoral dissertation, Southern Illinois University, 1975.

12.251 Davis, M. G. "Kentucky Library Association." *ELIS* 13 (1975): 421–23.

12.252 Deale, H. V. "MALC's Second Decade: Commitment to Communication." *CRL* 36 (1975): 143–51.

12.253 Hartje, G. N. *Missouri Library Association, 1900–1975.* Columbia, Mo.: Missouri Library Association, 1975.

12.254 Hazelton, R. A. "Maine Library Association." *ELIS* 16 (1975): 481–82.

12.255 Johnson, M. S. "Lutheran Church Library Association." *ELIS* 16 (1975): 363–66.

12.256 Meyer, M. "Kansas Library Association." *ELIS* 13 (1975): 399–400.

12.257 Morton, F. F. "Louisiana Library Association." *ELIS* 16 (1975): 346–47.

12.258 Piper, T. "The American Library Institute, 1905–1951: An Historical Study and an Analysis of Goals." Research Paper, University of Wisconsin, 1975.

12.259 Slanker, B. O. "Library Research Round Table." *ELIS* 15 (1975): 493–94.

12.260 Thompson, L. S. "Latter-Day Saints, Genealogical Society of the Church of Jesus Christ of." *ELIS* 14 (1975): 74–76.

12.261 Adkinson, B. W. "National Science Foundation—Science Information." *ELIS* 19 (1976): 154–77.

12.262 Ayrault, M. W., and Vann, S. K. "RTSD . . . after Twenty Years." *LRTS* 20 (1976): 301–14.

12.263 Beatty, W. K. "Medical Library Association." *ELIS* 17 (1976): 378–94.

12.264 Brahm, W. "New England Library Board." *ELIS* 19 (1976): 334.

12.265 Cohn, W. L. "An Overview of ARL Directors, 1933–1973." *CRL* 37 (1976): 137–44.

12.266 Conmy, P. T., and Coughlin, C. M. "The Principal Library Associations." In *A Century of Service: Librarianship in the United States and Canada,* edited by S. L. Jackson, E. B. Herling, and E. J. Josey. Chicago: American Library Association, 1976. Pp. 260–80.

12.267 Davis, D. G. "AALS: The Lost Years, 1925–1928." *JEL* 17 (1976): 98–105.

12.268 Drake, E. A. "Mississippi Library Association." *ELIS* 18 (1976): 198–200.

12.269 Duame, M. "Michigan Library Association." *ELIS* 18 (1976): 50–53.

12.270 Finney, L. C. "Maryland Library Association." *ELIS* 17 (1976): 194–97.

12.271 Folmer, F. "Texas Library Association." *HT* 3 (1976): 983.

12.272 Hale, C. E. "Association of College and Research Libraries, 1889–1960." Doctoral dissertation, Indiana University, 1976.

12.273 Harris, M. H. " 'An Idea in the Air'— How the ALA Was Born." *Library Association Record* 78 (1976): 302–04.

12.274 Hartje, G. N. "Missouri Library Association." *ELIS* 18 (1976): 203–09.

12.275 Hastings, G. "National Library Week." *ELIS* 19 (1976): 146–53.

12.276 Holley, E. G. "ALA at 100." *ALA Yearbook* 1 (1976): 1–32.

12.277 Johnson, B. D. "The California Library Association, 1895–1906: Years of Experimentation and Growth." *CalL* 37 (1976): 24–29.

12.278 Keenan, S., and Bearman, T. C. "National Federation of Abstracting and Indexing Services." *ELIS* 19 (1976): 84–90.

12.279 King, G. B. "Minnesota Library Association." *ELIS* 18 (1976): 150–54.

12.280 Koch, C. W. "A History of the American Association of School Librarians, 1950–1971." Doctoral dissertation, Southern Illinois University, 1976.

12.281 McKenzie, M. A. "New England Library Association." *ELIS* 19 (1976): 327–33.

12.282 Peterson, V. A. "Nebraska Library Association." *ELIS* 19 (1976): 208–19.

12.283 Polson, B. M. "Nevada Library Association." *ELIS* 19 (1976): 307–16.

12.284 Pond, P. B. "Development of a Professional School Library Association: American Association of School Librarians." *School Media Quarterly* 5 (1976): 12–18.

12.285 Price, L. C. "New Hampshire Library Association." *ELIS* 19 (1976): 335–36.

12.286 Reddy, S. R. "Massachusetts Library Association." *ELIS* 17 (1976): 259–64.

12.287 Rice, H. F. "New York Library Association." *ELIS* 19 (1976): 365–74.

12.288 Schultz, C. K. "ASIS: Notes on Its Founding and Development." *BASIS* 2 (1976): 49–51.

12.289 Sullivan, P. A. "Library Associations." *LibT* 25 (1976): 135–52.

12.290 Sullivan, P. A. *Carl H. Milam and the American Library Association.* New York: H.W. Wilson, 1976.

12.291 Thomison, D. "The A.L.A. Goes West: The 1891 San Francisco Conference." *CalL* 37 (1976): 30–35.

12.292 Walker, M. J. D. "New Mexico Library Association." *ELIS* 19 (1976): 336–42.

12.293 Warden, M. S. "Montana Library Association." *ELIS* 18 (1976): 263–68.

12.294 Wedgeworth, R., ed. *The ALA Yearbook*, Centennial edition. Chicago: American Library Association, 1976.

12.295 Weichlein, W. J. "The Music Library Association." *ELIS* 18 (1976): 457–63.

12.296 Whitten, J. N. "The Melvil Dui Marching and Chowder Association." *ELIS* 17 (1976): 437–39.

12.297 Whitten, J. N. "New York Library Club." *ELIS* 19 (1976): 374–76.

12.298 Wyche, B. "Texas Library Association Celebrates Seventy-fifth Birthday." *TL* 38 (1976): 147–52.

12.299 Bacelli, H. S., Tucker, M. S., and Fox, C. S. "Looking Back: An Archives History of NCLA." *NCL* 34 (1977): 3–12.

12.300 Caldwell, R. B. "The South Carolina State Library Group." *HBLib*: 1977 57–61.

12.301 Copeland, E. H. "North Carolina Library Association." *ELIS* 20 (1977): 163–67.

12.302 Crayton, J. E., and Wilson, L. "California Librarians Black Caucus." *HBLib*: 1977 77–81.

12.303 Davis, D. G. "Office for Library Education, ALA." *ELIS* 20 (1977): 332–35.

12.304 Diana, J. P. "Pennsylvania Library Association." *ELIS* 21 (1977): 485–96.

12.305 Eaton, K. G. "Oregon Library Association." *ELIS* 20 (1977): 465–68.

12.306 Guzzo, L. S. "The Medical Library Association: Its History and Activities." Research Paper, Texas Woman's University, 1977.

12.307 Harvard-Williams, P. "History of the International Federation of Library Associations and Institutions." *UNESCO Bulletin for Libraries* 31 (1977): 203–09.

12.308 Heilprin, L. B. "On the Core Goal of Our Society." *BASIS* 3 (1977): 19–21.

12.309 Herold, V. W. "Petroleum Division, Special Libraries Association." *ELIS* 22 (1977): 119–25.

12.310 Hill, H. M. "The Division of Librarians of the Virginia State Teachers Association." *HBLib*: 1977 62–65.

12.311 Jenkins, C., and Washington, E. "New York Black Librarians Caucus." *HBLib*: 1977 84–89.

12.312 Josey, E. J. "Black Caucus of the American Library Association." *HBLib*: 1977 66–77.

12.313 Kennedy, F. "Oklahoma Library Association." *ELIS* 20 (1977): 379–84.

12.314 King, S. K. "History and Work of the Social Responsibilities Round Table of the American Library Association." Research Paper, Texas Woman's University, 1977.

12.315 Lewis, L. S. "The Librarian's Section of the Georgia Teachers and Education Association." *HBLib*: 1977 51–53.

12.316 Marshall, A. P. "The North Carolina Negro Library Association." *HBLib*: 1977 54–57.

12.317 Munford, W. A. "The American Library Association and the Library Association: Retrospect, Problems, and Prospects." *AdLib* 7 (1977): 145–76.

12.318 Ollé, J. G. "The Library Association and the American Library Association: Their First Fifty Years." *Journal of Librarianship* 9 (1977): 247–60.

12.319 Pears, T. C. "The Pittsburgh Bibliophiles." *ELIS* 22 (1977): 271–72.

12.320 Robinson, C. C. "The Alabama Association of School Librarians." *HBLib*: 1977 47–51.

12.321 Rogers, A. R. "Ohio Library Association." *ELIS* 20 (1977): 350–62.

12.322 Turner, F. L. "A Tribute to Past [T.L.A.] Presidents." *TLJ* 53 (1977): 61–63.

12.323 Wilson, J., and Shepard, M. D. "Library and Archives Development Program: Organization of American States (OAS)." *ELIS* 21 (1977): 19–35.

12.324 Woods, A. L. "Chicago Area Black Librarians." *HBLib*: 1977 81–83.

12.325 Young, A. P. "World War I, ALA, and Censorship." *Newsletter on Intellectual Freedom* 26 (1977): 95–97, 123.

12.326 Anderson, G. A., and Runyon-Lancaster, K. E. "U.L.A.: History and Current Trends." *Utah Libraries* 21 (1978): 35–42.

12.327 Busbin, O. M. "A Survey of the Writings of the First Fifteen Women Presidents of the American Library Association." Master's thesis, Western Michigan University, 1978.

12.328 Clausman, G. J. "Then and Now: The Medical Library Association in Change, Comparison, and Controversy—Inaugural Address." *BMLA* 66 (1978): 172–74.

12.329 Dale, D. C. "ALA and Its First 100 Years, 1876–1976." In *Milestones to the Present: Papers from Library History Seminar V*, edited by H. Goldstein. Syracuse, N.Y.: Gaylord Professional Publications, 1978. Pp. 286–99.

12.330 Findlay, S. M. "The Tennessee Library Association, 1950–1975." Master's thesis, University of Tennessee, 1978.

12.331 Flanagan, L. N. "The Rhode Island Library Association: A History." *ELIS* 25 (1978): 384–99.

12.332 "History of Kentucky Association of School Librarians, 1946–1974." *KLAB* 42 (1978): 6–15.

12.333 Thomison, D. *A History of the American Library Association, 1876–1972.* Chicago: American Library Association, 1978.

12.334 Downs, R. B. "Assessing the American Library Association: A Review Essay." *JLH* 14 (1979): 191–99.

12.335 Edelstein, J. M. "The Bibliographical Society of America, 1904–1974." *PBSA* 73 (1979): 389–433.

12.336 Mount, E. "Science-Technology Division, Special Libraries Association." *ELIS* 26 (1979): 372–75.

12.337 Raymond, B. "ACONDA and ANACONDA Revisited: A Retrospective Glance at the Sounds of Fury of the Sixties." *JLH* 14 (1979): 349–62.

12.338 Sutherland, M. C., and Conway, W. E. "The Rounce and Coffin Club." *ELIS* 26 (1979): 160.

12.339 Theis, K. A. "The Association of College and Research Libraries: A History." Research Paper, Texas Woman's University, 1979.

12.340 Walters, P. L. "A History of the Amigos Bibliographic Council: 1972–1979." Research Paper, Texas Woman's University, 1979.

12.341 Aud, T. L., and McLeary, J. "A History of the Trustees and Friends of the SELA." *SEL* 30 (1980): 195–97.

12.342 Darling, M. J. "State Library Associations: The New Jersey Library Association." *ELIS* 29 (1980): 42–55.

12.343 Jay, D. F. "The History and Activities of the International Relations Round Table: A Report to the International Relations Assembly." *Leads* 22 (1980): 5, 8–9.

12.344 Kunkle, H. J., and Turner, F. L. "Texas Library Association." *ELIS* 30 (1980): 341–52.

12.345 Lorenz, J. G. "The Association of Research Libraries: A Five Year Review, 1975–1979." *Bowker Annual of Library and Book Trade Information* 25th ed. (1980): 140–45.

12.346 McKenna, F. E. "Special Libraries and the Special Libraries Association." *ELIS* 28 (1980): 386–443.

12.347 Martin, B. "A History of the School and Children's Librarians Section of the SELA." *SEL* 30 (1980): 191–94.

12.348 Martin, J. A. "Tennessee Library Association." *ELIS* 30 (1980): 284–88.

12.349 Rachow, L. A. "The Theatre Library Association." *ELIS* 29 (1980): 413–15.

12.350 Stormo, L., and Darling, D. "The South Dakota Library Association." *ELIS* 28 (1980): 277–98.

12.351 Tucker, E. E., ed. *The Southeastern Library Association: Its History and Its Honorary Members, 1920–1980.* Tucker, Ga.: Southeastern Library Association, 1980.

12.352 Walker, E. P. "South Carolina Library Association: 1915–1978." *ELIS* 28 (1980): 261–62.

12.353 Young, A. P. "Aftermath of a Crusade: World War I and the Enlarged Program of the American Library Association." *LQ* 50 (1980): 191–207.

12.354 Alexander, M. D. "Washington (State) Library Association." *ELIS* 32 (1981): 401–13.

12.355 Bradley, C. J. "The Music Library Association: The Founding Generation and Its Work." *MLAN* 37 (1981): 763–822.

12.356 Bryant, D. W. "The American Trust for the British Library." *HLB* 29 (1981): 298–306.

12.357 Burr, C. R. M. "Missouri Association for School Librarians: 1950–1975." Doctoral dissertation, Saint Louis University, 1981.

12.358 Fischer, E. T. "Virginia Library Association." *ELIS* 32 (1981): 381–83.

12.359 Geary, K. A. "Vermont Library Association." *ELIS* 32 (1981): 357–79.

12.360 Hensley, C. "The Resources and Technical Services Division at Twenty-Five." *LRTS* 25 (1981): 395–406.

12.361 Neal, J. G. "The American Merchant Marine Library Association: The First Decade of Its Development, 1921–1930." *American Neptune* 41 (1981): 5–24.

12.362 Rayward, W. B. "The Evolution of an International Library and Bibliographic Community." *JLH* 16 (1981): 449–62.

12.363 Runyon-Lancaster, K. E., and Anderson, G. A. "The Utah Library Association." *ELIS* 32 (1981): 307–14.

12.364 Wiegand, W. A. "American Library Association Executive Board Members, 1876–1917: A Collective Profile." *Libri* 31 (1981): 153–66.

12.365 Wiegand, W. A., and Greenway, G. "A Comparative Analysis of the Socioeconomic and Professional Characteristics of American Library Association Executive Board and Council Members, 1876–1917." *Library Research* 2 (1981): 309–25.

12.366 Young, A. P. *Books for Sammies: The American Library Association and World War I.* Pittsburgh: Beta Phi Mu, 1981.

12.367 Bennett, S. B. "Library Friends: A Theoretical History." In *Organizing the Library's Support: Donors, Volunteers, Friends,* edited by D. W. Krummel. Urbana: University of Illinois Graduate School of Library and Information Science, 1982. Pp. 23–32.

12.368 Davis, S. A. "Wisconsin Library Association." *ELIS* 33 (1982): 162–73.

12.369 Goff, K. E. "West Virginia Library Association." *ELIS* 33 (1982): 104–07.

12.370 Hindman, J. F. *The Catholic Library Association: The First Sixty Years, 1921–1981.* Haverford, Pa.: Catholic Library Association, 1982.

12.371 Lichtenwanger, W. "When *Notes* was Young: 1945–1960." *MLAN* 39 (1982): 7–30.

12.372 Murphy, M. "1941–1981: Forty Years of the Geography and Map Division in SLA." *SLAGMDB* 128 (1982): 2–9.

12.373 Pond, P. K. "The American Association of School Librarians: The Origins and Development of a National Professional Association for School Librarians, 1896–1951." Doctoral dissertation, University of Chicago, 1982.

12.374 Richardson, J. V. *Alice J. Appell and the Origin and Early Development of Beta Phi Mu: An Oral Interview.* Pittsburgh: Beta Phi Mu, 1982.

12.375 Zubatsky, D. S. " 'No Book Should Be out of Reach': The Role of the American Library Association in the Sharing of Resources for Research, 1922–1945." Doctoral dissertation, University of Illinois, 1982.

12.376 de Costa, S. "The Foundation and Development of IFLA, 1926–1939." *LQ* 52 (1982): 41–58.

12.377 Gutherie, V. G. "Founders of the Kentucky Library Association." *Kentucky Libraries* 47 (1983): 6–17.

12.378 Hannaford, C. "Church and Synagogue Library Association: Fifteen Years of Ecumenical Concern for Quality Service in Religious Libraries." *SL* 74 (1983): 271–77.

12.379 Palmer, J. W. "ALA's Film Office and the Film Advisor: Remembering a Neglected Pioneer." *Public Libraries [1970–]* 22 (1983): 75–76.

12.380 Virgo, J. A. C., and Schwedes, J. T. "Association of College and Research Libraries." *ELIS* 36 (1983): 16–25.

12.381 Williams, R. V., and Zachert, M. J. "Crisis and Growth: SLA, 1918–1919." *SL* 74 (1983): 254–64.

12.382 Williams, R. V., and Zachert, M. J. "Knowledge Put to Work: SLA at 75." *SL* 74 (1983): 370–82.

12.383 Baggett, C. "MLA: The First Fifty Years." *Mississippi Libraries* 48 (1984): 32–34.

12.384 Cox, A., and Lyons, M. "MLA Highlights, 1960–1983." *Mississippi Libraries* 48 (1984): 35.

12.385 Doerschuk, E. E. "Assembly of State Librarians." *ELIS* 37 (1984): 11–12.

12.386 Ellison, F. "History of GODORT in South Carolina." *South Carolina Librarian* 28 (1984): 13–15.

12.387 Farkas-Conn, I. S. "From Documentation to Information Science: The Origins and Early Development of the American Documentation Institute-American Society for Information Science." Doctoral dissertation, University of Chicago, 1984.

12.388 Holley, E. G. "The Influence of ARL on Academic Librarianship, Legislation, and Library Education." *ALAO* 3 (1984): 295–305.

12.389 McCarthy, S. A. "The ARL at Fifty." *ALAO* 3 (1984): 277–85.

12.390 Molholt, P. A. "Special Report on SLA: A 75th Anniversary Historical Review." *ALA Yearbook of Library and Information Services* 9 (1984): 278–79.

12.391 Sprudzs, A. "The International Association of Law Libraries and its 25 Years of Activities." *Law Librarian* 15 (1984): 50–53.

12.392 Welsh, W. J. "ARL/LC: 1932–1982." *ALAO* 3 (1984): 287–94.

12.393 Hartje, G. N. "Missouri Library Association, 1975–1985." *Show-Me Libraries* 37 (October/November 1985): 15–19.

12.394 Kraske, G. E. *Missionaries of the Book: The American Library Profession and the Origins of United States Cultural Diplomacy.* Westport, Conn.: Greenwood Press, 1985.

12.395 Krieger, T. "RQ: 1960 to 1985." *RQ* 25 (1985): 121–36.

12.396 Moore, R. E. "PNLA 1959–1984: A Chronology of Events to Commemorate 75 Years of Library Cooperation in the Pacific Northwest." *PNLAQ* 49 (1985): 5–13.

12.397 Redmond, A. D. "American Society for Information Science—History." *ELIS* 38 (1985): 11–31.

12.398 Ring, D. F. "Two Cultures: Libraries, the Unions, and the 'Case' of the Jefferson School of Social Science." *JLH* 20 (1985): 287–301.

12.399 Roberts, B. "The Arkansas Library Association." *ELIS* 38 (1985): 31–36.

12.400 Schultz, C. K. "ASIS Meetings: What Can We Learn from History?" *BASIS* 11 (1985): 10–12.

12.401 Wedgeworth, R. "IFLA, 1933–1985: A U.S. Perspective." *Bowker Annual of Library and Book Trade Information* 30th ed. (1985): 102–06.

12.402 Winger, H. W. "AALS Publishing in the 50s: Predecessors of *JEL*." *JELIS* 25 (1985): 245–61.

12.403 Beatty, W. K. "The Bright Thread: The *Bulletin's* 75th Anniversary." *BMLA* 74 (1986): 191–204.

12.404 Coleman, J. E. "ALA's Role in Adult and Literacy Education." *LibT* 35 (1986): 207–17.

12.405 Dyess, S. W. "A Backward Glance at the Texas Library Association: An Interview with Ray C. Janeway." *TLJ* 62 (1986): 108–12.

12.406 Morrison, P. D. "Fifty Years of PNLAQ—A Personal View: In Memory of Daniel Newberry, 1936–1986; Editor, 1979–1982." *PNLAQ* 51 (1986): 20–27.

12.407 Pettit, K. D. "The Bexar County Library Association: Fifty Years of Service." *TLJ* 62 (1986): 104–07.

12.408 Pierce, W. "In the Shadow of the Storm: The Texas Library Association and the Red Scare, 1950–1954." *TLJ* 62 (1986): 164–70.

12.409 Razer, B. A. "A History of the Arkansas Library Association." *ArkL* 43 (December 1986): 6–15.

12.410 Razer, B. A. "A Chapter in Arkansas Library History: When the American Library Association Came to Arkansas." *ArkL* 43 (March 1986): 23–31.

12.411 Torres, A. L. "The Social Responsibility Movement among Law Librarians: The Debate Revisited." *LLJ* 78 (1986): 405–24.

12.412 Vanderhoof, A. "Church and Synagogue Library Association in Texas." *TLJ* 62 (1986): 32–33.

12.413 Wiegand, W. A. *Politics of an Emerging Profession: The American Library Association, 1876–1917.* Westport, Conn.: Greenwood Press, 1986.

12.414 Wiegand, W. A. "Library Politics and the Organization of the Bibliographical Society of America." *JLH* 21 (1986): 131–57.

13.

Special Aspects of Librarianship

This chapter of the bibliography identifies materials relating to aspects of the library profession that do not lend themselves easily to categorization, but rather that touch on more than one major facet of library activity and, in some instances, may affect a wide array of programs, services, or collections. Citations whose content extends beyond types of libraries or specialized functions are divided into these three sections: (1) International Relations, (2) Technical Services, and (3) Public Services.

International Relations

Early works of special value to students of comparative librarianship begin with Wilhelm Munthe's *American Librarianship from a European Angle* (1939, **2.31**; listed in Chapter 2, "General Studies") and William Warner Bishop's "International Relations: Fragments of Autobiography" (1949, **15.164**; listed in Chapter 15, "Biographies of Individual Librarians and Library Benefactors"). The topics of comparative librarianship and American influence abroad overlap considerably, and readers interested in these aspects of librarianship should not overlook the works of one dominant figure, J. Periam Danton. His *United States Influence on Norwegian Librarianship 1890–1940* (1957, **13.4**) and *Book Selection and Collections: A Comparison of German and American University Libraries* (1963, **6.46**; listed in Chapter 6, "Academic Libraries") emerged as classics and were followed a decade later by his handbook, *The Dimensions of Comparative Librarianship* (1973, **13.30**).

The latter-day authority on international library history is W. Boyd Rayward, with an essay that presented some general observations (1976,

13.41); an article on the origins of an international bibliographic community (1981, **12.362**; listed in Chapter 12, "Library Associations"); a study of the reception of the Dewey Decimal Classification in Great Britain, Europe, and Australia (1983, **13.50**); and an article on the International Exposition and World Documentation Congress of 1937 (1983, **13.51**). Rayward's 1976 essay was nicely complemented by Vivian D. Hewitt (1976, **13.40**).

Specialized studies worthy of mention are Budd L. Gambee's writings on American participation at international conferences (1967, **13.8**; 1968, **13.13**; 1972, **13.27**; 1977, **13.44**), Margaret Chapman's study of American ideas in German librarianship (1971, **13.21**), Norman Horrocks's dissertation on the impact of the Carnegie Corporation on Australian librarianship (1971, **13.22**), Yukihisa Suzuki's study of American influence on Japanese libraries from 1860 to 1941 (1974, **13.37**), Beverly Brewster's study of overseas library technical assistance from 1940 to 1970 (1976, **13.38**), and an article by Mary Niles Maack on American influence on French librarianship from 1900 to 1950 (1985, **13.54**).

Five essays deal at least tangentially with library collections. Robert G. Vosper studied blanket orders in the United States and Great Britain (1980, **13.45**); Pamela Spence Richards examined an information-gathering system that was active during World War II (1981, **13.46**) and studied U.S. War Information Libraries in Australia, New Zealand, and South Africa (1982, **13.49**); Douglas W. Bryant evaluated the British Library's efforts at collecting library materials on America (1981, **12.356**; listed in Chapter 12, "Library Associations"); and Margaret McKinley reviewed international serials exchange activity at the University of California, Los Angeles for the years 1932 to 1986 (1986, **13.228**).

Arthur P. Young and Gary E. Kraske produced the major monographs of recent vintage, *Books for Sammies: The American Library Association and World War I* (1981, **12.366**) and *Missionaries of the Book: The American Library Profession and the Origins of United States Cultural Diplomacy* (1985, **12.394**), respectively, both listed in Chapter 12, "Library Associations." Interested readers should consult the entries in Chapter 12 that treat additional overseas activities of the American Library Association as well as pertinent publications by or about key figures listed in Chapter 15, "Biographies of Individual Librarians and Library Benefactors."

Technical Services

Not surprisingly, much of the historical writing that incorporates international developments discusses cataloging agreements established between North American and European librarians. Significantly, Anglo-American cataloging issues and agreed-upon codes were examined in a spate of essays written within a six-year span by Elizabeth L. Tate (1976, **13.164**), Wyllis E. Wright (1976, **13.165**), Margaret F. Maxwell (1977, **13.171**), Carol R. Kelm (1978, **13.175**), Alan Jeffreys (1980, **13.184**), and Robert D. Rodriguez (1981, **13.194**).

Cataloging and classification have attracted considerable attention, resulting in a number of scholarly articles. Among the most impressive of the general interpretive studies are those by Charles Martel (1926, **13.60**), Leo E. LaMontagne (1953, **13.87**), Wyllis E. Wright (1953, **13.88**), Thelma Eaton (1959, **13.100**), Vivian D. Palmer (1963, **13.107**), and David C. Weber (1964, **13.110**). More recent papers, most of them inspired by the centennial of the American Library Association, encompass the development of bibliographic networks and include the writings of Kathryn L. Henderson (1976, **13.152**), Doralyn J. Hickey (1976, **13.153**; 1977, **13.169**), Suzanne Massonneau (1976, **13.158**), Barbara Markuson (1976, **13.157**), Ann Schabas (1976, **13.161**), Edith Scott (1976, **13.162**), and Henriette D. Avram (1977, **13.167**).

The major works on cataloging, classification, and related matters are largely products of the 1980s, although Donald J. Lehnus's book-length study of famous catalogers and their writings appeared somewhat earlier (1974, **13.135**). Gordon Stevenson and Judith Kramer-Greene edited *Melvil Dewey: The Man and the Classification* (1983, **13.204**), which includes some historical papers among those presented at a seminar sponsored two years earlier by Forest Press. Francis Miksa produced a thoroughly researched monograph, *The Subject in the Dictionary Catalog from Cutter to the Present* (1983, **13.203**). Two collections of documentary sources are worth noting: Michael Carpenter and Elaine Svenonius, *Foundations of Cataloging: A Sourcebook* (1985, **13.215**), and Lois Mai Chan and others, *Theory of Subject Analysis: A Sourcebook* (1986, **13.216**).

Various specialized studies have been published on a wide range of cataloging topics. Important works include the writings of Mary B. Ruffin (1935, **13.63**), Sarah Corcoran (1936, **13.64**), Raynard C. Swank (1944, **13.74**), Jesse H. Shera (1951, **13.82**), Richard H. Shoemaker (1960, **13.105**), Jim Ranz (1964, **13.109**), and Robert B. Winans (1978, **13.178**) on bibliography and printed book catalogs; Ruth M. Heiss on card catalogs (1938, **13.67**); Velva J. Osborn (1944, **13.72**), William Carlson (1952, **13.84**), James R. Hunt (1964, **13.108**), and John M. Dawson (1967, **13.114**) on cooperative cataloging; Nancy P. Bates on the classification of maps (1954, **13.89**); Russell E. Bidlack (1957, **13.96**), Eugene E. Graziano (1959, **13.101**), Benjamin A. Custer (1972, **13.124**), John P. Comaromi (1976, **13.147**), and Comaromi with Mohinder P. Satija (1985, **13.218**) on the Dewey Decimal Classification; Jan Gossens on the Universal Decimal Classification (1982, **13.196**); Robert D. Rodriguez on subject analysis (1984, **13.210**; 1984, **13.211**); and John J. Boll on the literature of cataloging (1985, **13.213**). Further historical information on cataloging in the United States may be found in the biographical entries for key figures, in particular, Charles Ammi Cutter, Melvil Dewey, J. C. M. Hanson, Charles Coffin Jewett, and Esther J. Piercy, listed in Chapter 15, "Biographies of Individual Librarians and Library Benefactors."

An overview of the history of American cataloging must incorporate analyses of the nation's bibliographical flagship, the Library of Congress. Works by J. C. M. Hanson (1929, **13.62**), Alpheus L. Walter (1952, **13.85**), Leo E. LaMontagne (1961, **13.106**), Martha M. Evans (1969, **13.120**), Paul Edlund (1976, **13.150**), and Francis Miksa (1984, **13.208**) merit special attention.

Broader studies on the history of the Library of Congress and its role as a national leader are cited in Chapter 9, "Special Libraries."

Public Services

Reference services, library use, and bibliographic instruction have attracted much less historical attention than have technical services. The substantive general studies of reference work began with the writings of Louis Kaplan, who concentrated on the latter decades of the nineteenth century (1947, **13.232**; 1952, **13.234**), continued through Samuel Rothstein's highly regarded monograph, *The Development of Reference Services through Academic Traditions, Public Library Practice and Special Librarianship* (1955, **13.237**), and concluded with sound essays by Rothstein (1977, **13.245**) and Robert Wagers (1978, **13.248**).

More recent scholarship has become specialized, treating a particular aspect of public services, an individual institution or, alternatively, larger issues of library use. Boyd Childress scrutinized library use at the University of Virginia for the years 1878 to 1879 (1980, **6.728**; listed in Chapter 6, "Academic Libraries"); Norman D. Stevens analyzed library networking and resource sharing (1980, **2.289**; listed in Chapter 2, "General Studies"); David S. Zubatsky evaluated the role of the American Library Association in support of resource sharing from 1922 to 1945 (1982, **12.375**; listed in Chapter 12, "Library Associations"); Charles A. Bunge conducted a historical review of the literature of reference interviewing (1984, **13.250**); Margaret F. Stieg offered a careful overview of the "fee vs. free" debate in the provision of information services (1985, **13.253**); and, finally, M. Lynne Neufeld and Martha Cornog examined the history of online databases (1986, **13.254**), adding substantially to an earlier work by Martha E. Williams (1977, **13.172**).

The re-emergence of instruction in library use in the late 1960s and early 1970s stimulated historical research on this vital topic. Most of the relevant articles are identified in Chapter 6, "Academic Libraries," although Richard Rubin's study of Azariah Smith Root and bibliographic instruction (1977, **15.1529**) is cited in Chapter 15, "Biographies of Individual Librarians and Library Benefactors." Finally, much can be learned about the development of reference and other public service programs and, to a lesser extent, library use by examining the historical monographs devoted to major academic and public libraries.

International Relations

13.1 Kildal, A. "American Influence on European Librarianship." *LQ* 7 (1937): 196–210.

13.2 Stevens, R. D. *The Role of the Library of Congress in the International Exchange of Official Publications: A Brief History.* Washington, D.C.: Library of Congress, 1953.

13.3 Parker, J. A. "The Books Across the Sea Library in the United States: Its Establishment, Purposes, and Operation." Master's thesis, Pratt Institute, 1955, ACRL Microcard no. 80.

13.4 Danton, J. P. *United States Influence on Norwegian Librarianship, 1890–1940.* Berkeley: University of California Press, 1957.

13.5 Poste, L. I. "The Development of U.S. Protection of Libraries and Archives in Europe during World War II." Doctoral dissertation, University of Chicago, 1958.

13.6 Au, C. "American Impact on Modern Chinese Library Development." Master's thesis, University of Chicago, 1964.

13.7 Thompson, S. O. "The American Library in Paris: An International Development in the American Library Movement." *LQ* 34 (1964): 179–90.

13.8 Gambee, B. L. "The Great Junket: American Participation in the Conference of Librarians, London, 1877." *JLH* 2 (1967): 9–44.

13.9 Glazier, K. M. "United States Influence on Canadian Universities and Their Libraries." *CRL* 28 (1967): 311–16.

13.10 Wessells, H. E. "History of the International Relations Round Table." In *Foreign Service Directory of American Librarians*, 3d ed., edited by J. C. Phillips. Pittsburgh: University of Pittsburgh Book Center, 1967. Pp. ix–xi.

13.11 Williamson, I. R. "The Development of the United States Collection, Department of Printed Books, British Museum." *Journal of American Studies* 1 (1967): 79–86.

13.12 Daily, J. E. "Anglo-American Code." *ELIS* 1 (1968): 416–22.

13.13 Gambee, B. L. "Best Foot Forward: Representation of American Librarianship at World's Fairs, 1853–1904." In *Library History Seminar No. 3, Proceedings, 1968*, edited by M. J. Zachert. Tallahassee: JLH, 1968. Pp. 137–74.

13.14 Kirkegaard, P. "Anglo-Scandinavian Library Conferences." *ELIS* 1 (1968): 423–24.

13.15 Steig, L. F. "American Librarians Abroad, 1946–1965." *LQ* 38 (1968): 315–22.

13.16 Wormann, C. D. "Aspects of International Library Cooperation, Historical and Contemporary." *LQ* 38 (1968): 340–42.

13.17 Siggins, J. A. "American Influence on Modern Japanese Library Development." Master's thesis, University of Chicago, 1969.

13.18 Stroup, E. W. "The American Hauser and Their Libraries: An Historical Sketch and Evaluation." *JLH* 4 (1969): 239–52.

13.19 Bone, L. E. "The American Library in Paris: Fifty Years of Service." *ALib* 1 (1970): 279–83.

13.20 Moscowitz, R. "The History of the U.S.I.A. Overseas Library Program." Research Paper, Long Island University, 1970.

13.21 Chapman, M. "American Ideas in the German Public Libraries: Three Periods." *LQ* 41 (1971): 35–53.

13.22 Horrocks, N. "Carnegie Corporation of New York and Its Impact on Library Development in Australia: A Case Study of Foundation Influence." Doctoral dissertation, University of Pittsburgh, 1971.

13.23 Bixler, P. "The Charity of Books." *LibT* 20 (1972): 478–99.

13.24 Collett, J. "American Libraries Abroad: United States Information Agency Activities." *LibT* 20 (1972): 538–47.

13.25 Dale, D. C. "An American in Geneva: Florence Wilson and the League of Nations Library." *JLH* 7 (1972): 109–29.

13.26 Donovan, D. G. "Library Development and the U.S. Consultant Overseas." *LibT* 20 (1972): 506–14.

13.27 Gambee, B. L. "The Role of American Librarians at the Second International Library Conference, London, 1897." In *Library History Seminar No. 4, Proceedings, 1971*, edited by H. Goldstein and J. Goudeau. Tallahassee: Florida State University School of Library Science, 1972. Pp. 52–85.

13.28 Sullivan, P. A. "The International Relations Program of the American Library Association." *LibT* 20 (1972): 577–91.

13.29 Williams, E. E. "Farmington Plan." *ELIS* 8 (1972): 361–68.

13.30 Danton, J. P. *The Dimensions of Comparative Librarianship.* Chicago: American Library Association, 1973.

13.31 Liebaers, H. "Books, Libraries, Librarians—European and American Style." *JLH* 8 (1973): 18–22.

13.32 Sussman, J. *United States Information Service Libraries.* Urbana: University of Illinois Graduate School of Library Science, 1973.

13.33 Allardyce, A., Sternberg, I., and Christophers, R. A. "International Book Exchange." *ELIS* 12 (1974): 257–77.

13.34 Gelfand, M. A. "International Relations Round Table (IRRT)." *ELIS* 12 (1974): 434–35.

13.35 Greenaway, E. "International Relations Committee, ALA." *ELIS* 12 (1974): 432–34.

13.36 Krzys, R. "The International Library Information Center of the University of Pittsburgh." *ELIS* 12 (1974): 413–18.

13.37 Suzuki, Y. "American Influence on the Development of Library Services in Japan, 1860–1941." Doctoral dissertation, University of Michigan, 1974.

13.38 Brewster, B. J. *American Overseas Library Technical Assistance, 1940–1970.* Metuchen, N.J.: Scarecrow Press, 1976.

13.39 Dale, D. C., ed. *Carl H. Milam and the United Nations Library.* Metuchen, N.J.: Scarecrow Press, 1976.

13.40 Hewitt, V. D. "Services to Library Life Abroad." In *A Century of Service: Librarianship in the United States and Canada*, edited by S. L. Jackson, E. B. Herling, and E. J. Josey. Chicago: American Library Association, 1976. Pp. 321–40.

13.41 Rayward, W. B. "Librarianship in the New World and the Old: Some Points of Contact." *LibT* 25 (1976): 209–26.

13.42 Vosper, R. "A Century Abroad." *CRL* 37 (1976): 514–30.

13.43 Werdel, J. A., and Adams, S. "U.S. Participation in World Information Activities." *BASIS* 2 (1976): 44–48.

13.44 Gambee, B. L. *Return Engagement: The Role of American Librarians at the Second International Library Conference, London, 1897.* Urbana: University of Illinois Graduate School of Library Science, Occasional Paper no. 129, 1977.

13.45 Vosper, R. "The Blanket Order: Some Historical Footnotes and Conjectures." In *Shaping Library Collections for the 1980s*, edited by P. Spyers-Duran and T. Mann. Phoenix, Ariz.: Oryx Press, 1980. Pp. 4–17.

13.46 Richards, P. S. "Gathering Enemy Scientific Information in Wartime: The OSS and the Periodical Republication Program." *JLH* 16 (1981): 253–64.

13.47 Rochester, M. "American Influence in New Zealand Librarianship, as Facilitated by the Carnegie Corporation of New York." Doctoral dissertation, University of Wisconsin-Madison, 1981.

13.48 Price, P. P., ed. *International Book and Library Activities: The History of a U.S. Foreign Policy.* Metuchen, N.J.: Scarecrow Press, 1982.

13.49 Richards, P. S. "Information for the Allies: Office of War Information Libraries in Australia, New Zealand and South Africa." *LQ* 52 (1982): 325–47.

13.50 Rayward, W. B. "The Early Diffusion Abroad of the Dewey Decimal Classification: Great Britain, Australia, Europe." In *Melvil Dewey: The Man and the Classification*, edited by G. Stevenson and J. Kramer-Greene. Albany, N.Y.: Forest Press, 1983. Pp. 149–73.

13.51 Rayward, W. B. "The International Exposition and the World Documentation Congress, Paris, 1937." *LQ* 53 (1983): 254–68.

13.52 Benjamin, C. G. *U.S. Books Abroad: Neglected Ambassadors.* Washington, D.C.: Library of Congress, 1984.

13.53 Lin, S. C. "Historical Development of Library Education in China." *JLH* 20 (1985): 368–87.

13.54 Maack, M. N. "Americans in France: Cross-Cultural Exchange and the Diffusion of Innovations." *JLH* 21 (1986): 315–33.

Technical Services

1876–1919

13.55 Nelson, C. A. "The 'A.L.A.' Library Catalog, 1876–1894 [a poem]." *LJ* 19 (1894): 134.

13.56 Jordon, F. P. "History of Printed Catalog Cards." *PL* 9 (1904): 318–21.

13.57 Hanson, J. C. M. "The Subject Catalogs of the Library of Congress." *BALA* 3 (1909): 385–97.

1920–1949

13.58 Dewey, M. "Decimal Classification Beginnings." *LJ* 45 (1920): 151–54.

13.59 Datz, H. R. "A Pioneer: The Library Bureau." *LJ* 51 (1926): 669–70.

13.60 Martel, C. "Cataloging: 1876–1926." *BALA* 20 (1926): 492–98.

13.61 Chevalier, S. A. "The History of the Catalogue Department." *MoreB* 2 (1927): 215–19.

13.62 Hanson, J. C. M. "The Library of Congress and Its New Catalogue." In *Essays Offered to Herbert Putnam by His Colleagues and Friends on His Thirtieth Anniversary as Librarian of Congress, 5 April 1929*, edited by W. W. Bishop and A. Keogh. New Haven: Yale University Press, 1929. Pp. 178–94.

13.63 Ruffin, M. B. "Some Developments toward Modern Cataloging Practice in University Libraries as Exemplified in the Printed Book Catalogs of Harvard and Yale before 1876." Master's thesis, Columbia University, 1935.

13.64 Corcoran, S. R. "A Study of Cataloging Practice through 1830 as Shown in Printed Book Catalogs of Six Libraries in the City of New York." Master's thesis, Columbia University, 1936.

13.65 Hensel, E. M. "History of the Catalog Department of the University of Illinois Library." Master's thesis, University of Illinois, 1936.

13.66 Pettee, J. "The Development of Authorship Entry and the Formulation of Authorship Rules as Found in the Anglo-American Code." *LQ* 6 (1936): 270–99.

13.67 Heiss, R. M. "The Card Catalog in Libraries of the United States Before 1876." Master's thesis, University of Illinois, 1938.

13.68 Monrad, A. M. "Historical Notes on the Catalogues and Classifications of the Yale University Library." In *Papers in Honor of Andrew Keogh, Librarian of Yale University*, edited by M. C. Withington. New Haven, Conn.: Privately printed, 1938. Pp. 251–84.

13.69 Currier, T. F. "Cataloguing and Classification at Harvard, 1878–1938." *HLN* 29 (1939): 232–42.

13.70 Heiss, R. M. "The Card Catalog in Libraries of the United States before 1876."

Catalogers and Classifiers Yearbook 8 (1939): 125–26.

13.71 Currier, M. "Cataloguing at Harvard in the Sixties." *HLN* 32 (1942): 67–73.

13.72 Osborn, V. J. "A History of Cooperative Cataloging in the United States." Master's thesis, University of Chicago, 1944.

13.73 Stutsman, E. B. "Historical Development from 1792 to 1936 in the Printed Documents of Kentucky, with a View to Their Cataloging." Master's thesis, Columbia University, 1944, ACRL Microcard no. 8.

13.74 Swank, R. C. "Subject Catalogs, Classifications or Bibliographies? A Review of Critical Discussion, 1876–1942." *LQ* 14 (1944): 316–22.

13.75 Leidecker, K. F. "The Debt of Melvil Dewey to William Torrey Harris." *LQ* 15 (1945): 139–42.

13.76 Evans, L. H. "History and the Problem of Bibliography." *CRL* 7 (1946): 195–205.

13.77 Pettee, J. *Subject Headings: The History and Theory of the Alphabetical Subject Approach to Books.* New York: H.W. Wilson, 1946.

13.78 Schley, R. "Cataloging in the Libraries of Princeton, Columbia, and the University of Pennsylvania Before 1876." Master's thesis, Columbia University, 1946.

1950–1971

13.79 Servies, J. A. "Thomas Jefferson and His Bibliographic Classification." Master's thesis, University of Chicago, 1950.

13.80 Frarey, C. J. "Subject Heading Revision by the Library of Congress, 1941–1950." Master's thesis, Columbia University, 1951, ACRL Microcard no. 15.

13.81 Kipp, L. J., and Thomas, A. T. "The Creation of a Cataloging Economy: The Typing Section of the Widener Library [1892–1950]." *HLB* 5 (1951): 112–16.

13.82 Shera, J. H. "The Beginnings of Systematic Bibliography in America, 1642–1797." In *Essays Honoring Lawrence G. Wroth,* edited by The Committee on Publication. Portland, Me.: Anthoensen Press, 1951. Pp. 263–78.

13.83 Straka, M. "A Historical Review of the Cataloging Department of the Columbia University Libraries: 1883–1950." Master's thesis, Columbia University, 1951.

13.84 Carlson, W. H. "Cooperation: An Historical Review and a Forecast." *CRL* 13 (1952): 5–13.

13.85 Walter, A. L. "Fifty Years Young: Library of Congress Cards." *CRL* 13 (1952): 305–08.

13.86 Hitchcock, J. E. "The Yale Library Classification." *YULG* 27 (1953): 95–109.

13.87 LaMontagne, L. E. "Historical Background of Classification." In *Subject Analysis of Library Materials,* edited by M. Tauber. New York: Columbia University Press, 1953. Pp. 16–28.

13.88 Wright, W. E. "The Subject Approach to Knowledge: Historical Aspects and Purposes." In *Subject Analysis of Library Materials,* edited by M. Tauber. New York: Columbia University Press, 1953. Pp. 8–15.

13.89 Bates, N. P. "The History of the Classification and Cataloging of Maps as Shown in Printed Book Catalogues of Sixteen United States Libraries Issued fron 1827 through 1907." Master's thesis, University of North Carolina, 1954, University of Kentucky Press Microcard Series B, no. 15.

13.90 Oswald, J. F. "The Development of the Medical Subject Heading." Master's thesis, Drexel Institute of Technology, 1955.

13.91 Wilkins, M. J. "History and Evaluation of Subject Heading Approach in Medicine: A Study of Certain Medical Indexes Published in the United States." Master's thesis, Catholic University of America, 1955.

13.92 Devlin, E. "The Development of the Catalogue of the University of Pennsylvania Library (1829–1955)." *LC* 22 (1956): 19–28.

13.93 Dunkin, P. S. "Criticisms of Current Cataloging Practice (1941–1956)." *LQ* 26 (1956): 286–302.

13.94 Shera, J. H., and Egan, M. E. *The Classified Catalog: Basic Principles and Practices.* Chicago: American Library Association, 1956.

13.95 Tauber, M. F. "Board on Cataloging Policy and Research: Review of Its Work, 1951–1956." *Journal of Catalogers & Classifiers* 12 (1956): 229–33.

13.96 Bidlack, R. E. "The Coming Catalogue of Melvil Dewey's Flying Machine: Being the Historical Background of the A.L.A. Catalog." *LQ* 27 (1957): 137–60.

13.97 Nyhom, A. W. "The Final Solution to the Problem of Cataloging: A Note on the Contribution of Agnes M. Cole, 1873–1956." *WLB* 31 (1957): 247–49.

13.98 Baker, M. O. "American Library Catalogs a Hundred Years Ago." *WLB* 33 (1958): 284–85.

13.99 Reddie, J. N. "Author Headings of the Official Publications of the State of Ohio, 1900–1957." Master's thesis, Kent State University, 1958.

13.100 Eaton, T. "The Development of Classification in America." In *The Role of Classification in the Modern American Library,* edited by T. Eaton and D. E. Strout. Urbana: University of Illinois Graduate School of Library Science, 1959. Pp. 8–30.

13.101 Graziano, E. E. "Hegel's Philosophy as a Basis for the Dewey Classification Schedule." *Libri* 9 (1959): 45–52.

13.102 Kaser, J. "The Venerable History of Cataloging-in-Source." *Missouri Library Association Quarterly* 20 (September 1959): 76–81.

13.103 Thackston, F. V. "The Development of Cataloging in the Libraries of Duke University and the University of North Carolina from Their Establishment to 1953." Master's thesis, University of North Carolina, 1959, ACRL Microcard no. 124.

13.104 Trotier, A. "Cataloging in Source—the Story Up to Now." *IllL* 41 (1959): 426–31.

13.105 Shoemaker, R. H. "Some American Twentieth Century Book Catalogs: Their Purposes, Format, and Production Techniques." *LRTS* 4 (1960): 195–207.

13.106 LaMontagne, L. E. *American Library Classification: With Special Reference to the Library of Congress.* Hamden, Conn.: Shoe String Press, 1961.

13.107 Palmer, V. D. "A Brief History of Cataloging Codes in the United States, 1852–1949." Master's thesis, University of Chicago, 1963.

13.108 Hunt, J. R. "The Historical Development of Processing Centers in the United States." *LRTS* 8 (1964): 54–59.

13.109 Ranz, J. *The Printed Book Catalogue in American Libraries, 1723–1900.* Chicago: American Library Association, 1964.

13.110 Weber, D. C. "The Changing Character of the Catalog in America." In *Library Catalogs: Changing Dimensions*, edited by R. F. Strout. Chicago: University of Chicago Press, 1964. Pp. 20–33.

13.111 Gillespie, S. C. "An Analysis of Certain Notes Used by the Library of Congress in Cataloging Serial Publications, 1898–1942." Master's thesis, Emory University, 1965.

13.112 Savary, M. J. "The Latin American Cooperative Acquisitions Project (LACAP)." Research Paper, Long Island University, 1966.

13.113 Cronin, J. W. "History of *The National Union Catalog*, Pre–1956 Imprints." In *Prospectus for* The National Union Catalog, *Pre–1956 Imprints.* London: Mansell, 1967. Pp. 15–16.

13.114 Dawson, J. M. "A History of Centralized Processing." *LRTS* 11 (1967): 28–32.

13.115 Dougherty, R. M., and McKinnery, A. "Ten Years of Progress in Acquisitions: 1956–66." *LRTS* 11 (1967): 289–301.

13.116 Kebabian, B. "Bibliographic Quiddling." *LRTS* 11 (1967): 397–404.

13.117 Bates, P. N. H. "Subject Catalog Use Studies, 1953–1966." Master's thesis, University of Chicago, 1968.

13.118 Leonard, L. E. *Cooperative and Centralized Cataloging and Processing: A Bibliography, 1850–1967*. Urbana: University of Illinois Graduate School of Library Science, Occasional Paper no. 93, 1968.

13.119 Rowe, H. M. "A Comparative Historical Study of the Library Systems Concept As It Developed in the States of California and New York." Research Paper, University of Southern California, 1968.

13.120 Evans, M. M. "A History of the Development of Classification K (Law) at the Library of Congress." *LLJ* 62 (1969): 25–39.

13.121 Hanson, E. R., and Daily, J. E. "Catalogs and Cataloging." *ELIS* 4 (1970): 242–305.

13.122 Parker, R. H. "Charging Systems." *ELIS* 4 (1970): 468–79.

13.123 Pope, E. "Cataloging in Source." *ELIS* 4 (1970): 231–42.

1972–1986

13.124 Custer, B. A. "Dewey Decimal Classification." *ELIS* 7 (1972): 128–42.

13.125 Einhorn, N. R. "Exchange of Publications." *ELIS* 8 (1972): 282–89.

13.126 Immroth, J. P. "Expansive Classification." *ELIS* 8 (1972): 297–316.

13.127 Jackson, C. "The Library of Congress' National Program for Acquisitions and Cataloging: Its Historical Perspective." Master's thesis, University of Chicago, 1972.

13.128 Albrecht, T. J. "Evidence of an Early Union Catalogue in Texas." *TL* 35 (1973): 204–06.

13.129 Davis, E. R. "Author vs. Title: A Historical Treatment of the Conflict Over Choice of Entry for Serials Issued by Corporate Bodies." Master's thesis, University of Chicago, 1973.

13.130 Finn, T. M. "Hall and Co., G.K." *ELIS* 10 (1973): 284–89.

13.131 Rohdy, M. A. "Cataloging Anonymous Works: An Historical and Theoretical Study." Master's thesis, University of Chicago, 1973.

13.132 Sealock, R. B. "Forest Press, Inc." *ELIS* 9 (1973): 8–12.

13.133 Thorp, E. N. "The Fulbright Program, 1948–1968: University Lectureships and Advanced Research Awards in Library Science." Master's thesis, University of Chicago, 1973.

13.134 Evensen, R. L. "The Bibliographical Control of Art Exhibition Catalogs: An Historical and Comparative Analysis of Cataloging Rules and Library Procedures in France, Great Britain, and the United States." Master's thesis, University of Chicago, 1974.

13.135 Lehnus, D. J. *Milestones in Cataloging: Famous Catalogers and Their Writings, 1835–1969*. Littleton, Colo.: Libraries Unlimited, 1974.

13.136 Post, K. L. "History of the Ohio College Library Center from 1967–1972." Research Paper, Kent State University, 1974.

13.137 Stevenson, G. "The Historical Context: Traditional Classification Since 1950." *DLQ* 10 (1974): 11–20.

13.138 Avram, H. D. "Machine-Readable Cataloging (MARC) Program." *ELIS* 16 (1975): 380–413.

13.139 Bolef, D. "Mechanization of Library Procedures in a Medium-sized Medical Library: XVI. Computer-assisted Cataloging, the First Decade." *BMLA* 63 (1975): 272–82.

13.140 Grove, P. S. "The Bibliographic Organization of Nonprint Media." In *Nonprint Media in Academic Libraries*. Chicago: American Library Association, 1975. Pp. 1–51.

13.141 Hagler, R. "The Development of Cataloging Rules for Nonbook Materials." *LRTS* 19 (1975): 268–78.

13.142 Immroth, J. P. "Library of Congress Classification." *ELIS* 15 (1975): 93–200.

13.143 Manheimer, M. L. "Main Entry." *ELIS* 16 (1975): 470–80.

13.144 Miletic, I. "Major Cooperative Programs of Research Libraries: The Farmington Plan; the Public Law 480 Program and the National Program for Acquisitions and Cataloging." Research Paper, Queens College, 1975.

13.145 Pope, E. "Library Catalog Cards." *ELIS* 14 (1975): 448–64.

13.146 Batty, D. "Dewey Abroad: The International Use of the Dewey Decimal Classification." *QJLC* 33 (1976): 300–310.

13.147 Comaromi, J. P. *The Eighteen Editions of the Dewey Decimal Classification.* Albany, N.Y.: Forest Press Div., Lake Placid Educational Foundation, 1976.

13.148 Comaromi, J. P. "Knowledge Organized Is Knowledge Kept: The Dewey Decimal Classification, 1873–1976." *QJLC* 33 (1976): 311–31.

13.149 Cunha, G. M. "New England Document Conservation Center." *ELIS* 19 (1976): 322–25.

13.150 Edlund, P. "A Monster and a Miracle: The Cataloging Distribution Service of the Library of Congress, 1901–1976." *QJLC* 33 (1976): 383–421.

13.151 Heisey, T. M. "Early Catalog Code Development in the United States, 1876–1908." *JLH* 11 (1976): 218–48.

13.152 Henderson, K. L. " 'Treated with a Degree of Uniformity and Common Sense': Descriptive Cataloging in the United States, 1876–1975." *LibT* 25 (1976): 227–71.

13.153 Hickey, D. J. "Subject Analysis: An Interpretive Study." *LibT* 25 (1976): 273–91.

13.154 Hickey, D. J. "Margaret Mann Citation in Cataloging and Classification." *ELIS* 17 (1976): 161–65.

13.155 Immroth, J. P. "National Union Catalog." *ELIS* 19 (1976): 182–86.

13.156 Lewis, D. T. "The History of the Publishing of the *National Union Catalog*." Research Paper, Texas Woman's University, 1976.

13.157 Markuson, B. E. "Bibliographic Systems, 1945–1976." *LibT* 25 (1976): 311–28.

13.158 Massonneau, S. "Technical Services and Technology: The Bibliographical Imperative." In *A Century of Service: Librarianship in the United States and Canada,* edited by S. L. Jackson, E. B. Herling, and E. J. Josey. Chicago: American Library Association, 1976. Pp. 192–207.

13.159 Pitkin, G. M. *Serials Automation in the United States: A Bibliographic History.* Metuchen, N.J.: Scarecrow Press, 1976.

13.160 Saracevic, T. "Intellectual Organization of Knowledge: The American Contribution." *BASIS* 2 (1976): 16–17.

13.161 Schabas, A. H. "Technical Services and Technology: Technological Advance." In *A Century of Service: Librarianship in the United States and Canada,* edited by S. L. Jackson, E. B. Herling, and E. J. Josey. Chicago: American Library Association, 1976. Pp. 208–20.

13.162 Scott, E. "The Evolution of Bibliographic Systems in the United States, 1876–1945." *LibT* 25 (1976): 293–309.

13.163 Selmer, M. L. "Map Cataloging and Classification Methods: A Historical Survey." *SLAGMDB* 103 (1976): 7–12.

13.164 Tate, E. L. "International Standards: The Road to the Universal Bibliographic Control." *LRTS* 20 (1976): 16–24.

13.165 Wright, W. E. "The *Anglo-American Cataloging Rules*: A Historical Perspective." *LRTS* 20 (1976): 36–47.

13.166 Avram, H. D. "Production, Dissemination and Use of Bibliographic Data and Summary of the Conference." In *Prospects for Change in Bibliographic Control,* edited by A. Bookstein, H. H. Fussler, and H. F. Schmierer. Chicago: University of Chicago Press, 1977. Pp. 113–35.

13.167 Avram, H. D. "Production, Dissemination and Use of Bibliographic Data and Summary of the Conference." *LQ* 47 (1977): 347–69.

13.168 Folts, S. B. "Pittsburgh Regional Library Center." *ELIS* 22 (1977): 272–80.

13.169 Hickey, D. J. "Theory of Bibliographic Control in Libraries." *LQ* 47 (1977): 253–73.

13.170 Kilgour, F. G. "Ohio College Library Center." *ELIS* 20 (1977): 346–47.

13.171 Maxwell, M. F. "The Genesis of the Anglo-American Cataloging Rules." *Libri* 27 (1977): 238–62.

13.172 Williams, M. E. "Data-bases: A History of Developments and Trends from 1966 through 1975." *JASIS* 28 (1977): 71–78.

13.173 Allen, J. A. "The History of Automated Library Cooperation in Arkansas." *ArkL* 35 (September 1978): 15–18.

13.174 Comstock, N. "The Dewey Dichotomy." *WLB* 52 (1978): 400–407.

13.175 Kelm, C. R. "The Historical Development of the Second Edition of the *Anglo-American Cataloging Rules.*" *LRTS* 22 (1978): 22–33.

13.176 Myrick, W. J. "Access to Microforms: A Survey of Failed Efforts." *LJ* 103 (1978): 2301–04.

13.177 Scott, S. S. "Cataloging in Publication: History and Development." Research Paper, Texas Woman's University, 1978.

13.178 Winans, R. B. "Beginnings of Systematic Bibliography in America up to 1800:

Further Explorations." *PBSA* 72 (1978): 15–35.

13.179 Batty, D. "The Sheaf Catalog." *ELIS* 27 (1979): 312–19.

13.180 Sinkankas, G. M. "The Sears List of Subject Headings." *ELIS* 27 (1979): 160–79.

13.181 Axford, H. W. "An Historical Overview and an Assessment of Future Value." In *Shaping Library Collections for the 1980s,* edited by P. Spyers-Duran and T. Mann. Phoenix, Ariz.: Oryx Press, 1980. Pp. 18–31.

13.182 Custer, B. A. "The View from the Editor's Chair." *LRTS* 24 (1980): 99–105.

13.183 Gorman, M. " 'Let Us Now Praise . . .' A Reflective Look at Six Persons Who Greatly Influenced the Art of Cataloging." *ALib* 11 (1980): 201–03.

13.184 Jeffreys, A. "Cataloging and Classification: The Anglo-American Concorde." In *University Library History: An International Review,* edited by J. Thompson. New York: K.G. Saur, 1980. Pp. 149–69.

13.185 Lehnus, D. J. *Book Numbers: History, Principles, and Application.* Chicago: American Library Association, 1980.

13.186 London, G. "The Place and Role of Bibliographic Description in General and Individual Catalogues: A Historical Analysis." *Libri* 30 (1980): 253–84.

13.187 Maruskin, A. F. *OCLC, Inc.: Its Governance, Function, Financing and Technology.* New York: Marcel Dekker, Inc., 1980.

13.188 Miller, R. C. "Approval Plans: Fifteen Years of Frustration and Fruition." In *Shaping Library Collections for the 1980s,* edited by P. Spyers-Duran and T. Mann. Phoenix, Ariz.: Oryx Press, 1980. Pp. 43–53.

13.189 Poole, H. "Fremont Rider and His International Classification: An Interesting Tale of American Library History." *LRTS* 24 (1980): 106–13.

13.190 Stevens, C. H. "Solinet." *ELIS* 28 (1980): 107–10.

13.191 Ball, A. D. "The Universal Serials and Book Exchange, Inc." *ELIS* 32 (1981): 146–51.

13.192 Comaromi, J. P. *Book Numbers: A Historical Study and Practical Guide to Their Use.* Littleton, Colo.: Libraries Unlimited, 1981.

13.193 Hanson, E. R. "Union Catalogs." *ELIS* 31 (1981): 391–445.

13.194 Rodriquez, R. D. "Classification and Subject Indication: Highlights of the Anglo-American Debate, 1850–1950." *Libri* 31 (1981): 322–40.

13.195 Gorman, M. "1941: An Analysis and Appreciation of Andrew Osborn's 'The Crisis in Cataloging.'" *SerL* 6 (1982): 127–31.

13.196 Gossens, J. "Origins and Development of the Universal Decimal Classification." *International Forum on Information and Documentation* 7 (1982): 7–10.

13.197 Heifer, R. S. "Beginning of Course with A: A Study of Library Filing and the 1980 Filing Codes." Master's thesis, University of Chicago, 1982.

13.198 McMullin, B. J. "About the Size of It." *JLH* 17 (1982): 429–52.

13.199 Robertson, H. W. "Andrew Osborn and Serials Cataloging." *SerL* 6 (1982): 133–38.

13.200 Yu, P. C. "Berkeley's Exchange Program: A Case Study." *JLH* 17 (1982): 241–67.

13.201 Comaromi, J. P. "The Foundations of the Dewey Decimal Classification: The First Two Editions." In *Melvil Dewey: The Man and the Classification,* edited by G. Stevenson and J. Kramer-Greene. Albany, N.Y.: Forest Press, 1983. Pp. 135–47.

13.202 Freedman, M. J. "The Functions of the Catalog and the Main Entry as Found in the Work of Panizzi, Jewett, Cutter, and Lubetzky." Doctoral dissertation, Rutgers University, 1983.

13.203 Miksa, F. L. *The Subject in the Dictionary Catalog from Cutter to the Present.* Chicago: American Library Association, 1983.

13.204 Stevenson, G., and Kramer-Greene, J. *Melvil Dewey: The Man and the Classification.* Albany, N.Y.: Forest Press, 1983.

13.205 Stevenson, J. "The Classified Catalogue of the New York State Library in 1911." In *Melvil Dewey: The Man and the Classification,* edited by G. Stevenson and J. Kramer-Greene. Albany, N.Y.: Forest Press, 1983. Pp. 175–200.

13.206 McHugh, W. A. "The Publication of the First Edition of the *Union List of Serials.*" Master's thesis, University of Chicago, 1984.

13.207 Maciuszko, K. *OCLC: A Decade of Development, 1967–1977.* Littleton, Colo.: Libraries Unlimited, 1984.

13.208 Miksa, F. L. *The Development of Classification at the Library of Congress.* Urbana: University of Illinois Graduate School of Library and Information Science, Occasional Paper no. 164, 1984.

13.209 Morris, L. R. "The History of Computer Use in Libraries Based on Bibliographic Inferences." *Journal of Information Science* 9 (1984): 129–32.

13.210 Rodriguez, R. D. "Hulmes's Concept of Literary Warrant." *Cataloging and Classification Quarterly* 5 (1984): 17–26.

13.211 Rodriguez, R. D. "Kaiser's Systematic Indexing." *LRTS* 28 (1984): 163–74.

13.212 Bloss, M. E. "And in Hindsight . . . The Past Ten Years of Union Listing." *SerL* 10 (1985–1986): 141–48.

13.213 Boll, J. J. "Professional Literature on Cataloging—Then and Now." *LRTS* 29 (1985): 226–38.

13.214 Brown, R. C. "Online Computer Library Center (OCLC)." *ELIS* 38 (1985): 294–312.

13.215 Carpenter, M., and Svenonius, E., eds. *Foundations of Cataloging: A Sourcebook.* Littleton, Colo.: Libraries Unlimited, 1985.

13.216 Chan, L. M., Richmond, P. A., and Svenonius, E. *Theory of Subject Analysis: A Sourcebook.* Littleton, Colo.: Libraries Unlimited, 1985.

13.217 Cole, J. E., and Madison, O. M. A. "A Decade of Serials Cataloging." *SerL* 10 (1985–1986): 103–16.

13.218 Comaromi, J. P., and Satija, M. P. "History of the Indianization of the Dewey Decimal Classification." *Libri* 35 (1985): 1–20.

13.219 Cornog, M. "Out of the Shoebox and into the Computer: Serials Indexing 1975–1985." *SerL* 10 (1985–1986): 161–68.

13.220 Florance, V. "Access to U.S. Government Periodicals in Health Sciences Libraries: An Overview." *SerL* 10 (1985–1986): 215–23.

13.221 Gorman, M. "The Online Catalogue at the University of Illinois at Urbana-Champaign: A History and Overview." *Information Technology and Libraries* 4 (1985): 308–11.

13.222 Lanier, D., and Vogt, N. "The Serials Department, 1975–1985." *SerL* 10 (1985–1986): 5–11.

13.223 McIver, C. R. "The AACRs and Serials Cataloging." *SerL* 10 (1985–1986): 117–27.

13.224 Maruyama, L. S. "What Has Technology Done for Us Lately?" *SerL* 10 (1985–1986): 65–89.

13.225 Rohrback, P. T. *FIND: Automation at the Library of Congress, the First Twenty-Five Years.* Washington, D.C.: Government Printing Office, 1985.

13.226 Sadowski, F. E. "Serials Cataloging Developments, 1975–1985: A Personal View of Some Highlights." *SerL* 10 (1985–1986): 133–40.

13.227 Smith, D. A. "Processing Services 1905: Putting the Library's House in Order and the Country's Cataloging in Gear." *LRTS* 29 (1985): 248–63.

13.228 McKinley, M. M. "The Exchange Program at UCLA: 1932 through 1986." *Serials Review* 12 (1986): 75–80.

13.229 Walden, B. " *LAPT* at Ten." *Library Acquisitions: Practice and Theory* 10 (1986): 3–7.

Public Services

13.230 Short, O. C. "Development of the Municipal Reference Service in the Bureau of the Census." *SL* 28 (1937): 364–65.

13.231 Thompson, M. C. "History of the Reference Department of the University of Illinois Library." Master's thesis, University of Illinois, 1942.

13.232 Kaplan, L. "Early History of Reference Service in the United States." *LibR* 83 (1947): 286–90.

13.233 Dunn, A. "The Nature and Functions of Readers' Advisory Service as Revealed by a Survey of the Literature of the Field from 1935–1950." Master's thesis, Western Reserve University, 1950.

13.234 Kaplan, L. *The Growth of Reference Service in the United States from 1876 to 1891.* Chicago: Association of College and Research Libraries, 1952.

13.235 Rothstein, S. "The Development of the Concept of Reference Service in American Libraries, 1850–1900." *LQ* 23 (1953): 1–15.

13.236 McBride, M. "Reference Service for Congress before 1915." Master's thesis, Drexel Institute of Technology, 1955.

13.237 Rothstein, S. *The Development of Reference Services through Academic Traditions, Public Library Practice and Special*

Librarianship. Chicago: American Library Association, 1955.

13.238 Adams, E. M. "A Study of Reference Librarianship in the American College: 1876–1955." Master's thesis, East Texas State Teachers College, 1956.

13.239 Phelps, R. B. "Reference Services in Public Libraries: The Last Quarter Century." *WLB* 32 (1957): 281–85.

13.240 Kaplan, L. "Reference Services in University and Special Libraries Since 1900." *CRL* 19 (1958): 217–20.

13.241 Perrins, B. C. "Business and Industrial Reference Service by Academic Libraries, 1900–1965." Master's thesis, Southern Connecticut State College, 1967.

13.242 Bray, R. S. "Blind and Physically Handicapped, Library Service." *ELIS* 2 (1969): 624–37.

13.243 Gambee, B. L., and Gambee, R. R. "Reference Services and Technology." In *A Century of Service: Librarianship in the United States and Canada,* edited by S. L. Jackson, E. B. Herling, and E. J. Josey. Chicago: American Library Association, 1976. Pp. 169–91.

13.244 Walsh, R. R. "New England Deposit Library." *ELIS* 19 (1976): 317–22.

13.245 Rothstein, S. "Across the Desk: 100 Years of Reference Encounters." *Canadian Library Journal* 34 (1977): 391–93.

13.246 Galvin, T. J. "Reference Services and Libraries." *ELIS* 25 (1978): 210–26.

13.247 Nasri, W. Z. "Reprography." *ELIS* 25 (1978): 230–39.

13.248 Wagers, R. "American Reference Theory and the Information Dogma." *JLH* 13 (1978): 265–81.

13.249 Stevenson, G. *Rudolph Focke and the Theory of the Classified Catalog.* Urbana: University of Illinois Graduate School of Library Science, Occasional Paper no. 145, 1980.

13.250 Bunge, C. A. "Interpersonal Dimensions of the Reference Interview: A Historical Review of the Literature." *DLQ* 20 (1984): 4–23.

13.251 Farrington, J. W. "The Use of Microforms in Libraries: Concerns of the Last Ten Years." *SerL* 10 (1985–1986): 195–99.

13.252 Harrington, W. G. "A Brief History of Computer-Assisted Legal Research." *LLJ* 77 (1985): 543–56.

13.253 Stieg, M. F. "Fee vs. Free in Historical Perspective." *The Reference Librarian* 12 (1985): 93–103.

13.254 Neufeld, M. L., and Cornog, M. "Database History: From Dinosaurs to Compact Discs." *JASIS* 37 (1986): 183–90.

14.

Women in Librarianship

The literature dealing with the historical role of women in librarianship has developed considerably since the mid–1970s, justifying a separate chapter. The difficulties inherent in preparing a chapter of this nature suggest that not every reader will be pleased with the necessary choices.

This chapter brings together materials that address issues pertaining to women in the historical development of the profession, more precisely, publications that treat women's issues consciously as women's issues rather than merely the work of women in various library and library-related tasks. The latter are necessarily scattered throughout the bibliography. For example, C. S. Cummings's *Biographical-Bibliographical Directory of Women Librarians* (1976, **1.101**) along with other bibliographic contributions (1975, **1.95** ; 1979, **1.126**) appears in Chapter 1, "Historiography and Sources," with other reference items. J. C. Spruill (1935, **3.33**) and R. D. Lillard (1944, **3.263**) have published studies that are listed in Chapter 3, "Private Libraries and Reading Tastes." Other treatments of women's club libraries appear in Chapter 5, "Public Libraries," including work by Mrs. A. F. Bixby (1876, **5.555**), P. N. Hamner (1954, **5.559**), M. J. Hoesch (1955, **5.560**), and M. R. Burrell (1964, **5.363**). Citations to the lives of individual women are found in Chapter 15, "Biographies of Individual Librarians and Library Benefactors."

The paucity of citations before 1960 will surprise some and confirm the suspicions of others. After World War I, R. R. Bowker himself prepared an early series of brief articles (1920, **14.1**) that surveyed the role of women in the library profession and drew a mixed response from readers. A similar article by R. L. Power on women in special libraries complements the Bowker contribution (1920, **14.2**). Aside from a limited historical flashback at the time of the profession's fiftieth anniversary (1926, **14.3**), little of specifically historical treatment appeared until the groundbreaking thesis of Sharon Wells on "Feminization of the American Library Profession, 1876–1923" (1967, **14.5**), nearly fifty years later. This study was later extended by Margaret Ann Corwin to state and local library associations (1974, **14.11**).

275

The 1970s saw a burst of publication and were marked by three volumes that set the agenda for future research. *Women in the Library Profession* (1971, **14.10**) gave some historical treatment to various issues as five distinguished alumnae of the University of Michigan library school reflected on the past in papers commemorating the centennial of that university's first female student. There was some history, as well, in the 1973 Rutgers University-sponsored *Women in Librarianship: Melvil's Rib Symposium* (1975, **14.14**). The major work of the decade was the landmark anthology *The Role of Women in Librarianship, 1876–1976: The Entry, Advancement, and Struggle for Equalization in One Profession,* edited by Kathleen Weibel and Kathleen Heim (1979, **14.32**). Not only were the selected pieces arranged into five chronological divisions that sought to interpret the women's movement in the profession, but the extensive annotated bibliography of literature that touched on the subject, complete with indexes, provided a foundation for ongoing research efforts.

Original research had, in fact, already begun to flourish. Dee Garrison raised provocative ideas in "The Tender Technicians: The Feminization of Public Librarianship, 1876–1905" (1973, **5.146**), placed in context in Chapter 5, "Public Libraries," and her bicentennial survey (1976, **14.18**). Laurel A. Grotzinger emerged as a consistent researcher in the field (1978, **14.28**; 1978, **14.29**), while Anita Schiller (1974, **14.12**) and Jody Newmyer (1976, **14.21**) dealt with the sociological aspects of women's issues. Finally, dissertations dealing with specific topics began to appear, as exemplified by the work of Lelia Rhodes on black women librarians (listed and discussed in Chapter 2, "General Studies"; 1975, **2.192**) and of Brenda Branyan on women school librarians (1981, **14.34**).

A new level of scholarly activity became a reality in the 1980s. Mary Niles Maack's analysis of research needs (1982, **14.36**) and Mary Biggs's inquiry into "The Woman Question" (1982, **14.35**) opened new avenues for study. A later paper of Maack's dealt further with the use of comparative methodology (1985, **14.46**). In 1983 two publications appeared that included major papers by three library historians who have contributed regularly to this field. *The Status of Women in Librarianship: Historical, Sociological, and Economic Issues,* edited by Kathleen M. Heim (1983, **14.42**), included papers by Suzanne Hildenbrand on women in the history of the public library movement from 1876–1920 (**14.43**), by Barbara Elizabeth Brand on "Sex-Typing in Education for Librarianship, 1870–1920" (**14.38**), and Laurel A. Grotzinger on "Biographical Research on Women Librarians: Its Paucity, Perils, and Pleasures" (**14.40**). The same year a special issue of the *Journal of Library History* produced the papers of a 1982 program session of the American Library Association's Library History Round Table devoted to "Women in Library History: Liberating Our Past," chaired by Mary Niles Maack. This program and issue included articles by Grotzinger (1983, **14.41**), Hildenbrand (1983, **14.44**), and Brand (1983, **14.37**)—some of which built on the volume mentioned above. Phyllis Dain assessed the status of women's studies in American library history in a learned essay responding to the other papers (1983, **14.39**).

Library History Seminar VII (1985) featured a session on "Women in Professional Leadership: The American South," which included a general paper by Anne Firor Scott (1986, **14.52**) and a study of "Atlanta's Female Librarians, 1883–1915" (1986, **14.49**) by James V. Carmichael, Jr. Others have discovered the fruitful field of state and local women's studies, such as David Taylor, who studied Helena, Arkansas (1985, **14.47**), and Alice Rhoades, who profiled six Texas women who were library pioneers (1986, **14.50**). A final example of recent research that breaks down unexamined stereotypes is the article by Joanne Passet Bailey (1986, **14.48**) demythologizing the long-accepted imagined role of the male librarian-professor in midwestern colleges during the last quarter of the nineteenth century. Other studies of this kind remain to be done.

1920–1949

14.1 Bowker, R. R. "Women in the Library Profession." *LJ* 45 (1920): 545–49, 587–92, 635–40.

14.2 Power, R. L. "Women in Special Libraries." *LJ* 45 (1920): 691–95.

14.3 Hanaford, P. "Women Librarians Fifty Years Ago." *Libraries* 31 (1926): 270–71.

1950–1971

14.4 Elliot, L. R. "Salute to the Vanguard." *TLJ* 36 (1960): 7–10.

14.5 Wells, S. B. "The Feminization of the American Library Profession, 1876 to 1923." Master's thesis, University of Chicago, 1967.

14.6 Boaz, M. "And There Were Giantesses in Library Education." In *Women in the Library Profession: Leadership Roles and Contributions*, edited by University of Michigan School of Library Science Alumnus in Residence 1971. Ann Arbor: University of Michigan School of Library Science, 1971. Pp. 1–10.

14.7 Field, F. B. "Technical Services and Women." In *Women in the Library Profession: Leadership Roles and Contributions*, edited by University of Michigan School of Library Science Alumnus in Residence 1971. Ann Arbor: University of Michigan School of Library Science, 1971. Pp. 11–15.

14.8 Lynch, M. J. "Women in Reference Service." In *Women in the Library Profession: Leadership Roles and Contributions*, edited by University of Michigan School of Library Science Alumnus in Residence 1971. Ann Arbor: University of Michigan School of Library Science, 1971. Pp. 20–23.

14.9 Murdoch, F. "Standard Bearers for School Libraries." In *Women in the Library Profession: Leadership Roles and Contributions*, edited by University of Michigan School of Library Science Alumnus in Residence 1971. Ann Arbor: University of Michigan School of Library Science, 1971. Pp. 24–27.

14.10 *Women in the Library Profession: Leadership Roles and Contributions.* Ann Arbor: University of Michigan School of Library Science, 1971.

1972–1986

14.11 Corwin, M. A. "An Investigation of Female Leadership in State Library Organizations and Local Library Associations, 1876–1923." *LQ* 44 (1974): 133–44.

14.12 Schiller, A. R. "Women in Librarianship." *AdLib* 4 (1974): 103–47.

14.13 Tierney, C. M. "Women in American Librarianship: An Annotated Bibliography of Articles in Library Periodicals, 1920–1973." Research Paper, Kent State University, 1974.

14.14 Myers, M., and Scarborough, M., eds. *Women in Librarianship: Melvil's Rib Symposium.* New Brunswick: Rutgers University Graduate School of Library Service, 1975.

14.15 Schiller, A. R. "Sex and Library Careers." In *Women in Librarianship: Melvil's Rib Symposium*, edited by M. Myers and M. Scarborough. New Brunswick: Rutgers University Graduate School of Library Service, Bureau of Library and Information Science Research, 1975. Pp. 11–20.

14.16 Wallace, S. L. "Editor's Note [On the Role of Women in Libraries]." *QJLC* 32 (1975): 257–59, 412.

14.17 Burgh, A. E., and Beede, B. R. "American Librarianship." *Signs: Journal of Women in Culture and Society* 1 (1976): 943–55.

14.18 Garrison, D. "Women in Librarianship." In *A Century of Service: Librarianship in the United States and Canada*, edited by S. L. Jackson, E. B. Herling, and E. J. Josey. Chicago: American Library Association, 1976. Pp. 146–68.

14.19 Gerhardt, L. N. "Needed: A Monumental Checkup." *SchLJ* 22 (1976): 5.

14.20 Lemke, A. B. "Access, Barriers, Change: The ABC's of Women in Libraries." *SchLJ* 22 (1976): 17–19.

278

14.21 Newmyer, J. "The Image Problem of the Librarian: Femininity and Social Control." *JLH* 11 (1976): 44–67.

14.22 Gerhardt, L. N. "Before and Since—Angie." *SchLJ* 23 (1977): 6–8.

14.23 McCauley, E. B. "A Half Century before Dewey; Some Early Women Librarians in New England." *WLB* 51 (1977): 648–55.

14.24 Milden, J. W. "Women, Public Libraries, and Library Unions." *JLH* 12 (1977): 150–58.

14.25 Brand, B. E. "The Influence of Higher Education on Sex-Typing in Three Professions, 1870–1920: Librarianship, Social Work, and Public Health." Doctoral dissertation, University of Washington, 1978.

14.26 Detlefsen, E. G. "[Dewey's 'Splendid Women' and Their Impact on Library Education] Comment." In *Milestones to the Present: Papers from Library History Seminar V*, edited by H. Goldstein. Syracuse, N.Y.: Gaylord Professional Publications, 1978. Pp. 152–54.

14.27 Foner, P. S. "A Pioneer Proposal for a Women's Library." *JLH* 13 (1978): 157–59.

14.28 Grotzinger, L. A. "Dewey's 'Splendid Women' and Their Impact on Library Education." In *Milestones to the Present: Papers from Library History Seminar V*, edited by H. Goldstein. Syracuse, N.Y.: Gaylord Professional Publications, 1978. Pp. 125–52.

14.29 Grotzinger, L. A. "Women Who 'Spoke for Themselves.'" *CRL* 39 (1978): 175–90.

14.30 McMullen, H. "A Note on Early American Libraries for Women." *JLH* 13 (1978): 464–65.

14.31 Coleman, G. P. "Women's Rights and the Centralization of Libraries: A Note Concerning Collection Development." *JLH* 14 (1979): 73–76.

14.32 Weibel, K., and Heim, K. M., eds. *The Role of Women in Librarianship, 1876–1976: The Entry, Advancement, and Struggle for Equalization in One Profession*. Phoenix, Ariz.: Oryx Press, 1979.

14.33 Lundy, K. R. *Women View Librarianship: Nine Perspectives*. Chicago: American Library Association, 1980.

14.34 Branyan, B. M. *Outstanding Women Who Promoted the Concept of the Unified School Library and Audiovisual Programs, 1950 through 1975*. Fayetteville, Ark.: Hi Willow Research and Publishing, 1981.

14.35 Biggs, M. "Libraries and the 'Woman Question': An Inquiry into Conservatism." *JLH* 17 (1982): 409–28.

14.36 Maack, M. N. "Toward a History of Women in Librarianship: A Critical Analysis with Suggestions for Further Research." *JLH* 17 (1982): 164–85.

14.37 Brand, B. E. "Librarianship and Other Female-Intensive Professions." *JLH* 18 (1983): 391–406.

14.38 Brand, B. E. "Sex-Typing in Education for Librarianship, 1870–1920." In *The Status of Women in Librarianship: Historical, Sociological, and Economic Issues*, edited by K. M. Heim. New York: Neal-Schuman, 1983. Pp. 29–49.

14.39 Dain, P. "Women's Studies in American Library History: Some Critical Reflections." *JLH* 18 (1983): 450–63.

14.40 Grotzinger, L. A. "Biographical Research on Women Librarians: Its Paucity, Perils, and Pleasures." In *The Status of Women in Librarianship: Historical, Sociological, and Economic Issues*, edited by K. M. Heim. New York: Neal-Schuman, 1983. Pp. 139–90.

14.41 Grotzinger, L. A. "Biographical Research: Recognition Denied." *JLH* 18 (1983): 372–81.

14.42 Heim, K. M., ed. *The Status of Women in Librarianship: Historical, Sociological, and Economic Issues*. New York: Neal-Schuman, 1983.

14.43 Hildenbrand, S. "Revision versus Reality: Women in the History of the Public

Library Movement, 1876–1920." In *The Status of Women in Librarianship: Historical, Sociological, and Economic Issues,* edited by K. M. Heim. New York: Neal-Schuman, 1983. Pp. 7–27.

14.44 Hildenbrand, S. "Some Theoretical Considerations on Women in Library History." *JLH* 18 (1983): 382–90.

14.45 Fenster, V. R. *Out of the Stacks: Notable Wisconsin Women Librarians.* Madison, Wis.: Wisconsin Women Library Workers, 1985.

14.46 Maack, M. N. "Comparative Methodology as a Means for Assessing the Impact of Feminization and Professionalization on Librarianship." *International Library Review* 17 (1985): 5–16.

14.47 Taylor, D. "Ladies of the Club: An Arkansas Story." *WLB* 59 (1985): 324–27.

14.48 Bailey, J. P. "The Rule Rather Than the Exception': Midwest Women as Academic Librarians, 1875–1900." *JLH* 21 (1986): 673–92.

14.49 Carmichael, J. V. "Atlanta's Female Librarians, 1883–1915." *JLH* 21 (1986): 376–99.

14.50 Rhoades, A. J. "Early Women Librarians in Texas." *TL* 47 (1986): 46–53.

14.51 Rossiter, M. W. "Women and the History of Scientific Communication." *JLH* 21 (1986): 39–59.

14.52 Scott, A. F. "Women and Libraries." *JLH* 21 (1986): 400–405.

15.

Biographies of Individual Librarians and Library Benefactors

Well-researched scholarly writing has come to characterize biographical studies of librarians, but the earliest publications consisted of less useful works—often presented on the occasion of the subject's retirement or death. Examples of this genre include tributes to William Frederick Poole by the Newberry Library (1895, **15.1390**), John Shaw Billings by the New York Public Library (1915, **15.124**), and Herbert Putnam by the Library of Congress (1956, **15.1442**).

Following World War I the American Library Association, approaching its fiftieth anniversary, launched the American Library Pioneer Series which included seven brief studies: Harry M. Lydenberg on John Shaw Billings (1924, **15.128**), R. K. Shaw on Samuel Swett Green (1926, **15.761**), W. P. Cutter on Charles Ammi Cutter (1931, **15.438**), Linda A. Eastman on William Howard Brett (1940, **15.247**), Chalmers Hadley on John Cotton Dana (1943, **15.454**), Fremont Rider on Melvil Dewey (1944, **15.493**), and Joseph A. Boromé on Charles Coffin Jewett (1951, **15.961**). Several other volumes were planned, but they never materialized, and the series was completed by Emily M. Danton's collection of eighteen sketches issued as *Pioneering Leaders in Librarianship* (1953, **2.56**; listed in Chapter 2, "General Studies").

Although librarians have produced relatively few autobiographies, the genre has gained considerable momentum in recent years. Some of the earliest date from the turn of the century, having appeared as journal articles or commemorative pamphlets. One of the more engaging is *A Life with Men and Books* (1939, **15.206**) by Arthur E. Bostwick, the St. Louis Public Librarian; his successor, Charles H. Compton, followed with *Memories of a Librarian* (1954,

281

15.378). The memoirs of Sydney B. Mitchell were published posthumously in 1960 (**15.1235**). Lawrence Clark Powell and Louis Shores, important statesmen for the profession, recounted their experiences in *Fortune and Friendship: An Autobiography* (1968, **15.1414**) and *Quiet World: A Librarian's Crusade for Destiny* (1975, **15.1632**) respectively. These were followed, soon thereafter, by Gordon McShean's *Running a Message Parlor: A Librarian's Medium Rare Memoir about Censorship* (1977, **15.1165**) and Keyes D. Metcalf's *Random Recollections of an Anachronism, or Seventy-Five Years of Library Work* (1980, **15.1215**). Metcalf's sequel, *My Harvard Library Years, 1937–1955*, nearing completion at the time of his death, was edited by Edwin E. Williams (Cambridge, Mass.: Harvard College Library, 1988). Finally, Donald C. Gallup published *Pigeons on the Granite: Memories of a Yale Librarian* (New Haven, Conn.: Beinecke Rare Book & Manuscript Library, 1988).

A major development in the 1980s is the effort of Scarecrow Press to encourage prominent librarians and library educators to write autobiographies. Although the results are somewhat uneven in terms of literary style and candor of presentation, the program has considerable merit, and its potential for raising the historical consciousness of the profession should be evident. Scarecrow autobiographies issued through 1986 include Ralph E. Ellsworth's *Ellsworth on Ellsworth* (1980, **15.597**), Guy R. Lyle's *Beyond My Expectation: A Personal Chronicle* (1981, **15.1125**), William B. Ready's *Files on Parade: A Memoir* (1982, **15.1474**), Robert B. Downs's *Perspectives on the Past: An Autobiography* (1984, **15.556**), Johanna Tallman's *Check Out a Librarian* (1985, **15.1736**), and Lawrence Clark Powell's sequel, *Life Goes On: Twenty More Years of Fortune and Friendship* (1986, **15.1420**). Recently published or still in preparation are the memoirs of Martha Boaz, Mary Virginia Gaver, David Gerard, and Annie McPheeters.

Full-length, thoroughly documented scholarly biographies did not appear in comparative abundance until the 1960s. (Most of them originated as doctoral dissertations and a large percentage have not been issued by commercial publishers). Among the earliest of the full-length books was E. M. Fleming's study of R. R. Bowker (1952, **15.224**). A decade later Martha Boaz published her study of Althea Warren (1961, **15.1845**). These were soon followed by two outstanding works that substantially elevated the scholarly attributes of biographies about important librarians: Edward G. Holley's interpretation of Charles Evans (1963, **15.607**) and William L. Williamson's book on William Frederick Poole (1963, **15.1400**). Other major works appeared in the 1960s, including those by Laurel A. Grotzinger on Katharine Lucinda Sharp (1966, **15.1594**) and Maurice F. Tauber on Louis Round Wilson (1967, **15.1924**).

In the 1970s a flurry of interest produced several new scholarly biographies, accelerating the pace even faster than in the previous decade. Charles H. Baumann published his study of Angus Snead Macdonald (1972, **15.1142**), and J. D. Rhodehamel and R. F. Wood produced a book on Ina Coolbrith (1973, **15.385**). These were followed by Peggy Sullivan on Carl H. Milam (1976, **15.1228**), William Bentinck-Smith on Archibald Cary Coolidge (1976,

15.391), and Charles B. Sanford on the bibliophilic habits of Thomas Jefferson (1977, **15.950**).

The movement for more scholarly biographies was supported strongly by Libraries Unlimited, a commercial library science publisher that established the Heritage of Librarianship Series under the editorial guidance of Michael H. Harris. Each title in the series begins with an analytical essay evaluating the subject's contribution to librarianship; this extended interpretation is followed by reprints of the subject's more important articles and reports as well as a bibliography of publications by and about the subject. The series began in 1975 with works by Michael H. Harris on Charles Coffin Jewett (**15.963**) and John Y. Cole on Ainsworth Rand Spofford (**15.1695**). Three more were issued before the series ended—Francis L. Miksa on Charles Ammi Cutter (1977, **15.445**), Sarah K. Vann on Melvil Dewey (1978, **15.518**), and Wayne Cutler and Michael Harris on Justin Winsor (1980, **15.1968**). It is perhaps symbolic that the first major biography of the 1980s, the Cutler-Harris study of Winsor, was the last of a dying series. Significantly, the publishing output of the 1980s has resulted in only two substantial biographies of librarians. Marion Casey produced a thoroughly researched profile of Charles McCarthy (1981, **15.1133**), and Robert F. Byrnes wrote a biography of the professional life of Archibald Cary Coolidge, one chapter of which discusses the latter's library administrative work at Harvard (1982, **15.393**).

Much historical writing has emanated from graduate-level research. Numerous master's theses on librarians, benefactors, and library-related individuals offer the sole source of retrospective interpretations of their subjects, frequently figures of local, state, or regional importance. Lamentably, a number of scholarly biographies remain as dissertations, having yet to be edited for formal publication. The list is long enough to demonstrate continued interest in historical-biographical writing, the recent minimal output of publishers notwithstanding. Subjects treated are Justin Winsor by Joseph A. Boromé (1950, **15.1963**), Ernest Cushing Richardson by Lewis C. Branscomb (1954, **15.1483**), Raymond Cazallis Davis by John C. Abbott (1957, **15.472**), Malcolm Glenn Wyer by Paul M. Parham (1964, **15.1999**), William Warner Bishop by Claud G. Sparks (1967, **15.168**), Charles C. Williamson by Paul A. Winckler (1968, **15.1897**), J. C. M. Hanson by Edith Scott (1970, **15.820**), Abraham Cassel by Marlin L. Heckman (1971, **15.326**), George Ticknor by Harold M. Turner (1972, **15.1762**), Isadore Gilbert Mudge by John N. Waddell (1973, **15.1282**), Mary Josephine Booth by Richard W. Lawson (1975, **15.202**), Arthur A. Schomburg by Elinor D. Sinnette (1977, **15.1574**), the educational ideas of Melvil Dewey by Michael M. Lee (1979, **15.519**), John Griswold White by M. B. Y. Reece (1979, **15.1879**), Joseph Sabin by Gary D. Jensen (1980, **15.1551**), Mildred L. Batchelder by Dorothy J. Anderson (1981, **15.84**), Augusta Baker by Maxine M. Merriman (1983, **15.64**), and Azariah Smith Root by John Mark Tucker (1983, **15.1532**).

Types of literature other than book-length works indicate an abiding interest in life-writing. For the most part, these consist of interpretive articles on influential figures published in journals, in *festschriften,* and in other collected works. Two collections of special note appeared in 1983: Gordon Stevenson and Judith Kramer-Greene edited *Melvil Dewey: The Man and the Classification,* papers presented at a symposium sponsored by Forest Press, which includes biographical articles (1983 **15.525**); and Wayne A. Wiegand edited *Leaders in American Academic Librarianship, 1925–1975* (1983 **6.131**, listed in Chapter 6, "Academic Libraries"). The latter volume represents a departure from the tendency of academic library history to attract less scholarly attention than public library history.

Articles appearing in state, regional, and national library science and historical journals are too numerous to mention, the exceptions being Robert S. Martin's "Maurice F. Tauber's *Louis Round Wilson:* An Analysis of a Collaboration," which explains how one biography was written and edited (1984, **15.1932**) and Edwin S. Gleaves's evaluation of the genre of library science *festschriften* in "A Watch and Chain and a Jeweled Sword: The *Festschrift* and Librarianship" (1985, **2.345**; listed in Chapter 2, "General Studies").

As in other areas of historical scholarship, women and blacks are under-represented. Of the sixty-four previously mentioned subjects in this essay, eleven were females. For additional sources on the role of women in librarianship, consult Chapter 14, "Women in Librarianship." The most significant contribution to black biography is, in fact, a collection (almost entirely) of autobiographical essays edited by E. J. Josey, *The Black Librarian in America* (1970, **2.135**; listed and discussed in Chapter 2, "General Studies"). Master's theses had already been written on Thomas Fountain Blue (1955, **15.179**) and Susan Dart Butler (1959, **15.298**) when a collective biography was completed, Lelia G. Rhodes's study of the careers of fifteen black female librarians (1975, **2.192**; listed and discussed in Chapter 2, "General Studies"). Recent book-length studies include the aforementioned dissertations of Sinnette on Arthur Schomburg and Merriman on Augusta Baker. The University of Michigan School of Library Science published the reminiscences of Virginia Lacy Jones (1979, **15.980**); Jones was one of two blacks, along with Annette L. Phinazee, represented in *Women View Librarianship: Nine Perspectives* (1980, **14.33**; listed in Chapter 14, "Women in Librarianship"). The same year, Phinazee edited *The Black Librarian in the Southeast: Reminiscences, Activities, Challenges,* a collection of brief but insightful essays that contain a number of possibilities for future inquiry (1980, **2.287**; listed in Chapter 2, "General Studies").

Library historians have traditionally turned to major biographical reference sources as departure points for research. Publications such as the *National Cyclopedia of American Biography, Dictionary of American Biography (DAB), Encyclopedia of Library and Information Science,* and *Notable American Women* have provided both background information and bibliographical references. Reference librarians and researchers used these tools in the absence of a biographical source specifically designed for the library community. One of the earliest publications devoted to biographies of librarians was Alfred C. Potter and Charles K. Bolton's *The Librarians of Harvard College 1667–1877* consisting of sketches of sixty individuals (1897, **6.318**; listed in Chapter 6, "Academic Libraries"). "A Library Hall of Fame" (*LJ* 76 [March 15,1951]: 466–72), published in conjunction with the seventy-fifth anniversary of the American Library Association, served as a gentle reminder of who the nation's library pioneers had been, but it could hardly qualify as a reference work.

Thus, it was with considerable excitement that in 1978 the library community welcomed the *Dictionary of American Library Biography* (*DALB*, 1978, **1.125**; listed and discussed in Chapter 1, "Historiography and Sources") in which retrospective biography achieved for the profession a new level of intellectual maturity. Entries from this collection of essays appear separately under their respective subjects. The *DALB* was joined three years later by Rudolph Engelbarts's *Librarian Authors* (1981, **2.301**), a work that consists principally of biographical entries of 108 subjects, seventy-three of whom were from the United States. Like the *DALB*, entries from Engelbarts are listed in this chapter.

The *DALB* was admirably complemented in 1986 by Donald C. Dickinson's *Dictionary of American Book Collectors* (*DABC*) containing 359 biographical entries (1986, **2.359**; listed in Chapter 2, "General Studies"). The value of this work for library history lies in the fact that numerous important library acquisitions and donations began with the reading interests of devoted collectors. Together, the *DALB* and the *DABC* serve as reliable reference tools for students and scholars interested in the contributions of distinguished librarians, library educators, association officers, publishers, book collectors, and library benefactors. A supplement to the *DALB*, edited by Wayne A. Wiegand, was scheduled for publication by Libraries Unlimited in 1989.

While the present chapter attempts to provide a comprehensive list of biographies of librarians, equal coverage of library benefactors remains beyond the scope of this compilation. Many articles and books have been identified and are included, but the sources remain far too widely scattered to attempt more than introductory coverage for important benefactors. However, major figures who supported library growth and development such as George Ticknor, Andrew Carnegie, and many others are typically represented at least by a *Dictionary of American Biography* (*DAB*) entry and a standard book-length biography. Philanthropists and private collectors who have contributed large sums of money or significant collections number, perhaps, in the hundreds. Readers interested in biographical studies of these individuals should consult the numerous in-house newsletters, local papers, institutional journals, and other publications that describe the services and collections of individual libraries and library systems.

Abbot, Ezra

15.1 Bond, B. W. "Abbot, Ezra (Apr. 28, 1819–Mar. 21, 1884)." *DAB* 1 (1928): 10–11.

15.2 Estabrook, L. "Abbot, Ezra (1819–1884)." *DALB*: 1978 1–2.

Adams, Charles Kendall

15.3 Towne, J. E. "Charles Kendall Adams and the First University Library Building (Ann Arbor) (1881–1883)." *Michigan History Magazine* 37 (June 1953): 129–44.

Adams, Herbert Baxter

15.4 Cunningham, R. "Historian among the Librarians: Herbert Baxter Adams and Modern Librarianship." *JLH* 21 (1986): 704–22.

Adams, Joseph Quincy

15.5 McManaway, J. G., Dawson, G. E., and Willoughby, E. E. *Joseph Quincy Adams Memorial Studies.* Washington, D.C.: Folger Shakespeare Library, 1948.

Adams, Randolph Greenfield

15.6 "Librarian Authors: Randolph Greenfield Adams." *LJ* 58 (1933): 255.

15.7 Adams, R. G. "The Credo of the Late Director of the Wm. L. Clements Library, as Historian, Librarian and Bibliophile." *MAQR* 57 (1951): 310–17.

15.8 Storm, C. "Randolph Greenfield Adams: 1892–1951." *Antiquarian Bookman* 7 (1951): 1097–98.

15.9 Peckham, H. "Introductory Memoir." In *A Bibliography of Randolph G. Adams,* edited by Clements Library Association. Ann Arbor, Mich.: William L. Clements Library, 1962. Pp. 1–9.

15.10 Thompson, S. O. "Adams, Randolph Greenfield (Nov. 7, 1892–Jan. 4, 1951)." *DAB* Suppl. 5 (1977): 8–10.

15.11 Kaser, D. "Adams, Randolph Greenfield (1892–1951)." *DALB*: 1978 2–3.

15.12 "Adams, Randolph G." In *Librarian Authors: A Biobibliography,* by R. Engelbarts. Jefferson, N.C.: McFarland, 1981. Pp. 118–20.

Adams, Scott

15.13 Rogers, F. B. "Scott Adams." *BMLA* 55 (1967): 343–44.

15.14 Garfield, E. "Scott Adams and Medical Bibliography in an Age of Discontinuity—A Tribute to a Visionary Leader in the Field of Medical Information." *Current Contents* 26 (1983): 5–11.

15.15 Rogers, F. B. "Scott Adams, 1909–1982." *BMLA* 71 (1983): 245–48.

15.16 Rogers, F. B. "Adams, Scott." *ELIS* 38 (1985): 1–7.

Adkinson, Burton Wilbur

15.17 "Adkinson, Burton W(ilbur)." *CB* (1959): 1–3.

Adler, Cyrus

15.18 Goodwin, J. "Adler, Cyrus (1863–1940)." *DALB*: 1978 3–5.

Ahern, Mary Eileen

15.19 "Mary Eileen Ahern." *BB* 12 (1925): 125.

15.20 MacPherson, H. D. "Ahern, Mary Eileen (Oct. 1, 1860–May 22, 1938)." *NAW* 1 (1971): 25–26.

15.21 Dale, D. C. "Ahern, Mary Eileen (1860–1938)." *DALB*: 1978 5–7.

15.22 Mulac, C. M. " 'Librarian Militant': Mary Eileen Ahern and *Public Libraries*." Master's thesis, University of Chicago, 1978.

15.23 "Ahern, Mary Eileen." In *Librarian Authors: A Biobibliography*, by R. Engelbarts. Jefferson, N.C.: McFarland, 1981. Pp. 111–12.

15.24 Fain, E. "Ahern, Mary Eileen (1860–1938)." *ALAWE2*: 1986 36.

Akers, Susan Grey

15.25 Fair, E. M. "Susan Grey Akers." *BB* 22 (1958): 145–46.

Allen, Winnie

15.26 McLean, M. D. "A Tribute to Miss Winnie Allen, Founder of the Texas Historical Survey Committee." In *Papers Concerning Robertson's Colony in Texas*, edited by M. D. McLean. Fort Worth, Tex.: Texas Christian University Press, 1976. Pp. 7–19.

Allibone, Samuel Austin

15.27 Paltsits, V. H. "Allibone, Samuel Austin (Apr. 17, 1816–Sept. 2, 1889)." *DAB* 1 (1928): 218.

Anderson, Edwin Hatfield

15.28 Lydenberg, H. M. "Edwin Hatfield Anderson." *BB* 15 (1935): 121.

15.29 Hopper, F. F. "Edwin Hatfield Anderson." *BNYPL* 51 (1947): 389–90.

15.30 Freehafer, E. G. "Anderson, Edwin Hatfield (Sept. 27, 1861–Apr. 29, 1947)." *DAB* Suppl. 4 (1974): 18–19.

15.31 Metcalf, K. D. "Six Influential Academic and Research Librarians." *CRL* 37 (1976): 332–45.

15.32 Dain, P. "Anderson, Edwin Hatfield (1861–1947)." *DALB*: 1978 7–11.

15.33 "Anderson, Edwin Hatfield." In *Librarian Authors: A Biobibliography*, by R. Engelbarts. Jefferson, N.C.: McFarland, 1981. Pp. 20–21.

Andrews, Clement Walker

15.34 "Clement Walker Andrews." *BB* 11 (1921): 97.

15.35 Bay, J. C. "Dr. Clement Walker Andrews, 1858–1930." *Libraries* 36 (1931): 1–5.

15.36 Brown, C. H. "Clement Walker Andrews, 1858–1930." In *Pioneering Leaders in Librarianship*, edited by E. M. Danton. Chicago: American Library Association, 1953. Pp. 1–12.

15.37 Dale, D. C. "Andrews, Clement Walker (1858–1930)." *DALB*: 1978 11–13.

15.38 "Andrews, Clement Walker." In *Librarian Authors: A Biobibliography*, by R. Engelbarts. Jefferson, N.C.: McFarland, 1981. Pp. 26–27.

Andrews, Siri

15.39 Fuller, M. "Siri Andrews of Henry Holt and Company." *PW* 153 (1948): 1805–08.

Andrews, Thelma

15.40 Dyke, J. "H.S.U. Librarian." *NNT* 25 (April 1949): 49.

Andrews, William Loring

15.41 Nikirk, R. "Two American Book Collectors of the Nineteenth Century: William Loring Andrews and Beverly Chew." In *Book Selling and Book Buying: Aspects of the Nineteenth Century British and North American Book Trade*, edited by R. G. Landon. Chicago: American Library Association, 1979. Pp. 99–108.

Arbuthnot, May Hill

15.42 Miller, M. "Arbuthnot, May Hill (1884–1969)." *DALB*: 1978 13–14.

15.43 Miller, M. "Arbuthnot, May Hill (1884–1969)." *ALAWE2*: 1986 51–52.

Armstrong, Andrew Joseph

15.44 Herring, J. "Armstrong, Andrew Joseph." In *Handbook of Waco and McLennan County*, edited by D. Kelley. Waco, Tex.: Texian Press, 1972. P. 9.

15.45 Edwards, M. R. "Armstrong, Andrew Joseph." *HT* 3 (1976): 38.

Ash, Lee

15.46 Annan, G. L. "Lee Ash." *BB* 24 (1964): 49–51.

Asheim, Lester E.

15.47 Carner, C. R. "Lester Asheim." *BB* 24 (1963): 25–27.

15.48 Carnovsky, R. F. "[Lester Asheim] Biographical Sketch." In *As Much to Learn as to Teach: Essays in Honor of Lester Asheim*, edited by J. M. Lee and B. A. Hamilton. Hamden, Conn.: Shoe String Press, 1979. Pp. 16–24.

15.49 Holley, E. G. "Asheim, Lester E. (1914–)." *ALAWE2*: 1986 79–80.

Askew, Sarah Byrd

15.50 Severns, H. "Sarah B. Askew, 1863–1942." In *Pioneering Leaders in Librarianship*, edited by E. M. Danton. Chicago: American Library Association, 1953. Pp. 13–21.

15.51 Niemeyer, M. J. "Askew, Sarah Byrd (Feb. 15, 1877–Oct. 20, 1942)." *NAW* 1 (1971): 61–62.

15.52 McDonough, R. H. "Askew, Sarah Byrd (1863–1942)." *DALB*: 1978 14–16.

15.53 "Askew, Sarah Byrd." In *Librarian Authors: A Biobibliography*, by R. Engelbarts. Jefferson, N.C.: McFarland, 1981. Pp. 28–30.

Asplund, Julia Brown

15.54 Honea, A. B. "Julia Brown Asplund: New Mexico Librarian, 1875–1958." Master's thesis, University of Texas, 1967.

Ayer, Edward Everett

15.55 Ghent, W. J. "Ayer, Edward Everett (Nov. 16, 1841–May 3, 1927)." *DAB* 1 (1928): 448–49.

Babb, James Tinkham

15.56 "Babb, James T(inkham)." *CB* (1955): 32–34.

15.57 Liebert, H. W. "James T. Babb." *BB* 23 (1963): 217–19.

Bailey, Louis J.

15.58 Smith, D. E. "Louis J. Bailey." *BB* 17 (1943): 201–03.

Baillie, Herbert

15.59 Faxon, F. W. "Herbert Baillie." *BB* 13 (1927): 41–42.

Baker, Augusta

15.60 Baker, A. "My Years as a Children's Librarian." In *The Black Librarian in America*, edited by E. J. Josey. Metuchen, N.J.: Scarecrow Press, 1970. Pp. 117–23.

15.61 Flynn, J. J. "Augusta Baker." In *Negroes of Achievement in Modern America*. New York: Dodd, Mead, 1970. Pp. 98–103.

15.62 "Augusta Baker." *LJ* 99 (1974): 859–61.

15.63 Izard, A. R. "Augusta Baker, Coordinator of Children's Services of the New

York Public Library, Retired on March 1, 1974." *TN* 30 (1974): 352–55.

15.64 Merriman, M. M. "Augusta Baker: Exponent of the Oral Art of Storytelling; Utilizing Video as a Medium." Doctoral dissertation, Texas Woman's University, 1983.

15.65 Shaw, S. G. "Baker, Augusta (1911–)." *ALAWE2*: 1986 97–98.

Baker, James Biscoe

15.66 Clemons, H. "James Biscoe Baker." In *The University of Virginia Library*. Charlottesville: University of Virginia Library, 1954. Pp. 112–15.

Baldwin, Clara Frances

15.67 Countryman, G. A. "Clara F[rances] Baldwin [1871–1951]." *MinnL* 16 (1951): 291–92.

Baldwin, Emma V.

15.68 Quigley, M. C. "Emma V. Baldwin." *BALA* 42 (1948): 307–09.

15.69 Manley, M. C. "Emma Baldwin." *LJ* 77 (1952): 487.

Ballard, James Francis

15.70 McDaniel, W. B. "James Francis Ballard, 1878–1955." *BMLA* 44 (1956): 92–97.

15.71 Spector, B. "James Francis Ballard, 1878–1955." *Journal of the History of Medicine & Allied Sciences* 11 (1956): 339–41.

Ballinger, William Pitt

15.72 "Ballinger, William Pitt." *HT* 1 (1952): 104.

15.73 King, C. R. "William Pitt Ballinger: Texas Bibliophile." *TL* 31 (1969): 154–61.

Bancroft, Frederic

15.74 Cooke, J. E. "Manchester Liberal and Philanthropist." In *Frederic Bancroft, Historian*. Norman: University of Oklahoma Press, 1957. Pp. 126–42.

15.75 Cooke, J. E. "Bancroft, Frederic (Oct. 30, 1860–Feb. 22, 1945)." *DAB* Suppl. 3 (1973): 31–32.

Barker, Eugene Campbell

15.76 Pool, W. C. *Eugene C. Barker: Historian*. Austin: Texas State Historical Association, 1971.

15.77 Pool, W. C. "Barker, Eugene Campbell." *HT* 3 (1976): 59–60.

Barker, Tommie Dora

15.78 Hinton, F. D. "Tommie Dora Barker." *BB* 17 (1940): 41–42.

Barnard, Howard A.

15.79 Wallace, R. "Great Teacher of the Plains." *Reader's Digest* 49 (November 1946): 92–96.

Barnett, Claribel Ruth

15.80 Colcord, M. "Claribel Ruth Barnett." *BB* 18 (1944): 73–74.

Barrette, Lydia Margaret

15.81 Barrette, L. M. *There Is No End*. New York: Scarecrow Press, 1961.

Barrow, William J.

15.82 Roberson, D. D. "Barrow, William J. (1904–1967)." *ALAWE2*: 1986 101–02.

Bartlett, John Russell

15.83 Lockwood, F. C. "John Russell Bartlett [Thumbnail Sketches of Famous Arizona Desert Riders, 1538–1946]." *General Bulletin. University of Arizona* 11 (1946): 16–17.

Batchelder, Mildred L.

15.84 Anderson, D. J. "Mildred L. Batchelder: A Study in Leadership." Doctoral dissertation, Texas Woman's University, 1981.

15.85 Tarbox, R. "Batchelder, Mildred (1901–)." *ALAWE2*: 1986 102–03.

Bates, Joshua

15.86 Ticknor, G. "Joshua Bates." *AJE* 7 (1859): 270–72.

Bates, Mary E.

15.87 Sutherland, A. "Mary E. Bates." *BB* 18 (1945): 121–22.

Battle, William James

15.88 "Battle, William James." *HT* 3 (1976): 64.

Bauer, Harry Charles

15.89 Tucker, L. L. "Harry Charles Bauer." *BB* 21 (1954): 49–51.

Bay, Jens Christian

15.90 Bay, J. C. *The Fortune of Books: Essays, Memories and Prophecies of a Librarian.* Chicago: Walter M. Hill, 1941.

15.91 Taylor, K. L. *J. Christian Bay at Seventy: A Review and a Bibliography.* Chicago: John Crerar Library, 1941.

15.92 Henkle, H. H. "Bay, Jens Christian (1871–1962)." *DALB*: 1978 16–17.

15.93 "Bay, J. Christian." In *Librarian Authors: A Biobibliography,* by R. Engelbarts. Jefferson, N.C.: McFarland, 1981. Pp. 27–28.

Beals, Ralph Albert

15.94 Hadley, M. "Meet the New NYPL Director." *LJ* 71 (1946): 1437–38.

15.95 "The Talk of the Town [Ralph A. Beals]." *New Yorker* 22 (2 November 1946): 25–26.

15.96 "Beals, Ralph A(lbert) Mar. 29, 1899–." *CB* (1947): 38–39.

15.97 Hutchins, R. M. "Ralph Beals: The University of Chicago Years." *BNYPL* 59 (1955): 314–15.

15.98 "Ralph A. Beals." *BNYPL* 59 (1955): 3–15.

15.99 Miller, W. T. "Beals, Ralph Albert (Mar. 29, 1899–Oct. 14, 1954)." *DAB* Suppl. 5 (1977): 46–47.

15.100 Shera, J. H. "Beals, Ralph Albert (1899–1954)." *DALB*: 1978 17–21.

Beckley, John James

15.101 Berkeley, E., and Berkeley, D. S. *John Beckley: Zealous Partisan in a Nation Divided.* Philadelphia: American Philosophical Society, 1973.

15.102 Berkeley, E., and Berkeley, D. S. "The First Librarian of Congress: John Beckley." *QJLC* 32 (1975): 83–110.

15.103 Berkeley, E., and Berkeley, D. S. "Beckley, John James (1757–1807)." *DALB*: 1978 20–21.

Beer, William

15.104 "William Beer." *BB* 12 (1923): 2.

15.105 Tinker, E. L. "William Beer, 1849–1927." *PBSA* 20 (1926): 77–84.

15.106 Deynoodt, M. "List of Writings of William Beer." *LHQ* 11 (1928): 65–66.

15.107 Tinker, E. L. "William Beer, 1849–1927." *LHQ* 11 (1928): 59–65.

15.108 Kendall, I. R. "Beer, William (May 1, 1849–Feb. 1, 1927)." *DAB* 2 (1929): 138–39.

15.109 Kraus, J. W. *William Beer and the New Orleans Libraries, 1891–1927.* Chicago: Association of College and Research Libraries, 1952.

15.110 Kraus, J. W. "Beer, William (1849–1927)." *DALB*: 1978 21–23.

Belden, Charles Francis Dorr

15.111 Redstone, E. H. "Charles Francis Dorr Belden." *BB* 14 (1933): 205–06.

15.112 Palmer, R. C. "Belden, Charles Francis Dorr (1870–1931)." *DALB*: 1978 23–24.

Bell, James Ford

15.113 Gough, R. "Bell, James Ford (Aug. 16, 1879–May 7, 1961)." *DAB* Suppl. 7 (1981): 46–47.

Bell, Janet Elizabeth

15.114 Chou, M. P. "In Memoriam: Janet Elizabeth Bell, 1910–1983." *HLAJ* 40 (1983): 1–15.

Bentley, Harold

15.115 Doyle, H. G. "Harold Bentley." *Hispania* 30 (1947): 80.

Berelson, Bernard Reuben

15.116 "Berelson, Bernard (Reuben)." *CB* (1961): 42–44.

15.117 Asheim, L. E. "Bernard Berelson (1912–1979)." *LQ* 50 (1980): 407–09.

Berenson, Bernard

15.118 Sprigge, S. *Berenson, a Biography.* London: Allen and Unwin, 1960.

15.119 Gilmore, M. P. "Berenson, Bernard (June 26, 1865–Oct. 6, 1959)." *DAB* Suppl. 6 (1980): 55–57.

Bertram, James

15.120 Bobinski, G. S. "James Bertram and Alvin S. Johnson: Two Important but Little Known Figures in Library History." In *Library History Seminar No. 3, Proceedings, 1968,* edited by M. J. Zachert. Tallahassee: JLH, 1968. Pp. 35–46.

15.121 Bobinski, G. S. "Bertram, James (1872–1934)." *DALB*: 1978 24–25.

Billings, John Shaw

15.122 *Memorial Meeting in Honor of the Late Dr. John Shaw Billings, April 25, 1913.* New York: New York Public Library, 1913.

15.123 Mitchell, S. W. "Biographical Memoir of John Shaw Billings." *Science* 38 (1913): 827–33.

15.124 Garrison, F. H., ed. *John Shaw Billings: A Memoir.* New York: New York Public Library, 1915.

15.125 Hasse, A. R. "Bibliography of the Writings of John Shaw Billings, 1861–1913." In *John Shaw Billings: A Memoir,* edited by F. H. Garrison. New York: New York Public Library, 1915. Pp. 411–22.

15.126 Hurd, H. M. "Dr. John Shaw Billings, Bibliographer and Librarian." *BMLA* 5 (1915–16): 35–40.

15.127 "As It Was in the Beginning: John Shaw Billings." *PL* 29 (1924): 463.

15.128 Lydenberg, H. M. *John Shaw Billings: Creator of the National Medical Library and Its Catalogue, First Director of the New York Public*

Library. Chicago: American Library Association, 1924.

15.129 Willcox, W. F. "John Shaw Billings and Federal Vital Statistics." *American Statistical Association Journal* 21 (1926): 257–66.

15.130 Willcox, W. F. "Billings, John Shaw (Apr. 12, 1838–Mar. 11, 1913)." *DAB* 2 (1929): 266–69.

15.131 Lydenberg, H. M. "John Shaw Billings, 1838–1913." *BB* 14 (1931): 117–20.

15.132 Garrison, F. H. "Billings: A Maker of Modern Medicine." In *Lectures on the History of Medicine, 1926–1932.* Philadelphia: W.B. Saunders, 1933. Pp. 187–200.

15.133 Griffith, T. J. "High Points in the Life of Dr. John Shaw Billings." *IMH* 30 (1934): 325–30.

15.134 Lydenberg, H. M. "John Shaw Billings and the New York Public Library." *Bulletin of the History of Medicine* 6 (1938): 377–86.

15.135 Thornton, J. L. "John Shaw Billings." In *Mirror for Librarians.* London: Grafton, 1948. Pp. 101–02.

15.136 Banta, R. E. "John Shaw Billings: 1838–1913." In *Indiana Authors and Their Books, 1816–1916.* Crawfordsville, Ind.: Wabash College, 1949. Pp. 30–32.

15.137 Fulton, J. H. "John Shaw Billings." In *The Great Medical Bibliographers: A Study in Humanism,* by J. H. Fulton. Philadelphia: University of Pennsylvania Press, 1951. Pp. 67–75.

15.138 Curran, J. A. "John Shaw Billings, Medical Genius of the 19th Century." *BMLA* 42 (1954): 163–71.

15.139 Bradway, F. "Bibliography of the Writings of John Shaw Billings." In *Selected Papers of John Shaw Billings,* compiled by F. B. Rogers. Chicago: Medical Library Association, 1965. Pp. 285–300.

15.140 Rogers, F. B. "The Life of John Shaw Billings." In *Selected Papers of John Shaw Billings,* compiled by F. B. Rogers. Chicago: Medical Library Association, 1965. Pp. 11–13.

15.141 Cummings, M. M. "Books, Computers, and Medicine: Contributions of a Friend of Sir William Osler." *Medical History* 10 (1966): 130–37.

15.142 Vitz, C. "Three Master Librarians." *Cincinnati Historical Society Bulletin* 26 (1968): 343–60.

15.143 Rogers, F. B. "Billings, John Shaw." *ELIS* 2 (1969): 464–66.

15.144 Dain, P. "Billings, John Shaw (1838–1913)." *DALB:* 1978 25–31.

15.145 "Billings, John Shaw." In *Librarian Authors: A Biobibliography,* by R. Engelbarts. Jefferson, N.C.: McFarland, 1981. Pp. 60–64.

15.146 Rogers, F. B. "Billings, John Shaw (1838–1913)." *ALAWE2:* 1986 122–24.

Binkley, Robert Cedric

15.147 Fisch, M. H. "Robert Cedric Binkley, Historian in the Long Armistice." In *Selected Papers of Robert C. Binkley.* Cambridge: Harvard University Press, 1948. Pp. 3–46.

15.148 Schellenberg, T. R. "Binkley, Robert Cedric (Dec. 10, 1897–Apr. 11, 1940)." *DAB* Suppl. 2 (1958): 40–41.

Birdsall, John

15.149 Looscan, A. B. "Life and Service of John Birdsall." *SHQ* 26 (1922): 44–57.

15.150 Kemp, L. W. "Birdsall, John." *HT* 1 (1952): 165.

15.151 Houghton, D. K. "Birdsall, John." *HT* 3 (1976): 83.

Bisbee, Marvin Davis

15.152 Jenkins, F. W. "Marvin Davis Bisbee, 1845–1913." *BB* 8 (1915): 212–13.

Biscoe, Walter Stanley

15.153 Wynar, B. S., and Loomis, K. C. "Biscoe, Walter Stanley (1853–1933)." *DALB*: 1978 32–33.

Bishop, William Warner

15.154 Bishop, W. W. *Backs of Books and Other Essays in Librarianship*. Baltimore: Williams and Wilkins, 1926.

15.155 "William Warner Bishop, 'To Whom Honor Is Due.' " *BB* 15 (1933): 21–22.

15.156 Lydenberg, H. M., and Keogh, A., eds. *William Warner Bishop: A Tribute*. New Haven: Yale University Press, 1941.

15.157 Bishop, W. W. "Some Chicago Librarians of the Nineties: Fragments of Autobiography." *LQ* 14 (1944): 339–48.

15.158 Bishop, W. W. "Rome and Brooklyn, 1889–1902: Fragments of Autobiography." *LQ* 15 (1945): 324–38.

15.159 Bishop, W. W. "Princeton, 1902–07: Fragments of Autobiography." *LQ* 16 (1946): 211–24.

15.160 Bishop, W. W. "College Days, 1889–93: Fragments of Autobiography." *MAQR* 54 (1948): 340–52.

15.161 Bishop, W. W. "The Library of Congress, 1907–15: Fragments of Autobiography." *LQ* 18 (1948): 1–23.

15.162 Bishop, W. W. "Some Recollections of William Lawrence Clements and the Formation of His Library." *LQ* 18 (1948): 185–91.

15.163 Bishop, W. W. "The American Library Association: Fragments of Autobiography [1896–1918]." *LQ* 19 (1949): 36–45.

15.164 Bishop, W. W. "International Relations: Fragments of Autobiography." *LQ* 19 (1949): 270–84.

15.165 Bishop, W. W. "The American Library Association. II. Fragments of Autobiography [1918–1942]." *LQ* 21 (1951): 35–41.

15.166 Kaser, D. "William Warner Bishop: Contributions to a Bibliography." *LQ* 26 (1956): 52–60.

15.167 Mohrhardt, F. E. "Dr. William Warner Bishop (1871–1955): Our First International Librarian." *WLB* 32 (1957): 207–15.

15.168 Sparks, C. G. "William Warner Bishop." Doctoral dissertation, University of Michigan, 1967.

15.169 Sparks, C. G. "Bishop, William Warner (1871–1955)." *DALB*: 1978 33–36.

15.170 "Bishop, William Warner." In *Librarian Authors: A Biobibliography*, by R. Engelbarts. Jefferson, N.C.: McFarland, 1981. Pp. 64–66.

15.171 Sparks, C. G. "Bishop, William Warner." *ALAWE2*: 1986 125–26.

Bjerregaard, Carl Henrik Andreas

15.172 Lydenberg, H. M. "Bjerregaard, Carl Henrik Andreas (May 24, 1845–Jan. 28, 1922)." *DAB* 2 (1929): 307–08.

Bledsoe, Beulah Floy

15.173 Munn, K. "In Memorium: Beulah Floy Bledsoe." *HTL* 4 (1935): 145–46.

Bliss, Henry Evelyn

15.174 "Bliss, Henry E(velyn)." *CB* (1953): 75–77.

15.175 Anderson, M. J. "Bliss, Henry Evelyn (1870–1955)." *DALB*: 1978 36–39.

15.176 Mueller, J. G. "Bliss, Henry (1870–1955)." *ALAWE2*: 1986 126–27.

Blue, Thomas Fountain

15.177 Blue, T. F. "Hamptonian as Librarian." *Southern Workman* 53 (1923): 368–69.

15.178 Jackson, W. V. "Some Pioneer Negro Library Workers." *LJ* 64 (1939): 215–17.

15.179 Wright, L. T. "Thomas Fountain Blue, Pioneer Librarian, 1866–1935." Master's thesis, Atlanta University, 1955.

15.180 "Thomas Fountain Blue (1866–1935)." *HBLib*: 1977 31–32.

15.181 Wright, L. T. "Blue, Thomas Fountain (1866–1935)." *DALB*: 1978 39–41.

Bogle, Sarah C. N.

15.182 Vann, S. K. "Bogle, Sarah Comly Norris (Nov. 17, 1870–Jan. 11, 1932)." *NAW* 1 (1971): 187–88.

15.183 Sullivan, P. A. "Bogle, Sarah Comly Norris (1870–1932)." *DALB*: 1978 41–43.

15.184 "Bogle, Sarah C.N." In *Librarian Authors: A Biobibliography*, by R. Engelbarts. Jefferson, N.C.: McFarland, 1981. Pp. 40–41.

15.185 Dale, D. C. "Bogle, Sarah (1870–1932)." *ALAWE2*: 1986 128–29.

Boland, Edward R.

15.186 Conmy, P. T. "Edward R. Boland SJ—Librarian and Curator." *CLW* 56 (1984): 210–12.

Bolton, Charles Knowles

15.187 Shipton, C. K. "Charles Knowles Bolton." *PAAS* 60 (1950): 170–73.

15.188 Kelly, R. E. "Bolton, Charles Knowles (1867–1950)." *DALB*: 1978 43–44.

Bolton, Herbert Eugene

15.189 Kemble, J. H. "Bolton, Herbert Eugene." *HT* 3 (1976): 94–95.

15.190 Bannon, J. F. "Bolton, Herbert Eugene." *DAB* Suppl. 5 (1977): 76–78.

15.191 Bannon, J. F. *Herbert Eugene Bolton: The Historian and the Man.* Tucson: University of Arizona Press, 1978.

Bontemps, Arna Wendell

15.192 "Bontemps, Arna (Wendell) Oct. 13, 1902–." *CB* (1946): 59–61.

15.193 Bontemps, A. "Why I Returned." In *The South Today,* edited by W. Morris. New York: Harper and Row, 1965. Pp. 102–14.

15.194 Fuller, H. W. "Arna Bontemps, Bibliography." *Black World* 2 (September 1971): 78–79.

15.195 Conroy, J. "Memories of Arna Bontemps, Friend and Collaborator." *AL* 5 (1974): 602–06.

15.196 Shockley, A. A. "Arna Bontemps (1902–1973)." *HBLib*: 1977 161–62.

15.197 Smith, J. C. "Bontemps, Arna Wendell (1902–1973)." *DALB*: 1978 44–47.

15.198 Alexander, S. C. "Arna Bontemps: The Formative Years." *Black Books Bulletin* 7 no. 3 (1981): 32–35.

Boorstin, Daniel Joseph

15.199 Annunziata, F. "Daniel J. Boorstin." *Dictionary of Literary Biography* 17 (1983): 79–85.

15.200 "Boorstin, Daniel J(oseph)." *CB* (1984): 37–40.

15.201 Wiegand, W. A. "Boorstin, Daniel J. (1914–)." *ALAWE2*: 1986 130–32.

Booth, Mary Josephine

15.202 Lawson, R. W. "Mary Josephine Booth: A Lifetime of Service, 1904–1945." Doctoral dissertation, Indiana University, 1975.

15.203 Lawson, R. W. "Mary Josephine Booth: A Gallant Lady, a Superb Librarian." *IllL* 60 (1978): 504–10.

Borden, William A.

15.204 Nagar, M. L. *First American Library Pioneer in India.* Colombia, Mo.: South Asian Publications, 1983.

Bostwick, Arthur Elmore

15.205 "Arthur Elmore Bostwick." *BB* 10 (1919): 85.

15.206 Bostwick, A. E. *A Life with Men and Books.* New York: H.W. Wilson, 1939.

15.207 Boromé, J. A. "Bibliography of Arthur Elmore Bostwick, 1860–1942." *BB* 18 (1944): 62–66.

15.208 Doud, M. "Arthur E. Bostwick, 1860–1942." In *Pioneering Leaders in Librarianship,* edited by E. M. Danton. Chicago: American Library Association, 1953. Pp. 22–33.

15.209 Doud, M. "Recollections of Arthur E[lmore] Bostwick." *WLB* 27 (1953): 818–25.

15.210 Doud, M. "Recollection of Arthur E. Bostwick." *WLB* 27 (1953): 818–25.

15.211 Cunningham, L. L. "Contributions of Arthur Elmore Bostwick to the Library Profession." Master's thesis, Indiana University, 1962.

15.212 Boromé, J. A. "Bostwick, Arthur Elmore (Mar. 8, 1860–Feb. 13, 1942)." *DAB* Suppl. 3 (1973): 90–91.

15.213 Davis, D. G. "Bostwick, Arthur Elmore (1860–1942)." *DALB*: 1978 47–50.

15.214 "Bostwick, Arthur Elmore." In *Librarian Authors: A Biobibliography,* by R. Engelbarts. Jefferson, N.C.: McFarland, 1981. Pp. 66–69.

Bostwick, Lucy Hampton

15.215 McPharlin, P. "Bostwick and Thornley: Librarians and Publishers." *PW* 150 (1946): 3206–09.

Bowerman, George Franklin

15.216 Putnam, H. "George Franklin Bowerman." *BB* 16 (1936): 1–2.

15.217 Eastman, L. A. "Who Says That They Have Retired?" *LJ* 72 (1947): 1125–26.

15.218 Bowerman, G. F. "Some Reminiscences by Dr. George F. Bowerman, Chief Librarian, D.C. Public Library, 1904–1940." *DCL* 26 (1955): 3–7.

15.219 Bowerman, G. F. *Some Memories, 1868–1956.* N.p.: Privately printed, 1956.

15.220 Tabb, W. "Bowerman, George Franklin (1868–1960)." *DALB*: 1978 50–52.

Bowker, Richard Rogers

15.221 Foster, W. E. "Five Men of '76." *BALA* 20 (1926): 312–23.

15.222 "Richard Rogers Bowker." *BB* 12 (1926): 185–86.

15.223 Melcher, F. G. "Among the Founders." *LJ* 76 (1951): 1959–63.

15.224 Fleming, E. M. *R.R. Bowker: Militant Liberal.* Norman: University of Oklahoma, 1952.

15.225 Ferguson, M. J. "Richard Rogers Bowker, 1848–1933." In *Pioneering Leaders in Librarianship,* edited by E. M. Danton. Chicago: American Library Association, 1953. Pp. 34–47.

15.226 Landau, R. A. "Richard Rogers Bowker." *ELIS* 3 (1970): 148–55.

15.227 Miele, M. F. "Bowker, Richard Rogers (1848–1933)." *DALB*: 1978 52–55.

15.228 "Bowker, R.R." In *Librarian Authors: A Biobibliography,* by R. Engelbarts. Jefferson, N.C.: McFarland, 1981. Pp. 116–18.

15.229 McMullen, H. "Bowker, R.R. (1848–1932)." *ALAWE2*: 1986 134–35.

Boyd, Anne Morris

15.230 Bonn, G. S. "Boyd, Anne Morris (1884–1974)." *DALB*: 1978 55–56.

Boyd, Julian Parks

15.231 *Julian P. Boyd: A Bibliographic Record Compiled and Offered by His Friends on the Occasion of His Tenth Anniversary as Librarian of Princeton University.* Princeton: Princeton University Library, 1950.

15.232 "Boyd, Julian P(arks)." *CB* (1975): 58–61.

Brademas, John

15.233 "Brademas, John." *CB* (1977): 77–80.

Bradshaw, Lillian Moore

15.234 "Bradshaw, Lillian Moore." *CB* (1970): 46–48.

Bray, Robert Stuart

15.235 "Bray, Robert S(tuart)." *CB* (1966): 28–30.

15.236 Cylke, F. K. "Bray, Robert S." *ELIS* 36 (1983): 51–54.

Bray, Thomas

15.237 Thornton, J. L. "Thomas Bray." In *Mirror for Librarians.* London: Grafton, 1948. Pp. 53–54.

15.238 Nasri, W. Z. "Bray, Thomas." *ELIS* 3 (1970): 163–65.

15.239 Laugher, C. T. "Bray, Thomas (1658–1730)." *DALB*: 1978 56–58.

15.240 "Bray, Thomas." In *Librarian Authors: A Biobibliography,* by R. Engelbarts. Jefferson, N.C.: McFarland, 1981. Pp. 8–10.

15.241 Laugher, C. T. "Bray, Thomas (1658–1730)." *ALAWE2*: 1986 136–37.

Brett, William Howard

15.242 Faxon, F. W. "William Howard Brett, 1846–1918." *BB* 10 (1918): 69.

15.243 "William Howard Brett, Librarian of the Cleveland Public Library." *Open Shelf [Cleveland Public Library]* (September–October 1918): 1–24.

15.244 "William Howard Brett: In Memoriam." *LJ* 43 (1918): 793–807.

15.245 "As It Was in the Beginning: William Howard Brett." *PL* 30 (1925): 306–08.

15.246 Eastman, L. A. "Brett, William Howard (July 1, 1846–Aug. 24, 1918)." *DAB* 3 (1929): 20–21.

15.247 Eastman, L. A. *Portrait of a Librarian: William Howard Brett.* Chicago: American Library Association, 1940.

15.248 Vitz, C. "William Howard Brett." *BALA* 34 (1940): 250, 301–02.

15.249 Vitz, C. "William Howard Brett." *WLB* 25 (1950): 297–303, 313.

15.250 Vitz, C. "William Howard Brett." *ELIS* 3 (1970): 260–69.

15.251 Cramer, C. H. "Brett, William Howard (1846–1918)." *DALB*: 1978 58–61.

15.252 "Brett, William Howard." In *Librarian Authors: A Biobibliography*, by R. Engelbarts. Jefferson, N.C.: McFarland, 1981. Pp. 21–23.

15.253 Ring, D. F. "Fighting for Their Hearts and Minds: William Howard Brett, the Cleveland Public Library, and World War I." *JLH* 18 (1983): 1–20.

15.254 Gaines, E. J. "Brett, William Howard (1846–1918)." *ALAWE2*: 1986 139–40.

Brientnall, Joseph

15.255 Bloore, S. "Joseph Brientnall, First Secretary of the Library Company." *PMHB* 59 (1935): 42–56.

Brigham, Clarence Saunders

15.256 "Brigham, Clarence S(aunders)." *CB* (1959): 43–44.

15.257 Hench, J. B. "Brigham, Clarence Saunders (1877–1963)." *DALB*: 1978 61–63.

Brigham, Johnson

15.258 "Johnson Brigham." *BB* 13 (1928): 85–86.

15.259 Wright, L. M. "Johnson Brigham—Librarian." *Palimpsest* 33 (1952): 225–56.

Brockenbrough, William Henry

15.260 Clemons, H. "William Henry Brockenbrough." In *The University of Virginia Library*. Charlottesville: University of Virginia Library, 1954. Pp. 101–05.

Brode, Mildred Hooker

15.261 "Brode, Mildred H(ooker)." *CB* (1963): 45–47.

Brooks, Hallie Beacham

15.262 Miller, R. "One Georgia Librarian, Hallie Beacham Brooks Remembers—1930 to 1977." *GL* 14 (1977): 29–37.

Brotherton, Nina C.

15.263 Edge, S. A. "Nina C. Brotherton." *Massachusetts Library Association Bulletin* 39 (1949): 48.

Brown, Alberta Louise

15.264 "Brown, Alberta L(ouise)." *CB* (1958): 63–65.

Brown, Charles Harvey

15.265 Spaulding, F. "Charles Harvey Brown." *BB* 16 (1937): 21–22.

15.266 Crawford, H. "Bibliography of Charles Harvey Brown." *CRL* 8 (1947): 380–84.

15.267 Tauber, M. F. "Charles Harvey Brown: The Man." *CRL* 8 (1947): 293.

15.268 Thompson, L. S. "Brown, Charles Harvey (1875–1960)." *DALB*: 1978 63–65.

15.269 Holley, E. G. "Mr. ACRL: Charles Harvey Brown (1875–1960)." *Journal of Academic Librarianship* 7 (1981): 271–78.

15.270 Holley, E. G. "Charles Harvey Brown." *LAAL*: 1983 11–48.

Brown, Dee

15.271 Courtemanche-Ellis, A. "Meet Dee Brown: Author, Teacher, Librarian." *WLB* 52 (1978): 552–61.

Brown, Demarchus Clariton

15.272 Banta, R. E. "Brown, Demarchus Clariton: 1857–1926." In *Indiana Authors and Their Books, 1816–1916*. Crawfordsville, Ind.: Wabash College, 1949. P. 44.

Brown, Harold Gibson

15.273 Murphy, M. " 'Clean Books for Clean People': The Legacy of Harold Gibson Brown." *Mississippi Libraries* 43 (1979): 81–82.

Brown, Walter Lewis

15.274 Bartlett, L. "Walter L. Brown." *BB* 14 (1931): 66–67.

15.275 Rooney, P. M. "Brown, Walter Lewis (1861–1931)." *DALB*: 1978 65–66.

Brown, Zaidee Mabel

15.276 Donnelly, J. R. "Zaidee Mabel Brown." *BB* 18 (1945): 169–70.

Bryan, James Edmund

15.277 "Bryan, James E(dmund)." *CB* (1962): 54–55.

Buck, Paul Herman

15.278 "Buck, Paul H(erman)." *CB* (1955): 77–78.

Buck, Solon Justus

15.279 McCoy, D. R. "Buck, Solon Justus (1884–1962)." *ALAWE2*: 1986 142–43.

Budington, William Stone

15.280 "Budington, William S(tone)." *CB* (1964): 58–60.

Buffington, Willie Lee

15.281 Carr, L. D. "The Reverend Willie Lee Buffington's Life and Contributions to the Development of Rural Libraries in the South." Master's thesis, Atlanta University, 1958.

Buffum, Mary F.

15.282 Taylor, M. D. "Miss Mary F. Buffum." *LJ* 71 (1946): 1703–04.

Bugbee, Lester Gladstone

15.283 Barker, E. C. "Lester Gladstone Bugbee: Teacher and Historian." *SHQ* 49 (1945): 1–32.

Bullen, Henry Lewis

15.284 Mallison, D. W. "Henry Lewis Bullen and the Typographic Library and Museum of the American Type Founders Company." Doctoral dissertation, Columbia University, 1976.

Burchard, John Ely

15.285 "Burchard, John E(ly)." *CB* (1958): 68–70.

Burges, Richard Fenner

15.286 Strickland, R. W. "Richard Fenner Burges." *SHQ* 48 (1945): 558–60.

15.287 "Burges, Richard Fenner." *HT* 1 (1952): 246.

Burr, George Lincoln

15.288 "George Lincoln Burr." *PAAS* n.s. 42 (1938): 168–70.

15.289 Bainton, R. H. "George Lincoln Burr: His Life." In *George Lincoln Burr: His Life, Selections from His Writings,* edited by L. O. Gibbons. Ithaca: Cornell University Press, 1943. Pp. 3–143.

15.290 Powicke, F. M. "An American Scholar: George Lincoln Burr." In *Ways of Medieval Life and Thought: Essays and Addresses.* Boston: Beacon Press, 1951. Pp. 249–55.

15.291 Evans, A. P. "Burr, George Lincoln (Jan. 30, 1857–June 27, 1938)." *DAB* Suppl. 2 (1958): 75–76.

Butler, Pierce

15.292 Bell, B. I. "Pierce Butler, Professor and Priest." *LQ* 22 (1952): 174–76.

15.293 "Bibliography of Pierce Butler." *LQ* 22 (1952): 165–69.

15.294 Pargellis, S. M. "Pierce Butler—A Biographical Sketch." *LQ* 22 (1952): 170–73.

15.295 Wilson, L. R. "Pierce Butler, 1886–1953." *NCL* 11 (1953): 70.

15.296 Ash, L. "Butler, Pierce (1886–1953)." *DALB*: 1978 66–67.

15.297 Shera, J. H. "Butler, Pierce (1886–1953)." *ALAWE2*: 1986 148–49.

Butler, Susan Dart

15.298 Bolden, E. E. M. "Susan Dart Butler—Pioneer Librarian." Master's thesis, Atlanta University, 1959.

15.299 "Susan Dart Butler (1888–1959)." *HBLib*: 1977 32–33.

15.300 Jones, V. L. "Butler, Susan Dart (1888–1959)." *DALB*: 1978 68–69.

Byam, Milton S.

15.301 Byam, M. S. "A Librarian Grows in Brooklyn." In *The Black Librarian in America,* edited by E. J. Josey. Metuchen, N.J.: Scarecrow Press, 1970. Pp. 50–68.

Canfield, James Hulme

15.302 Butler, N. M. "In Memoriam—Dr. James Hulme Canfield." *National Education Association Journal of Proceedings and Addresses* 47 (1909): 105–07.

15.303 Wright, E. H. "Canfield, James Hulme (Mar. 18, 1847–Mar. 29, 1909)." *DAB* 3 (1929): 472.

15.304 Fisher, D. C. "A Librarian's Creed: James Hulme Canfield." *CLC* 2 (1952): 2–12.

Carey, Miriam E.

15.305 Jones, P. "Miriam E. Carey, 1858–1937." In *Pioneering Leaders in Librarianship,* edited by E. M. Danton. Chicago: American Library Association, 1953. Pp. 48–60.

15.306 "Carey, Miriam E." In *Librarian Authors: A Biobibliography,* by R. Engelbarts. Jefferson, N.C.: McFarland, 1981. Pp. 38–39.

Carlson, William Hugh

15.307 Carlson, W. H. *In a Grand and Awful Time.* Corvallis: Oregon State University Press, 1967.

Carlton, William N. C.

15.308 Carlton, W. N. C. "After Forty Years (1893–1933): Some Memories and Reflections." *Massachusetts Library Club Bulletin* 23 (1933): 43–48.

Carnegie, Andrew

15.309 Hendrick, B. J. "Carnegie, Andrew (Nov. 25, 1835–Aug. 11, 1919)." *DAB* 3 (1929): 499–506.

15.310 "Andrew Carnegie, the Patron Saint of Libraries." *KLAB* 27 (1963): 8–19.

15.311 Ollé, J. G. "Andrew Carnegie: The 'Unloved Benefactor.' " *LW* 70 (1969): 255–62.

15.312 Belfour, S. "Andrew Carnegie." *ELIS* 4 (1970): 192–200.

15.313 Wall, J. F. *Andrew Carnegie.* New York: Oxford University Press, 1970.

15.314 Bobinski, G. S. "Carnegie, Andrew (1835–1919)." *DALB*: 1978 69–73.

15.315 "Carnegie, Andrew." In *Librarian Authors: A Biobibliography,* by R. Engelbarts. Jefferson, N.C.: McFarland, 1981. Pp. 113–14.

15.316 Deitch, J. "Benevolent Builder: Appraising Andrew Carnegie." *WLB* 59 (1984): 16–22.

15.317 Kiddoo, K. "Andrew Carnegie and the Library Movement." *ABBW* 76 (1985): 64–68.

15.318 Bobinski, G. S. "Carnegie, Andrew (1835–1919)." *ALAWE2*: 1986 166–67.

Carnovsky, Leon

15.319 Haygood, W. C. "Leon Carnovsky: A Sketch." *LQ* 38 (1968): 422–28.

15.320 "Leon Carnovsky: A Bibliography." *LQ* 38 (1968): 429–41.

15.321 Winger, H. W. "Carnovsky, Leon (1903–1975)." *DALB*: 1978 73–74.

15.322 Winger, H. W. "Carnovsky, Leon (1903–1975)." *ALAWE2*: 1986 167–68.

Carr, Deborah Edith Wallbridge

15.323 "Deborah Edith Wallbridge Carr." *BB* 12 (1924): 65–66.

Carr, Henry James

15.324 "Henry James Carr." *BB* 11 (1921): 77.

15.325 Wiegand, W. A. "Carr, Henry James (1849–1929)." *DALB*: 1978 74–76.

Cassel, Abraham Harley

15.326 Heckman, M. L. "Abraham Harley Cassel: Nineteenth-Century American Book Collector." Doctoral dissertation, University of Chicago, 1971.

Castañeda, Carlos Eduardo

15.327 Almaraz, F. D. "The Making of a Boltonian: Carlos E. Castañeda of Texas—the Early Years." *Red River Valley Historical Review* 1 (1947): 329–50.

15.328 Almaraz, F. D. "Carlos Eduardo Castañeda: Mexican-American Historian, the Formative Years, 1896–1927." *Pacific Historical Review* 42 (1973): 619–34.

15.329 Spell, L. M. "Castañeda, Carlos Eduardo." *HT* 3 (1976): 150.

15.330 Almaraz, F. D. "Carlos E. Castañeda's Rendezvous with a Library: The Latin American Collection, 1920–1927—The First Phase." *JLH* 16 (1981): 315–28.

Castagna, Edwin

15.331 Powell, L. C. "Edwin Castagna." *LJ* 87 (1962): 3390–91.

15.332 "Castagna, Edwin." *CB* (1964): 74–76.

Certain, Casper Carl

15.333 Lowrie, J. E. "Certain, Casper Carl (1885–1940)." *DALB*: 1978 76–77.

Chadwick, James Read

15.334 "In Memoriam: James Read Chadwick, M.D.—A Sketch of His Life." *Medical Library and Historical Journal* 4 (1906): 113–25.

15.335 Viets, H. R. "Chadwick, James Read (Nov. 2, 1844–Sept. 23, 1905)." *DAB* 3 (1929): 588.

Cheney, Frances Neel

15.336 Green, E. "Frances Neel Cheney." *BB* 24 (1963): 1–3.

15.337 Gleaves, E. S. "A Frances Neel Cheney Chronology." In *Reference Services and Library Education: Essays in Honor of Frances Neel Cheney*, edited by E. S. Gleaves and J. M. Tucker. Lexington, Mass.: Lexington Books, 1983. Pp. 19–22.

15.338 Gleaves, E. S. " 'Pleased to Teach and Yet Not Proud to Know': A Profile of the Life and Career of Frances Neel Cheney." In *Reference Services and Library Education: Essays in Honor of Frances Neel Cheney*, edited by E. S. Gleaves and J. M. Tucker. Lexington, Mass.: Lexington Books, 1983. Pp. 5–18.

15.339 Marshall, J. D. "FNC in Print: A Bibliography of Works by and about Frances Neel Cheney." In *Reference Services and Library Education: Essays in Honor of Frances Neel Cheney*, edited by E. S. Gleaves and J. M. Tucker. Lexington, Mass.: Lexington Books, 1983. Pp. 267–91.

Cheney, John Vance

15.340 Greever, G. "Cheney, John Vance (Dec. 29, 1848–May 1, 1922)." *DAB* 4 (1930): 53.

Chew, Beverly

15.341 Nikirk, R. "Two American Book Collectors of the Nineteenth Century: William Loring Andrews and Beverly Chew." In *Book Selling and Book Buying: Aspects of the Nineteenth Century British and North American Book Trade*, edited by R. G. Landon. Chicago: American Library Association, 1979. Pp. 99–108.

Childs, James Bennett

15.342 Wisdom, D. F. "Childs, James Bennett." *ELIS* 37 (1984): 20–33.

Clapp, Verner Warren

15.343 "Clapp, Verner W(arren)." *CB* (1959): 67–68.

15.344 Mohrhardt, F. E. "Clapp, Verner Warren (1901–1972)." *DALB*: 1978 77–81.

15.345 Hallstein, A. L. "Clapp, Verner W." *ELIS* 39 (1985): 79–86.

15.346 Wagman, F. H. "Clapp, Verner W. (1901–1972)." *ALAWE2*: 1986 197–99.

Clark, George Thomas

15.347 Conmy, P. T. "George Thomas Clark, the California Library Association's Illustrious Number Two." *CalL* 37 (1976): 5–13.

Clark, Geraldine

15.348 Clark, G. "A Paralysis of Will: A School Library Administrator's Viewpoint." In *The Black Librarian in America*, edited by E. J. Josey. Metuchen, N.J.: Scarecrow Press, 1970. Pp. 290–96.

15.349 "Clark, James Benjamin." *HT* 1 (1952): 355.

Clark, William Andrews, Jr.

15.350 Conway, W. E. "Books, Bricks, and Copper: Clark and His Library." In *William Andrews Clark, Jr.: His Cultural Legacy. Papers Read at a Clark Library Seminar, 7 November 1981*, edited by W. E. Conway and R. Stevenson. Los Angeles: William Andrews Clark Memorial Library, University of California, Los Angeles, 1985. Pp. 3–27.

Clarke, Sarah Freeman

15.351 Olsson, N. W., ed. "Visit to Wisconsin in 1843." *WMH* 31 (1948): 452–60.

Clay, Margaret

15.352 Morison, C. K. "Margaret Clay." *BALA* 48 (1954): 15–16, 34.

Clements, William L.

15.353 Bishop, W. W. "Some Recollections of William Lawrence Clements and the Formation of His Library." *LQ* 18 (1948): 185–91.

15.354 Maxwell, M. F. *Shaping a Library: William L. Clements as Collector.* Amsterdam: N. Israel, 1973.

Clemons, Harry

15.355 Dalton, J. "Clemons, Harry (1879–1968)." *DALB*: 1978 81–83.

Clift, David Horace

15.356 Babb, J. T. "David Horace Clift." *BB* 20 (1952): 177–78.

15.357 "Clift, David H(orace)." *CB* (1952): 111–12.

15.358 "Two Decisive Decades—1952–1972: Special Issue Honoring David Clift." *ALib* 3 (1972): 701–815.

15.359 Shields, G. R. "Clift, David Horace (1907–1973)." *DALB*: 1978 83–87.

15.360 Shields, G. R. "Clift, David H. (1907–1973)." *ALAWE2*: 1986 206–07.

Cobb, William Henry

15.361 Persons, F. T. "Cobb, William Henry (Apr. 2, 1846–May 1, 1923)." *DAB* 4 (1930): 247–48.

Cogswell, Joseph Green

15.362 "J.G. Cogswell." *American Bibliopolist* 6 (September–October 1874): 120.

15.363 Ticknor, A. E. *Life of Joseph Green Cogswell, as Sketched in His Letters.* Cambridge, Mass.: Riverside Press, 1874.

15.364 Lydenberg, H. M. "A Forgotten Trail Blazer." In *Essays Offered to Herbert Putnam by His Colleagues and Friends on His Thirtieth Anniversary as Librarian of Congress, 5 April 1929*, edited by W. W. Bishop and A. Keogh. New Haven: Yale University Press, 1929. Pp. 302–14.

15.365 Mackall, L. L. "Goethe's Letter to Joseph Green Cogswell." In *Essays Offered to Herbert Putnam by His Colleagues and Friends on His Thirtieth Anniversary as Librarian of Congress, 5 April 1929*, edited by W. W. Bishop and A. Keogh. New Haven: Yale University Press, 1929. Pp. 315–26.

15.366 Lane, W. C. "Cogswell, Joseph Green (Sept. 27, 1786–Nov. 26, 1871)." *DAB* 4 (1930): 273–74.

15.367 Turner, H. M. "Cogswell, Joseph Green (1786–1871)." *DALB*: 1978 87–91.

Colcord, Mabel

15.368 "Mabel Colcord." *BB* 19 (1949): 225.

Cole, Fred C.

15.369 Mohrhardt, F. E. "Cole, Fred C. (1912–)." *ALAWE2*: 1986 207.

Cole, George Watson

15.370 "George Watson Cole." *BB* 10 (1919): 117.

15.371 "List of the Printed Productions of George Watson Cole, 1870–1935." *BB* 15 (1936): 183–86; 16 (1936): 11–12; 16 (1937): 32–35.

15.372 Damon, T. F. "Cole, George Watson (Sept. 6, 1850–Oct. 10, 1939)." *DAB* Suppl. 2 (1958): 111–12.

15.373 Woodward, D. H. "Cole, George Watson (1850–1939)." *DALB*: 1978 91.

Colelazer, Henry

15.374 Bidlack, R. E. "Henry Colelazer, the University of Michigan's First Librarian: Custodian of a Handful of Books." *MAQR* 62 (1956): 157–71.

Collins, Leslie Morgan

15.375 Shockley, A. A. "Leslie Morgan Collins (1914–)." *HBLib*: 1977 163.

Compton, Charles H.

15.376 "Salute to Charles H. Compton." *LJ* 71 (1946): 779–81.

15.377 Bauer, H. C. "Charles Herrick Compton." *BALA* 48 (1954): 139–44.

15.378 Compton, C. H. *Memories of a Librarian.* St. Louis: St. Louis Public Library, 1954.

15.379 Price, P. P. "Compton, Charles Herrick (1880–1966)." *DALB*: 1978 91–94.

Coney, Donald

15.380 Swank, R. C. "Coney, Donald (1901–1973)." *DALB*: 1978 94–95.

Connor, Robert D. W.

15.381 Jones, H. G. "Connor, Robert D.W. (1878–1950)." *ALAWE2*: 1986 219.

Cook, Everett R.

15.382 Cook, E. R. *Everett R. Cook: A Memoir,* edited by J. Riggs and M. Lawrence. Memphis: Memphis Public Library, 1971.

Coolbrith, Ina

15.383 Dickson, S. "Ina Coolbrith." In *San Francisco Is Your Home.* Stanford: Stanford University, 1947. Pp. 171–78.

15.384 Hunt, R. D. "Ina Coolbrith." In *California's Stately Hall of Fame.* Stockton, Calif.: College of the Pacific, 1950. Pp. 553–57.

15.385 Rhodehamel, J. D., and Wood, R. F. *Ina Coolbrith: Librarian and Laureate of California.* Provo, Utah: Brigham Young University Press, 1973.

15.386 Hurst, L. "Ina Coolbrith: Forgotten as Poet . . . Remembered as Librarian." *PNLAQ* 41 (1977): 4–11.

15.387 Wood, R. F. "Coolbrith, Ina Donna (1841–1928)." *DALB*: 1978 95–97.

Coolidge, Archibald Cary

15.388 Currier, T. F. "Archibald Cary Coolidge." *LJ* 53 (1928): 131–33.

15.389 Emerton, E. "Coolidge, Archibald Cary (Mar. 6, 1866–Jan. 14, 1928)." *DAB* 4 (1930): 393–95.

15.390 Olsen, R. A. "Archibald Cary Coolidge and the Harvard University Library, 1910–1928." Research Paper, Long Island University, 1967.

15.391 Bentinck-Smith, W. *Building a Great Library: The Coolidge Years at Harvard.* Cambridge: Harvard University Press, 1976.

15.392 Byrnes, R. F. "Archibald Cary Coolidge and 'Civilization's Diary': Building the Harvard University Library." *ALAO* 1 (1982): 21–42.

15.393 Byrnes, R. F. *Awakening American Education to the World: The Role of Archibald Cary Coolidge, 1866–1928.* Notre Dame, Ind.: University of Notre Dame Press, 1982.

Coolidge, Thomas Jefferson

15.394 Whitehill, W. M. "Coolidge, Thomas Jefferson (Sept. 17, 1893–Aug. 6, 1959)." *DAB* Suppl. 6 (1980): 124–25.

Coon, Ethel L.

15.395 "Librarian to the Industry." *American Bee Journal* 89 (1949): 528.

Copeland, Emily America

15.396 Copeland, E. A. "Lady Emily." In *The Black Librarian in America,* edited by E. J. Josey. Metuchen, N.J.: Scarecrow Press, 1970. Pp. 77–91.

Cory, John Mackenzie

15.397 "Cory, John Mackenzie." *CB* (1949): 123–25.

Cossitt, Frederick

15.398 Holden, A. H. "Frederick Cossitt." *Memphis Commercial Appeal* (18 December 1932): .

Coulter, Edith Margaret

15.399 Parker, W. E. "Chronological List of the Writings of Edith M. Coulter." *CalL* 24 (1963): 103–04.

15.400 Powell, L. C. *The Example of Miss Edith M. Coulter.* Sacramento: California Library Association, 1969.

15.401 Powell, L. C. "Coulter, Edith Margaret (1880–1963)." *DALB*: 1978 97–98.

Countryman, Gratia Alta

15.402 "Gratia A. Countryman." *BB* 11 (1922): 137.

15.403 Potter, G. L. "Gratia Countryman, Pioneer." *WLB* 28 (1954): 470–71.

15.404 Dyste, M. C. "Gratia Alta Countryman, Librarian." Master's thesis, University of Minnesota, 1965.

15.405 Rohde, N. F. "Countryman, Gratia Alta (1866–1953)." *DALB*: 1978 98–100.

Crane, Evan Jay

15.406 Dikeman, R. K. "Crane, Evan Jay (1889–1966)." *DALB*: 1978 100–102.

Craver, Harrison Warwick

15.407 Cabeen, S. K. "Craver, Harrison Warwick (1875–1951)." *DALB*: 1978 102–03.

Crerar, John

15.408 Goodspeed, T. W. *John Crerar.* Chicago: John Crerar Library, 1939.

Cronin, John W.

15.409 Clapp, V. W., and Welsh, W. J. "The Age of Cronin: Aspects of the Accomplishment of John W. Cronin, Library of Congress, 1925–1968." *LRTS* 12 (1968): 385–405.

Crunden, Frederick Morgan

15.410 Bostwick, A. E. *Frederick Morgan Crunden: A Memorial Bibliography.* St. Louis: St. Louis Public Library, 1924.

15.411 Foster, W. E. "Frederick Morgan Crunden." *BB* 12 (1924): 85–86.

15.412 "As It Was in the Beginning." *PL* 30 (1925): 138–42.

15.413 Drumm, S. M. "Crunden, Frederick Morgan (Sept. 1, 1847–Oct. 28, 1911)." *DAB* 4 (1930): 583.

15.414 Doane, B. "Frederick M[organ] Crunden [1847–1911]." *WLB* 29 (1955): 446–49, 452.

15.415 Gambee, B. L. "Crunden, Frederick Morgan (1847–1911)." *DALB*: 1978 103–05.

15.416 "Crunden, Frederick Morgan." In *Librarian Authors: A Biobibliography*, by R. Engelbarts. Jefferson, N.C.: McFarland, 1981. Pp. 72–74.

Cullen, Thomas Stephen

15.417 Robinson, J. *Tom Cullen of Baltimore.* New York: Oxford University Press, 1949.

15.418 Corner, G. W. "Cullen, Thomas Stephen (Nov. 20, 1868–Mar. 4, 1953)." *DAB* Suppl. 5 (1977): 146–48.

Culver, Essae Martha

15.419 Morton, F. F. "Culver, Essae Martha (1882–1973)." *DALB*: 1978 105–07.

Cummings, Martin M.

15.420 Colaianni, L. A. "Cummings, Martin M." *ALAWE2*: 1986 235–37.

Cunningham, Eileen Roach

15.421 Kaser, D. "Cunningham, Eileen Roach (1894–1965)." *DALB*: 1978 107–08.

Cunningham, William D.

15.422 Cunningham, W. D. "Rock Chalk, Jayhawk; Oh, Excuse Me, Rock Chalk, Blackhawk." In *The Black Librarian in America*, edited by E. J. Josey. Metuchen, N.J.: Scarecrow Press, 1970. Pp. 284–89.

Currier, Thomas Franklin

15.423 Ford, E. G., Tucker, M. M., and Wood, M. P. "Thomas Franklin Currier." *ALA Cataloging and Classification Yearbook* 9 (1940): 18–20.

15.424 Lydenberg, H. M. "T. Franklin Currier and Selective Cataloguing at Harvard." *HLN* 4 (1941): 8–15.

15.425 Osborn, A. D. "T. Franklin Currier: Cataloger and Bibliographer Par Excellence." *LJ* 71 (1946): 1530–31.

15.426 "Thomas Franklin Currier." *PAAS* 56 (1946): 165–67.

15.427 Roxas, S. A. "Thomas Franklin Currier." *ELIS* 6 (1971): 375–79.

Curry, Arthur Ray

15.428 Winship, S. G. "Arthur Ray Curry: A Biography." Master's thesis, University of Texas, 1966.

Curtis, Florence Rising

15.429 Davis, D. G. "Curtis, Florence Rising (1873–1944)." *DALB*: 1978 108–09.

Cushing, Edward Hopkins

15.430 Cushing, E. B. "Edward Hopkins Cushing: An Appreciation by His Son." *SHQ* 25 (1922): 261–73.

15.431 "Cushing, Edward Hopkins." *HT* 1 (1952): 449.

Cushing, Harvey

15.432 Fulton, J. F. *Harvey Cushing, a Biography*. Springfield, Ill.: Charles C. Thomas, 1946.

Cutter, Charles Ammi

15.433 Foster, W. E. "Charles Ammi Cutter: A Memorial Sketch." *LJ* 28 (1903): 697–703.

15.434 Green, S. S. "Charles Ammi Cutter." *BB* 8 (1914): 59–60.

15.435 "As It Was in the Beginning." *PL* 29 (1924): 236–40.

15.436 Foster, W. E. "Five Men of '76." *BALA* 20 (1926): 312–23.

15.437 Ashley, F. W. "Cutter, Charles Ammi (Mar. 14, 1837–Sept. 6, 1903)." *DAB* 5 (1930): 15–16.

15.438 Cutter, W. P. *Charles Ammi Cutter*. Chicago: American Library Association, 1931.

15.439 Thornton, J. L. "Charles Ammi Cutter." In *Mirror for Librarians*. London: Grafton, 1948. Pp. 87–88.

15.440 Morse, C. R. "A Biographical, Bibliographical Study of Charles Ammi Cutter, Librarian." Master's thesis, University of Washington, 1961.

15.441 Little, A. E. "Charles Ammi Cutter, Librarian at Forbes Library, Northampton, Massachusetts, 1894–1903." Master's thesis, University of North Carolina, 1962.

15.442 Immroth, J. P. "Charles Ammi Cutter." *ELIS* 6 (1971): 380–87.

15.443 Horiuchi, I. "Charles Ammi Cutter." *Library and Information Science [Mita Society]* 10 (1972): 187–94.

15.444 Miksa, F. L. "Charles Ammi Cutter: Nineteenth-Century Systematizer of Libraries." Doctoral dissertation, University of Chicago, 1974.

15.445 Miksa, F. L., ed. *Charles Ammi Cutter: Library Systematizer*. Littleton, Colo.: Libraries Unlimited, 1977.

15.446 Miksa, F. L. "Cutter, Charles Ammi (1837–1903)." *DALB*: 1978 109–15.

15.447 "Cutter, Charles Ammi." In *Librarian Authors: A Biobibliography*, by R. Engelbarts. Jefferson, N.C.: McFarland, 1981. Pp. 57–60.

15.448 Miksa, F. L. "Cutter, Charles Ammi (1837–1903)." *ALAWE2*: 1986 238–40.

Dana, John Cotton

15.449 "John Cotton Dana." *BB* 10 (1918): 25.

15.450 Dana, J. C. *Suggestions*. Boston: F.W. Faxon Co., 1921.

15.451 Genzmer, G. H. "Dana, John Cotton (Aug. 19, 1856–July 1, 1929)." *DAB* 5 (1930): 56–58.

15.452 Johnson, H., and Winser, B. "Bibliography: John Cotton Dana, Author." *LQ* 7 (1937): 68–98.

15.453 Kingdon, F. *John Cotton Dana, a Life*. Newark, N.J.: Newark Public Library and Museum, 1940.

15.454 Hadley, C. *John Cotton Dana: A Sketch*. Chicago: American Library Association, 1943.

15.455 Sabine, J. E., and Frebault, M. "John Cotton Dana, 1856–1929: A Remembrance." *Newark Public Library News* 12 (October 1956): 71, 74–76.

15.456 *John Cotton Dana [1856–1929], the Centennial Convocation: Addresses by Arthur T. Vanderbilt and L. Quincy Mumford, with a Prefatory Note by James E. Bryan*. New Brunswick: Rutgers University Press, 1957.

15.457 Lansberg, W. R. "John Cotton Dana, 1856–1929." *WLB* 31 (1957): 542.

15.458 Hauserman, D. D. "John Cotton Dana: The Militant Minority of One." Master's thesis, New York University, 1965.

15.459 Cohen, L. G. "John Cotton Dana's Library Services for Children in Springfield, Massachusetts." Master's thesis, Southern Connecticut State College, 1966.

15.460 Sabine, J. E. "John Cotton Dana in Newark: I Remember, I Remember." *Antiquarian Bookman* 41 (3–10 June 1968): 2124–25.

15.461 Sabine, J. E. "John Cotton Dana." *ELIS* 6 (1971): 417–23.

15.462 Stevens, N. D. "Dana, John Cotton (1865–1929)." *DALB*: 1978 115–20.

15.463 "Dana, John Cotton." In *Librarian Authors: A Biobibliography*, by R. Engelbarts. Jefferson, N.C.: McFarland, 1981. Pp. 69–72.

15.464 Vormelker, R. L. "Dana, John Cotton (1856–1929)." *ALAWE2*: 1986 244–46.

Danton, J. Periam

15.465 *J. Periam Danton: A Bibliography.* Berkeley: School of Librarianship, University of California, 1976.

Darrach, Marjorie J.

15.466 Marshall, M. L. "Marjorie J. Darrach." *BMLA* 38 (1950): 272.

David, Charles Wendell

15.467 Riggs, J. B. *Charles Wendell David: Scholar, Teacher, Librarian.* Philadelphia: Union Catalogue of the Philadelphia Metropolitan Area, Inc., 1965.

Davis, Mary Gould

15.468 Sword, E. D. "Mary Gould Davis: Her Contribution to Storytelling." Master's thesis, Southern Connecticut State College, 1972.

Davis, Raymond Cazallis

15.469 Bishop, W. W. "Raymond Cazallis Davis, 1836–1919." *BB* 11 (1920): 23–24.

15.470 Finney, B. A. "As It Was In the Beginning: Raymond C. Davis." *PL* 29 (1924): 406–12.

15.471 Finney, B. A. "Davis, Raymond Cazallis (June 23, 1836–June 10,1919)." *DAB* 5 (1930): 142–43.

15.472 Abbott, J. C. "Raymond Cazallis Davis and the University of Michigan General Library, 1877–1905." Doctoral dissertation, University of Michigan, 1957.

15.473 Abbott, J. C. "Davis, Raymond Cazallis (1836–1919)." *DALB*: 1978 120–22.

Dean, Lucille

15.474 "Lady and the Cowboys." *American Magazine* 144 (August 1947): 114–15.

DeGolyer, Everette Lee

15.475 "DeGolyer, Everette Lee." *National Cyclopedia of American Biography* 43 (1961): 12–14.

15.476 Tinkle, L. *Mr. De: A Biography of E.L. DeGolyer.* Boston: Little, Brown, 1970.

15.477 Tinkle, L. "DeGolyer, Everette Lee." *HT* 3 (1976): 234–35.

Deinard, Ephraim

15.478 Newman, L. I. "Solomon Roubin and Ephraim Deinard, Cataloguers of the Hebraica in the Sutro Library in San Francisco." In *Semitic and Oriental Studies*, edited by W. J. Fischel. Berkeley: University of California Press, 1951. Pp. 355–64.

Delaney, Sadie Peterson

15.479 Sprague, M. D. "Dr. Sadie Peterson Delaney, 'Great Humanitarian.'" *Service* 15 (June 1951): 17–18, 25–26.

15.480 Cantrell, C. H. "Sadie P. Delaney: Bibliotherapist and Librarian." *SEL* 6 (1956): 105–09.

15.481 "Sadie Peterson Delaney (1889–1959)." *HBLib*: 1977 34–35.

15.482 Jones, V. L. "Delaney, Sadie Peterson (1889–1959)." *DALB*: 1978 122–24.

Densmore, Frances

15.483 Schusky, E. L. "Densmore, Frances (May 21, 1867–June 5, 1957)." *DAB* Suppl. 6 (1980): 161–63.

Dewey, Melvil

15.484 "Melvil Dewey." *BB* 9 (1917): 133.

15.485 "As It Was in the Beginning." *PL* 30 (1925): 72–80.

15.486 Foster, W. E. "Five Men of '76." *BALA* 20 (1926): 312–23.

15.487 Gray, A. "That Darned Literary Fellow across the Lake." *American Magazine* 103 (April 1927): 56–59, 128–32.

15.488 Dawe, G. *Melvil Dewey: Seer, Inspirer, Doer, 1851–1931.* Lake Placid, N.Y.: Lake Placid Club, 1932.

15.489 Haynes, B. G. "Melvil Dewey." Master's thesis, George Peabody College for Teachers, 1932.

15.490 Jast, L. S. "Recollections of Melvil Dewey." *LibR* 31 (1934): 285–90.

15.491 Williamson, C. C. "Melvil Dewey, Creative Librarian." In *Fifty Years of Education for Librarianship,* Papers Presented at the Celebration of the Fiftieth Anniversary of the University of Illinois Library School, 2 March 1943. Urbana: University of Illinois Press, 1943. Pp. 1–8.

15.492 Lydenberg, H. M. "Dewey, Melvil (Dec. 10, 1851–Dec. 26, 1931)." *DAB* Suppl. 1 (1944): 241–44.

15.493 Rider, F. *Melvil Dewey.* Chicago: American Library Association, 1944.

15.494 Thornton, J. L. "Melvil Dewey." In *Mirror for Librarians.* London: Grafton, 1948. Pp. 143–47.

15.495 Burger, B. "He Lived as If He Were Always Catching Trains: Melvil Dewey." *North Country Life* 5 (Spring 1951): 26–28, 43.

15.496 Dewey, G. "Dewey 1851–1951." *LJ* 76 (1951): 1964–65.

15.497 Ferguson, M. J. " 'Diamond' Dewey." *DCL* 11 (1951): 2–4.

15.498 Melcher, F. G. "Among the Founders." *LJ* 76 (1951): 1959–63.

15.499 "Melvil Dewey (1851–1931)." *Nature* 168 (1951): 981–82.

15.500 Gropp, A. E. "Key to Knowledge Turns South." *Rotarian* 83 (October 1953): 30–32.

15.501 Kennedy, R. F. "Who Was Melvil Dewey?" *Indian Librarian* 8 (1953): 8–13.

15.502 Pinkowski, E. "Father of Modern Librarians: Melvil Dewey." In *Forgotten Fathers.* Philadelphia: Sunshine Press, 1953. Pp. 3–21.

15.503 Trautman, R. L. "Melvil Dewey and the 'Wellesley Half Dozen.' " *CLC* 3 (1954): 9–13.

15.504 MacLeod, R. D. "Melvil Dewey and His Famous School." *LibR* 135 (1960): 479–84.

15.505 Hassenforder, J. "Trois Pionniers des Bibliothèques Publiques, Edward Edwards, M. Dewey, Eugene Morel: Étude Biographique Comparée." *Education et Bibliothèque* 11 (1964): 11–40.

15.506 Gunjal, S. R. "Melvil Dewey and His Achievements." *Herald of Library Science* 4 (1965): 39–45.

15.507 Harlow, N. "Who's Afraid of Melvil Dewey?" *PNLAQ* 31 (1966): 10–17.

15.508 Takeuchi, S. "Dewey in Florida." *JLH* 1 (1966): 127–32.

15.509 Grotzinger, L. A. "Melvil Dewey: The 'Sower.' " *JLH* 3 (1968): 313–28.

15.510 Rayward, W. B. "Melvil Dewey and Education for Librarianship." *JLH* 3 (1968): 297–312.

15.511 Rockwood, R. H. "Melvil Dewey and Librarianship." *JLH* 3 (1968): 329–41.

15.512 Linderman, W. B. "Melvil Dewey." *ELIS* 7 (1972): 142–60.

15.513 Kumar, P. S. G. "Dewey and Ranganathan: A Perspective." *Herald of Library Science* (1973): 163–68.

15.514 Horiuchi, I. "Melvil Dewey." *Library and Information Science [Mita Society]* 12 (1974): 143–53.

15.515 Frost, J. E. "Wakers and Shakers." *Alabama Librarian* 27 (1975): 2–5.

15.516 Dale, D. C. "A Nineteenth-Century Cameo: Melvil Dewey in 1890." *JLH* 13 (1978): 48–56.

15.517 Vann, S. K. "Dewey, Melvil (1851–1931)." *DALB*: 1978 124–34.

15.518 Vann, S. K., ed. *Melvil Dewey: His Enduring Presence in Librarianship.* Littleton, Colo.: Libraries Unlimited, 1978.

15.519 Lee, M. M. "Melvil Dewey (1851–1931): His Educational Contributions and Reforms." Doctoral dissertation, Loyola University of Chicago, 1979.

15.520 "Dewey, Melvil." In *Librarian Authors: A Biobibliography,* by R. Engelbarts. Jefferson, N.C.: McFarland, 1981. Pp. 54–57.

15.521 Elliott, A. "Melvil Dewey: A Singular and Contentious Life." *WLB* 55 (1981): 666–71.

15.522 Garrison, D. "Dewey the Apostle." In *Melvil Dewey: The Man and the Classification,* edited by G. Stevenson and J. Kramer-Greene. Albany, N.Y.: Forest Press, 1983. Pp. 29–47.

15.523 Metcalf, K. D. "Reminiscences of Melvil Dewey." In *Melvil Dewey: The Man and the Classification,* edited by G. Stevenson and J. Kramer-Greene. Albany, N.Y.: Forest Press, 1983. Pp. 3–8.

15.524 Miksa, F. L. "Dewey and the Corporate Ideal." In *Melvil Dewey: The Man and the Classification,* edited by G. Stevenson and J. Kramer-Greene. Albany, N.Y.: Forest Press, 1983. Pp. 49–100.

15.525 Stevenson, G., and Kramer-Greene, J. *Melvil Dewey: The Man and the Classification.* Albany, N.Y.: Forest Press, 1983.

15.526 Comaromi, J. P. "Dewey, Melvil (1851–1931)." *ALAWE2*: 1986 248–50.

Dickinson, Asa Don

15.527 Gambee, B. L. "Dickinson, Asa Don (1876–1960)." *DALB*: 1978 134–35.

Dickinson, George Sherman

15.528 Bradley, C. J. "Dickinson, George Sherman (1888–1964)." *DALB*: 1978 135–37.

Dienst, Alex

15.529 Barker, E. C. "Dienst, Alex." *HT* 1 (1952): 502.

Ditzion, Sidney Herbert

15.530 Shera, J. H. "Ditzion, Sidney Herbert (1908–1975)." *DALB*: 1978 137–38.

Dix, William Shepherd

15.531 "Dix, William Shepherd." *CB* (1969): 126–28.

15.532 Bryant, D. W. "A Tribute to Bill Dix, 1910–1978." *WLB* 52 (1978): 614–15.

15.533 Harris, M. H., and Tourjee, M. A. "William Shepherd Dix: Symbolic Leadership and

Academic Librarianship." *Journal of Academic Librarianship* 8 (1982): 221–26.

15.534 Harris, M. H., and Tourjee, M. A. "William S. Dix." *LAAL*: 1983 50–71.

15.535 Kaser, D. "Dix, William Shepherd." *ELIS* 36 (1983): 182–86.

15.536 Tuttle, H. W. "Dix, William S. (1910–1978)." *ALAWE2*: 1986 251–52.

Dobie, J. Frank

15.537 Bode, W. *A Portrait of Pancho; The Life of a Great Texan: J. Frank Dobie*. Austin: Pemberton Press, 1965.

15.538 Dugger, R., ed. *Three Men in Texas: Bedichek, Webb, Dobie; Essays by Their Friends in the "Texas Observer"*. Austin: University of Texas Press, 1967.

15.539 Owens, W. A. *Three Friends: Roy Bedichek, J. Frank Dobie, Walter Prescott Webb*. Garden City, N.Y.: Doubleday, 1969.

15.540 Tinkle, L. *An American Original: The Life of J. Frank Dobie*. Boston: Little, Brown, 1978.

Doe, Janet

15.541 Annan, G. L. "Janet Doe." *BMLA* 36 (1948): 413–14.

15.542 "A Bibliography of Janet Doe." *BMLA* 45 (1957): 281–84.

Doms, Keith

15.543 "Doms, Keith." *CB* (1971): 104–06.

Dondale, Marion Frances

15.544 Babcock, H. "Marion Frances Dondale." *BMLA* 41 (1953): 287–89.

Doren, Electra Collins

15.545 Hollingsworth, V. "Dedicated Life: Memories of a Great Librarian—Electra Collins Doren." *WLB* 28 (1954): 782–87.

15.546 Kingery, R. E. "Doren, Electra Collins (1861–1927)." *DALB*: 1978 138–39.

Douglas, Mary Teresa Peacock

15.547 Johnson, M. F. K. "Douglas, Mary Teresa Peacock (1903–1970)." *DALB*: 1978 139–41.

15.548 Gambee, B. L. "A Firm Persuasion: The Career of Mary Peacock Douglas." *NCL* 43 (1985): 72–86.

Downs, Robert Bingham

15.549 "Downs, Robert B(ingham)." *CB* (1952): 158–61.

15.550 Harwell, R. "Robert Bingham Downs." *BB* 23 (1960): 25–27.

15.551 Suen, M. T. "Robert Bingham Downs and Academic Librarianship." Master's thesis, Southern Connecticut State College, 1967.

15.552 Gunning, C. "Publications of Robert B. Downs." In *Research Librarianship: Essays in Honor of Robert B. Downs*, edited by J. Orne. New York: R.R. Bowker, 1971. Pp. 141–62.

15.553 Duyka, A. A. "Robert Bingham Downs: His Life and Works." Research Paper, Texas Woman's University, 1976.

15.554 "Downs, Robert Bingham." In *Librarian Authors: A Biobibliography*, by R. Engelbarts. Jefferson, N.C.: McFarland, 1981. P. 158.

15.555 Young, A. P. "Robert B. Downs." *LAAL*: 1983 73–93.

15.556 Downs, R. B. *Perspectives on the Past: An Autobiography*. Metuchen, N.J.: Scarecrow Press, 1984.

15.557 Downs, R. B. *Books in My Life.* Washington, D.C.: Center for the Book, Library of Congress, 1985.

15.558 Kraus, J. W. "Downs, Robert B. (1903–)." *ALAWE2*: 1986 255–56.

Draper, Lyman Copeland

15.559 Thwaites, R. G. "Lyman Copeland Draper—A Memoir." *Wicsonsin State Historical Society Collections* 12 (1892): 1–19.

15.560 Schafer, J. "Draper, Lyman Copeland (Sept. 4, 1815–Aug. 26, 1891)." *DAB* 5 (1930): 441–42.

15.561 Hesseltine, W. B. *The Story of Lyman Copeland Draper.* Madison, Wis.: State Historical Society of Wisconsin, 1954.

15.562 Conaway, C. W. "Draper, Lyman Copeland (1815–1891)." *DALB*: 1978 141–43.

15.563 Mattern, C. J. "Lyman Copeland Draper: An Archivist's Reappraisal." *AAr* 45 (1982): 444–54.

Drury, Francis Keese Wynkoop

15.564 Gleaves, E. S. "Drury, Francis Keese Wynkoop (1878–1954)." *DALB*: 1978 143–45.

Du Bois, Isabel

15.565 Orion, W. H. "Who Says That They Have Retired?" *LJ* 72 (1947): 1549.

Dudgeon, Matthew Simpson

15.566 Samore, T. "Dudgeon, Matthew Simpson (1871–1949)." *DALB*: 1978 145–46.

Duke, James Buchanan

15.567 Mitchell, B. "Duke, James Buchanan (Dec. 23, 1856–Oct. 10, 1925)." *DAB* 5 (1930): 497–98.

Dunkin, Paul Shaner

15.568 Carnovsky, R. F. "Paul S. Dunkin." *LRTS* 12 (1968): 447–49.

15.569 Hickey, D. J. "Dunkin, Paul Shaner (1905–1975)." *DALB*: 1978 147–48.

15.570 Hickey, D. J. "Dunkin, Paul S. (1908–1975)." *ALAWE2*: 1986 257–58.

Dunn, Jacob Piatt

15.571 Banta, R. E. "Dunn, Jacob Piatt: 1855–1924." In *Indiana Authors and Their Books, 1816–1916.* Crawfordsville, Ind.: Wabash College, 1949. P. 94.

Durrie, Daniel Steele

15.572 Butler, J. D. "Daniel Steele Durrie." *Proceedings of the State Historical Society of Wisconsin* 39 (1892): 73–81.

15.573 Smith, W. M. "Durrie, Daniel Steele (Jan. 2, 1819–Aug. 31, 1892)." *DAB* 5 (1930): 551–52.

Eames, Wilberforce

15.574 Paltsits, V. H. "Wilberforce Eames, American Bibliographer." *BNYPL* 59 (1955): 505–19.

15.575 Robertson, W. D., and Holley, E. G. "Eames, Wilberforce (1855–1937)." *DALB*: 1978 148–53.

15.576 "Eames, Wilberforce." In *Librarian Authors: A Biobibliography,* by R. Engelbarts. Jefferson, N.C.: McFarland, 1981. Pp. 104–06.

Eastlick, John Taylor

15.577 Chapman, E. D. "John Taylor Eastlick." *BB* 23 (1960): 1–3.

Eastman, Linda Anne

15.578 "Linda A. Eastman." *BB* 13 (1926): 1.

15.579 Eastman, L. A. "Who Says That They Have Retired?" *LJ* 72 (1947): 1125.

15.580 Wright, A. E. "Linda A. Eastman: Pioneer in Librarianship." Master's thesis, Kent State University, 1952.

15.581 Phillips, C. O. "Linda Anne Eastman: Librarian." Master's thesis, Western Reserve University, 1953.

15.582 Cramer, C. H. "Eastman, Linda Anne (1867–1963)." *DALB*: 1978 153–55.

15.583 Fenster, V. R. "Eastman, Linda Anne, July 17, 1867–April 5, 1963." *Notable American Women: The Modern Period*: 1980 215–16.

Eastman, Mary Huse

15.584 Frank, W. P. "Mary Huse Eastman." *BB* 21 (1953): 25–26.

Eaton, Anne Thaxter

15.585 Sayers, F. C. "Anne Eaton of Lincoln School." *HB* 23 (1947): 331–39.

15.586 Sassé, M. "Eaton, Anne Thaxter (1881–1971)." *DALB*: 1978 155–56.

Eaton, John

15.587 Miksa, F. L. "Eaton, John (1829–1906)." *DALB*: 1978 156–57.

15.588 Miksa, F. L. "Eaton, John (1829–1906)." *ALAWE2*: 1986 259.

Edgar, Neal Lowndes

15.589 Harrick, R. D. "Neal Lowndes Edgar, 1927–1983." *Technical Services Quarterly* 3 (1985–1986): 141–44.

Edmands, John

15.590 Montgomery, T. L. "Edmands, John (Feb. 1, 1820–Oct. 17, 1915)." *DAB* 6 (1931): 21–22.

15.591 Clapp, V. W., and First, E. W. "A.L.A. Member No. 13: A First Glance at John Edmands." *LQ* 26 (1956): 1–22.

15.592 Wessells, M. B. "Edmands, John (1820–1915)." *DALB*: 1978 157–58.

Edmonds, Cecil

15.593 Razer, B. A., and Thwing, V. "A Chapter in Arkansas Library History; Cecil Edmonds and Operation Library." *ArkL* 43 (June 1986): 33–43.

Egan, Margaret Elizabeth

15.594 Shera, J. H. "Egan, Margaret Elizabeth (1905–1959)." *DALB*: 1978 158–59.

Elliott, Leslie Robinson

15.595 Benson, S. H. "Leslie Robinson Elliott: His Contribution to Theological Librarianship." Master's thesis, University of Texas, 1965.

15.596 Wills, K. C. "Librarian L.R. Elliott and Baptist History." *Baptist History and Heritage* 6 (1971): 156–63.

Ellsworth, Ralph E.

15.597 Ellsworth, R. E. *Ellsworth on Ellsworth: An Unchronological, Mostly True Account of Some Moments of Contact between "Library Science" and Me, since Our Confluence in 1931, with Appropriate Sidelights.* Metuchen, N.J.: Scarecrow Press, 1980.

15.598 Johnson, E. R. "Ralph E. Ellsworth." *LAAL*: 1983 95–123.

Elmendorf, Theresa West

15.599 Faxon, F. W. "Theresa West Elmendorf." *BB* 14 (1931): 93–94.

15.600 Rooney, P. M. "Elmendorf, Theresa Hubbell West (1855–1932)." *DALB*: 1978 159–60.

15.601 "Elmendorf, Theresa West." In *Librarian Authors: A Biobibliography*, by R. _Engelbarts. Jefferson, N.C.: McFarland, 1981. Pp. 23–24.

15.602 Thomison, D. "Elmendorf, Theresa West (1855–1932)." *ALAWE2*: 1986 265–66.

Emrich, Duncan

15.603 "Emrich, Duncan (Black Macdonald)." *CB* (1955): 180–82.

Esterquest, Ralph Theodore

15.604 Bryant, D. W. "Ralph T. Esterquest." *BB* 23 (1960): 49–51.

15.605 Eastlick, J. T. "Esterquest, Ralph Theodore (1912–1968)." *DALB*: 1978 160–61.

Estes, Eleanor

15.606 "Estes, Eleanor." *CB* (1946): 185–86.

Evans, Charles

15.607 Holley, E. G. *Charles Evans: American Bibliographer*. Urbana: University of Illinois Press, 1963.

15.608 Holley, E. G. "Evans, Charles (1850–1935)." *DALB*: 1978 162–67.

15.609 "Evans, Charles." In *Librarian Authors: A Biobibliography*, by R. Engelbarts. Jefferson, N.C.: McFarland, 1981. Pp. 106–07.

15.610 Holley, E. G. "Evans, Charles (1850–1935)." *ALAWE2*: 1986 272–73.

Evans, Luther Harris

15.611 Clapp, V. W. "Luther H. Evans." *BB* 24 (1964): 97–103.

15.612 Sittig, W. J. "Luther Evans: Man for a New Age." *QJLC* 33 (1976): 251–67.

15.613 "Evans, Luther Harris." In *Librarian Authors: A Biobibliography*, by R. Engelbarts. Jefferson, N.C.: McFarland, 1981. P. 156.

15.614 Milum, B. L. "Evans, Luther (1902–1981)." *ALAWE2*: 1986 274.

Exall, May Dickson

15.615 Dibrell, J. "Exall, Mrs. May Dickson." *HT* 1 (1952): 605–06.

Fair, Ethel Marion

15.616 Aldrich, G. L. "Ethel Marion Fair." *BB* 20 (1951): 81–83.

Fairchild, Mary Salome Cutler

15.617 "As It Was in the Beginning." *PL* 29 (1924): 349–52.

15.618 Wyer, J. I. "Fairchild, Mary Salome Cutler (June 21, 1855–Dec. 20, 1921)." *DAB* 6 (1931): 254–55.

15.619 Boromé, J. A. "Fairchild, Mary Salome Cutler (June 21, 1855–Dec. 20, 1921)." *NAW* 1 (1971): 593–94.

15.620 Gambee, B. L. "Fairchild, Mary Salome Cutler (1855–1921)." *DALB*: 1978 167–70.

15.621 "Fairchild, Mary Salome Cutler." In *Librarian Authors: A Biobibliography*, by R. Engelbarts. Jefferson, N.C.: McFarland, 1981. Pp. 41–42.

Fargo, Lucile Foster

15.622 McGuire, A. B. "Fargo, Lucile Foster (1880–1962)." *DALB*: 1978 170–71.

Faust, Clarence Henry

15.623 "Faust, Clarence H(enry)." *CB* (1952): 181–83.

Faxon, Frederick Winthrop

15.624 "Frederick Winthrop Faxon." *BB* 14 (1932): 185–86.

15.625 Cveljo, K. "Faxon, Frederick Winthrop (1866–1936)." *DALB*: 1978 171–72.

Fellows, Jennie Dorcas

15.626 Getchell, M. W. "Dorkas Fellows, Cataloger and D.C. Editor." *Catalogers and Classifiers Handbook* 8 (1940): 14–19.

15.627 McMullen, H. "Fellows, Jennie Dorcas (1873–1938)." *DALB*: 1978 173–74.

Ferguson, Milton James

15.628 Brown, T. G. "Dr. Milton James Ferguson." *BB* 17 (1942): 129–30.

15.629 Breivik, P. S. "Ferguson, Milton James (1879–1954)." *DALB*: 1978 174–76.

Findly, Elizabeth

15.630 Oregon University, School of Librarianship. *Honoring Elizabeth Findly: Writings to Honor the Retirement of Elizabeth Findly.* Eugene: University of Oregon, School of Librarianship, 1974.

Fiske, Daniel Willard

15.631 Fowler, M. "Willard Fiske as a Bibliographer." *PBSA* 12 (1918): 89–96.

15.632 Hermannsson, H. "Willard Fiske and Icelandic Bibliography." *PBSA* 12 (1918): 97–106.

15.633 White, H. S. "A Sketch of the Life and Labors of Professor Willard Fiske." *PBSA* 12 (1918): 69–88.

15.634 White, H. S. *Willard Fiske, Life and Correspondence: A Biographical Study.* New York: Oxford University Press, 1925.

15.635 White, H. S. "Fiske, Daniel Willard (Nov. 11, 1831–Sept. 17, 1904)." *DAB* 6 (1931): 417.

15.636 Vevstad, J. "Boksamleren Professor Willard Fiske." *Bokvennen* 5 (1935): 1–4.

15.637 Williams, R. J. *Jennie McGraw Fiske: Her Influence upon Cornell University.* Ithaca: Cornell University Press, 1949.

15.638 Bierds, B. K. "Daniel Willard Fiske: His Professional Career and Its Influence on the Growth of the Cornell University Libraries." Research Paper, Long Island University, 1966.

15.639 Pitschmann, L. A. "Fiske, Daniel Willard." *ELIS* 38 (1985): 176–83.

Fitzgerald, Frances Emmett

15.640 Conmy, P. T. "Frances Emmett Fitzgerald, 1901–1961, Librarian of Many Parts." *CLW* 57 (1986): 205–07.

Fitzgerald, Hugh Nugent

15.641 Crane, E. "Fitzgerald, Hugh Nugent." *HT* 1 (1952): 605.

Fleming, Richard Tudor

15.642 Frantz, J. B. "Tribute to Richard T. Fleming at Memorial Services March 16, 1973." *LCT* 6 (1973): 16–23.

15.643 Frantz, J. B. "Fleming, Richard Tudor." *HT* 3 (1976): 298.

Fletcher, William Isaac

15.644 Faxon, F. W. "William Isaac Fletcher (1844–1917)." *BB* 9 (1917): 181–82.

15.645 Jones, E. L. "As It Was in the Beginning." *PL* 29 (1924): 522–26.

15.646 Bobinski, G. S. "William Isaac Fletcher: An Early American Library Leader." *JLH* 5 (1970): 101–18.

15.647 Bobinski, G. S. "Fletcher, William Isaac (1844–1917)." *DALB*: 1978 176–79.

15.648 "Fletcher, William I." In *Librarian Authors: A Biobibliography*, by R. Engelbarts. Jefferson, N.C.: McFarland, 1981. Pp. 107–09.

Flexner, Jennie Maas

15.649 Edge, S. A. "Jennie M. Flexner." *BB* 17 (1940): 1–2.

15.650 Johnston, E. "Jennie M. Flexner, 1882–1944." In *Pioneering Leaders in Librarianship*, edited by E. M. Danton. Chicago: American Library Association, 1953. Pp. 61–73.

15.651 Edge, S. A. "Flexner, Jennie Maas (Nov. 6, 1882–Nov. 17, 1944)." *NAW* 1 (1971): 633–34.

15.652 Ditzion, S. H. "Flexner, Jennie Maas (Nov. 6, 1882–Nov. 17, 1944)." *DAB* Suppl. 3 (1973): 280–81.

15.653 Monroe, M. E. "Flexner, Jennie Maas (1882–1944)." *DALB*: 1978 179–82.

15.654 "Flexner, Jennie Maas." In *Librarian Authors: A Biobibliography*, by R. Engelbarts. Jefferson, N.C.: McFarland, 1981. Pp. 93–95.

Fling, Margaret

15.655 Tingley, D. F. "Margaret Fling: The Historian's Librarian." *Illinois Historical Journal* 77 (1984): 249–54.

Flint, Weston

15.656 Meyer, H. H. B. "Flint, Weston (July 4, 1835–Apr. 6, 1906)." *DAB* 6 (1931): 475–76.

Fogarty, John E.

15.657 Healey, J. S. *John E. Fogarty: Political Leadership for Library Development*. Metuchen, N.J.: Scarecrow Press, 1974.

15.658 Healey, J. S. "Fogarty, John E. (1913–1967)." *DALB*: 1978 182–83.

Foik, Paul Joseph

15.659 Byrne, P. R. "Paul Joseph Foik, C.S.C." *CLW* 12 (1941): 183.

15.660 Clancy, R. J. "Foik, Paul Joseph." *HT* 1 (1952): 614–15.

15.661 Bresie, M. "Paul J. Foik, C.S.C., Librarian-Historian." Master's thesis, University of Texas, 1964.

15.662 Bresie, M. "Foik, Paul Joseph (1879–1941)." *DALB*: 1978 183–84.

Folger, Henry Clay

15.663 Genzmer, G. H. "Folger, Henry Clay (June 18, 1857–June 11, 1930)." *DAB* 6 (1931): 487–88.

15.664 *Henry C. Folger, 18 June 1857–11 June 1930*. New Haven, Conn.: Privately printed, 1931.

15.665 Knachel, P. A. "Folger, Henry Clay." *ELIS* 8 (1972): 578–82.

15.666 Knachel, P. A. "Folger, Henry Clay (1857–1930)." *ALAWE2*: 1986 282–83.

Folsom, Charles

15.667 Parsons, T. "Memoir of Charles Folsom." *PMHS* 13 (1875): 26–42.

15.668 Lane, W. C. "Folsom, Charles (Dec. 24, 1794–Nov. 8, 1872)." *DAB* 6 (1931): 493–94.

Folsom, George

15.669 "George Folsom." *Proceedings of the American Academy of Arts and Sciences* 9 (1874): 237–38.

Forbes, George Washington

15.670 Jackson, W. V. "Some Pioneer Negro Library Workers." *LJ* 64 (1939): 215–17.

15.671 "George Washington Forbes (1864–1927)." *HBLib:* 1977 28–29.

Force, Peter

15.672 Martz, D. J. "Force, Peter (1790–1868)." *ALAWE2:* 1986 283–84.

Foster, William Eaton

15.673 Sherman, C. E. "William E. Foster, 1851–1930." *BB* 14 (1930): 41–45.

15.674 Sherman, C. E. "William E. Foster: Liberal Librarian." *WLB* 30 (1956): 449–53, 467.

15.675 Healey, J. S. "Foster, William Eaton (1851–1930)." *DALB:* 1978 184–86.

15.676 "Foster, William E." In *Librarian Authors: A Biobibliography,* by R. Engelbarts. Jefferson, N.C.: McFarland, 1981. Pp. 83–85.

Fowler, Julian Sabin

15.677 Lang, R. "Julian Sabin Fowler." *BB* 18 (1945): 145–47.

Franklin, Benjamin

15.678 Becker, C. L. "Franklin, Benjamin (Jan. 17, 1706–Apr. 17, 1790)." *DAB* 6 (1931): 585–98.

15.679 Nasri, W. Z. "Franklin, Benjamin." *ELIS* 9 (1973): 84–89.

15.680 Miller, C. W. "Franklin and the Booksellers." *ABBW* 60 (1977): 2610–12.

15.681 Harris, M. H. "Franklin, Benjamin (1706–1790)." *DALB:* 1978 186–88.

15.682 Clark, R. W. *Benjamin Franklin: A Biography.* New York: Random House, 1983.

15.683 Adams, T. A. "Franklin, Benjamin (1706–1790)." *ALAWE2:* 1986 292–94.

Franklin, Louise

15.684 Pettigrew, C. L. "Louise Franklin: The Education of a Texas Librarian." Master's thesis, University of Texas, 1967.

Franklin, Robert D.

15.685 Munn, R. R. "Robert D. Franklin." *BB* 23 (1961): 121–23.

Fraser, Ian Forbes

15.686 "Fraser, Ian Forbes." *CB* (1954): 287–88.

Freedley, George Reynolds

15.687 "Freedley, George (Reynolds)." *CB* (1947): 215–16.

15.688 Correll, L. "American Theatre Librarianship: Focus on Leadership of George R. Freedley." *JLH* 6 (1971): 317–26.

Freehafer, Edward Geier

15.689 "Freehafer, Edward G(eier)." *CB* (1955): 215–16.

Freeman, Marilla Waite

15.690 McDonald, G. D. "Marilla Waite Freeman." *BB* 19 (1947): 29–31.

15.691 Vormelker, R. L. "Freeman, Marilla Waite (1871–1961)." *DALB*: 1978 188–91.

Frick, Bertha Margaret

15.692 Stevens, J. E. "Frick, Bertha Margaret (1894–1975)." *DALB*: 1978 191–92.

Fuller, Margaret Harwell

15.693 "Fuller, Margaret H(arwell)." *CB* (1959): 137–38.

Fulton, John Farquhar

15.694 "Bibliography of John Farquhar Fulton." *Journal of the History of Medicine & Allied Sciences* 17 (1962): 51–71.

15.695 Muirhead, A. "Portrait of a Bibliophile IX: John Farquhar Fulton, 1899–1960." *BC* 11 (1962): 427–36.

15.696 Muirhead, A. "John Fulton—Book Collector, Humanist, and Friend." *Journal of the History of Medicine & Allied Sciences* 17 (1962): 2–15.

15.697 Thomson, E. H. "Fulton, John Farquhar (Nov. 1, 1899–May 29, 1960)." *DAB* Suppl. 6 (1980): 222–24.

Fussler, Herman Howe

15.698 Shera, J. H. "Herman Howe Fussler." *LQ* 53 (1983): 215–53.

15.699 Winger, H. W. "In Honor of Herman Howe Fussler." *LQ* 53 (1983): 213–14.

15.700 McElderry, S. "Fussler, Herman Howe (1914–)." *ALAWE2*: 1986 294–95.

Fyan, Loleta Dawson

15.701 "Fyan, Loleta D(awson)." *CB* (1951): 221–23.

15.702 Hagerman, D. T. "Loleta Dawson Fyan." *BB* 23 (1961): 73–75.

Garfield, Eugene

15.703 Griffith, B. "Garfield, Eugene." *ALAWE2*: 1986 298–99.

Garrison, George Pierce

15.704 Barker, E. C. "Garrison, George Pierce." *HT* 1 (1952): 673–74.

Gates, Doris

15.705 Montgomery, E. R. "Doris Gates." In *The Story behind Modern Books*. New York: Dodd, 1949. Pp. 125–29.

Gaver, Mary Virginia

15.706 "Gaver, Mary Virginia." *CB* (1966): 122–24.

15.707 Jones, M. L. "Gaver, Mary (1906–)." *ALAWE2*: 1986 300–301

Gay, Frank Butler

15.708 Kerr, R. A. "Frank Butler Gay (1856–1934)—Bibliophile." *Trinity College Library Gazette* 1 (February 1955): 18–21.

Gerould, James Thayer

15.709 Gilchrist, D. B. "James Thayer Gerould." *BB* 15 (1935): 101.

15.710 Heyl, L. "James Thayer Gerould: Some Recollections of an Association." *Princeton University Library Chronicle* 14 (1953): 91–93.

15.711 Harvey, J. F. "Gerould, James Thayer (1872–1951)." *DALB*: 1978 192–94.

Gerould, Winifred Gregory

15.712 Haas, M. L. "Gerould, Winifred Gregory (1885–1955)." *DALB*: 1978 194–95.

Gibson, Robert William, Jr.

15.713 "Gibson, Robert W(illiam), Jr." *CB* (1969): 161–63.

Gilchrist, Donald Bean

15.714 Hayes, C. D. "Gilchrist, Donald Bean (1892–1939)." *DALB*: 1978 195–96.

Gillett, Charles Ripley

15.715 Slavens, T. P. "Incidents in the Librarianship of Charles Ripley Gillett." *JLH* 4 (1969): 321–29.

15.716 Slavens, T. P. "Gillett, Charles Ripley (1855–1948)." *DALB*: 1978 196–97.

Gillis, James Louis

15.717 Brewitt, T. R. "James L. Gillis, 1857–1917." In *Pioneering Leaders in Librarianship*, edited by E. M. Danton. Chicago: American Library Association, 1953. Pp. 74–84.

15.718 "James L. Gillis Centennial." *CalL* 18 (1957): 220–38.

15.719 Mumm, B., and Ottley, A. "James L. Gillis in Print." *NNCL* 52 (1957): 654–58.

15.720 Halligan, J. T. "James Louis Gillis, California State Librarian, 1899–1917: His Role and Influence in the Growth of California Libraries." Research Paper, Long Island University, 1962.

15.721 Held, R. "Gillis, James Louis (1857–1917)." *DALB*: 1978 197–200.

15.722 "Gillis, James L." In *Librarian Authors: A Biobibliography*, by R. Engelbarts. Jefferson, N.C.: McFarland, 1981. Pp. 30–32.

Gillis, Mabel Ray

15.723 Warren, A. "Mabel Ray Gillis." *CalL* 12 (1951): 196–99, 224.

15.724 Conmy, P. T. "Mabel Ray Gillis, California State Librarian: The Fulfillment of the Destiny of Inheritance." *NNCL* 63 (1968): 284–94.

15.725 Boaz, M. "Gillis, Mabel Ray (1882–1961)." *DALB*: 1978 200.

Gilman, Daniel Coit

15.726 Mitchell, S. C. "Gilman, Daniel Coit (July 6, 1831–Oct. 13, 1908)." *DAB* 7 (1931): 299–303.

15.727 Young, A. P. "Daniel Coit Gilman and the Formative Period of American Librarianship." *LQ* 45 (1975): 117–40.

15.728 Young, A. P. "Daniel Coit Gilman (1831–1908)." *DALB*: 1978 200–203.

Githens, Alfred Morton

15.729 Oehlerts, D. E. "Githens, Alfred Morton (1876–1973)." *DALB*: 1978 203–04.

Gitler, Robert L.

15.730 Bevis, D. "Robert L. Gitler." *BB* 22 (1957): 25–27.

Gjelsness, Rudolph H.

15.731 Bidlack, R. E. "Gjelsness, Rudolph H. (1894–1968)." *DALB*: 1978 204–05.

15.732 Bidlack, R. E. "Gjelsness, Rudolph H. (1894–1968)." *ALAWE2*: 1986 312–13.

Gleason, Eliza Atkins

15.733 Josey, E. J. "Gleason, Eliza Atkins." *ALAWE2*: 1986 313–14.

Goldman, Edwin Franko

15.734 Jackson, R. "Goldman, Edwin Franko (Jan. 1, 1878–Feb. 21, 1956)." *DAB* Suppl. 6 (1980): 241–43.

Goldstein, Isaac A.

15.735 "Goldstein, Isaac A." In *Handbook of Waco and McLennan County*, edited by D. Kelley. Waco, Tex.: Texian Press, 1972. P. 112.

Gonzalez, Efren William

15.736 "Gonzalez, Efren W(illiam)." *CB* (1971): 160–62.

Goodrich, Francis Lee Dewey

15.737 Podolnick, S. "The Administration of the Library of the College of the City of New York by Francis L.D. Goodrich from 1930–1945." Research Paper, Long Island University, 1966.

15.738 Harvey, J. F. "Goodrich, Francis Lee Dewey (1877–1962)." *DALB*: 1978 205–07.

Goodrich, Nathaniel Lewis

15.739 Fay, L. E. "Nathaniel Lewis Goodrich." *BB* 19 (1946): 1–3.

15.740 Goodrich, N. L. "Report on 38 Years." *DCLB* 5 (April 1950): 35–40.

Goodwin, John Edward

15.741 Coldren, F. A. "John Edward Goodwin." *CLB* 6 (1944): 27.

15.742 Mitchell, S. B. "John Edward Goodwin." *CRL* 5 (1944): 278–81.

15.743 Salinas, A. "John Edward Goodwin: University Librarian." Master's thesis, University of Texas, 1966.

15.744 Powell, L. C. "John E. Goodwin, Founder of the UCLA Library: An Essay Toward a Biography." *JLH* 6 (1971): 265–74.

15.745 Powell, L. C. "Goodwin, John Edward (1876–1948)." *DALB*: 1978 207–08.

Goree, Edwin Sue

15.746 Johnson, L. C. "Edwin Sue Goree, 1884–1961." *TLJ* 37 (1961): 70–72.

15.747 Porter, M. L. R. "Edwin Sue Goree, a Biography." Master's thesis, University of Texas, 1965.

15.748 Porter, P. "Edwin Sue Goree: A Name Synonymous with Libraries in Texas." *TL* 45 (1984): 95–99.

Gould, Charles Henry

15.749 Lomer, G. R. "Charles Henry Gould, 1855–1919." *BB* 13 (1927): 22.

15.750 Crouch, K. "Gould, Charles Henry (1855–1919)." *DALB*: 1978 208–10.

Graff, Everett Dwight

15.751 Pargellis, S. M. "Everett D. Graff: An Appreciation." *Newberry Library Bulletin* 5 (1960): 187–89.

15.752 Towner, L. W. "Graff, Everett Dwight (Aug. 7, 1885–Mar. 11, 1964)." *DAB* Suppl. 7 (1981): 294–95.

Graham, Bessie

15.753 Campbell, M. M. "Bessie Graham, Bibliophile." Master's thesis, Texas State College for Women, 1953.

15.754 Platon, M. J. "Graham, Bessie (1881–1966)." *DALB*: 1978 210–11.

Graham, Clarence Reginald

15.755 "Graham, Clarence R(eginald)." *CB* (1950): 189–90.

15.756 Thompson, L. S. "Skip Graham." *BALA* 47 (1953): 246–47, 273–74.

Green, Bernard Richardson

15.757 Dobbs, K. W. "Green, Bernard Richardson (1843–1914)." *DALB*: 1978 211–12.

Green, Samuel Swett

15.758 Coombs, Z. W. *Samuel Swett Green, Worcestor Free Public Library, Worcester, Mass.: Director, 1867–1871, Librarian, 1871–1909.* Worcester, Mass.: F.S. Blanchard, 1909.

15.759 Green, S. S. "Samuel Swett Green: Some Autobiographical Sketches of Incidents in His Life." *LJ* 38 (1913): 666–70.

15.760 Faxon, F. W. "Samuel Swett Green, 1837–1918." *BB* 10 (1919): 102–03.

15.761 Shaw, R. K. *Samuel Swett Green.* Chicago: American Library Association, 1926.

15.762 Ashley, F. W. "Green, Samuel Swett (Feb. 20, 1837–Dec. 8, 1918)." *DAB* 7 (1931): 557–58.

15.763 Thornton, J. L. "Samuel Swett Green." In *Mirror for Librarians.* London: Grafton, 1948. Pp. 92–93.

15.764 Trombley, M. F. X. "Samuel Swett Green: His Contribution to the Worcester, Massachusetts Free Public Library." Master's thesis, Southern Connecticut State College, 1972.

15.765 Gambee, B. L. "Green, Samuel Swett (1837–1918)." *DALB*: 1978 212–16.

15.766 "Green, Samuel Swett." In *Librarian Authors: A Biobibliography,* by R. Engelbarts. Jefferson, N.C.: McFarland, 1981. Pp. 52–54.

Greenaway, Emerson

15.767 Taylor, T. "Emerson Greenaway." *BB* 22 (1957): 49–51.

15.768 "Greenaway, Emerson." *CB* (1958): 174–75.

Greene, Belle da Costa

15.769 "Belle of the Books." *Time* 53 (11 April 1949): 76–78.

15.770 Miner, D. E., ed. *Studies in Art and Literature for Belle da Costa Greene.* Princeton: Princeton University Press, 1954.

15.771 Miner, D. E., and Haight, A. L. "Greene, Belle da Costa (Dec. 13, 1883–May 10, 1950)." *NAW* 2 (1971): 83–85.

15.772 Wilson, M. T. "Greene, Belle da Costa (Dec. 13, 1883–May 10, 1950)." *DAB* Suppl. 4 (1974): 344–46.

15.773 White, M. D. "Greene, Belle da Costa (1883–1950)." *DALB*: 1978 216–18.

Greener, Richard Theodore

15.774 Woodson, C. G. "Greener, Richard Theodore (Jan. 30, 1844–May 2, 1922)." *DAB* 7 (1931): 578–79.

Gregorian, Vartan

15.775 Deitch, J. "Portrait: Vartan Gregorian." *WLB* 56 (1981): 278–79.

15.776 Allen, J. "The Library's Social Lion: On the Go with Gregorian." *New York* 17 (16 January 1984): 34–42.

15.777 "Gregorian, Vartan." *CB* (1985): 158–61.

Griffin, Appleton Prentiss Clark

15.778 Ashley, F. W. "Griffin, Appleton Prentiss Clark (July 24, 1852–Apr. 16, 1926)." *DAB* 7 (1931): 617.

15.779 Haskell, J. D. "Griffin, Appleton Prentiss Clark (1852–1926)." *DALB*: 1978 218–20.

Griffin, Etta Josselyn

15.780 Stevenson, V. F. *Etta Josselyn Griffin: Pioneer Librarian for the Blind.* Washington, D.C.: National Library for the Blind, 1959.

Griffith, Reginald Harvey

15.781 Osborne, M. T., ed. *The Great Torch Race: Essays in Honor of Reginald Harvey Griffith.* Austin: University of Texas Press, for the Conference of College Teachers of English of Texas and the Humanities Research Center, 1961.

15.782 Clapp, S. L. C., and Ratchford, F. E. "Griffith, Reginald Harvey." *HT* 3 (1976): 359–60.

Griggs, Lillian Baker

15.783 Young, L. B. "Griggs, Lillian Baker (1876–1955)." *DALB:* 1978 220–21.

15.784 Young, B. I. "Lillian Baker Griggs." *LAAL:* 1983 125–46.

Grothaus, Julia

15.785 Drummond, D. R. "Julia Grothaus, San Antonio Librarian." Master's thesis, University of Texas, 1964.

Grover, Wayne C.

15.786 McCoy, D. R. "Grover, Wayne C. (1906–1970)." *ALAWE2:* 1986 316–17.

Gscheidle, Gertrude E.

15.787 Strable, E. G. "Gertrude E. Gscheidle." *BB* 21 (1954): 97–99.

Guerrier, Edith

15.788 King, J. E. "Edith Guerrier." *BB* 18 (1943): 1–3.

Guild, Reuben Aldridge

15.789 "Reuben Guild." *PAAS* n.s. 13 (1900): 126–30.

15.790 Koopman, H. L. "Reuben Aldridge Guild, 1822–1899." *BB* 8 (1915): 119–20.

15.791 Genzmer, G. H. "Guild, Reuben Aldridge (May 4, 1822–May 13, 1899)." *DAB* 8 (1932): 42–43.

Gunter, Lillian

15.792 Nichols, M. I. "Lillian Gunter: Pioneer Texas County Librarian, 1870–1926." Master's thesis, University of Texas, 1958.

15.793 Nichols, I. C., and Nichols, M. I. "Lillian Gunter: Texas County Legislation, 1914–1919." *JLH* 8 (1973): 11–17.

15.794 Nichols, M. I. "Lillian Gunter: County Librarian." *TL* 39 (1977): 129–44.

Haas, Warren J.

15.795 Duda, F. "Haas, Warren J." *ALAWE2:* 1986 322.

Hackett, Charles Wilson

15.796 "Hackett, Charles Wilson." *HT* 1 (1952): 752.

Hadley, Chalmers

15.797 "Chalmers Hadley." *BB* 12 (1925): 105.

15.798 "In Memory of Chalmers Hadley." *Guide Post* 33 (1958): 1–30.

15.799 Harris, M. H., King, T. E., and Starkey, E. D. "Hadley, Chalmers (1872–1958)." *DALB:* 1978 222–23.

Haines, Helen E.

15.800 Haines, H. E. "Through Time's Bifocals." *CalL* 12 (1950): 85–86, 114–15.

15.801 Hyers, F. H. "Helen E. Haines." *BB* 20 (1951): 129–31.

15.802 Sive, M. R. "Helen E. Haines, 1872–1961: An Annotated Bibliography." *JLH* 5 (1970): 146–64.

15.803 Harlan, R. D. "Helen E. Haines." *ELIS* 10 (1973): 278–84.

15.804 Harlan, R. D. "Haines, Helen Elizabeth (1872–1961)." *DALB*: 1978 223–26.

15.805 Edmonds, A. C. "Haines, Helen Elizabeth, Feb. 9, 1892–Aug. 26, 1961." *Notable American Women: The Modern Period*: 1980 298–99.

15.806 "Haines, Helen E." In *Librarian Authors: A Biobibliography*, by R. Engelbarts. Jefferson, N.C.: McFarland, 1981. Pp. 154–56.

15.807 Warncke, R. "Haines, Helen (1872–1951)." *ALAWE2*: 1986 322–23.

Hall, Mary Evelyn

15.808 Pond, P. B. "Hall, Mary Evelyn (1874–1956)." *DALB*: 1978 226–27.

Hallidie, Andrew Smith

15.809 Kahn, E. M. "Andrew Smith Hallidie." *CHSQ* 19 (1940): 144–56.

15.810 Kahn, E. M. "Andrew Hallidie as Writer and Speaker." *CHSQ* 25 (1946): 1–16.

15.811 Mood, F. "Andrew S. Hallidie and Librarianship in San Francisco, 1868–79." *LQ* 16 (1946): 202–10.

Hamer, Philip M.

15.812 Holmes, O. W. "Hamer, Philip M. (1891–1971)." *ALAWE2*: 1986 324–26.

Hamlin, Talbot Faulkner

15.813 Placzek, A. K. "Hamlin, Talbot Faulkner (June 16, 1889–Oct. 7, 1956)." *DAB* Suppl. 6 (1980): 272–73.

Hammond, George P.

15.814 Farquhar, F. P. P. "George P. Hammond's Publications." In *G.P.H.: An Informal Record of George P. Hammond and His Record in the Bancroft Library.* Berkeley: University of California, 1965. Pp. 83–106.

Handy, Daniel Nash

15.815 Christianson, E. B. *Daniel Nash Handy and the Special Library Movement.* New York: Special Libraries Association, Insurance Division, 1980.

Hanson, James C. M.

15.816 Bishop, W. W. "J. C. M. Hanson and International Cataloging." *LQ* 4 (1934): 165–68.

15.817 Butler, P. "Bibliography of James C. M. Hanson." *LQ* 4 (1934): 131–35.

15.818 Starr, H. K. "Mr. Hanson and His Friends." *LQ* 4 (1934): 329–33.

15.819 McMullen, H. "J. C. M. Hanson, 1864–1943." In *Pioneering Leaders in Librarianship*, edited by E. M. Danton. Chicago: American Library Association, 1953. Pp. 85–96.

15.820 Scott, E. "J. C. M. Hanson and His Contribution to Twentieth Century Cataloging." Doctoral dissertation, University of Chicago, 1970.

15.821 Scott, E. "J. C. M. Hanson." *ELIS* 10 (1973): 304–11.

15.822 Scott, E. "Hanson, James Christian Meinich (Mar. 13, 1864–Nov. 8, 1943)." *DAB* Suppl. 3 (1973): 326–27.

15.823 Hanson, J. C. M. *What Became of Jens? A Study in Americanization Based on the Reminiscences of J. C. M. Hanson, 1864–1943*, edited by O. M. Hovde. Decorah, Iowa: Luther College Press, 1974.

15.824 Immroth, J. P. "Hanson, James Christian Meinich (1864–1943)." *DALB*: 1978 227–30.

15.825 "Hanson, J. C. M." In *Librarian Authors: A Biobibliography*, by R. Engelbarts. Jefferson, N.C.: McFarland, 1981. Pp. 88–91.

15.826 Scott, E. "Hanson, J. C. M. (1864–1943)." *ALAWE2*: 1986 332–33.

Harrer, Gustave Adolphus

15.827 Grieder, E. M. "Gustave Adolphus Harrer." *BB* 23 (1961): 97–99.

Harris, Bertha Bell

15.828 "Quién et Quién." *LJ* 72 (1947): 840–41.

Harris, Mildred Alston

15.829 Stovel, L. "Appreciation of Mildred Harris." *Volta Review* 52 (1950): 257, 292–94.

Harris, Thaddeus Mason

15.830 Frothingham, N. L. "Memoir of Thaddeus Mason Harris." *Collections of the Massachusetts Historical Society* ser. 4, 2 (1854): 130–55.

15.831 Frothingham, N. L. *Memoir of Rev. Thaddeus Mason Harris, D.D.* Boston: Crosby, Nichols, and Co., 1854.

15.832 Hawthorne, N. "The Ghost of Dr. Harris." *Living Age* 224 (1900): 345–49.

15.833 Parkes, H. B. "Harris, Thaddeus Mason (July 7, 1768–Apr. 3, 1842)." *DAB* 8 (1932): 320–21.

Harris, Thaddeus William

15.834 Howard, L. O. "Harris, Thaddeus William (Nov. 12, 1795–Jan. 16, 1856)." *DAB* 8 (1932): 321–22.

Harris, William Torrey

15.835 Leidecker, K. F. *Yankee Teacher: The Life of William Torrey Harris.* New York: Philosophical Library, 1946.

15.836 Dillon, L. D., and Miksa, F. L. "Harris, William Torrey (1835–1909)." *DALB*: 1978 230–32.

Harrison, Alice Sinclair

15.837 Herring, B. G. "Alice S. Harrison, Pioneer School Librarian, 1882–1967." Master's thesis, University of Texas, 1968.

15.838 Herring, B. G. "Harrison, Alice Sinclair (1882–1967)." *DALB*: 1978 232–33.

Harrison, Joseph LeRoy

15.839 Faxon, F. W. "Joseph LeRoy Harrison." *BB* 14 (1932): 165.

Harrisse, Henry

15.840 Robertson, W. D. "Harrisse, Henry (1829–1910)." *DALB*: 1978 233–34.

Hart, Gilbert

15.841 Hutchinson, V. L. "Gilbert Hart (1828–1912), the Man and His Library." *Vermont Quarterly* 20 (1952): 108–12.

Haskell, Daniel Carl

15.842 Lydenberg, H. M. "Daniel Carl Haskell." *BB* 19 (1948): 169–71.

Hasse, Adelaide Rosalie

15.843 Childs, J. B. "Adelaide Rosalie Hasse." *ELIS* 10 (1973): 373–77.

15.844 Grotzinger, L. A. "Hasse, Adelaide Rosalie (1868–1953)." *DALB*: 1978 234–36.

15.845 Grotzinger, L. A. "Women Who 'Spoke for Themselves'." *CRL* 39 (1978): 175–90.

15.846 Stubbs, W. R. "Adelaide R. Hasse: First Public Documents Librarian." *IllL* 62 (1980): 672–75.

15.847 Corbin, J. "The Strange Case of Adelaide Hasse." *WLB* 55 (1981): 756–57.

15.848 Grotzinger, L. A. "Hasse, Adelaide (1868–1953)." *ALAWE2*: 1986 333–35.

Haven, Samuel Foster

15.849 Miksa, F. L. "Haven, Samuel Foster (1806–1881)." *DALB*: 1978 236–37.

Haycraft, Howard

15.850 "Haycraft, Howard." *CB* (1941): 371–72.

Hayes, Rutherford Platt

15.851 Perling, J. J. "Sons of Rutherford B. Hayes." In *Presidents' Sons: The Prestige of Name in a Democracy*. New York: Odyssey Press, 1947. Pp. 187–201.

Hayes, Webb Cook

15.852 Perling, J. J. "Sons of Rutherford B. Hayes." In *Presidents' Sons: The Prestige of Name in a Democracy*. New York: Odyssey Press, 1947. Pp. 187–201.

Haykin, David Judson

15.853 Ellinwood, L. "Haykin, David Judson (1896–1958)." *DALB*: 1978 237–38.

Hazeltine, Mary Emogene

15.854 Nienstedt, J. E. "Mary Emogene Hazeltine." *LJ* 74 (1949): 1303.

15.855 Haygood, W. C. "Hazeltine, Mary Emogene (May 5, 1868–June 16, 1949)." *NAW* 2 (1971): 170–71.

15.856 Fenster, V. R. "Hazeltine, Mary Emogene (1868–1949)." *DALB*: 1978 238–40.

15.857 "Hazeltine, Mary Emogene." In *Librarian Authors: A Biobibliography*, by R. Engelbarts. Jefferson, N.C.: McFarland, 1981. Pp. 42–43.

Henne, Frances E.

15.858 Hannigan, J. A. "Henne, Frances E. (1906–1985)." *ALAWE2*: 1986 335–36.

Henry, Edward Atwood

15.859 Kuhlman, A. F. "Edward Atwood Henry." *BB* 20 (1952): 153–54.

Henry, William Elmer

15.860 Henry, W. E. *Through Seventy-Seven Years, November 1857–November 1934, His Own Story*. Seattle: University of Washington Library, 1934.

Herbert, Clara Wells

15.861 Bowerman, G. F. "Who Says That They Have Retired?" *LJ* 72 (1947): 972–73.

Herrick, Edward Claudius

15.862 Starr, H. E. "Herrick, Edward Claudius (Feb. 24, 1811–June 11, 1862)." *DAB* 8 (1932): 586–87.

Hewins, Caroline Maria

15.863 "Caroline M. Hewins of Hartford." *BB* 11 (1920): 42.

15.864 "As It Was in the Beginning: Caroline M. Hewins, Lover of Children." *PL* 30 (1925): 246–50.

15.865 Root, M. E. S. "Caroline Maria Hewins, 1846–1926." In *Pioneering Leaders in Librarianship,* edited by E. M. Danton. Chicago: American Library Association, 1953. Pp. 97–107.

15.866 Miller, B. M., ed. *Caroline M. Hewins: Her Book.* Boston: Horn Book, 1954.

15.867 Deksnis, A. "Caroline Maria Hewins: Pioneer in the Development of Library Service for Children." Master's thesis, Southern Connecticut State College, 1959.

15.868 Lindquist, J. D. "Hewins, Caroline Maria (Oct. 10, 1846–Nov. 4, 1926)." *NAW* 2 (1971): 189–91.

15.869 Gambee, B. L. "Hewins, Caroline Maria (1846–1926)." *DALB*: 1978 240–43.

15.870 "Hewins, Caroline M." In *Librarian Authors: A Biobibliography,* by R. Engelbarts. Jefferson, N.C.: McFarland, 1981. Pp. 98–100.

15.871 Gambee, B. L. "Hewins, Caroline M. (1846–1926)." *ALAWE2*: 1986 337–38.

Hewitt, Vivian Davidson

15.872 Hewitt, V. D. "A Special Librarian by Design." In *The Black Librarian in America,* edited by E. J. Josey. Metuchen, N.J.: Scarecrow Press, 1970. Pp. 253–71.

Heye, George Gustav

15.873 Schusky, E. L. "Heye, George Gustav (Sept. 16, 1874–Jan. 20, 1957)." *DAB* Suppl. 6 (1980): 289–90.

Hicks, Frederick G.

15.874 "Bibliography of Books and Articles by Frederick G. Hicks." *LLJ* 37 (1944): 19–24.

15.875 Roalfe, W. R. "Frederick G. Hicks [1875–1956]: Scholar-Librarian." *LLJ* 50 (1957): 88–98.

Hill, Frank Pierce

15.876 "Hill, Frank Pierce." *BB* 10 (1918): 1.

15.877 Breivik, P. S. "Hill, Frank Pierce (1855–1941)." *DALB*: 1978 243–44.

Hirshberg, Herbert Simon

15.878 Strong, G. F. "Herbert Simon Hirshberg." *BB* 17 (1941): 105–07.

15.879 Kaltenbach, M. "Hirshberg, Herbert Simon (1879–1955)." *DALB*: 1978 244–47.

Hodges, Nathaniel Dana Carlile

15.880 Abell, J. R. "Hodges, Nathaniel Dana Carlile (1852–1927)." *DALB*: 1978 247–48.

Hofer, Philip

15.881 Bentinck-Smith, W. "Prince of the Eye: Philip Hofer and the Harvard Library." *HLB* 32 (1984): 317–47.

Holcombe, Thomas Beverly

15.882 Clemons, H. "Thomas Beverly Holcombe." In *The University of Virginia Library.*

Charlottesville: University of Virginia Library, 1954. Pp. 105–08.

Holley, Edward G.

15.883 "Holley, Edward G(ailon)." *CB* (1974): 179–81.

15.884 Bobinski, G. S. "Holley, Edward G. (1927–)." *ALAWE2*: 1986 338–39.

Holmes, Thomas James

15.885 Holmes, T. J. *The Education of a Bibliographer: An Autobiographical Essay.* Cleveland: Western Reserve University Press, 1957.

15.886 Keys, T. E. "Thomas James Holmes, Bibliographer, Bookbinder, and Librarian 1875–1959." *BMLA* 47 (1959): 325–29.

Holte, Clarence L.

15.887 "Clarence Holte's Search into the Black Past." *Ebony* 25 (April 1970): 95–102.

15.888 Hunter, C. "7,000 Books on Blacks Fill a Home." *New York Times* (18 March 1972): 33.

15.889 Walton, H. "Literary Works of a Black Bibliophile: Clarence L. Holte." *Negro Educational Review* 29 (1978): 237–48.

Homes, Henry Augustus

15.890 Peterson, A. E. "Homes, Henry Augustus (Mar. 10, 1812–Nov. 3, 1887)." *DAB* 9 (1932): 191–92.

15.891 Christoph, P. R. "Homes, Henry Augustus (1812–1887)." *DALB*: 1978 248–49.

Hoole, William Stanley

15.892 Hoole, W. S. "Autobiographical Note." *Alabama Librarian* 3 (1952): 6.

15.893 Hoole, M. D. "William Stanley Hoole, Student-Teacher-Librarian-Author."

Master's thesis, Florida State University, 1958.

15.894 "Hoole, William Stanley." In *Librarian Authors: A Biobibliography,* by R. Engelbarts. Jefferson, N.C.: McFarland, 1981. Pp. 156–57.

Hopper, Franklin Ferguson

15.895 Lydenberg, H. M. "Franklin Ferguson Hopper, 1878–1950." *BNYPL* 55 (1951): 159–61.

15.896 Cory, J. M., and Murphy, L. P. "Hopper, Franklin Ferguson (1878–1950)." *DALB*: 1978 249–50.

Hosmer, James Kendall

15.897 "As It Was in the Beginning." *PL* 29 (1924): 130–32.

15.898 Countryman, G. A. "James Kendall Hosmer." *BB* 13 (1929): 193–94.

15.899 Brown, R. A. "Hosmer, James Kendall (1834–1927)." *DALB*: 1978 250–51.

Hostetter, Anita Miller

15.900 Logsdon, R. H. "Hostetter, Anita Miller (1889–1963)." *DALB*: 1978 251–53.

Howe, Harriet Emma

15.901 Boaz, M., Eastlick, J. T., and Grotzinger, L. A. "Howe, Harriet Emma (1881–1965)." *DALB*: 1978 253–55.

Howe, Mark Antony de Wolfe

15.902 Howe, H. *The Gentle Americans, 1864–1960: Biography of a Breed.* New York: Harper and Row, 1965.

15.903 Whitehill, W. M. "Howe, Mark Antony de Wolfe (Aug. 23, 1864–Dec. 6, 1960)." *DAB* Suppl. 6 (1980): 306–07.

Howland, Arthur Charles

15.904 Setton, K. M. "Arthur Charles Howland (1869–1952)." *LC* 18 (1952): 77–79.

Huff, William H.

15.905 Brown, N. B. "Wiliam H. Huff: A Tribute." *SerL* 7 (1983): 19–24.

Hunt, Clara Whitehill

15.906 Schuman, P. G. "Hunt, Clara Whitehill (1871–1958)." *DALB*: 1978 255–56.

Hunt, Hannah

15.907 Kaltenbach, M., and Rowell, J. A. "Hunt, Hannah (1903–1973)." *DALB*: 1978 256–57.

Hunter, Kate

15.908 Harrell, C. "Kate Hunter: Palestine's Guardian Angel." *TL* 47 (1986): 78–79.

Huntington, Henry Edwards

15.909 Vincent, J. M. "Huntington, Henry Edwards (Feb. 27, 1850–May 23, 1927)." *DAB* 9 (1932): 414–16.

15.910 Thorpe, J. "Huntington, Henry E. (1850–1927)." *ALAWE2*: 1986 346–47.

Hutchins, Frank Avery

15.911 Marvin, C. "As It Was in the Beginning: Frank Avery Hutchins." *PL* 30 (1925): 186–92.

15.912 Kent, A. E. "Frank Avery Hutchins: Promoter of 'The Wisconsin Idea.' " *WLB* 30 (1955): 73–77.

15.913 Lyman, H. H. "Hutchins, Frank Avery (1851–1914)." *DALB*: 1978 257–59.

15.914 "Hutchins, Frank Avery." In *Librarian Authors: A Biobibliography,* by R. Engelbarts. Jefferson, N.C.: McFarland, 1981. Pp. 32–34.

Hutchins, Margaret

15.915 Patterson, C. D. "Hutchins, Margaret." *ELIS* 11 (1974): 123–27.

15.916 Cheney, F. N. "Hutchins, Margaret (1884–1961)." *DALB*: 1978 259–60.

15.917 Lynch, M. J. "Hutchins, Margaret (1884–1961)." *ALAWE2*: 1986 347–48.

Ideson, Julia Bedford

15.918 Smither, H. W. "Julia Bedford Ideson." In *[Philosophical Society of Texas] Proceedings 1945.* Dallas: The Society, 1946. Pp. 56–58.

15.919 McSwain, M. B. "Julia Bedford Ideson, Houston Librarian, 1880–1945." Master's thesis, University of Texas, 1966.

15.920 Franklin, L. "Ideson, Julia Bedford." *HT* 3 (1976): 427.

15.921 McSwain, M. B. "Ideson, Julia Bedford (1880–1945)." *DALB*: 1978 260–61.

Iles, George

15.922 Brown, W. L. "As It Was in the Beginning: George Iles." *PL* 30 (1925): 367–68.

Ireland, Norma Olin

15.923 Ewing, M. J. "Norma Olin Ireland." *BB* 19 (1948): 141–43.

Isom, Mary Frances

15.924 Pipes, N. B. "Isom, Mary Frances (Feb. 27, 1865–Apr. 15, 1920)." *DAB* 9 (1932): 516–17.

15.925 Johansen, D. O. *The Library and the Liberal Tradition.* Corvallis: Friends of the Library, Oregon State College, 1959.

15.926 Van Horne, B. "Mary Frances Isom: Creative Pioneer in Library Work in the Northwest." *WLB* 33 (1959): 409–16.

15.927 "Isom, Mary Frances (Feb. 27, 1865– Apr. 15, 1920)." *NAW* 2 (1971): 258–59.

15.928 Kingsbury, M. E. " 'To Shine in Use': The Library and War Service of Oregon's Pioneer Librarian, Mary Frances Isom." *JLH* 10 (1975): 22–34.

15.929 Kingsbury, M. E. "Isom, Mary Frances (1865–1920)." *DALB:* 1978 261–63.

15.930 "Isom, Mary Frances." In *Librarian Authors: A Biobibliography,* by R. Engelbarts. Jefferson, N.C.: McFarland, 1981. Pp. 34–35.

Jackson, Eugene Bernard

15.931 "Jackson, Eugene B(ernard)." *CB* (1961): 218–20.

Jackson, J. Arthur

15.932 Jackson, W. V. "Some Pioneer Negro Library Workers." *LJ* 64 (1939): 215–17.

Jackson, Miles M.

15.933 Jackson, M. M. "An Odyssey in Black: Fragments of an Autobiography." In *The Black Librarian in America,* edited by E. J. Josey. Metuchen, N.J.: Scarecrow Press, 1970. Pp. 43–49.

Jackson, Sidney Louis

15.934 Jackson, C. O. "Jackson, Sidney Louis." *ELIS* 36 (1983): 237–39.

Jackson, William Alexander

15.935 Bond, W. H. "Introduction." In *Records of a Bibliographer: Selected Papers of William Alexander Jackson,* edited by W. H. Bond. Cambridge: Belknap Press of Harvard University, 1967. Pp. 1–29.

15.936 Bond, W. H. "William Alexander Jackson Bibliography of Published Writings." In *Records of a Bibliographer: Selected Papers of William Alexander Jackson,* edited by W. H. Bond. Cambridge: Belknap Press of Harvard University, 1967. Pp. 31–43.

15.937 Jackson, W. A. *Records of a Bibliographer: Selected Papers.* Cambridge: Harvard University Press, 1967.

15.938 Bond, W. H. "Jackson, William Alexander (July 25, 1905–Oct. 18, 1964)." *DAB* Suppl. 7 (1981): 386–87.

Jacobs, John Hall

15.939 "Turns of a Bookworm." *Time* 52 (6 September 1948): 40–41.

15.940 "Biographical Sketch [John Hall Jacobs]." *SEL* 14 (1964): 56.

15.941 Rheay, M. L. "Jacobs, John Hall." *ELIS* 13 (1975): 166–69.

15.942 Wynar, B. S., and Loomis, K. C. "Jacobs, John Hall (1905–1967)." *DALB:* 1978 263–64.

James, Hannah Packard

15.943 Poland, M. "Hannah Packard James,1835–1903." *BB* 8 (1914): 91–92.

15.944 "As It Was in the Beginning." *PL* 29 (1924): 176–78.

15.945 Costello, J. M., and Holley, E. G. "James, Hannah Packard (1835–1903)." *DALB:* 1978 264–66.

Jameson, J. Franklin

15.946 Hench, J. B. "Jameson, J. Franklin (1859–1937)." *ALAWE2:* 1986 403.

Jefferson, Thomas

15.947 Long, O. W. *Thomas Jefferson and George Ticknor: A Chapter in American Scholarship.* Williamstown, Mass.: McClelland Press, 1933.

15.948 Malone, D. "Jefferson, Thomas (Apr. 2/13, 1743–July 4, 1826)." *DAB* 10 (1933): 17–35.

15.949 Adams, R. G. "Thomas Jefferson, Librarian." In *Three Americanists: Henry Harrisse, Bibliographer; George Brinley, Book Collector; Thomas Jefferson, Librarian.* Philadelphia: University of Pennsylvania Press, 1939. Pp. 69–96.

15.950 Sanford, C. B. *Thomas Jefferson and His Library: A Study of His Literary Interests and of Religious Attitudes Revealed by Relevant Titles in His Library.* Hamden, Conn.: Archon Books, 1977.

15.951 Harmeling, D., and Harris, M. H. "Jefferson, Thomas (1743–1826)." *DALB:* 1978 266–68.

15.952 Ladenson, A. " 'I Cannot Live Without Books': Thomas Jefferson, Bibliophile." *WLB* 52 (1978): 624–31.

Jennings, Judson Toll

15.953 "Judson Toll Jennings." *BB* 12 (1926): 165.

15.954 Youngs, W. O. "Jennings, Judson Toll (1872–1948)." *DALB:* 1978 268–69.

15.955 "Jennings, Judson." In *Librarian Authors: A Biobibliography,* by R. Engelbarts. Jefferson, N.C.: McFarland, 1981. Pp. 35–37.

Jesse, William Herman

15.956 Bassett, R. J. "Jesse, William Herman (1908–1970)." *DALB:* 1978 269–71.

Jewett, Charles Coffin

15.957 Trask, W. B. "Charles Coffin Jewett." *New England Historical and Genealogical Register* 22 (1868): 365–66.

15.958 Guild, R. A. "Biographical Notice of Charles Coffin Jewett." In *Annual Report of the Board of Regents of the Smithsonian Institution 1867.* Washington, D.C.: Government Printing Office, 1872. Pp. 128–30.

15.959 Guild, R. A. "Memorial Sketch of Professor Charles Coffin Jewett." *LJ* 12 (1887): 507–11.

15.960 Lane, W. C. "Jewett, Charles Coffin (Aug. 12, 1816–Jan. 9, 1868)." *DAB* 10 (1933): 65–66.

15.961 Boromé, J. A. *Charles Coffin Jewett (1816–68).* Chicago: American Library Association, 1951.

15.962 Harris, M. H. "An 1845 Overture to the Librarian's Creed: Farsighted Bibliophile Promotes the Free Flow of Information." *ALib* 6 (1975): 404.

15.963 Harris, M. H., ed. *The Age of Jewett: Charles Coffin Jewett and American Librarianship, 1841–1868.* Littleton, Colo.: Libraries Unlimited, 1975.

15.964 Harris, M. H. "Jewett, Charles Coffin (1816–1868)." *DALB:* 1978 271–74.

15.965 Purcell, B. L. "Charles Coffin Jewett: A Man Ahead of His Times." Research Paper, Texas Woman's University, 1979.

15.966 "Jewett, Charles Coffin." In *Librarian Authors: A Biobibliography,* by R. Engelbarts. Jefferson, N.C.: McFarland, 1981. Pp. 51–52.

15.967 Shank, R. "Jewett, Charles Coffin." *ALAWE2:* 1986 410–12.

Joeckel, Carleton Bruns

15.968 Harding, T. S. "Joeckel, Carleton Bruns (1886–1960)." *DALB:* 1978 274–76.

15.969 Powers, M. L. "Joeckel, Carleton B. (1886–1960)." *ALAWE2*: 1986 412–14.

Johnson, Alvin S.

15.970 Bobinski, G. S. "James Bertram and Alvin S. Johnson: Two Important but Little Known Figures in Library History." In *Library History Seminar No. 3, Proceedings, 1968,* edited by M. J. Zachert. Tallahassee: JLH, 1968. Pp. 35–46.

15.971 Bobinski, G. S. "Johnson, Alvin S. (1874–1971)." *DALB*: 1978 276–78.

Jones, Clara Stanton

15.972 "Detroit's Top Librarian." *Ebony* 27 (November 1971): 115–23.

15.973 "Jones, Clara Stanton." *CB* (1976): 201–04.

Jones, Gardner Maynard

15.974 "Gardner Maynard Jones." *BB* 13 (1928): 105.

Jones, John Price

15.975 Furlong, P. J. "Jones, John Price (Aug. 12, 1877–Dec. 23, 1964)." *DAB* Suppl. 7 (1981): 400–401.

Jones, Mary

15.976 Maxwell, M. F. "The Lion and the Lady: The Firing of Miss Mary Jones." *AL* 9 (1978): 268–72.

Jones, Perrie

15.977 Morton, H. C. "Perrie Jones." *BALA* 48 (1954): 324–28.

Jones, Samuel Minot

15.978 Walker, C. S. *Samuel Minot Jones: The Story of an Amherst Boy.* Amherst, Mass.: [The Jones Library], 1922.

Jones, Virginia Lacy

15.979 Jones, V. L. "A Dean's Career." In *The Black Librarian in America,* edited by E. J. Josey. Metuchen, N.J.: Scarecrow Press, 1970. Pp. 19–42.

15.980 Jones, V. L. *Reminiscences in Librarianship and Library Education: With Words of Appreciation by Friends and Colleagues in Celebration of the Conferring upon Dean Jones the Honorary Degree Doctor of Letters by the University of Michigan in Ann Arbor, August 19, 1979.* Ann Arbor: University of Michigan School of Library Science, 1979.

15.981 Marshall, A. P. "Jones, Virginia Lacy (1912–1984)." *ALAWE2*: 1986 414.

Jordan, Casper LeRoy

15.982 Jordan, C. L. "I Have Paid My Dues." In *The Black Librarian in America,* edited by E. J. Josey. Metuchen, N.J.: Scarecrow Press, 1970. Pp. 98–114.

Jordan, John Woolf

15.983 Jackson, J. "Jordan, John Woolf (Sept. 14, 1840–June 11, 1921)." *DAB* 10 (1933): 215.

Josephson, Aksel Gustav Salomon

15.984 Foos, D. D. "Aksel G.S. Josephson, 1860–1944, Precursor." In *Library History Seminar No. 4, Proceedings, 1971,* edited by H. Goldstein and J. Goudeau. Tallahassee: Florida State University School of Library Science, 1972. Pp. 195–202.

15.985 Childs, J. B. "Josephson, Aksel Gustav Salomon." *ELIS* 13 (1975): 310–13.

15.986 Foos, D. D. "Josephson, Aksel Gustav Salomon (1860–1944)." *DALB*: 1978 278–80.

Josey, E. J.

15.987 Josey, E. J. "A Dreamer—With a Tiny Spark." In *The Black Librarian in America*, edited by E. J. Josey. Metuchen, N.J.: Scarecrow Press, 1970. Pp. 297–323.

Josselyn, Robert

15.988 Gage, L. J. "The Editors and Editorial Policies of the *Texas Star Gazette*, 1849–1879." Master's thesis, University of Texas, 1959.

15.989 Skinner, A. E. "Robert Josselyn: State Librarian." *TL* 40 (1978): 126–35.

15.990 Skinner, A. E. "Swante Palm on Robert Josselyn." *TL* 40 (1978): 136–37.

Kaiser, John Boynton

15.991 Schein, B. "John Boynton Kaiser." *BB* 21 (1953): 1–3.

15.992 Newark, N. J., Free Public Library. *An Annotated Bibliography of the Writings of John Boynton Kaiser, Published 1911 to 1958: Prepared on the Occasion of His Retirement as Director, April 15, 1943–July 2, 1958, of the Newark Public Library.* Newark, N.J.: Newark Public Library, 1958.

15.993 Bryan, J. E. "Kaiser, John Boynton (1887–1973)." *DALB*: 1978 280–82.

Kaiser, Walter Herbert

15.994 Dinnan, L. T. "Kaiser, Walter Herbert (1910–1971)." *DALB*: 1978 282–84.

Kean, John Vaughn

15.995 Clemons, H. "Kean, John Vaughn." In *The University of Virginia Library*. Charlottesville: University of Virginia Library, 1954. Pp. 91–93.

Keck, Lucile Liebermann

15.996 "Keck, Lucile L(iebermann)." *CB* (1954): 369–70.

Kell, Frank

15.997 Williams, J. W. "Kell, Frank." *HT* 1 (1952): 941–42.

Kelso, Tessa

15.998 Geller, E. "Tessa Kelso: Unfinished Hero of Library Herstory." *ALib* 6 (1975): 347.

Kemp, Louis Wiltz

15.999 Taylor, V. H. "Louis W. Kemp, 1881–1956." *TL* 18 (1956): 206–08.

15.1000 Gilchrist, G. "Kemp, Louis Wiltz." *HT* 3 (1976): 468–69.

Keogh, Andrew

15.1001 "Andrew Keogh." *BB* 12 (1925): 145.

15.1002 Babb, J. T. "Andrew Keogh: His Contribution to Yale [1899–1938]." *YULG* 29 (1954): 47–60.

15.1003 Rollins, C. P. "Andrew Keogh (November 14, 1869–February 13, 1953)." *YULG* 28 (1954): 139–43.

15.1004 Libbey, D. C. "Keogh, Andrew (1869–1953)." *DALB*: 1978 284–85.

Keppel, Frederick Paul

15.1005 Wilson, L. R. "Frederick P. Keppel, 1875–1943." *LQ* 14 (1944): 55–56.

15.1006 Sullivan, P. A. "Keppel, Frederick Paul (1875–1943)." *DALB*: 1978 285–86.

15.1007 Brown, G. P. "Keppel, Frederick Paul (1875–1943)." *ALAWE2*: 1986 417–18.

Kerr, Willis Holmes

15.1008 Claremont College. *Willis Holmes Kerr, Librarian Emeritus Claremont College.* Claremont, Calif.: Claremont College, 1952.

15.1009 Kerr, W. H. "My Life with Books." *CalL* 13 (1952): 203–04, 236.

Keys, Thomas Edward

15.1010 Keys, T. E. "Past Presidents I Have Known." *BMLA* 63 (1975): 49–59, 216–22.

Kidder, Ida Angeline

15.1011 Carlson, W. H. "Ida Angeline Kidder: Pioneer Western Land-Grant Librarian." *CRL* 29 (1968): 217–23.

Kilgour, Frederick G.

15.1012 Kilgour, F. G. *Collected Papers of Frederick G. Kilgour,* 2 vols. Dublin, Ohio: OCLC, 1984.

15.1013 Kaser, D. "Kilgour, Frederick G. (1914–)." *ALAWE2*: 1986 420.

Kinder, Katharine Louise

15.1014 "Kinder, Katharine L(ouise)." *CB* (1958): 298–99.

King, Valentine Overton

15.1015 "King, Valentine Overton." *HT* 1 (1952): 960.

15.1016 Huff, M. "Introduction." In *Valentine Overton King's Index to Books about Texas before 1889; A Facsimile of the Original in the Collection of the Texas State Library,* by V. O. King. Austin: Texas State Library, 1976. Pp. v–vi.

Kingsbury, Mary A.

15.1017 Clark, M. B. "Mary A. Kingsbury, Pioneer." *WLB* 26 (1951): 50–51.

Kinkeldey, Otto

15.1018 Smith, C. S. "Otto Kinkeldey." *MLAN* 6 (1948): 27–37.

15.1019 Lang, P. H. "[Three Distinguished Septuagenarian Musicologists]." *Musical Quarterly* 37 (1951): 71–75.

15.1020 Bradley, C. J. "Kinkeldey, Otto (1878–1966)." *DALB*: 1978 286–89.

Kinsey, Alfred Charles

15.1021 Christenson, C. V. "Kinsey, Alfred Charles (June 23, 1894–Aug. 25, 1956)." *DAB* Suppl. 6 (1980): 342–44.

Kirkpatrick, Oliver Austin

15.1022 Shockley, A. A. "Oliver Austin Kirkpatrick (1911–)." *HBLib*: 1977 162.

Klaerner, Christian

15.1023 "Klaerner, Christian." *HT* 1 (1952): 968.

Klahre, Ethel Susan

15.1024 "Klahre, Ethel S(usan)." *CB* (1962): 234–40.

Klingelsmith, Margaret Center

15.1025 Lingelbach, A. L. "Klingelsmith, Margaret Center (Nov. 27, 1859–Jan. 19, 1931)." *DAB* 10 (1933): 444–45.

Knapp, Patricia L. Bryan

15.1026 Monroe, M. E. "Knapp, Patricia L. Bryan (1914–1972)." *DALB*: 1978 289–90.

Knight, Hattie Madson

15.1027 Rabner, L. B. "Hattie Madson Knight: Leader, Educator, Librarian—Professional Years, 1941–1973." Research Paper, Brigham Young University, 1976.

Knox, Dudley Wright

15.1028 Spector, R. "Knox, Dudley Wright (June 21, 1877–June 11, 1960)." *DAB* Suppl. 6 (1980): 348–49.

Koch, Theodore Wesley

15.1029 Goodrich, F. L. D. "Theodore Wesley Koch." *BB* 16 (1939): 189.

15.1030 Goodrich, F. L. D. "Theodore Wesley Koch, 1871–1941." *CRL* 3 (1941): 67–70.

15.1031 Snyder, F. B. *Theodore Wesley Koch: An Address.* Evanston, Ill.: Northwestern University Press, 1941.

15.1032 "Theodore Wesley Koch: Northwestern's Great Librarian, 1919–1941." *John Evans Club Newsletter* (Summer 1972): 3–4.

15.1033 Erickson, R. "Koch, Theodore Wesley (1871–1941)." *DALB*: 1978 290–94.

Koopman, Harry Lyman

15.1034 Faxon, F. W. "Harry Lyman Koopman." *BB* 13 (1929): 169.

15.1035 Jonah, D. A. "Koopman, Harry Lyman (1860–1937)." *DALB*: 1978 294–95.

Kreisler, Fritz

15.1036 Braverman, S. "Kreisler, Fritz (Feb. 2, 1875–Jan. 29, 1962)." *DAB* Suppl. 7 (1981): 443–45.

Kroeger, Alice Bertha

15.1037 MacPherson, H. D. "Kroeger, Alice Bertha (May 2, 1864–Oct. 31, 1909)." *NAW* 2 (1971): 348–49.

15.1038 Grotzinger, L. A. "Kroeger, Alice Bertha (1864–1909)." *DALB*: 1978 295–98.

15.1039 "Kroeger, Alice Bertha." In *Librarian Authors: A Biobibliography*, by R. Engelbarts. Jefferson, N.C.: McFarland, 1981. Pp. 92–93.

Kuhlman, Augustus Frederick

15.1040 Matthews, J. P. "A.F. Kuhlman—A Bibliographic View." *SEL* 11 (1961): 313–18.

Lacy, Mary G.

15.1041 Sherman, C. B. "Mary G. Lacy." *BB* 17 (1940): 21–22.

Laich, Katherine Wilhelmina Schlegel

15.1042 "Laich, Katherine (Wilhelmina Schlegel)." *CB* (1972): 268–70.

15.1043 Hewitt, J. A. "Lancaster, F. Wilfred (1933–)." *ALAWE2*: 1986 429.

Lancaster, Joseph

15.1044 Huson, H. "Lancaster, Joseph." *HT* 2 (1952): 18.

Lancour, Harold

15.1045 Nasri, W. Z. "Lancour, Harold." *ELIS* 37 (1984): 195–201.

Landowska, Wanda Aleksandra

15.1046 Restout, D. "Landowska, Wanda Aleksandra (July 5, 1879–Aug. 16, 1959)." *DAB* Suppl. 6 (1980): 357.

Lane, William Coolidge

15.1047 "William Coolidge Lane." *BB* 11 (1921): 57.

15.1048 Wiegand, W. A. "Lane, William Coolidge (1859–1931)." *DALB*: 1978 298–301.

Larkey, Sanford Vincent

15.1049 McDaniel, W. B. "Sanford Vincent Larkey." *BMLA* 37 (1949): 257–58.

Larned, Josephus Nelson

15.1050 Olmsted, J. B. "Joseph Nelson Larned." *Buffalo Historical Society Publications* 19 (1915): 3–33.

15.1051 Brown, W. L. "Josephus Nelson Larned." *BB* 13 (1928): 125–26.

15.1052 Shearer, A. H. "Larned, Josephus Nelson (May 11, 1836–Aug. 15, 1913)." *DAB* 11 (1933): 2.

15.1053 Ditzion, S. H. "The Social Ideas of a Library Pioneer: Josephus Nelson Larned, 1836–1913." *LQ* 13 (1943): 112–31.

15.1054 Ditzion, S. H. "Josephus Nelson Larned, 1836–1913." In *Pioneering Leaders in Librarianship*, edited by E. M. Danton. Chicago: American Library Association, 1953. Pp. 108–19.

15.1055 Young, B. "Josephus Nelson Larned and the Public Library Movement." *JLH* 10 (1975): 323–40.

15.1056 Smith, E. W. "Larned, Josephus Nelson (1836–1913)." *DALB*: 1978 301–05.

15.1057 "Larned, Josephus Nelson." In *Librarian Authors: A Biobibliography*, by R. Engelbarts. Jefferson, N.C.: McFarland, 1981. Pp. 120–21.

Learned, William Setchel

15.1058 Boaz, M. "Learned, William Setchel (1876–1950)." *DALB*: 1978 305.

Leavitt, Mollie

15.1059 Lydenberg, H. M. "Memories of Mollie Leavitt." *BNYPL* 51 (1947): 328–31.

Lee, Mollie Huston

15.1060 Moore, R. N. "Mollie Huston Lee: A Profile." *WLB* 49 (1975): 432–39.

LeFevre, Alice Louise

15.1061 Lowrie, J. E. "LeFevre, Alice Louise (1898–1963)." *DALB*: 1978 306–07.

Legler, Henry Eduard

15.1062 Roden, C. B. "Henry Eduard Legler." *BB* 14 (1930): 21–22.

15.1063 Kellogg, L. P. "Legler, Henry Eduard (June 22, 1861–Sept. 13, 1917)." *DAB* 11 (1933): 148–49.

15.1064 Field, P. I., and Warren, A. "Henry Eduard Legler, 1861–1917." In *Pioneering Leaders in Librarianship*, edited by E. M. Danton. Chicago: American Library Association, 1953. Pp. 120–29.

15.1065 Colson, J. C. "Legler, Henry Eduard (1861–1917)." *DALB*: 1978 307–10.

15.1066 "Legler, Henry Eduard." In *Librarian Authors: A Biobibliography*, by R. Engelbarts. Jefferson, N.C.: McFarland, 1981. Pp. 74–76.

Leigh, Robert Devore

15.1067 Bryan, A. I. "Leigh, Robert Devore (1890–1961)." *DALB*: 1978 310–13.

Leland, Waldo Gifford

15.1068 Hench, J. B. "Leland, Waldo Gifford (1879–1966)." *ALAWE2*: 1986 449–50.

Lenox, James

15.1069 Lydenberg, H. M. "Lenox, James (Aug. 19, 1800–Feb. 17, 1880)." *DAB* 11 (1933): 172–73.

15.1070 Stevens, H. *Recollections of James Lenox and the Formation of His Library.* New York: New York Public Library, 1951.

Lester, Robert MacDonald

15.1071 Sullivan, P. A. "Lester, Robert MacDonald (1889–1969)." *DALB*: 1978 313–14.

Lewis, Chester Milton

15.1072 "Lewis, Chester M(ilton)." *CB* (1956): 375–77.

Lewis, Wilmarth Sheldon

15.1073 Lewis, W. S. *One Man's Education.* New York: Alfred A. Knopf, 1967.

Leypoldt, Frederick

15.1074 Beswick, J. W. *The Work of Frederick Leypoldt: Bibliographer and Publisher.* New York: R.R. Bowker, 1942.

15.1075 Melcher, F. G. "Among the Founders." *LJ* 76 (1951): 1959–63.

15.1076 McMullen, H. "Leypoldt, Frederick (1835–1884)." *DALB*: 1978 314–16.

Lilly, Josiah Kirby

15.1078 Neu, I. D. "Lilly, Josiah Kirby (Nov. 18, 1861–Feb. 8, 1948)." *DAB* Suppl. 4 (1974): 499–500.

Linderfelt, Klas August

15.1079 Wiegand, W. A. "The Wayward Bookman: The Decline, Fall, and Historical Obliteration of an ALA President, Parts I & II." *ALib* 8 (1977): 134–37, 197–200.

15.1080 Wiegand, W. A. "Linderfelt, Klas August (1847–1900)." *DALB*: 1978 316–17.

Lippincott, J. B.

15.1081 Fitzsimmons, R. "Lippincott, J. B. (1813–1886)." *ALAWE2*: 1986 499–501.

Little, George Thomas

15.1082 Dunnack, H. E. "George Thomas Little (1857–1915)." *BB* 9 (1917): 157–59.

Littlefield, George Washington

15.1083 Haley, J. E. "Littlefield, George Washington." *DAB* 6 (1933): 300–301.

15.1084 Haley, J. E. *George W. Littlefield, Texan.* Norman: University of Oklahoma Press, 1943.

15.1085 "Littlefield, George Washington." *HT* 2 (1952): 66.

Lloyd, John Uri

15.1086 Simons, C. M. *John Uri Lloyd: His Life and Works, 1849–1936; With a History of the Lloyd Library.* Cincinnati: C.M. Simons, 1972.

Locke, George Herbert

15.1087 Hill, F. P. "George Herbert Locke, M.A., LL.D." *BB* 15 (1934): 41–42.

15.1088 Anderson, M. J. "Locke, George Herbert (1870–1937)." *DALB*: 1978 317–19.

15.1089 "Locke, George Herbert." In *Librarian Authors: A Biobibliography,* by R. Engelbarts. Jefferson, N.C.: McFarland, 1981. Pp. 76–77.

15.1090 Anderson, M. "Locke, George (1870–1937)." *ALAWE2*: 1986 501–02.

Logan, James

15.1091 Tolles, F. B. *James Logan and the Culture of Provincial America.* Boston: Little, Brown, 1957.

15.1092 Wolf, E. *James Logan, 1674–1751, Bookman Extraordinary.* Philadelphia: Library Company of Philadelphia, 1971.

Logasa, Hannah

15.1093 Pulling, H. A. "Hannah Logasa." *BB* 22 (1956): 1–3.

15.1094 Norell, I. P. "Logasa, Hannah (1879–1967)." *DALB*: 1978 319–22.

Long, Walter Ewing

15.1095 "Long, Walter Ewing." *HT* 3 (1976): 537.

Longfellow, Henry Wadsworth

15.1096 Johnson, C. L. "Henry W. Longfellow, Librarian [Bowdoin College, 1829–35]." *CRL* 15 (1954): 425–29.

15.1097 Michener, R. "Henry Wadsworth Longfellow: Librarian of Bowdoin College, 1829–1835." *LQ* 43 (1973): 215–26.

Lord, Milton Edward

15.1098 Briggs, W. B. "Milton Edward Lord." *BB* 17 (1941): 61–62.

15.1099 "Lord, Milton E(dward)." *CB* (1950): 351–52.

Lorde, Andre

15.1100 Shockley, A. A. "Andre Lorde (1934–)." *HBLib*: 1977 165.

Lorenz, John George

15.1101 "Lorenz, John G(eorge)." *CB* (1966): 246–48.

Loughran, Vernon

15.1102 Loughran, V. "Pioneering in Platte County, or the Exciting Adventure of a Library Extension Worker." *Wyoming Library Roundup* 11 (June 1956): 9–13.

Lovett, Eddie

15.1103 "Farmer Librarian's Bumper Crop of Books." *Ebony* 29 (December 1973): 85–88, 92.

Lowe, John Adams

15.1104 O'Flynn, M. E. "John Adams Lowe: Administrator and Library Planner." Master's thesis, Drexel Institute of Technology, 1955.

Lowrie, Jean Elizabeth

15.1105 "Lowrie, Jean E(lizabeth)." *CB* (1973): 262–64.

Lubetzky, Seymour

15.1106 Carpenter, M. "Lubetzky, Seymour (1898–)." *ALAWE2*: 1986 502–03.

Ludington, Flora Belle

15.1107 Bevis, D. "Flora B. Ludington." *BB* 21 (1956): 193–95.

15.1108 Johnson, M. L. "Flora Belle Ludington: A Biography and Bibliography." *CRL* 25 (1964): 375–79.

15.1109 Edmonds, A. C. "Ludington, Flora Belle (1898–1967)." *DALB*: 1978 322–24.

15.1110 Grotzinger, L. A. "Women Who 'Spoke for Themselves.'" *CRL* 39 (1978): 175–90.

Luhn, Hans Peter

15.1111 Harvey, J. F. "Luhn, Hans Peter (1896–1964)." *DALB*: 1978 324–26.

15.1112 Furth, S. E. "Luhn, Hans Peter (1864–1964)." *ALAWE2*: 1986 503–04.

Lummis, Charles Fletcher

15.1113 Gordon, D. "Aggressive Librarian: Charles Fletcher Lummis." *WLB* 45 (1970): 399–405.

15.1114 Gordon, D. *Charles F. Lummis: Crusader in Corduroy.* Los Angeles: Cultural Assets Press, 1972.

15.1115 Gordon, D. "Lummis, Charles Fletcher (1859–1928)." *DALB*: 1978 326–28.

Lydenberg, Harry Miller

15.1116 Fulton, D., ed. *Bookmen's Holiday: Notes and Studies Gathered in Tribute to Harry Miller Lydenberg.* New York: New York Public Library, 1943.

15.1117 Evans, L. H. "The Little Man Who Isn't Here: Or the Caboose That Pushed the Streamliner." *LJ* 72 (1947): 152–54.

15.1118 Fulton, D. "Harry Miller Lydenberg." *BALA* 47 (1953): 145–47, 167.

15.1119 Stam, D. H. "A Bibliography of the Published Writings of Harry Miller Lydenberg, 1942–1960." *BNYPL* 64 (1960): 298–302.

15.1120 Metcalf, K. D. "Six Influential Academic and Research Librarians." *CRL* 37 (1976): 332–45.

15.1121 Dain, P. "Harry M. Lydenberg and American Library Resources: A Study in Modern Library Leadership." *LQ* 47 (1977): 451–69.

15.1122 Dain, P. "Lydenberg, Harry Miller (1874–1960)." *DALB*: 1978 329–33.

15.1123 Dain, P. "Lydenberg, Harry Miller (Nov. 18, 1874–Apr. 16, 1960)." *DAB* Suppl. 6 (1980): 398–400.

Lyle, Guy R.

15.1124 Wilson, G. P. "Guy R. Lyle." *BB* 20 (1950): 57–58.

15.1125 Lyle, G. R. *Beyond My Expectation: A Personal Chronicle.* Metuchen, N.J.: Scarecrow Press, 1981.

15.1126 Dare, P. "Guy R. Lyle." *LAAL*: 1983 148–66.

McAnally, Arthur Monroe

15.1127 Downs, R. B. "McAnally, Arthur Monroe (1911–1972)." *DALB*: 1978 347–49.

McCarthy, Charles

15.1128 Plunkett, H. "McCarthy of Wisconsin: The Career of an Irishman Abroad as It Appeals to an Irishman at Home." *Nineteenth Century* 77 (1915): 1335–47.

15.1129 Fitzpatrick, E. A. *McCarthy of Wisconsin*. New York: Columbia University Press, 1944.

15.1130 Donnan, E., and Stock, L. F., eds. "Letters: Charles McCarthy to J. Franklin Jameson." *WMH* 33 (1949): 64–86.

15.1131 Casey, M. "Charles McCarthy's 'Idea': A Library to Change Government." *LQ* 44 (1974): 29–41.

15.1132 Casey, M. "McCarthy, Charles (1873–1921)." *DALB*: 1978 349–50.

15.1133 Casey, M. *Charles McCarthy, Librarianship and Reform*. Chicago: American Library Association, 1981.

McCarthy, Stephen

15.1134 Oehlerts, D. E. "Stephen McCarthy." *LAAL*: 1983 168–82.

15.1135 Oehlerts, D. E. "McCarthy, Stephen (1908–)." *ALAWE2*: 1986 505–06.

McClung, Calvin Morgan

15.1136 Mellen, G. F. "Calvin Morgan McClung and His Library." *Tennessee Historical Magazine* 7 (1921): 3–26.

McCombs, Charles Flowers

15.1137 Sawyer, R. A. "Charles Flowers McCombs, 1887–1947." *BNYPL* 52 (1948): 450–53.

McCrum, Blanche Prichard

15.1138 Kondayan, B. R. "Blanche Prichard McCrum: A Small Giant." *Journal of Academic Librarianship* 8 (1982): 68–75.

15.1139 Kondayan, B. R. "Blanche P. McCrum." *LAAL*: 1983 185–210.

McDiarmid, Errett Weir

15.1140 "McDiarmid, Errett Weir." *CB* (1948): 397–99.

15.1141 McCulley, K. M. "Dr. Errett Weir McDiarmid's Application of His Philosophy of Library Administration in the University of Minnesota Library, 1943–1951." Master's thesis, University of North Carolina, 1963.

Macdonald, Angus Snead

15.1142 Baumann, C. H. *Angus Snead Macdonald*. Metuchen, N.J.: Scarecrow Press, 1972.

15.1143 Baumann, C. H. "Macdonald, Angus Snead (1883–1961)." *DALB*: 1978 333–35.

McDonald, Gerald D.

15.1144 Fall, J. "Gerald D. McDonald." *BB* 23 (1962): 169–71.

McDonough, Roger Henry

15.1145 "McDonough, Roger H(enry)." *CB* (1968): 237–38.

McDowell, John H.

15.1146 Woods, A. "John H. McDowell." *Theatre Studies* 20 (1973–1974): 5–8.

MacGregor, Ellen

15.1147 Eason, H. H. "Ellen MacGregor." *WLB* 28 (1954): 646.

15.1148 "MacGregor, Ellen." *CB* (1954): 430–31.

McGuire, Alice Rebecca Brooks

15.1149 Sparks, C. G., and Moore, M. R. "McGuire, Alice Rebecca Brooks (1902–1975)." *DALB*: 1978 350–52.

Mack, John B.

15.1150 Mack, J. B. *Nobody Promised Me.* Chicago: Children's Press, 1970.

MacKaye, Julia Gunther

15.1151 "MacKaye, Julia (Josephine) Gunther." *CB* (1949): 382–83.

McKenna, Francis Eugene

15.1152 "McKenna, F(rancis) E(ugene)." *CB* (1966): 253–56.

15.1153 Matarazzo, J. M. "McKenna, F.E." *ELIS* 36 (1983): 361–63.

McKim, Charles Follen

15.1154 Oehlerts, D. E. "McKim, Charles Follen (1847–1909)." *DALB*: 1978 352, 435–37.

MacLeish, Archibald

15.1155 "MacLeish, Archibald." *CB* (1959): 279–81.

15.1156 Goldschmidt, E. "Archibald Mac-Leish: Librarian of Congress." *CRL* 30 (1969): 12–24.

15.1157 Goldschmidt, E., ed. *Champion of a Cause: Essays and Addresses on Librarianship by Archibald MacLeish.* Chicago: American Library Association, 1971.

15.1158 Benco, N. L. "Archibald MacLeish: The Poet Librarian." *QJLC* 33 (1976): 233–49.

15.1159 Maier, K. S. "A Fellowship in German Literature: Thomas Mann, Agnes Meyer, and Archibald MacLeish." *QJLC* 36 (1979): 385–400.

15.1160 "MacLeish, Archibald." In *Librarian Authors: A Biobibliography*, by R. Engelbarts. Jefferson, N.C.: McFarland, 1981. P. 156.

15.1161 Cole, J. Y. "MacLeish, Archibald (1892–1982)." *ALAWE2*: 1986 507–08.

15.1162 Drabeck, B. A., and Ellis, H. E. *Archibald MacLeish: Reflections.* Boston: University of Massachusetts Press, 1986.

McMurtrie, Douglas Crawford

15.1163 Cveljo, K., and White, M. D. "McMurtrie, Douglas Crawford (1888–1944)." *DALB*: 1978 352–55.

MacPherson, Harriet Dorothea

15.1164 Harvey, J. F. "MacPherson, Harriet Dorothea (1892–1967)." *DALB*: 1978 336–37.

McShean, Gordon

15.1165 McShean, G. *Running a Message Parlor: A Librarian's Medium-Rare Memoir about Censorship.* Palo Alto, Calif.: Ramparts Press, 1977.

Madison, James

15.1166 Rutland, R. A. "Madison's Bookish Habits." *QJLC* 37 (1980): 176–91.

Magruder, Patrick

15.1167 Gordon, M. K. "Patrick Magruder: Citizen, Congressman, Librarian of Congress." *QJLC* 32 (1975): 154–71.

15.1168 Gordon, M. K. "Magruder, Patrick (1768–1819)." *DALB*: 1978 337–39.

Manchester, Earl N.

15.1169 Henry, E. A. "Earl N. Manchester." *BB* 19 (1948): 113–14.

Mann, Horace

15.1170 O'Connell, J. J. "Horace Mann's Influence on School Libraries in Massachusetts." Master's thesis, Massachusetts State College, 1934.

15.1171 Jones, E. K. "Horace Mann and the Early Libraries of Massachusetts." *Massachusetts Library Association Bulletin* 27 (1937): 19–21.

15.1172 King, C. S. "Horace Mann's Influence on South American Libraries." *History of Education Quarterly* 1 (1961): 16–26.

15.1173 Downs, R. B. "Books and Libraries." In *Horace Mann: Champion of Public Schools*. Boston: Twayne Publishing, 1974. Pp. 58–68.

Mann, Margaret

15.1174 Wead, E. "Margaret Mann—A Bibliography." *Catalogers and Classifiers Yearbook* 7 (1938): 15–18.

15.1175 Shaw, D. R. "Life and Work of Margaret Mann." Master's thesis, Drexel Institute of Technology, 1950.

15.1176 Grotzinger, L. A. "Margaret Mann: The Preparatory Years." *JEL* 10 (1970): 302–15.

15.1177 Grotzinger, L. A. "The Protofeminist Librarian at the Turn of the Century: Two Studies." *JLH* 10 (1975): 195–213.

15.1178 Grotzinger, L. A. "Mann, Margaret (1873–1960)." *DALB*: 1978 339–42.

15.1179 Grotzinger, L. A. "Women Who 'Spoke for Themselves.' " *CRL* 39 (1978): 175–90.

15.1180 Rinehart, C. "Mann, Margaret (1873–1960)." *ALAWE2*: 1986 516–17.

Mapp, Edward

15.1181 Mapp, E. "From My Perspective: A Social Responsibility." In *The Black Librarian in America*, edited by E. J. Josey. Metuchen, N.J.: Scarecrow Press, 1970. Pp. 184–90.

Marriott, Alice Lee

15.1182 "Marriott, Alice (Lee)." *CB* (1950): 382–83.

Marshall, Alfred Prince

15.1183 Marshall, A. P. "The Search for Identity." In *The Black Librarian in America*, edited by E. J. Josey. Metuchen, N.J.: Scarecrow Press, 1970. Pp. 173–83.

Martel, Charles

15.1184 Childs, J. B. "Martel, Charles (Mar. 5, 1860–May 15, 1945)." *DAB* Suppl. 3 (1973): 509–11.

15.1185 Childs, J. B., and Cole, J. Y. "Martel, Charles (1860–1945)." *DALB*: 1978 342–45.

15.1186 "Martel, Charles." In *Librarian Authors: A Biobibliography*, by R. Engelbarts. Jefferson, N.C.: McFarland, 1981. Pp. 91–92.

15.1187 Scott, E. "Martel, Charles (1860–1945)." *ALAWE2*: 1986 518–19.

Martin, Allie Beth Dent

15.1188 "Martin, Allie Beth." *CB* (1975): 264–66.

15.1189 Kennedy, F. "Martin, Allie Beth Dent (1914–1976)." *DALB*: 1978 345–47.

15.1190 Woodrum, P. "Martin, Allie Beth (1914–1976)." *ALAWE2*: 1986 519.

Martin, Mary P.

15.1191 Wetzel, N. P. "Mary P. Martin and the Canton Public Library, 1884–1928: A Study in Library Leadership." Master's thesis, Kent State University, 1969.

Martin, Naomi

15.1192 Scheuber, Mrs. C. "In Memoriam: Naomi Martin." *HTL* 4 (1935): 1466.

Mathis, Sharon Bell

15.1193 Shockley, A. A. "Sharon Bell Mathis (1937–)." *HBLib*: 1977 165–66.

Maze, Adele Henry

15.1194 Maze, A. H. "Librarian Tells of 35 Years' Service in South Oak Park." *IllL* 36 (1954): 137–39.

Mearns, David Chambers

15.1195 "Mearns, David C(hambers)." *CB* (1961): 302–03.

Meehan, John Silva

15.1196 McDonough, J. "John Silva Meehan: A Gentleman of Amiable Manners." *QJLC* 33 (1976): 3–28.

15.1197 McDonough, J. "Meehan, John Silva (1790–1863)." *DALB*: 1978 355–57.

Meigs, Return Jonathan

15.1198 Faulkner, R. W. "Return Jonathan Meigs: Tennessee's First State Librarian." *THQ* 42 (1983): 151–64.

Melcher, Daniel

15.1199 Larrick, N. "Daniel Melcher." *BB* 24 (1966): 225–28, 248.

15.1200 Grannis, C. B. "Melcher, Daniel (1912–1985)." *ALAWE2*: 1986 542.

Melcher, Frederic Gershom

15.1201 Masten, H. A., ed. "In Tribute to Frederic G. Melcher." *TN* 20 (1964): 177–207.

15.1202 Melcher, D. "Fred Melcher as I Knew Him." *BALA* 61 (1967): 56–62.

15.1203 Grannis, C. B. "Melcher, Frederic Gershom (1879–1963)." *DALB*: 1978 358–59.

15.1204 Peters, J. "Melcher, Frederic Gershom (Apr. 12, 1879–Mar. 9, 1963)." *DAB* Suppl. 7 (1981): 524–25.

15.1205 Tanselle, G. T. "Melcher, Frederic G. (1879–1963)." *ALAWE2*: 1986 542–44.

Merrill, Elmer Drew

15.1206 Salk, D. S. "Merrill, Elmer Drew (Oct. 15, 1876–Feb. 25, 1956)." *DAB* Suppl. 6 (1980): 449–50.

Merrill, James Cushing

15.1207 Phalen, J. M. "Merrill, James Cushing (Mar. 26, 1853–Oct. 27, 1902)." *DAB* 12 (1933): 560–61.

Merrill, Julia Wright

15.1208 Vitz, C. "Julia Wright Merrill." *BALA* 40 (1946): 96–97.

15.1209 Stevens, R. E. "Merrill, Julia Wright (1881–1961)." *DALB*: 1978 359–60.

Merrill, William Stetson

15.1210 Krummel, D. W., and Williamson, W. L. "Merrill, William Stetson (1866–1969)." *DALB*: 1978 360–61.

Merritt, LeRoy Charles

15.1211 Danton, J. P. "Merritt, LeRoy Charles (1912–1970)." *DALB*: 1978 361–63.

Metcalf, Clarence Sheridan

15.1212 Gordon, R. "Clarence Sheridan Metcalf." *BB* 20 (1950): 1–3.

Metcalf, Keyes DeWitt

15.1213 Osborn, A. D. "Keyes D. Metcalf." *BB* 18 (1944): 48–50.

15.1214 Williams, E. E. "The Metcalf Administration, 1937–1955, and Keyes D. Metcalf: A Bibliography of Published Writings." *HLB* 17 (1969): 113–42.

15.1215 Metcalf, K. D. *Random Recollections of an Anachronism, or Seventy-Five Years of Library Work.* New York: Readex Books, 1980.

15.1216 Horner, S. J. "Spotlighting a Nonagenerian Achiever: Keyes DeWitt Metcalf." *WLB* 55 (1981): 353–57.

15.1217 "Metcalf, Keyes DeWitt." In *Librarian Authors: A Biobibliography,* by R. Engelbarts. Jefferson, N.C.: McFarland, 1981. P. 159.

15.1218 Hernon, P. "Keyes DeWitt Metcalf." *LAAL*: 1983 213–35.

15.1219 McEldowney, W. J. "Keyes D. Metcalf and New Zealand." *New Zealand Libraries* 44 (1985): 197–202.

15.1220 Kaser, D. "Metcalf, Keyes D. (1889–1983)." *ALAWE2*: 1986 544–45.

Meyer, Herman H. B.

15.1221 Bishop, W. W. "H. H. B. Meyer." *BB* 15 (1935): 141.

15.1222 Cole, J. Y. "Meyer, Herman H. B. (1864–1937)." *DALB*: 1978 363–64.

Milam, Carl Hastings

15.1223 Wilson, L. R. "Carl H. Milam." *LJ* 70 (1945): 331–33.

15.1224 Ulveling, R. A. "Carl H. Milam." *BALA* 42 (1948): 203.

15.1225 Danton, E. M. "Carl Hastings Milam." *BALA* 53 (1959): 753–62.

15.1226 Fontaine, E. O. "People and Places of the Milam Era." *BALA* 58 (1964): 363–71.

15.1227 Dale, D. C., ed. *Carl H. Milam and the United Nations Library.* Metuchen, N.J.: Scarecrow Press, 1976.

15.1228 Sullivan, P. A. *Carl H. Milam and the American Library Association.* New York: H.W. Wilson, 1976.

15.1229 Sullivan, P. A. "Milam, Carl Hastings (1884–1963)." *DALB*: 1978 364–66.

15.1230 "Milam, Carl H." In *Librarian Authors: A Biobibliography,* by R. Engelbarts. Jefferson, N.C.: McFarland, 1981. Pp. 96–98.

15.1231 Milczewski, M. A. "Milam, Carl H. (1884–1963)." *ALAWE2*: 1986 557–58.

Miller, Charles

15.1232 Miller, C. E. " 'Exit Smiling' Reflections Culled from the Autobiography of Charles Miller, Librarian of the Mercantile

Library of St. Louis (ca. 1890)." *Missouri Historical Society Bulletin* 6 (October 1949): 44–52.

Mitchell, Sydney Bancroft

15.1233 Sayers, F. C. "Who Says That They Have Retired?" *LJ* 72 (1947): 906–07.

15.1234 Powell, L. C. "Mitchell of California." *WLB* 28 (1954): 778–81, 790.

15.1235 Mitchell, S. B. *Mitchell of California; the Memoirs of Sydney B. Mitchell: Librarian, Teacher, Gardener.* Berkeley: California Library Association, 1960.

15.1236 Powell, L. C. "Mitchell, Sydney Bancroft (1878–1951)." *DALB*: 1978 366–67.

15.1237 "Mitchell, Sydney B." In *Librarian Authors: A Biobibliography,* by R. Engelbarts. Jefferson, N.C.: McFarland, 1981. Pp. 50–51.

Moe, Philip Severin

15.1238 Fleming, T. P. "Philip S. Moe, 1908–1948." *BMLA* 36 (1948): 433.

Mohrhardt, Foster Edward

15.1239 "Mohrhardt, Foster E(dward)." *CB* (1967): 292–94.

15.1240 Vosper, R. "Mohrhardt, Foster E. (1907–)." *ALAWE2*: 1986 559–61.

Montague, Gilbert Holland

15.1241 Urofsky, M. I. "Montague, Gilbert Holland (May 27, 1880–Feb. 4, 1961)." *DAB* Suppl. 7 (1981): 547–48.

Montgomery, Thomas Lynch

15.1242 "Thomas Lynch Montgomery, Litt. D., 1862–1929." *BB* 14 (1932): 141–42.

15.1243 Krash, R. D. "Montgomery, Thomas Lynch (1862–1929)." *DALB*: 1978 367–68.

Monti, Minne Sweet

15.1244 Hershey, F. E. "Minne Sweet Monti: Her Life and Influence." Master's thesis, Western Reserve University, 1957.

Moore, Anne Carroll

15.1245 Williams, M. "Anne Carroll Moore." *BB* 18 (1946): 221–23.

15.1246 Sawyer, R. "Anne Moore of Limerick, Maine, Minister without Portfolio." *HB* 26 (1950): 245–51.

15.1247 Akers, N. M. "Anne Carroll Moore; A Study of Her Work with Children's Libraries and Literature." Master's thesis, Pratt Institute, 1951.

15.1248 Evans, E. "Anne Carroll Moore Fills Eighty Years." *PW* 160 (1951): 306–07.

15.1249 Power, L. S. "Recollections of Anne Carroll Moore (Children's Librarian in New York Since 1906)." *BNYPL* 60 (1956): 623–27.

15.1250 Strang, M. "Good Labor of Old Days." *BNYPL* 60 (1956): 537–50.

15.1251 Forsee, A. "Anne Carroll Moore: Librarian From Limerick." In *Women Who Reached for Tomorrow.* Philadelphia: Macrae Smith, 1960. Pp. 36–55.

15.1252 Estes, E., Dalphin, M., and Baker, A. "Tribute to Anne Carroll Moore." *TN* 18 (1961): 31–41.

15.1253 Poor, A. M. "Anne Carroll Moore: The Velvet Glove of Librarianship." Master's thesis, Southern Connecticut State College, 1966.

15.1254 Sayers, F. C. *Anne Carroll Moore: A Biography.* New York: Atheneum, 1972.

15.1255 Fasick, A. M. "Moore, Anne Carroll (1871–1961)." *DALB*: 1978 368–71.

15.1256 Kenney, A. L. "Moore, Anne Carroll, July 12, 1871–Jan. 20, 1961." *Notable American Women: The Modern Period*: 1980 489–90.

15.1257 "Moore, Anne Carroll." In *Librarian Authors: A Biobibliography*, by R. Engelbarts. Jefferson, N.C.: McFarland, 1981. Pp. 102–04.

15.1258 Mycue, D. J. "Moore, Anne Carroll (July 12, 1871–Jan. 20, 1961)." *DAB* Suppl. 7 (1981): 550–51.

15.1259 Baker, A. "Moore, Anne Carroll (1871–1961)." *ALAWE2*: 1986 561–62.

Moore, George Henry

15.1260 Wall, A. J. "Moore, George Henry (Apr. 20, 1823–May 5, 1892)." *DAB* 13 (1934): 125–26.

Moore, Mrs. John Trotwood

15.1261 Faulkner, R. W. "Mrs. John Trotwood Moore, 1875–1957." *Tennessee Librarian* 34 (1982): 41–49.

Moore, Nathaniel Fish

15.1262 Haight, B. I. *A Memorial Discourse of Nathaniel F. Moore, LL.D.: Sometime President of Columbia College.* New York: C.A. Kittle, printer, 1874.

15.1263 Pine, J. B. "Nathaniel F. Moore, LL.D." *Columbia University Quarterly* 5 (1903): 182–91.

15.1264 Thomas, M. H. "Moore, Nathaniel Fish (Dec. 25, 1782–Apr. 27, 1872)." *DAB* 13 (1934): 134–35.

Morgan, John Pierpont (1837–1913)

15.1265 Atwood, A. W. "Morgan, John Pierpont (Apr. 17, 1837–Mar. 31, 1913)." *DAB* 13 (1934): 175–80.

15.1266 Satterlee, H. L. *J. Pierpont Morgan, An Intimate Portrait.* New York: Macmillan, 1934.

15.1267 Taylor, F. H. *Pierpont Morgan as Collector and Patron, 1837–1913.* New York: Pierpont Morgan Library, 1957.

15.1268 Jackson, S. *J.P. Morgan: A Biography.* New York: Stein and Day, 1983.

15.1269 Hendricks, D. D. "Morgan, J. Pierpont (1837–1913)." *ALAWE2*: 1986 564–65.

Morgan, John Pierpont (1867–1943)

15.1270 Forbes, J. D. *J.P. Morgan, Jr., 1867–1943.* Charlottesville: University Press of Virginia, 1981.

Moriarty, John Helenbeck

15.1271 Dowden, K. "Moriarty, John Helenbeck (1903–1971)." *DALB*: 1978 371–72.

Morison, Nathaniel Holmes

15.1272 *Memorial of Nathaniel Holmes Morison (1815–1890), First Provost of the Peabody Institute (1867–1890).* Baltimore: Press of I. Friedenwald, 1892.

Morley, Linda Huckel

15.1273 Vormelker, R. L. "Morley, Linda Huckel (1881–1972)." *DALB*: 1978 372–73.

Morsch, Lucile M.

15.1274 Wheeler, J. L. "Lucile Morsch." *Journal of Catalogers & Classifiers* 7 (1951): 73–75.

15.1275 "Morsch, Lucile M." *CB* (1958):377–79.

15.1276 Cole, J. Y. "Morsch, Lucile M." *ELIS* 18 (1976): 277–83.

15.1277 Richmond, P. A. "Morsch, Lucile M. (1906–1972)." *DALB*: 1978 373–77.

Morton, Florrinell Francis

15.1278 "Morton, Florrinell F(rancis)." *CB* (1961): 325–27.

Moser, Fritz

15.1279 "Moser, Fritz." *CB* (1955): 432–33.

Moses, Louise J.

15.1280 Moses, L. J. "The Black Librarian: Untapped Resource." In *The Black Librarian in America*, edited by E. J. Josey. Metuchen, N.J.: Scarecrow Press, 1970. Pp. 137–41.

Mudge, Isadore Gilbert

15.1281 Evans, A. P. "God Almighty Hates a Quitter." *CLC* 2 (1952): 13–18.

15.1282 Waddell, J. N. "The Career of Isadore G. Mudge: A Chapter in the History of Reference Librarianship." Doctoral dissertation, Columbia University, 1973.

15.1283 Waddell, J. N. "Mudge, Isadore Gilbert." *ELIS* 18 (1976): 287–91.

15.1284 Grotzinger, L. A. "Women Who 'Spoke for Themselves.' " *CRL* 39 (1978): 175–90.

15.1285 Waddell, J. N., and Grotzinger, L. A. "Mudge, Isadore Gilbert (1875–1957)." *DALB*: 1978 377–79.

15.1286 Dain, P. "Mudge, Isadore Gilbert, Mar. 14, 1875–May 16, 1957." *Notable American Women: The Modern Period*: 1980 503–04.

15.1287 Cohen, P. "Mudge, Isadore Gilbert (1875–1957)." *ALAWE2*: 1986 567–68.

Mulford, Clarence Edward

15.1288 Faulk, O. B. "Mulford, Clarence Edward (Feb. 3, 1883–May 10, 1956)." *DAB* Suppl. 6 (1980): 466–67.

Mullin, Francis A.

15.1289 Conmy, P. T. "The Ultimate Professionalization of the Catholic University Library: Father Mullin and Eugene Willging." *CLW* 56 (1985): 416–18.

Mumford, Lawrence Quincy

15.1290 "Mumford, L(awrence) Quincy." *CB* (1954): 481–83.

15.1291 Rogers, R. D. "LQM of LC." *BB* 25 (1968): 161–65.

15.1292 Powell, B. E. "Lawrence Quincy Mumford: Twenty Years of Progress." *QJLC* 33 (1976): 269–87.

15.1293 Lorenz, J. G. "Mumford, L. Quincy (1903–1982)." *ALAWE2*: 1986 568–69.

Munn, Ralph

15.1294 Hadley, C. "Ralph Munn." *BB* 16 (1938): 125–26.

15.1295 Berneis, R. F. "Munn, Ralph (1894–1975)." *DALB*: 1978 379–81.

15.1296 Doms, K. "Munn, Ralph (1894–1975)." *ALAWE2*: 1986 570–72.

Murray, Daniel A. P.

15.1297 Jackson, W. V. "Some Pioneer Negro Library Workers." *LJ* 64 (1939): 215–17.

15.1298 Harris, R. L. "Daniel Murray and The Encyclopedia of the Colored Race." *Phylon: The Atlanta University Review of Race and Culture* 37 (1976): 270–82.

15.1299 "Daniel A.P. Murray (1852–1925)." *HBLib*: 1977 27–28.

15.1300 Cole, J. Y. "Murray, Daniel Alexander Payne (1852–1925)." *DALB*: 1978 381–82.

Nash, Herbert Charles

15.1301 Conmy, P. T. "Stanford's Herbert Charles Nash, Fourth President of California Library Association." *CalL* 39 (1978): 39–45.

Nelson, Charles Alexander

15.1302 Williamson, C. C. "Nelson, Charles Alexander (Apr. 14, 1839–Jan 13, 1933)." *DAB* 13 (1934): 413–14.

15.1303 Miksa, F. L. "Nelson, Charles Alexander (1839–1933)." *DALB:* 1978 382–83.

Nolan, Edward J.

15.1304 Conmy, P. T. "Edward J. Nolan, Scientist, Librarian, and a Founder of the American Library Association." *CLW* 56 (1984): 66–67.

Norton, Andre

15.1305 "Norton, Andre." *CB* (1958): 411–12.

Norton, Charles Benjamin

15.1306 Krummel, D. W. "Norton, Charles Benjamin (1825–1891)." *DALB:* 1978 383–84.

Norton, Margaret

15.1307 Mitchell, T. W. "Norton, Margaret (1891–1984)." *ALAWE2:* 1986 606–07.

Nourse, Louis Martin

15.1308 Hyle, D. F. "Louis Martin Nourse." *BB* 17 (1942): 177–78.

Noyes, Marcia C.

15.1309 "Reception Honoring Marcia C. Noyes." *BMLA* 34 (1946): 340–46.

Noyes, Stephen Buttrick

15.1310 Miksa, F. L. "Noyes, Stephen Buttrick (1833–1885)." *DALB:* 1978 384–87.

O'Reilly, Aidan

15.1311 Ernest, B. *As a Star for All Eternity: A Story of Brother Aidan O'Reilly, CSC.* Notre Dame, Ind.: Dujaríe Press, 1948.

Oberly, Eunice Rockwood

15.1312 Allen, J. M. "Eunice Rockwood Oberly, 1878–1921." In *Pioneering Leaders in Librarianship,* edited by E. M. Danton. Chicago: American Library Association, 1953. Pp. 130–40.

15.1313 "Oberly, Eunice Rockwood." In *Librarian Authors: A Biobibliography,* by R. Engelbarts. Jefferson, N.C.: McFarland, 1981. Pp. 25–26.

Oboler, Eli Martin

15.1314 Oboler, E. M. "Twenty Years an Idaho Librarian: A Personal Report." *Idaho Librarian* 21 (July 1969): 95–99.

Olcott, Frances Jenkins

15.1315 Thompson, J. A. "As It Was in the Beginning: Frances Jenkins Olcott." *PL* 30 (1925): 417–22.

15.1316 Woolls, B. "Olcott, Frances Jenkins (1872–1963)." *DALB:* 1978 387–88.

Oltman, Florine Alma

15.1317 "Oltman, Florine (Alma)." *CB* (1970): 327–28.

Orne, Jerrold

15.1318 Poole, H. "Jerrold Orne: A Biography." In *Academic Libraries by the Year 2000: Essays Honoring Jerrold Orne,* edited by H. Poole. New York: R.R. Bowker, 1977. Pp. 1–6.

15.1319 DuMont, R. R. "Jerrold Orne: A Biographical Sketch." *Journal of Academic Librarianship* 8 (1982): 20–25.

15.1320 DuMont, R. R. "Jerrold Orne." *LAAL*: 1983 237–60.

Osborn, Andrew D.

15.1321 Bagnall, A. G. "Andrew Osborn in New Zealand." *SerL* 6 (1982): 115–16.

15.1322 Bryan, H. "The Three Careers of Andrew Osborn." *SerL* 6 (1982): 107–13.

15.1323 Gellatly, P. "Introduction." *SerL* 6 (1982): 87–88.

15.1324 Hotimsky, C. M. "Andrew D. Osborn and Education for Librarianship in Canada." *SerL* 6 (1982): 117–25.

15.1325 Katz, B. "Osborn and That Elusive Definition." *SerL* 6 (1982): 143–44.

15.1326 Mason, E. "Andrew Osborn and the Library World of His Time." *SerL* 6 (1982): 95–106.

15.1327 Melin, N. "Andrew Osborn: The Serials Specialist." *SerL* 6 (1982): 139–42.

15.1328 Metcalf, K. D. "Andrew D. Osborn." *SerL* 6 (1982): 89–94.

15.1329 Morrison, P. D., and Cooksey, E. B. "Andrew D. Osborn: A Bio-bibliography." *SerL* 6 (1982): 145–58.

Osborn, George A.

15.1330 Cameron, D. F. "George A. Osborn Was Champion of Best College Practices." *LJ* 72 (1947): 1481, 1484.

Overton, Florence

15.1331 Hopper, F. F. "Florence Overton, 1870–1948." *BNYPL* 52 (1948): 355–56.

Owen, Thomas McAdory

15.1332 Ketchersid, A. L. "Thomas McAdory Owen: Archivist." Master's thesis, Florida State University, 1961.

Page, Frederick Winslow

15.1333 Clemons, H. "Frederick Winslow Page." In *The University of Virginia Library*. Charlottesville: University of Virginia Library, 1954. Pp. 115–18.

Palm, Swante

15.1334 Barron, A. D. "Sir Swante Palm." *Alcalde* 5 (1917): 473–79.

15.1335 Evans, M. "Sir Swante Palm's Legacy to Texas." *American Scandinavian Review* 37 (1949): 41–45.

15.1336 Ransom, H. H. "A Renaissance Gentleman in Texas: Notes on the Life and Library of Swante Palm." *SHQ* 53 (1950): 225–38.

15.1337 Rosenquist, C. M. "Palm, Swante." *HT* 2 (1952): 326–27.

15.1338 Dickerson, D. L. "Swante Palm's Legacy for Texans." *TL* 29 (1967): 16–22.

15.1339 Rogers, A. E. "Swante Palm: Nineteenth Century Texas Book Collector." *TLJ* 43 (1967): 68–69, 88–92.

Paltsits, Victor Hugo

15.1340 Hill, R. W. "Victor Hugo Paltsits." *BNYPL* 56 (1952): 554–56.

15.1341 Norton, M. C. "Victor Hugo Paltsits." *AAr* 16 (1953): 137–40.

15.1342 Brown, R. A. "Paltsits, Victor Hugo (1867–1952)." *DALB*: 1978 388–89.

Pargellis, Stanley M.

15.1343 Pargellis, S. M. "On Being a Librarian." *American Oxonian* 40 (1953): 3–8.

15.1344 Billington, R. A. "Stanley Pargellis." In *Essays in History and Literature Presented by Fellows of the Newberry Library to Stanley*

Pargellis, edited by H. Bluhm. Chicago: Newberry Library, 1965. Pp. 3–18.

15.1345 Krummel, D. W. "The Writings of Stanley Pargellis." In *Essays in History and Literature Presented by Fellows of the Newberry Library to Stanley Pargellis,* edited by H. Bluhm. Chicago: Newberry Library, 1965. Pp. 221–31.

15.1346 Krummel, D. W. "Pargellis, Stanley (1898–1968)." *DALB:* 1978 389–91.

Patten, Frank Chauncy

15.1347 Ideson, J. B. "Frank Chauncy Patten: An Appreciation." *Library Service News* (April 1934): 35–37.

15.1348 Gardner, M. C. "In Memoriam: Frank Chauncy Patten." *HTL* 4 (1935): 143–44.

15.1349 Jordan, M. "Frank Chauncy Patten: The Galveston Years." Master's thesis, University of Texas, 1966.

Patton, John Shelton

15.1350 Clemons, H. "John Shelton Patton." In *The University of Virginia Library.* Charlottesville: University of Virginia Library, 1954. Pp. 118–22.

Paylore, Patricia

15.1351 Paylore, P. "The Chief Librarian and Book Knowledge." *CRL* 15 (1954): 313–16.

Pearson, Edmund Lester

15.1352 Pearson, E. L. *The Library and the Librarian: A Selection of Articles from the Boston Evening Transcript* and Other Sources. Woodstock, Vt.: Elm Tree Press, 1910.

15.1353 Hyland, L. "An Interpretation of Edmund Lester Pearson—Librarian Extraordinary, to Which Is Added a Bibliography of His Works." Master's thesis, Carnegie Institute of Technology, 1952.

15.1354 Durnell, J. "An Irrepressible Deceiver." *PNLAQ* 36 (1971): 17–23.

15.1355 Pearson, E. L. *The Librarian: Selections from the Column of That Name,* edited by J. B. Durnell and N. D. Stevens. Metuchen, N.J.: Scarecrow Press, 1976.

15.1356 Stevens, N. D. "Pearson, Edmund Lester (1880–1937)." *DALB:* 1978 392–93.

15.1357 "Pearson, Edmund Lester." In *Librarian Authors: A Biobibliography,* by R. Engelbarts. Jefferson, N.C.: McFarland, 1981. Pp. 112–13.

Peck, Adolph L.

15.1358 Eastman, W. R. "Adolph L. Peck (1847–1911)." *BB* 9 (1916): 86.

Pennypacker, Mrs. Percy V.

15.1359 "Pennypacker, Mrs. Percy V." *HT* 2 (1952): 360.

Peoples, William Thaddeus

15.1360 "William Thaddeus Peoples." *BB* 9 (1916): 61.

Perkins, Frederick Beecher

15.1361 Wessells, M. B. "Perkins, Frederick Beecher (1828–1899)." *DALB:* 1978 393–94.

Perry, Hally Ballinger Bryan

15.1362 Caldwell, Mrs. J. S. "Perry, Hally Ballinger Bryan." *HT* 3 (1976): 724.

Perry, James Whitney

15.1363 Perry, R. "Perry, James Whitney." *ELIS* 22 (1977): 66–68.

Perry, Margaret

15.1364 Shockley, A. A. "Margaret Perry (1933–)." *HBLib*: 1977 164.

Persons, Frederick Torrel

15.1365 Babcock, F. K. "Frederick Torrel Persons and Church Architecture." *American Congregational Association Bulletin* 2 (1951): 3–14.

Pettee, Julia

15.1366 Raeppel, J. E. "Julia Pettee." *BALA* 47 (1953): 417–19.

15.1367 Pearson, L. "The Life and Work of Julia Pettee, 1872–1967." *American Theological Library Association Newsletter* 18, no. 2 suppl. (14 November 1970): 25–92.

15.1368 Rinehart, C. "Pettee, Julia (1872–1967)." *DALB*: 1978 394–95.

Pfeuffer, Somers V.

15.1369 "Pfeuffer, Somers V." *HT* 2 (1952): 371.

Pierce, Cornelia Marvin

15.1370 Brisley, M. A. "Cornelia Marvin Pierce: Pioneer in Library Extension." *LQ* 38 (1968): 125–53.

15.1371 Mickey, M. B. "Pierce, Cornelia Marvin (1873–1957)." *DALB*: 1978 395–98.

Piercy, Esther June

15.1372 Castagna, E. "Esther Piercy, My Friend and Colleague." *LRTS* 11 (1967): 261–62.

15.1373 Cronin, J. M. "Esther Piercy and the Cataloging-in-Source Experiment." *LRTS* 11 (1967): 263–64.

15.1374 Dunkin, P. S. "Piercy, Esther June (1905–1967)." *DALB*: 1978 398–99.

Pintard, John

15.1375 Sullivan, L. E. "Books, Power, and the Development of Libraries in the New Republic: The Prison and Other Journals of John Pintard of New York." *JLH* 21 (1986): 407–24.

Plummer, Mary Wright

15.1376 Brown, W. L. "A Library Life: A Symposium in Honor of the Memory and in Gratitude for the Work and Influence of Mary Wright Plummer." *LJ* 41 (1916): 865–81.

15.1377 Moore, A. C. "Mary Wright Plummer, 1856–1916." *BB* 14 (1930): 1–3.

15.1378 Lydenberg, H. M. "Plummer, Mary Wright (Mar. 8, 1856–Sept. 21, 1916)." *DAB* 15 (1935): 17.

15.1379 Banta, R. E. "Plummer, Mary Wright: 1856–1916." In *Indiana Authors and Their Books, 1816–1916.* Crawfordsville, Ind.: Wabash College, 1949. P. 257.

15.1380 Hamilton, R. H. "Plummer, Mary Wright (Mar. 8, 1856–Sept. 21, 1916)." *NAW* 3 (1971): 77–78.

15.1381 Karlowich, R. A., and Sharify, N. "Plummer, Mary Wright (1856–1916)." *DALB*: 1978 399–402.

15.1382 "Plummer, Mary Wright." In *Librarian Authors: A Biobibliography,* by R. Engelbarts. Jefferson, N.C.: McFarland, 1981. Pp. 100–102.

15.1383 Davis, D. G. "Plummer, Mary Wright (1856–1916)." *ALAWE2*: 1986 648–49.

Polk, Mary

15.1384 Perez, C. B. "Mary Polk: Library Pioneer." *Library Mirror* 2 (1931): 24–26.

15.1385 Lopez, L. L. "Mary Polk—Library Pioneer." *Journal of Philippine Librarianship* 3 (1970): 61–72.

Pollack, Ervin Harold

15.1386 Branscomb, L. C., and Mersky, R. M. "Pollack, Ervin Harold (1913–1972)." *DALB*: 1978 402–03.

Poole, Fitch

15.1387 Bolton, C. K. "Poole, Fitch (June 13, 1803–Aug. 19, 1873)." *DAB* 15 (1935): 65–66.

Poole, Reuben Brooks

15.1388 Kraus, J. W. "Poole, Reuben Brooks (1834–1895)." *DALB*: 1978 404.

Poole, William Frederick

15.1389 Chicago Literary Club. *In Memoriam William Frederick Poole.* Chicago: Chicago Literary Club, 1894.

15.1390 Newberry Library, Board of Trustees. *Memorial Sketch of Dr. William Frederick Poole.* Chicago: Newberry Library, 1895.

15.1391 "Publications of William Frederick Poole." In *Memorial Sketch of Dr. William Frederick Poole.* Chicago: Newberry Library, 1895. Pp. 29–34.

15.1392 Holbrook, Z. S. "Dr. Poole and the New England Clergy." *Bibliotheca Sacra* 57 (1900): 282–308.

15.1393 Fletcher, W. I. "William Frederick Poole, 1821–1894." *BB* 8 (1914): 30–31.

15.1394 Davis, R. C. "Some Library Reminiscences." *PL* 22 (1917): 180–82.

15.1395 Johnson, A. "As It Was in the Beginning: An Interview with Dr. W. F. Poole." *PL* 29 (1924): 72–73.

15.1396 Foster, W. E. "Five Men of '76." *BALA* 20 (1926): 312–23.

15.1397 Roden, C. B. "The Boston Years of Dr. W.F. Poole." In *Essays Offered to Herbert Putnam by His Colleagues and Friends on His Thirtieth Anniversary as Librarian of Congress, 5 April 1929,* edited by W. W. Bishop and A. Keogh. New Haven: Yale University Press, 1929. Pp. 388–94.

15.1398 Roden, C. B. "Poole, William Frederick (Dec. 24, 1821–Mar. 1, 1894)." *DAB* 15 (1935): 66–67.

15.1399 Kessler, S. H. "William Frederick Poole, Librarian-Historian." *WLB* 28 (1954): 788–90.

15.1400 Williamson, W. L. *William Frederick Poole and the Modern Library Movement.* New York: Columbia University Press, 1963.

15.1401 Vitz, C. "Three Master Librarians." *Cincinnati Historical Society Bulletin* 26 (1968): 343–60.

15.1402 Metcalf, K. D. "Six Influential Academic and Research Librarians." *CRL* 37 (1976): 332–45.

15.1403 Williamson, W. L. "Poole, William Frederick." *ELIS* 23 (1978): 94–117.

15.1404 Williamson, W. L. "Poole, William Frederick (1821–1894)." *DALB*: 1978 404–12.

15.1405 "Poole, William Frederick." In *Librarian Authors: A Biobibliography,* by R. Engelbarts. Jefferson, N.C.: McFarland, 1981. Pp. 123–25.

15.1406 Ladenson, A. "Poole, William Frederick (1821–1894)." *ALAWE2*: 1986 651–53.

Porter, Dorothy B.

15.1407 Lubin, M. A. "Important Figure in Black Studies: Dr. Dorothy B. Porter." *CLA Journal* 16 (1973): 514–18.

Posner, Ernst

15.1408 Bryan, M. L. M. "Posner, Ernst (1892–1980)." *ALAWE2*: 1986 654–55.

Powell, Benjamin Edward

15.1409 "Powell, Benjamin E(dward)." *CB* (1959): 366–67.

Powell, Lawrence Clark

15.1410 Marshall, B. "Lawrence Clark Powell: An Alchemist of Books." *BB* 20 (1953): 225–27.

15.1411 Harlow, N. "Lawrence Clark Powell." *BALA* 48 (1954): 553–55.

15.1412 "Powell, Lawrence Clark." *CB* (1960): 318–20.

15.1413 Rosenberg, B. *Checklist of the Published Writings of Lawrence Clark Powell.* Los Angeles: University of California, 1966.

15.1414 Powell, L. C. *Fortune and Friendship: An Autobiography.* New York: R.R. Bowker, 1968.

15.1415 "Powell, Lawrence Clark." In *Librarian Authors: A Biobibliography,* by R. Engelbarts. Jefferson, N.C.: McFarland, 1981. Pp. 157–58.

15.1416 Wiegand, W. A. "Lawrence Clark Powell." *LAAL*: 1983 263–87.

15.1417 Zeitlin, J. "Lawrence Clark Powell: A Bookman in the Library Community." *ABBW* 73 (1984): 4727–30.

15.1418 Marshall, J. D., ed. *Books Are Basic: The Essential Lawrence Clark Powell.* Tucson: University of Arizona Press, 1985.

15.1419 Eshelman, W. R. "Powell, Lawrence Clark (1906–)." *ALAWE2*: 1986 656–57.

15.1420 Powell, L. C. *Life Goes On: Twenty More Years of Fortune and Friendship.* Metuchen, N.J.: Scarecrow Press, 1986.

Power, Effie Louise

15.1421 Becker, M. B. "Effie Louise Power: Pioneer in the Development of Library Services for Children." Master's thesis, Western Reserve University, 1950.

15.1422 Berneis, R. F. "Power, Effie Louise (1873–1969)." *DALB*: 1978 412–14.

15.1423 Kingsbury, M. E. "Power, Effie Louise (1873–1969)." *ALAWE2*: 1986 657–59.

Pratt, Enoch

15.1424 Hart, R. H. *Enoch Pratt: The Story of a Plain Man.* Baltimore: Enoch Pratt Free Library, 1935.

Prentis, Robert Riddick

15.1425 Clemons, H. "Robert Riddick Prentis." In *The University of Virginia Library.* Charlottesville: University of Virginia Library, 1954. Pp. 108–10.

Price, Miles Oscar

15.1426 Pimsleur, M. G., and Cohen, M. L. "Price, Miles Oscar (1890–1968)." *DALB*: 1978 414–15.

Prime, L. Margueriete

15.1427 Troxel, W. "Margueriete Prime." *BMLA* 39 (1951): 227–28.

Pritchard, Martha Caroline

15.1428 Smith, S. S. "Pritchard, Martha Caroline (1882–1959)." *DALB*: 1978 415–17.

Pugh, John Jones

15.1429 "John Jones Pugh." *BB* 17 (1941): 81–82.

Purdy, George Flint

15.1430 Sullivan, H. A. "Purdy, George Flint (1905–1969)." *DALB*: 1978 417–18.

Putnam, Herbert

15.1431 "Herbert Putnam." *BB* 10 (1918): 56–57.

15.1432 Belden, C. F. D. "The Library Service of Herbert Putnam in Boston." In *Essays Offered to Herbert Putnam by His Colleagues and Friends on His Thirtieth Anniversary as Librarian of Congress, 5 April 1929*, edited by W. W. Bishop and A. Keogh. New Haven : Yale University Press, 1929. Pp. 10–14.

15.1433 Bowker, R. R. "The Appointment of Herbert Putnam as Librarian of Congress." In *Essays Offered to Herbert Putnam by His Colleagues and Friends on His Thirtieth Anniversary as Librarian of Congress, 5 April 1929*, edited by W. W. Bishop and A. Keogh. New Haven: Yale University Press, 1929. Pp. 15–21.

15.1434 Countryman, G. A. "Mr. Putnam and the Minneapolis Public Library." In *Essays Offered to Herbert Putnam by His Colleagues and Friends on His Thirtieth Anniversary as Librarian of Congress, 5 April 1929*, edited by W. W. Bishop and A. Keogh. New Haven: Yale University Press, 1929. Pp. 5–9.

15.1435 Utley, G. B. "The Library War Service and Its General Director." In *Essays Offered to Herbert Putnam by His Colleagues and Friends on His Thirtieth Anniversary as Librarian of Congress, 5 April 1929*, edited by W. W. Bishop and A. Keogh. New Haven: Yale University Press, 1929. Pp. 474–91.

15.1436 Lewis, L. *A Tribute to Dr. Herbert Putnam, Librarian of Congress, by Hon. Lawrence Lewis of Colorado before the House of Representatives, February 17, 1939.* Washington, D.C.: Government Printing Office, 1939.

15.1437 Mearns, D. C. "Herbert Putnam, Librarian of the United States—the Minneapolis Years." *WLB* 29 (1954): 59–63.

15.1438 Dickinson, A. D. "Recollections of Herbert Putnam." *WLB* 30 (1955): 311–15.

15.1439 Mearns, D. C. "Herbert Putnam: Librarian of the U.S." *DCL* 26 (1955): 22–24.

15.1440 Bay, J. C. "Herbert Putnam, 1861–1955." *Libri* 6 (1956): 201–07.

15.1441 Jones, H. D. "Herbert Putnam: [A Bibliography]." In *Herbert Putnam, 1861–1955: A Memorial Tribute.* Washington, D.C.: Library of Congress, 1956. Pp. 53–80.

15.1442 Mearns, D. C. "Herbert Putnam and His Responsible Eye." In *Herbert Putnam, 1861–1955: A Memorial Tribute.* Washington, D.C.: Library of Congress, 1956. Pp. 1–52.

15.1443 Kreig, C. J. "Herbert Putnam's Philosophy of Librarianship." Master's thesis, Long Island University, 1970.

15.1444 Metcalf, K. D. "Six Influential Academic and Research Librarians." *CRL* 37 (1976): 332–45.

15.1445 Waters, E. N. "Herbert Putnam: The Tallest Little Man in the World." *QJLC* 33 (1976): 151–75.

15.1446 Waters, E. N. "Putnam, [George] Herbert (Sept. 20, 1861–Aug. 14, 1955)." *DAB* Suppl. 5 (1977): 554–55.

15.1447 Childs, J. B. "Putnam, Herbert." *ELIS* 25 (1978): 31–37.

15.1448 Cole, J. Y. "Putnam, George Herbert (1861–1955)." *DALB*: 1978 418–22.

15.1449 Wiegand, W. A. "Herbert Putnam's Appointment as Librarian of Congress." *LQ* 49 (1979): 255–82.

15.1450 "Putnam, Herbert." In *Librarian Authors: A Biobibliography*, by R. Engelbarts. Jefferson, N.C.: McFarland, 1981. Pp. 87–88.

15.1451 Cole, J. Y. "Putnam, Herbert (1861–1955)." *ALAWE2*: 1986 687–88.

Quarles, James Hays

15.1452 "Quarles, James Hays." In *Handbook of Waco and McLennan County*, edited by D. Kelley. Waco, Tex.: Texian Press, 1972. P. 220.

Quigley, Margery Closey

15.1453 Angoff, A. "Margery Quigley, 1885–1968." *Teaneck Points of Reference* 3 (May 1968): 7–8.

15.1454 Curley, A. "Quigley, Margery Closey (1886–1968)." *DALB*: 1978 422–23.

Ragsdale, Smith

15.1455 Bradfield, O. R. "Ragsdale, Smith." *HT* 2 (1952): 429.

Raines, Cadwell Walton

15.1456 Winkler, E. W. "Raines, Cadwell Walton." *HT* 2 (1952): 431.

15.1457 Winfrey, D. H. "Life of Early Librarian Sketched." *TL* 24 (1962): 76–77.

15.1458 Christie, C. C. "Cadwell Walton Raines, 1839–1906: Historian and Librarian." Master's thesis, University of Texas, 1966.

15.1459 Christie, C. C. "Cadwell Walton Raines: State Librarian." *TL* 34 (1972): 191–203.

Ranck, Samuel H.

15.1460 "Samuel H. Ranck." *BB* 11 (1923): 177.

15.1461 Wheeler, J. L. "Samuel H. Ranck." *Michigan Librarian* 7 (1941): 6.

Randall, Dudley

15.1462 Shockley, A. A. "Dudley Randall (1914–)." *HBLib*: 1977 162–63.

Raney, McKendree Llewellyn

15.1463 Harding, T. S. "Raney, McKendree Llewellyn (1877–1964)." *DALB*: 1978 423–27.

Ransom, Harry Hunt

15.1464 Taylor, B. "Harry Ransom as Library Builder." *TLJ* 62 (1986): 28–30.

Ratchford, Fannie Elizabeth

15.1465 Wiley, A. N. "Fannie Elizabeth Ratchford." *BB* 20 (1950): 29–31.

15.1466 Wiley, A. N. "Fannie Elizabeth Ratchford." *TLJ* 27 (1951): 15–19.

15.1467 "Ratchford, Fannie Elizabeth." *HT* 3 (1976): 779–80.

Rathbone, Josephine Adams

15.1468 Horton, M. "Josephine Adams Rathbone: A.L.A. President, 1931–1932." *BB* 15 (1934): 81.

15.1469 Fenneman, N. "Recollections of Josephine Adams Rathbone." *WLB* 23 (1949): 773–74.

15.1470 Shirley, W. "Josephine Adams Rathbone." *WLB* 34 (1959): 199–204.

15.1471 Boromé, J. A. "Rathbone, Josephine Adams (Sept. 10, 1864–May 17, 1941)." *NAW* 3 (1971): 118–19.

15.1472 Davis, D. G. "Rathbone, Josephine Adams (1864–1941)." *DALB*: 1978 427–29.

15.1473 "Rathbone, Josephine Adams." In *Librarian Authors: A Biobibliography*, by R. Engelbarts. Jefferson, N.C.: McFarland, 1981. Pp. 43–44.

Ready, William B.

15.1474 Ready, W. B. *Files on Parade: A Memoir.* Metuchen, N.J.: Scarecrow Press, 1982.

Ricard, Herbert Frederic

15.1475 "Borough Historians [Herbert Frederic Ricard]." *New Yorker* 29 (7 November 1953): 31–33.

Rice, Paul North

15.1476 "Rice, Paul North." *CB* (1947): 536–38.

15.1477 Lydenberg, H. M. "Paul North Rice: The Man and the Librarian." *BNYPL* 57 (1953): 389–91.

15.1478 Kingery, R. E. "Rice, Paul North (1888–1967)." *DALB*: 1978 429–30.

Richards, John Stewart

15.1479 "Richards, John S(tewart)." *CB* (1955): 507–08.

15.1480 Youngs, W. O. "John Stewart Richards." *BB* 22 (1959): 193–94.

Richardson, Ernest Cushing

15.1481 "Ernest Cushing Richardson." *BB* 10 (1919): 133.

15.1482 Branscomb, L. C. "Ernest Cushing Richardson, 1860–1939." In *Pioneering Leaders in Librarianship,* edited by E. M. Danton. Chicago: American Library Association, 1953. Pp. 141–52.

15.1483 Branscomb, L. C. "A Bio-bibliographic Study of Ernest Cushing Richardson, 1860–1939." Doctoral dissertation, University of Chicago, 1954.

15.1484 Currie, R. "Ernest Cushing Richardson." Research Paper, University of North Carolina School of Library Science, 1966.

15.1485 Hadidian, D. Y. "Ernest Cushing Richardson,1860–1939." *CRL* 33 (1972): 122–26.

15.1486 Branscomb, L. C. "Richardson, Ernest Cushing (1860–1939)." *DALB*: 1978 430–35.

15.1487 "Richardson, Ernest Cushing." In *Librarian Authors: A Biobibliography,* by R. Engelbarts. Jefferson, N.C.: McFarland, 1981. Pp. 125–27.

15.1488 Young, A. P. "Richardson, Ernest C. (1860–1939)." *ALAWE2*: 1986 707–09.

Richardson, Henry Hobson

15.1489 Oehlerts, D. E. "Richardson, Henry Hobson (1838–1886)." *DALB*: 1978 435–37.

Richardson, Sid Williams

15.1490 Frantz, J. B. "Richardson, Sid Williams (Apr. 25, 1891–Sept. 30, 1959)." *DAB* Suppl. 6 (1980): 339–41.

Richmond, James Theodore

15.1491 Jansma, H. "Arkansas Lives: The Book Man and the Library; A Chapter in Arkansas Library History." *ArkL* 39 (December 1982): 28–31.

Richmond, Ted

15.1492 Cessna, R. "Library in the Wilderness." *Christian Science Monitor Magazine* (5 April 1947): 6.

Ricord, Frederick William

15.1493 "Frederick William Ricord." *Proceedings of the New Jersey Historical Society* 2 (1902): 194–95.

15.1494 Genzmer, G. H. "Ricord, Frederick William (Oct. 7, 1819–Aug. 12, 1897)." *DAB* 15 (1935): 587–88.

Rider, Arthur Fremont

15.1495 Rider, F. *And Master of None: An Autobiography in the Third Person.* Middletown, Conn.: Godfrey Memorial Library, 1955.

15.1496 Parker, W. W. "Rider, Arthur Fremont (1885–1962)." *DALB: 1978* 437–39.

15.1497 "Rider, Fremont." In *Librarian Authors: A Biobibliography,* by R. Engelbarts. Jefferson, N.C.: McFarland, 1981. Pp. 159–60.

15.1498 Young, A. P. "Rider, Arthur Fremont (1885–1962)." *ALAWE2: 1986* 709–10.

Ridington, John

15.1499 Faxon, F. W. "John Ridington." *BB* 15 (1936): 161.

Ring, Elizabeth L.

15.1500 Ring, Mrs. R. "Ring, Elizabeth L." *HT* 3 (1976): 797.

Robbins, Thomas

15.1501 Love, W. D. *Reverend Thomas Robbins, D.D.: An Address Delivered before the Connecticut Historical Society, Hartford, October 2, 1906.* Hartford, Conn.: Connecticut Historical Society, 1906.

15.1502 Land, W. G. "Robbins, Thomas (Aug. 11, 1777–Sept. 13, 1856)." *DAB* 15 (1935): 645–46.

15.1503 Harlow, T. R. "Thomas Robbins, Clergyman, Book Collector, and Librarian." *PBSA* 61 (1967): 1–11.

Robertson, James Alexander

15.1504 Hill, R. R. "Dr. James Alexander Robertson." *Hispanic American Historical Review* 19 (1939): 127–29.

15.1505 Wilgus, A. C., ed. *Hispanic American Essays: A Memorial to James Alexander Robertson.* Chapel Hill: University of North Carolina Press, 1942.

15.1506 Whitaker, A. P. "Robertson, James Alexander (Aug. 19, 1873–Mar. 20, 1939)." *DAB* Suppl. 2 (1958): 560–61.

Robertson, William Spence

15.1507 Humphreys, R. A. "Robertson, William Spence (Oct. 7, 1872–Oct. 24, 1955)." *DAB* Suppl. 5 (1977): 577–78.

Robinson, Carrie C.

15.1508 Robinson, C. C. "First by Circumstance." In *The Black Librarian in America,* edited by E. J. Josey. Metuchen, N.J.: Scarecrow Press, 1970. Pp. 275–83.

Robinson, Edgar Stewart

15.1509 Bauer, H. C. "Edgar Stewart Robinson." *BB* 21 (1956): 217–19.

Robinson, Otis Hall

15.1510 Holley, E. G. "Robinson, Otis Hall (1835–1912)." *DALB: 1978* 439–41.

Rockwell, William Walker

15.1511 Slavens, T. P. "William Walker Rockwell and the Development of the Union Theological Seminary Library." *JLH* 11 (1976): 26–43.

Roden, Carl Bismarck

15.1512 "Chicago's Book Boss." *Newsweek* 32 (8 November 1948): 88.

15.1513 Fleming, J. B. "Carl B. Roden—No Mere Keeper of Books." *LJ* 75 (1950): 2138–39.

15.1514 Shuman, B. A. "Roden, Carl Bismarck (1871–1956)." *DALB*: 1978 441–43.

15.1515 Adkins, M. R. "Carl Bismarck Roden and the Chicago Public Library." Master's thesis, University of Chicago, 1979.

Rogan, Edgar Huntley

15.1516 Vogel, J. B. "History of Caldwell County Newspapers." Master's thesis, University of Texas, 1947.

15.1517 "Rogan, Edgar Huntley." *HT* 2 (1952): 498.

Rogan, Octavia F.

15.1518 Banks, K. "Octavia F. Rogan, Texas Librarian." Master's thesis, University of Texas, 1963.

Rogers, Frank Bradford

15.1519 Mohrhardt, F. E. "Frank Bradford Rogers." *LJ* 87 (1962): 2836–38.

Rogers, Frank Bradway

15.1520 "Rogers, Frank B(radway)." *CB* (1962): 359–61.

15.1521 Brodman, E. "Rogers, Frank Bradway (1914–)." *ALAWE2*: 1986 710–11.

Rogers, Rutherford David

15.1522 "Rogers, Rutherford David." *CB* (1962): 361–63.

Rollins, Charlemae

15.1523 Saunders, D. "Charlemae Rollins." *BALA* 49 (1955): 68–70.

Roorbach, Orville Augustus

15.1524 Haas, M. L. "Roorbach, Orville Augustus (1803–1861)." *DALB*: 1978 443–44.

Roosevelt, Franklin Delano

15.1525 Stewart, W., and Pollard, C. "Franklin D. Roosevelt, Collector." *Prologue* 1 (1969): 13–28.

Root, Azariah Smith

15.1526 "Azariah Smith Root." *BB* 11 (1920): 1.

15.1527 Bishop, W. W. "Azariah Smith Root." *PBSA* 22 (1928): 66–68.

15.1528 Rubin, R. "Azariah Root's Concept of Education for Librarianship." Research Paper, Kent State University, 1976.

15.1529 Rubin, R. "Azariah Smith Root and Library Instruction at Oberlin College." *JLH* 12 (1977): 250–61.

15.1530 Johnson, H. F. "Root, Azariah Smith (1862–1927)." *DALB*: 1978 444–46.

15.1531 Tucker, J. M. "Azariah Smith Root and Social Reform at Oberlin College." *JLH* 16 (1981): 280–91.

15.1532 Tucker, J. M. "Librarianship as a Community Service: Azariah Smith Root at Oberlin College." Doctoral dissertation, University of Illinois, 1983.

Rose, Ernestine

15.1533 Seldin, B. "Rose, Ernestine (1880–1961)." *DALB*: 1978 447–48.

Rosenbach, Abraham Simon Wolf

15.1534 Rosenbach, A. S. W. *Books and Bidders: The Adventures of a Bibliophile.* Boston: Little, Brown, 1927.

15.1535 Rosenbach, A. S. W. *A Book Hunter's Holiday: Adventures with Books and Manuscripts.* Boston: Houghton Mifflin, 1936.

15.1536 Wolf, E., and Fleming, J. F. *Rosenbach: A Biography.* Cleveland: World Publishing Co., 1960.

15.1537 Wolf, E. "Rosenbach, Abraham Simon Wolf (July 22, 1876–July 1, 1952)." *DAB* Suppl. 5 (1977): 586–88.

Rosenbach, Philip Hyman

15.1538 Wolf, E. "Rosenbach, Philip Hyman (Sept. 29, 1863–Mar. 5, 1953)." *DAB* Suppl. 5 (1977): 586–88.

Rosenberg, Henry

15.1539 [Rogan, O. F.] "Rosenberg, Henry." *DAB* 8 (1933): 166–67.

15.1540 Morgan, W. M. "Rosenberg, Henry." *HT* 2 (1952): 504–05.

Rosenwald, Julius

15.1541 Mann, L. L. "Rosenwald, Julius (Aug. 12, 1862–Jan. 6, 1932)." *DAB* 16 (1935): 170–71.

Rotan, Kate Sturm McCall

15.1542 "Rotan, Kate Sturm McCall." In *Handbook of Waco and McLennan County,* edited by D. Kelley. Waco, Tex.: Texian Press, 1972. Pp. 234–36.

Rothrock, Mary Utopia

15.1543 Suddarth, E. "Mary Utopia Rothrock." *BB* 22 (1957): 73–75.

15.1544 Deaderick, L. "Rothrock, Mary Utopia (1890–1976)." *DALB*: 1978 448–49.

Roubin, Solomon

15.1545 Newman, L. I. "Solomon Roubin and Ephraim Deinard, Cataloguers of the Hebraica in the Sutro Library in San Francisco." In *Semitic and Oriental Studies,* edited by W. J. Fischel. Berkeley: University of California Press, 1951. Pp. 355–64.

Rowell, Joseph Cummings

15.1546 Kurts, B. *Joseph Cummings Rowell, 1853–1938.* Berkeley: University of California Press, 1940.

Rudolph, Alexander Joseph

15.1547 Miksa, F. L. "Rudolph, Alexander Joseph (c.1850–1917)." *DALB*: 1978 449–50.

Rush, Charles Everett

15.1548 Winslow, A. "Charles Everett Rush." *BB* 18 (1946): 193–94.

15.1549 Logsdon, R. H. "Rush, Charles Everett (1885–1958)." *DALB* 1978 450–52.

Sabin, Joseph

15.1550 Roscoe, S. "Sabin, Joseph (1821–1881)." *DALB*: 1978 452–55.

15.1551 Jensen, G. D. "Joseph Sabin and His *Dictionary of Books Relating to America.*" Doctoral dissertation, George Washington University, 1980.

15.1552 Asaf, A. "Sabin, Joseph (1821–1881)." *ALAWE2*: 1986 720–21.

St. John, Francis Regis

15.1553 Byam, M. S. "St. John, Francis Regis (1908–1971)." *DALB*: 1978 455–56.

15.1554 Summers, F. W. "St. John, Francis R. (1908–1971)." *ALAWE2*: 1986 721–22.

Sanders, Minerva Lewis

15.1555 Smith, E. "Minerva Sanders, 1837–1912." In *Pioneering Leaders in Librarianship*, edited by E. M. Danton. Chicago: American Library Association, 1953. Pp. 153–64.

15.1556 Sassé, M. "Sanders, Minerva Amanda Lewis (1837–1912)." *DALB*: 1978 456–58.

15.1557 "Sanders, Minerva." In *Librarian Authors: A Biobibliography*, by R. Engelbarts. Jefferson, N.C.: McFarland, 1981. Pp. 24–25.

Santmeyer, Helen Hooven

15.1558 "Santmeyer, Helen Hooven." *CB* (1985): 357–60.

Saunders, Frederick

15.1559 Harlow, A. F. "Saunders, Frederick (Aug. 14, 1807–Dec. 12, 1902)." *DAB* 16 (1935): 381–82.

Savord, Catherine Ruth

15.1560 Vormelker, R. L. "Savord, Catherine Ruth (1894–1966)." *DALB*: 1978 458–60.

Sayers, Frances Clarke

15.1561 Sayers, F. C. "A Skimming of Memory." *HB* 52 (1976): 270–75.

15.1562 Ragsdale, W. "Sayers, Frances Clarke (1897–)." *ALAWE2*: 1986 726–27.

Scheide, John Hinsdale

15.1563 Bryan, M. R. "Portrait of a Bibliophile XVII: The Scheide Library." *BC* 21 (1972): 489–502.

Schellenberg, Theodore R.

15.1564 Evans, F. B. "Schellenberg, Theodore R. (1903–1970)." *ALAWE2*: 1986 729–30.

Schenk, Rachel Katherine

15.1565 Crawford, H. "Rachel K. Schenk." *BB* 23 (1962): 145–46.

15.1566 Crawford, H. "Schenk, Rachel Katherine (1899–1973)." *DALB*: 1978 460–61.

Scheuber, Jennie Scott

15.1567 Taylor, R. N. "Jennie Scott Scheuber: An Approach to Librarianship." Master's thesis, University of Texas, 1968.

15.1568 Taylor, R. N. "Fort Worth's First Librarian." *TL* 42 (1980): 9–03.

Schick, Mary Elizabeth

15.1569 Standlee, M. W. "The Book Lady." *Military Surgeon* 111 (1952): 44–49.

Schomburg, Arthur A.

15.1570 Williamson, H. A. *Arthur A. Schomburg, the Freemason*. New York: Williamson Masonic Collection, 1941.

15.1571 "Arthur A. Schomburg: 'The Sherlock Holmes of Negro History' (1874–1938)." In *World's Great Men of Color*, vol. 2, edited by J. H. Clarke. New York: Macmillan, 1972. Pp. 449–53.

15.1572 Joyce, D. F. "Arthur Alonzo Schomburg: A Pioneering Black Bibliophile." *JLH* 10 (1975): 169–77.

15.1573 "Arthur Alphonso Schomburg (1874–1938)." *HBLib*: 1977 25.

15.1574 Sinnette, E. D. V. "Arthur Alfonso Schomburg, Black Bibliophile and Curator: His Contribution to the Collection and Dissemination of Materials about Africans and People of African Descent." Doctoral dissertation, Columbia University, 1977.

15.1575 Sinnette, E. D. V. "Schomburg, Arthur Alfonso (1874–1938)." *DALB*: 1978 461–63.

Schwab, John Christopher

15.1576 Day, C. "Schwab, John Christopher (Apr. 1, 1865–Jan. 12, 1916)." *DAB* 16 (1935): 480.

Schwartz, Jacob, Jr.

15.1577 Vann, S. K. "Schwartz, Jacob, Jr. (1846–19—)." *DALB*: 1978 463–65.

Scoggin, Margaret Clara

15.1578 "Scoggin, Margaret C(lara)." *CB* (1952): 520–22.

15.1579 "Take a Bow, Margaret Scoggin." *PW* 161 (1952): 1190–91.

15.1580 Lowy, B. "Margaret C. Scoggin (1905–1968): Her Professional Life and Work in Young Adult Librarianship." Research Paper, Long Island University, 1970.

15.1581 Lowy, B. "Scoggin, Margaret Clara (1905–1968)." *DALB*: 1978 465–67.

15.1582 Chelton, M. K. "Scoggin, Margaret Clara (1905–1968)." *ALAWE2*: 1986 751–53.

Sears, Minnie Earl

15.1583 Whitmore, H. E. "Sears, Minnie Earl (1873–1933)." *DALB*: 1978 467–68.

15.1584 Gates, B. "Sears, Minnie Earl (1873–1933)." *ALAWE2*: 1986 753.

Seaver, William N.

15.1585 Bigelow, R. P. "William N. Seaver." *BB* 19 (1947): 85–87.

Severance, Henry Ormal

15.1586 Hanna, F. M., comp. *Henry Ormal Severance, Librarian, 1907–1937.* Columbia: University of Missouri Library Staff, 1937.

15.1587 Compton, C. H. "Henry Ormal Severance." *BB* 16 (1938): 81–83.

Sewell, Emma Winifred

15.1588 "Sewell, (Emma) Winifred." *CB* (1960): 373–74.

Sewell, Herbert M.

15.1589 Franklin, R. D. "Herbert M. Sewell." *BB* 22 (1958): 97–99.

Seymour, Evelyn May

15.1590 Vann, S. K. "Seymour, Evelyn May (1857–1921)." *DALB*: 1978 468–70.

Shaffer, Kenneth R.

15.1591 Kipp, L. J., and Kipp, R. C. "Kenneth R. Shaffer." *BB* 22 (1959): 169–71.

Sharp, Katharine Lucinda

15.1592 Utley, G. B. "Sharp, Katharine Lucinda (May 25, 1865–June 1, 1914)." *DAB* 17 (1935): 24–25.

15.1593 Howe, H. E. "Katharine Lucinda Sharp, 1865–1914." In *Pioneering Leaders in Librarianship,* edited by E. M. Danton. Chicago: American Library Association, 1953. Pp. 165–72.

15.1594 Grotzinger, L. A. *The Power and the Dignity: Librarianship and Katharine Sharp.* Metuchen, N.J.: Scarecrow Press, 1966.

15.1595 Phelps, R. B. "Sharp, Katharine Lucinda (May 25, 1865–June 1, 1914)." *NAW* 3 (1971): 272–73.

15.1596 Grotzinger, L. A. "Sharp, Katharine Lucinda (1865–1914)." *DALB*: 1978 470–73.

15.1597 Grotzinger, L. A. "Women Who 'Spoke for Themselves.'" *CRL* 39 (1978): 175–90.

15.1598 "Sharp, Katharine Lucinda." In *Librarian Authors: A Biobibliography,* by R. Engelbarts. Jefferson, N.C.: McFarland, 1981. Pp. 44–45.

15.1599 Grotzinger, L. A. "Sharp, Katharine (1865–1914)." *ALAWE2*: 1986 759–60.

Shaw, Charles Bunsen

15.1600 Josey, E. J. "Shaw, Charles Bunsen (1894–1962)." *DALB*: 1978 473–76.

Shaw, Ralph Robert

15.1601 "Shaw, Ralph R(obert)." *CB* (1956): 570–72.

15.1602 Tauber, M. F. "Ralph Robert Shaw." *BB* 23 (1962): 193–95.

15.1603 Stevens, N. D. "Shaw, Ralph Robert (1907–1972)." *DALB*: 1978 476–81.

15.1604 Thompson, L. S. "Shaw, Ralph Robert." *ELIS* 27 (1979): 309–11.

15.1605 Turner, I. B. "Ralph Shaw." *LAAL*: 1983 289–319.

15.1606 Gaver, M. V. "Shaw, Ralph (1907–1972)." *ALAWE2*: 1986 760–62.

Shaw, Spencer C.

15.1607 Shaw, S. C. "'Not What You Get, But What You Give.'" In *The Black Librarian in America,* edited by E. J. Josey. Metuchen, N.J.: Scarecrow Press, 1970. Pp. 142–69.

Shearer, Augustus Hunt

15.1608 Hoffman, H. "Augustus Hunt Shearer." *BB* 16 (1939): 149–51.

Shedlock, Marie L.

15.1609 Kingsbury, M. E. "Shedlock, Marie L. (1854–1935)." *DALB*: 1978 481–82.

Sheehan, Helen Beebe

15.1610 Conmy, P. T. "Sister Helen Beebe Sheehan, Librarian of Many Parts." *CLW* 56 (1984): 115–17, 120.

Shera, Jesse Hauk

15.1611 "Shera, Jesse H(auk)." *CB* (1964): 409–11.

15.1612 Ruderman, L. P. "Jesse Shera: A Bio-Bibliography." Master's thesis, Kent State University, 1968.

15.1613 Molz, R. K. "Jesse Shera." *BB* 26 (1969): 33–36.

15.1614 Brookes, B. C. "Jesse Shera and the Theory of Bibliography." *Journal of Librarianship* 5 (1973): 233–45, 258.

15.1615 "Shera, Jesse Hauk." In *Librarian Authors: A Biobibliography,* by R. Engelbarts. Jefferson, N.C.: McFarland, 1981. P. 160.

15.1616 Rawski, C. H. "Shera, Jesse Hauk." *ELIS* 38 (1985): 348–71.

15.1617 Kaltenbach, M. "Shera, Jesse H. (1903–1982)." *ALAWE2*: 1986 762–64.

Sherman, Clarence Edgar

15.1618 Adams, V. M. "Sherman, Clarence Edgar (1887–1974)." *DALB*: 1978 482–83.

Shettles, Elijah Leroy

15.1619 Dobie, J. F. "E.L. Shettles, Man, Bookman, and Friend." *SHQ* 44 (1941): 350–56.

15.1620 "Shettles, Elijah L." *HT* 2 (1951): 605.

15.1621 Shettles, E. L. *The Recollections of a Long Life,* edited with an introduction by A. P. McDonald. Foreword by J. F. Dobie. [Nashville: Blue and Grey Press, 1973].

Shipton, Clifford Kenyon

15.1622 Brown, R. A. "Shipton, Clifford Kenyon (1902–1973)." *DALB*: 1978 483–84.

Shirley, William Wayne

15.1623 Shirley, W. "An American Librarian's Heritage." *Florida State University Studies* 12 (1953): 141–56.

15.1624 Marshall, J. D. "As I Remember Wayne Shirley." *JLH* 9 (1974): 293.

15.1625 Rush, N. O. "Wayne Shirley, 1900–1973: An Appreciation." *JLH* 9 (1974): 294–95.

15.1626 Shores, L. "Wayne Shirley: In Memoriam." *JLH* 9 (1974): 291–92.

15.1627 Marshall, J. D. "Shirley, William Wayne (1900–1973)." *DALB*: 1978 484–85.

Shockley, Ann Allen

15.1628 Shockley, A. A. "A Soul Cry for Reading." In *The Black Librarian in America,* edited by E. J. Josey. Metuchen, N.J.: Scarecrow Press, 1970. Pp. 225–33.

15.1629 Josey, E. J. "Ann Allen Shockley (1927–)." *HBLib*: 1977 163–64.

Shoemaker, Richard

15.1630 Thompson, S. O. "Shoemaker, Richard (1907–1970)." *DALB*: 1978 485–87.

Shores, Louis

15.1631 Marshall, J. D. *Louis Shores: A Bibliography.* Tallahassee: Beta Phi Mu, Gamma Chapter, Florida State University Library School, 1964.

15.1632 Shores, L. *Quiet World: A Librarian's Crusade for Destiny.* Hamden, Conn.: Archon Books, 1975.

15.1633 Marshall, J. D. *Louis Shores, Author Librarian: A Bibliography.* Tallahassee: Gamma Chapter, Beta Phi Mu, School of Library Science, Florida State University, 1979.

Shortess, Lois F.

15.1634 Theriot, B. C. "A Study of the Contributions of Lois F. Shortess to Louisiana's Public School Library Development." Master's thesis, University of Southwestern Louisiana, 1968.

Shuey, Leila Bliss

15.1635 Trible, B. M. "In Memoriam: Leila Bliss Shuey." *HTL* 4 (1935): 145.

Shuler, Ellis William

15.1636 Geiser, S. W. "Ellis William Shuler, Ph.D., LL.D." *Field and Laboratory* 21 (1953): 5–10.

15.1637 Trent, R. M. "Ellis William Shuler and the (Southern Methodist) University Libraries (1915–50)." *Field and Laboratory* 21 (1953): 10–12.

Sibley, John Langdon

15.1638 Peabody, A. P. *Memoire of John Langdon Sibley.* Cambridge, Mass.: John Wilson & Son, 1886.

15.1639 Potter, A. C. "Sibley, John Langdon (Dec. 29, 1804–Dec. 9, 1885)." *DAB* 17 (1935): 147–48.

15.1640 Shipton, C. K. "John Langdon Sibley, Librarian." *HLB* 9 (1955): 236–61.

15.1641 Harris, M. H., and Harmeling, D. "Sibley, John Langdon (1804–1885)." *DALB*: 1978 487–89.

Simmons, Ethel

15.1642 Rogan, O. F. "More Tribute to a Texas Librarian." *TLJ* 28 (1952): 91–92.

15.1643 Dulaney, M. "Ethel Simmons." *TLJ* 32 (1956): 33.

Skinner, Mark

15.1644 Utley, G. B. "An Early 'Friend' of Libraries." *LQ* 12 (1942): 725–30.

Slaughter, Henry Proctor

15.1645 "Henry Proctor Slaughter (1871–1958)." *HBLib*: 1977 25–26.

15.1646 Jackson, M. M. "Slaughter, Henry P." *ELIS* 27 (1979): 432–34.

Smith, Ashbel

15.1647 Smither, H. W. "Smith, Ashbel." *HT* 2 (1952): 620–21.

15.1648 Friend, L. B. "Ashbel Smith: Library of a Regent." *LCT* 7 (Summer 1962): 41–63.

15.1649 Silverthorne, E. *Ashbel Smith of Texas: Pioneer, Patriot, Statesman, 1805–1886.* College Station: Texas A&M University Press, 1982.

Smith, Carleton Sprague

15.1650 "Smith, Carleton Sprague." *CB* (1960): 388–90.

15.1651 Morgan, P. "Smith, Carleton Sprague (b New York, 8 Aug. 1905)." *New Grove Dictionary of American Music* 4 (1986): 244–45.

Smith, Charles Wesley

15.1652 Robinson, E. S. "Charles Wesley Smith." *BB* 19 (1949): 197–99.

15.1653 Gershevsky, R. H. "Charles W. Smith, 1877–1956: An Affectionate Tribute." *PNLAQ* 20 (1956): 156–57.

15.1654 Johnson, A. F. "Smith, Charles Wesley (1877–1956)." *DALB*: 1978 489–90.

Smith, Elva Sophrenia

15.1655 Hodges, M. "Smith, Elva Sophrenia (1871–1965)." *DALB*: 1978 490–91.

Smith, Henry Boynton

15.1656 Slavens, T. P. "The Librarianship of Henry B. Smith, 1851–1877." *LHR* 1 (December 1974): 1–41.

Smith, Henry Preserved

15.1657 Slavens, T. P. "The Librarianship of Henry Preserved Smith, 1913–1925." In *Library History Seminar No. 4, Proceedings, 1971*, edited by H. Goldstein and J. Goudeau. Tallahassee: Florida State University School of Library Science, 1972. Pp. 183–94.

Smith, Jessie Carney

15.1658 Smith, J. C. "The Four Cultures." In *The Black Librarian in America*, edited by E. J. Josey. Metuchen, N.J.: Scarecrow Press, 1970. Pp. 191–204.

Smith, Joel Sumner

15.1659 O'Meara, E. J., and Blanshard, R. Y. "Joel Sumner Smith (1830–1903)." *YULG* 55 (1981): 128–39.

Smith, John Jay

15.1660 Jackson, J. "Smith, John Jay (June 16, 1798–Sept. 23, 1881)." *DAB* 17 (1935): 303–04.

Smith, Lloyd Pearsall

15.1661 Abbot, G. M. "Some Recollections of Lloyd P. Smith." *LJ* 12 (1887): 545–46.

15.1662 Abbot, G. M. "Lloyd Pearsall Smith, (1822–1886)." *BB* 9 (1916): 37–38.

15.1663 Jackson, J. "Smith, Lloyd Pearsall (Feb. 6, 1822–July 2, 1886)." *DAB* 17 (1935): 317.

15.1664 Roscoe, S. "Smith, Lloyd Pearsall (1822–1886)." *DALB*: 1978 491–93.

Smither, Harriet Wingfield

15.1665 Winfrey, D. H. "Smither, Harriet Wingfield." *HT* 3 (1976): 896.

Snelling, Henry Hunt

15.1666 Olmstead, A. J. "Snelling, Henry Hunt (Nov. 8, 1817–June 24, 1897)." *DAB* 17 (1935): 379–80.

Sohier, Elizabeth Putnam

15.1667 Wellman, H. C. "Elizabeth Putnam Sohier, 1847–1926." In *Pioneering Leaders in Librarianship*, edited by E. M. Danton. Chicago: American Library Association, 1953. Pp. 173–78.

Solberg, Thorvald

15.1668 "Thorvald Solberg." *BB* 12 (1923): 21.

15.1669 Sittig, W. J. "Solberg, Thorvald (1852–1949)." *DALB*: 1978 493–95.

Sonneck, Oscar George Theodore

15.1670 Egli, C. "Sonneck, Oscar George Theodore (Oct. 6, 1873–Oct. 30, 1928)." *DAB* 17 (1935): 395–96.

15.1671 Kinkeldy, O. "Oscar George Theodore Sonneck (1873–1928)." *Notes* 11, 2nd ser. (1953): 25–32.

15.1672 Moore, D. T. "Oscar G. Sonneck and His Contributions to Music Librarianship and Bibliography." Master's thesis, Southern Connecticut State College, 1973.

15.1673 Bradley, C. J. "Sonneck, Oscar George Theodore (1873–1928)." *DALB*: 1978 495–99.

15.1674 Newsom, J. "Sonneck, Oscar George Theodore." *New Grove Dictionary of Music and Musicians* 17 (1980): 525.

15.1675 Bradley, C. J. "Oscar G.T. Sonneck: Architect of the 'National Music Collection.'" *JLH* 16 (1981): 293–304.

15.1676 Lichtenwanger, W., ed. *Oscar Sonneck and American Music*. Urbana: University of Illinois Press, 1983.

Soule, Charles Carroll

15.1677 Faxon, F. W. "Charles Carroll Soule." *BB* 9 (1917): 109–10.

15.1678 Faxon, F. W. "As It Was in the Beginning." *PL* 30 (1925): 541–44.

Spain, Frances Lander

15.1679 "Spain, Frances Lander." *CB* (1960): 392–93.

Spell, Lota Mae

15.1680 Benson, N. L. "Spell, Lota Mae." *HT* 3 (1976): 913–14.

Spencer, Anne

15.1681 Shockley, A. A. "Anne Spencer (1881–1975)." *HBLib*: 1977 160–61.

Spingarn, Arthur B.

15.1682 Ivy, J. W. "Arthur B. Spingarn—Humanist and Bookman." *Crisis* 73 (1966): 100–102.

15.1683 "Arthur B. Spingarn: A Short Biography." *Crisis* 79 (1972): 56.

15.1684 Ivy, J. W. "Arthur B. Spingarn—Humanist and Bookman." *Crisis* 79 (1972): 52–56.

15.1685 Moon, H. L. "Arthur B. Spingarn: Civil Rights Patriarch." *Crisis* 79 (1972): 50–51.

Spofford, Ainsworth Rand

15.1686 Putnam, H. "Ainsworth Rand Spofford: A Librarian Past." *The Independent* 65 (1908): 1149–55.

15.1687 *Ainsworth Rand Spofford, 1825–1908: A Memorial Meeting at the Library of Congress.* New York: Printed for the District of Columbia Library Association by the Webster Press, 1909.

15.1688 Slade, W. A. "As It Was in the Beginning." *PL* 29 (1924): 293–96.

15.1689 Miller, C. H. "Ainsworth Rand Spofford, 1825–1908." Master's thesis, George Washington University, 1938.

15.1690 Schubach, B. W. "Ainsworth Rand Spofford and the Library of the United States." Master's thesis, Northern Illinois University, 1965.

15.1691 Grisso, K. M. "Ainsworth R. Spofford and the American Library Movement, 1861–1908." Master's thesis, Indiana University, 1966.

15.1692 Mearns, D. C. "Ainsworth the Unforgettable." *QJLC* 25 (1968): 1–5.

15.1693 Vitz, C. "Three Master Librarians." *Cincinnati Historical Society Bulletin* 26 (1968): 343–60.

15.1694 Cole, J. Y. "Ainsworth Spofford and the Copyright Law of 1870." *JLH* 6 (1971): 34–40.

15.1695 Cole, J. Y., ed. *Ainsworth Rand Spofford: Bookman and Librarian.* Littleton, Colo.: Libraries Unlimited, 1975.

15.1696 Cole, J. Y. "Ainsworth Rand Spofford: The Valiant and Persistent Librarian of Congress." *QJLC* 33 (1976): 93–115.

15.1697 Cole, J. Y. "Spofford, Ainsworth Rand (1825–1908)." *DALB*: 1978 499–501.

15.1698 Cole, J. Y. "Spofford, Ainsworth Rand." *ELIS* 28 (1980): 443–52.

15.1699 "Spofford, Ainsworth Rand." In *Librarian Authors: A Biobibliography,* by R. Engelbarts. Jefferson, N.C.: McFarland, 1981. Pp. 86–87.

15.1700 Cole, J. Y. "Spofford, Ainsworth Rand (1825–1908)." *ALAWE2*: 1986 782–84.

Stallmann, Esther Laverne

15.1701 Douglass, R. R. "Stallmann, Esther Laverne (1903–1969)." *DALB*: 1978 501–03.

Stanton, Madeline E.

15.1702 Blankfort, J. R. "Madeline Earle Stanton and the Historical Library of the Yale Medical Library." Master's thesis, Southern Connecticut State College, 1976.

Stark, Miriam Lutcher

15.1703 Ratchford, F. E. "Stark, M.L." *HT* 2 (1952): 659.

Starks, Samuel W.

15.1704 Jackson, W. V. "Some Pioneer Negro Library Workers." *LJ* 64 (1939): 215–17.

15.1705 "S.W. Starks (1866–1908)." *HBLib*: 1977 27.

15.1706 Jordan, C. L. "Starks, Samuel W. (1865?–1908)." *DALB*: 1978 503–04.

Stearns, Lutie Eugenia

15.1707 Tannenbaum, E. "The Library Career of Lutie Eugenia Stearns." *WMH* 39 (1956): 159–65.

15.1708 Stearns, L. E. "My Seventy-Five Years: Part I, 1866–1914." *WMH* 42 (1959): 211–18.

15.1709 Stearns, L. E. "My Seventy-Five Years: Part II, 1914–1942." *WMH* 42 (1959): 282–87.

15.1710 Stearns, L. E. "My Seventy-Five Years: Part III, Increasingly Personal." *WMH* 43 (1959–1960): 97–105.

15.1711 Haygood, W. C. "Stearns, Lutie Eugenia (Sept. 13, 1866–Dec. 25, 1943)." *NAW* 3 (1971): 353–54.

15.1712 Colson, J. C. "Stearns, Lutie Eugenia (1866–1943)." *DALB*: 1978 504–05.

15.1713 "Stearns, Lutie E." In *Librarian Authors: A Biobibliography*, by R. Engelbarts. Jefferson, N.C.: McFarland, 1981. Pp. 47–50.

Stearns, Raymond Phineas

15.1714 Brindenbaugh, C. "Raymond Phineas Stearns." *PMHS* 83 (1971): 157–60.

Steiner, Bernard Christian

15.1715 "Bernard Christian Steiner." *BB* 11 (1922): 117.

15.1716 Wroth, L. C. "Steiner, Bernard Christian (Aug. 13, 1867–Jan. 12, 1926)." *DAB* 17 (1935): 561–62.

15.1717 Wessells, M. B. "Steiner, Bernard Christian (1867–1926)." *DALB*: 1978 505–06.

Steiner, Lewis Henry

15.1718 Phalen, J. M. "Steiner, Lewis Henry (May 4, 1827–Feb. 18, 1892)." *DAB* 17 (1935): 562–63.

Stephenson, John Gould

15.1719 Wood, R. G. "Librarian-at-Arms: The Career of John G. Stephenson." *LQ* 19 (1949): 263–69.

15.1720 Carter, C. "John Gould Stephenson: Largely Known and Much Liked." *QJLC* 33 (1976): 77–91.

15.1721 Cole, J. Y. "Stephenson, John Gould (1828–1883)." *DALB*: 1978 506–08.

Stevenson, Burton Egbert

15.1722 Vince, T. L. "Stevenson, Burton Egbert (1872–1962)." *DALB*: 1978 508–10.

Stiles, Ezra

15.1723 Lutz, C. E. "Ezra Stiles and the Library." *YULG* 56 (1981): 13–21.

Stillwell, Margaret Bingham

15.1724 Stillwell, M. B. *Librarians Are Human: Memories In and Out of the Rare-Book World, 1907–1970.* Boston: Colonial Society of Massachusetts, 1973.

Stowe, Calvin Ellis

15.1725 Hilgert, E. "Calvin Ellis Stowe: Pioneer Librarian of the Old West." *LQ* 50 (1980): 324–51.

Strecker, John Kern

15.1726 Brandes, G. "John Kern Strecker." *HTL* 4 (1935): 144–45.

15.1727 "Strecker, John Kern." In *Handbook of Waco and McLennan County,* edited by D. Kelley. Waco, Tex.: Texian Press, 1972. Pp. 254–55.

Street, Alfred Billings

15.1728 Wyer, J. I. "Street, Alfred Billings (Dec. 18, 1811–June 2, 1881)." *DAB* 18 (1936): 134–35.

Strohm, Adam Julius

15.1729 Hughes, H. L. "Adam Strohm." *BB* 15 (1933): 1–2.

15.1730 Dalligan, A. C. "Strohm, Adam Julius (1870–1951)." *DALB*: 1978 510–11.

Stuckert, Beatrice Stackhouse

15.1731 Potts, A. J. "The Life and Librarianship of Beatrice Stackhouse Stuckert, Director of the Haddonfield Public Library, Haddonfield, New Jersey." Research Paper, Glassboro State College, 1972.

Sullivan, Maud Durlin

15.1732 "In Memory of Mrs. Maud Durlin Sullivan." *NNT* 20 (February 1944): 3–4.

15.1733 Lea, T. "Maud Durlin Sullivan." *LJ* 69 (1944): 244–46.

15.1734 Lea, T. *Maud Durlin Sullivan, 1872–1944: Pioneer Southwestern Librarian.* [El Paso]: Printed by Carl Hertzog of El Paso for the Class of 1962, School of Library Service, University of California, Los Angeles, 1962.

Swem, Earl Gregg

15.1735 Wessells, M. B. "Swem, Earl Gregg (1870–1965)." *DALB*: 1978 511–12.

Tallman, Johanna E.

15.1736 Tallman, J. E. *Check Out a Librarian.* Metuchen, N.J.: Scarecrow Press, 1985.

Tate, Binnie L.

15.1737 Tate, B. "Traffic on the Drawbridge." In *The Black Librarian in America,* edited by E. J. Josey. Metuchen, N.J.: Scarecrow Press, 1970. Pp. 124–29.

Taube, Mortimer

15.1738 Shera, J. H. "Taube, Mortimer (1910–1965)." *DALB*: 1978 512–13.

15.1739 White, H. S. "Taube, Mortimer (1910–1965)." *ALAWE2*: 1986 797–98.

Tauber, Maurice Falcolm

15.1740 Szigethy, M. C. *Maurice Falcolm Tauber: A Bio-Bibliography, 1934–1973.* Metuchen, N.J.: Published for Beta Phi Mu, Nu Chapter, Columbia University School of Library Service. Scarecrow Press, 1974.

15.1741 Maier, K. S. "Maurice F. Tauber." *LAAL*: 1983 321–45.

15.1742 Martin, R. S. "Maurice F. Tauber's *Louis Round Wilson:* An Analysis of a Collaboration." *JLH* 19 (1984): 373–89.

15.1743 Sharify, N. "Tauber, Maurice (1908–1980)." *ALAWE2*: 1986 798–99.

Teggart, Frederick John

15.1744 Nisbet, R. "Teggart, Frederick John (May 9, 1870–Oct. 12, 1946)." *DAB* Suppl. 4 (1974): 823–25.

15.1745 Conmy, P. T. "Frederick John Teggart: Librarian, Historian and Prophet of Social Institutions, Third President of California Library Association." *CalL* 38 (1977): 11–17.

Thacher, John Boyd

15.1746 Wyer, J. I. "Thacher, John Boyd (Sept. 11, 1847–Feb. 25, 1909)." *DAB* 18 (1936): 388–89.

Thomas, Isaiah

15.1747 Vail, R. W. G. "Thomas, Isaiah (Jan. 19, 1749–Apr. 4, 1831)." *DAB* 18 (1936): 435–36.

15.1748 McCorison, M. A. "Isaiah Thomas, the American Antiquarian Society, and the Future." *PAAS* 91 (1981): 27–37.

Thompson, Alleen

15.1749 "Thompson, Alleen." *CB* (1965): 422–24.

Thomson, John

15.1750 "John Thomson." *BB* 8 (1915): 177.

Thomson, O. R. Howard

15.1751 Crocker, M. E. "Dr. O. R. Howard Thomson." *BB* 16 (1937): 61–62.

Thornley, Fant Hill

15.1752 McPharlin, P. "Bostwick and Thornley: Librarians and Publishers." *PW* 150 (1946): 3206–09.

Thwaites, Reuben Gold

15.1753 Turner, F. J. *Reuben Gold Thwaites: A Memorial Address*. Madison, Wis.: State Historical Society of Wisconsin, 1914.

15.1754 Nunns, A. A. "Reuben Gold Thwaites, 1853–1913." *BB* 13 (1929): 146–47.

15.1755 Kellogg, L. P. "Thwaites, Reuben Gold (May 15, 1853–Oct. 22, 1913)." *DAB* 18 (1936): 521–22.

15.1756 Lord, C. L. "Thwaites, Reuben Gold (1853–1913)." *DALB*: 1978 513–15.

15.1757 "Thwaites, Reuben Gold." In *Librarian Authors: A Biobibliography*, by R. Engelbarts. Jefferson, N.C.: McFarland, 1981. Pp. 109–11.

Ticknor, George

15.1758 "George Ticknor." *PMHS* 20 (1884): 384–91.

15.1759 Long, O. W. *Thomas Jefferson and George Ticknor: A Chapter in American Scholarship*. Williamstown, Mass.: McClelland Press, 1933.

15.1760 Ford, J. D. M. "Ticknor, George (Aug. 1, 1791–Jan. 26, 1871)." *DAB* 18 (1936): 525–28.

15.1761 Tyack, D. B. *George Ticknor and the Boston Brahmins*. Cambridge: Harvard University Press, 1967.

15.1762 Turner, H. M. "George Ticknor and the American Library Movement." Doctoral dissertation, New York University, 1972.

15.1763 Harris, M. H. "Ticknor, George (1791–1871)." *DALB*: 1978 515–16.

Tilton, Edward Lippincott

15.1764 Oehlerts, D. E. "Tilton, Edward Lippincott (1861–1933)." *DALB*: 1978 516–17.

Timothee, Louis

15.1765 Friedman, W. "The First Librarian of America." *LJ* 56 (1931): 902–03.

15.1766 Blumenthal, W. H. "First Librarian of Colonial America." *American Notes and Queries* 1 (1963): 83–84.

Titcomb, Mary Lemist

15.1767 Wilkinson, M. S. "Mary L. Titcomb, 1857–1931." In *Pioneering Leaders in Librarianship*, edited by E. M. Danton. Chicago: American Library Association, 1953. Pp. 179–87.

15.1768 Braunagel, J. "Titcomb, Mary Lemist (1857–1932)." *DALB*: 1978 518–19.

Tompkins, Miriam Downing

15.1769 Edge, S. A. "Miriam A. Tompkins." *BB* 18 (1943): 25–26.

15.1770 Shapiro, R. "Tompkins, Miriam Downing (1892–1954)." *DALB*: 1978 519–21.

Toner, Joseph Meredith

15.1771 Bierring, W. L. "Joseph Meredith Toner, M.D." In *A History of the American Medical Association, 1847 to 1947*, edited by M. Fishbein. Philadelphia: Saunders, 1947. Pp. 623–24.

Tory, Jesse

15.1772 Teggart, J. F. "An Early Champion of Free Libraries." *LJ* 23 (1898): 617–18.

Totten, Herman L.

15.1773 Totten, H. L. "Put Sinews in the Wings of the Eagle." In *The Black Librarian in America*, edited by E. J. Josey. Metuchen, N.J.: Scarecrow Press, 1970. Pp. 216–24.

Towles, Susan Starling

15.1774 "Susan Starling Towles Makes Distinctive Contribution." *LJ* 74 (1949): 811–12.

Tremaine, Marie

15.1775 Murray, F. B. "Marie Tremaine." *BB* 19 (1949): 253–55.

Troxel, Wilma

15.1776 Prime, L. M. "Wilma Troxel." *BMLA* 42 (1954): 363–64.

Tsuffis, Mary Lee Toomes

15.1777 Tsuffis, M. L. T. "The Alternative to Invisibility." In *The Black Librarian in America*, edited by E. J. Josey. Metuchen, N.J.: Scarecrow Press, 1970. Pp. 237–46.

Tucker, Harold Walton

15.1778 Solomita, J. "Tucker, Harold Walton (1915–1973)." *DALB*: 1978 521–22.

Tyler, Alice Sarah

15.1779 "Alice S. Tyler." *BB* 13 (1927): 61.

15.1780 Richardson, C. E. "Alice Sarah Tyler: A Biographical Study." Master's thesis, Western Reserve University, 1951.

15.1781 Scott, C. R. "Alice Sarah Tyler, 1859–1944." In *Pioneering Leaders in Librarianship*, edited by E. M. Danton. Chicago: American Library Association, 1953. Pp. 188–96.

15.1782 Focke, H. M. "Tyler, Alice Sarah (Apr. 27, 1859–Apr. 18, 1944)." *NAW* 3 (1971): 493–94.

15.1783 Focke, H. M. "Tyler, Alice Sarah (1859–1944)." *DALB*: 1978 522–25.

15.1784 "Tyler, Alice Sarah." In *Librarian Authors: A Biobibliography*, by R. Engelbarts. Jefferson, N.C.: McFarland, 1981. Pp. 45–47.

Uhler, Philip Reese

15.1785 Howard, L. O. "Uhler, Philip Reese (June 3, 1835–Oct. 21 1913)." *DAB* 19 (1936): 106–07.

Ulveling, Ralph Adrian

15.1786 Conmy, P. T. "Ralph Adrian Ulveling, 1902–1980, Public Librarian." *CLW* 56 (1985): 66–68.

Upham, Warren

15.1787 Emmons, W. H. "Upham, Warren (Mar. 8, 1850–Jan. 29, 1934)." *DAB* 19 (1936): 124–25.

Usher, Elizabeth Reuter

15.1788 "Usher, Elizabeth R(euter)." *CB* (1967): 426–28.

Utley, George Burwell

15.1789 Roden, C. B. "George B. Utley." *BB* 15 (1934): 61–62.

15.1790 "George Burwell Utley." *Newberry Library Bulletin* 6 (December 1946): 19.

15.1791 Doane, G. H. "George Burwell Utley, 1876–1946." In *The Librarians' Conference of 1853: A Chapter in American History,* by G. B. Utley. Chicago: American Library Association, 1951. Pp. v–xi.

15.1792 Boromé, J. A. "Utley, George Burwell (Dec. 3, 1876–Oct. 4, 1946)." *DAB* Suppl. 4 (1974): 845–46.

15.1793 Blazek, R. "Utley, George Burwell (1876–1946)." *DALB*: 1978 525–27.

15.1794 "Utley, George B." In *Librarian Authors: A Biobibliography,* by R. Engelbarts. Jefferson, N.C.: McFarland, 1981. Pp. 95–96.

15.1795 Young, A. P. "Utley, George Burwell (1876–1946)." *ALAWE2*: 1986 839–40.

Utley, Henry Munson

15.1796 "Henry M. Utley." *BB* 9 (1916): 1.

15.1797 Tucker, F. R. "Utley, Henry Munson (1836–1917)." *DALB*: 1978 527–29.

Vail, Robert William Glenroie

15.1798 Goff, F. R. "Vail, Robert William Glenroie (1890–1966)." *DALB*: 1978 529–30.

Van Hoesen, Henry Bartlett

15.1799 Brigham, H. O. "Henry Bartlett Van Hoesen." *BB* 16 (1938): 105–06.

15.1800 Brown, H. G. "Van Hoesen, Henry Bartlett (1885–1965)." *DALB*: 1978 530–32.

15.1801 "Van Hoesen, Henry Bartlett." In *Librarian Authors: A Biobibliography,* by R. Engelbarts. Jefferson, N.C.: McFarland, 1981. P. 154.

Van Name, Addison

15.1802 Klemin, A. "Van Name, Addison (Nov. 15, 1835–Sept. 29, 1922)." *DAB* 19 (1936): 201–02.

15.1803 Schiff, J. A. "Van Name, Addison (1835–1922)." *DALB*: 1978 532–34.

Van Patten, Nathan

15.1804 Koch, T. W. "Nathan Van Patten." *BB* 16 (1939): 169.

15.1805 Hansen, R. W. "Van Patten, Nathan (1887–1956)." *DALB*: 1978 535–36.

Van Vechten, Carl

15.1806 Schuyler, G. S. "Phylon Profile, XXII: Carl Van Vechten." *Phylon: The Atlanta University Review of Race and Culture* 11 (1950): 362–68.

15.1807 Kellner, B. *Carl Van Vechten and the Irreverent Decades.* Norman: University of Oklahoma Press, 1968.

15.1808 Kellner, B. *A Bibliography of the Work of Carl Van Vechten*. Westport, Conn.: Greenwood Press, 1980.

15.1809 Lueders, E. "Van Vechten, Carl (June 17, 1880–Dec. 21, 1964)." *DAB* Suppl. 7 (1981): 753–55.

Vandale, Earl

15.1810 Haley, J. E. *Earl Vandale on the Trail of Texas Books*. Canyon, Tex.: Palo Duro Press, 1965.

15.1811 Carroll, M. J. "Vandale, Earl." *HT* 3 (1976): 1058.

Vattemare, Nicolas Marie Alexandre

15.1812 "Strange Career of an Artist." *Hours at Home* (October 1868): 534–39.

15.1813 Vattemare, H. "Notices of the Life of Alexandre Vattemare, Founder of the System of International Exchange." *Historical Magazine* 4, 2nd ser. (1868): 297–300.

15.1814 Winsor, J. "M. Vattemare and the Public Library System." *LW* 10 (1879): 185–86.

15.1815 Winsor, J. "The Results of Vattemare's Library Scheme." *LW* 10 (1879): 281–82.

15.1816 Quincy, J. P. "The Character and Services of Alexandre Vattemare." *PMHS* 21 (1884): 260–72.

15.1817 Quincy, J. P. "Conversations with Alexandre Vattemare." *PMHS* 1, 2nd ser. (1884): 260–72.

15.1818 Haraszti, Z. "Alexandre Vattemare." *MoreB* 2 (1927): 257–66.

15.1819 Richards, E. M. "Vattemare, Nicolas Marie Alexandre (Nov. 8, 1796–Apr. 7, 1864)." *DAB* 19 (1936): 231–32.

15.1820 Richards, E. M. "Alexandre Vattemare and His System of International Exchanges." *BMLA* 32 (1944): 413–48.

15.1821 Gambee, B. L. "Vattemare, Nicolas-Marie-Alexandre (1796–1864)." *DALB*: 1978 536–37.

Vinton, Frederic

15.1822 Gerould, J. T. "Vinton, Frederic (Oct. 9, 1817–Jan. 1, 1890)." *DAB* 19 (1936): 283.

15.1823 Miksa, F. L. "Vinton, Frederic (1817–1890)." *DALB*: 1978 537–38.

Vitz, Carl

15.1824 Compton, C. H. "Carl Vitz." *BB* 21 (1955): 121–23.

Vogelson, Helen E.

15.1825 Schenk, G. K. "Who Says That They Have Retired?" *LJ* 72 (1947): 907–08.

Vormelker, Rose L.

15.1826 Magner, M. J. "The Businessman's Librarian—Rose L. Vormelker." Master's thesis, Western Reserve University, 1957.

15.1827 Taylor, J. K. "Rose L. Vormelker." *BB* 22 (1959): 217–19.

15.1828 Gabriel, P. "Rose L. Vormelker, 1895–1970." Research Paper, Kent State University, 1971.

Vosper, Robert Gordon

15.1829 "Vosper, Robert G(ordon)." *CB* (1965): 439–41.

15.1830 Milum, B. L. "Robert G. Vosper." *LAAL*: 1983 347–71.

15.1831 Shank, R. "Vosper, Robert G. (1913–)." *ALAWE2*: 1986 846.

Wagman, Frederick Herbert

15.1832 "Wagman, Frederick H(erbert)." *CB* (1963): 450–52.

Walker, Caroline Burnite

15.1833 Andrews, S. M. *Caroline Burnite Walker, a Pioneer in Library Work with Children.* Cleveland: Sturgis Printing Co., 1950.

15.1834 Sassé, M. "Walker, Caroline Burnite (1875–1936)." *DALB*: 1978 538–40.

Walker, Estelle Paxton

15.1835 Galick, V. G. "Estelle Paxton Walker: Personality Unlimited." *BALA* 48 (1954): 421–23, 449–50.

Wall, Alexander J.

15.1836 Wall, L. B. *Entre Nous: An Intimate Portrait of Alexander J. Wall.* New York: New York Historical Society, 1949.

Walter, Frank Keller

15.1837 Bay, J. C. "Frank K. Walker in Retrospect." *CRL* 4 (1943): 309–11.

15.1838 Vitz, C. "Frank Keller Walter." *BB* 18 (1944): 97–99.

15.1839 Shove, R. H. "Walter, Frank Keller (1874–1945)." *DALB*: 1978 540–42.

Waples, Douglas

15.1840 Richardson, J. V. "Douglas Waples (1893–1978)." *JLH* 15 (1980): 76–83.

15.1841 Monroe, M. E. "Waples, Douglas (1893–1978)." *ALAWE2*: 1986 847–48.

Warncke, Ruth

15.1842 Martin, R. "Ruth Warncke: Preacher at Heart." *BALA* 48 (1954): 271–74.

Warren, Althea Hester

15.1843 Hyers, F. H. "Althea Warren." *BB* 17 (1942): 153–54.

15.1844 Garbutt, K. K. "Who Says That They Have Retired?" *LJ* 72 (1947): 905–06.

15.1845 Boaz, M. *Fervent and Full of Gifts: The Life of Althea Warren.* New York: Scarecrow Press, 1961.

15.1846 *Althea Warren, Librarian,* Keepsake no. 3. N.p.: California Library Association, 1962.

15.1847 Boaz, M. "Warren, Althea Hester (1886–1958)." *DALB*: 1978 542–43.

15.1848 "Warren, Althea." In *Librarian Authors: A Biobibliography,* by R. Engelbarts. Jefferson, N.C.: McFarland, 1981. Pp. 77–80.

Watson, Genevieve

15.1849 Grotzinger, L. A. "Women Who 'Spoke for Themselves.'" *CRL* 39 (1978): 175–90.

Watson, Katherine Williams

15.1850 Means, F. C. "Katherine Watson of Denver." *HB* 25 (1949): 250.

Watterson, George

15.1851 Kennedy, J. A. *George Watterson, Novelist, "Metropolitan Author," and Critic.* Washington, D.C.: Catholic University of America, 1933.

15.1852 Ashley, F. W. "Watterson, George (Oct. 23, 1783–Feb. 4, 1854)." *DAB* 19 (1936): 555–56.

15.1853 Matheson, W. "George Watterson: Advocate of the National Library." *QJLC* 32 (1975): 371–88.

15.1854 Gwinn, N. E. "Watterson, George (1783–1854)." *DALB*: 1978 543–46.

Weitenkampf, Frank

15.1855 Roth, E. E. "Weitenkampf, Frank (1866–1962)." *DALB*: 1978 546–47.

Welch, Eleanor Weir

15.1856 Schmidt, K. A. "Deucedly Independent: A Bibliographical Overview of the Library Career of Eleanor Weir Welch." *LQ* 55 (1985): 300–315.

Wellman, Hiller Crowell

15.1857 "Hiller Crowell Wellman." *BB* 11 (1922): 153.

15.1858 Dougherty, H. T. "Hiller C. Wellman to Retire." *Massachusetts Library Association Bulletin* 38 (1948): 53–54, 60.

15.1859 Humphry, J. A. "Wellman, Hiller Crowell (1871–1956)." *DALB*: 1978 547–48.

Wertenbaker, William

15.1860 Clemons, H. "William Wertenbaker." In *The University of Virginia Library*. Charlottesville: University of Virginia Library, 1954. Pp. 93–101.

West, Elizabeth Howard

15.1861 Hester, G. A. "Elizabeth Howard West, Texas Librarian." Master's thesis, University of Texas, 1965.

15.1862 Winfrey, D. H. "West, Elizabeth Howard." *HT* 3 (1976): 1097–98.

Westfall, Edward Dixon

15.1863 Cameron, M. B. "Edward Dixon Westfall: An Appreciation." *SHQ* 50 (1946): 288–90.

15.1864 Sexton, K., and Sexton, I. "Edward Dixon Westfall: Early Texas Climatologist, Philosopher, and Philanthropist." *SHQ* 68 (1964): 1–13.

15.1865 Sexton, I., and Sexton, K. "Westfall, Edward Dixon." *HT* 3 (1976): 1101.

Wheeler, Joseph Lewis

15.1866 Lydenberg, H. M. *Joseph Lewis Wheeler, Pathfinder and Pioneer.* Baltimore: Enoch Pratt Free Library, 1945.

15.1867 "Three Tributes to Joseph Lewis Wheeler." *LJ* 70 (1945): 283–85.

15.1868 "Tribute to Dr. Wheeler." *Between Librarians* 12 (1945): 7–8.

15.1869 Compton, C. H. "Joseph L. Wheeler." *BB* 21 (1955): 169–71.

15.1870 Bell, M. V. "Joseph L. Wheeler: A Bibliography." *BB* 23 (1961): 127–32.

15.1871 Wheeler, J. L. "Happy Days." *Maryland Libraries* 27 (1961): 5–7.

15.1872 Edwards, M. A. "I Once Did See Joe Wheeler Plain." *JLH* 6 (1971): 291–302.

15.1873 Warner, L. H. "Wheeler, Joseph Lewis (1884–1970)." *DALB*: 1978 549–52.

15.1874 Castagna, E. "Wheeler, Joseph L. (1884–1970)." *ALAWE2*: 1986 848–49.

Wheeler, Warren Gage

15.1875 Freiberg, M. "Warren Gage Wheeler." *PMHS* 94 (1982): 88–90.

White, Herbert Spencer

15.1876 "White, Herbert S(pencer)." *CB* (1968): 430–32.

White, John Griswold

15.1877 "John Griswold White." *Open Shelf* [Cleveland Public Library] 2 (June 1929): 1–28.

15.1878 Roberts, I. B. "Biography of John Griswold White." *Gambit* 8 (June 1930): 1–11.

15.1879 Reece, M. B. Y. "John Griswold White, Trustee, and the White Collection in the Cleveland Public Library." Doctoral dissertation, University of Michigan, 1979.

Whitehill, Walter Muir

15.1880 McCord, D. "Walter Muir Whitehill." *BB* 22 (1958): 121–23.

15.1881 "Whitehill, Walter Muir." *CB* (1960): 457–59.

15.1882 *Walter Muir Whitehill: Director and Librarian, Boston Athenaeum, 1946–1973. A Bibliography and Verses by Friends Presented on His Retirement.* Boston: Boston Athenaeum, 1974.

Whitney, James Lyman

15.1883 Whitney, J. L. "Reminiscences of an Old Librarian." *LJ* 34 (1909): 471–75.

15.1884 Swift, L. "James Lyman Whitney, M.A. (1835–1910)." *BB* 8 (1915): 152–54.

15.1885 Lord, M. E. "Whitney, James Lyman (Nov. 28, 1835–Sept. 25, 1910)." *DAB* 20 (1936): 161.

Whitten, Sam Gerald

15.1886 Gay, D. "Sam Whitten: In Memoriam." *TLJ* 62 (1986): 8–11.

Widener, Harry Elkins

15.1887 Bolton, C. K. "Widener, Harry Elkins (Jan. 3, 1885–Apr. 15, 1912)." *DAB* 20 (1936): 184–85.

Wilcox, Sebron Sneed

15.1888 Garcia, R. O. "Wilcox, Sebron Sneed." *HT* 3 (1976): 1110.

Willerford, Frederick P.

15.1889 Willerford, F. P. "NYPL and the Impossible Dream." In *The Black Librarian in America,* edited by E. J. Josey. Metuchen, N.J.: Scarecrow Press, 1970. Pp. 205–15.

Willging, Eugene

15.1890 Conmy, P. T. "The Ultimate Professionalization of the Catholic University Library: Father Mullin and Eugene Willging." *CLW* 56 (1985): 416–18.

Williams, Edward Christopher

15.1891 Jackson, W. V. "Some Pioneer Negro Library Workers." *LJ* 64 (1939): 215–17.

15.1892 Josey, E. J. "Edward Christopher Williams: A Librarian's Librarian." *JLH* 4 (1969): 106–22.

15.1893 "Edward Christopher Williams (1871–1929)." *HBLib:* 1977 30–31.

15.1894 Josey, E. J. "Williams, Edward Christopher (1871–1929)." *DALB:* 1978 552–53.

Williams, John Fletcher

15.1895 Blegen, T. C. "Williams, John Fletcher (Sept. 25, 1834–Apr. 28, 1895)." *DAB* 20 (1936): 275–76.

Williamson, Charles Clarence

15.1896 Reece, E. J. "C.C. Williamson: A Record of Service to American Librarianship." *CRL* 4 (1943): 306–08.

15.1897 Winckler, P. A. "Charles Clarence Williamson (1877–1965): His Professional Life and Work in Librarianship and Library Education in the United States." Doctoral dissertation, New York University, 1968.

15.1898 Metcalf, K. D. "Six Influential Academic and Research Librarians." *CRL* 37 (1976): 332–45.

15.1899 Winckler, P. A. "Williamson, Charles Clarence (1877–1965)." *DALB*: 1978 553–58.

15.1900 Winckler, P. A. "Williamson, Charles C." *ELIS* 33 (1982): 149–62.

15.1901 Churchwell, C. D. "Williamson, Charles C. (1877–1965)." *ALAWE2*: 1986 850–52.

Wilson, Florence

15.1902 Dale, D. C. "An American in Geneva: Florence Wilson and the League of Nations Library." *JLH* 7 (1972): 109–29.

Wilson, Halsey William

15.1903 Peet, C. "Profile: A Mousetrap in the Bronx." *New Yorker* 14 (29 October 1938): 25–28.

15.1904 "Retouching the Profile." *WLB* 13 (1939): 250–51.

15.1905 "Wilson, H(alsey) W(illiam)." *CB* (1948): 679–82.

15.1906 Wilson, H. W. "Random Reminiscences." *WLB* 22 (1948): 779–83.

15.1907 Pollack, J. H. "Giant of Bibliographers." *Saturday Review* 34 (3 February 1951): 32–34.

15.1908 "Halsey William Wilson, May 12, 1868–March 1, 1954." *WLB* 28 (1954): 665–68.

15.1909 Haycraft, H. "Mr. Wilson—An Informal Reminiscence." *WLB* 29 (1954): 52–57.

15.1910 "H.W.W. Himself . . . and the Women behind Him." *WLB* 47 (1973): 510–11.

15.1911 Plotnik, A. "Halsey William Wilson." *ELIS* 10 (1973): 273–78.

15.1912 Dain, P. "Wilson, Halsey William (May 12, 1868–Mar. 1, 1954)." *DAB* Suppl. 5 (1977): 752–54.

15.1913 Plotnik, A. "Wilson, Halsey William (1868–1954)." *DALB*: 1978 558–61.

15.1914 "Wilson, H.W." In *Librarian Authors: A Biobibliography,* by R. Engelbarts. Jefferson, N.C.: McFarland, 1981. Pp. 115–16.

15.1915 Skinner, A. E. "Wilson, H.W. (1868–1954)." *ALAWE2*: 1986 852–54.

Wilson, Louis Round

15.1916 *Louis Round Wilson: Papers in Recognition of a Distinguished Career in Librarianship.* Chicago: University of Chicago Press, 1942.

15.1917 Randall, W. M. "Louis R. Wilson and the Graduate Library School." *LQ* 12 (1942): 645–50.

15.1918 Rush, C. E. "Another Pioneer Is Honored in His Own Country [Louis R. Wilson]." *LQ* 12 (1942): 675–78.

15.1919 Thornton, M. I. "Bibliography of Louis Round Wilson." *LQ* 12 (1942): 339–42.

15.1920 Barker, T. D. "Louis Round Wilson: A Tribute." *SEL* 1 (1951): 75–89.

15.1921 Tauber, M. F. "The Contributions of Louis Round Wilson to Librarianship [Since 1901]." *WLB* 31 (1956): 315–23.

15.1922 Tauber, M. F. *Louis R. Wilson: A Biographic Sketch.* Chapel Hill: Friends of the [University of North Carolina] Library, 1956.

15.1923 Johnson, W. H. "Louis R. Wilson, Teacher." *NCL* 18 (1959): 21–22.

15.1924 Tauber, M. F. *Louis Round Wilson: Librarian and Administrator.* New York: Columbia University Press, 1967.

15.1925 Mathis, G. R., ed. "Louis Round Wilson's Decision to Remain at the University of North Carolina." *JLH* 4 (1969): 256–64.

15.1926 *Louis Round Wilson Bibliography: A Chronological List of Works and Editorial Activities Presented on the Occasion of His Centennial Celebration, December 2, 1976.* Chapel Hill: University of North Carolina Library, 1976.

15.1927 Weaver, F. A. *Louis Round Wilson: The Years Since 1955.* [Chapel Hill: University of North Carolina Friends of the Library, 1976].

15.1928 Danton, J. P. "Louis Round Wilson, 1876–1979." *LQ* 50 (1980): 283–86.

15.1929 "Wilson, Louis Round." In *Librarian Authors: A Biobibliography,* by R. Engelbarts. Jefferson, N.C.: McFarland, 1981. P. 161.

15.1930 Shera, J. H. "Louis Round Wilson (1876–1979): The Last of the Pioneers." *JLH* 17 (1982): 65–77.

15.1931 Richardson, J. V. "Louis Round Wilson." *LAAL:* 1983 373–99.

15.1932 Martin, R. S. "Maurice F. Tauber's *Louis Round Wilson:* An Analysis of a Collaboration." *JLH* 19 (1984): 373–89.

15.1933 Martin, R. S. "Louis Round Wilson's *Geography of Reading:* An Inquiry into Its Origins, Development, and Impact." *JLH* 21 (1986): 425–44.

15.1934 Weaver, F. A. "Wilson, Louis Round (1876–1979)." *ALAWE2:* 1986 854–55.

Winchell, Constance Mabel

15.1935 "Winchell, Constance M(abel)." *CB* (1967): 465–68.

15.1936 Whyte, E. "Constance M. Winchell: Reference Librarian." Research Paper, Long Island University, 1971.

15.1937 "Winchell, Constance M." In *Librarian Authors: A Biobibliography,* by R. Engelbarts. Jefferson, N.C.: McFarland, 1981. P. 154.

15.1938 Lynch, M. J. "Winchell, Constance M." *ALAWE2:* 1986 855–56.

Windsor, Phineas Lawrence

15.1939 Downs, R. B. "Windsor, Phineas Lawrence (1871–1965)." *DALB:* 1978 561–64.

Wing, Donald Goddard

15.1940 Cveljo, K. "Wing, Donald Goddard (1904–1972)." *DALB:* 1978 564–66.

15.1941 Crist, T. J. "Wing, Donald Goddard (1904–1972)." *ALAWE2:* 1986 856–57.

Winkler, Ernest William

15.1942 Friend, L. B. "E.W. Winkler and the Texas State Library." *TL* 24 (1962): 89–114.

15.1943 Friend, L. B. "From a Librarian's Chronicle." *LCT* 4 (1972): 67–71.

15.1944 Friend, L. B. "Winkler, Ernest William." *HT* 3 (1976): 1120–21.

Winser, Beatrice

15.1945 Manley, M. C. "Beatrice Winser, Administrator and Friend." *LJ* 72 (1947): 1481.

15.1946 Coffey, K. "Winser, Beatrice (Mar. 11, 1869–Sept. 14, 1947)." *NAW* 3 (1971): 630–32.

15.1947 Sabine, J. E. "Winser, Beatrice (1869–1947)." *DALB:* 1978 566–68.

Winship, George Parker

15.1948 Whitehill, W. M. "George Parker Winship (1871–1952)." *PMHS* 71 (1953–57): 366–75.

15.1949 Whitehill, W. M. "Winship, George Parker (July 29, 1871–June 22, 1952)." *DAB* Suppl. 5 (1977): 755–56.

15.1950 Koda, P. S. "Winship, George Parker (1871–1952)." *DALB*: 1978 568–70.

Winslow, Amy

15.1951 Greenaway, E. "Amy Winslow." *BB* 20 (1952): 201–03.

Winsor, Justin

15.1952 Cutter, C. A. "Justin Winsor." *Nation* 65 (1897): 335.

15.1953 Lane, W. C., and Tillinghast, W. "Justin Winsor, Librarian and Historian, 1831–1897." *LJ* 23 (1897): 7–13.

15.1954 Channing, E. "Justin Winsor." *AHR* 3 (1898): 197–202.

15.1955 Scudder, H. E. "Memoir of Justin Winsor." *PMHS* 12 (1899): 457–82.

15.1956 Yust, W. F. *A Bibliography of Justin Winsor.* Cambridge: Library of Harvard University, 1902.

15.1957 Foster, W. E. "Justin Winsor, 1831–1897." *BB* 8 (1914): 2–3.

15.1958 Davis, R. C. "Some Library Reminiscences." *PL* 22 (1917): 180–82.

15.1959 "As It Was in the Beginning." *PL* 29 (1924): 13–15.

15.1960 Foster, W. E. "Five Men of '76." *BALA* 20 (1926): 312–23.

15.1961 Adams, J. T. "Winsor, Justin (Jan. 2, 1831–Oct. 22, 1897)." *DAB* 20 (1936): 403–04.

15.1962 Kilgour, F. G. "Justin Winsor." *CRL* 3 (1941): 64–66.

15.1963 Boromé, J. A. "The Life and Letters of Justin Winsor." Doctoral dissertation, Columbia University, 1950.

15.1964 Brundin, R. E. "Justin Winsor of Harvard and the Liberalizing of the College Library." *JLH* 10 (1975): 57–70.

15.1965 Metcalf, K. D. "Six Influential Academic and Research Librarians." *CRL* 37 (1976): 332–45.

15.1966 Sharma, R. N. "Winsor: The Quintessential Librarian." *WLB* 51 (1976): 48–52.

15.1967 Cutler, W., and Harris, M. H. "Winsor, Justin (1831–1897)." *DALB*: 1978 570–72.

15.1968 Cutler, W., and Harris, M. H. *Justin Winsor: Scholar Librarian.* Littleton, Colo.: Libraries Unlimited, 1980.

15.1969 "Winsor, Justin." In *Librarian Authors: A Biobibliography,* by R. Engelbarts. Jefferson, N.C.: McFarland, 1981. Pp. 127–28.

15.1970 Koelsch, W. A. "'A Profound Though Special Erudition': Justin Winsor as Historian of Discovery." *PAAS* 93 (1983): 55–94.

15.1971 Brundin, R. E. "Winsor, Justin (1831–1897)." *ALAWE2*: 1986 857–58.

Winston, William Aylett

15.1972 Clemons, H. "William Aylett Winston." In *The University of Virginia Library.* Charlottesville: University of Virginia Library, 1954. Pp. 110–12.

Winthrop, James

15.1973 Shipton, C. K. "Winthrop, James (Mar. 28, 1752–Sept. 26, 1821)." *DAB* 20 (1936): 407–08.

Wire, George Edwin

15.1974 Beatty, W. K. "Medicine, Law, Librarianship: The Unique Contribution of George Edwin Wire." *LLJ* 68 (1975): 82–91.

Wister, Owen

15.1975 Mason, J. "Owen Wister, Boy Librarian." *QJLC* 26 (1969): 200–212.

Wood, Mary Elizabeth

15.1976 Clemons, H. "Wood, Mary Elizabeth (Aug. 22, 1861–May 1, 1931)." *DAB* 20 (1936): 469–70.

15.1977 Chiu, A. K. "Wood, Mary Elizabeth (Aug. 22, 1861–May 1, 1931)." *NAW* 3 (1971): 647–48.

15.1978 Huang, G. W. "Miss Mary Elizabeth Wood: Pioneer of the Library Movement in China." *LHR* 1 (December 1974): 42–54.

15.1979 Huang, G. W. "Miss Mary Elizabeth Wood: Pioneer of the Library Movement in China." *Journal of Library and Information Science* 1 (1975): 67–78.

15.1980 Winkelman, J. H. "Mary Elizabeth Wood (1861–1931): American Missionary-Librarian to Modern China." *Journal of Library and Information Science* 943 (1982): 62–76.

Woods, Bill Milton

15.1981 "Woods, Bill M(ilton)." *CB* (1966): 454–56.

15.1982 Jackson, E. B. "Woods, Bill Milton (1924–1974)." *DALB*: 1978 573–75.

Woodworth, Florence

15.1983 Dewey, M. "As It Was in the Beginning." *PL* 30 (1925): 482–84.

Work, Monroe Nathan

15.1984 "Monroe Nathan Work (1866–1945)." *HBLib*: 1977 26–27.

15.1985 McMurry, L. O. "Black Intellectual in the South: Monroe Nathan Work, 1866–1945." *Phylon: The Atlanta University Review of Race and Culture* 26 (1980): 333–44.

15.1986 McMurry, L. O. *Recorder of the Black Experience: A Biography of Monroe Nathan Work.* Baton Rouge: Louisiana State University Press, 1985.

Works, George Alan

15.1987 Richardson, J. V. "George Alan Works (1877–1957); 'Seeking Neither Fame Nor Fortune.'" *JLH* 19 (1984): 298–304.

Wright, Louis Booker

15.1988 "Wright, Louis B(ooker)." *CB* (1950): 627–29.

15.1989 Hard, F. "Louis B. Wright: A Biographical Sketch." In *Louis B. Wright: A Bibliography and an Appreciation.* Charlottesville: University Press of Virginia, 1968. Pp. 1–75.

15.1990 Knachel, P. A. "Louis B. Wright." *PAAS* 94 (1984): 36–40.

Wright, Purd B.

15.1991 Compton, C. H. "Purd B. Wright Used Talents at Both Local and National Levels." *LJ* 72 (1947): 1049.

Wright, Wyllis Eaton

15.1992 Fulton, D. "Wyllis Eaton Wright." *BB* 20 (1951): 105–07.

Wroth, Lawrence Counselman

15.1993 Adams, M. W., and Black, J. D. "List of the Published Writings of Lawrence C. Wroth to December 31, 1950." In *Essays Honoring Lawrence C. Wroth.* Portland, Me.: Anthoensen Press, 1951. Pp. 485–504.

15.1994 Black, J. D. "Wroth, Lawrence Counselman (1884–1970)." *DALB*: 1978 575–76.

Wyer, James Ingersoll

15.1995 "James Ingersoll Wyer." *BB* 12 (1924): 41.

15.1996 Cregan, F., and Strube, J. "James Ingersoll Wyer: Writings in Librarianship and Education, 1899–1942." In *New York State Library School Register, 1887–1926*. New York: New York State Library School Association, 1959. Pp. 45–51.

15.1997 Paulson, P. J. "Wyer, James Ingersoll (1869–1955)." *DALB*: 1978 576–79.

Wyer, Malcolm Glenn

15.1998 Nichol, I. "Malcolm Glenn Wyer." *LJ* 76 (1951): 933.

15.1999 Parham, P. M. "Malcolm Glenn Wyer, Western Librarian: A Study in Leadership and Innovation." Doctoral dissertation, University of Denver, 1964.

15.2000 Wyer, M. G. *Books and People: Short Anecdotes from a Long Experience*. Denver: Old West, 1964.

15.2001 Gripton, J., and Bangoura, L. *Dr. Malcolm Wyer—A Bio-Bibliographical Study*. Denver: University of Denver, 1967.

15.2002 Wynar, B. S., and Loomis, K. C. "Wyer, Malcolm Glenn (1877–1965)." *DALB*: 1978 579–82.

15.2003 "Wyer, Malcolm Glenn." In *Librarian Authors: A Biobibliography*, by R. Engelbarts. Jefferson, N.C.: McFarland, 1981. Pp. 82–83.

Yarmolinsky, Avraham

15.2004 Lydenberg, H. M. "Avraham Yarmolinsky." *BNYPL* 59 (1955): 107–32.

Yonge, Ena Laura

15.2005 Kline, N. M. "Yonge, Ena Laura (1895–1971)." *DALB*: 1978 582–84.

Young, John Russell

15.2006 Broderick, J. C. "John Russell Young: The Internationalist as Librarian." *QJLC* 33 (1976): 117–49.

15.2007 Broderick, J. C. "Young, John Russell (1840–1899)." *DALB*: 1978 584–86.

Yust, William F.

15.2008 Hodges, B. E. "William F. Yust." *LJ* 73 (1948): 411.

Zimmerman, Carma Russell

15.2009 Schenk, G. K. "Carma Russell Zimmerman." *BB* 21 (1955): 145–47.

Index to Authors

The Index to Authors cites each individual author, editor, or compiler of a work regardless of the total number of authors responsible for that work. The index also cites corporate authors such as libraries, associations, academic institutions, and governmental agencies.

Entries are arranged alphabetically by author. The number with each entry refers to the number of the bibliographic entry.

Digit(s) preceeding the period identify the chapter; digit(s) following the period refer to the number of the entry within the chapter.

Casey, G.M., 2.142, 2.246
Casey, G.M., ed., 2.181
Casey, M., 1.137, 2.296, 15.1131, 15.1132, 15.1133
Casey, P.A., 5.606
Castañeda, C.E., 6.650
Castagna, E., 5.469, 15.1372, 15.1874
Castegnetti, N.R., 4.258
Cater, H.D., 9.167
Cavitt, L.C., 9.25
Cazden, R.E., 3.365, 3.373, 4.295
Cecil, H.L., 7.24
Cessna, R., 15.1492
Chadbourn, E.S., 9.371
Chadbourne, E.H., 4.273
Chadwick, J.R., 9.379, 9.381, 9.384
Chalker, W.J., 8.29
Chamberlain, L.C., 6.209
Chan, L.M., 13.216
Chancellor, J., 5.43
Chandler, A., 5.372
Chandley, J.T., 5.441
Chang, H.C., 2.170
Channing, E., 15.1954
Chapin, V.J., 5.685
Chapman, E.D., 15.577
Chapman, M., 13.21
Chapman, M.L., 12.209
Charpentier, A.A., 12.154
Chase, E., 6.625
Chase, E.H., 5.786
Chase, V., 4.225
Cheeseman, M., 9.368
Chelton, M.K., 15.1582
Chenery, F.L., 9.198
Cheney, A.P., 9.152
Cheney, E.P., 6.585
Cheney, F.N., 8.22, 15.916
Chevalier, S.A., 13.61
Chicago Literary Club., 15.1389
Chichester, M., 5.686
Childress, B., 6.104, 6.644, 6.728
Childs, J.B., 9.579, 9.581, 9.632, 15.843, 15.985,15.1184, 15.1185, 15.1447
Chin, J., 12.174
Chinard, G., 9.77
Chinard, G., ed., 3.201
Chipley, L., 3.404
Chisholm, M., 11.132
Chisum, E.D., 6.749, 6.750
Chitwood, J.R., 5.373
Chiu, A.K., 15.1977
Chong, N.S., 2.331
Chou, M.P., 15.114
Christenson, C.V., 15.1021
Christianson, E.B., 9.32, 9.40, 15.815

Christie, C.C., 15.1458, 15.1459
Christoph, P.R., 15.891
Christophers, R.A., 13.33
Chudacoff, N.F., 9.237
Church, F.E., 6.9
Churchwell, C.D., 11.124, 15.1901
Cincinnati Young Men's Mercantile LibraryAssociation., 4.135
Cincinnati. Public Library., 5.826
Clack, C.Y., 8.73
Clack, D.H., 2.262
Clairmont, S.A., 12.210
Clancy, M.M., 6.246
Clancy, R.J., 15.660
Clapp, S.L.C., 15.782
Clapp, V.W., 2.143, 9.534, 15.409, 15.591, 15.611
Clare, F., 11.25
Claremont College., 15.1008
Clark, C., 5.744
Clark, E.S., 5.634
Clark, G., 15.348
Clark, H., 9.663
Clark, J.B., 6.681
Clark, M.B., 15.1017
Clark, R.B., 5.532
Clark, R.L., ed., 10.85
Clark, R.M., 9.268
Clark, R.W., 15.682
Clark, S.N., 6.1, 9.316, 9.498
Clark, T.D., 3.403, 4.276
Clarke, J.A., 11.174
Clarke, J.H., 5.821
Clarke, M.G.M., 6.190
Clarke, O., 9.328
Clausen, M.P., 10.68
Clausman, G.J., 12.328
Clayton, H., 6.53
Clayton, S.A.H., 5.407
Clement, E.G., 12.248
Clemons, H., 3.93, 6.718, 15.66, 15.260, 15.882,15.995, 15.1333, 15.1350, 15.1425, 15.1860, 15.1972, 15.1976
Cleveland, D.B., 2.237
Clift, D.H., 12.74
Clift, D.H., ed., 12.75
Cline, G.S., 2.263, 6.122
Clinefeller, R.W., 6.562
Clive, J., 3.297
Clopine, J., 2.48
Close, V.L., 2.247
Clower, G.W., 3.116
Clute, M., 5.384
Clymer, B.F., 9.440
Coates, A., 9.350
Coats, N.M., 9.181

Copeland, E.H., 12.301
Copeland, M.T., 6.378
Copp, R.V.H., 4.315
Corbin, J., 15.847
Corbin, J.B., 2.280
Corcoran, S.R., 13.64
Corner, G.W., 15.418
Cornog, M., 13.219, 13.254
Cornwall, A.W., 9.262
Correll, L., 1.69, 15.688
Corsaro, J., 5.732, 6.518
Corwin, E.K., 12.22
Corwin, M.A., 14.11
Cory, J.M., 15.896
Costello, J.M., 15.945
Couch, C.R., 9.97
Coughlan, M., 7.111
Coughlin, B., 5.429
Coughlin, C.M., 12.266
Coulter, E.M., 6.156
Council of National Library
    Associations., 12.67
Countryman, G.A., 12.32, 15.67, 15.898,
    15.1434
Courtemanche-Ellis, A., 15.271
Coville, B., 6.519
Cowles, L.H., 9.73
Cox, A., 12.384
Cox, D.J., 12.250
Cox, J.W., 9.239
Cox, M., 12.43
Cox, R.J., 1.152, 10.72, 10.73, 10.97,
    10.120,10.121, 10.122, 10.155
Coyte, D.E., 9.352
Cramer, C.H., 5.897, 11.150, 15.251,
    15.582
Crammer, J.C., 5.832
Crandall, J.C., 3.347
Crane, E., 15.641
Cranford, J.P., 6.543
Crawford, A., 9.588
Crawford, D.R., 12.227
Crawford, H., 15.266, 15.1565, 15.1566
Crawford, L., 7.78
Crawford, M.C., 4.78
Crayton, J.E., 12.302
Creek, A.B., 9.310
Cregan, F., 15.1996
Crenshaw, M.V., 5.27
Cret, P.P., 9.57
Crist, L.L., 3.179
Crist, T.J., 15.1941
Crittenden, J.L.J., 5.336
Crocker, M.E., 15.1751
Cronin, J.M., 15.1373
Cronin, J.W., 13.113

Crook, M.R., 4.235
Cropper, M.S., 9.353
Cross, W.O., 3.208
Crouch, K., 15.750
Crouch, M.L., 5.956
Crumpacker, G.F., 5.433
Cuadra, C.A., 5.154
Culbertson, D.S., 12.228
Culp, B.A., 4.185
Culp, P.M., 5.1035, 5.1036
Culver, E.M., 5.446, 8.37
Cummings, C.S., comp., 1.101
Cummings, M.M., 15.141
Cummins, L.T., 10.112
Cunha, G.M., 13.149
Cunning, E.T., 9.425
Cunningham, L.L., 15.211
Cunningham, R., 15.4
Cunningham, W.D., 15.422
Curless, M., 5.420
Curley, A., 5.639, 15.1454
Curran, J.A., 15.138
Currie, R., 15.1484
Currier, L.G., 8.50
Currier, M., 9.168, 13.71
Currier, T.F., 13.69, 15.388
Curry, A.R., 2.29
Curry, J.L., 5.320
Curry, W.L., 2.73
Curtis, C.M., 5.628
Cushing, E.B., 15.430
Cushing, J.D., 4.342
Cushman, A.B., 4.338
Custer, B.A., 13.124, 13.182
Cutler, S.B., 4.105
Cutler, W., 15.1967, 15.1968
Cutliffe, M.R., 1.38
Cutter, C.A., 5.641, 6.314, 15.1952
Cutter, W.P., 15.438
Cveljo, K., 15.625, 15.1163, 15.1940
Cylke, F.K., 9.603, 9.652, 15.236

Dabagh, J., 12.155
Daily, J.E., 13.12, 13.121
Dain, P., 1.116, 2.265, 5.156, 5.765, 5.775,
    14.39,15.32, 15.144, 15.1121, 15.1122,
    15.1123, 15.1286, 15.1912
Dain, P., ed., 11.201
Dale, D.C., 1.102, 9.596, 12.329, 13.25,
    15.21,15.37, 15.185, 15.516, 15.1902
Dale, D.C., comp., 1.153
Dale, D.C., ed., 13.39, 15.1227
Dale, E.E., 3.264, 3.284, 3.338
Dallas, Texas. Public Library., 5.1005
Dalligan, A.C., 15.1730
Dalphin, M., 4.144, 15.1252

Fowler, S.P., 4.98
Fox, C.S., 12.299
Fox, K., 5.623
Fox, M.H., 10.65
Francis, W.W., 12.25
Frank, W.P., 15.584
Franklin Typographical Society, Boston.,
　9.48
Franklin, H.R., 5.166, 5.313
Franklin, L., 15.920
Franklin, R.D., 15.1589
Franklin, W.D., 5.680
Frantz, J.B., 15.642, 15.643,
　15.1490
Frantz, J.C., 9.583
Frantz, R.W., 5.115
Frarey, C.J., 13.80
Frebault, M., 15.455
Freedly, G., 12.144
Freedman, M.J., 13.202
Freehafer, E.G., 15.30
Freeman, A., 3.166
Freeman, J., 4.227
Freestone, R., 5.177
Freiberg, M., 15.1875
French, J.C., 6.295
Freund, C.E., 9.418
Freund, E., 5.733
Friedman, W., 15.1765
Friend, L.B., 6.660, 8.72, 8.75,
　15.1648, 15.1942,15.1943,
　15.1944
Friis, H.R., 9.687
Friley, C.E., 6.266
Frost, J., 12.145
Frost, J.E., 15.515
Frothingham, N.L., 15.830,
　15.831
Fruin, R., 10.13
Fry, A., 9.435
Fry, B.M., 9.539
Fry, J.W., 2.184, 6.575
Fulcino, S.A., 2.171
Fuller, H.M., 6.187
Fuller, H.W., 15.194
Fuller, M., 15.39
Fullerton, M.G., 6.267
Fulton, D., 15.1118, 15.1992
Fulton, D., ed., 15.1116
Fulton, J.F., 9.63, 9.410, 9.411, 9.449,
　15.432
Fulton, J.H., 15.137
Fulton, S., 5.1022
Fund, C.K., 5.549
Fung, M.C., 9.688
Furlong, P.J., 15.975

Furth, S.E., 15.1112
Fyock, E.R., 11.85

Gabriel, P., 15.1828
Gabriel, R.H., 9.540
Gage, L.J., 15.988
Gaines, E.J., 5.574, 15.254
Gaiser, B.F., 5.436
Galbreath, C.B., 5.820, 8.3
Galbreath, C.B., comp., 5.819
Galick, V.G., 5.533, 15.1835
Gallant, E.F., 5.630
Galloway, M.L., 7.41
Gallup, D., 6.198
Galpin, W.F., 6.470, 6.476
Galvin, T.J., 11.86, 11.143, 11.202, 13.246
Gambee, B.L., 1.138, 7.94, 7.97, 13.8,
　13.13, 13.27,13.44, 13.243, 15.415,
　15.527, 15.548, 15.620, 15.765,
　15.869,15.871, 15.1821
Gambee, R.R., 13.243
Gambrell, H.P., 4.142, 4.191, 4.289,
　6.661
Ganey, M.M., 5.997
Gankoski, I.F., 5.883
Gapp, K.S., 6.450
Gara, L., 2.61
Garbutt, K.K., 15.1844
Garceau, O., 5.72
Garcia, R.O., 15.1888
Gardiner, J.H., 6.320
[Gardner, H.B.], 5.946
Gardner, M.C., 15.1348
Gardner, O.M., 5.794
Gardner, R.K., 2.96
Garfield, E., 15.14
Garfinkle, N., 3.298
Garnett, R., 5.645
Garoogian, R., 5.780
Garrison, B.S., 5.809
Garrison, D., 5.134, 5.145, 5.146, 5.157,
　5.167, 5.191, 14.18, 15.522
Garrison, F.H., 15.132
Garrison, F.H., ed., 15.124
Garrison, G., 11.108
Gartland, H.J., 9.568
Garvey, S.K., 11.67
Garwig, P.L., 9.21
Gaskill, G.A., 4.175
Gaston, M., 7.98
Gates, B., 15.1584
Gates, E.S., 7.66
Gates, J.K., 5.229
Gaver, M.V., 15.1606
Gavurin, E.A., 5.766
Gay, D., 15.1886

Hatch, O.W., 4.252
Hauserman, D.D., 15.458
Hausmann, A.F., 5.294
Hausrath, D.C., 9.666
Haverstick, D.C., 4.81
Havlik, R.J., 2.113
Havron, H.J., 5.884
Hawkins, H., 6.305
Hawkins, J.A.W., 6.676
Hawks, G.P., 7.112
Hawthorne, N., 15.832
Haycraft, H., 15.1909
Hayden, E.C., 5.1090
Hayes, C.D., 6.490, 6.503, 15.714
Hayes, J.S., 4.68
Hayes, P.F., 2.121
Hayes, R.M., 1.148
Haygood, W.C., 5.654, 15.319, 15.855,
    15.1711
Haynes, B.G., 15.489
Hazeltine, R.E., 5.833
Hazelton, P.A., 9.346
Hazelton, R.A., 12.254
Healey, J.S., 15.657, 15.658, 15.675
Heaney, H.J., 1.98
Heaps, W.A., 7.24
Heard, J.M., 5.478
Heard, J.N., 10.23
Hecht, A., 5.312
Heck, R.S., 5.379
Heckel, J.W., 12.83
Heckman, M.L., 6.245, 15.326
Hedbavny, L., 4.192
Hedges, H.A., 5.772
Hedlin, E., 10.133, 10.160
Hedrick, L.F., 9.647
Hedrick, U.P., 3.225
Hegel, R., 6.191
Heidtmann, T., 6.616
Heifer, R.S., 13.197
Heilprin, L.B., 12.308
Heim, H.R., 5.881
Heim, K.M., 11.151
Heim, K.M., ed., 14.32, 14.42
Heindel, S.W., 6.544
Heisey, T.M., 13.151
Heiss, R.M., 13.67, 13.70
Heisser, W.A., 6.150
Heister, C.G., 9.690
Heizmann, L.J., 5.942
Held, R., 4.240, 4.242, 4.263, 4.341, 5.263,
    15.721
Helicher, K., 9.681
Helms, C.E., 5.561
Hembree, M.M., 7.18
Hemmer, P.B., 5.451

Hemphill, W.E., ed., 3.266
Hench, J.B., 2.316, 15.257, 15.946, 15.1068
Hench, M., 9.333
Henderson, J.D., 5.135, 5.267, 12.49
Henderson, K.L., 13.152
Henderson, T.B., 5.380
Hendrick, B.J., 15.309
Hendricks, D.D., 15.1269
Hendrickson, R.M., 12.120
Henke, E.M., 5.911
Henkle, H.H., 9.110, 9.452, 15.92
Henne, F., 7.51
Henry, E.A., 6.19, 15.1169
Henry, W.E., 5.409, 15.860
Hensel, E.M., 13.65
Hensley, C., 12.360
Hensley, H.C., 5.247, 5.248
Hepworth, B.M., 2.204, 5.1045
Herdman, M.M., 5.57
Herling, E.B., ed., 2.210
Hermannsson, H., 15.632
Herner, S., 2.334
Hernon, P., 6.123, 9.642, 9.694, 15.1218
Herold, J.V., 12.125
Herold, V.W., 12.309
Heron, D.W., 6.274
Heron, D.W., ed., 2.302
Herrick, C.A., 3.198
Herrick, C.C., 5.381
Herrick, D., 9.654
Herrick, M.D., 6.288
Herrin, B.R., 7.115
Herring, B.G., 15.837, 15.838
Herring, J., 6.683, 14.44
Hershey, F.E., 15.1244
Hertz, R.S., 2.145
Hertzel, D.H., 2.347
Heskin, M.K., 9.171
Hess, H., comp., 9.148
Hess, J.D., 5.408
Hesseltine, W.B., 2.61, 15.561
Hesseltine, W.B., ed., 10.37
Hester, G.A., 15.1861
Hewett, W.T., 6.462
Hewins, C.M., 5.283
Hewitt, J.A., 15.1043
Hewitt, V.D., 13.40, 15.872
Heyl, L., 15.710
Hibbs, J.E., 5.905
Hickey, D.J., 13.153, 13.154, 13.169,
    15.569, 15.570
Hickman, R.W., 6.375
Higgins, M.H., 9.26
High, W.M., 5.813, 10.88
Hildenbrand, S., 14.43, 14.44
Hilgert, E., 15.1725

Laubach, H., 9.286
Laudine, M., 6.158
Laugher, C.T., 4.31, 15.239, 15.241
Laughlin, J.L., 8.87
Law, R.A., 9.53
Lawler, J., 2.44
Lawrence, D.E., 9.274
Lawson, L.G., 5.900
Lawson, R.W., 15.202, 15.203
Lawson, V., 11.111
Lazerow, S., 2.175
Lea, J., 9.149
Lea, T., 15.1733, 15.1734
Leach, S., 6.90
Leach, S.G., ed., 1.141
Learned, W.S., 5.31
Leary, L., 3.401
Leary, W.M., 2.114
Leasure, M.F., 9.290
Lee, J.B., 6.670
Lee, M.M., 15.519
Lee, R.E., 5.116, 5.203, 5.1003
Lehnus, D.J., 2.154, 13.135, 13.185
Leidecker, K.F., 13.75, 15.835
Leigh, R.D., 5.75
Leinoff, T., 12.192
Leland, W.G., 9.560, 10.16, 10.22
Lemieux, D.J., 9.275
Lemkau, H.L., 9.475
Lemke, A.B., 14.20
Lemke, D.H., 6.76
Lemley, D.E., 7.36
Lenfest, G.E., 5.608
Lengelsen, R., 5.385
Lenhart, J.M., 9.193
Lentz, L., 6.703
Leonard, G., 4.147
Leonard, G.M., 9.217
Leonard, H.V., 6.548
Leonard, I.A., 3.60
Leonard, L.E., 13.118
Lester, C.B., 5.1075
Lester, E.L., 5.93
Lester, R.M., 5.58, 5.92
Lethbridge, M.C., 9.621
Leverette, S., 12.86
Levine, L.E., 8.64
Levy, R.G., 5.55
Lewis, D.F., 5.414
Lewis, D.T., 13.156
Lewis, J.F., 4.112
Lewis, L., 15.1436
Lewis, L.L., 6.194
Lewis, L.S., 12.315
Lewis, M.E., 5.834
Lewis, R.A., 5.891

Lewis, W.D., 6.200
Lewis, W.P., 5.615
Lewis, W.S., 4.170, 15.1073
Libbey, D.C., 9.165, 15.1004
Library Company of Philadelphia., 4.218
Library of Congress., 9.673, 9.674
Licandro, M.L., 5.720
Lichtenstein, J., 5.233, 5.241
Lichtenwanger, W., 12.371
Lichtenwanger, W., ed., 15.1676
Liebaers, H., 13.31
Lieberman, I., 11.171
Liebert, H.W., 15.57
Liebman, S.W., 3.368
Lillard, R.D., 3.263
Lin, S.C., 13.53
Lincoln, M.E., 5.572
Lind, L.R., 6.256
Linderman, W.B., 6.475, 11.99, 15.512
Lindquist, J.D., 15.868
Lindquist, V., 5.386
Line, B.W., 2.97
Line, M.B., 2.283
Lingelbach, A.L., 15.1025
Lingelbach, W.E., 9.62, 9.83
Lingfelter, M.R., 5.921
Linton, R.C., 3.185
Lippman, M., 2.123
List, B.T., 6.545
Little, A.E., 15.441
Little, E.N., 3.299
Littlefield, G.E., 3.194
Litto, F.M., 3.339
Liu, N., 6.51
Livingood, J.W., 4.133
Livingston, H.E., 4.16
Lloyd, D.D., 9.561
Lo, H., 5.747
Lockwood, F.C., 15.83
Loeh, B.B., 5.1087
Logsdon, R.H., 15.900, 15.1549
Logsdon, R.L., 8.83, 8.84
Lohrer, A., 11.28, 12.160
Lomer, G.R., 15.749
London, G., 13.186
Long, F., 5.889
Long, H.C., 5.33
Long, H.G., 7.93
Long, L.E., 2.74
Long, O.W., 15.947, 15.1759
Longhway, M.W., 5.567
Longworth, R.O., 5.607
Lonie, C.A., 5.562
Lonn, E., 4.111
Loomis, K.C., 15.153, 15.942, 15.2002
Looscan, A.B., 15.149

Index to Institutions

The Index to Institutions cites institutions in bibliographic entries when such information is contained as part of the author or the title of the entry. Index entries are arranged alphabetically by the name of the institution and the number given refers to the number of the bibliographic entry.

Special forms of entry are as follows. Private libraries are listed under the last name of the collector. Universities and departments within universities are listed under current rather than previous forms. College and university libraries appear under the name of the parent institution unless the bibliographic citation identifies a named library, for example, the Agassiz Natural History Library, Harvard University, which appears under "Agassiz." Subgroups of associations are listed under the name of the subgroup, for example, International Relations Round Table, American Library Association, which appears under "International." When subgroups are indexed, an entry number is given both under the subgroup and under its parent organization. Archives are listed separately except for archives of individual states, which are listed with state libraries. States are identified for public libraries only when such information is contained in the bibliographic entry, for example, Salem, Ohio Public Library.

Index to Essays

The Index to Essays provides dictionary access to the narratives that introduce each of the fifteen chapters. This index lists authors (using the same criteria as the Index to Authors), titles of publications (i.e., books, journals, articles, book chapters, dissertations, unpublished works, etc.), and subjects. Entries are interfiled alphabetically; each entry gives a page number rather than an entry number.

Abbott, John C., 283
Abbott, George, 56
Abraham, Mildred, 37
Academic libraries, 3, 35, 127–30; architecture of, 128; bibliographic instruction in, 129; black, 18–19; budgets and financing in, 128; collection development in, 127–29; college (as distinguished from university), 127, 129; colonial, 5, 127–29; cooperation among, 128; and curriculum development, 128; departmental libraries in, 179; "Golden Age" of, 128; governance in, 128; growth of, 127–29; histories of, 262; law libraries in [See Law libraries]; liberal arts colleges, 129; medical libraries in, [See Medical libraries]; mid-nineteenth century, 128; organization in, 128; public services in, 128–29; reference work in, 129; teachers colleges, 129; technical processing in, 128; technology in, 128; university (as

distinguished from college), 129. *See also* Higher education; Literary society libraries
Addison, Joseph, 38
Administration 18, 127–28
"Advances in American Library History," 75
"ALA at 100," 241
ALA World Encyclopedia of Library and Information Services (2d ed), 5
Aldrich, Frederic D., 165
Allen, Walter C., 18
"Ambivalence and Paradox: The Social Bonds of the Public Library," 78
American Antiquarian Society, library, 180; Program in the History of the Book in American Culture, 38
"American Archival History: Its Development, Needs, and Opportunities," 218
American Archivist, 215–17
American Association for State and Local History, 173

453

"Atlanta's Female Librarians, 1883–1915," 277
Audiovisual programs, 166, 242. *See also* School libraries; School media centers
Austin, Texas, circulating libraries in, 57
Australia, Carnegie Corporation influence in, 260; Dewey Decimal Classification in, 260; U. S. War Information Service Libraries in, 260
Autobiographies *See* Librarians, autobiographies of
Avram, Henriette D., 261

Babylon, Eugenia R., 174
Bach, Harry, 5
Backus, Joyce, 57
Bailey, Joanne Passet, 277
Bailyn, Bernard, 165
Baker, Augusta, 19, 283–84
Baker, Hugh, 37
Baltimore Public Library, 77. *See also* Enoch Pratt Free Library
Baltimore, social libraries in, 56
Banned Books, 17
Barr, Larry J., 5, 17, 174
Barr, Mary, 38
Barrington, Jean W., 18
Batchelder, Mildred L., 283
Bates, Nancy P., 261
Baumann, Charles H., 282
Bay, J. Christian, 180
Baylor University Library, 130
Beck, Nelson, 76
Beneath the Footnote, 216
Benidt, Bruce, 77
Bentinck-Smith, William, 282
Berkshire Republican Library at Stockbridge, 57
Berner, Richard C., 216
Berninghausen, David K., 17
Best, John Hardin, 165
Bestor, Arthur E., Jr., 128
Beyond My Expectation: A Personal Chronicle, 282
Bibliographic essays, 3, 5
Bibliographic instruction, 129, 262. *See also* Instruction in library use; Library use; Public services; Reference services
Bibliographic networks, 261. *See also* Library cooperation; Resource sharing
Bibliography, 261. *See also* Printed book catalogs
Bibliography of Library Economy, 1876 to 1920, 6
Bidlack, Russell, 57, 129, 261
Biggs, Mary, 276

Billings, John Shaw, 281
Biographical-Bibliographical Directory of Women Librarians, 275
Biographical research, 77, 281–84; and doctoral dissertations, 282–84. *See also* Historical research; History; Life-writing; Psychohistory; Research methods
"Biographical Research on Women Librarians: Its Paucity, Perils, and Pleasures," 276
Biographies of librarians and library benefactors 281–85. *See also* Black librarianship; *Festschriften*; Librarians; Women in librarianship
Biography, collective, 284; commemorative, 281; retrospective, 284–85; scholarly, 282–83
Bishop, William Warner, 259, 283
Bixby, Mrs. A.F., 275
Black Academic Libraries and Research Collections: An Historical Survey, 19
"Black Academic Libraries Founded Prior to 1900," 19
The Black Librarian in America, 19, 284
The Black Librarian in the Southeast: Reminiscences, Activities, Challenges, 284
Black librarianship, 18–19; academic libraries in, 18–19; autobiographies in, 19, 284; biographies in, 19, 284; in Brooklyn, 19; chronology of, 16; doctoral dissertations in, 19, 284; in Kentucky, 165; librarians in, 19; library associations in, 19; library education in, 19; public libraries in, 19; and racial integration, 18–19; school libraries in, 165; services in, 76; women in, 276. *See also* Blacks, library services for; Minorities
Blacks, library services for, 18–19, 76. *See also* Black librarianship; Minorities
Blanket orders, 260
Blazek, Ron, 77
Blegen, Theodore C., 37
Blue, Thomas Fountain, 284
Boaz, Martha, 282
Bobinski, George S., 5, 16, 76
Boll, John J., 261
Bolton, Charles K., 57, 284
Bonk, Sharon C., 18
Book catalogs. *See* Printed book catalogs
Book collecting and collectors, 36–37, 285
"Book Collections of Five Colonial College Libraries: A Subject Analysis," 128
Book Company of Durham, 57

Krug, Judith, 17
Krummel, Donald W., 18
Kruty, Paul, 18
Kruzas, Anthony T., 181

Lamberton, E. V., 36
LaMontagne, Leo E., 261
Lane, Margaret, 165
"Language and the Printed Word,"
  36
Lanier, Gene D., 166
Larsen, John C., 174
Laugher, Charles T., 55
Laughlin, Jeannine L., 174
Law libraries, 179, 181. See also
  Correctional institutions
"Law Libraries and Librarians: A
  Revisionist History," 181
Lawson, Richard W., 283
Leach, Steven G., 5
Leaders in American Academic Librarian-
  ship, 1925–1975, 128, 284
Leavitt, Arthur H., 216
Lee, Michael M., 283
Lee, Robert, 76
Lehnus, Donald J., 261
Leland, Waldo Gifford,
  217
Lemley, Dawson E., 166
Leonard, Grace, 57
Lewis, John F., 57
Liberal arts colleges, 129. See also
  Academic libraries; Higher educa-
  tion; Literary society libraries
Librarian Authors, 285
Librarians, 3–4, 16, 281–85;
  autobiographies of, 19; biographies
  of, 261, 281–85; black, 18–19, 284;
  catalog, 261; image in literature, 16; of
  the Indiana State Library, 174; at international conferences, 260; in
  Midwestern colleges, 277; oral history
  interviews of, 6; public librarians, 77;
  reference librarians, 284; reprints of
  articles and reports by, 283; school
  librarians, 166, 276. See also
  Biographies of librarians and library
  benefactors; Biography; Black
  librarianship; Festschriften; Women in
  librarianship
"The Librarians of Harvard College
  1667–1877," 284
Libraries, "Golden Age" of, 16, 128; and
  international relations, 259–60; and
  oversees technical assistance, 260;
  and racial integration, 18–19

Libraries & Culture (collected work), 16;
  (journal), 5. See also Journal of Library
  History
Libraries and Librarianship in the West: A
  Brief History, 15
Libraries, Books, & Culture, 16
Libraries for Teaching, Libraries for
  Research: Essays for a Century, 128
Libraries in American Periodicals before
  1876: A Bibliography with Abstracts and
  an Index, 5–6
Libraries Unlimited, 5, 283, 285;
  Heritage of Librarianship Series, 283
Library and information science educa-
  tion. See Education for librarianship
Library architecture, 5, 18, 128
Library associations, 241–42; anniver-
  sary commemorations of, 241–42;
  black, 19; doctoral research in,
  241–42; local, 242; master's research
  in, 242; national, 241–42; regional,
  241; specialized, 242; state, 241–42,
  275; women in, 275
"Library Associations in the United
  States and British Commonwealth,"
  241
"Library Associations: Their History
  and Influence," 241
Library benefactors, 5, 37, 281–85
Library Bill of Rights, 17
The Library Book: Centennial History of
  the Minneapolis Public library, 77
Library Company of Philadelphia, 56
Library cooperation, 128, 261. See also
  Bibliographic networks; Resource
  sharing
Library education. See Education for
  librarianship
Library Education: An International
  Survey, 227
Library governance. See Administration
Library growth, 127–29
"A Library Hall of Fame," 285
Library History (monograph), 4
Library History: An Examination
  Guidebook (2d ed.), 4
Library History Round Table, 4, 18, 276.
  See also American Library Associa-
  tion, Library History Round Table
Library History Seminar VII, 4, 277
Library History Seminar VI, 4
Library history seminars, 4, 15, 277
The Library in America: A Celebration in
  Words and Pictures, 16
The Library in Society, 16
Library legislation, 17

Nicholson, J.B., 56
North Carolina Library Commission, 174
Norton, Margaret Cross, 217
Notable American Women, 284
Notices of Public Libraries in the United States of America, 16
Nunis, Doyce, 37

Oboler, Eli M., 241
O'Connor, Sister M.V., 56
O'Connor, Thomas F., 130
Oehlerts, Donald E., 5, 18
Ogden, Sherelyn, 18
Ohio, school libraries in, 165; social libraries in, 56; state library services in, 174
Ohio State University Library, 130
Ohio Valley, reading tastes in, 37
Oliphant, J. Orin, 130
Olle, James G., 4
O'Loughlin, M.A.J., 241
Online databases, 262. *See also* Reference services
Open Shelves and Open Minds: A History of the Cleveland Public Library, 77
Orians, G.H., 38
Origins of American Academic Librarianship, 128
Origins of the American College Library, 1638–1800, 127
Osborn, Velva J., 261
Osburn, Charles B., 129

Palmer, Vivian D., 217
Paltsits, Victor H., 217
The Paperbound Book in America, 37
Parham, Paul M., 283
Parnassus on Main Street: A History of the Detroit Public Library, 77
Parochial libraries, 55; in Maryland, 55
Patton & Miller (architectural firm), 18
Peckham, Howard, 37
Peden, William, 37
Peirce, Neal R., 173
Pennsylvania, private libraries in, 36; school libraries in, 165; social libraries in, 56
"Perceptions of the Academic Library: Midwestern College Libraries as They Have Been Depicted in College Histories," 128
Perspectives on the Past: An Autobiography, 282
Peterson, Kenneth G., 17, 130
Philadelphia Public Library, 77

Philanthropy, 127
Phinazee, Annette L., 19, 284
Photocopying, 17
Piercy, Esther J., 261
Pigeons on the Granite: Memories of a Yale Librarian, 282
Pioneering Leaders in Librarianship, 281
Plantation libraries, 36
Pomfret, John E., 180
Pond, Patricia K., 242
Poole, William Frederick, 77, 281–82
Pope, Alexander, 38
The Popular Book: A History of America's Literary Taste, 37
Posner, Ernst, 215–17
Potter, Alfred C., 284
Powell, Benjamin E., 127
Powell, Lawrence Clark, 282
Power, R.L., 275
Predecessors of the public library, 55–58, 76. *See also* Circulating libraries; Reading rooms; School district libraries; Social libraries
Predeek, Albert, 15
Preservation and conservation of materials, 18
Presidential libraries, 182. *See also* Government libraries and programs
"The Prevalence of Libraries in the United States before 1876: Some Regional Differences," 17
Princeton University, libraries, 130; society libraries, 129
Printed book catalogs, 261 *See also* Bibliography
Printing and Society in Early America, 38
Prison libraries. *See* Correctional institutions
Private libraries, 35–37, 180; of lawyers, 179, 181; in Louisiana, 36; in Maryland, 36; medical libraries, 179, 181; in Pennsylvania, 36; in South Carolina, 36; in southern plantations, 36; in St. Louis, 36; in Virginia, 36. *See also* Scholarly libraries
Private Libraries in Creole St. Louis, 36
The Professionalization of Education for Librarianship, 228
Professions, history of the, 228
Progress and Problems in Education for Librarianship, 228
Provenance, 218
Providence Athenaeum, 57
Psychohistory, 3–4. *See also* Biographical research; Historical research; Lifewriting; Research methods

The bibliographic information for this book was stored, sorted, and retrieved using Advanced Revelation database managment system for microcomputers, by Revelation Technologies, Inc. The data was then exported to Xerox Ventura Publisher Version 2.0 for page composition.